Time Out

Seville & Andalucía

timeout.com/andalucia

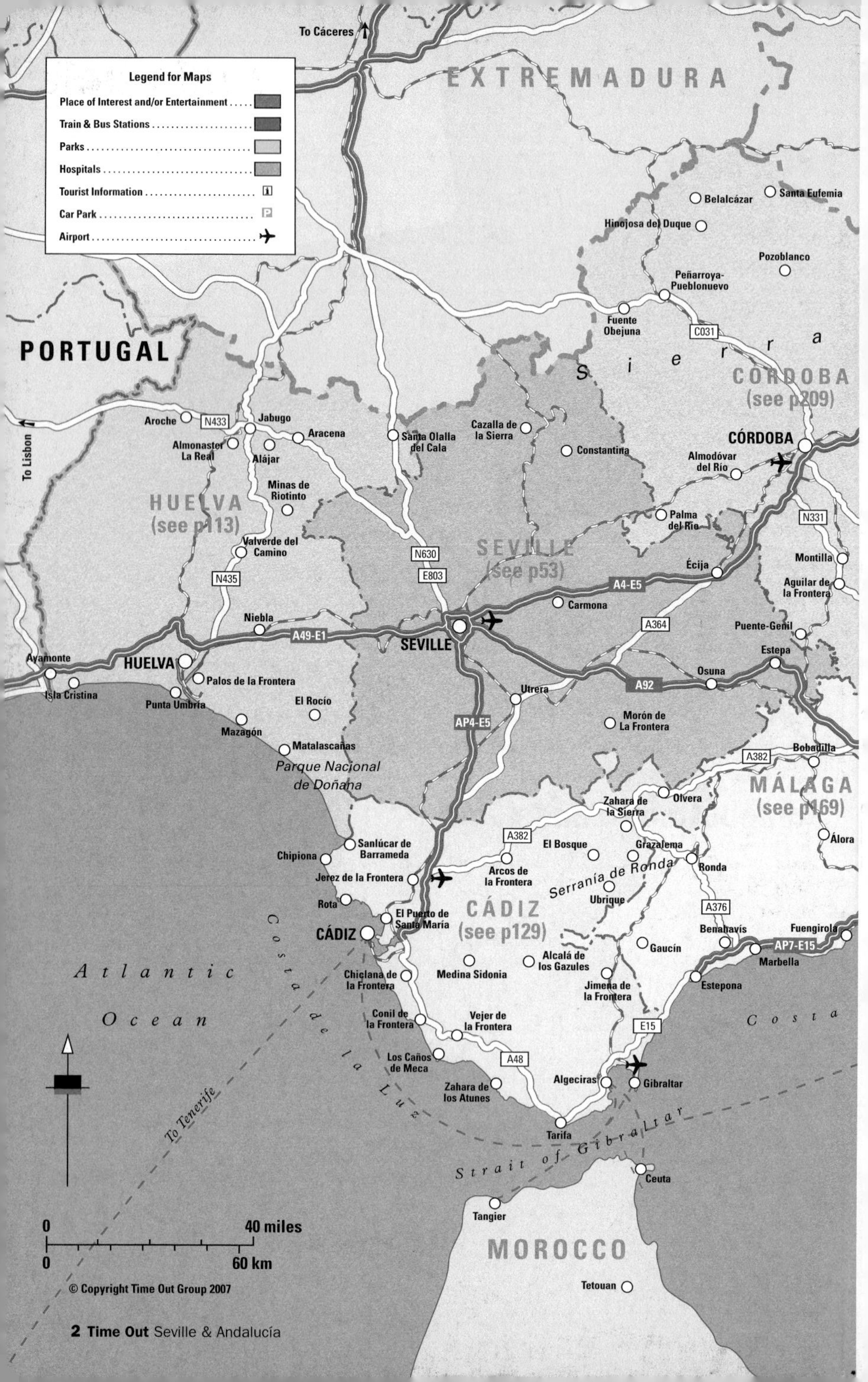
Legend for Maps
Place of Interest and/or Entertainment
Train & Bus Stations
Parks
Hospitals
Tourist Information
Car Park
Airport
To Cáceres
EXTREMADURA
PORTUGAL
To Lisbon
Belalcázar
Santa Eufemia
Hinojosa del Duque
Pozoblanco
Peñarroya-Pueblonuevo
Fuente Obejuna
C031
Sierra
CÓRDOBA (see p209)
CÓRDOBA
Almodóvar del Río
Aroche
N433
Jabugo
Aracena
Almonaster La Real
Alájar
Santa Olalla del Cala
Cazalla de la Sierra
Constantina
Minas de Riotinto
HUELVA (see p113)
Valverde del Camino
N435
N630
E803
SEVILLE (see p53)
Palma del Río
N331
Montilla
Écija
Aguilar de la Frontera
A4-E5
Carmona
Niebla
A49-E1
SEVILLE
A364
Puente-Genil
Estepa
Ayamonte
HUELVA
Isla Cristina
Palos de la Frontera
Punta Umbría
El Rocío
Osuna
A92
Utrera
AP4-E5
Morón de La Frontera
Mazagón
Matalascañas
Parque Nacional de Doñana
A382
Bobadilla
MÁLAGA (see p169)
Olvera
Zahara de la Sierra
A382
El Bosque
Grazalema
Álora
Sanlúcar de Barrameda
Chipiona
Arcos de la Frontera
Ronda
Jerez de la Frontera
Serranía de Ronda
Ubrique
Rota
CÁDIZ (see p129)
A376
El Puerto de Santa María
CÁDIZ
Benahavís
Fuengirola
AP7-E15
Marbella
Gaucín
Medina Sidonia
Alcalá de los Gazules
Chiclana de la Frontera
Jimena de la Frontera
Estepona
Atlantic Ocean
Costa de la Luz
Conil de la Frontera
Vejer de la Frontera
E15
Costa
Los Caños de Meca
A48
Zahara de los Atunes
Algeciras
Gibraltar
To Tenerife
Tarifa
Strait of Gibraltar
Ceuta
Tangier
0
40 miles
0
60 km
MOROCCO
Tetouan

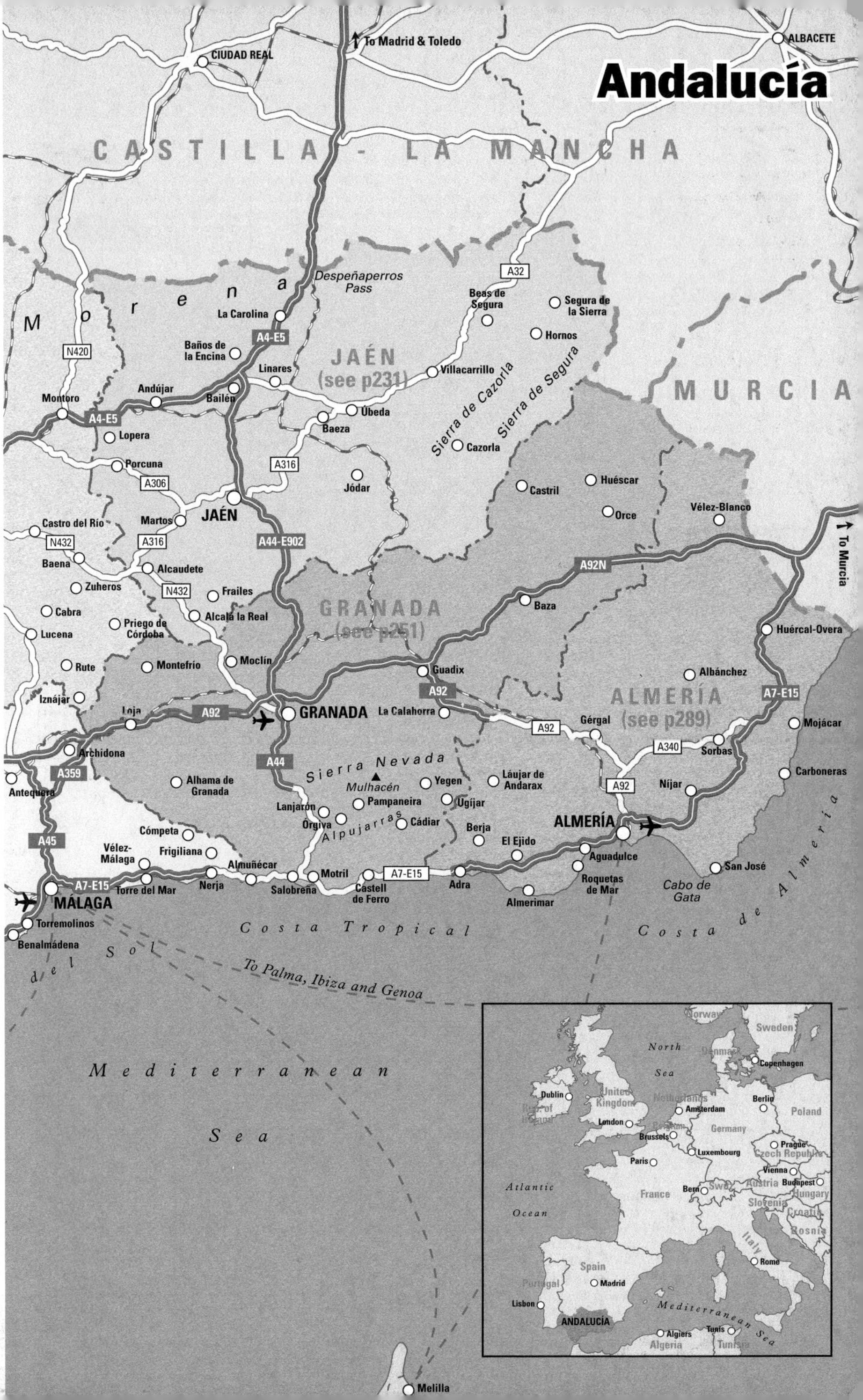

Andalucía
To Madrid & Toledo
ALBACETE
CIUDAD REAL
CASTILLA - LA MANCHA
MURCIA
To Murcia
Morena
Despeñaperros Pass
La Carolina
A4-E5
Baños de la Encina
N420
Linares
JAÉN (see p231)
Montoro
Andújar
Bailén
Lopera
Porcuna
A306
A316
Úbeda
Baeza
Jódar
Villacarrillo
A32
Beas de Segura
Segura de la Sierra
Hornos
Sierra de Cazorla
Sierra de Segura
Cazorla
Castril
Huéscar
Orce
Vélez-Blanco
Castro del Río
N432
Martos
JAÉN
A44-E902
Baena
Alcaudete
Zuheros
Frailes
Cabra
Alcalá la Real
Lucena
Priego de Córdoba
Rute
Montefrío
Moclín
Iznájar
GRANADA (see p251)
A92N
Baza
Huércal-Overa
Guadix
Albánchez
ALMERÍA (see p289)
A7-E15
Loja
A92
GRANADA
La Calahorra
Gérgal
Mojácar
Archidona
A359
A44
Sierra Nevada
Mulhacén
A340
Sorbas
Carboneras
Antequera
Alhama de Granada
Yegen
Láujar de Andarax
Níjar
Lanjarón
Pampaneira
Ugíjar
Órgiva
Alpujarras
Cádiar
Berja
ALMERÍA
A45
Cómpeta
Vélez-Málaga
Frigiliana
Almuñécar
El Ejido
Aguadulce
Torre del Mar
Nerja
Salobreña
Motril
Castell de Ferro
Adra
Roquetas de Mar
Almerimar
San José
Cabo de Gata
MÁLAGA
Torremolinos
Benalmádena
Costa del Sol
Costa Tropical
Costa de Almería
To Palma, Ibiza and Genoa
Mediterranean Sea
Melilla
Norway
Sweden
North Sea
Denmark
Copenhagen
Dublin
Rep. of Ireland
United Kingdom
London
Netherlands
Amsterdam
Berlin
Poland
Brussels
Germany
Luxembourg
Prague
Czech Republic
Paris
Vienna
Austria
Budapest
Hungary
Atlantic Ocean
France
Bern
Switz.
Slovenia
Croatia
Bosnia
Italy
Rome
Spain
Madrid
Portugal
Lisbon
Mediterranean Sea
ANDALUCÍA
Algiers
Tunis
Algeria
Tunisia

Published by Time Out Guides Ltd, a wholly owned subsidiary of Time Out Group Ltd.
Time Out and the Time Out logo are trademarks of Time Out Group Ltd.

Previous editions 2002, 2004.

10 9 8 7 6 5 4 3 2 1

This edition first published in Great Britain in 2007 by Ebury Publishing
Ebury Publishing is a division of The Random House Group Ltd,
20 Vauxhall Bridge Road, London SW1V 2SA

Random House Australia Pty Limited 20 Alfred Street, Milsons Point, Sydney, New South Wales 2061, Australia
Random House New Zealand Limited 18 Poland Road, Glenfield, Auckland 10, New Zealand
Random House South Africa (Pty) Limited Isle of Houghton, Corner Boundary Road & Carse O'Gowrie, Houghton 2198, South Africa

Random House UK Limited Reg. No. 954009

Distributed in USA by Publishers Group West
1700 Fourth Street, Berkeley, California 94710

Distributed in Canada by Publishers Group Canada
250A Carlton Street, Toronto, Ontario M5A 2L1

For further distribution details, see www.timeout.com

ISBN 10: 1-904978-68-1
ISBN 13: 9781904978688

A CIP catalogue record for this book is available from the British Library

Colour reprographics by Wyndeham Icon, 3 & 4 Maverton Road, London E3 2JE

Printed and bound in Germany by Appl

Papers used by Ebury Publishing are natural, recyclable products made from wood grown in sustainable forests

Time Out Guides Limited
Universal House
251 Tottenham Court Road
London W1T 7AB
Tel + 44 (0)20 7813 3000
Fax + 44 (0)20 7813 6001
Email guides@timeout.com
www.timeout.com

Editorial
Editor Sally Davies
Deputy Editor Simon Coppock
Consultant Editor Michael Jacobs
Sub Editors Ismay Atkins, Edoardo Albert
Listings Editors Alex Phillips, Roberto Rama, Dylan Simanowitz
Map Researcher Alex Phillips
Proofreader Angela Jameson-Potts
Indexer Anna Norman

Editorial/Managing Director Peter Fiennes
Series Editor Ruth Jarvis
Deputy Series Editor Lesley McCave
Business Manager Gareth Garner
Guides Co-ordinator Holly Pick
Accountant Kemi Olufuwa

Design
Art Director Scott Moore
Art Editor Pinelope Kourmouzoglou
Senior Designer Josephine Spencer
Graphic Designer Henry Elphick
Digital Imaging Dan Conway
Ad Make-up Jenni Prichard

Picture Desk
Picture Editor Jael Marschner
Deputy Picture Editor Tracey Kerrigan
Picture Researcher Helen McFarland

Advertising
Sales Director Mark Phillips
International Sales Manager Ross Canadé
International Sales Executive Simon Davies

Marketing
Group Marketing Director John Luck
Marketing Manager Yvonne Poon
Marketing & Publicity Manager, US Rosella Albanese

Production
Group Production Director Mark Lamond
Production Manager Brendan McKeown
Production Coordinator Caroline Bradford

Time Out Group
Chairman Tony Elliott
Managing Director Mike Hardwick
Financial Director Richard Waterlow
TO Magazine Ltd MD David Pepper
Group General Manager/Director Nichola Coulthard
TO Communications Ltd MD David Pepper
Group Art Director John Oakey
Group IT Director Simon Chappell

Contributors
Introduction Jonathan Cox. **History** Adam Coulter (*What have the Moors done for us?* Chris Moss). **Andalucía Today** Stephen Burgen, Adam Coulter. **Literary Andalucía** Michael Jacobs. **Architecture** Helen Crawshaw, Jonathan Cox. **Food & Drink** Adam Coulter. **Festivals & Events** Adam Coulter. **Seville City** Adam Coulter, Sally Davies, Nadia Feddo (*Thrills, spills & polka-dot frills* Michael Jacobs; *How to be a flamenco fashionista* Jo Williams). **Seville Province** Kirsten Foster, Martin Hastings. **Huelva City & the Coast** Kirsten Foster, Sally Davies. **Sierra Aracena** Kirsten Foster, Jo Williams. **Cádiz City** Adam Coulter, Martin Hastings. **North of Cádiz** Adam Coulter, Martin Hastings (*Bring on the dancing horses* Tara Stevens). **East of Cádiz** Jonathan Cox, Guy Hunter-Watts. **Costa de la Luz** Tara Stevens. **Gibraltar** Tara Stevens. **Málaga City** Tara Stevens (*All the fun of the feria* Michael Kessler). **Costa del Sol** Tara Stevens (*Sign language* Kip Tobin). **East of Málaga** Tara Stevens. **North of Málaga** Helen Crawshaw, Jonathan Cox. **West of Málaga** Jonathan Cox, Guy Hunter-Watts. **Córdoba City** Kirsten Foster, Amanda White; *additional reviews* Annie Bennett. **Around Córdoba** Martin Hastings, Amanda White. **Jaén City** Adam Coulter, Jonathan Cox. **North & South of Jaén** Jonathan Cox (*World power* Michael Jacobs). **East of Jaén** Jonathan Cox, Sally Davies. **Granada City** Nadia Feddo. **Around Granada** Sophie Blacksell, Jonathan Cox (*Keeping cavey* Alex Johnson). **Sierra Nevada & the Alpujarras** Sophie Blacksell, Tara Stevens. **Costa Tropical** Tara Stevens. **Almería City** Jonathan Cox. **Costa de Almería** Jonathan Cox, Sally Davies. **Almería Interior** Jonathan Cox. **Directory** Adam Coulter, Jonathan Cox. **Province Introductions** Jonathan Cox. **Additional reviews throughout** Sally Davies, Jo Williams.

Maps JS Graphics (john@jsgraphics.co.uk).

Photography by Karl Blackwell, except: page 14 Christie's Images / Corbis; page 19 Private Collection, Ken Welsh / The Bridgeman Art Library; page 22 akg-images; page 24 AFP / Getty Images; pages 31, 280 Granada Tourist Board; pages 48, 51 Costa del Sol Tourist Board; page 118 Herminio M. Muñiz; page 137 Cadiz Turismo; page 145 Courtesy of the Real Escuela.

The following image was provided by the featured establishment/artist: page 58.

The Editor would like to thank Maria Utrera in Málaga; Manuel Iglesias, Daniel Navarro, Ignacio Rivero and Antonio Rodríguez in Huelva; Amanda Cobertt in Seville; Manuel de la Varga in Cádiz; Paco Ramírez in Córdoba; Esmeralda Castillo and Maria José Arredondo in Jaén; Inma Muñoz and Francisco Titos in Granada, and Emily Herreras-Griffiths and Francisco Álvarez at the Spanish Tourist Board in London. Thanks also to Laura Baena, Faiza Bahna, Alex Crichton, Felipe Guardiola, Roser Marimon, John O'Donovan, Carolina Oficialdegui, Silvana Presta, Gabriel Quesada, Andrew Shaw and Marion Voege.

The Editor travelled courtesy of Bravo Car Hire (966 46 04 18/www.bravocarhire.com).

Contents

Introduction

For many northern Europeans, Andalucía is a second (and, increasingly frequently, a first) home. The Brits and the Germans, in particular, have had a love affair with southern Spain for more than 40 years. Yet the waves of holidaymakers and expats of the last few decades are only the latest in almost three millennia of foreign invasions.

Since ancient times this immense and immensely varied region has held an allure, a mystique, a whiff of the exotic. Nowhere does Europe come closer to Africa – literally and metaphorically. Many aspects of its flora and fauna, its history, culture and architecture span two continents, and it's this unique blending that has long given the region its distinctive flavour. Educated travellers have, for the last two centuries, been seduced by this exoticism, and particularly the legacy of the Moors, whose 700-year presence in Spain remains etched in stone and stucco across the region.

Another major draw today is that Andalucía is popularly seen as the quintessence of Spain. Here is the home of virtually everything perceived of as stereotypically Spanish – the blood and machismo of the bullfight, the fire and passion of flamenco, fragrant orange blossom, wild-eyed gypsies, tapas, sherry... Clichéd these images may be, but they remain defining features of the region.

And then there's Andalucía extraordinary natural beauty and diversity. It's perfectly possible to ski in pristine alpine scenery in the morning, and then drive through a multi-hued desert to reach unspoiled beaches in time for a late afternoon swim.

Of course, it's not all light and loveliness. The region has no shortage of problems – severe rural poverty, racial tensions, a coastline that has, in large part, been irredeemably ruined by overdevelopment – but, as a visitor, the former two issues will rarely be encountered and the latter can easily be avoided.

For a tourist, Andalucía really has got it all. Whatever type of holiday you seek, you can find it somewhere here. Bucket-and-spaders can soak up the rays, swig sangría and party all night long on the Costa del Sol; more individualistic sun-seekers choose to head for the Costa de la Luz or the Cabo de Gata for low-key resorts and endless white-sand beaches. Urban sophisticates can bar-hop the hip hangouts of Granada, Málaga, Córdoba and Sevilla, while more tradition-minded folk might prefer to crawl classic trapped-in-amber tapas bars in the very same cities. The culturally inclined can follow in the footsteps of the Moors, via extraordinary castles, palaces and mosques; those who favour physical over cerebral pleasures can windsurf off Tarifa's famed beaches, scuba dive off Gibraltar or hike and ski among Spain's highest peaks, the Sierra Nevada.

But be warned: this place is a drug. Once visited, you'll find yourself wistfully enquiring after local property prices, and dreaming of that perfect place in the sun.

ABOUT TIME OUT GUIDES

This is the third edition of *Time Out Seville & Andalucía*, one of an expanding series of Time Out guides produced by the people behind the successful listings magazines in London, New York and Chicago. Our guides are all written by resident experts who strive to provide you with all the most up-to-date information you'll need to explore the region, whether you're a local or a first-time visitor.

THE LIE OF THE LAND AND MAPS

In order to make this guide as easy to navigate as possible, we have divided it into sections corresponding to the eight provinces that make up Andalucía. A map of the entire region can be found at the front of the guide (*see pp2-3*). Seville is mapped on pp54-55; a map of its province is on p104. Each of the other chapters start with a map of the region, but there are also detailed maps of the most important cities and towns. These have full grid referencing and pinpoint the specific locations of hotels (❶) and restaurants, cafés and bars (❶).

ESSENTIAL INFORMATION

For all the practical information you might need for visiting the area – including visa and customs information, disabled access, emergency telephone numbers, a list of useful websites and the lowdown on the local transport network – turn to the Directory chapter at the back of this guide. It starts on p307.

THE LOWDOWN ON THE LISTINGS

We've tried to make this book as useful as possible. Addresses, phone numbers, transport information, opening times and admission prices are all included in the listings. However, businesses can change their arrangements at any time. Before you go out of your way, we'd strongly advise you to call and check opening times and other particulars. While every effort has been made to ensure the accuracy of the information contained in this guide, the publishers cannot accept responsibility for any errors it may contain.

PRICES AND PAYMENT

We have noted whether venues such as hotels and restaurants in major towns and cities accept the following major cards: American Express (AmEx), Diners Club (DC), MasterCard (MC) and Visa (V). Many businesses will also accept other cards, such as Switch/Maestro and Delta, and travellers' cheques.

The prices we've supplied in this guidebook should be treated as guidelines, not gospel. If prices vary wildly from those we've quoted, ask whether there's a good reason. If not, go elsewhere. Then please let us know. We aim to give the best and most up-to-date advice, so we want to know if you've been badly treated or overcharged.

TELEPHONE NUMBERS

All telephone numbers in this guide include the relevant three-figure provincial code, which must always be dialled, regardless of whether you are within or outside the province in question. The international dialling code for Spain is 34.

To dial numbers as given in this book from abroad, use your country's exit code (00 in the UK, 011 in the US), followed by 34 (the country code for Spain) and then the number as printed. For more details of phone codes and charges, *see p322.*

LET US KNOW WHAT YOU THINK

We hope you enjoy *Time Out Seville & Andalucía*, and we'd like to know what you think of it. We welcome tips for places that you consider we should include in future editions and take notice of your criticism of our choices. You can email us at guides@timeout.com.

Prices in restaurants

Within this guide you will see that we have denoted the price range of each restaurant we mention with between one and four euro symbols. These correspond approximately to the following price brackets for a full meal per person (in Gibraltar, £ = under £15, etc):

€	= under €15
€€	= €15-€20
€€€	= €25-€35
€€€€	= over €35

Advertisers

We would like to stress that no establishment has been included in this guide because it has advertised in any of our publications and no payment of any kind has influenced any review. The opinions given in this book are those of Time Out writers and entirely independent.

There is an online version of this book, along with guides to over 100 international cities, at **www.timeout.com**.

Time Out
Travel Guides
Worldwide
All our guides are written by a team of local experts with a unique and stylish insider perspective. We offer essential tips, trusted advice and honest reviews for everything you need to know in the city.
Over 50 destinations available at all good bookshops and at timeout.com/shop
Time Out
Guides
Amsterdam
Athens
Bangkok
Barcelona
Beijing
Berlin
Boston
Brussels
Budapest
Buenos Aires
California
Cape Town
Chicago
Croatia
Dubai
Dublin
Edinburgh
Florence
Havana
Hong Kong
Istanbul
Las Vegas
Lisbon
London
Los Angeles
Madrid
Mallorca
Marrakech
Miami
Milan
Mumbai & Goa
Naples
New Orleans
New York
Paris
Patagonia
Prague
Rio de Janeiro
Rome
San Francisco
Seville & Andalucía
Shanghai
Singapore
South of France
Stockholm
Sydney
Tokyo 東京
Toronto
Turin
Vancouver
Venice
Vienna
Washington, DC

Time Out Marrakech
Time Out Miami
Time Out Milan
Time Out Mumbai & Goa
Time Out Naples
Time Out New Orleans
Time Out New York
Time Out Paris
Time Out Patagonia
Time Out Prague
Time Out Rio de Janeiro
Time Out Rome
Time Out San Francisco
Time Out Seville & Andalucía
Time Out Shanghai
Time Out Singapore
Time Out South of France
Time Out Stockholm
Time Out Sydney
Time Out Tokyo 東京
Time Out Toronto
Time Out Turin
Time Out Venice
Time Out Vienna
Time Out Washington, DC
Time Out Amsterdam
Time Out Athens
Time Out Bangkok
Time Out Barcelona
Time Out Beijing
Time Out Berlin
Time Out Boston
Time Out Brussels
Time Out Budapest
Time Out Buenos Aires
Time Out California
Time Out Cape Town
Time Out Chicago
Time Out Copenhagen
Time Out Croatia
Time Out Dubai
Time Out Dublin
Time Out Edinburgh
Time Out Florence
Time Out Havana
Time Out Hong Kong
Time Out Istanbul
Time Out Las Vegas
Time Out Lisbon
Time Out London
Time Out Los Angeles
Time Out Madrid
Time Out Mallorca
Time Out Marrakech
Time Out Miami
Time Out Milan
Time Out Mumbai & Goa
Time Out Naples
Time Out New Orleans
Time Out New York
Time Out Paris
Time Out Patagonia
Time Out Prague
Time Out Rio de Janeiro
Time Out Rome
Time Out San Francisco
Time Out Seville & Andalucía
Time Out Shanghai
Time Out Singapore
Time Out South of France
Time Out Stockholm
Time Out Sydney
Time Out Tokyo 東京
Time Out Toronto
Time Out Turin
Time Out Venice
Time Out Vienna
Time Out Washington, DC
Time Out Amsterdam
Time Out Athens
Time Out Bangkok
Time Out Barcelona
Time Out Beijing
Time Out Berlin
Time Out Boston
Time Out Brussels
Time Out Budapest
Time Out Buenos Aires
Time Out California
Time Out Cape Town
Time Out Chicago
Time Out Copenhagen
Time Out Croatia
Time Out Dubai
Time Out Dublin
Time Out Edinburgh
Time Out Florence
Time Out Havana
Time Out Hong Kong
Time Out Istanbul

In Context

Features

Gunsmiths at the **Alhambra**.

History

Fought over for centuries and admired for longer.

Andalucía has always had a character distinct from the rest of Spain. Invaders – trekking through the emptiness of the Castilian plains, or across from the deserts of North Africa, or sailing to the Mediterranean's westernmost reaches – saw it as a kind of paradise. Rolling hills, lush forests, fertile plains, bountiful seas and a mild climate have attracted everyone from the Greeks and Phoenicians of antiquity to the package tourists of today. The concept of Andalucía as a geographical area is most popularly attributed to the Moors. Although the name 'al-Andalus' was used freely to refer to the entire Moorish kingdom, which stretched as far north as the Pyrenees at one time, it is most strongly associated with the geographical area we know today, which the Moors singled out as 'Yesira al-andalus' ('the Island of al-Andalus').

Andalucía's shape is dictated by geography – it is largely cut off from the rest of Spain by a mountain range, the Sierra Morena, and for centuries there was only one entry point by land from the north: the Despeñaperros Pass, a dramatic gorge through the otherwise impenetrable sierra. To the west the River Guadiana provides the logical border with Portugal, while to the east the Sierra de los Filabres separates Andalucía from Murcia. Only in the far north-west, where the province of Huelva meets Extremadura, has the border been more fluid.

PREHISTORIC ANDALUCÍA (60,000 BC-1100 BC)

The region has a rich prehistory, and is scattered with early archaeological sites and artefact-packed local museums to prove it. The earliest evidence of human habitation in Spain is Neanderthal Man, or, rather, Woman – a 60,000-year-old female skeleton that was uncovered on Gibraltar.

Andalucía also abounds in cave paintings. Perhaps the most impressive are those in the Cueva de la Pileta, in the Serranía de Ronda, which date from c25,000 BC; images of animals, fish and magic symbols are etched in charcoal, yellow and red on the walls. Skeletons of Palaeolithic Man and pottery fragments have also been discovered here. The paintings in the Cueva de Nerja in Málaga province, and the

Cueva de Tajo de las Figueras, near Benalup de Sidonia in Cádiz province, date from a similar period and contain neolithic artefacts.

Southern Spain boasts the oldest dolmens in western Europe, on the outskirts of Antequera in Málaga province. These enormous megalithic tombs date back as far as 4500 BC; their interiors are covered with etchings and paintings.

'It was the arrival of the Phoenicians that would mark out a new era.'

The Bronze Age in Andalucía (from c2600 BC) is best represented by the settlement at Los Millares in Almería province, one of the most important of its kind in Europe. Finds from the area reveal a people who made bronze and stone weapons and tools, grew crops, and hunted as well as bred animals. The culture lasted some 800 years, but, despite its apparent sophistication, appears to have had little lasting influence on the region. Instead, it was the arrival of the Phoenicians that would mark out a new era of development in southern Spain.

TARTESSUS, PHOENICIANS AND CARTHAGINIANS (1100 BC-201 BC)

The Phoenicians are popularly said to have first landed in Andalucía at Cádiz (Gadir, as they knew it) in about 1100 BC. Originating in what is now Lebanon, these bold seafarers were interested in trade with the native Iberians rather than conquest, and were especially keen to get their hands on the region's great mineral wealth. In exchange, they, and subsequent Greek traders, brought with them two crops that have done more to shape Andalucía's landscape and subsequent history than any others – the grape and the olive.

The period of Phoenician influence in the region (during which they founded a series of coastal towns such as Málaga, Almuñecar and Adra) coincided with the golden age of the kingdom of Tartessus. This most mysterious and least documented of Andalucian civilisations supposedly covered all or most of the region at this time. For the Greeks, who first made landfall near Málaga in 636 BC, Tartessus was a promised land in the west, overflowing with natural wealth and ruled over by a powerful king called Arganthonius. Although some archaeological finds associated with the Tartessians have been discovered (including the treasure of Carambola, now in the Museo Arqueológico in Seville), historians and archaeologists are still struggling to establish more details of the dominion and culture of this legendary kingdom.

What is known is that during this period native Iberians prospered from trade with the Phoenicians and began to develop a parallel inland culture in hilltop settlements, found primarily in the east of the region. Towns were mainly residential and contained few public buildings. Two terracotta sculptures of women, the Dama de Baza and the Dama de Elche, represent a high point of the Iberian cultural legacy. Both pieces date from about 400 BC and were found in Granada province, although they are now on display in Madrid. The best collection of fifth-century BC Iberian sculptures, though, was unearthed near Porcuna and now rests in the Museo Provincial in Jaén.

The decline of Tartessus from about 550 BC had a detrimental effect on the Phoenicians, with whom the Tartessians had enjoyed an excellent trading relationship, and many Phoenician colonies disappeared at this time. Those that survived expanded under the rule of Carthage, a former Phoenician colony in modern-day Tunisia, whose dominion spread throughout the western Mediterranean.

Carthage appears to have crushed the power of Tartessus, but its aggressive expansionist policies were to be its undoing. The newly powerful Romans became increasingly concerned about events in the west, leading to the First Punic War of 264-241 BC, and the subsequent loss to the Carthaginians of many of their possessions in the western Mediterranean. Despite this setback, Carthage continued to expand across the Iberian peninsula from a new capital at Cartegena in Murcia. By 237 BC it had gained military control over most of Spain.

The Second Punic War was precipitated by Hannibal, the Carthaginian commander in Spain, who in 219 BC attacked Saguntum (now Sagunto, near Valencia), a Roman ally, before marching on to invade Italy. In retaliation, the Romans landed at modern Tarragona in Catalonia, with an army of 15,000 troops and headed south, conquering successive coastal towns and bringing an end to Carthaginian rule on the Iberian peninsula.

THE ROMANS (201 BC-AD 409)

By 201 BC, Rome was in control of most of present-day Spain. Occupation was not easy, however; guerrilla warfare was widespread across the peninsula (though less so in Andalucía), with frequent struggles between rival factions and challenges to Roman rule in both provinces. It was not until Julius Caesar's decisive victory against the supporters of Pompey at Munda near Bailén in 45 BC that an uneasy peace was established.

There followed a period of colonisation in which Roman towns, populated by Roman citizens, were established. Under the Emperor

Augustus the peninsula was divided again, this time into three provinces: Lusitania, encompassing modern Portugal; Hispania Citerior, covering the centre and Catalonia; and Baetica, roughly equivalent to modern Andalucía and part of Extremadura. The capital of Baetica was Córdoba.

Baetica played a key role in the development and prosperity of the Roman Empire, both commercially and culturally. Thanks to their long history of interaction with other cultures, the native inhabitants of the south took far more readily to Roman rule than elsewhere in Spain. Baetica was also the richest of the three provinces, producing olive oil, minerals from the Sierra Morena, wool and wine. The well-preserved town of Baelo Claudio, in Cádiz province, was the peninsula's major centre for production of *garum* (a fishy relish made from tuna, which was exported all over the Empire).

The emperors Trajan, Hadrian and Theodosius were born in Itálica (the first Roman city in Spain and now the region's most famous Roman ruins) and the intellectuals Seneca and Lucan were from Córdoba.

Roman bridges at Córdoba and Andújar, amphitheatres at Ronda la Vieja and Cádiz, and city walls and a necropolis at Carmona all testify to the Romans' lasting impact on Andalucía. They provided the region with a good transport infrastructure, developed a strong agricultural base, and established Latin as the foundation of the Spanish language, thus linking the peninsula to the rest of Europe.

VANDALS AND VISIGOTHS (AD 409-711)

However, as civil war wracked Italy in the late fourth and early fifth centuries, so decline set in across the Empire. In AD 409 tribes from northern Europe – the Vandals, Alans and Sueves – sensing an opportunity for plunder and colonisation, poured over the Pyrenees and settled in Spain and Portugal.

The Vandals quickly established themselves in Baetica, and although they left little in the way of monuments, they may have lent their name to the region – Vandalusia. In AD 416, while the rest of Spain fell to the semi-Romanised Visigoths from Gaul, the Vandals consolidated their power in the south, stubbornly refusing to budge until 429 when they headed south to North Africa. A treaty between Rome and the Visigoths in 456 led to a second invasion by the latter, and by the 470s the whole peninsula was under direct Visigoth rule.

The Visigoths were military men first and foremost, statesmen a poor second. They kept the majority of their subjects servile and relied on support from landowners in times of war. Despite frequent plots, counterplots and regicides, the Visigoths muddled along for three centuries under a succession of kings who varied in their ability to bind the country together.

Among the most significant rulers were Athanagild (554-67), who moved the capital from Seville to Toledo in central Spain, and his successor Leovigild (569-86), who reconquered much of the land around the Guadalquivir valley, which had been lost to Byzantine forces earlier in the sixth century. The zenith of Visigothic culture in Andalucía was the scholarship of St Isidore (560-636) from Seville.

'It is hard to overstate the influence and legacy of the Moorish occupation.'

The death of Leovigild's Catholic son Recared in 601 led to a century of political instability in the kingdom, culminating in civil war in 710, when Roderic, Duke of Baetica, usurped the Visigoth throne. Opponents of Roderic gained the support of Muslims from North Africa, and the new king was defeated by an Arab army in 711.

THE MOORS (711-1212)

It is hard to overstate the profound influence and lasting legacy of the Moorish occupation of Spain on Andalucía. The architecture and the landscape, the language and the food – all were shaped by more than 700 years of Islamic culture. At times, the Moors controlled almost the whole of the Iberian peninsula, but it is Andalucía (or al-Andalus as they knew it) that carries their mark most strongly.

In 710 a Moroccan officer called Tarif made an excursion across the Straits to the tip of land that now bears his name, Tarifa. A year later an army of 7,000 men led by Tariq ibn-Zayad made the same crossing, and, with the help of Visigoths opposed to King Roderic, won a historic battle at Barbate, on the River Guadelete. They went on to conquer the rest of the peninsula (apart from the mountains of Asturias in northern Spain) with remarkable ease within five years.

Historians still debate whether the word 'conquer' is the correct way to describe the Moorish occupation. It is not improbable that much of the population welcomed these relatively enlightened invaders, who tolerated both the Jewish and the Christian religions, encouraged cross-faith marriages and gave areas limited autonomy in return for taxes.

Power shifted between Tariq and his governor, Musa ibn Nusayr, during the early years, finally settling on Musa's son, Abd al-

What have the Moors done for us?

The English word 'Moor' comes from the Spanish '*moro*', meaning 'coloured' – though some historians argue it refers specifically to Mauretania. The word has been used indiscriminately for centuries to refer to Muslims, Persians and Indians, as well as the Berbers who made up the bulk of the Islamic forces that invaded Spain in 711 and were to change the face of the country, but particularly the region of Andalucía, forever.

The romantic, and sometimes rather vague, 'Moorish' archi-tour has been easy to export. Many travellers visit Andalucia specifically – or solely – to see Granada's Alhambra (*pictured*) and Generalife and Córdoba's Mezquita. They may tag on the ruins of Medina Azahara outside Córdoba and pause, briefly, at the Pass of the Moor's Sigh on the Sierra Nevada – reputedly where Boabdil, the last Moorish ruler, looked back on all he had lost.

Many Spanish etymologies find their root in the period when Hispania was a province of al-Andalus ('Land of the Vandals') and all words beginning with 'al' are of Arabic origin. Irrigation, agriculture, music, dance and food were touched by the scientific and cultural genius of the Moors. The use of saffron and cumin and the popularity of communal dishes – such as paella, *migas* (fried breadcrumbs or semolina), and *gachas* (a kind of wheat porridge) – hark back to the period of *la convivencia*, when the various cultures of Muslims, Christians, Jews and converts to Islam co-existed across the whole of central and southern Spain.

However, the nostalgic vision of Islamic Spain as a golden land of peace and tolerance – a vision perpetuated by the French, British and American Romantic travellers who 'rediscovered' Andalucía in the early 1800s (*see p21*) – is a misleading one. War, not peace, was the norm for much of the period. The initial Berber submission of Spain was fast and brutal and was followed by decades of factional fighting before the emergence of the Umayyads; later came the feuding of the 11th-century taifa states and two further Berber conquests. There were rumblings of Arab-Christian warfare during almost the entire period. Some historians have come to see the initial invasion as a liberation from the incumbent Visigoths, but it was as much a conquest and colonisation as the Christian Reconquista.

The issue of Arab-Christian coexistence has come to the fore in recent years. Three days after the bombings on the Madrid railway system on March 11, 2004, the Conservative Prime Minister José María Aznar lost power. In a speech later that year, Aznar alluded to the year 711 and claimed that 'Spain's problem with al-Qaeda starts in the eighth century... when a Spain recently invaded by the Moors refused to become just another piece in the Islamic world and began a long battle to recover its identity.'

Aznar's position had some similarities, however, to that of those on the opposite side of the debate such as Ayman al-Zawahiri, Osama bin Laden's right-hand man. When the US invaded Afghanistan, al-Zawahiri had pronounced: 'Let the whole world know that we shall never accept that the tragedy of Al Andalus should be repeated.'

These inflammatory statements not only play right into the hands of Spain's still formidable right wing, but have also led to 19th-century Romantic attitudes towards the Islamic past being taken up under the banner of political correctness. It may be tempting to look back on Moorish Spain as a model of mutual tolerance – but closer inspection reveals this to be an oversimplification.

Aziz, in 714. He promptly made Seville the capital of the Emirate in Spain, but after his assassination in 716, the capital moved to Córdoba, where it remained until the 11th century. For several decades, warring factions of Berbers, Syrians, Egyptians and Yemenis threatened to tear the fragile state apart. However, the arrival in 756 of a young prince from the Umayyad dynasty in Damascus, Abd al-Rahman, united these disparate elements and brought peace and prosperity to the region.

By the time of Abd al-Rahman's death in 788, al-Andalus stretched from the Mediterranean to the Pyrenees. His successors consolidated this power, and in 929 Abd al-Rahman III proclaimed himself the legitimate descendant of Mohammed, and ruler of an autonomous Caliphate, independent of Baghdad.

Andalucía now entered its greatest period of cultural, philosophical, scientific and artistic innovation. Urban life boomed and Córdoba soon became the largest city in Europe, a centre for study and for trade. Universities, mosques and palaces were built, including the Mezquita and the royal city of Medina Azahara. The countryside, too, underwent something of a renaissance, thanks to advanced irrigation techniques that made full use of the land.

The Moorish Golden Age was not to last. By 1008 al-Andalus was on the point of collapse, riven by financial, military and political crises. Much of the blame can be pinned on Abu al-Mansur, or Almanzor, who seized power from the boy Caliph Hisham II and led a series of bloody and ultimately fruitless military campaigns that squandered the wealth, and diluted the power, of the state. He spent profligately, rewarding his friends, paying off his enemies and dramatically increasing the size of the army.

On his death in 1002, al-Mansur was succeeded briefly by his son Abd al-Malik, who held the Caliphate together despite rising tensions until 1008. After this date, though, the disintegration of al-Andalus was swift. By 1031, when the Caliphate was abolished, the region had fragmented into 30 separate states, or *taifas*, run by different princes all jostling for political power, and Seville had replaced Córdoba as the most important city. Civil disobedience and riots were rife, and the once-subdued Christian kingdoms to the north were making ever more daring raids into al-Andalus.

In 1085 the King of Castilla and León, Alfonso VI, with the help of the warrior El Cid, captured Toledo. It was a significant loss for the *taifa* kings, who requested assistance from Morocco to defend their rapidly shrinking state. Enter the Almoravids, a fundamentalist fighting force, made up mainly of fanatical Berber tribesmen. By 1110, under the leadership of Yusuf ibn-Tashufin, al-Andalus was reunited, but this time under strict Islamic rule: Christianity was suppressed, and wine and poetry banned; tensions rose and civil strife again became the norm.

The Almoravid era was brought to a swift end some 50 years later by the invasion of the Almohads from Morocco. Led by a Muslim preacher named ibn-Tumart, the Almohads, whose name means 'Upholders of the Divine Unity', were even more fundamentalist than their predecessors. After several forays across the Straits and years of political turmoil, they had gained control of al-Andalus by 1173.

The following years saw an extension of the Almohad state as far as Lisbon in the west, Madrid in the north and the Balearic Islands in the Mediterranean. It was also a period of cultural and literary activity, which saw the building of the Giralda in Seville and the emergence of two great philosophers, ibn Rushd, better known as Averroës, and Maimonides, both of whom lived in Córdoba.

However, Christian forces were massing in the north, and by 1212 were in a position to launch an attack on the Almohads. Under the leadership of Alfonso VIII, the Christian armies secured a decisive victory on the plains of Las Navas de Tolosa, just to the south of the Despeñaperros Pass, thus opening the gateway to Andalucía, and signalling the beginning of the end for Moorish rule in Spain.

THE RECONQUISTA (1212-1492)

Under the crusading zeal of Iago (James) I of Aragón (1213-76), Fernando III of Castilla (1217-52) and Sancho II of Portugal (1223-48), the next 40 years saw almost the whole of al-Andalus fall into Christian hands during the early stages of the controversially named Reconquista (Reconquest): the Balearics and Badajoz in 1230; Córdoba in 1236; Valencia in 1238 and, in 1248, the big prize of Seville.

It was now that the word 'Mudéjar' ('persons allowed to remain') was first used to refer to Muslims living under Christian rule. As the Christians' grip on the region tightened, so did their religious bigotry: forced conversions and expulsions became commonplace, and the status of resident Moors was gradually eroded.

Conquered land was parcelled out in huge swathes to victorious noblemen, imposing a socially and economically ruinous system of immense estates (known as '*latifundia*'), absentee landlords and dispossesed masses. Incredibly, the pattern of land-ownership in Andalucía is not greatly different today, and continues to be a major source of economic and (to a lesser extent) political instability.

How things used to be: a map of Andalucía from 1638.

By 1248 just one Muslim state remained. The Nasrid Kingdom of Granada was founded by Mohammed ibn Yusuf ibn Nasr (known as Mohammed I) in 1237, and, amazingly, managed to survive (though often precariously) for a further 250 years. Stretching from the Mediterranean coast of Almería to Gibraltar, it repelled Christian invaders with a chain of castles along its borders, and with military back-up from Morocco. Most of the time, however, skilful diplomacy kept the infidels at bay. Life inside this tiny kingdom recalled the Golden Age of al-Andalus: the arts flourished and construction began on the world's most beautiful Moorish monument – the Alhambra.

Granada's fate was sealed by the marriage of Fernando II of Aragón and Isabel of Castilla in 1469 (who became known collectively as Los Reyes Católicos – literally, 'the Catholic Kings'), resulting in the union of the two most powerful Christian kingdoms in Spain. Fernando and Isabel's fundamentalist Catholic views would not tolerate religious diversity, and so they set about conquering the Moorish kingdom.

Málaga fell to Christian forces in 1487, followed by Baeza and Almería in 1489. In 1491 the Christians began an eight-month siege of Granada that culminated in its surrender. On 1 January 1492 Boabdil, last king of the Nasrid dynasty, handed over the keys of Granada to Fernando and Isabel, surrendering Moorish rule on the peninsula once and for all. As he left the outskirts he turned for one last look at his beloved city, at a spot now known as El Suspiro del Moro, 'the Moor's Sigh'.

THE SPANISH EMPIRE (1492-1700)

The two centuries following the taking of Granada are traditionally known as Spain's Golden Age – a period of unparalleled Christian wealth, expansionism and artistic achievement.

'By 1570 Seville was the largest city in Europe after Venice and Rome.'

In 1492 Cristóbal Colón (Christopher Columbus) set sail across the Atlantic from the coast of Huelva province and discovered the Americas. Within ten years the *conquistadores* had conquered much of the continent and established an enormous empire for their rulers in Spain. Gold, silver and precious stones poured into the region via Cádiz and up the Guadalquivir to Seville, which became one of the wealthiest and fastest-growing metropolises in Europe. By 1570 it was the largest city in Europe after Venice and Rome.

Meanwhile, Boabdil and his followers had decamped to the Alpujarras to set up a small community of about 250,000 people. The terms of surrender had guaranteed religious rights to Granada's former citizens, but this policy was soon reversed. Fernando and Isabel unleashed a wave of religious persecution and set up the Inquisition. Some 40,000 Jews fled the country after an edict in 1492, and in 1499 the fanatical Cardinal Cisneros ordered the forced baptism of 60,000 Muslims in Granada, resulting in a two-year revolt in the Alpujarras.

The Spanish reacted by sailing across the Straits and capturing the towns of Ceuta and Melilla on the Moroccan coast (both of which Spain still possesses), in an attempt to ensure no Muslim invasions could take place. Moorish clothing and speech were banned in Spain and unconverted Muslims were expelled; the Moors who remained became known as *moriscos*.

Carlos I (1516-56; more commonly known as Carlos V, or Charles V, the Holy Roman Emperor) spent most of his reign squandering Spain's new-found wealth in defence of his vast empire, which included the Netherlands and large chunks of France, as well as the Americas. Wars, poor governance and inflation took their toll, and by the time his son Felipe II (1556-98) succeeded to the throne, the country was almost bankrupt. Wealth continued to be concentrated in the hands of a few nobles whose enormous estates were worked by serf-like peasants who had no rights to the land.

In 1568 Felipe II determined to extinguish the last vestiges of Moorish culture in Spain. His decision sparked a revolt in the Alpujarras that was finally quashed in 1571, with the expulsion of a huge number of *moriscos* to North Africa. (It is said there are houses in Morocco that still contain the keys to the owners' 16th-century homes in Granada.) Felipe III (1598-1621) went one better, ordering the expulsion from Spain of all descendants of the Moors.

The consequences were not just personally disastrous for those exiled unfortunates, but also for the *vegas* (plains) that they had irrigated so skilfully and kept so productive. What had once been one of the wealthiest and most cultured corners of Europe now became one of its poorest and most backward. In hardship, the country turned to religion and developed many of the Catholic festivals and celebrations that are such a feature of the Andalucían calendar today.

By the 1620s money from the Americas was drying up and Spaniards were getting tired of financing profligate monarchs. Plagues devastated populations across Spain, particularly in Seville, and uprisings and skirmishes by disenchanted subjects broke out across the country, leading to the loss of Portugal in 1640. (The Netherlands and Spanish possessions in France were also lost.) Yet even despite its economic and political decline, Andalucía was the cradle for some of the finest Spanish artists of the century – Velázquez, Zurbarán and Murillo were all born in the region.

When Felipe IV (1621-65) died, he left a bitterly divided country under the leadership of the weak Carlos II. The French launched a series of raids in the 1690s and put increasing pressure on Carlos to appoint a French successor to the Spanish throne. Just before his death in 1700 Carlos complied, naming the Bourbon Duke of Anjou as the future king of Spain, Felipe V (1700-46).

REVIVAL (1700-92)

During the 18th century Spain appeared to rally under Bourbon rule; some cities in Andalucía, particularly Cádiz, even prospered as trade with the Americas revived. However, the reign of Felipe V was to have dire consequences for the Spanish succession and to lead to French occupation of Spain in the following century.

Soon after Felipe became king, war broke out between Spain and Archduke Charles of Austria, who had a rival claim to the Spanish throne. Charles was supported by Dutch and British forces, which captured Gibraltar in 1704. The Treaty of Utrecht (1713) ended the War of the Spanish Succession and recognised Felipe as the legitimate King of Spain, but at the expense of the Spanish Empire: Austria took the Spanish Netherlands and Spanish possessions in Italy, while the British claimed Menorca and broke Spain's monopoly on the slave trade to the Americas.

Fernando VI (1746-59) built up the Spanish navy, which took part in a brief war with the British in 1748 over American trade. This was followed by Spain's involvement in the Seven Years War (1761-63) and the War of American Independence (1779-83), during which Menorca and Florida were recaptured from the British, and Gibraltar lay under siege for a year.

The succession of Carlos III (1759-88) signalled an upturn in the fortunes of Andalucía, with wide-scale resettlement in the deserted countryside and the founding of new planned immigrant towns, among them La Carolina, La Louisiana and Olivares, just south of the Sierra Morena. A new age of enlightenment saw the emergence of various groups dedicated to improved farming techniques and mass education. Carlos also attempted to reform local government, particularly in Andalucía, where he ordered common lands to be redistributed as smallholdings to the poor and landless. He also oversaw a road-building programme to link disparate parts of the country, and exercised a more tolerant attitude towards the gypsies.

Peace with Britain in 1783 saw Spain's fortunes revive further: trade between Andalucía and the Americas was booming and the economy experienced ten years of sustained growth.

A DIVIDED COUNTRY (1792-1931)

The upheaval following the French Revolution was to bring development and progress within Spain to a halt. The weak Carlos IV (1788-1808) presided over a rapidly disintegrating Empire and a poverty-stricken country, with effective power in the hands of his chief minister Manuel Godoy. Godoy compromised with the French, attracting the enmity of the British, who blockaded the coast, effectively cutting off trade between Spain and the Americas and leading to a sharp decline in Cádiz's fortunes.

When the joint Spanish and French fleets were decisively defeated by Nelson at the Battle of Trafalgar off the coast of Cádiz province in 1805, Godoy was blamed for the defeat and was overthrown. Carlos abdicated in 1808, and the Emperor of France, Napoleon Bonaparte, seized the opportunity to gain control of Spain. Carlos and his son Fernando were escorted out of the country by French troops, and the Spanish crown was given to Napoleon's brother Joseph.

French rule was hugely unpopular with the Spanish populace: spontaneous riots broke out across the country on 2 May 1808 and were brutally suppressed by French troops. Meanwhile, local administrators raised armies against the French occupiers. The British could not accept French hegemony in Spain, and landed in Portugal, starting the Peninsular War. The first major battle took place at Bailén in Córdoba province in 1808, where a Spanish army unexpectedly defeated the French.

The Spanish court and what remained of its government fled to Cádiz, where in 1812 it established a parliament (Cortes) and published a liberal Spanish constitution that was to become a talisman of democratic Spain. A year later, Spanish, Portuguese and British forces, led by the Duke of Wellington, forced Joseph back into France, and Fernando VII (1814-33) returned as king. In the meantime, most of Spain's American colonies had broken free of colonial rule, and the last Spanish pretence of playing a world role evaporated.

Although a fledgling Spanish democracy had been born during the French occupation, too many non-liberal pro-monarchist factions remained powerful around the country for it to survive: the Cortes was abolished and its leading liberals were put to death – acts of conservative despotism that sowed the seeds for the eventual Civil War.

A succession crisis led to the First Carlist War (1833-39), a civil war that was repeated in 1872-76 in the Second Carlist War, during which time (1873-74) Spain briefly experienced its First Republic.

Andalucía, at the vanguard of the political reforms of the early 19th century, was left more backward and impoverished than ever by their suppression: peasants continued to struggle to eke an existence from land they did not own; foreigners ran the agriculture and mining operations; and Cádiz was again reduced to an insignificant port. It was perhaps inevitable, then, that the region would be open to new political ideas, among them anarchism, which came to Andalucía in 1870. The backwardness of the region contributed to its political radicalism, and led in 1910 to the establishment of the anarcho-syndicalist union, the CNT.

Violence in the shape of terrorism and banditry continued unchecked, particularly in the lawless mountain areas. This atmosphere contributed to the modern view of Andalucía as a land of romance, exoticism and danger. Foreign writers, among them Washington Irving and Richard Ford, were attracted to the region and helped perpetuate this image.

Meanwhile, the last fragments of the Spanish Empire were slipping away. By the end of the 19th century Spain had lost Cuba, its last American colony, and was faced with political unrest at home, despite the introduction of universal male suffrage in 1892.

'Conservative forces saw dictatorship as the solution to Spain's problems.'

Political strife was compounded by the lack of continuity in government, with no fewer than 34 administrations holding power between 1902 and 1923. General Primo de Rivera attempted to assert stability on the country by carrying out a military coup in 1923.

For a brief period, prosperity seemed to be returning. Spain still had international pretensions, as the 1929 Expo in Seville was intended to prove, but the fair left the city bankrupt and political and economic tensions re-emerged. Primo de Rivera's dictatorship collapsed and Alfonso XIII abdicated in 1931.

With this a dangerous precedent had been set – conservative forces increasingly begin to see military might and dictatorship as the solution to Spain's problems.

FROM REPUBLIC TO CIVIL WAR (1931-39)

The Second Republic was established on 14 April 1931. It was Spain's first genuine democracy and was greeted with widespread celebrations in the street. In Andalucía it was met with jubilation by the poor labourers, who for the first time could look forward to a landowning future, and horror by landowners.

Expectations were high – too high for the new government to deliver. Caught between the hopes of the deprived and the fears of the conservatives, the nation again began to fray. Strikes were called, unemployment soared and divisions occurred within the Republican movement, foreshadowing the split in the Civil War between the anarchists and the socialists. The Right, meanwhile, was divided between traditional conservatives and the fascist Falangist party, established in 1933 by José Antonio Primo de Rivera. Elections in 1934 saw the Republicans replaced by a radical right-wing government. Peasant unrest grew, and whispers of an army coup were rife.

The 1936 election was won by the left-wing Popular Front alliance, but this only caused the violence to escalate, with assassinations and bloody reprisals on both sides. The scene was set for outright civil war.

The Civil War (1936-39) was the most divisive, bloody and bitter episode in modern Spanish history, involving not simply Nationalists versus Republicans, but also landowners versus peasants, anarchists versus communists, and the Catholic Church versus libertarians. It is also widely regarded as a prelude to World War II, since the non-intervention of both Britain and France and an embargo on arms imports from the United States allowed Hitler, Mussolini and Stalin to use Spain as a testing ground for their latest aircraft and military equipment. Foreign troops gained combat experience in the field, and modern military techniques such as Blitzkrieg bombing were first employed. (The most infamous example of the latter was the destruction of Guernica.)

The war was also the last 'romantic', idealised war in Europe. It was popularly regarded the world over as a fight against fascism and attracted hundreds of foreign volunteers, known as the International Brigades, to join the left-wing Republican cause.

Although subsequently many historians regarded the outbreak of war as inevitable, its scale and scope were unexpected at the time. In fact, when General Francisco Franco launched his Nationalist military uprising in Spanish Morocco on 17 July 1936 he did not expect the coup to last more than a few days, so confident was he of success. Preliminary signs were good for the Nationalists, with Ceuta and Melilla secured by that evening, allowing safe passage by German transport planes from Africa to the ports of Andalucía the following morning.

On 18 July the rebel forces captured Cádiz, Jerez, Algeciras and La Línea, encouraged in no small part by landowners of the huge Andalucían estates. Seville, Huelva and

Granada – where rebel troops razed the Albaicín district to the ground – all fell a few days later.

Granada was the scene of one of the most infamous episodes of the war, which galvanised intellectuals and artists in France and Britain to oppose the Nationalist rebels. Federico García Lorca, who had returned to his home town just a few days before the uprising, was arrested by Nationalist forces and taken to the village of Víznar, where he was shot. His body was never found and his death remained a forbidden topic in Spain until after Franco's death.

The Nationalists' initial swift progress through Andalucía met with firm resistance at Málaga and all points east. Elsewhere in Spain, Galicia and most of Castilla and León had fallen, but the rest of the country, including Madrid, Barcelona and Valencia, remained loyal to the Republicans.

In the second week of August, however, the Nationalists began to head east, capturing Córdoba and most of Granada province, before heading south to Ronda, where they exacted swift and bloody retribution on its citizens, throwing many into the town's gorge, as re-created in Ernest Hemingway's *For Whom the Bell Tolls*. By the end of September the Nationalists had pressed deep into eastern Andalucía and now controlled the provinces of Huelva, Cádiz, Seville and Córdoba and large parts of Granada and Málaga. Only Almería and Jaén remained under Republican command.

Málaga held out until February 1937, when Nationalist forces were joined by 10,000 Italian fascist troops and air cover from the Legionary Air Force. They attacked from all sides, including a naval bombardment by the Nazi warship *Admiral Graf Spee*, and within three days were at the city's outskirts. The Republican force of 12,000 militia, a third of whom had no rifles, was powerless to defend the city. The Nationalist atrocities committed in Málaga were some of the most horrific in the whole war: 3,500 people were killed in six days and a further 16,500 over the next seven years. By 1938 it is estimated that 150,000 people Andalucíans had been murdered by the Nationalists. The fall of Málaga signalled the end of the war in the south, and the two provinces which had held out against the Nationalists – Jaén and Almería – remained largely unaffected by the fighting in the north of the country until the end of the war.

Elsewhere in Spain the Republicans were gradually losing territory in a series of bitter, bloody battles, and both sides suffered terrible losses during the winter of 1937, which was one of the coldest on record. Thoroughly demoralised, the Republicans offered little resistance when the Nationalists advanced east towards the Mediterranean coast in spring 1938. They did, however, launch one last disastrous counter-offensive at the Battle of the Ebro on 25 July 1938, resulting by November in the loss of 70,000 Republican troops and a large part of the Republican air defences.

On 26 January 1939 the Nationalists triumphantly entered Barcelona, and on 27 March the Republican frontline spontaneously disappeared as the Nationalists took Madrid, thereby gaining control of the whole country.

REPRESSION AND REFORM (1939-75)

The Civil War was followed by a brutal period of retribution. Anyone with left-wing sympathies was targeted, resulting in mass imprisonments, show trials and executions. Many Republicans fled to refugee camps in France; towns were left in ruins, and the remaining citizens were reduced to near-starvation. Andalucía in particular saw mass emigration that decimated the countryside population.

Franco became chief of state and head of government in September 1939 and declared his shattered country neutral when hostilities broke out in the rest of Europe later that month. He then set about eradicating everything he believed had 'infected' the country during its experiment with democracy and liberalism. Strikes were banned on penalty of death, wages were reduced to 1936 levels and all the land that had been redistributed under the agrarian reforms of the early 1930s was given back to its original owners. Democrats, atheists, liberals, communists, Jews, anarchists, Freemasons – all were targeted and persecuted. The Catholic Church, in contrast, was elevated to an unprecedented level of importance, playing a part in almost every aspect of public life.

'By the mid 1950s inflation was rife and a series of strikes spread across the country.

Spain became insular and isolated during the 1940s, choosing to stay clear of the world stage. However, Franco's attempts at national self-sufficiency didn't work, and by the end of the decade it became obvious that the economy had to be liberalised. In 1953 Franco handed over Spanish land to the USA in exchange for US$625 million. The US used the land to establish a number of military bases, among them Rota in Cádiz province. Two years later Spain rejoined the United Nations.

By the mid 1950s the Spanish economy had still not improved, inflation was rife and a series of strikes spread across the country. The government reacted with further liberal economic reforms, including the introduction of industrial programmes in the major cities and a dam project in Andalucía, intended to stop the crippling cycle of floods and famine.

The key initiative, however, was the development of the Costa del Sol as a first experiment in mass tourism. It led to increased prosperity for Andalucía – at least for those who lived along the coast. Throughout the 1960s Spain enjoyed growth rates twice as high as other countries in the European Economic Community. Annual tourist numbers increased from four million to 14 million during that decade, and tourist spending leapt from less than £80 million to more than £500 million.

By the early 1970s Spain was industrially and economically on a par with the rest of western Europe. Politically and culturally, however, it was still lagging behind. Renewed regionalism and a rediscovery of officially forbidden customs and languages became widespread. Student riots broke out and were brutally suppressed by the authorities, and the Basque separatist group ETA was formed.

The last two years of Franco's rule were characterised by social unrest and the dictator's gradual descent into Parkinson's disease. Finally, the king-in-waiting, Juan Carlos, was nominated by Franco as his successor.

MODERN ANDALUCÍA (FROM 1975)

Franco died in November 1975 and Juan Carlos was crowned two days later. The monarch was committed to democracy, but was aware that the country was still riven by rival factions. He successfully manoeuvred to replace the old Francoist Prime Minister Carlos Arrias Navarro with Adolfo Suárez, who was also committed to reform. After victory in the 1977 elections, Suárez steered the country towards democracy and drafted a modern constitution, approved by 88 per cent of voters in December 1978.

Just three years after the dictator's death, the Franco regime had been dismantled and replaced with a modern democracy. The army, however, was still fiercely loyal to Franco's memory, and unhappy at the pace of change. On 23 February 1981 Lieutenant Colonel Antonio Tejero led an attempted coup on the parliament. Miscalculations by Tejero and the intervention of the king as commander-in-chief of the armed forces meant that the coup failed, but its consequences were far-reaching.

Spaniards, outraged at Tejero's actions, made their disapproval felt in the elections of 1982, when the left-wing PSOE, led by the Sevillian Felipe González, swept to victory. The pace of change following the elections was rapid, and with a *sevillano* in charge of the government, Andalucía returned to the forefront of Spanish policy and politics. In 1986 Spain joined the European Community and NATO, regional autonomy was granted, democracy was consolidated and the arts flourished.

Felipe González, former prime minister.

In 1992 the quincentenary of Columbus's discovery of the Americas was marked by high-profile celebrations all over Spain: Seville put on another hugely expensive Expo; a high-speed train link, known as the Alta Velocidad España (AVE), was constructed between Andalucía and Madrid; Barcelona got ready to host the Olympic Games; and Madrid was made European City of Culture.

This enormous national spending spree led to a recession and a loss of support for the PSOE, which was compounded by damaging stories about high-level corruption. The 1996 elections saw victory for the first right-wing government since Franco's death, the Partido Popular led by José María Aznar. Spain's complex labour laws were revised and the economy was further liberalised under the conservatives, who won a second term in 2000.

In Andalucía there has been a general swing to the right since the mid 1990s. The PP made substantial gains in 2003 municipal elections, despite huge opposition to the Iraq War, and would almost certainly have remained in power had it not been for the Madrid bombing of 11 March 2004. Instead, the PSOE's José Luis Rodríguez Zapatero became the new Prime Minister, but grumbles about his rise to power being influenced by terrorism have since been silenced thanks to a strong performance at the top and a likeable public persona.

Key events

PREHISTORY TO THE PHOENICIANS

c60,000 BC Evidence of Neanderthal Man on Gibraltar.
c25,000 BC Prehistoric man occupies caves in Málaga province.
2600 BC Copper Age settlement at Los Millares in Almería.
1100 BC Phoenicians land at Cádiz.
c1500-550 BC Kingdom of Tartessus dominant in the Guadalquivir valley.
500-400 BC Carthage colonises south Spain.
241-201 BC Iberian Peninsula falls to the Romans in the Punic Wars.

ROMANS, VANDALS AND VISIGOTHS

205 BC Founding of Itálica, first Roman city on the Iberian Peninsula.
27 BC Southern Iberia becomes Roman province of Baetica; Córdoba is its capital; start of Golden Age of Roman Empire in Spain.
AD 409 Vandals invade Spain from the north and settle in Baetica.
AD 456-711 Second Visigoth invasion leads to colonisation of the Peninsula.

THE MOORS

710 Tarif crosses the Straits from Morocco to the Andalucían coast at Tarifa.
711-16 Tariq ibn-Zayad defeats Visigoths and goes on to conquer the rest of the Peninsula.
716 Córdoba becomes capital of al-Andalus.
756 Abd al-Rahman unites al-Andalus, heralding the Moorish Golden Age in Spain; construction of Córdoba's Mezquita begun.
929 Abd al-Rahman III establishes the Córdoban Caliphate.
1031 Caliphate abolished; al-Andalus is divided into 30 *taifa* kingdoms.
1085 Loss of Toledo to Alfonso VI.
1110 Al-Andalus reunited under the Almoravids from North Africa.
1160 Almohad invasion.
1173-1211 Expansion and consolidation of Almohad kingdom; Seville's Giralda is built.
1212 Alfonso VIII defeats the Almohads at Las Navas de Tolosa.

THE RECONQUISTA

1214-48 Christian forces take control of major cities in Andalucía; Seville falls in 1248.
1237-1492 Nasrid Kingdom of Granada. Moorish arts flourish; the Alhambra is built.
1487-92 Fernando and Isabel take control of major cities in the Nasrid kingdom, culminating in the surrender of Granada.

THE SPANISH EMPIRE

1492 Columbus discovers the Americas; Spanish Empire is established.
1499-1501 First Alpujarran uprising.
1520 Carlos I becomes Holy Roman Emperor Carlos V. Start of Spanish Golden Age.
1568-71 Second Alpujarran uprising.
1609 Expulsion of *moriscos* from Spain.
1649 Great plague in Seville.
1700 Succession of Bourbon Duke of Anjou as Felipe V of Spain, triggering the War of the Spanish Succession.
1704 British forces capture Gibraltar.
1713 Spain loses territory to Britain and Austria by the Treaty of Utrecht.
1759 Succession of Carlos III heralds an age of enlightened despotism in Spain.

A DIVIDED COUNTRY

1805 Battle of Trafalgar.
1808 Napoleon seizes power and gives the Spanish crown to his brother Joseph, precipitating the Peninsular War.
1812 The Cortes in Cádiz produces the first Spanish constitution.
1813-14 French driven from Spain by British and Dutch forces, ending the Peninsular War; Fernando VII is restored to the throne.
1833-36 First Carlist War.
1834 Andalucía divided into eight provinces.
1872-76 Second Carlist War.
1873-74 First Republic.
1892 Universal male suffrage introduced.
1929 Expo in Seville.

FROM REPUBLIC TO DICTATORSHIP

1931 Second Republic established.
1936-39 Civil War.
1939 General Franco becomes chief of state and head of government.
1953 Spanish land sold to USA for use as military bases.
1950s-60s Development of the Costa del Sol begins. Economic revival in Spain.

MODERN ANDALUCÍA

1975 Franco dies; Juan Carlos becomes king.
1981 Attempted army coup leads to victory for socialist Sevillian Felipe González in the 1982 elections.
1992 Quincentenary of Columbus's discovery of the Americas; Expo in Seville.
2002 Euro replaces the peseta.
2004 Madrid bombings; socialist José Luis Rodríguez Zapatero wins elections.

Andalucía Today

The playground of Europe – at a certain cost.

Arriving at Málaga airport, and driving west along the Costa del Sol, most first-time visitors to Andalucía are overwhelmed by the scale of development. Mile upon mile of hotels, apartment complexes, resorts, holiday villas, golf courses, marinas, amusement parks and casinos stretch monotonously back from the beach and into the hills. And the construction shows little sign of slowing down – in 2005 over 300,000 new homes were built on the Spanish coast, with an equal number scheduled for 2006.

Most Andalucíans don't see a problem: tourism is the industry that transformed this region in the 1960s from poverty-ravaged rural backwater to Europe's cheap 'n' cheerful summer playground, and tourism is the industry that, by and large, keeps it alive today. On the dark side, however, the demand for holiday homes has made the Costa del Sol the favourite destination for Europe's money launderers. The construction business, aided by offshore financial services in Gibraltar, is the ideal way to clean up the millions accrued through arms smuggling, drug trafficking and, increasingly, prostitution. In a separate development, the mayor and a host of other officials and businessmen were arrested in Marbella in 2006, charged with corruption and influence-peddling. According to the prosecution, one man controlled all planning permissions for the Marbella region, which he sold off to developers, using some of the proceeds to pay off officials and pocketing millions. All the accused deny all the charges.

THE TOURISTS

Annually, Spain attracts 50 million visitors, 14 per cent of whom holiday in Andalucía. Add to these seven million foreigners the 13 million Spaniards who head south for their holidays every year and the scale and importance of tourism to Andalucía is immediately apparent.

But package tourists are becoming increasingly discerning and, as a result, many coastal towns are smartening themselves up. Once-dirty beaches are being cleaned, swish promenades are being built and ugly tower blocks torn down. The result is that the Costa del Sol is no longer a cheap destination. Ironically, this investment – combined with a rising euro, so-called 'destination fatigue' and stiff competition from emerging markets such as Turkey and Bulgaria – could price it out of the cheap sun and beach market.

Yet the developers build on, and no one with the power to do so seems inclined to say 'enough', especially as – unofficially – the major political parties are partly funded through the commissions they charge construction companies. The days of unchecked building might be over, but the trend for creating land-hungry, low-rise *urbanizaciones*, five-star resorts, golf courses and luxury marinas has resulted in just as much, if not more, ecological damage.

Few of the lessons that should have been learned from the wholesale concreting over of the Costa del Sol seem to have been absorbed, and the region's few remaining stretches of unspoiled coastline – such as the once-pristine

Costa de la Luz, and parts of the supposedly protected Cabo de Gata in Almería – seem likely to fall before the regiment of bulldozers.

It is dawning on the regional government that it is not economically or socially healthy for the region for such a great proportion of tourist euros go to the coast, while much of the interior remains poor and underdeveloped. Government is now pushing for upmarket tourists to spend euros inland; *turismo rural* is the buzz-phrase, with an increasing number of visitors seeking out villas away from the coast.

THE FARMERS

Head inland, far from the coast and the cities, and you'll see little prosperity. Unemployment stands at a hefty 17.2 per cent, and much of the work is still seasonal, relying primarily on the olive harvest. Outside this period the unemployment rate in many areas runs at more than twice that of the rest of Spain and, as more young people are drawn to the coast for employment, the villages continue to empty out.

Andalucía is not wholly dependent on tourism, though – farming is also a key pillar of the regional economy. Spain has the third-largest grape harvest in the world; in Andalucía this is centred on wine and sherry production, mainly in Cádiz province. Production has, though, suffered in recent years due to a fall in exports to the UK, the biggest sherry market, and consequently Jerez and other towns heavily reliant upon sherry production have seen a sharp rise in unemployment.

Andalucía is pioneering wind-farming, solar power and hydro-electricity.

Jaén and southern Córdoba provinces form the world's largest olive-producing area, but the dangers of relying on an economic monoculture are becoming apparent. Competition from North Africa has badly affected production; EU subsidies are due to be slashed as Spain already exceeds its subsidy quota by 50 per cent, leading to a glut of olive oil; and health fears regarding the chemicals used to treat the trees might soon affect sales.

The one undoubted boom area in farming is in Almería province, where the *plasticultura* industry (growing produce under plastic), which supplies most of the year-round fruit and veg to northern Europe, is thriving. Yet this too has plenty of adverse environmental and social consequences caused by the demands on natural resources and the influx of foreign workers – not to mention the aesthetic horrors of an entire coastline under plastic.

Livestock farming is important – Andalucía supports a million cattle, including cows for meat and milk, and, of course, fighting bulls (*toros bravos*). Pig breeding is also huge, but the market for pork is confined mainly to Spain. Fish stocks, as everywhere in Europe, have been severely depleted. Even staples like tuna, which traditionally kept entire villages along the Costa de la Luz employed, are becoming scarce. Ironically, 'tuna ranching' (farming), which also attracts high EU subsidies, is contributing to the decline of wild tuna stocks.

There is little heavy industry in the region today. Mining in Huelva (even the famed Río Tinto mines) is minimal, oil-refining is confined to Algeciras and shipbuilding to near Cádiz. Salt-mining remains big business, however.

Andalucía is also pioneering renewable energy projects – wind-farming in Tarifa (which has spread to the Alpujarras and the Sierra Sur de Jaén, scarring the countryside without reducing the need for nuclear power stations), solar power in Almería and hydro-electricity in Málaga.

LOS INMIGRANTES

Despite an imperial past, Spain, unlike the rest of western Europe, has never assimilated a non-Spanish population, largely because the country was pretty much a closed shop until the late 1960s. Even now most non-whites in Spain are illegal immigrants, either hawking stuff on the streets or working in the *plasticultura* farms.

Andalucía's proximity to Africa means that it has a high proportion of the country's illegal immigrants. The previous government's response was predictably tough: repealing a law that would have led to the naturalisation of many immigrants; denying work or residency permits to anyone already working; and tightening up external border controls. Despite this, boat-loads of hopefuls continue to attempt to cross the narrow but treacherous Strait of Gibraltar to Andalucía. Many hundreds have died in the attempt, but since patrols were stepped up on the strait, immigrants now attempt the longer and still more dangerous trip from Mauritania to the Canary Isles.

At the other extreme is immigration of another kind – northern Europeans buying up second homes. It is estimated that there are some half a million foreign homeowners in Andalucía alone. Once confined to the coast, it now seems that no part of Andalucía is out of bounds for Brits and Germans trying to get away from it all. Although locals benefit from the original sale, non-property-owners and young people are increasingly unable to afford to buy, and it's not uncommon to find villages almost entirely populated by foreigners.

THE CRIMINALS

The Costa del Sol has long been known as the Costa del Crime, but while this was once the stuff of comedy shows about a couple of bank robbers from Bethnal Green, in recent years Andalucía has been attracting bigger and nastier fish. It is the preferred haunt for Russian and other eastern European gangsters who readily merge into their own communities on the *costa* while finding ready outlets for money laundering. Where once they treated Spain as a place to relax and run operations at home but at a safe distance, increasingly they do business in Spain itself. This is particularly evident in the huge rise in the number of prostitutes, over 95 per cent of whom are immigrants, many from the former eastern bloc. A recent report claimed that prostitution in Andalucía generated €2 billion a year. In the past two years, police on the Costa del Sol have confiscated hundreds of properties and hundreds of millions in cash – including money linked to Russian oligarchs – in raids related to money laundering and property scams.

THE ROCK

The continuing saga of Gibraltar's future has been put on the back burner once again after a fraught period a couple of years ago. In 2002 Tony Blair and the then Spanish Prime Minister José María Aznar tried to sew up a quick solution with a joint sovereignty deal. But no deal can go ahead without agreement from the inhabitants of the Rock, and that is not going to happen in a hurry: a referendum in November 2002 resulted in a 99 per cent 'No' vote.

The British government knows that for a joint sovereignty deal to have any chance of returning a 'Yes' vote, it must be seen as a permanent agreement and not as a stepping-stone to full Spanish sovereignty.

In the Anglo-Gibraltar talks held March 2006 to revise the 1969 constitution, Gibraltar inserted a new clause referring to 'self-determination' but the British government says this will not affect its international status. Meanwhile, the socialist government of José Luis Zapatero has been too busy dealing with the question of Catalan and Basque autonomy to give the problems of the Rock more than its most cursory attention. However, the irony of the continued existence of Ceuta and Melilla, the Spanish protectorates in Morocco, seems lost on all Madrid governments, whatever their political stripe.

THE POLITICAL LANDSCAPE

President Manuel Chaves secured a fifth term for himself and the socialist PSOE in the 2004 regional elections, creating history in the process by forming the first regional government in Spain with more women than men (eight to six). One of his first declarations was a pledge to improve the 'quality of democracy' in Andalucía by creating a register of MPs' wealth and interests, and improving communications with senior cabinet members and the public, a public recognition – made more urgent by the Marbella scandal – that politics in the region has been scarred by nepotism and backhanders, and a canny way to tell the populace that he has no intention, after so long in power, of becoming complacent.

Chaves also pledged to both improve relations with Madrid and keep up the pressure to ensure Andalucía is high on the central government's agenda – improving the region's infrastructure is his main priority. He had a difficult eight years while the PP (Partido Popular) were in power in Madrid – they adopted a confrontational stance towards all the powerful autonomous regions – but Chaves has in fellow socialist Zapatero a more conciliatory negotiating partner. He has also identified the creation of new companies and investment in innovation as two other key priorities and, to that end, has created a new Department of Equality and Innovation. Many of the bigger infrastructure projects, such as the extension of the AVE high-speed train link from Seville to Málaga (due by 2007) and a new metro service in Seville, as well as ongoing road-building schemes, have also received a boost under the Zapatero regime. Andalucía has, on the back of the revised Statute of Autonomy brought about in Catalonia, itself gained more fiscal autonomy.

THE FUTURE

Aside from improvements in infrastructure, communications with the rest of the world have also improved: there are now hundreds more direct flights (many of them with budget airlines) to Jerez, Granada, Málaga, Almería and Seville. The type of tourist may be changing, but the numbers stay the same, and the new, more upmarket visitors spend more money: talk of the death of tourism in Andalucía is certainly premature.

Andalucía retains a cultural identity that sets it apart from the rest of Spain, yet it is also being drawn ever closer to the rest of the country. The region may still celebrate its romantic roots with wild abandon, but it is now also aware of its role within the national story. Sadly, the spectre of global terrorism now hangs heavy over the region. But a renewed political will and an ongoing modernisation drive could see Andalucía regain its historical position as a major player in Europe.

Becquer surveys Parque de María Luisa. *See p31.*

Literary Andalucía

From Lorca to Rushdie, this is a region that has captured many literary hearts.

Andalucía, a land encapsulating all the romantic clichés of Spain, has inspired some of the greatest foreign writings on the country. But it is also a place whose seductive beauty has nurtured many of Spain's finest poets.

THE POETS OF AL-ANDALUS

The first of the major Andalucían writers were the poets of the Islamic period, beginning with those from the intensely competitive *taifa* kingdoms. The intellectual giant of this period was **Ibn Hazm** (994-1064), a Córdoba-born polymath who moved to Almería at the time of the collapse of the Caliphate, and wrote one of the most translated works from Muslim Spain, *The Ring of the Dove*. This extraordinary book, which is partly a Neo-Platonic treatise on love, partly an autobiography, and partly a collection of the author's own poems, offers a penetrating psychological portrait of the human heart, as well as interesting titbits about the sexual customs and preferences of the time. Córdoban men, for instance, really did prefer blondes.

Love was a major preoccupation of the other Islamic poets of the 11th century, including, most famously, **Ibn Zaydun** (1003-70), a Córdoban writer whose life and work were dominated by his passion for the daughter of Caliph al-Mustakfi, Princess Walladah, herself a poetess. When she abandoned him for a wealthier and more influential lover, he wrote a vituperative piece about his rival (a man as 'worthless as a fly or mosquito') that had him thrown briefly into jail. A more positive outcome of his rejection was a poem in which the unending anguish of his loss was expressed through constant repetition of the same rhyme. It has since become one of the most famous love poems in the Arab language.

Another celebrated love affair of this time was the relationship between the poet ruler of Seville, **al-Mutamid** (reigned 1069-91), and a woman called Itimad. His feverish love poems addressed to her ('I am pining because of being separated from you/Inebriated with the wine of my longing for you') were succeeded in later life by works conveying a general nostalgia for the past and for Andalucía. By then he had been exiled to the remote Moroccan village of Agmat, where his mausoleum is still a place of pilgrimage for sentimental *sevillanos*.

The 11th and 12th centuries also saw the emergence of some of the finest of Spain's Jewish poets (an excellent English anthology is David Goldstein's *The Jewish Poets of Spain 900-1250*, Harmondsworth, 1971), who, though writing in Hebrew, followed classical Arabic forms of verse. **Samuel Ha-Nagrid**, who was born in Córdoba in 993, and rose to become vizier to the Zirids in Granada, was a master of martial verse, and the only Jew ever to lead a Muslim army. Whereas he evoked the *taifa* kingdoms at their height, the collapse of these kingdoms after 1089 was brilliantly conveyed by **Judah Ha-Levi**, who, after long stays in Lucena, Seville and Granada, set off to the Middle East, where, according to legend, he was killed at the moment of reaching the gates to Jerusalem.

The last phase in the history of al-Andalus, the period of the Nasrids, was marked in literature by poets whose verse is inscribed in plaster all over the walls of the Alhambra. Among these writers was the Loja-born **Ibn al-Khatib** (1313-71), a vizier to both Yusuf I and Muhammad V, and whose varied and prolific output included the historical work *The Shining Rays of the Full Moon*, one of the major sources for our knowledge of the Nasrid Golden Age.

But the greatest of those poets who turned the Alhambra into what has been called the most sumptuous book of verse ever produced, was Ibn al-Khatib's ruthless protégé **Ibn Zamrak** (1333-92). Born to a Granadan ironworker, and an early beneficiary of the city's newly founded *madrasa* (a collegiate institution with bursaries for the poor), Ibn Zamrak supplanted his mentor as vizier by spreading rumours that led to the man's flight to Morocco and eventual murder by strangling. As with all but one of the Alhambra poets, Ibn Zamrak met a violent death, being killed with all his family on the orders of Yusuf II. The sordid political manoeuvrings of his life and times were in ironic contrast to his lyrical, panegyric verse, which is flooded with references to nuptial diadems, paradisal gardens, serene full moons and other 'enfolding wonders'.

AFTER THE RECONQUISTA

The legends of the last days of Nasrid Spain were assimilated by the Christians, giving rise in c1550 to one of the most popular 16th-century novels, the anonymous *Story of the Abencerrage and the Beautiful Jarifa*. In the meantime, the spirit of Christian triumphalism that set in during the reigns of Carlos V and Felipe II was reflected in the rhetorical, Italianate verse of **Fernando de Herrera** (1534-97), known to his contemporaries as 'The Divine'. A *sevillano* who spent all his life in his native city (which he called, in his poem 'Seville', 'not a city but a universe'), Herrera acquired much of his great learning through belonging to one of Spain's earliest known intellectual salons or *tertulias*.

It was also attended by Columbus's great grandson, Álvaro Colón, whose wife Leonor was the subject of many of Herrera's tedious outpourings of platonic love. A rather more down-to-earth regular at this *tertulia* was **Baltasar del Alcázar** (1530-1606), a poet whose racy, light verse – which was never intended for publication – captures the sense of humour for which the Sevillians are famous. 'Three things', begins one of his best-known works, 'keep my heart love's captive:/the fair Inés, smoked ham/and aubergines with cheese'.

Beyond the refinements of the *tertulia*, a pungent, vibrant and crime-ridden Seville was the setting for lively theatrical activity. The rough-and-ready plays of the Seville-born actor, writer and manager **Lope de Rueda** (c1505-65) were a prelude to the popular drama of the Spanish Shakespeare, **Lope de Vega** (1562-1635), whose comedy *El Arenal de Sevilla* captures the vitality and cosmopolitanism of the city's port. But no writer evoked Seville's Golden Age better than **Miguel de Cervantes** (1547-1616), who spent much of the 1580s and '90s in Andalucía, living an itinerant existence, still hoping to make a name as a playwright. His knowledge of Andalucía, in particular the lowlife of Seville (a place he described as 'the asylum of the poor and refuge of the outlaw'), is apparent in the entertaining short stories that make up his *Exemplary Novels* (1616).

The only leading Golden Age writer actually native to Andalucía was the poet **Luis de Góngora** (1561-1627). Born to a wealthy and cultured Córdoban family, he would celebrate his city in a poem ('To Córdoba') whose lines are inscribed today on a plaque facing the Roman bridge: 'Oh mighty wall, oh towers crowned with honour, majesty and gallantry! Oh great river, great king of Andalucía, with your noble, if not golden sands!' After a dissolute youth of whoring, gambling and theatre-going, first as a student at Salamanca University, and then as a prebendary at

Córdoba Cathedral, Góngora moved to Madrid, and developed an increasing melancholy and austerity. As a poet he became the master of a learned style pejoratively referred to in its time as *culteranismo*. Extremely artificial, full of obscure references, and with a Latinate syntax and vocabulary, it was the antithesis of the fresh and simple effects that his contemporary Lope de Vega aimed to achieve. Góngora's masterpiece is the long and incomplete pastoral work *Solitudes* (the 1961 English translation by EM Wilson is even less intelligible than the original), which probably drew greatly from memories of the Córdoban countryside.

Writing at the same time as Góngora were a great number of minor Andalucían poets; for instance, the Utrera-born and Seville-based **Rodrigo Caro** (1573-1647), an archaeologist and antiquary who is best remembered for a poem bemoaning the fast disappearance of the Roman settlement of Itálica ('These empty fields before you,/Fabio, this parched mound of earth,/Were once, alas, the famed Itálica').

THE ROMANTIC 19TH CENTURY

It was not until the early 19th century that Andalucía saw again a major flowering of literary talent, and this time it was Moorish rather than Roman ruins that drew the attention of writers. Almost all the main figures involved in the Romantic discovery of Andalucía were British and French travellers, attracted to Spain by improved communications, and the enormous publicity the country received in the wake of the Peninsular War (not to mention the wealth of works of art to be had on the cheap). The great focus of attention was the Alhambra in Granada, then a collapsing monument overrun by gypsies and vagrants.

François Renée Chateaubriand, who visited Granada in 1807, transformed *The Story of the Abencerrage and the Beautiful Jarifa* into his novel *The Last of the Abencerrages* (1827), an international bestseller that heralded a spectacular revival of interest in Nasrid Spain. Two years later a young American diplomat, **Washington Irving**, then researching a book on the conquest of Granada, took up quarters in the Alhambra, which inspired his enormously successful and largely fictional concoction later entitled *Tales of the Alhambra* (1832).

So great was the tourist appeal of Spain from the 1830s that Byron's publisher, John Murray, commissioned in 1839 a volume on the country for the popular series Murray's Handbooks. (Byron was himself an enthusiast of Andalucía, especially the women of Cádiz.) The writer who took on the commission was **Richard Ford**, an aristocrat based in Seville and Granada from 1830 to 1833. The resulting *Handbook to Spain*

Federico García Lorca. *See p32.*

(1845) strengthened the misleading view that Andalucía was the quintessential Spanish region, but nevertheless remains the most detailed and scholarly guide to Spain ever written. But it is much more than this. Ford was a brilliant descriptive writer, whose lyricism was tempered by a sense of humour that frequently makes you laugh out loud.

Two other outstanding literary achievements by foreign travellers are **George Borrow**'s *The Bible in Spain* (1842) and **Théophile Gautier**'s *Journey to Spain* (1841). Borrow was a delightfully perverse traveller who noticeably avoided both the Alhambra and other British tourists, preferring the company of gypsies and lowlifes. Gautier, despite having the conventional orientalist biases of his generation, had a vividly pictorial descriptive style that the Spanish essayist and novelist Azorín would later praise for helping Spaniards achieve 'a poetic understanding' of their country.

Initially, Spanish writers lagged behind their foreign contemporaries in exploiting Andalucían orientalist subject matter. The Alhambra, for instance, would not properly be celebrated in Spanish verse until the publication in 1852 of the two-volume *Granada* by the Castilian poet and playwright **José Zorrilla** (1817-93), a man later to be crowned Spain's national poet in a ceremony that took place in the Court of the Lions. The Sevillian **Gustavo Adolfo Bécquer** (1836-70; **photo** *p29*), by far the greatest of this region's native Romantic writers, made no reference to al-Andalus in his works, lived for much of his short and unhappy life outside Andalucía, and devoted himself to themes of thwarted love, misery and solitude. His sparse poems were not brought together until after his death, in a publication, *Rimas*, that became the most popular book of Spanish verse until Lorca's *Romancero Gitano*.

Among Bécquer's Andalucían contemporaries, those who wrote about their region mainly concentrated on those local manners and customs – from fiestas to flamenco – that most appealed to the burgeoning tourist market. One of these so-called *costumbristas* was the Málaga-born **Serafín Estébanez Calderón** (1799-1867), whose *Andalucían Scenes* (1847) featured the first lengthy description of a gypsy festival in Triana. Another was the adopted Sevillian **Fernán Caballero** (the pseudonym of Swiss-born Cecilia Boehl von Faber; 1796-1877), a pioneering compiler of regional folk songs, and the author of the much-translated novel of Andalucían life, *The Seagull* (1856).

But only the French writer, **Prosper Mérimée**, in his novella *Carmen* (1845), was able to turn to such typical *costumbrista* subjects as bullfights, bandits and gypsies, and create out of these a work of fiction that truly seized the European imagination.

The 19th-century craze for Andalucía (which reached new heights with Bizet's 1875 musical version of Mérimée's tale) was finally accompanied, from the 1870s onwards, by a renascence of native literature. The Guadix novelist **Pedro Antonio de Alarcón** (1833-91) popularised the wild mountainous district of the Alpujarras with his humorous short story *The Three-Cornered Hat* (1874), while a psychologically more penetrating portrait of Andalucían village life was given in the novels of the Cabra-born **Juan Valera** (1824-1905). An unequalled prose poem to Granada, *Granada the Beautiful* (1896), was written by the locally born **Ángel Ganivet** (1865-98).

THE 20TH CENTURY TO TODAY

Above all, it was poetry that flourished in the early 20th century. The Seville-born **Antonio Machado** (1875-1939) – a leading member, like Ganivet, of the Generation of 1898 group – was the most important Spanish poet immediately prior to Lorca. After a flirtation in Paris with modernism and the bohemian life, he gave this all up to become a provincial schoolteacher. The death of his young wife and muse Leonor in the Castilian town of Soria prompted him to move back to Andalucía in 1913, where he lived as an exile. While working in the small town of Baeza in Jaén province, he continued to dream about the stark and empty Castilian countryside, and in 1917 brought out a much expanded edition of his greatest collection of verse, the *Campos de Castilla*, which is filled with musings on that landscape, and on the passing of old glories. The folkloric Andalucían themes that he rigorously avoided were the speciality of his brother, **Manuel Machado** (1874-1947).

Often considered as a link between one literary generation and the next was the Nobel-prizewinning poet **Juan Ramón Jímenez** (1881-1958). His best-loved work was a book ostensibly for children, *Platero and I* (1914), a series of prose poems describing life in the author's native town of Moguer de la Frontera.

The group – essentially of poets – who called themselves the Generation of 1927 (after their admiration for the then much-neglected Góngora, who died in 1627) included several Andalucíans, notably the Seville-born **Luis Cernuda** (1902-63) and **Federico García Lorca** (1898-1936; **photo** *p31*). Whereas the former left Andalucía at a very early age, and rarely referred to the region in his works, Lorca's poems and plays were not only heavily influenced by local folk culture, but also did much to perpetuate the romantic clichés about Andalucía, including a sentimental veneration of its Islamic past. *See p264* **The Lorca trail**.

No Andalucían writer since Lorca has gained much of a reputation outside Spain. However, important and successful writers from elsewhere have continued to be lured by the region and its history. A number of recent novelists have been as fascinated as their Romantic predecessors by the eclipse of Nasrid civilisation, including **Amin Maalouf** in his memorable *Leo the African* (1986), **Tariq Ali** in the lightweight *Shadows of the Pomegranate Tree* (1992) and **Salman Rushdie** in *The Moor's Last Sigh* (1996), which gave new life to the tired legends about Boabdil. The Islamic legacy in Spain has also obsessed the Catalan novelist **Juan Goytisolo** (born 1928), the author of one of the starkest post-war travel accounts about Andalucía, *Campo de Níjar* (1959).

Laurie Lee, in *A Rose for Winter* (1955) and *As I Walked Out One Midsummer's Morning* (1969), evoked Andalucía in rich poetic prose; but he lacked the in-depth knowledge of the region that is such a feature of the writings of the Hispanist and Bloomsbury associate **Gerald Brenan**. The latter's *South From Granada* (1957), an idiosyncratic account of his time spent living in the remote Alpujarran village of Yegen, was the first of a number of British books dedicated to Andalucían rural life, of which the most charming recent examples are **Michael Jacobs**' *Factory of Light* and **Chris Stewart**'s *Driving over Lemons* trilogy.

Ronda la Vieja.

Architecture

Where Moorish meets Gothic, Renaissance and baroque.

The legacy of the Moors has bewitched so many writers on Andalucía that it is easy believe that nothing worthwhile existed in southern Spain before their arrival at Tarifa in 711. Yet Andalucía is one of the archaeologically richest regions on the continent, and there's plenty of evidence left of the succession of civilisations that have sought to control this strategically important, mineral-rich land.

There are stunning late-palaeolithic cave paintings at **La Pileta**, near Ronda, neolithic dolmens at **Antequera** (among the most impressive to be found anywhere in the world), an outstanding Bronze Age settlement at **Los Millares** in Almería province and Phoenician tombs at **Almuñécar**, but, unsurprisingly, it was the Romans who left the greatest number of ancient remains.

The most significant Roman site is **Itálica**, just outside Seville, which was founded in 205 BC as the first Roman town in Spain. It grew to become a sizeable port and city (birthplace of Hadrian and Trajan) and was lavishly endowed with grand public buildings, such as an amphitheatre, bathhouse and theatre. The site hasn't fared well over the years, and is curiously lacking in atmosphere, though the amphitheatre has now been restored. Other important Roman settlements have been uncovered at **Baelo Claudia**, near Tarifa, and **Ronda la Vieja/Acinipo**, close to Ronda. At **Carmona** there's one of the most important Roman necropolises outside Italy; **Córdoba**'s Roman bridge still spans the Guadalquivir; **Cádiz** has an impressive amphitheatre. The list goes on…

SENSE AND SENSUALITY: THE MOORS

There is no doubt, however, that the biggest architectural draws in Andalucía are the mosques, castles and palaces built by the Moors during their seven centuries in southern Spain.

In both architectural and artistic terms, Andalucía's most important Moorish dynasty was that of the **Umayyads**. Originally from Damascus, the old capital of Islam, they were ousted by a new faction called the Abbasids. The Umayyads then fled to Córdoba in 756, whereupon their leader, Abd al-Rahman, proclaimed himself the first ruler of the independent emirate of al-Andalus. As well as relative social stability and economic prosperity, the invaders brought with them

Torre del Oro, Seville. *See p35.*

the best traditions of Islamic architecture and decoration, and quickly set about building in an imposing, confident manner now broadly known as the Umayyad (or Caliphal) style.

'The Mezquita is packed with imaginative borrowings and inspired innovation.'

One of the great triumphs of this essentially unintellectual style was to fuse classical and Islamic elements, while bringing a new sensuality into architecture – a direct reflection of society at the time, which, according to contemporary literature and poetry, eschewed serious religious contemplation in favour of music, drinking, games of chess and making love. This sensuality manifested itself in a rejection of strict rules of proportion and space in favour of more intangible structures, and in mysterious plays on light and shadow and intricate decorative effects on a grand scale.

The Umayyad style is exemplified par excellence by the **Mezquita**, Córdoba's Great Mosque, which was started around 780, and enlarged and embellished over the next 200 years. It's packed with imaginative borrowings and inspired innovation. Of the former, the Visigothic horseshoe arch is everywhere, as are re-used Roman and Visigothic capitals; the mosaics are strongly Byzantine-influenced; and the arcading (one row of arches on top of another), which was unprecedented in a mosque, was inspired by Roman aqueducts.

There are also plenty of novel and distinctly Islamic elements – alternating bands of brick and ashlar masonry, the use of calligraphy as the principal decorative element, employing stone rather than stucco, and the highly suggestive (rather than hierarchic) use of space.

By the mid tenth century, a period known as the '**Umayyad baroque**', architectural complexity was reaching a peak, and the Mezquita's features from this time (in the royal gallery of the Caliph) include elaborate decorative arcading, with interlaced arches, arches with semicircular segments cut out of them and the earliest use of 'honeycomb' effects. The decoration around the *mihrab* (prayer niche) is spectacularly ornate – star-shaped vaulting, mosaics and a stunning dome. The blurring between structure and decoration was to be immensely influential on Muslim architecture in the coming centuries.

Another good example of the Umayyad style lies just east of Córdoba on the peaceful lower slopes of the Sierra Morena: the ruined **Medina Azahara** palace-city. Originally intended as a summer palace for Abd al-Rahman III, the complex consisted of several palaces, extensive gardens, a zoo, an aviary, a weapons production site and a mosque – it was inspired by monumental Roman constructions, particularly the palace-city of Diocletian at Split. Building started in 936 at huge expense: engraved basins were imported from Constantinople and Syria; marble was brought from Almería and Carthage; and – the most lavish touch of all – the roof tiles were covered in gold and silver, a decadent symbol of Arabic glory.

Unfortunately, the city was largely destroyed when the Umayyads were ousted from Córdoba in 1009, and for centuries the plundered site was left to disintegrate. In recent years, however, an extensive reconstruction and restoration programme has put Medina Azahara back on the map. The centrepiece is an ornately decorated hall that gives visitors an excellent idea of the scale and style of the various buildings that made up this important complex. The carvings are some of the finest of the period, and are notable for their bird and Tree of Life forms, rather than for their scripts.

After the collapse of Umayyad al-Andalus in the early 11th century, the power vacuum was eventually filled by the **Almoravids**, and then the **Almohads**, both strict, morally rigid Berber tribes from North Africa, who between them ruled until the early 13th century. Initially, they had a far more severe, simple view of what architecture should be, and reacted against the decorative excesses of the Umayyads. They were superb military architects – much of the **Alcazaba** in Almería, the most impressive Moorish fortress in Spain after the Alhambra, dates from the Almohad period, as does Seville's **Torre del Oro**.

Yet even these austere rulers seem to have eventually softened, as can be seen in the exquisite **Giralda minaret** in Seville, now incorporated into the cathedral. Completed by the Almohads in 1195, it is a wonderful example of Maghreb architecture, the second movement associated with Islam in southern Spain, yet is far more ornate than any comparable Almohad structure in North Africa. The tower is a breathtaking display of graceful proportions, trellis-like brick patterning and elegant arabesques. In typical Maghreb style, which became increasingly elaborate as time went on, the square form (the shape of all Andalucían minarets) is awash with decoration and colour, the latter changing subtly with the light.

The last stage of Muslim architecture in Andalucía came with the founding of the **Nasrid dynasty** in Granada in the early 13th century, by which time much of al-Andalus had already been lost to the Christians. That a Moorish state survived at all for the next 250 years is remarkable; that created the extraordinary **Alhambra** is astonishing.

Part private residence, part bureaucratic offices, the halls and courtyards of the Alhambra contain none of the architectural innovations that mark out the Mezquita, but, instead, are a brilliant recapitulation of all that went before. Times being far harder than in the days of the Umayyads, however, it is the cheaper material of stucco (a slow-setting plaster) that is largely employed. The use of stucco reached new heights of complexity, particularly during the period of the so-called '**Nasrid baroque**' under Mohammed V in the mid 14th century, when designs fused Kufic (old Islamic script) and Neskhi (modern Islamic). Another development was remarkable stucco *muqarnas* ceilings (sometimes known as stalactite or honeycomb ceilings) – that in the Alhambra's **Sala de las Dos Hermanas** (Hall of the Two Sisters) is the most elaborate of its kind in the Islamic world. (There are also fine examples in Seville's Alcázar.)

Granada itself was the only purpose-built Islamic town in Andalucía (Córdoba was built on Roman foundations), and the maze of alleyways and whitewashed houses swarming over the Albaicín hill below the Alhambra are the most perfectly preserved Moorish quarter in the region. At the foot of the hill is **El Bañuelo**, the 11th-century Arab baths, the oldest civic building in Granada and most complete Moorish bathhouse in Spain. Another remarkable survival, not far from the cathedral, is the 14th-century **Casa del Carbón**, the only surviving wheat exchange of its period in Spain.

Outside of the big cities, there are plenty of other relics from Moorish times. One outstanding example can be found in northern Huelva province, where the small town of **Almonaster La Real** possesses a perfect gem of Islamic architecture in the form of a tenth-century mosque. The building was turned into a church by conquering Castilians in the 13th century (as were countless other mosques), but the original Arabic structure was left intact, including incorporated bits of an earlier Visigothic church and Roman stonework.

TRIUMPHALISM AND SYNTHESIS: THE GOTHIC

The 500-year Moorish domination of Andalucía came to an end in 1212 at the Battle of Las Navas de Tolosa, where a Christian army under Alfonso VII defeated the Almohads. With the new conquerors came fresh architectural ideas and energy. The **Gothic** style, which originated in France, reached Andalucía in the 13th century. Its progress was slow, but once it had gained a foothold, it remained the dominant architectural form until the 16th century, and a defiant statement of the triumph of Christianity.

Thanks to some important technical innovations, the new Gothic constructions tended to be much larger than their Moorish predecessors. Like most significant European buildings of this period, they were characterised by flying buttresses, intricate window tracery, ribbed ceilings and pointed arches, but they differed from their contemporaries in several ways. The cathedrals, for example, tended to be wider than others in Europe because they were often built on the sites of square mosques.

Furthermore, the choir and chapel containing the high altar could often be found in the middle of the church rather than at one end. New cathedrals were designed with lots of side chapels and, uniquely, contained *retablos*, three-part sculptural altarpieces that frequently filled the whole width of the nave behind the altar. The point of the *retablo*, a Spanish invention, was to illustrate Christ's teachings and stories with elaborately carved or painted biblical scenes. The best Gothic example is in Seville's cathedral, a masterpiece created by the Flemish sculptor Pieter Dancart in 1482 with more than 1,000 gilded and painted biblical figures.

The Christian conquerors may have found the Moors' religion intolerable, but they had far more time for their artistic and architectural traditions, which strongly influenced the incoming Gothic style. Obvious Muslim borrowings included profusely decorated surfaces and lashings of rich furnishings, as well as the use of decorative strips of lettering. The most popular ceilings – known as *artesonado* ceilings – were also borrowed directly from the Moors, and the Christians continued to use skilled Arab artisans to build them. The employment of Muslims to decorate Christian structures in Islamic style became known as the **Mudéjar** tradition. Their work was characterised by elaborately carved wooden inlays imitating traditional Muslim leatherwork, and remained fashionable until the 17th century.

The best example of Gothic architecture in Andalucía is the **Catedral** in **Seville**. Built on the site of the great Almohad mosque, it was completed in 1504, and is the largest cathedral in the world. Its impressive exterior features a great rose window, double buttresses and a 'fence' of Roman columns joined by chains. Inside, the key quality is size rather than grace, although it does contain some impressive tombs, including those of Alfonso the Wise, Pedro the Cruel and Christopher Columbus.

There are dozens of other Gothic churches throughout the region. One of the most charming is the simple, unambitious church of **Santa Ana** in Seville, built under Pedro the Cruel. Elsewhere, the straightforward, elegant parish churches of **Córdoba** are well worth a visit, as are the cathedrals at **Jerez de la Frontera** and **Málaga**, both of which combine Gothic, Renaissance and baroque styles.

Andalucía's Gothic period moved into its final and most extravagant phase under Fernando and Isabel, who finally completed the *reconquista* when they took Granada in 1492. The style that developed under their patronage is known as **Isabelline Gothic** or **Gothic Plateresque**, a highly decorative (*platero* means 'silversmith' in Spanish), exuberant extension of the early Gothic form. The movement roughly corresponded with the French Flamboyant and English Perpendicular styles, and was characterised by lace-like ornament, low-relief sculptures, sinuously curved arches and tracery, and playful, naturalistic detail. For supreme examples of this late Gothic flamboyance, see the façade of the **Palacio de Jabalquinto** in Baeza in Jaén province, or, better still, Fernando and Isabel's own burial chapel, the **Capilla Real** in Granada. Here, the greatest architect of the time, **Enrique de Egas** (1445-1534), gave his passion for unrestrained Gothicism a free rein, perfectly illustrated by the splendid north portal, which now stands inside the adjacent cathedral. The chapel, which wasn't completed until 1527, is made all the more interesting by the fact that the men working with Egas favoured a more measured, classical style usually associated with the later Renaissance period. The result is a building that skilfully balances fantastical, late Gothic elements with other more restrained features, such as the classical archway through which you enter the building from the street.

HARMONY AND PURITY: THE RENAISSANCE

The Gothic movement proved remarkably resilient in Andalucía, overlapping with the new ideas of the Italian-born **Renaissance** in the early 16th century. The latter brought about a return to the ancient Roman and Greek ideals of harmony and proportion. Columns, arcaded interior courtyards and classical shapes (squares, circles, triangles) made a big comeback, although, as in the Gothic period, many new buildings were still imbued with geometric Muslim-style decorative effects.

Spanish Renaissance architecture can be roughly divided into three periods: classical Plateresque, purist Renaissance and Herreresque (though the latter only had a very limited impact in Andalucía). As the name suggests, the **classical Plateresque** movement was a continuation and development of the Gothic Plateresque style. Decorative rather than structural (another legacy of the region's Islamic past), the movement endowed buildings with highly intricate designs resembling those of silverware, and façades were given round-arch portals bordered by columns and stone sculpture.

In contrast, the **purist Renaissance** style steered clear of excessive ornamentation in favour of simple, classical harmony, as exemplified in the **Palacio de Carlos V** in the **Alhambra**. Here, architect **Pedro Machuca**, who had trained in Italy, created an imposing square block notable for its deliberate lack of ornamentation and the unprecedented classical severity of its design.

However, it was the last phase, called **Herreresque** after the architect **Juan de Herrera** (1530-97), that was the plainest of the three – Herrera's was responsible for the austere San Lorenzo de El Escorial monastery near Madrid. De Herrera's only work in the region is **La Lonja** in Seville.

Just as there were several different periods of Renaissance architecture, so there were several big-name architects associated with the movement. The first was **Diego de Siloé** (1495-1563) who, with Jacopo Florentino, designed the enormous **Monasterio de San Jerónimo** in Granada, combining Gothic proportions with classical detailing. De Siloé was also ultimately responsible for **Granada**'s **cathedral**, the first plans for which were drawn up by the Gothicist Enrique de Egas. Deemed too old-fashioned by Carlos V, Egas's design was cast aside in favour of de Siloé's, who set about building an uncompromisingly classical structure that contrasted sharply with Egas's homely chapel next door. Inside, the effect is one of intense drama, created not only by the vast size of the space and towering circular chancel, but also by a giant order of classical columns intended to support barrel vaulting that was, in the end, changed to Gothic vaulting in the late 16th century. The sense of theatre is further emphasised by the fact that the whole place is painted white. In **Almería** there's another cathedral partially designed by de Siloé, and a third in **Guadix**, the latter an austere, grey reminder of one's Christian duty.

De Siloé's successor, **Andrés de Vandelvira** (1509-75), quickly established himself as a worthy heir. His **cathedral** at **Málaga** has all the drama of that in Granada, while its counterpart in **Jaén** is a giant construction that dwarfs the town below. Vandelvira was a prolific builder who spanned all three phases of Renaissance architecture, particularly in the neighbouring towns of Úbeda and Baeza in Jaén province, where he constructed some of the finest ensembles of Renaissance architecture in the country. Thanks to a thriving textile industry and the fact that it was home to Carlos V's hugely influential secretary, Francisco de los Cobos y Molina, **Úbeda** was chosen as the site for Vandelvira's best work: the **Sacra Capilla del Salvador del Mundo**, where de los Cobos y Molina is buried. The chapel was started by de Siloé but executed by Vandelvira and, unusually, remains close to its original state to this day, with most of its 16th-century furnishings and a handsome *retablo* by **Alonso Berruguete**, Spain's leading Renaissance sculptor and a pupil of Michelangelo. The chapel stands on one of Andalucía's most beautiful squares, **Plaza de Vázquez de Molina**, lined on every side by remarkable Renaissance buildings.

Nearby, **Baeza** doesn't possess quite the quantity of Renaissance treasures as Úbeda, but the influence of Vandelvira's delicate classicism makes itself felt in its immaculately preserved streets. The tiny **Plaza del Pópulo** is a tiny Renaissance gem of a square.

Don't miss Architecture

Roman

The remains of the city of **Itálica** (*see p80*), birthplace of Hadrian and Trajan, lie just outside Seville. Other important Roman sites include **Baelo Claudia** (*see p158*), near Tarifa, and the theatre at **Ronda La Vieja** (*see p207*), not far from Ronda.

Moorish

Córdoba's astonishing **Mezquita** (*see p212*) is the prime example of Umayyad period architecture. The later Almohads were masters of military building, as seen in the **Alcazaba** in Almería (*see p292*). Andalucía's iconic structure is undoubtedly Granada's **Alhambra** (*see p255*), whose stucco splendours are the greatest legacy of the last Moorish dynasty, the Nasrids.

Gothic

Seville's 15th-century **Catedral** (*see p68*) is the region's finest Gothic building. In Granada, Enrique de Egas's **Capilla Real** (*see p266*) showcases the flamboyant late Isabelline Gothic style.

Renaissance

The **Palacio de Carlos V** (*see p260*) in Granada exemplifies the unadorned classical harmony of the pure Renaissance style. More dramatic and theatrical is Diego de Siloé's towering **Catedral** (*see p266*), also in Granada. The exquisite towns of **Úbeda** (*see p245*) and **Baeza** (*see p242*) contain possibly the finest ensembles of Renaissance architecture in Spain.

Baroque

The **Monasterio de la Cartuja** (*see p267*) in Granada drips with some of the most extraordinary examples of baroque exuberance in the country. A clutch of fine churches and a remarkable fountain have earned **Priego de Córdoba** (*see p228*) the title of capital of Andalucían baroque.

Another Renaissance masterpiece is the **Colegiata de Santa María de la Asunción** in the beautifully preserved town of **Osuna** in eastern Seville province. It was begun in 1534 and, though not finally completed until the 18th century, remains a coherent and essentially early-16th-century structure. The airy interior houses exquisite 16th- and 17th-century furnishings and a staggering 16th-century pantheon of the Dukes of Osuna, itself a miniature church complete with tiny choir stalls.

The Italian influence was felt in town planning, military architecture and garden design, as well as in individual *palacios* and churches. During the 16th century, **Granada**'s **Plaza Nueva** was constructed and the lower city took on a completely new identity as an Italianate Renaissance town. Italian architects and craftsmen were responsible for two of Andalucía's finest castles: **La Calahorra** in Granada province and **Vélez Blanco** in Almería province, both built in the early 16th century and the first important examples of Italian Renaissance design outside Italy. La Calahorra houses a magnificent (if crumbling) Italian Renaissance courtyard. In **Seville**, the Moorish gardens of the **Alcázar** acquired new Italian-style features including classical statues, grottoes and the perfectly balanced arcaded pavilion known as the **Pabellón de Carlos V**.

EXUBERANCE AND EXCESS: THE BAROQUE

If the Renaissance period was largely characterised by sober, restrained design, the **baroque** movement that followed was precisely the opposite. Typically flamboyant and naturalistic in approach, it was a direct reaction against the classical Renaissance form and made extensive use of colour, ornament and decoration. However, while Italian baroque architecture was defined by innovations such as dynamic ground plans, the Spanish version was really only 'baroque' in the sense of being exuberantly ornamental. The structures of the buildings remained remarkably conventional.

'Andalucía became one of the European centres of the baroque style.'

Gathering steam in the 17th century, and reaching a peak of opulence in the 18th century with the so-called **churrigueresque** style (named after a family of sculptors and architects from Salamanca called Churriguera, who were, ironically, the least 'churrigueresque' of the churrigueresque architects), Andalucía became one of the European centres of the baroque style. The Spanish movement affected the look of present-day Andalucía as much as the Muslim period, reaching even the most isolated villages and endowing rural areas with unexpectedly lavish buildings. In the parish church of **San Mateo** in **Lucena** (in southern Córdoba province), for example, there is a Sagrario chapel decorated with an intricacy on a par with the best baroque buildings in Granada and Seville. The overall result was a plethora of delightful constructions displaying unprecedented decorative freedom in a uniquely Spanish mode that also incorporated diverse references to previous architectural styles.

One of the most memorable exponents of the new style was **Alonso Cano** (1601-67). Known as the 'Spanish Michelangelo' for his remarkable ability to paint, sculpt and design buildings, he was responsible for the unique 17th-century façade of **Granada**'s **cathedral**. This early baroque construction, with its three tall arches, illustrates the stylistic transition from classical Renaissance to the new Spanish approach, simultaneously displaying elements of baroque ornamentation over Renaissance roots. Cano also provided some of the sculptures for the extraordinary baroque façade of the monastery of **La Cartuja** outside **Jerez**.

In Seville, **Leonardo de Figueroa** (1650-1730) was responsible for the churches of **El Salvador** and **San Luis**, the **Colegio San Telmo** and what is now the **Museo de Bellas Artes** (the latter being a very early and restrained version of baroque). Others, like **Vicente Acero**, developed the baroque style into rococo forms, with conspicuous constructions such as the façade of the **cathedral** at **Guadix** and José de Bada's church of **San Juan de Dios** in Granada.

Visitors to Granada can admire one of the most sumptuous creations of the period in all Spain: the dazzling gold and marble chancel by **Francisco Hurtado Izquierdo** (1669-1725) in the **Monasterio de la Cartuja**. The sacristy, where not a single bit of the wall is left undecorated, is also an exhilarating experience, as is the nearby **Charterhouse**, which achieves astonishing levels of architectural flamboyance.

Other buildings of note include the **Palacio del Marqués de la Gomera** in **Osuna** with its strange, asymmetrical skyline, inspired by German rococo illustrations, and the wedding cake-like Sagrario chapel in the delightful town of **Priego de Córdoba**, a soaring, circular construction with plaster-coated balconies that have now been restored to their original sparkling white. The same town possesses another rather surprising baroque structure: a public fountain with mythological statues showered by more than 100 jets of water.

Plaza de Vázquez de Molina. *See p37.*

REVIVALISM AND ECLECTICISM: TO THE PRESENT

After the excitement of the baroque movement came a period of relative, neo-classical calm and a return to the cleaner, more serene architectural principles of Ancient Greece and Rome. A general economic decline in Andalucía, however, meant that the style, popular the mid 18th century and lasted until the early 19th century, did not take hold with anything the same force as previous movements. **Cádiz** has the biggest neo-classical heritage in Andalucía: apart from its huge, ungainly cathedral, which was completed in 1856, there are scores of houses and churches bearing testament to this short-lived, underfunded architectural period.

'The recent tendency has been to revive almost every historical style.'

The 19th and 20th centuries witnessed further serious economic decline in the region and a concomitant lack of architectural development. Displaying a yearning for the glory of days gone by, the tendency in recent years has been to revive almost every historical style, particularly that of the Moors.

Seville's Ibero-American Exhibition of 1929 left the city with a number of grandiose neo-Moorish/neo-Renaissance buildings, most notably the majestic **Hotel Alfonso XIII** and the extraordinary **Plaza de España**, with its huge sweep of tiles depicting the 40 regions of Spain. A more recent example of neo-Moorish is the city's former **Estación de Córdoba**, a 19th-century railway station that was converted into an exhibition venue in 1992. Other neo-Moorish structures include the **Alhambra Palace Hotel** in **Granada** and the **Palacio de Orleans y Borbón** in **Sanlúcar de Barrameda**, but little splashes of Islamicism, often in the form of decorative tile-work, are found everywhere, from railway stations and markets to bus stations and cottages.

One of Andalucía's rare 20th-century buildings worthy of note is the **Fundación de Rodríguez-Acosta** in **Granada**, an extraordinarily original construction (dating from the second and third decades of the century) that anticipated postmodernism and has been admired by many leading architects of today, such as Rafael Moneo.

The buildings erected for **Seville**'s **1992 Expo** were rather less permanent than those built for the 1929 exhibition – most were demolished or removed afterwards – though some were genuinely forward-looking (such as Nicholas Grimshaw's British Pavilion). The Expo's greatest architectural legacy was the two bridges contructed by **Santiago Calatrava**: the crossbow-shaped **Puente de la Barqueta** and the lyre-like **Puente del Alamillo**. The former has become a symbol of the 'new Andalucía', as eloquent as the Giralda was of the old region. Exciting contemporary buildings continue to be a rarity in Andalucía, however, with urban regeneration given a greater priority than new building – Córdoba's Plaza de la Corredera and the Alameda de Hércules in Seville, for instance, have been transformed in recent years.

Food & Drink

A plate of prawns and a glass of cold *fino* is just the start.

Few people come to southern Spain for the food. Old stereotypes die hard, and, while Andalucía's reputation for sun and scenic beauty is unassailable, many first-time visitors assume the trade-off is a monotonous, oily diet of fried fish and gazpacho. As with most stereotypes, there's an element of truth to it – olive oil is ubiquitous, many menus across the region are strikingly similar and there are a fair few bad restaurants out there. Yet the curious gastronome is far more likely to return from their holiday with their preconceptions in tatters.

Spain's ongoing culinary revolution has been slow to reach the far south, but it is now starting to make a mark (particularly in the cities of Málaga and Córdoba). Fine-dining restaurants may be relatively few as yet, but many of those that are here are very fine indeed. However, it's the pleasures of simple local cooking that are likely to provide your most satisfying culinary reminiscences – nibbling on a skewer of freshly grilled sardines at a beachside *chiringuito*, perhaps, or tucking into a platter of tender, locally raised lamb chops, accompanied by vegetables plucked from the cook's own garden, on the terrace of a mountain village *venta*.

ESSENTIAL FLAVOURS AND DISHES

Andalucía's best-known dish is gazpacho, and all its many regional variations. In its traditional form it comes as a tomato, olive oil and garlic-based soup, served cold, often with ice cubes, and a selection of chopped onions, peppers, cucumber, croutons and egg to sprinkle on top. Each region has its own interpretation: Málaga's *ajo blanco*, made with almonds and grapes; Antequera's *pimentón*, made with red peppers; Córdoba's thick *salmorejo* (made without water); Huelva's *gazpacho verde*, using parsley rather than tomatoes; and Cádiz's *sopa de picadillo*, which is spicier.

The region is also famous for its olives (*aceitunas*), which come in a multitude of forms: green, black, marinated in garlic and olive oil or vinegar, or stuffed with anchovies and peppers. Their extract – olive oil – is an intrinsic part of Spanish cuisine and is used in or on almost every Andalucían dish. Although some visitors complain about Spanish food being too 'greasy', it is important to realise that the Spaniards view olive oil almost as a dish in its own right; mopping-up some leftover oil on the plate with a hunk of bread is often the tastiest part of the meal.

Jamón (cured ham) is another Andalucían speciality that can be found in every bar in Spain, usually hanging in shanks from the ceiling. It comes in a variety of forms and at wildly different prices. The standard *jamón serrano* is the cheapest and is what usually ends up in sandwiches (*bocadillos*), while that from Jabugo in Huelva province is generally regarded as the finest and is the most expensive. This is *pata negra*, or *jamón ibérico*, made from free-range black pigs fed only on acorns; the finest cut is awarded '*cinco jotas*' or five 'j's and costs much the same as gold. High in the Alpujarras in Granada, the village of Trevélez produces snow-cured *jamón*, which is half the price of Jabugo ham, although it isn't in the same league.

Each region, each town, sometimes each village in Andalucía has a different speciality. The inland provinces of Córdoba, Jaén and Seville concentrate on hearty meat meals, often in the form of stews (*cocidos*) like *estofado* flavoured with cloves, or game dishes, such as venison, partridge, rabbit and wild boar. *Rabo de toro*, made with oxtail, onions and tomatoes, is a Córdoban favourite, while the province's Jewish and Moorish heritage is revealed in dishes such as *caldereta*, a lamb stew with almonds. Granada and Jaén's wonderfully refreshing *remojón* (a salad of salt cod, oranges and olives) is another legacy of the Moors. The list goes on…

MEAT, FISH AND SEAFOOD

Meat, be it beef, lamb or pork, is served straight up and simple; presentation is not a strong point in Andalucía, and even the most elaborate-sounding meat dish on the menu will often be served with just a handful of chips. The pig is big in the region, and pork is the number-one meat of the south (particularly in the sierras). Pork products will be found on just about every menu – from *lomo* (loin) to *jamón* via a dozen variations on sausage (such as *chorizo* – paprika-spiked sausage; and *morcilla* – blood pudding). Lamb is favoured very young and milk-fed; as a consequence, it is tender but somewhat lacking in flavour. *Ternera* (strictly, veal) is likewise preferred over beef, though is not necessarily milk-fed.

It's always worth trying the local game, which is common in season in mountainous areas in particular – Córdoba province, for example, is known for its wild boar and Jaén province for partridge.

Fish and seafood can be found all over Andalucía, but it is predominantly in the coastal provinces of Huelva, Cádiz and Málaga that these are at their best. Cádiz, and nearby towns like Sanlúcar and El Puerto, are recognised as having the finest seafood and the best fish restaurants in the region, with the freshest and priciest catches coming from the Bay of Cádiz itself. Be aware that much of the fish you will encounter is peculiar to the coasts off which it's caught and doesn't have an English translation. Most fresh fish is grilled; shellfish may be served more elaborately: steamed, perhaps, in garlic and chilli, or boiled, as in Cádiz and Huelva, and flavoured with herbs. Inland and outside the main cities, the best fish you're likely to find is fresh trout, which teems in the sierra rivers in Huelva and Jaén.

Common across all of Andalucía is *arroz marinera*. It is basically the Andalucían version of paella, but far more soup-like and with more emphasis on seafood than the Valencian dish. Another ubiquitous seafood favourite is *zarzuela*, which is similar to bouillabaisse.

VEGETABLES AND FRUIT

Although Almería supplies most of the rest of Europe with year-round veg and fruit, vegetables do not feature prominently in Andalucían cuisine and are often served as separate dishes rather than with the main meal. Of the cooked dishes, *espinacas con garbanzos* (spinach with chickpeas) is probably the best known across the region, along with grilled mushrooms, often in garlic and olive oil, another popular dish. Specialities include asparagus from the Trigueros region of Huelva, served with onions, coriander and lemon.

As for fruit, Huelva province is famed for its strawberries, and Málaga province for its fat, juicy muscatel grapes. More unusual fruit to look out for includes (in autumn) the *chirimoya* (custard fruit) and the delicious sweet, tomato-lookalike *caquis*.

Vegetarians should note that many ostensibly vegetable-only dishes, such as *huevos a la flamenca* (eggs and vegetables), may be sprinkled with *jamón*. Salads (*ensaladas*) are served all over the region and are usually much more substantial than those served in the UK. A house salad, for example, will generally consist of tuna, egg, asparagus, carrot, olives, onion and a lot of olive oil, as well as lettuce and tomato. It's not easy to find much variety in salads – they tend to be essentially the same throughout Spain.

DESSERTS

Dessert is not Spain's forte, and this certainly applies in Andalucía. More often than not your only sweet choices will be fresh fruit, or a pud from the freezer in the corner of the restaurant with the Menorquina logo emblazoned on it. This company seems to have cornered the entire dessert market, supplying *helado* (ice-cream), *flan* or *tocinos de cielo* (both types of crème caramel), and *natillas* (custard) to all the restaurants in the region.

Having said that, there are also some Andalucían specialities worth looking out for, especially in Granada, where the Moorish influence has lingered the longest: try delicious *alfajores* (a type of pastry made with honey and almonds, similar to baklawa) or *piononos* (almond-based cakes soaked in liqueur). In Cádiz province the *crema de jerez* (sherry pudding) is worth ordering, and in Málaga *peras al vino* (pears baked in red wine) is another great way to finish a meal. Other desserts include *yemas* (candied egg yolks) and *tocino del cielo* (crème caramel).

Cheese is rarely served after a meal, but as a tapa, and there are few well-known varieties. Most are produced on a village-by-village basis and are unlikely to be found outside the local area. The one exception is pedroches from Córdoba (a soft goat's cheese, kept in oil and flavoured with herbs).

DRINK

Sherry is the quintessential Andalucían drink. Forget the outmoded British view of it as sweet, dark-coloured mouthwash associated with vicars and aged aunts. Sherry in Andalucía

Food glossary

For a glossary of common tapas, *see p45* **Tapas tips**.

ESSENTIALS

desayuno breakfast; **almuerzo** lunch; **cena** dinner.**carta** menu; **menú del día** set menu; **primer plato (entrante)** starter; **segundo plato** main course; **postre** dessert; **plato combinado** one-course meal.
pan bread; **mantequilla** butter; **sal** salt; **pimienta** pepper; **mostaza** mustard; **ketchup/salsa de tomate** ketchup; **aceite** oil; **vinagre** vinegar; **aceitunas** olives.
cubiertos cutlery; **cuchilla** knife; **tenedor** fork; **cuchara** spoon; **plato** plate; **botella** bottle; **vaso** glass.**la cuenta** the bill; **servicio incluído** service included; **propina** tip.

COOKING STYLES AND TECHNIQUES

en adobo marinated; **al ajillo** with olive oil and garlic; **caliente** hot; **al chilindrón** a spicy tomato, pepper, ham, onion and garlic sauce; **crudo** raw; **escabechado/en escabeche** marinated in vinegar with bay and garlic; **estofado** braised; **frio** cold; **frito** fried; **guisado** stewed; **hervido** boiled; **al horno/ asado** baked/roasted; **a la marinera** (fish or shellfish) cooked with garlic, onions and white wine; **a la parilla** charcoal grilled; **picante** spicy; **al pil-pil** flash-fried in sizzling oil and garlic; **a la plancha/brasa** grilled; **relleno** stuffed; **a la Romana** deep-fried in batter; **en salsa** in sauce or gravy; **al vapor** steamed; **muy hecho** well done; **medio hecho/regular** medium; **poco hecho** rare.

EGGS (HUEVOS)

huevos fritos fried eggs; **revuelto** scrambled eggs; **tortilla francesa** plain omelette; **tortilla de patatas/española** Spanish potato omelette.

FISH AND SHELLFISH (PESCADO Y MARISCOS)

almejas clams; **almendritas** small cuttlefish; **anchoas** anchovies; **anchoba** a type of mackerel; **anguila** eel; **angulas** baby eels; **atún/bonito** tuna; **bacalao** salt cod; **berberechos** cockles; **besugo** sea bream; **bogavante** lobster; **bonito** light tuna; **boquerones** anchovies; **caballa** mackerel; **calamares (en su tinta)** squid (in their own ink); **camarones** shrimps; **cangrejo** crab; **chipirones** baby squid; **choco** cuttlefish; **cigalas** crayfish; **coquinas** small clams; **corbina** sea bass; **dorada** gilthead bream; **erizo** sea urchin; **gambas** prawns; **langosta** spiny lobster; **langostinos** langoustines; **lenguado** sole; **lubina** sea bass; **mejillones** mussels; **merluza** hake; **mero** Mediterranean sea bass/grouper; **navajas** razor clams; **neceros** small crabs; **ostras** oysters; **pargo** bream; **perca** perch; **percebes** barnacles; **pescaditos** whitebait; **pez espada** swordfish; **pijota** whiting; **pulpo** octopus; **puntillitas** tiny squid; **quisquillas** small shrimp; **rape** monkfish; **róbalo** sea perch; **robaballo** turbot; **salmón** salmon; **salmonete** red mullet; **sardinas** sardines; **sargo** bream; **sepia** cuttlefish; **trucha** trout; **vieiras** scallops; **zarzuela** fish stew.

MEAT, POULTRY, GAME AND CHARCUTERIE (CARNE, AVES, CAZA Y EMBUTIDOS)

albóndigas meatballs; **bistec** steak; **buey/ternera** (cuts **entrecot** entrecôte, **filete** fillet, **solomillo** tenderloin) beef; **cabrito** kid; **callos** tripe; **cerdo** pork; **chorizo** spicy sausage; **choto** kid; **chuletas** chops; **chuletón** large steak; **cochinillo** roast suckling pig; **cocido** stew; **codorniz** quail;

comes in a variety of styles (from ultra dry to syrupy sweet), is the perfect foil for a seafood tapa and is often drunk ice-cold with a full meal, a habit unique to the region. Production is centred on the 'sherry triangle' the three points of which are the towns of Jerez, Sanlúcar de Barrameda and El Puerto de Santa María. Most Spanish brandies also come from this area – among the best-known are Soberano, Carlos I and III, and Gran Duque de Alba.

A similar drink to sherry is produced in Montilla in southern Córdoba province (from which the name *amontillado* – meaning 'in the style of Montilla' – derives). Montilla is created in a comparable way to sherry, but with the significant difference that no alcohol is added to aid the fermentation process, so it is not fortified. Also, the main grape variety used is Pedro Ximénez (which is only used to make sweet dessert styles in Jerez) rather than *palamino*. In terms of flavour, Montilla has even more toasted, nutty flavours than sherry; its richness works wonders with the local food.

The wines of Andalucía are relatively few and are generally not highly regarded. The little wine that is produced in the region's wine-

conejo rabbit; **cordero** lamb; **costillas** ribs; **empanada** pasty; **estofado** stew; **faisán** pheasant; **gallina** chicken; **higado** liver; **jabalí** wild boar; **jamón (serrano)** cured ham; **jamón york** cooked ham; **lengua** tongue; **liebre** hare; **lomo** loin (usually pork); **morcilla** blood sausage; **oca** goose; **pato** duck; **pavo** turkey; **pechuga** breast; **perdiz** partridge; **pichón** pigeon; **pinchito** small kebab; **pollo** chicken; **rabo de toro** oxtail; **riñones** kidneys; **salchicha** sausage; **salchichón** salami; **sesos** brains; **tocino** bacon; **vaca** beef; **venado** venison.

VEGETABLES AND PULSES (VERDURES Y LEGUMBRES)

ajo garlic; **alcachofas** artichokes; **arroz** rice; **berenjena** aubergine/eggplant; **calabacines** courgettes/zucchini; **cebolla** onion; **champiñones** mushrooms; **col** cabbage; **endivias** chicory/endive; **ensalada mixta** mixed salad; **ensalada verde** green salad; **espárragos** asparagus; **espinacas** spinach; **fríjoles/habichuelas** red kidney beans; **garbanzos** chickpeas; **guisantes** peas; **habas** broad beans; **judías blancas** haricot beans; **judías verdes** green (French) beans; **judiones** large haricot beans; **lechuga** lettuce; **lentejas** lentils; **maíz** sweetcorn; **patatas** potatoes; **patatas fritas** chips/french fries; **pepinillos** gherkins; **pepino** cucumber; **pimientos** (red/green/yellow) peppers; **puerro** leek; **remolacha** beetroot; **repollo** cabbage; **setas** wild mushrooms; **zanahoria** carrot.

FRUIT (FRUTA)

aguacate avocado; **albaricoque** apricot; **cerezas** cherries; **ciruelas** plums; **frambuesas** raspberries; **fresas** strawberries; **granada** pomegranate; **higos** figs; **macedonia** fruit salad; **manzana** apple; **melocotón** peach; **melón** melon; **naranja** orange; **nectarina** nectarine; **pera** pear; **piña** pineapple; **plátano** banana; **pomelo** grapefruit; **sandía** watermelon; **tomate** tomato; **uvas** grapes.

DESSERTS (POSTRES)

arroz con leche rice pudding; **flan** crème caramel; **helado** ice-cream; **tarta** cake.

DRINKS (BEBIDAS)

agua (con gas/sin gas) water (sparkling/still); **aguardiente** aniseed spirit; **amontillado** dry, amber-coloured sherry; **anis** aniseed; **café (con leche)** coffee (with milk); **cortado** small coffee with a little milk; **café americano** weak coffee; **café solo** espresso; **carajillo** Irish coffee; **cerveza** beer; **fino** pale, dry sherry; **con hielo** with ice; **infusión de manzanilla** camomile tea; **leche** milk; **manzanilla** pale, very dry sherry; **oloroso** dark, strong, sometimes sweet sherry; **té (con leche)** tea (with milk); **vino (de la casa)** (house) wine; **vino blanco** white wine; **vino rosado** rosé; **vino tinto** red wine; **zumo** juice.

OUR CLIMATE NEEDS
A HELPING HAND TODAY
Be a smart traveller. Help to offset your carbon emissions from your trip by pledging Carbon Trees with Trees for Cities.
All the Carbon Trees that you donate through Trees for Cities are genuinely planted as additional trees in our projects.
Trees for Cities is an independent charity working with local communities on tree planting projects.
www.treesforcities.org Tel 020 7587 1320
Trees for Cities
Charity registration number 1032154

Tapas tips

The original tapa was a small dish that the *camarero* (barman) would place over your drink – hence the name: lid. The reason for this practice is unclear: in most versions of the story it was to keep the flies off; but perhaps it was also the combination of poverty and heat, which made eating a large meal impractical. Either way, the important thing was that the snack was free.

Nowadays, tapas have evolved from those humble beginnings to become practically an art form in Seville and Granada. In some cities (Granada and Jaén for example) you will often automatically be given a tapa whenever you order a drink; in most other places expect to pay a couple of euros for most tapas.

There are four basic sizes of tapa: a *pincho* (more or less a mouthful), a *tapa* (a saucerful or so – though, traditionally, the same size as a *pincho*), a *media-ración* (half a plateful) and a *ración* (a plateful). Not all of these will always be offered.

The tapas list will be displayed on a menu at the bar, on a board on the wall or, most likely, you just take your pick of what you fancy from trays under a glass counter. If you eat at the bar, you'll pay the price on the menu; if you eat at a table or outside on the *terraza*, you'll end up paying about 25 per cent more. Settle the bill once you have finished eating, rather than when you order.

CLASSIC TAPAS

aceitunas (rellenos) olives (stuffed); **albóndigas** meatballs; **almendras saladas** salted almonds; **boquerones en vinagre** fresh anchovies in vinegar; **calamares rellenos** stuffed baby squid; **calamares a la romana** fried battered squid rings; **calamares en su tinta** squid cooked in its ink; **chanquetes** tiny transparent fish, served battered; **chorizo al vino** spicy sausage in red wine; **croquetas** potato croquettes (sometimes with tuna, ham, chicken, etc); **empanadas** flat pies, usually with a tuna filling; **empanadillas** small fried pasties, usually with a tomato and tuna filling; **ensaladilla rusa** Russian salad (potatoes, onions, red peppers, usually tuna and other ingredients in mayonnaise); **flamenquines** ham and pork rolls in breadcrumbs; **fritura de pescado** flash-fried fish; **gambas al ajillo** prawns in garlic; **huevos rellenos** stuffed, cold hard-boiled eggs; **jamón serrano** cured ham; **mejillones al vapor** steamed mussels; **pan con tomate** bread rubbed with fresh tomato and olive oil; **patatas ali oli** potatoes in garlic mayonnaise; **patatas bravas** potatoes in a spicy tomato sauce, sometimes known as *papas bravas*; **pimientas de Padrón** fried, hot small green peppers; **pincho moruno** grilled meat brochette; **pisto manchego** ratatouille with meat (usually ham) and egg; **pollo al ajillo** chicken in garlic and olive oil; **revuelto** scrambled eggs; **riñones al jerez** kidneys in sherry; **sobrassada** soft Mallorcan paprika sausage; **tortilla española** Spanish omelette.

growing regions – the Villaviciosa area of Córdoba; parts of Seville; east of Úbeda, in Jaén province; the Condado de Huelva area; southern Granada; and Sanlúcar – is rarely found outside the area in which it is grown, with most restaurants serving well-known bottles from Rioja, Valdepeñas and Jumilla (in neighbouring Murcia), instead. However, this situation might be (very slowly) changing. Under the label Príncipe Alfonso, the Cortijo de las Monjas estate near Ronda, owned by socialite Alfonso von Hohenlohe, has produced first-rate reds from tempranillo grapes combined with French varieties (and with expert French help). It is up to other enterprising individuals to follow his lead. (Note that many red wines are served cold, especially during the summer.)

Andalucía's very strong and sweet (and mostly underrated) dessert wines, made from the moscatel and Pedro Ximénez grapes, are particularly good, and once enjoyed huge popularity in England (particularly in Elizabethan times, when they were known as 'Malaga-sack'). The main growing regions are the Axarquía, east of Málaga, and between Estepona and the border with Cádiz province,

MALAGA
DULCE

Alfonso
González

and the results are wines that are dark golden in colour and smell raisin-rich, with distinct flavours of chocolate and toffee.

Other tipples include *sangría*, which can be found all over the region, particularly in tourist areas (its variant *tinto de verano*, on the other hand, is drunk by locals too – ask for it with *casera blanca*, a fizzy drink less sweet than lemonade), and *aguardiente* (anis), which comes in a variety of different forms, sweet or dry, but is always very strong and is often drunk at breakfast (by locals). The best-known brands are Zalamea from Huelva, Rute from Córdoba and Cazalla de la Sierra from Seville.

Spaniards love beer (*cerveza*), and Andalucía produces three fine brands – Cruzcampo from Seville, Alhambra from Granada and Alcázar from Jaén. The former can be found all over the region, while the latter two are largely restricted to their respective provinces. Beer is usually served as a *caña* (on tap), and comes in glasses of about a third of a pint. A *tubo* is roughly half a pint and a *pinta* is a pint, but this measurement is rarely seen outside the British bars along the Costa del Sol (though, if you want a larger glass, ask for a *litrona* or a *jarra*).

You can rely on drinking excellent fresh coffee in Spain, without a grain of powder or a freeze-dried granule in sight (and that applies to decaffeinated – *descafeinado* – too, which is widely available). *Café con leche* (coffee with milk) is the Spanish equivalent of a *café au lait*; a *cortado* has the same amount of coffee but less milk, while a *café solo* is the equivalent of an espresso. *Té* (tea) is not common and will be served weak and black unless you specify otherwise, in which case you will also be given warm milk. *Té infusíon* is the name for herbal tea.

EATING HABITS AND PLACES TO EAT

Eating out is one of the delights of visiting Andalucía and should be enjoyed at an unhurried pace. The locals spend a large part of their lives socialising in bars and cafés, and you should do the same. Children are welcome everywhere and at any time of the day or night – it's not uncommon to see young families out dining at midnight.

Andalucíans do not generally go in for large breakfasts. A coffee, sometimes with a shot of *coñac*, a *magdalena*, perhaps a croissant with butter and *mermelada* (jam) and a fruit juice, is usually sufficient. *Chocolate* (hot chocolate) with *churros* (fried doughnut strips that are dipped into the drink) is a popular alternative all over the region. By far the most popular Andalucían breakfast dish, though, is *tostada* (toast), served in the west of the region with spiced lard (*manteca colorada*) and in the east with tomatoes and olive oil.

Visitors will probably have to alter their eating habits to correspond to local schedules: do not expect lunch before 2pm or dinner before 10pm or 11pm, unless you want to eat in a deserted restaurant (or a touristy one). Tapas can be relied on, though, to be available through the day and evening, should hunger strike.

The range of places to eat can be confusing for the first-time visitor. *Cervecerías* and *tascas* are both bars where you can get a basic meal and/or tapas. Often there's a *comedor* (dining room) attached, serving simple, cheap food. You can order from the *carta* (menu) or the *menú del día* (set menu). The *menú* will usually consist of a choice of three courses plus a drink and bread, and can represent excellent value for money. A *plato combinado* is a cheaper, single-dish option, which will usually consist of meat, chips and perhaps an egg. *Bocadillos* (baguette sandwiches) are usually filled with meat, cheese or tortilla. Beware: if you ask for a 'sandwich', you will get two anaemic slices of white bread with processed cheese and ham inside.

'*Ventas* are great fun on a Sunday when whole families visit for a prolonged lunch.'

Ventas are cheap, family-run establishments that serve up local dishes at reasonable prices. They are great fun on a Sunday when whole families visit for a prolonged lunch. *Mesones*, *bodegas* and *tabernas* are more like inns or pubs and will be slightly pricier, though most will serve tapas and *raciones* as well as full meals.

Restaurantes are officially rated with forks (rather than stars), usually according to price rather than quality. They usually offer a set menu at lunchtime in addition to à la carte, although upmarket establishments may have a *menú de degustación* that offers a number of dishes from the à la carte menu. Restaurant prices are still reasonable in most places compared to the rest of Europe, with an average meal for two plus wine costing about €30-€40. In some of the main cities and upmarket tourist areas, however, prices can skyrocket.

Seafood eateries come in two main guises – *marisquerías*, which are often pricey but are good quality; and *chiringuitos*, small beachside grills that you'll find dotted all along the coast.

In Spain, few people leave much of a tip (*propina*), though it's common to round the bill up. You will also find tax (IVA) added at seven per cent in some posher places. Wine is, however, relatively cheap. *Vino de la casa* is usually drinkable (at worst), and you can get some really fine wines for a fraction of the price you'd pay in a UK or US restaurant.

Festivals & Events

No saint is insignificant – it's always time for a *feria*.

Andalucians will jump on any excuse to let their hair down. Whatever time of year you visit you will stumble across some sort of fiesta during your stay. Many of the region's festivals are notable for their blending of religious and secular elements to create an unforgettably charged atmosphere. Their ubiquity and passion may have contributed to the seductive image of Andalucía abroad, but they are also intrinsic to the region's complex culture.

INFORMATION

For listings of the major events in the region get a copy of *52 and a half weeks*, available from most major tourist offices. There is also a monthly listings guide to the region called *¿Que Hacer? What's On?*. For details of all the festivals mentioned below, contact the relevant local tourist office. Look, too, on the website www.andalucia.org. Below we list the main festivals by type.

► For more on Cádiz's carnival, *see p137*; for Seville's Holy Week and *feria, see p71*, and for Málaga's *feria, see p176*.

CARNAVAL

Most towns in Andalucía celebrate Carnaval, a Catholic festival centred around Shrove Tuesday. The carnival is a last free-for-all before the abstentions and prohibitions of Lent, with everyone donning masks and fancy dress, and local politicans roundly lampooned. The implicit anarchy of the festival led Franco to abolish Carnaval in 1937, although it continued under a different name in several towns.

Today, **Carnaval** in **Cádiz** is one of Spain's most dazzling and exciting events, signalling the start of the festive season in Andalucía with ten days of mayhem and fun all over the city, including floats, parades, costumes, live music and lots of drinking (*see p137* **Party on**). It is followed by the **Carnaval de la Concha Fina** in **La Línea**, a four-day event with bands, music and a masked ball, for which the whole town wears fancy dress. Smaller versions of Carnaval can be found across Andalucía; the one in **El Puerto de Santa María** is lively.

SEMANA SANTA

Semana Santa (Holy Week; 2-8 April 2007, 17-23 March 2008) is celebrated with great fervour. Elaborate religious processions are organised by local brotherhoods, known as *cofradías*, with effigies of Christ on the Cross and the Virgin Mary in mourning carried through the streets from the local church, through emotional and passionate crowds. The image of the Virgin or Christ is placed on a float, known as a *paso*, and carried by *costaleros*, who either walk on each side of it (as in Málaga) or underneath it (as in Seville). The procession is led by *penitentes*, known as *nazarenos* in Seville, who are dressed in the same conical white hoods worn by the Inquisition and latterly by the Ku Klux Klan. The *paso* leaves the church in which it has been stored and makes its way through the streets, usually accompanied by a band, although in some cases the procession may be silent. Maundy Thursday and Good Friday are the high points of the week, after which celebrations wane over the Easter weekend.

Though the celebrations are ostensibly religious, for many participants it's the worship of the images themselves, rather than what they represent, that is most important. Certainly in Seville there is much rivalry between the various brotherhoods in terms of who is carrying the most beautiful/moving/well-dressed Virgin.

The (possibly apocryphal) origins of the festival can be traced back to 1521, when Don Fadrique, the first Marquis of Tarifa, came back from the Holy Land and introduced the *Via Crucis*, or Stations of the Cross, to Seville. The idea caught on, and each year more and more people participated. The exact form of today's processions dates back to the early 20th century.

Semana Santa is celebrated in every town and village across the region, but is at its most impressive in **Seville**, **Málaga**, **Granada** and **Córdoba**. **Jerez** and **Úbeda** also have striking processions, while **Baena** wins the prize for the loudest celebrations thanks to its deafening drum-rolling competition.

CORPUS CHRISTI

Corpus Christi, celebrating the presence of the body of Christ in the Communion host, has been a religious holiday in Spain since the 13th century. Celebrations kick off on the Wednesday after Trinity Sunday when balconies and buildings of towns and cities are bedecked with flowers. On the following day, Corpus Christi itself (which falls in May or June), a solemn procession carries images of the infant Jesus and various saints through streets strewn with cypress branches and flowers.

Corpus Christi is celebrated everywhere in Andalucía, most famously in **Granada**. In **Seville**, the key events are the procession of the enormous silver monstrance from the cathedral in the early hours of Thursday morning, and 'Los Seises', a dance that takes place on the steps of the cathedral. The dance dates from the 13th century and involves a group of ten children dressed in page-boy outfits accompanied by a band. **Ronda**, **Vejer de la Frontera** and **Zahara de la Sierra** also have big Corpus Christi celebrations.

ROMERÍAS

Hugely popular across Andalucía, *romerías* are community pilgrimages to shrines around which fiestas are held. Although most regional *romerías* lead to a local shrine a few miles from the town, the name remembers those pilgrims, or *romeros*, who walked all the way to Rome. May is the most popular month for *romerías*.

On the last Sunday of April, the people of **Andújar** in Jaén process from the town to the sanctuary of the **Virgen de la Cabeza**, overlooking the wild hills of the Sierra Morena. The pilgrimage has its origins in the 13th century, and now involves around half a million people. It is followed shortly afterwards by another important Jaén pilgrimage, on the first two days of May, to the shrine of **Nuestra Señora de la Estrella**, north of **Úbeda**. Pilgrims sing songs called *mayos* to the Virgin during the night and bid for the privilege of carrying her into the hermitage.

In **Huelva**, the **Romería de San Benito Abad** takes place on 4-6 May and includes songs, hymns and traditional dances such as the *fandango*. It often coincides with the **Romería de Santa Eulalia** in **Almonaster La Real** in northern Huelva on the first weekend in May, for which the townsfolk dress up in traditional garb, while *cofradías* compete to create the finest crosses.

The **Romería de San Isidro** on 17 May involves more than 500 horse riders and decorated carts travelling to the Sierra de San Pablo in Seville for boozing and traditional dancing. San Isidro is the patron saint of farmers, and his feast day is celebrated on 15 May in many rural villages with a procession through the fields and a fiesta. **Montefrío** in Granada province is a good example.

The biggest and most important pilgrimage of the year, however, is the **Romería del Rocío**, which takes place at Whitsun in May or June, and culminates at the Huelvan village of **El Rocío**. The three traditional routes start at Sanlúcar, Huelva and Triana in Seville, and involve up to a million people.

Later in the summer, on 5 August, the atmospheric **Romería de la Virgen de las Nieves** sets off from the village of **Trevélez** in the Alpujarras and heads up to a small shrine on the peak of Mulhacén, the highest mountain on the Iberian Peninsula, to celebrate the Virgin of the Snows. As the summer draws to a close, the people of Baeza, complete with carriages and horsemen, take part in the **Romería del Cristo de la Yedra** to return the Virgen del Rosel to her shrine (last Sunday in August or the first in September). The **Romería de Nuestra Señora de los Ángeles** is on 8 September, when brotherhoods on horseback from neighbouring villages dress up in traditional costume and process to the sanctuary of the Virgin in **Aracena** in northern Huelva, while the last *romería* of the season is the **Romería de Cristo del Paño** on 5 October in **Moclín** in Granada province – the most important in eastern Andalucía after the Andújar *romería*.

SAINTS' DAYS AND OTHER FESTIVALS

Every village and town has one or two patron saints, whose feast days are a perfect excuse for a fiesta. Despite the religious origin, such events usually incorporate secular celebrations.

The **Fiesta de los Reyes** on the evening of 5 January marks the visit of the three wise men to the infant Jesus and is celebrated throughout Spain. Three men dressed as kings ride through the town in a procession, scattering sweets to the children. In Málaga the event is known as the **Cabalgata de los Reyes Magos**.

The feast of San Juan on 24 June is an important festival in many regions of Spain. In Vejer de la Frontera effigies representing evil are burnt on a big fire in the main square. The fires are known as the **Candelas de San Juan** and conclude with a flaming effigy of a bull that is paraded around the town accompanied by fireworks. On the coast, San Juan celebrations take the form of bonfires and fireworks.

For the coastal towns, the **Virgen del Carmen**, patron of sailors, is one of the most important saints. On 16 July statues of the Virgin are borne across the water in decorated boats, accompanied by music and fireworks. The old fishermen's quarter of Los Boliches in Fuengirola and the town of Estepona have particularly atmospheric celebrations.

In August (13-15), the **Fiesta de Guadalquivir** in **Sanlúcar de Barrameda** celebrates the **Virgen de la Caridad** with bullfights and flamenco, while the people of **Mojácar** honour their patron **San Agustín** with a five-day fiesta at the end of the month.

Highlights of September include the **Virgen de la Luz** festival in **Tarifa** and the **Dia del Señor** festival in **Órgiva**, a noisy event dominated by fireworks and processions. Finally, the **Fiestas de Otoño** in **Jerez de la Frontera** celebrate the city's co-patron saints, the Virgen de la Merced and San Dionisio, with a prestigious horse festival in late October and early November. The highlights are the Parada Hipica, in which more than 1,000 riders in traditional costume parade, and the horse races in the Plaza del Arenal.

MAY FESTIVALS

Throughout May a series of festivals enlivens the streets of **Córdoba**. The first of these is the **Cruz de Mayo**, which is celebrated in a number of towns and villages across Andalucía, culminating in the **Fiesta de Santa Cruz** on the third of the month. Crosses decorated with flowers are set up in town squares as the centrepiece for drinking, dancing and singing, before eventually being set alight. The most notable celebrations are in Córdoba, Granada, Conil de la Frontera (Cádiz), Vilacarillo (Jaén) and Ubrique (Cádiz). Once every three years, the Cruz de Mayo celebrations coincide with Córdoba's **Concurso Nacional de Arte Flamenco**, a prestigious week-long flamenco competition. This is followed in the second week of May by Córdoba's **Festival de los Patios**, in which home-owners compete for the prize for the most beautifully decorated patio. The map provided by the tourist office will help you find competing courtyards, which are open to the public during the day. At the same time is the **Cata del Vino** wine-tasting festival. Córdoba's festive month concludes with a fiesta, processions and bullfights to celebrate **Nuestra Señora de la Salud** from 25 May to 2 June.

SUMMER FERIAS

Every town and village in Andalucía has its own *feria*. *Ferias* originated in the Middle Ages as livestock and produce fairs, but nowadays their purpose is pleasure rather than business, and they share many characteristics with local fiestas, including dressing up, drinking, bullfights, equestrian events and dancing.

The **Feria de Abril** in **Seville** is one of the first of the annual *ferias* and is a welcome antidote to the solemnity of Semana Santa. It takes place two weeks after the end of Easter and is one of the most colourful events in Spain, described by writer Michael Jacobs as 'the ultimate secular manifestation of the baroque spirit of Andalucía'.

Horses have replaced livestock at the *feria*, largely thanks to the influence of the **Feria del Caballo** in **Jerez de la Frontera**, an older but much smaller event in early to mid May, in which locals dress up in traditional costume and compete in various equestrian events.

The Feria de Abril also marks the peak of the main bullfighting season, which begins at Easter and lasts until the **Feria de San Lucas** in mid October. This fair in **Jaén** features fights on horseback, a carriage procession and lots of competitions and events.

Marbella kicks off Málaga province's party season with the five-day **Feria de San Bernabé** during the second week of June. This is followed by *ferias* in **Conil de la Frontera** (Cádiz) on 30 June, and the **Feria de San Francisco Solano** (Montilla in south Córdoba) in the second week of July.

In August, things really hot up, with town fairs in **Aroche** (Huelva), **Grazalema** (eastern Cádiz) and the spectacular **Feria de Málaga** all taking place in the third week. Málaga's nine-day bash, with a night fair and bullfights, rivals Cádiz's Carnaval as one of the wildest events in all Andalucía. Also in the third week of August is the **Feria de Algeciras**, one of the biggest bashes in Cadíz province. At the end of the month, the Virgen del Mar, patroness of Almería, is celebrated in a ten-day *feria* with floats and flowers, sports events, a flamenco festival and bullfighting. August finishes with the **Feria de Agosto** in **Antequera**, involving more bullfights, horse-drawn carriage competitions and concerts.

In the first two weeks of September, attention turns to **Ronda** for the town *feria* and the **Fiestas de Pedro Romero**. Two weeks of festivities are heralded by a traditional bullfight in 18th-century costume, known as the '*goyesca*'.

Next up is the **Feria de San Miguel**, celebrated in various places across Seville province on the last weekend in September. In the city of Seville the fair dates back to 1875, when it replaced the cattle fair that had been lost to the Feria de Abril. It was suspended under Franco and not revived until 2001; now it's held on the same site as the April *feria*, and includes *casetas* (marquees), a portable bullring, rides and exhibitions. **Úbeda**'s **San Miguel** festival is much the same but on a smaller scale.

Coinciding with the end of the bullfighting season is the horse parade at the **Feria del Rosario** in **Fuengirola**. The *feria* season finishes with the **Feria de San Pedro de Alcántara** in mid October.

MOORS AND CHRISTIANS

In **Granada** the feast of **San Basilio** (1-2 January) celebrates the entry of Fernando and Isabel into the city in 1492, signifying the end of Moorish rule in Andalucía. To the south-east of the city, the Alpujarras became the last refuge of the Spanish Moors in the 15th century and is now one of the best regions to see pageants re-creating battles between Moors and Christians. Re-enactments take place in **Pampaneira** on 3 May and in **Trevélez** on 13-14 June to celebrate San Antonio, although the most famous pageant is at **Válor** in September, which uses a 19th-century script to tell the story of local *morisco* rebel Aben Humaya.

Feria de Málaga.

You can also catch *moros y cristianos* events in **Mojácar** and **Vélez Blanco** in Almería province, as part of the **Santo Cristo de la Yedra** celebrations during the second week of August. The fiesta dates to the 16th century.

FLAMENCO FESTIVALS

It should come as no surprise that flamenco features prominently in Andalucía's cultural calendar. The first flamenco festival was held in Córdoba in 1956 and the custom soon spread to other towns and cities. Festivals and competitions are now held in the summer months throughout each of the eight provinces.

Almería's **Peña de Taranto** in the first week of May attracts some of the biggest names in flamenco. This is followed by the **Alhaurín de la Torre** festival in Málaga province (23-26 June), which incorporates processions and one of the region's best flamenco competitions (the **Torre del Cante**).

Throughout July, the town of **Sanlúcar de Barrameda** in Cádiz comes alive to the sound of flamenco at the annual **Feria de Flamenco**. The **Caracolá de Lebrija**, one of the oldest and most famous of Andalucía's flamenco festivals, takes place in the second half of July in Lebrija, between Seville and Jerez.

In the province of Cádiz a new flamenco festival is held over the summer at the castle in **Tarifa** (www.flamencotarifa.com), while in **Vejer de la Frontera** locals celebrate the Virgen de la Oliva with a flamenco festival that attracts leading singers and dancers (10-24 August). Throughout September, during the **Fiesta de Bulería**, flamenco fills the streets of **Jerez de la Frontera**.

CULTURAL AND SPORTING EVENTS

Flamenco also makes an appearance at the **Festival de Danza** in **Jerez** in late February/ early March and at the **Festival Internacional de Musica y Danza** in **Granada** from late June to early July. This month-long event is one of Spain's most important cultural festivals, showcasing performers from around the world.

The **Festival Internacional de la Guitarra** attracts global stars like Paco de Lucía and BB King to **Córdoba** in early July. It is followed by **Seville**'s **Festival de Música, Danza y Teatro de Itálica**, which runs until the middle of August among the Roman ruins of Itálica near Seville, and **Málaga**'s **Festival de Teatro**, a drama festival in the city's Roman theatre. At the end of July, **Etnosur**, a festival of leading international folk musicians, takes place in **Alcalá La Real** in Jaén province.

The **Colombinas** festival in **Huelva** on 3 August celebrates the discovery of the New World with sports events, bullfighting, cultural performances and a dance festival.

Once every two years, **Seville** hosts the **Festival Internacional de Música y Danza** for two weeks in September (next 2008).

In contrast to these prestigious events is the informal **Festival de Verdiales**, which takes place on 28 December at the Puerta de la Torre on the C3310 road towards Almogía, north-west of Málaga city. Groups of elaborately dressed local musicians, known as '*pandas*', compete on stage and take part in spontaneous jamming sessions while bottles of potent Málaga wine and *aguadiente* are passed around.

In addition to the *corridas* that form an essential element of so many local festivals, the region's calendar also supports any number of equestrian events. Among the best known are **Las Carreras de Caballos en la Playa** on Sanlúcar de Barrameda's beach in late August; these famous horse races attract thousands of onlookers and punters.

For something very different, speed freaks can see a stage of the **World Motorcycle Championships**, held in **Jerez** in early May.

FOOD AND WINE FESTIVALS

Although copious amounts of food and drink are a prominent part of almost all of Andalucía's festivals, towns or regions known for a particular delicacy also have specific events to celebrate their speciality. One of the largest of these is the **Fiesta de Urta** in **Rota** on the coast of Cádiz province in the second week of August. More than 100,000 people attend this four-day feast to find out who can create the best dish from the town's most famous fish.

Hams are among the region's most prized delicacies. The snow-cured *jamón serrano* of **Trévelez** is celebrated in the town on the feast of **San Antonio** on 15 August, while Huelva's superlative *jamón jabugo* gets its own **Feria de Jamón** in **Aracena** in late September. The feast of **San Martín** (11 November) is the traditional time to slaughter the pigs to make these hams. The fiesta, known as **La Matanza** – literally, 'the killing' – occurs in rural towns and villages throughout the region, and involves slaughtering, butchering and sausage-making, accompanied by much eating and drinking.

A less traumatic event is the **Feria de la Tapa** in **Sanlúcar** in mid October. The whole of the main square is transformed into an open-air restaurant where visitors can sample the best tapas the town has to offer.

The **Fiesta de la Aceituna** in **Martos** in Jaén celebrates the province's number-one crop, with a symbolic olive pressing and a flamenco festival in the first week of December.

The first major wine festival of the season is in **Montilla** at the end of April – a chance to sample Córdoban *amontillado*. To understand the differences between Andalucían wines, aficionados should then head to the **Feria de la Manzanilla** in **Sanlúcar de Barrameda** in the last week of May, where the townsfolk, dressed in traditional garb, celebrate their unique sherry with dancing, parades and a horse fair.

Around 6,000 people descend on **Cómpeta** in eastern Málaga province for the **Noche del Vino** on 15 August; the town's famed sweet wines are drunk copiously, accompanied by flamenco and food. The grape harvest, known as **La Vendimia**, takes place in late August and September, and is often accompanied by a fiesta. Some of the most famous events take place at **Montilla** and **Jerez**, where the beginning of the harvest is marked by the crushing of grapes on the cathedral steps.

Seville Province

Seville

Further Afield

Features

Maps

Seville

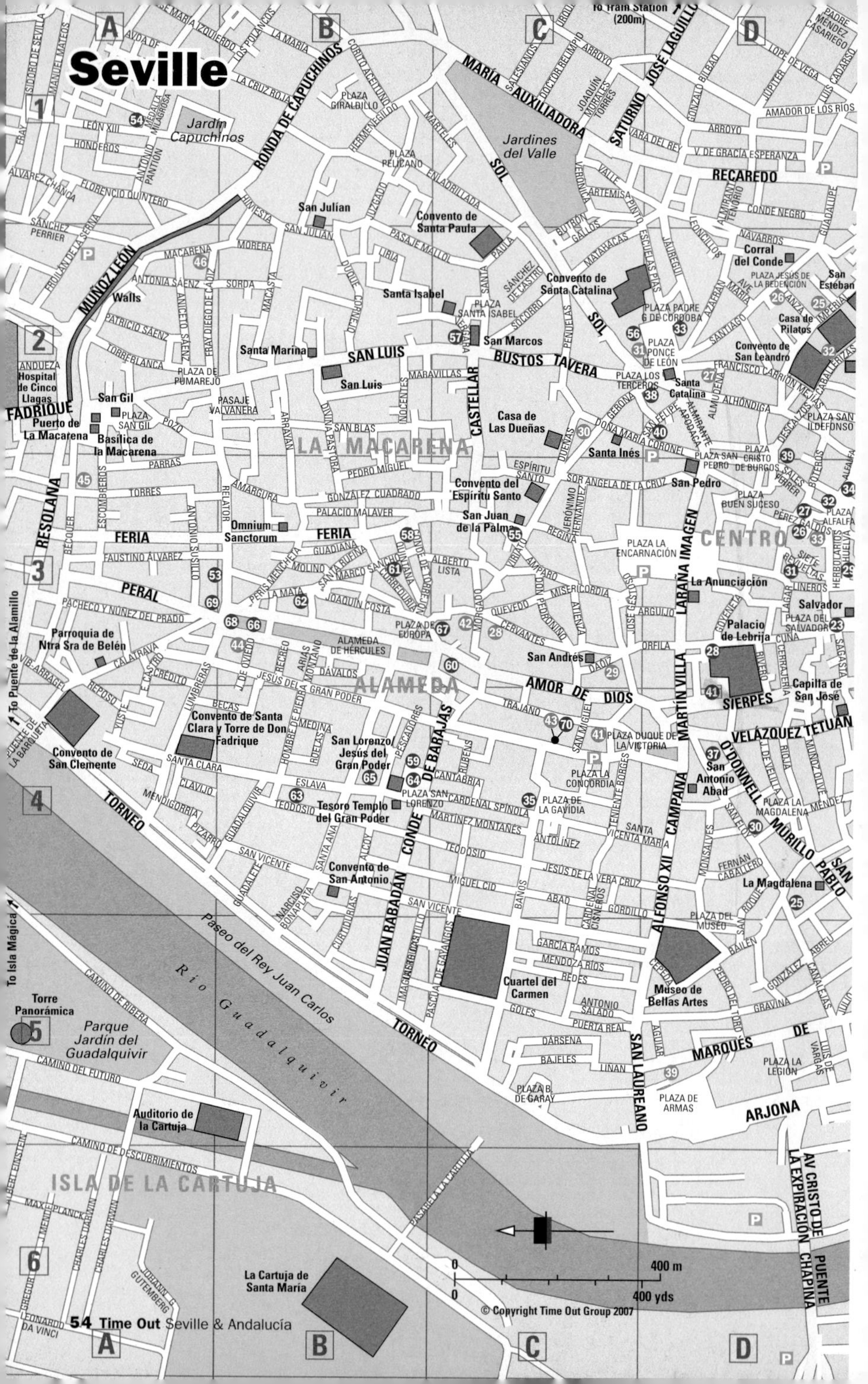
Seville
A
B
C
D
1
2
3
4
5
6
To Train Station (200m)
Jardín Capuchinos
Jardines del Valle
RONDA DE CAPUCHINOS
MARÍA AUXILIADORA
JOSÉ LAGUILLO
SATURNO
SOL
RECAREDO
MUÑOZ LEÓN
FADRIQUE
RESOLANA
FERIA
PERAL
SAN LUIS
BUSTOS TAVERA
CASTELLAR
LARAÑA IMAGEN
MARTÍN VILLA
AMOR DE DIOS
SIERPES
VELÁZQUEZ TETUÁN
O'DONNELL
MURILLO
SAN PABLO
CAMPANA
ALFONSO XII
CONDE DE BARAJAS
JUAN RABADÁN
TORNEO
SAN LAUREANO
MARQUÉS DE
ARJONA
AV CRISTO DE LA EXPIRACIÓN
PUENTE CHAPINA
San Julián
Convento de Santa Paula
Convento de Santa Catalina
Corral del Conde
San Esteban
Casa de Pilatos
Convento de San Leandro
Santa Isabel
San Marcos
Santa Marina
San Luis
Santa Catalina
Casa de Las Dueñas
Santa Inés
San Pedro
Walls
Hospital de Cinco Llagas
San Gil
Puerto de La Macarena
Basílica de la Macarena
LA MACARENA
Convento del Espíritu Santo
San Juan de la Palma
Omnium Sanctorum
CENTRO
La Anunciación
Salvador
Palacio de Lebrija
Capilla de San José
San Andrés
ALAMEDA
ALAMEDA DE HÉRCULES
PLAZA DE EUROPA
PLAZA LA ENCARNACIÓN
PLAZA DUQUE DE LA VICTORIA
PLAZA LA CONCORDIA
PLAZA DE LA GAVIDIA
Parroquia de Ntra Sra de Belén
Convento de San Clemente
Convento de Santa Clara y Torre de Don Fadrique
San Lorenzo/ Jesús del Gran Poder
Tesoro Templo del Gran Poder
Convento de San Antonio
San Antonio Abad
La Magdalena
Cuartel del Carmen
Museo de Bellas Artes
PLAZA DE ARMAS
PLAZA LA LEGIÓN
Paseo del Rey Juan Carlos
Río Guadalquivir
To Puente de la Barqueta
To Puente de la Alamillo
To Isla Mágica
Torre Panorámica
Parque Jardín del Guadalquivir
CAMINO DEL FUTURO
Auditorio de la Cartuja
CAMINO DE DESCUBRIMIENTOS
ISLA DE LA CARTUJA
PASARELA LA CARTUJA
La Cartuja de Santa María
0
400 m
0
400 yds
© Copyright Time Out Group 2007

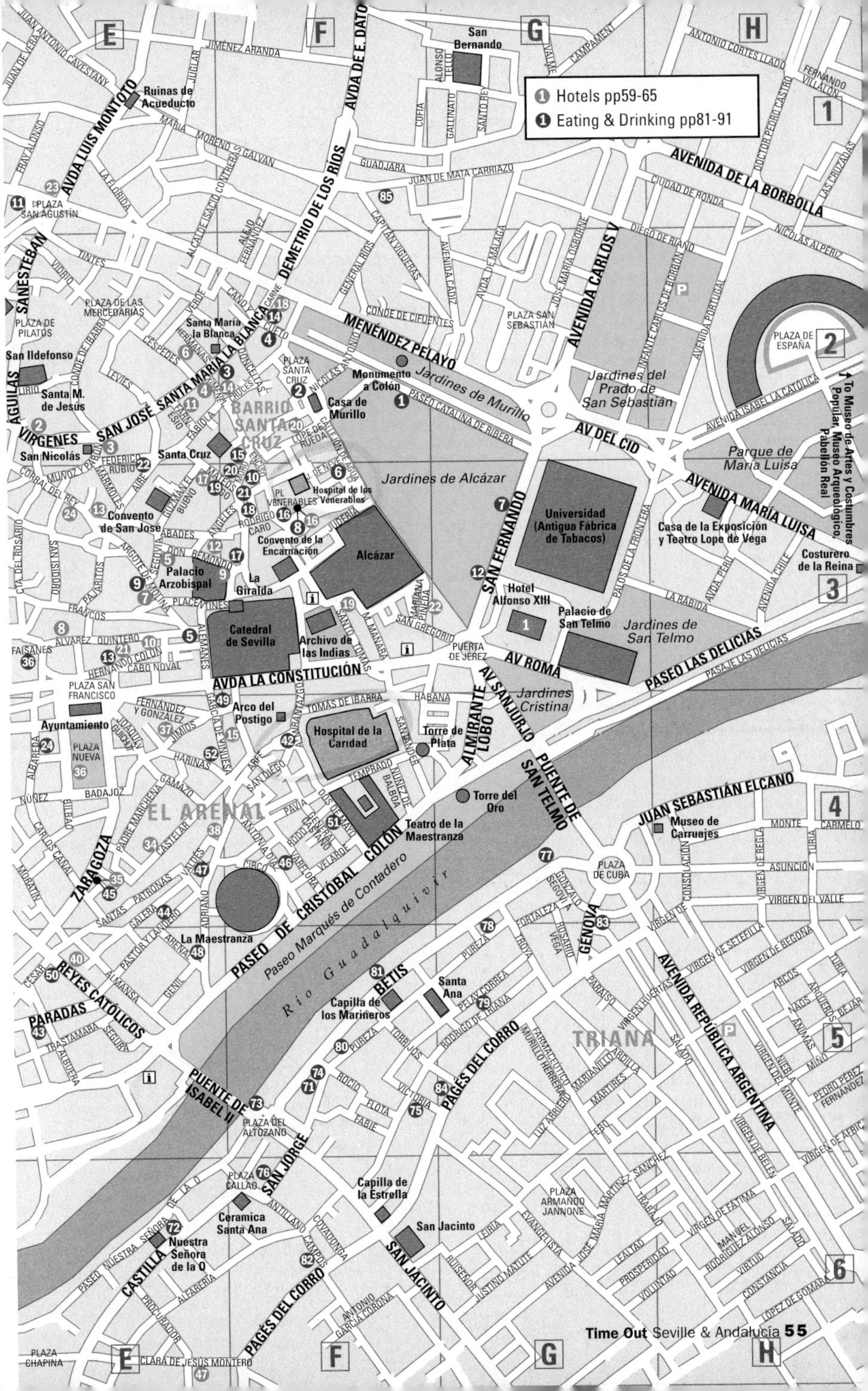
E
F
G
H
1
2
3
4
5
6
Hotels pp59-65
Eating & Drinking pp81-91
San Bernando
Ruinas de Acueducto
Jiménez Aranda
Juan Antonio Cavestany
Avda Luis Montoto
Maria Moreno Galvan
Avda de E. Dato
Demetrio de los Rios
Guadjara
Juan de Mata Carriazo
Antonio Cortes Llado
Fernando Villalón
Doctor Pedro Castro
Avenida de la Borbolla
Ciudad de Ronda
Diego de Riano
Nicolás Alperiz
Las Cruzadas
Plaza San Agustín
Sanesteban
Plaza de Pilatos
San Ildefonso
Santa M. de Jesús
Águilas
Virgenes
San Nicolás
San José
Santa Maria la Blanca
Santa Maria la Blanca
Plaza de las Mercedarias
Barrio Santa Cruz
Santa Cruz
Convento de San José
Palacio Arzobispal
La Giralda
Plaza Santa Cruz
Casa de Murillo
Monumento a Colón
Hospital de los Venerables
Convento de la Encarnación
Alcázar
Catedral de Sevilla
Archivo de las Indias
Menéndez Pelayo
Jardines de Murillo
Paseo Catalina de Ribera
Jardines de Alcázar
Conde de Cifuentes
Plaza San Sebastián
Avenida Carlos V
Jardines del Prado de San Sebastián
Plaza de España
To Museo de Artes y Costumbres Populares, Museo Arqueológico, Pabellón Real
Av del Cid
Avenida Isabel la Católica
Parque de María Luisa
Avenida María Luisa
Casa de la Exposición y Teatro Lope de Vega
Costurero de la Reina
San Fernando
Universidad (Antigua Fábrica de Tabacos)
Hotel Alfonso XIII
Palacio de San Telmo
Jardines de San Telmo
Paseo las Delicias
Puerta de Jerez
Av Roma
Jardines Cristina
Avda la Constitución
Plaza San Francisco
Ayuntamiento
Plaza Nueva
Arco del Postigo
Hospital de la Caridad
Torre de Plata
Almirante Lobo
Av Sanjurjo
Torre del Oro
Puente de San Telmo
El Arenal
Teatro de la Maestranza
La Maestranza
Paseo de Cristobal Colón
Paseo Marqués de Contadero
Río Guadalquivir
Juan Sebastián Elcano
Museo de Carruajes
Plaza de Cuba
Zaragoza
Reyes Católicos
Paradas
Betis
Capilla de los Marineros
Santa Ana
Triana
Avenida República Argentina
Puente de Isabel II
Plaza del Altozano
San Jorge
Pagés del Corro
Plaza Callao
Ceramica Santa Ana
Capilla de la Estrella
San Jacinto
Nuestra Señora de la O
Castilla
Plaza Armando Jannone
Avenida José Maria Martinez Sanchez
Plaza Chapina
Clara de Jesús Montero

Introduction

The life and *sol* of Andalucía.

Writer Rafael Cansinos-Assens called Seville the city 'where all men wish they had been born', and it is hard not to feel envious of the *sevillanos*. Theirs may not be the grandest or most modern of cities, but its vivacity and fun-loving spirit have earned it the soubriquet 'the Capital of Happiness'. This *alegría* is most easily observed in the city's 4,000 tapas bars and *tabernas* – overflowing with lively chat, cold *fino* sherry and saucers stacked with fresh fried fish. Every *sevillano* knows that the best place to eat is up at the counter, because it puts you in prime position for talking with everyone.

The eagerness of locals of all generations to uphold traditions means that Seville enjoys a distinctive and highly evolved local culture; even the surliest teenager looks forward to the week-long party of the Feria de Abril – for which it's not unusual to blow the bank on an elaborate outfit – and rather than being ousted by hip hop or techno, flamenco is currently enjoying a surge of renewed interest, with plenty of young performers experimenting with fusion styles. Even in an age of dwindling church attendance, crowds for Semana Santa (Holy Week) remain so dense that it seems the whole city has come out to admire the slowly shuffling floats and it is still considered a great honour to be part of a procession. Of course, there are, as the singer Carlos Cano pointed out, 'miserable *sevillanos*, boring *sevillanos*, who don't like the Feria and who don't like the Rocío…', but he was from Granada and they have a major reputation for dourness there.

Parties aside, Seville has plenty to see, although it must be enjoyed in the same way as the tapas: a variety of intense flavours in small portions. Apart from its three most famous monuments – the Giralda, Catedral and Alcázar – there are lots of little-visited sights, an elegant shopping area, buzzing nightlife and, of course, the ever-popular bullfighting and flamenco.

With a population of 800,000, Seville is a very manageable size and the most interesting areas are within walking distance of each other. In the Barrio de Santa Cruz there's the Arabic heritage of whitewashed alleys, tiled patios, fruit trees and the Alcázar. The centre is an imposing 17th-century collection of palaces, basilicas, the bullring and fountains, funded with booty from the New World. To the south, there's the extravagance of 1920s Seville, when they built

grand parks, hotels, museums and imposing boulevards for the 1929 Expo. The 1992 Expo, its modern mirror image, was built on the Isla Cartuja, where futuristic white buildings and bridges throw arty shapes over the water.

Current efforts are concentrated on the new metro and further pedestrianisation, which the city council is promoting under the banner 'Seville, building a dream'; progress has been continually hampered by funding problems or archaeological discoveries, leaving the slogan open to much wilful misinterpretation.

Despite this, Seville is well aware of its charms and prices can be a a good 25 per cent higher than you would pay in the rest of the province. Hotels are particularly expensive, prohibitively so for Semana Santa and the Feria de Abril, but if you aren't scared off by crowds and the complete disruption of opening hours and services, the back-to-back Semana Santa/ Feria de Abril celebrations are unforgettable. Even if you skip the parties, spring is the best time to visit: it is comfortably warm and every tree and plant is in blossom – the purple haze of jacarandas along the banks of the Guadalquivir and in the parks is strikingly beautiful. By June, term is over at the university and the nightlife starts winding down; in July and August the city is a ghost town as locals flee to the countryside to escape the infernal heat and, as low hotel prices reflect, all but the hardiest tourists try to resist Seville's charms.

History

One of the most traditional cities in Spain, Seville shows an unexpected knack for 21st-century thinking.

Seville's origins are murky, and the only thing that anyone knows for sure is that the city was founded by Hercules. The hero was engaged in the tenth of his 12 labours – stealing the cattle of Geryon – when, as the Quintero brothers explained in their comic poem *The History of Seville*, he became bored and decided to look for a place to open up a tavern. Hercules stopped in his tracks when he came to one beautiful spot, known today as the Alameda de Hércules, and marked the future city with six columns.

According to the official line, archaeological findings show the province of Seville to have been populated since around 5,000 BC, although the indigenous Iberian tribes did not settle in the fertile Guadalquivir valley until 800 BC. They began trading with Phoenician merchants who soon took over the settlements; this civilisation is thought to be the semi-mythical Tartessus, a mysterious culture referred to by the Bible and Greek historians, which was said to have provided precious metals for the temple of King Solomon. Apparently a peaceful and cultured race, the Tartessians left behind a few precious golden fingerprints in the form of the Carambolo jewellery, but little else. Their descendants called the settlement Hispalis, a name attributed to the wooden piles driven into the ground as building foundations.

During the Second Punic War, Scipio Africanus led the Roman invaders to victory in 206 BC. Under Roman rule Hispalis grew in size and significance and, together with the nearby military community of Itálica, became the political nerve centre of Baetica, the Spanish division of the Roman Empire. Julius Cesar named the city Iulia Romula Hispalis and filled it with forums, baths and temples: the area that now contains the cathedral is still sometimes referred to as the acropolis.

After the Roman Empire fell into decline, Christianity was legalised and Hispalis was taken over by a string of Visigothic invaders. By the time of Archbishop San Isidro in the sixth and seventh century it had settled down to become a leading cultural centre and Isidro's *Etymologies* was in its time regarded as the sum of all the knowledge of antiquity.

Over 500 years of Moorish rule followed the initial Islamic invasion in 711; Baetica became al-Andalus while Hispalis became known as Isibilya. Although Isibilya was of great cultural and political importance, Córdoba was the main seat of power until constant infighting caused the collapse of the caliphate in 1031. Isibilya finally rose to prominence after the 12th-century takeover by the Almohad tribe, who made it their capital and built the Alcázar, a huge mosque (where the cathedral stands today) and the Giralda.

When the city was conquered by Christian forces in 1248 a significant decline followed when most of the city's Muslim population fled as a wave of religious persecution was unleashed by Fernando III. The city was left with Mudéjares (converted Muslims, the name means 'those who were allowed to stay'), 24,000 new Christian settlers and a briefly thriving Jewish population. It remained a favoured city for subsequent rulers, however, including the infamous Pedro I 'The Cruel', who enlarged the royal residences in the Alcázar, employing a huge force of Moorish craftsmen.

It was the jackpot discovery of the Americas in 1492 that signalled the city's arrival on the world stage. Called the New Jerusalem and the Babylon of the West, Seville soon became the *Puerto y Puerta de las Indias* (Port and Gateway to the Indies), and its monopoly on American trade for the best part of two centuries saw it grow to become the largest and richest city in Spain. With money came culture and over this period Seville nurtured world-class artists such as Velázquez, Murillo, Valdés Leal, Roldán and the architect Juan de Oviedo. The population exploded from 50,000 to over 150,000 between 1500 and 1600, forcing the construction of a baroque and Renaissance city over the medieval layout; the many palace-homes built during this period boast splendid façades in contrast to the more inward-looking Muslim dwellings.

Dark times were just around the corner, however, and in 1649 a great plague killed off half the population. Meanwhile, the river Guadalquivir was quietly silting up and by the late 1600s, sandbars had made it impassable for the huge trade galleons, and the head of the Indies fleet transferred to Cádiz, signalling the end of the party for Seville. The widespread devastation of the 1755 Lisbon earthquake, said to be so fierce that the bells of the Giralda pealed on their own, and another plague in 1800 further weakened the city and Seville was easy prey for invading Napoleonic troops: the French occupied the city from 1810 to 1812.

Seville attempted to re-establish itself with the huge Ibero-American Exhibition of 1929. It had a signficant impact on the appearance of the city – the Parque de María Luisa and the Plaza de España were one result – but left the city in deep debt for over half a century.

The 1930s saw great bloodshed and Seville fell almost immediately in the Civil War, becoming Franco's first major prize in 1936. The decades of grinding poverty that followed were known as *los años de plomo* (the 'years of lead') and although the city's status gradually revived, it remained the capital of one of the most backward regions of Spain.

Seville's fortunes perked up in the 1980s when the Socialists, led by native *sevillano* Felipe González, came to power. One of the most significant events of his term of office was the enormous spending spree that presaged Expo '92, timed to mark the 500th anniversary of Columbus' voyage. Although it was to bankrupt the city once again, the Expo's legacy included the Santa Justa train station, the high-speed AVE rail connection to Madrid, the Maestranza theatre and new bridges across the Guadalquivir. The pavilions were built on the Isla Cartuja, a vast complex of almost exaggeratedly modern buildings which, after many embarrassing years as a white elephant, is finally gaining credibility as an area for business, cultural activities and clubbing.

Thrills, spills and polka-dot frills

The Andalucían capital of Seville, proverbially represented as a city of exotic sensuality and endless leisure, has bizarrely emerged in recent years as a popular setting for thrillers. The first person to see its possibilities as such was Murcia-born journalist turned novelist Arturo Pérez-Reverte, the most translated Spanish writer of today, if also perhaps the most overrated. His much-reprinted *The Seville Communion* involves a handsome and computer-literate priest who has been sent to investigate a couple of mysterious deaths at the bogus church of 'Our Lady of the Tears'. As a thriller, it may be less than successful; but it can be enjoyed as a portrait of the Seville that seduces most of its visitors.

Pérez-Reverte is an aficionado of the city, and he amiably incorporates into the narrative its most obvious attractions, from celebrated café La Campana on C/Sierpes, to restaurants in the tourist-congested Barrio de Santa Cruz. He also brings together a cast of *sevillano* stereotypes that include the slimy *señorito* (toff), the impoverished aristocrat, and the stunning young woman named after the most popular of the city's devotional images, the Virgin of the Macarena.

A far grimmer and more disturbing view of Seville can be glimpsed in the works of the British crime writer Robert Wilson, who has written a series of novels involving Inspector Javier Falcón. The first of these was the powerful and, at times, unbearably grotesque *The Blind Man of Seville*, in which Falcón is introduced as a recently separated man suffering from middle-aged angst and other ailments. Wilson knows Seville well, and has taken the trouble to research local corruption, and the workings of the city's police force. The atmosphere of his first Falcón novel also benefits from the author's evocation of the chaos accompanying the Holy Week festivities.

The *sevillanos*, touchy about how their city is represented, have taken violent offence to the way the place emerges in Dan Brown's *The Digital Fortress*, which opens with the unlikely image of a Japanese computer genius having an ostensible heart attack in the Plaza de España. The novel, first translated into Spanish early in 2006 following the unexpected success of *The Da Vinci Code*, has an author's note in the Spanish edition saying that Seville is his favourite European city, that he has been there no fewer than four times, and has even learnt to dance *sevillanas*.

Such professed intimacy has not prevented Brown from making such howlers as dating the 14th-century cathedral to the 11th century, and upsetting the *sevillanos* with his vision of the city as a third-world place with squalid hospitals and malfunctioning buses. Needless to say, their anger at Brown has not been reflected in sales of the book: for much of 2006 it was the bestselling book in Seville.

Where to Stay

Seville's hotels and *hostales* are often pretty but always pricey.

Hotel Alfonso XIII. *See p60.*

Seville's accommodation scene has improved dramatically over the last few years, although it is still generally geared towards the upper end of the market; you will notice a marked hike in hotel prices compared to the rest of the province. Seville has pioneered *casa particular* and *palacio* conversions, and exquisite former private homes have been turned into boutique-style hotels. But the city still struggles to provide good-quality rooms in the lower price categories, with *pensiones* and *hostales* often significantly overpriced.

Given the age of many of the converted buildings, it is wise to remember that rooms will often overlook interior patios rather than the street (which can be a blessing in noisy Seville); old houses were built to keep the light and heat out, so rooms tend to be dark and gloomy with small windows.

In terms of room rates, Seville has four seasons: low season includes July and August when prices drop but temperatures go through the roof; mid season is from March to June (excluding the fiestas) and from September to mid November; high season is Semana Santa; and very high, or 'extra', is the Feria de Abril. As well as being prohibitively expensive to stay in the city during high or extra periods, it is almost impossible to find any accommodation at all unless you book months in advance.

Finding hotels tucked down narrow backstreets can be a problem and the city council has responded with signs pointing the way to nearly every hotel. They respect the one-way traffic system and can be followed by car.

If you are staying centrally, avoid the hotel breakfasts and venture out to one of the many nearby bars for a far better deal and much more atmosphere.

Note: the hotels listed below are arranged in descending order of price for a double room within each area.

Barrio de Santa Cruz

Hotel Alfonso XIII

C/San Fernando 2 (954 91 70 00/www.westin.com). **Rates** (incl breakfast) €400-€486 single; €518-€679 double; €1,107-€1,926 suites. **Credit** AmEx, DC, MC, V. **Map** p55 G3 ❶

This five-star hotel, once the finest in all Spain, has been taken over by an international chain, whose bland and incongruous Americanisms have diluted its unique character. But it's still a beautiful place, built by King Alfonso for the 1929 Expo as accommodation for the royal family, visiting heads of state, leading matadors and the like. Breakfast includes champagne and caviar, and its two top-class restaurants – one Japanese, the other international – are popular with wealthy *sevillanos*. **Photo** *p59.*

Casa Numero 7

C/Virgenes 7 (954 22 15 81/21 45 27/www.casanumero7.com). **Rates** (incl breakfast) €189-€294 single/double. **Credit** MC, V. **Map** p55 E2 ❷

Staying here is more like being a visitor to someone's private mansion than a guest in a hotel. The six guest rooms (ask for the yellow room) are individually designed and furnished, with original paintings and antiques. The roof terrace has views of the Giralda and in the breakfast room a white-gloved butler serves the best scrambled eggs in Seville.

Hotel Petit Palace Santa Cruz

C/Muñoz y Pabón 18 (954 22 10 32/www.hthoteles.com). **Rates** €96-€268 double; €128-€300 triple; €150-€321 quadruple. **Credit** AmEx, DC, MC, V. **Map** p55 E2 ❸

This 17th-century mansion on a quiet backstreet was converted into a modern boutique hotel in April 2006. The 46 comfortable rooms, spread over three floors, are decorated in minimalist monochrome with flat-screen TVs, fine bathrooms and the odd historical touch, such as the stunning coffered ceiling in room 007. The staff are young and friendly, and free internet access is provided in the lobby.

Hotel Rey Alfonso X

C/Ximénez Enciso 35 (954 21 00 70/www.reyalfonsox.com). **Rates** €128-€193 single; €131-€214 double; €214-€289 suite. **Credit** AmEx, DC, MC, V. **Map** p55 E2 ❹

Very modern and extremely stylish, this well-located four-star boasts a rooftop pool with views over the cathedral. The 18th-century tiles in the reception are balanced by cutting-edge designer bathrooms and understated decor. The 35 rooms either look on to a quiet patio or out to the noisy square, but they are all soundproofed and have little balconies.

Los Seises

C/Segovia 6 (954 22 94 95/www.hotellosseises.com). **Rates** €140-€172 single; €172-€219 double. **Credit** AmEx, DC, MC, V. **Map** p55 E3 ❺

This 16th-century former archbishop's palace is like a miniature museum, stuffed full of Roman and Arab artefacts. The en suite rooms are comfortable and tastefully designed, and there's an excellent restaurant, not to mention a rooftop swimming pool with views of the Giralda. The in-house restaurant, La Cocina de los Seises, is set in a pretty courtyard.

Las Casas de la Judería

Callejón de Dos Hermanas 7 (954 41 51 50/www.casasypalacios.com). **Rates** €96-€198 single; €144-€284 double; €251-€428 suite. **Credit** AmEx, DC, MC, V. **Map** p55 E2 ❻

Over the years this historic hotel has expanded to include a whole series of houses and palaces in the Jewish quarter, and has the feel of an exclusive gated community, with romantic patios filled with fountains, plants and antiques. Be aware that the quality of the 118 rooms varies enormously and the maze-like corridors connecting them can mean a long walk to breakfast.

Convento La Gloria

C/Argote de Molina 26-28 (954 29 36 70/www.hotelconventolagloria.com). **Rates** €86-€136 single; €128-€203 double. **Credit** AmEx, DC, MC, V. **Map** p55 E3 ❼

It doesn't look like any vows of poverty were taken at this lavishly decorated 15th-century nunnery, encrusted with *azulejos*, coffered ceilings and artwork. It was converted into a hotel in 2003 and, while six of the 35 rooms have face-on views of the Giralda, some of the darker rooms can feel a little cell-like. Guests get discounts at the excellent Don Raimundo restaurant downstairs (*see p83*) and can have breakfast in the beautiful street-level café.

Las Casas de los Mercaderes

C/Álvarez Quintero 9-13 (954 22 58 58/www.casasypalacios.com). **Rates** €82-€171 single; €120-€150 double. **Credit** AmEx, DC, MC, V. **Map** p55 E3 ❽

This very pretty 18th-century building has been converted into a stylish hotel. Rooms are arranged around a patio, complete with columned arcades, galleries, mosaic tiling and an elaborate stained-glass roof. While the rooms themselves can't claim to match this, they are very comfortable; however, some – especially those that open on to the central courtyard – can feel a little gloomy.

Doña María

C/Don Remondo 19 (954 22 49 98/www.hdmaria.com). **Rates** €69-€176 single; €107-€256 double. **Credit** AmEx, DC, MC, V. **Map** p55 E/F3 ❾

Originally the property of Samuel Levy, the right-hand man of Pedro I 'the Cruel', this palatial home was once connected to the Alcázar via subterranean passages. But what really sells it, besides its antique fittings and four-poster beds, is the swimming pool on the roof. It's an extremely comfortable hotel, and reasonably priced considering its perfect location.

Hotel Alminar

C/Álvarez Quintero 52 (954 29 39 13/www.hotelalminar.com). **Rates** €60-€140 single; €90-€195 double; €110-€245 superior double. **Credit** AmEx, DC, MC, V. **Map** p55 E3 ❿

Just a minute's walk from the cathedral on a quiet pedestrian street, this charming little boutique hotel opened in 2005. Modern but not aggressively trendy, rooms have bags of style, with dark latticed woods, creamy fabrics, and chrome and marble bathrooms; rooms 31 and 32 ('superior' doubles) have their own terraces with views of the Giralda. The tiny lobby is improved by complimentary water, tea and coffee. Friendly service.

Hotel Amadeus

C/Farnesio 6 (954 50 14 43/www.hotelamadeus sevilla.com). **Rates** €69 single; €85-€149 double; €139-224 junior suite. **Credit** DC, MC, V. **Map** p55 E2 ⓫

An 18th-century home has been converted into a tasteful hotel with a musical theme. You are serenaded in the light-filled entrance, and pianos, sheet music and paintings of famous composers are dotted around the rooms and public areas. Each of the 14 rooms has a pretty design, and there is a roof terrace with views of the Giralda.

YH Giralda

C/Abades 30 (954 22 83 24/www.yh-hoteles.com). **Rates** €64-€148 single/double; €85-€200 triple; €92-€206 suite. **Credit** AmEx, DC, MC, V. **Map** p55 E/F3 ⓬

Despite the misleading name, this has nothing to do with youth hostels. It is, however, one of very few mansion conversions – in this case an 18th-century abbot's home – that won't break the *banco*, with stylish decor and fittings. Rooms, although generally on the small side, are simple and elegant with modern flourishes. Try to avoid those set around the ventilation shaft at the back of the hotel.

Hostal Callejón del Agua

C/Corral del Rey 23 (954 21 91 89/www.callejon delagua.es). **Rates** (incl breakfast) €106-€128 double. **Credit** AmEx, DC, MC, V. **Map** p55 E3 ⓭

This charming little *hostal* opened in 2006 and occupies a renovated 19th-century *casa-palacio*. Each of the 16 comfortable rooms is named after a different *paso* (float) from Semana Santa and decorated with pink and white stripes, floral upholstery and, on the first floor, intricate wrought-iron window grilles. Free coffee and newspapers are available in the pleasant reception area and there's a roof terrace.

Hotel Alcántara

C/Ximénez Enciso 28 (954 50 05 95/www.hotel alcantara.net). **Rates** €55-€112 single; €70-€140 double; €85-€165 triple. **Credit** AmEx, DC, MC, V. **Map** p55 F3 ⓮

In terms of value, style and location, this converted 18th-century converted mansion is hard to beat. Not easy to find, it is accessed through an old coach entrance set on a quiet backstreet near the Jardines de Murillo. The rooms are airy, spacious and decorated in white and cool shades of grey, while the bathrooms are surprisingly large for a city that generally favours the phonebox approach to bathroom architecture.

Hotel Simón

C/García de Vinuesa 19 (954 22 66 60/www. hotelsimonsevilla.com). **Rates** €48-€64 single; €74-€101 double; €107-€129 suite. **Credit** DC, MC, V. **Map** p55 E4 ⓯

Just across from the cathedral, this is another hotel housed in an 18th-century conversion, with columns, foliage and a large amount of antique furniture and fittings (think gilded mirrors, chandeliers, carpets and cabinets full of silver). Although the first-floor rooms have some very pretty tilework, the bedrooms are nothing special, and the cramped former servants' quarters on the top floor are to be avoided.

Hotel Hosteria del Laurel

Plaza de los Venerables 5 (954 22 02 95/www.hosteria dellaurel.com). **Rates** €52-€88 single; €74-€120 double. **Credit** AmEx, DC, MC, V. **Map** p55 F3 ⓰

The inn that inspired Don José Zorillo to conjure up Don Juan Tenorio during his stay here in 1844, and each of the 21 rooms is named after a character in his play. Comfortable rooms open on to a mellow square or small interior patios enlivened with fountains and flowers. All rooms have marble floors and good-sized en suite bathrooms.

Hostal Goya

C/Mateos Gago 31 (954 21 11 70/www.hostalgoya sevilla.com). **Rates** €50-€80 single; €80-€110 double. **Credit** MC, V. **Map** p55 F3 ⓱

This 19-room townhouse is a good low-budget option. The gold façade looks grand, but inside it's a cosy, simple affair made memorable by the friendly and helpful staff. Recent renovations mean that all rooms are now en suite with TV, phones, air-conditioning and heating.

Hotel Puerta de Sevilla

Puerta de la Carne 2 (954 98 72 70/www.hotelpuerta desevilla.com). **Rates** €50-€130 single; €65-€147 double. **Credit** AmEx, DC, MC, V. **Map** p55 F2 ⓲

This small and exceptionally friendly hotel is one of those perfect finds, just so long as rose-printed chintz and striped pastel wallpaper are to your taste. The good-value rooms have balconies overlooking the street and, although of a modest size, they are clean, comfortable and well maintained.

Hostal Van Gogh

C/Miguel de Mañara 4 (954 21 08 64/www.grupo-piramide.com). **Rates** €56-€145 double. **Credit** AmEx, DC, MC, V. **Map** p55 F3 ⓳

One of a pair of *hostales* under the same management, offering decent value and locations convenient for the cathedral and the Alcázar. The Van Gogh is designed in bright colours and festooned with pot plants; although not large, the en suite rooms are clean and comfy, and most have air-conditioning. The Hostal Picasso is nearby at C/San Gregorio 1.

Hotel Murillo

C/Lope de Rueda 9 (954 21 60 95/www.hotel murillo.com). **Rates** €48-€95 single; €60-€120 double. **Credit** AmEx, DC, MC, V. **Map** p55 F2 ⓴

Las Casas del Rey de Baeza.

Named after and dedicated to the Sevillian artist, this two-star has fairly standard rooms and smallish bathrooms, but there's a pleasant, old-fashioned feel to it and the common areas are impressive. Owned by the same people are the nearby Apartamentos Murillo (C/Reinosa 6, 954 21 09 59, www.apartamentosmurillo.com), which are more modern and excellent value for families.

Hotel San Francisco

C/Álvarez Quintero 38 (954 50 15 41/www.sanfranciscoh.com). **Rates** €40-€73 single; €50-€110 double; €62-€122 triple. **Credit** AmEx, DC, MC, V. **Map** p55 E3 ㉑
Located just around the corner from the cathedral, this adequate one-star has diminutive but clean en suite rooms, all with TV, air-conditioning and central heating. The rather austere decoration has a classic Sevillian air with dark wood furniture and tiled floors. The busy pedestrian street can be noisy; ask for one of the rooms that give on to the interior patio or the quieter backstreet.

Hostal Arias

C/Mariana Pineda 9 (954 21 83 89/www.hostalarias.com). **Rates** €34-€80 single; €46-€90 double; €62-€120 triple. **Credit** DC, MC, V. **Map** p55 F3 ㉒
A good-value, functional, comfortable *hostal* in an excellent location, literally round the corner from the Alcázar. Despite the pretty tiling in the lobby, the rooms are plain, with chintzy bedspreads and furnishings, but it's all spanking clean. All rooms have air-conditioning, heating and bathroom.

Hostal Puerta Carmona

Plaza San Agustín 5 (954 98 83 10). **Rates** €50-€75 double. **Credit** DC, MC, V. **Map** p55 E1 ㉓
Good-value *hostal* in a tastefully converted 19th-century townhouse located on the edge of the Barrio de Santa Cruz. The interior is distinctively modern and airy, with sophisticated touches like marble tables, tiled floors and bow windows on the first floor. En suite rooms have TV and air-con.

Hostal Sierpes

C/Corral del Rey 22 (954 22 49 48/www.hsierpes.com). **Rates** €35-€60 single; €50-€104 double; €60-€132 triple. **Credit** AmEx, MC, V. **Map** p55 E3 ㉔
At the heart of the action, this *pensión* is also good value, with its attractive, airy lobby. Most of the rooms are surprisingly big and light, and ranged around a small patio, although the decor is forgettable and a little threadbare. There's a garage and a decent restaurant attached.

Centro

Hotel Casa Imperial

C/Imperial 29 (954 50 03 00/www.casaimperial.com). **Rates** €214-€449 suites; €337-€556 triple. **Credit** AmEx, DC, MC, V. **Map** p54 D2 ㉕
This 16th-century *palacio*, originally owned by the Villafranco family (you can see their coat of arms carved into the entrance), has been turned into an exquisite, rambling five-star hotel made up of a series of beautiful interconnecting patios. Each luxury guest room is individually designed, with tiled floors, big beds and chunky antique furniture. Many bathrooms have sunken baths and twin washbasins. Rates include the use of a nearby gym and pool.

Las Casas del Rey de Baeza

Plaza Jesús de la Redención 2, off C/Santiago (954 56 14 96/www.hospes.es). **Rates** €139-€294 single; €160-€321 double; €321-€535 suite. **Credit** AmEx, DC, MC, V. **Map** p54 D2 ㉖
Converted from a pretty old *corral de vecinos* (workers' flats around a central patio), this place oozes luxurious cool, decorated with slate, teak, hessian and subtle hues. Superior rooms and suites come with hi-fis and DVD players (CDs and DVDs are free to borrow), and the sitting rooms have free internet access and books, with huge leather sofas in which to enjoy them. A hammock next to the rooftop pool is a stunning place for a sundowner, and there are plans to open a spa in 2007.

La Casa del Maestro.

La Casa del Maestro

C/Almudena 5 (954 50 00 07/www.lacasadel maestro.com). Closed 2wks Aug. **Rates** (incl breakfast) €96-€192 single; €107-€199 double; €123-€267 suite. **Credit** AmEx, DC, MC, V. **Map** p54 D2 ㉗

La Casa del Maestro is a hidden gem with bags of character, located in a quiet street. The house once belonged to renowned guitarist Niño Ricardo and the sympathetic conversion is full of pictures of El Maestro and other flamenco greats. The guest rooms are on the small side but comfortable, with big beds and fluffy pillows, while the bathrooms are decorated in perky blue and white porcelain. At the centre of the building is a pretty patio and small dining room where guests can enjoy breakfast and free internet access.

Hotel Cervantes

C/Cervantes 10 (954 90 02 80/www.hotel-cervantes.com). **Rates** €93-€182 single; €107-€214 double. **Credit** AmEx, DC, MC, V. **Map** p54 C3 ㉘

A recently built three-star with a plant-festooned, light-filled patio covered over with a glass ceiling. It's off the tourist trail, near the newly trendy Alameda, but still only ten minutes' walk from the cathedral. The rooms are all of a decent size and pleasantly, if uninspiringly, decorated; all have a minibar and air-conditioning.

Hotel Casona de San Andrés

C/Daóiz 7 (954 91 52 53/www.casonadesanandres.com). **Rates** €45-€50 single; €100-€160 double; €120-€180 triple. **Credit** MC, V. **Map** p54 C3 ㉙

A romantic mood pervades in this lovingly converted 19th-century mansion, with its carved dark wood furniture, leaded windows and wrought-iron balustrades. The brightest and most spacious rooms have balconies overlooking the square and original mosaic floors, but those giving on to the back patio are somewhat lacking in light and privacy. There is a roof terrace with sun loungers set around a stained-glass skylight.

Hotel Don Pedro

C/Gerona 22 (954 29 33 33/www.hoteldonpedro.net). **Rates** €50-€75 single; €65-€128 double. **Credit** AmEx, DC, MC, V. **Map** p54 C2 ㉚

A good-value two-star in a converted 18th-century palace on a quiet street just a few doors down from the famed El Rinconcillo tapas bar (*see p85*). Although the public spaces are very pretty and atmospheric, the bedrooms are merely functional, with comfortable but bland decor. Breakfast is served on the pretty patio.

Casa Baco

Plaza Ponce de León 15 (954 56 50 50/www.baco.es/hotel.htm). **Rates** €44.94-€85 single; €66.34-€133 double. **Credit** AmEx, DC, MC, V. **Map** p54 C/D2 ㉛

Part of the Baco delicatessen and restaurant chain, this hotel might not quite live up to the charm of its lovely façade and lobby but it's certainly more than adequate. Its 25 rooms are clean and neat with dark wood and pink upholstery, and all are en suite with air-conditioning. Those overlooking the patio are quieter than those over the busy square.

Hostal Atenas

C/Caballerizas 1 (954 21 80 47/www.hostal-atenas.com). **Rates** €32-€42 single; €58-€101 double; €74-€128 triple. **Credit** AmEx, DC, MC, V. **Map** p54 D2 ㉜

This is a good budget option, with plenty of plants and tiles, and clean, comfortable rooms.

Casa Sol y Luna

C/Pérez Galdós 1A (954 21 06 82/www.casasoly luna1.com). **Rates** €22-€32 single; €38-€80 double; €60-€90 triple. **No credit cards**. **Map** p54 D3 ㉝

This converted *casa-palacio* offers history, atmosphere and superlatively friendly service at rock-bottom prices. The best of the ten rooms is No.7, with its painted ceiling, *azulejos* and carved wooden dado. Some rooms are en suite, but others are served by large communal bathrooms. Most give on to a central patio and salon area, which can be noisy.

El Arenal

Hotel Vincci La Rábida

C/Castelar 24 (954 50 12 80/www.vinccihoteles.com). **Rates** €120-€300 single; €120-€345 double; €250-€490 suite. **Credit** AmEx, DC, MC, V. **Map** p55 E4 34

Tucked into the streets of El Arenal, halfway between the bullring and the cathedral, this 80-room, chain hotel is fine as long as you are not hoping for a chatty, family-style welcome. The rooms, set in an 18th-century palace, are arranged around two patios, but the labyrinthine interior structure means some rooms can only be reached by changing lifts. The rooftop terrace has great views.

Hotel Taberna del Alabardero

C/Zaragoza 20 (954 56 06 37/www.tabernadelalabardero.com). Closed Aug. **Rates** (incl breakfast) €123-€139 single; €139-€267 double; €160-€310 junior suite. **Credit** AmEx, DC, MC, V. **Map** p55 E4 35

This four-star in the 19th-century home of poet Juan Antonio Cavestany has been converted into one of the most tastefully designed small hotels in Seville. The seven elegant rooms, all with jacuzzi, are ranged round a patio draped in vines and flooded with light.

Hotel Inglaterra

Plaza Nueva 7 (954 22 49 70/www.hotelinglaterra.es). **Rates** €133-€235 double; €321 junior suite. **Credit** AmEx, DC, MC, V. **Map** p55 E4 36

For once the rooms outdo the lobby, so don't let the rather grotty statue of a bearskin-wearing guard by the entrance put you off. Rooms were completely renovated in 2006 and are very comfortable, with marble bathrooms, automatic blinds and warm wooden furnishings. There's a large sofa lounge in the lobby and an Irish pub, the Trinity, along with several small conference rooms.

Petit Palace Marqués de Santa Ana

C/Jimios 9-11 (954 22 18 12/www.hthoteles.com). **Rates** €96-€299 single/double. **Credit** AmEx, DC, MC, V. **Map** p55 E4 37

This recently opened hotel sits in a mid 19th-century building with a lovely roof terrace. The lounge manages to blend an arcaded patio with streamlined modern decor, while the look in the rooms is sharp and crisp, with lots of dark wood, dramatic lighting effects and magenta ceilings to offset the neutral palette. The high-tech rooms are business-oriented, with laptops, plasma TVs and exercise bikes.

Hotel Adriano

C/Adriano 12 (954 29 38 00/www.adrianohotel.com). **Rates** €85-€160 single; €107-€181 double. **Credit** MC, V. **Map** p55 E4 38

The excellent Hotel Adriano is strangely little known and a good place to seek rooms during busy times such as Semana Santa. Above a spacious lobby with pillars, striped sofas and a café, the 34 spotless rooms are kitted out in classic dark furniture with pelmetted curtains and marble floors, and the superior rooms have impressive high-post beds.

Hotel NH Plaza de Armas

C/Marqués de Paradas s/n (954 90 19 92/www.nh-hotels.com). **Rates** €106-€244 single/double; €187-€294 suite. **Credit** AmEx, DC, MC, V. **Map** p54 D5 39

The impressive curve of the building, the minimalist lobby and artworks, and the gentle brown and beige furnishings are verging on iconoclasm in what is, in design and hotelling terms, a conservative city. Function rooms make it one of the centre's few good business hotels, and there's a pool, satellite TV and babysitting for tourists.

Hotel Puerta de Triana

C/Reyes Católicos 5 (954 21 54 04/www.hotelpuertadetriana.com). **Rates** (incl breakfast) €64-€90 single; €85-€139 double; €128-€160 triple. **Credit** AmEx, DC, MC, V. **Map** p55 E5 40

Just a few streets away from the Maestranza bullring and the river, this hotel is spacious and comfortable. Although on a wide and noisy avenue, only eight of the 65 rooms are street facing and the rest look over the quiet interior patios. The public spaces are all elegant and well maintained and the rooms, while not particularly memorable, are of a decent size and have good, modern bathrooms.

La Alameda

Casa Romana

C/Trajano 15 (954 91 51 70/www.hotelcasaromana.com). **Rates** €117-€230 single; €253-€325 double; €550 junior suite. **Credit** AmEx, DC, MC, V. **Map** p54 C4 41

An incredible amount of care has gone into this boutique hotel, from the cold glass of *fino* offered to new arrivals to fresh flowers in the bathroom. Built on the site of an old Roman palace, each of the 24 rooms is named after a Roman emperor and decorated in warm and harmonious colours with hemp matting. Guests can take their breakfast or drinks up on the roof terrace, which has great views and a jacuzzi.

Hotel Corregidor

C/Morgado 17, corner of C/Amor de Dios (954 38 51 11/www.vimehoteles.com). **Rates** €74-€155 single; €84-€168 double; €119-€238 triple. **Credit** AmEx, DC, MC, V. **Map** p54 C3 42

At the end of a tiny cobbled passageway, the Corregidor is easy to walk past but, once inside, it's an oasis of tranquillity, with an exquisite patio and an airy, elegant lobby with a bar. The rooms were once famously grotty but a recent facelift and a back extension has left them all peachily painted, albeit in a rather forgettable corporate style. Popular with tour groups so the lobby can get mobbed at times.

Espacio Azahar

C/Jesús del Gran Poder 28 (954 38 4109/www.espacioazahar.com). **Rates** €63-€80 single; €85-€139 double. **Credit** AmEx, DC, MC, V. **Map** p54 C4 43

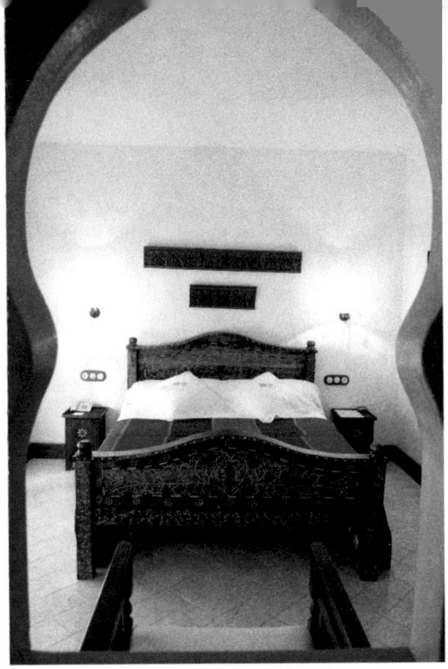

Alcoba del Rey.

The 'Orange Blossom Space' is enviably located in a beautiful late 19th-century townhouse by Aníbal González. Its 14 spacious rooms are decorated in light yellow, blue or white, and combine mosaic floors and wrought-iron bedsteads with the technological comfort of Wi-Fi and plasma TVs. There's also a café, restaurant and roof terrace bar.

Aparthotel Patios de la Alameda

Alameda de Hercules 56 (954 90 49 99, www.patiosdelaalamenda.com). **Rates** €64-€131 single; €82-€165 double. **Credit** AmEx, DC, MC, V. **Map** p54 B3 44

These modern and comfy two-person apartments are set around airy, flower-filled patios and represent excellent value for money, with a kitchen, bathroom, bedroom, sofa bed and living room, all cleaned daily and with 24-hour reception service.

La Macarena

Alcoba del Rey

C/Bécquer 9 (954 91 58 00/www.alcobadelrey.com). **Rates** (incl breakfast) €107-€182 single; €127-€266 double. **Credit** AmEx, DC, MC, V. **Map** p54 A3 45

This pretty Moorish-style boutique hotel opened in 2005. Rooms are all different but may contain huge tiled baths, diaphanous drapes, Moroccan rugs or Alhambra-style plasterwork. The common areas are tastefully decked out with kilims, candles and trickling fountains, while there is a rooftop terrace with a Bedouin-style *haima* acting as a bar.

Hostal La Muralla

C/Fray Diego de Cádiz 39 (954 37 10 49/hmuralla@terra.es). **Rates** €42-€86 single/double; €64-€107 triple. **Credit** MC, V. **Map** p54 A2 46

If you want to be in the heart of La Macarena, this is a good budget option, hard by the old city walls.

Triana

Hotel Monte Triana

C/Clara de Jesús Montero 24 (954 34 31 11/www.hotelesmonte.com). **Rates** €133-€181 single/double. **Credit** AmEx, DC, MC, V. **Map** p55 E6 47

Like the rather dull cream façade, the rooms are not memorable but certainly in very good condition, with plenty of light and good bathrooms. Most of them overlook the attractive interior patio and are very peaceful. The friendly and efficient staff are especially worthy of mention.

Outside the city

El Bulli Hotel Hacienda Benazuza

Sanlúcar La Mayor (955 70 33 44/www.hbenazuza.com). **Rates** €353-463 double; €463-€594 junior suite; €1,166-€1,278 suite. **Credit** AmEx, DC, MC. V.

Located 19 kilometres (12 miles) west of the city is superstar chef Ferran Adrià's first foray into the world of hotels. The famed force behind Catalonia's El Bulli restaurant has created the ultimate fairy-tale fantasy lodgings. From the sumptuous suites, where once the Catholic monarchs rested their heads, and secluded cottages with bubbling alfresco hot tubs, to the sunbeds that shelter like teak-wood cattle beneath the trees, the Hacienda Benazuza is a serious contender for the sexiest hotel on earth. And, of course, the food is a key part of the experience – chef Rafa Morales flirts and seduces with a 33-course tasting menu that easily rivals that of the mother restaurant up north. Meanwhile, El Bulli Breakfast – a seven-course extravaganza – gives guests the wake-up call of their lives. Inevitably, all this indulgence comes with a hefty price tag.

Sightseeing

The immense cathedral and exquisite Alcázar palace are only the beginning of Seville's sightseeing treasures.

Seville is a big city and requires at least a week to explore thoroughly. It would be impossible to see all the sights in a day or even two, especially in midsummer when temperatures soar, so take your time, and make the most of Seville's charms. To avoid total confusion when cross-referencing maps, be aware that some map-makers place the city facing north while others have it facing east. Orientate yourself by the position of the Guadalquivir river.

The cathedral & around

Signposted by the **Giralda**, this area is the epicentre of Seville and throngs with tourists who have come to admire the city's two biggest draws: the **cathedral** and the exquisite Mudéjar palace and gardens of the **Alcázar**. Due to their size and complexity, these two monuments alone could easily take a day to visit.

By the Giralda minaret, now the belltower for the cathedral, Plaza Virgen de los Reyes centres around a fountain designed by José Lafita. On the north side of the square is the **Palacio Arzobispal**, with its beautiful baroque façade, twin patios and a 17th-century jasper staircase. It served as a barracks during the Napoleonic invasion in 1810. Across the square is the **Convento de la Encarnación**, founded in 1591 and containing a collection of sculptures.

Between the cathedral and the Alcázar lies the Plaza del Triunfo, with its monument to the Virgin of the Immaculate Conception. It was built in gratitude after Seville survived the devastation of the 1755 earthquake that destroyed much of nearby Lisbon, an escape that was attributed to Seville's fervent devotion to the Virgin. On her feast day, 8 December, local *tuna* (minstrel) groups gather round the statue at dawn to pay homage. On the west side of this square, backing on to traffic-choked Avda de la Constitución, is the **Archivo de Las Indias** – the old Lonja (Stock Exchange) that houses the archives from Spain's adventures in the New World.

Alcázar

Patio de Banderas s/n (954 50 23 23/www.patronato-alcazarsevilla.es). **Open** *Apr-Sept* 9.30am-7pm Tue-Sat; 9.30am-5pm Sun. *Oct-Mar* 9.30am-5pm Tue-Sat; 9.30am-1.30pm Sun. **Admission** €7; free concessions. **Credit** AmEx, DC, MC, V. **Map** p55 F3.

The fortress palace of Pedro I ('the Cruel') contains the finest examples of 14th-century Moorish architecture outside the Alhambra. It goes back to the

Alcázar. *See p66.*

eighth century, but most of the design you see today dates from the 1360s, when Pedro installed himself and his mistress María de Padilla here.

You enter the complex through the Puerta de León, which contains traces of the original Almohad wall and opens on to a courtyard where Pedro received visitors and passed judgement on offenders. On the left is the Sala de Justicia, built by Alfonso XI of Castilla in around 1330, with a beautiful coffered ceiling and exquisite plasterwork. The Patio del Yeso (Plaster Courtyard) is the only surviving part of the original 12th-century palace.

From the Patio de la Montería (Hunting Courtyard), you can contemplate the wonderful Mudéjar façade of the palace, built by Pedro in 1364. It is a perfect synthesis of the different cultural and architectural styles that were present in Andalucía at that time. Muslim artists from Granada worked alongside Mudéjar carpenters from Toledo; Christian and Kufic inscriptions were carved side by side; and graceful Mudéjar columns bear heraldic lions and castles signifying Pedro's kingdom.

To the right of the palace lies the rather dreary Casa de la Contratación, where Fernando and Isabel planned much of the conquest of the Americas – there's a stunning painting here by Alejo Fernández of the Virgin protecting the navigators. Pass through here to the interior of the palace and its breathtaking designs. In keeping with Moorish custom, the palace is divided into public and private domains. Among the public areas is the Patio de las Doncellas, named after Christian maidens who were presented to the Moors as an annual peace offering.

The arches are supported by matching marble columns, and the 14th-century tiling is perhaps the prettiest in the Alcázar complex. A gallery was added by Carlos V on the occasion of his marriage in 1525. This leads on to the Salón de Embajadores (Hall of Ambassadors), which is quite overwhelming in its beauty and craftsmanship. Take time to gaze at the wooden dome, gilded and painted with spots of bright red, green, blue and gold, and decorated with stalactite designs. The balconies were added later by Felipe II.

Pass through the bedroom next door to reach the intimate Patio de las Muñecas, once the living room of the palace and named after two tiny dolls' faces carved into the honeycombed arches. The columns were taken from the ruins of the Moorish palace outside Córdoba, Medina Azahara. Numerous other bedrooms and salas, as well as an entire palace, were tacked on to the east side of the complex by Carlos V. The classical-style rooms are full of Flemish tapestries and unlikely to hold your attention, so continue to the gardens, which are among the loveliest in all Spain. Huge palms tower over the paths, flowers and fish ponds, and birdsong fills the air in all seasons. The gardens are a combination of Moorish design and later Italian influence, resulting in trickling streams and little fountains interspersed with gaudy grottoes and wildly staring sculptures. There is also a small maze at the far end. Near here is the Pabellón de Carlos V, a gem of Spanish Renaissance architecture, with a marvellous combination of classical and Moorish elements.

Archivo de Las Indias

Avda de la Constitución 3 (954 21 12 34). **Open** 10am-4pm Mon-Sat; 10am-2pm Sun. **Admission** free. **Map** p55 F3.

In 1785, after Seville had been usurped by Cádiz as the centre of trade with the Americas, Carlos III converted the former Lonja (stock exchange) into a huge

Woolly thinking

As you stroll around Seville, you won't miss a strange emblem on lamp-posts, manhole covers, municipal buildings, and even the base of Columbus's tomb. It looks like 'NO-8-DO', with the figure eight representing a looped skein of wool or *madeja*. The pun reads 'NO-madeja-DO' or 'no me ha dejado' – literally 'she never abandoned me' – and was famously uttered by Alfonso the Wise after the city remained loyal to him in a battle with his son Sancho during the 13th century. The phrase still conjures up pride in the people of Seville, and the *madeja* has become an enduring symbol of the city.

storehouse to hold the records for the four centuries of the Spanish Empire. Reopened in June 2005 after many years of restoration, the Archivo de las Indias (Archive of the Indies) consists of almost 40,000 documents – currently being digitalised – stored on a staggering five miles of 18th-century mahogany shelves. The archives include maps, drawings, trade documents, plans of South American towns, letters from Magellan and Cortés, George Washington, Cervantes and the star exhibit: Columbus's log. Although only licensed researchers can get their hands on the documents, the public is free to admire the Renaissance building, designed by Juan de Herrera (architect of the similarly austere El Escorial outside Madrid) in 1572, and which includes a superb marble staircase and breathtaking vaulted ceilings on the upper floor. There are rotating displays of various maps and documents.

Catedral & La Giralda

Avda de la Constitución s/n (954 21 49 71/www.catedralsevilla.org). **Open** *July, Aug* 9.30am-3.30pm Mon-Sat; 2.30-6pm Sun. *Sept-June* 11am-5pm Mon-Sat; 2.30-6pm Sun. **Admission** €7.50; €2 concessions; free under-12s; free to all Sun. **No credit cards. Map** p55 F3.

It's the sheer size of Seville's Brobdingnagian cathedral that first takes your breath away. Not just the height of its emblematic structure, the Giralda minaret, but the sheer mass of the building. Théophile Gautier called it 'a hollow mountain, an upside-down valley', adding that 'Notre Dame could walk with its head high down Seville cathedral's centre aisle'. Allow a few minutes to walk around outside to marvel at the size of the Roman pillars, connected by huge metal chains, and at the enormous double flying buttresses.

Until the early 1400s the Christians of Seville worshipped in the 12th-century Almohad mosque, which was adapted for use as a church by Fernando III in 1248. By 1401 the building was beginning to show signs of wear and tear so the church authorities pulled it down and replaced it with a magnificent new structure, an unsurpassed monument to the Christian faith, 'a church which those who see it finished will think we were mad for attempting'. Nothing like it had been built before. Although it was Gothic in design, the shape of the cathedral had no clear precedents, and the architects – all 17 of them – were constrained by the floorplans of the original mosque. Construction began in 1434 and was completed, incredibly, by 1517. Today, the cathedral is considered the largest church in the world – bigger in volume than St Peter's in Rome.

The building's Moorish past is most evident at the original entrance to the old mosque, the Almohad-style Puerta del Perdón, whose 12th-century bronze doors have inscriptions from the Koran. This gateway leads into the Patio de los Naranjos, where orange trees follow the outline of the original mosque courtyard; the fountain in the centre and some of the walls date from this period. The east wall contains the Biblioteca Colombina, a library of manuscripts from Christopher Columbus's journeys, founded by his son.

Once inside the cathedral, you'll notice the tops of columns soaring towards the ceiling and enormous arches sweeping across the tops of the naves. The sheer scale would no doubt have cowed the original worshippers: at its highest point, the central nave rises to almost 43m (140ft), supported by columns that are 3.6m (12ft) thick. The *retablo* of the high altar is the largest and richest in the world. Depicting 45 carved and gilded scenes from the life of Christ, it is deemed to be one of the finest examples of Gothic woodcarving anywhere and, most remarkably of all, was the life's work of a single craftsman, Pierre Dancart.

The chapels along the sides of the building contain works such as Murillo's *Vision of St Anthony* and *Baptism of Christ*; Zurbarán's *retablo* of the life of St Paul; and, in the Sacristía de los Cálices, Goya's *Saints Justa and Refina*.

The centrepiece of the cathedral is the main altar in the Capilla Mayor, an extraordinary work begun in 1482 and completed a century later. It contains more than 1,000 sculptures in wood and gold depicting biblical scenes. Behind the Capilla Mayor, against the eastern wall, is the Capilla Real, housing the ornate tomb of Fernando III, his wife Beatrice and his son Alfonso the Wise. On the south side is another impressive tomb, held aloft by four pallbearers representing the kingdoms of Castilla, León, Navarra and Aragón, and containing at least some of the remains of Christopher Columbus, as finally verified by DNA testing in 2006.

To the left of the tomb lies the Sacristía Mayor, a huge space topped by a dome dating to 1528. It's full of art, including an impressive Deposition by 16th-century Flemish-born Pedro de Campaña, which greatly influenced Velázquez. The centrepiece, though, is an incredible 3m-high (10ft) 16th-century monstrance made entirely of silver. East of the main sacristy is the stunning Sala Capitular (Chapter House). Conceived in 1558 (although not completed until 1591), it represents the first oval design by a Renaissance architect. The domed ceiling, with an Immaculate Conception by Murillo, and the beautiful marble floor make this an architectural gem.

At the north-east corner of the cathedral lies the entrance to the Giralda, the symbol of Seville and a landmark visible from almost anywhere in the city. The minaret of the original mosque, it was built between 1172 and 1195. It was originally topped by four shiny globes, designed to catch the light and be visible from far beyond the city, but these fell during a 13th-century earthquake and were replaced in 1568 by a spire and a weathervane, El Giraldillo, from which the tower takes its name. Despite the masculine name, the figure is of a woman (a pretty weighty one of 2,000kg/4,400lbs of cast bronze), representing Faith as a Christian version of Pallas Minerva.

Despite being more than 91m (300ft) high, the Giralda is surprisingly easy to climb due to gently inclining ramps inside. These were designed to allow the muezzin to ride his horse to the top.

Barrio de Santa Cruz

The streets twisting away east from the cathedral and Alcázar make up the old Jewish quarter and are the most atmospheric part of the city. Here you'll find tiny squares studded with orange trees and jasmine; narrow, whitewashed streets filled with needle-sharp sunlight and shadows; plant-covered patios behind iron railings; and shady bars serving *fino*, cured ham and cold beers. This whole area was drastically restored in the 1920s by the founder of the *parador* hotels, the Marquis of Vega-Inclán, Spain's first minister of tourism. Unfortunately, it can feel like a theme park in high season, all jammed with tour groups.

If you're here in summer, try to visit early in the morning, before 9am, when you'll find the streets practically deserted. The prettiest lanes are those backing on to the north-east wall of the Alcázar. Follow C/Judería and C/Vida as they twist and turn along to Plaza de Doña Elvira, a beautiful square fringed by orange trees and with a pretty fountain in the middle; it's home to the Corral de Comedías, where playwright Lope de Rueda began his career.

Running alongside the walls of the palace gardens is the Callejón de Agua, a lovely tree-shaded street whose name derives from the watercourse that ran along the top of the wall. Leading off it are C/Pimienta (Pepper Street), supposedly named after an incident involving a Jewish spice merchant who found a pepper tree growing outside his front door, and C/Susona, where, according to legend, a beautiful Jewish girl and her entire family were killed by her Christian lover (in fact, she betrayed her family to the Christians, then killed herself). A plaque records the incident. The *callejón* leads to Plaza Alfaro, inspiration for the balcony scene between the young lovers in the *Barber of Seville*; continue along to the **Jardines de Murillo**, a slender landscaped park of ancient peepul trees, lady of the night and jasmine, with shaded corners and water features. These ornamental gardens are the old orchards and vegetable plots that once formed part of the Alcázar. In 1911 they were donated to the city and named after its favourite son, Murillo, who lived nearby (*see below*). Between the palms is a monument to Christopher Columbus – one of four in the city – with a bronze sculpture of the caravel that carried him to the New World in 1492. The two Corinthian columns, symbolising the columns of Hercules, are topped by a lion and globe, symbolising the Spanish Empire.

Plaza Alfaro almost adjoins one of the prettiest squares in the barrio, Plaza Santa Cruz. In the centre, flowers and orange trees surround a wrought-iron cross, known as **La Cerrajería**, indicating where the original church once stood; it was pulled down by the French in 1810. In one corner of the square is **La Albahaca**, the former home of the architect Talavera and now a fine restaurant (*see p81*), while at C/Santa Teresa 8 is the last home of

Barrio de Santa Cruz.

Casa de Pilatos.

the *sevillano* artist Murillo, the **Casa de Murillo**, now a bookshop owned by the Andalucían government. Visitors may enter the patio and look at the occasional exhibitions.

The church of **Santa Cruz** (C/Mateos Gago s/n, no phone), with a façade by Juan Talavera, is a minute's walk away, and almost opposite on C/Aire are some new **Arab baths** (C/Aire 15, 955 01 00 25, www.airedesevilla.com), set in a 16th-century palace built by the Viceroy of the Indies. The last original hammam in Seville disappeared in the 17th century.

C/Aire runs into C/Mármoles, which is named after the **Monolitos Romanos**, the three Roman columns that remain from what is thought to have been an enormous temple to the goddess Diana. Nearby is the **Convento de San José** (C/Gúzman el Bueno 10), a 16th-century church that contains beautiful Mudéjar decoration. A further minute to the east, through Plaza de las Cruces, is the church of **Santa María la Blanca** (C/Santa María la Blanca 5), a Visigothic temple that was used as a synagogue in the 13th century before being converted into a church in 1391. Further alterations took place in 1659 and the heavy baroque plasterwork is striking. Inside are wonderful *azulejos* and a Murillo Last Supper.

C/Santa María la Blanca opens up into a small square with a number of good bars and restaurants; it marks the northern edge of the barrio. The streets and houses beyond retain little of Santa Cruz's unique atmosphere, but it's worth pressing on to the north-east to see Seville's prettiest mansion, the **Casa de Pilatos** on C/Esteban. At the westerly border of the Santa Cruz, on the cusp of the Centro district, lies a valuable addition to the city's museums, the **Museo del Baile Flamenco**.

Casa de Pilatos

Plaza de Pilatos 1 (954 22 52 98). **Open** *Mar-Sept* 9am-7pm daily. *Oct-Feb* 9am-6pm daily. **Admission** *Ground floor & gardens* €5. *Both floors & gardens* €8. **No credit cards. Map** p54 D2.

The house's name (according to one theory) comes from the mistaken belief that it was built to the same dimensions as Pontius Pilate's house, after one of the original owners went to Jerusalem on a pilgrimage. Work was started in 1481 by Don Pedro Enríquez, a former governor of Andalucía, but it was his son, Don Fadrique, who redesigned it in a mixture of Mudéjar, Renaissance and Gothic styles. The entrance is via a marble triumphal arch to the porticoed *apeadero*, where carriages waited, and into the central courtyard with its harmonious mixture of architectural styles. It is surrounded by a series of irregular arches topped with Gothic balustrades. The corners are occupied by three statues of the goddesses Minerva, Ceres and Athene, and the central fountain was imported from Genoa in Italy.

Several rooms are entered via the main patio, beyond which lie pretty gardens with Italian-style loggias, small pools and statuary. To the right, the Praetorium Room has a beautiful coffered ceiling, marquetry and 16th-century *muqarna* cones (stalactite designs). The stairs leading to the upper floors are magnificent – a dazzling array of tiles in light blues, greens and reds, covered by a coffered ceiling with more stalactites; these floors are occupied and can only be visited on a guided tour. They contain paintings and frescoes, including the *Apotheosis of Hercules* ceiling by Francisco Pacheco, the mentor of Velázquez, and three paintings by *sevillano* artist Sebastián de Llanos Valdés.

Hospital de los Venerables

Plaza de los Venerables 8 (954 56 26 96/www.focus.abengoa.es). **Open** 10am-2pm, 4-8pm daily. **Admission** €4.75; €2.40 concessions. **No credit cards. Map** p55 F3.

One of the most beautifully restored pieces of baroque *sevillano* architecture, Los Venerables was built as a nursing home for old and sick priests on the initiative of a local canon in 1676 and contains perhaps the prettiest patio in Andalucía. Four tiled staircases lead down to a sunken terracotta courtyard with a tiny fountain at its centre and orange trees in each corner. The rose-coloured patio is surrounded by slender marble arcades and first-floor balconies, set off by pretty tilework. The murals in the single-nave church are outstanding: most impressive are the *trompe l'oeil* ceiling mural of *The Triumph of the Cross* in the Sacristy and *The*

Apotheosis of San Fernando that presides over the main altar; the Greek frieze reminds visitors that they should 'fear God and honour his priests'. There are also excellent sculptures of San Pedro and San Fernando at the foot of the nave beneath the choir.

Bought and restored by the FOCUS cultural foundation in the 1980s, the hospital's ground floor and first-floor infirmaries (the upper floor was used in the winter months) host excellent temporary exhibitions on Seville art and history, while the church is an auditorium regularly used for concerts, including a cycle of organ music each January. **Photo** *p74*.

Museo del Baile Flamenco

C/Manuel Rojas Marcos 3 (954 34 03 11/www.museoflamenco.com). **Open** *Apr-Oct* 9am-7pm daily. *Nov-Mar* 9am-6pm daily. **Admission** €10; €6 concessions. **Credit** AmEx, DC, MC, V. **Map** p55 E3.

This beautifully designed museum and interactive space opened in 2006 and provides a much-needed introduction to the history, techniques and practice of flamenco dance. Housed in a huge 18th-century building, the museum is fluid rather than static, with visitors free to watch the flamenco dance workshops and classes, attend seminars or use the library; performances take place on the hidden hydraulic stage (snoop under the carpet in the patio café) with full drop-down lighting rigs and backdrops.

At the heart of the museum, on the first floor, are touch screens, sound showers and even olfactory cues to explain the lives of flamenco greats and follow the dance's evolution from the domestic patio to the tablao stage show. With six languages supplementing the visual displays, the difference between, say, farrucas and tangos or the meaning of different hand movements is clearly explained and shows all the technique and hard work behind the duende (the spirit underlying pure flamenco). Excellent costume displays show the impossibly tiny waist of Antonio Gades' trousers or the dress worn by Cristina Hoyos, the museum's founder and artistic director, at the inauguration of the Barcelona Olympic Games. Art includes Colita's emotive photographs and a series of lively pencil portraits by Miguel Alcalá.

Centro

The **Plaza San Francisco** is the logical place to start a tour of central Seville. This smart square was rebuilt at the same time as the **Ayuntamiento** (town hall, now housing the municipal **Museo de la Logia**) and is where the autos-da-fé were held between the 15th and 18th century. It's at the heart of the festivities for Semana Santa and Corpus Christi when it is filled with seating for local dignitaries and richly decorated with velvet banners. On New Year's Eve, crowds traditionally gather in **Plaza Nueva**, on the other side of the Ayuntamiento, and count down to midnight by the clock over the main entrance.

Holy spree

SEMANA SANTA

Holy Week celebrations are not unique to Seville, but they are at their finest and most moving here. The build-up lasts for weeks: you'll see *cofradías* (brotherhoods) practising for the processions and bands warming up everywhere.

Events officially begin on Palm Sunday, with the streets thronged and the bars open all night. Processions begin at noon at their respective churches, head to the cathedral, through it and back again. This continues until Thursday evening, when the men dress up in dark suits and the women don their black mantillas for the three most important processions of the week: **El Gran Poder, La Esperanza de Triana** and **La Macarena**, which head off from their respective churches at midnight. The processions fizzle out on Good Friday, with just four on Easter Saturday.

As an outsider it's difficult to know what's going on, where to look and why people may be cheering or crying. Fortunately, there is an excellent pocket guide published by the tourist office, which provides information on the terminology, routes and timing. *See also p48.*

FERIA DE ABRIL

The more sombre atmosphere of Semana Santa is blown away in the second half of the month by the Feria de Abril, a week-long round of parades, dressing-up, dancing, bullfighting and drinking. The fairground takes up a large area in Los Remedios, although space restrictions may force it to move in the future.

The *feria* is still dominated by *casetas* (marquees), the setting for business deals when the *feria* was a cattle fair, but now used for socialising. Some *casetas* are public, but most are owned by companies or families – you'll need an invitation to get in. They contain little more than ample supplies of sherry or *manzanilla* and crowds of people. During the day the fairground and much of the rest of the city is a riot of colour: women wear stunning flamenco creations in bright colours, while the men, dressed in traditional leather trousers and waistcoats, ride groomed horses around town. As the day wears on, the dancing of *sevillanas* begins and continues until dawn. *See also p50.*

The unspeakable in pursuit of the edib

Forget football stars, Spain's real macho heroes are the chaps who take on the big black bulls. And it's in steaming Seville that the definitive bullfight, in the definitive bullring, can be seen. Although the pitting of *hombre* against *toro* is far from exclusive to Andalucía, it was here that the form and substance of the *corrida* were developed, and here that its spiritual heart remains. If you can overcome any squeamishness and moral objections you might have, and want to experience first-hand what it's all about, here's what to expect...

In the *venta de taquillas* (ticket office) you'll find little maps of the bullring hanging on the wall. There are two things to decide: how near you want to be to the action and whether you want to be in the *sol* (sun) or *sombra* (shade). *Sol* is always cheaper than *sombra*, as most of the action takes place in shadow.

To smell the bulls and catch every last expression of the matadors, choose a seat in the first three rows, known as *filas*. These seats, which are actually little more than concrete benches, are pretty uncomfortable and allow a close-up view of the action that is definitely not for the squeamish. The next few rows back are known as *tendidos*. They offer a little more comfort (they have backs, at least), but you can expect to have to put up with a lot of people, including the beer vendors, walking past. Beyond here is the *balcón*, where the seats are cheaper the further back you sit.

THE CORRIDA

A typical *corrida* lasts for at least a couple of hours, during which time six bulls are killed. The show begins with a procession, accompanied by a band, in which you see the entire cast of characters: the three matadors, their *cuadrillas* (helpers) – two mounted *picadores* and three *banderilleros* – followed by the mule teams who will carry off the dead animals.

Once the ring is cleared the fight begins in earnest. First the bull storms in, snorting and magnificent. He is goaded by *banderilleros* with capes, partly to tire him, and partly to ascertain how angry he is.

Next come the *picadores* on horseback. For many observers, this is the most objectionable part of the *corrida*. Although the horses are covered in heavy padding and blindfolded, they are well aware of what's going on, and it's a shocking sight when one is tossed and gored on the bull's horns. The horses' silence has nothing to do with their stoicism: their vocal cords are cut before they come into the ring. The idea of this part of the fight is to allow the *picador* to stab the bull's neck, thus weakening its muscles and forcing it to lower its head, making the kill easier for the matador.

A horn sounds, the ring is cleared and in march the *banderilleros*, whose job it is to stick three sets of *banderillas* (thin poles with barbed ends, festooned in bright ribbons) into the bull's shoulders. This can

North of here, the main shopping streets of the city all lie parallel – C/Sierpes, C/Tetuán and C/Cuna – which also contain a number of good bars and restaurants. C/Cuna, or Cradle Street, was named after the foundling hospital that once stood there. Between Sierpes and Tetuán is the exquisite, tiny **Capillita de San José** (C/Jovellanos 10), one of the best examples of baroque architecture in the city, while a couple of minutes' walk to the west is the church of **La Magdalena** (C/San Pablo s/n). The church was rebuilt by Leonardo de Figueroa at the end of the 17th century and the beginning of the 18th, and contains a *Life of Dominic* by Zurbarán. A little to the west lies the Convento de la Merced, now the **Museo de Bellas Artes**.

Head back east from the museum along C/Alfonso XII to see the rest of the Centro. The **Palacio de Lebrija** on C/Cuna has three ornate patios and a collection of Roman artefacts from the nearby settlement of Itálica. Close by is the church of **La Anunciación** (C/Laraña), which flanks the Plaza de la Encarnación, and further east, the Gothic **San Pedro** (Plaza de San Pedro) where local boy Velázquez was baptised, and **Santa Catalina** (Plaza de Santa Catalina s/n), whose tower is a copy of the Giralda. Just behind here, on C/Gerona, is Seville's oldest tapas bar, **El Rinconcillo** (*see p85*).

From the west corner of Plaza San Pedro walk down the tiny C/Padre Luis María Llop to see the **Casa Natal de Velázquez**, the house at No.4 where the great *sevillano* painter was born in 1599. The house is closed to the public, but has a commemorative plaque.

Continuing west away from San Pedro, C/Sales Ferrer takes you to the perpetually

be nerve-wracking to watch, and involves an enormous amount of skill and courage – though, again, animal rights groups contest that the odds are unfairly stacked against the bull, who is soon bleeding heavily and dizzy through lack of oxygen.

The fourth and final act begins as the matador strides on in brilliantly coloured garb, carrying the traditional cape (pink on one side, gold on the other). At this point all chatter ceases and you can hear the swoosh of the cape and the matador's words as he whispers to the bull, '*Vamos toro... vamos toro...* '. The skill of a professional matador can be mesmerising: he may choose to 'flirt' with the bull, placing his arm across its back and circling with it in a danse macabre, or he may get the animal to come closer and closer to him as it charges the cape. Often the matador will contemptuously turn his back on the animal and walk away. When the matador judges it's time to dispatch the bull, he grabs his sword and holds it under the cape, readying himself. He needs the animal right in front of him, head bowed, to thrust the sword between its shoulders and through to its heart for a quick kill.

If the matador is accurate and swift, there is little blood; the animal pauses and there is total silence in the ring; it sways slightly, staggers, its front legs give way and it collapses. However, if the kill is not clean, things can get very messy indeed: the bull will start staggering around, glassy-eyed, throwing up gallons of blood all over the pristine yellow sand while the matador either tries to finish the job himself with a second sword or instructs one of his men to stab the bull in the brain with a tiny dagger. Either way, it's horribly distressing to watch.

Finally, the bull is dragged away, the sand is cleaned and the crowd make clear their feelings – by either shouting abuse or waving white handkerchiefs in approval. The president will then decide whether the matador should be awarded one ear, both ears, or both ears and a tail, if the matador's performance has been especially impressive.

The whole event is repeated a further five times until the entire cast (minus the bulls) comes on for a few laps of honour. If they've done well, the audience will shower them with red roses. After a particularly fine show, the matador may be carried out on the shoulders of his *cuadrillas* and led through the main door of the bull ring. This rarely happens in Seville, where the aficionados are considered the most discerning in Spain.

lively **Plaza Alfalfa**, full of bars, cafés and small alternative shops. This tiny square gets its curious name from the old haymarket that used to be held here. Heading west from here along C/Alcaicería will take you towards **Plaza del Salvador**, dominated by its church (954 21 16 79, www.colegialsalvador.org, closed for restoration), converted from the ninth-century mosque of Ibn Addabas in 1672. The inside is dominated by a baroque *retablo* and various wooden carvings, including Cristo del Amor by Juan de Mesa and Señor de la Pasión and San Cristóbal, both by Juan Martínez Montañes, who is commemorated by a statue in the square. The minaret (now a belltower) and a central patio are from the original mosque.

Ayuntamiento

Plaza Nueva 1 (954 59 01 01). **Open** *Museum* 10am-5pm daily. *Building* (by pre-booked guided tour only) 5.30pm, 6pm Tue-Thur; noon Sat. Closed mid July-mid Sept. **Admission** *Museum* €2. *Building* free with passport/ID. **No credit cards**. **Map** p55 E4.

Work on the town hall began in 1527 under Diego de Riaño and the elaborate eastern façade on Plaza San Francisco is one of the earliest and most important pieces of early Spanish Plateresque. After the San Francisco monastery was demolished in 1835, the city council used the extra space to extend the town hall towards the west, with a new main entrance on what is now known as Plaza Nueva. Built in 1891, the new extension was neo-classical in style and simply wrapped around most of the original building. The guided tour (in Spanish only) of the interior of the building shows off several impressive chambers, but the star of the show is the deeply coffered ceiling of the lower council chamber; embedded with the busts of 36 monarchs, it ends with Carlos V in one corner, wearing his emperor's crown. The gracious rooms on the upper floor hold

Hospital de los Venerables. See p70.

artwork by Valdés Leal, Juan de Espinal and Domínguez Bécquer, among others.

The small municipal museum, **Museo de la Logia**, opened in 2006 and briefly charts 3,000 years of Seville's history. The entrance is on the Plaza de San Francisco through heavy red curtains that open on to the old loggia of the Ayuntamiento – this narrow gallery displays reproductions of treasures such as the eighth-century BC golden jewellery found at Carámbolo and the eighth-century Moorish keys to the city, as well as the maces that appear in Seville's coat of arms, maps and documents. Changing exhibitions of art from the Ayuntamiento's holdings include Velázquez's outstanding *Imposition of the Chasuble of San Ildefonso*.

Museo de Bellas Artes

Plaza del Museo 9 (954 22 07 90/www.juntadeandalucia.es/cultura/museos/MBASE). **Open** 2.30-8.30pm Tue; 9am-8.30pm Wed-Sat; 9am-2.30pm Sun. **Admission** €1.50; free with EU passport. **No credit cards. Map** p54 D5.

The Fine Arts Museum has a collection of mainly Spanish art that is regarded as the finest outside the Prado in Madrid. The museum was founded in 1835 and is housed in the beautiful Convento de la Merced, rebuilt by Juan de Oviedo in 1612 and renovated by Leonardo de Figueroa in 1724. The galleries are arranged on two floors around three pretty courtyards. Highlights on the ground floor include an El Greco, a lively portrait of his son; the wooden St Jerome by Pietro Torregiano, and a gruesome picture of the severed head of John the Baptist by Núñez Delgado. Through a courtyard and past the impressive main staircase, Room 5 was once the church of the convent, where murals by Domingo Martínez cover the domed ceiling and form an appropriately grand setting for some of the museum's key pieces: Zurbarán's *Apotheosis of St Thomas* along with some of Murillo's most famous works.

The upper floor is dedicated to the baroque, especially works from the *sevillano* masters Valdés Leal, Ribera, Zurbarán and the indefatigable Murillo. One of many highlights is Zubarán's *Saint Hugo in the Refectory* – depicting the monks' vow to renounce meat, it was painted for La Cartuja (*see p80*).

Palacio de Lebrija

C/Cuna 8 (954 22 78 02/www.palaciodelebrija.com). **Open** *June-Sept* 10.30am-1.30pm, 5-8pm Mon-Fri; 10am-2pm Sat. *Oct-May* 10.30am-1.30pm, 4.30-7.30pm Mon-Fri; 10am-2pm Sat. **Admission** *Ground floor* €4. *Both floors* (incl tour) €8. **No credit cards. Map** p54 D3.

Belonging to the family of the Countess of Lebrija, this palatial mansion dates from the 15th and 16th centuries and is a magpie's nest of borrowed treasures. The palace is particularly famous for its mosaic flooring and has over 580 square metres (6,240 square feet) of Roman mosaic. When the Countess renovated the palace in the early 1900s, she rebuilt the rooms to fit around her most priceless treasures; the centrepiece is the stunning principal courtyard, surrounded by Moorish arches and fine *azulejos,* which holds a huge Roman mosaic of the god Pan lifted from the Itálica ruins and superior to anything you will find at the original site. Other highlights are the coffered ceiling of the stairway (from the palaces of the Dukes of Arcos in Marchena near Seville), a Renaissance frieze and *azulejo* borders (from a convent). All the rooms off the courtyard are filled with priceless archaeological pieces, including some original marbles from the Medina Azahara (*see p226*) in Córdoba, and 18th-century tiles. Upstairs are the sumptuously decorated rooms of the Countess's private winter residence, peppered with everything from Persian stone arches to paintings by Van Dyck.

El Arenal

The name of this district refers to the open sandy area by the riverbank where the city walls receded inland. This was once the city's port area and although there are no longer caravels and trade boats clogging the water, the Guadalquivir river remains a hub, with several terrace bars, river cruisers and even canoes. As with many ports, it was also Seville's red-light district and had a justified reputation for smuggling, thievery and violence. The area was built up in the 19th century to provide more housing and, although it is not as chocolate-box pretty as Santa Cruz, it feels a lot more authentic, mainly due to the lack of tourists. It's a good area in which to lose yourself for a few hours, dipping into the many excellent tapas bars and restaurants.

El Arenal is the bullfighting neighbourhood and its main sight is **La Maestranza**, Seville's bullring on the Paseo de Colón – an enormous complex containing offices, apartments and, at the western end, a museum and ticket office. Nearby there are three statues: the bullfighters Curro Romero and, opposite, Pepe Luís Vásquez, as well as one of the gypsy Carmen who, according to the works by Merimée and Bizet, was killed on this spot by José, while her lover, the bullfighter Escamillo, was fighting just yards away in the Maestranza.

A short walk down the riverside Paseo de Colón is Seville's main theatre, **Teatro de la Maestranza** (*see p102*). Like many of the buildings designed for the 1992 Expo, it is rather austere and forbidding, although the colossal flat-capped cupola adds a touch of whimsy. The *sevillanos* were quick to christen it La Magefesa, after a popular brand of pressure cooker. On C/Santander is the **Torre de Plata** (Tower of Silver), a Moorish watchtower, while the better-known **Torre del Oro** (Tower of Gold) stands on the riverbank close by. Just behind on C/Temprado, the 13th-century arches of the huge royal shipyards, **Las Reales Atarazanas**, give a glimpse of Seville's glorious trading days, although some of them were converted into the **Hospital de la Caridad** (now a museum) in the 17th century.

Hospital de la Caridad

C/Temprado 3 (954 22 32 33). **Open** 9am-1.30pm, 3.30-7.30pm Mon-Sat; 9am-1pm Sun. **Admission** €5. **No credit cards. Map** p55 F4.

An undervisited treasure trove, the Hospital de la Caridad is built on land that belonged to the Hermandad de Santa Caridad, an obscure fraternity dedicated to burying abandoned corpses and the bodies of the condemned. This all changed in 1661 with the admission of Miguel de Mañara, the rakish son of a wealthy landowner, who transformed it into a lavishly decorated baroque church and charity hospital, which still functions as a nursing home today. Mañara (who may have been the inspiration for Don Juan) was a dedicated philanderer, frittering away his fortune until, at the age of 34 (legend has it), he had a vision of his own death. He dedicated the rest of his life and his inheritance to rebuilding the church and an adjoining charity hospital for the poor and needy. Despite these good deeds, Mañara's self-penned epitaph ends, 'Here lie the bones and ashes of the worst man who ever lived on this earth. Pray for his soul.' It is placed on the ground at the church entrance, as it was Mañara's wish that all those who entered walk over him.

However keen on self-denial Mañara may have been, he didn't stint on art; the complex houses the best collection of paintings and sculpture in Seville after the Museo de Bellas Artes. Some of the finest works were commissioned directly by Mañara and reflect his obsession with death and the rejection of worldly wealth; these include two rather disturbing pieces by Juan de Valdés Leal in the church entrance.

Murillo, a good friend of Mañara, was commissioned to produce a series of 11 paintings on the theme of mercy for the chapel, although only seven of them survived the looting during the Napoleonic occupation. Murillo also designed the distinctive tiles on the church's main façade, representing Faith, Hope and Charity and, below, St George and St James. The third great *sevillano* artist commissioned by Mañara was Pedro Roldán, who carved the wonderful *Burial of Christ* scene at the centre of the jaw-dropping – though rather dusty – *retablo* of the high altar. The figures were later painted by Valdés Leal.

Plaza de Toros de la Real Maestranza

Paseo de Colón 18. Corrida ticket sales: C/Adriano 37 (corrida tickets 954 56 07 59/www.plazadetoros delamaestranza.com/museum 954 22 45 77/www. realmaestranza.com). **Open** 9.30am-7pm daily (9.30am-3pm on fight days). **Admission** *Corridas* €7.50-€125. *Museum* €4. **No credit cards. Map** p54 F4.

The so-called Cathedral of Bullfighting holds 13,500 people; it's not as big as Las Ventas in Madrid but is regarded by aficionados as the most beautiful and important in the world. It was begun in 1761 under the orders of its current owners, the Real Maestranza de Caballería, and was constructed over the next 119 years. Delays contributed to its oval shape, as architects and builders attempted to work around new buildings. Despite the size of La Maestranza, its incredible acoustics allow you to hear everything that takes place, wherever you are sitting. The Museo de la Maestranza contains the heads of slain animals, gory oil paintings, posters, matadors' jackets and other *toro*-related memorabilia. The bullfighting season begins on Easter Monday, continues daily through the Feria de Abril, and then on Sundays and holidays from May to October.

Las Reales Atarazanas

C/Temprado 1 (954 22 51 05). **Open** 10am-2pm, 6-8pm Tue-Sat; 10am-2pm Sun. **Admission** free. **Map** p55 F4.

Built in 1252 by King Alfonso I 'The Wise', as Seville was on the verge of becoming Spain's major port, these royal shipyards lay just outside the wall that originally joined the Torre del Oro, the Torre de Plata and the Puertas del Carbón and Aceite, where coal and oil entered the city. Built in Almohad style, the shipyard's 17 naves lay perpendicular to the riverbanks. After the river silted up, some of the naves were turned over to the Hospital de la Caridad (*see above*) while others were used variously as a customs house, a fishing market and a munitions warehouse. In 1945 five of the Mudéjar naves on the south flank were demolished to make way for government buildings; in 1993, the seven remaining naves were impressively renovated, partly for use as a cultural space, and are open to the public.

Torre del Oro

Paseo de Colón s/n (954 22 24 19). **Open** 10am-2pm Tue-Fri; 11am-2pm Sat, Sun. Closed Aug. **Admission** €2; free to all Tue. **No credit cards. Map** p55 G4.

The 'golden tower' was built by the Almohads in 1220 to mark the edge of the city's defences and was originally connected to the Alcázar by a wall. If the city came under attack, a series of underwater chains and mechanisms would be stretched across the river from the tower to a small keep, the Torre de Abdelazi in Triana, to stop enemies entering; an idea that proved useless when the chain was broken during the conquest of Seville by the invading Christian fleet in 1248. The tower's name has uncertain origins, but two popular theories are that in Moorish times the tower was covered in golden-coloured tiles that reflected the sunlight; later, it became the unloading spot for gold and other treasure from the New World. These days its jaundiced sheen comes from unsubtle yellow lights that come on after dusk.

The tower has been used as a chapel, medieval prison, gunpowder warehouse, and even a post office, but it is now a small naval museum with two floors of maps and paintings from Seville's days as a major port, along with artefacts ranging from whole dessicated sharks to anchors.

La Alameda & La Macarena

North of the centre, La Macarena is somewhat rundown and slightly seedy in parts, but retains a strong character and has not become too touristy, despite having several monuments worth searching out. It has long been a solidly working-class area and, like Triana, was once home to the gypsy population, although is now being colonised by middle-class incomers.

La Alameda, in the north-west, was for a long time the city's red-light district, but is now an up-and-coming area, full of alternative shops, bars, discos and a fledgling gay scene, centred around the long, rectangular **Alameda de Hércules**. Once polluted marshland, it was developed in 1574 into a smart tree-lined promenade. The two columns at the southern end support statues of Hercules and Caesar, considered the founding fathers of the city, while at the other end are statues of flamenco greats. The Alameda really comes alive at night, when punters spill out on to the pavements drinking beers, munching tapas and talking until the small hours get big again. In 2006 the Alameda was under massive renovation with plans for pedestrianisation and fountains. Symbolic of the whole clean-up operation, a shiny new police station has replaced the old cinema at the north end of the boulevard, although it's doubtful how much will really change: at night the spillover from surrounding bars reaches the station and stoned students hang out just a bong's throw from the main doors.

From the southern end, heading west down C/Conde de Barajas will bring you to the 17th-century church of **San Lorenzo** and the more modern **Jesús del Gran Poder** (both on Plaza San Lorenzo). A short walk north and you arrive at the **Convento de Santa Clara** and the **Torre de Don Fadrique** (C/Santa Clara 40, 954 37 99 05, closed for renovation), a 13th-century tower probably built by Fernando III's son to protect his palace. C/Santa Clara leads to the **Monasterio de San Clemente** (C/Reposo 9, 954 37 80 40, closed for renovation), the city's oldest monastery, which was built over a Moorish palace. Inside is one of the finest baroque *retablos* in the city.

From here you can see the graceful **Puente de la Barqueta** (built for the 1992 Expo) crossing the Guadalquivir. South-west along the river is the restored area of Torneo, once a backwater but now the city's summer nightlife area, packed with bars and discos.

From the monastery, the main road C/Resolana runs east along the line of the old city walls past the **Hospital de Cinco Llagas**, a Renaissance hospital that is now home to the Andalucían parliament. Opposite are part of the old walls and the Puerta de Córdoba, the gateway into the La Macarena barrio. It was built by the Almoravids in the 12th century and strengthened by later rulers. Beside it is the **Basílica de la Macarena**, which contains the Virgen de la Macarena, the most revered of all the Semana Santa effigies.

There are a number of other churches in the immediate vicinity: **San Gil** (C/San Gil s/n), with its Mudéjar tower and ceiling; **San Luis** (C/San Luis 37), a superb example of *sevillano* baroque; the 13th-century Gothic-Mudéjar **Santa Marina** (C/San Luis 31), restored by Pedro I after an earthquake and featuring fine plasterworks and stalactite designs; the 14th-century **San Julián** (C/San Hermenegildo); and **San Marcos** (Plaza San Marcos), with a Mudéjar tower.

Basílica de la Macarena

C/Bécquer 1 (954 90 18 00/www.hermandaddelamacarena.org). **Open** *Church* 9am-2pm, 5-9pm daily. *Museum* 9.30am-2pm, 5-8pm daily. **Admission** *Museum* €3; €1.50 concessions. **No credit cards. Map** p54 A2.

Built in 1949, the brightly painted church is itself nothing special: it is the Macarena virgin, designed by Luisa Roldán in the last part of the 17th century, that people come to see. Hers is the image that attracts the most weeping and wailing during the Easter processions, as she is transported on a solid silver *paso*, accompanied by an image of Christ that

Plaza de España.

was carved by Felipe de Morales Nieto in 1654. The church museum contains fabulously gaudy jewels and outfits worn by the Virgin on her days out.

Convento de Santa Paula

C/Santa Paula 11 (954 53 63 30). **Open** *Museum* 10am-1pm Tue-Sun. **Admission** *Museum* €2. **No credit cards. Map** p54 C2.

Also in the area is the Convento de Santa Paula, the only closed convent in Seville that can be officially visited (at least, its museum can). Built in the late 15th century, it is worth seeing for its beautiful 17th-century coffered ceiling, and for the entrance portal, decorated by Millán in 1504, and covered in glazed tiles by Pisano. Seek out the gilded *retablo* depicting St John the Evangelist by Alonso Cano (1635), which incorporates a wonderful sculpture of the saint by Montañes. The museum has paintings by artists such as Zurbarán and Alonso Vázquez. You can buy the nuns' delicious home-made dulces and jams too.

The Parque de María Luisa & the Plaza de España

Beyond the gardens of the Alcázar to the south is a busy roundabout known as the **Puerta de Jerez**. This was originally the gateway to the trade route to Jerez and was built as part of the Moorish fortifications. Demolished completely in 1864, the gateway was replaced by a fountain dedicated to Seville as a goddess and circled by 11 playfully peeing cherubs, hence its local nickname, *los meones* ('the pissers'). All that remains of the gateway is a plaque bearing the famous paean to Seville: 'Hercules built me, Julius Caesar fortified me with walls and high towers…'.

To the south of the Puerta de Jerez are numerous other buildings of note, including the **Teatro Lope de Vega** (Avda de María Luisa s/n, *see p102*), the ultra-posh **Hotel Alfonso XIII** (C/San Fernando, *see p59*) and the **Antigua Fábrica de Tabacos** (Avda San Fernando 4), now owned by the university but once the tobacco factory where Merimée and Bizet's beautiful gypsy Carmen worked.

Spreading further south along the riverbanks is the **Parque de María Luisa (photo** *p79*), a truly delightful expanse of palms, cypresses, water features, formal rose gardens and Andalucían tiled patios. It is named after Princess María Luisa de Orleans who donated part of the land of the splendid baroque **Palacio San Telmo** (Avda Roma s/n, 955 03 55 00, closed for renovation) to the city. There are plenty of places to sit in the shade and listen to the ferocious cooing of the park's doves, and gardening fans can follow the 'botanic itinerary' of 127 species, exotic and indigenous, mapped out on signs for a self-guided walk. The peace is currently somewhat disturbed by the roadworks for the new metro system.

Constructed for the 1929 Ibero-American Expo, the whole concept is much better integrated with the city than the Isla de Cartuja (site of the 1992 Expo), chiefly because its grand, opulent buildings were created to last. Today, the majority are embassies, but there are still a number that are open to the public. One of the most beautiful is the pink-and-yellow-striped pavilion that now houses a tourist office. Probably the most pleasant way to visit the park is by horse-drawn carriage. Pick one up from Plaza del Triunfo for a 45-minute tour (about €30, agree your price before getting in).

On the north-east side of the park is the **Plaza de España**, a huge, semicircular complex of buildings decorated in bright tiles representing each of the 40 regions of Spain.

It's a stunning sight, and a good spot to read. Little boats can be hired to potter around on a canal that echoes the arc of the structure. Beyond the Plaza in the Prado de San Sebastián is **La Noria Panorámica**, Seville's equivalent to the London Eye, inaugurated in May 2006.

To the south of the park, two of the fair's most impressive mansions have been converted into museums: the **Museo Arqueológico** and the **Museo de Costumbres Populares**.

Museo Arqueológico

Plaza de América s/n (954 23 24 01/www.juntadeandalucia.es/cultura). **Open** 2.30-8.30pm Tue; 9am-8.30pm Wed-Sat; 9am-2.30pm Sun. **Admission** €1.50; free with EU passport or student ID. **No credit cards**. **Map** p55 off H2.

A chronological visit through the 27 rooms begins in the basement, which covers palaeolithic Spain through to the start of the Roman occupation. Copper Age artefacts include a collection of idols, characterised by their large sun-shaped eyes and thought to be the oldest representations of divinity on Spanish soil. In the protohistory section the star exhibit is the Carámbolo Treasure: 21 pieces of gold Tartessian jewellery from El Carámbolo, Ébora and Mairena, including a necklace, bracelets and pieces from a crown dating from the sixth century BC. The designs show clear oriental connections, thus raising questions about the identity of these ancient Andalucians. The items on display are copies; the originals are in secret vaults of the Banco de España.

Upstairs, the main galleries are devoted to the Roman era, with statues and fragments rescued from the nearby ancient site of Itálica. Highlights include a third-century BC mosaic from Écija, sculptures of locally born emperors, Trajan and Hadrian, and a world-class collection of bronze tablets bearing Roman laws. The rooms continue on to Moorish Spain with Visigothic relics and artefacts discovered at the Medina Azahara in Córdoba (*see p226*).

Museo de Costumbres Populares

Plaza de América 3 (954 23 25 76). **Open** 2.30-8.30pm Tue; 9am-8.30pm Wed-Sat; 9am-2.30pm Sun. **Admission** €1.50; free with EU passport or student ID. **No credit cards**. **Map** p55 off H2.

Located in the beautiful Mudéjar pavilion built for the 1929 Expo, the museum of popular customs houses a somewhat random collection of everything from Semana Santa costumes to postcards and kitchen implements. The most cogent collections are the 6,000 pieces of lace and embroidery and the countless posters and lithographs for the Feria de Abril. More accessible are the simulated scenes such as the workshops of luthiers, ironmongers and the entire cooperage of Claudio Bernal, the last barrel-maker in the city. New acquisitions include a vast collection of antique dolls and toys and a selection of ceramic holy water stoups dating back to the 15th century. Temporary exhibitions on the first floor usually mirror current events such as Semana Santa. Classical and folk concerts are hosted in the leafy patio on weekends in April, May and September.

La Noria Panorámica

Jardines del Prado de San Sebastián (954 61 95 12/www.noriapanoramicadesevilla.com). **Open** 10am-midnight daily. **Tickets** €8; €5-€6 concessions; free under-5s. **Credit** AmEx, DC, MC, V. **Map** p55 G2.

A new and flashily modern (if woefully underused) big wheel from the people behind the London Eye. La Noria has 42 capsules, which offer great views from up to 60m (200ft) during their rather rapid 12-minute rotation. Entire capsules (for eight) can be hired for €48 or there is a VIP capsule (for four, €75) whose leather interior holds a curiously redundant plasma TV, DVD player and telephone.

Triana

Separated from the centre of the city by the Guadalquivir, the barrio of Triana takes its name from the Emperor Trajan, who was born in nearby Itálica (*see p80*). Once a notoriously rough area, the district has been smartened up considerably over the past few years and its eastern section, flanking the river between two bridges, is nearly as full of tourists and tapas bars as Santa Cruz. This is more due to its fame as Seville's old gypsy quarter and the spiritual heart of the flamenco tradition than any must-see monuments; although it still retains some traditions, relatively few gypsies live here these days. Triana is one of the many starting points for the Romería del Rocío, the most important pilgrimage in the Andalucían calendar (*see p49*), and is where the weeping Virgen de la Esperanza – one of the most-adored virgins of the city – begins her Semana Santa procession.

From 1171 Triana was connected to the city by a pontoon bridge, which was replaced by the steel Puente de Isabel II in 1854. Cross the bridge – known to *sevillanos* as the **Puente de Triana** – to reach the charming Plaza Altozano, lined with bars and restaurants, and on to nearby Plaza Callao, where at No.12 you'll find the beautiful tiled façade of the **Ceramica Santa Ana**, the oldest of the city's remaining factories and recently saved from demolition for housing. Since Roman times, when clay was gathered from the banks of the river to make amphoras, Triana has been famous for its pottery and has long been the centre of *azulejo* production in the city.

North-west along C/Castilla lies the 17th-century church of **Nuestra Señora de la O** (C/Castilla). The chapel has a stunning crucified Christ by Francisco Antonio Gijón, known popularly as El Cacharro. It was supposedly inspired by the dead body of a gypsy singer killed outside in a street brawl and is one of the most popular processions of Semana Santa. Five hundred years ago, the most infamous building in Seville was located just south of here, on the site of the current food market. The Castillo de Triana was the residence of the Inquisition until it was formally abolished in 1820. You could continue north from C/Castillo to Isla de Cartuja, or double back towards the church of **San Jacinto** (C/Pagés del Corro s/n).

Running south-east along the riverbank from the Puente de Triana is **C/Betis**, whose lively bars and restaurants have excellent views of the city centre across the water. Halfway along is the church of **Santa Ana** (C/Pureza). The oldest church in Triana, it was built by Alfonso X in 1276 and houses a masterful 16th-century *retablo* richly carved by Alejo Fernández and painted by Pedro de Campaña, a double row of choir stalls carved in 1620 and a silver monstrance from 1726. Legend has it that the church's baptismal font, la Pila de los Gitanos, is where the gifts of flamenco singing and dancing are bestowed upon infants who are christened there. The gypsy quarter used to spread out through the streets and squares behind the church. Wander around and you'll spot some of the original gypsy *corrales*, communal houses centred around a courtyard.

Isla de Cartuja

Until the early 1990s the **Isla de Cartuja**, north of Triana on the west bank of the river, was filled with slum dwellings. The city resolved to clear it up for the 1992 Expo, displacing a lot of the residents in the process, many of whom now live in the shanty towns that ring the city. An enormous public works programme was begun, which involved not only building the Expo, but also creating the necessary infrastructure to welcome the world and beautify the entire city.

Parque de María Luisa. *See p77.*

The fair itself was meant to be a joint effort with the US, but in the event Seville was left to finance the extravaganza itself. Over six months the Expo attracted a whopping 42.5 million visitors, but even these hordes were not enough to cover costs, and the city was left with debts of some €360 million. Politicians may argue that the Expo was a success, but many *sevillanos* believe it was just a waste of money.

However, even the staunchest critics cannot deny the Expo's legacy: not the island itself, but the infrastructure that came with it. The Santa Justa train station formed a terminus for a new high-speed train link to Madrid, and an international airport, San Pablo, was built to bring foreign visitors to the city. Four new bridges were constructed to link the site to the city, including the **Puente de Alamillo**, designed by Santiago Calatrava. Perhaps the single most striking example of modern architecture in Andalucía, this 250-metre (820-foot) bridge consists of a single leaning pylon held in place with cables attached to different points along its length. Its lyre-like shape has become a symbol of Seville. The original plan for a matching bridge on the other side of the island was dropped due to budget constraints.

After the Expo much of the site lay unused and fell into disrepair, but today many of the buildings have been reappropriated as offices and a university faculty. In an effort to draw more people over the water, other pavilions have been converted into museums such as the new **Pabellón de la Energía Viva** (*see p95*), concert venues and other public spaces.

The only major attraction on the island is the 14th-century Carthusian monastery, **La Cartuja de Santa María**, with its modern art gallery, although anyone with young children will probably be bullied into spending a day at the **Isla Mágica** (*see p96*).

La Cartuja de Santa María

Isla de Cartuja (955 03 70 83/www.caac.es). **Open** *Apr-Sept* 10am-9pm Tue-Fri; 11am-8pm Sat; 10am-3pm Sun. *Oct-Mar* 10am-8pm Tue-Fri; 11am-8pm Sat; 10am-3pm Sun. **Admission** €3; free Tue. **No credit cards. Map** p54 B6.

Built in 1400 by the Archbishop of Seville, Gonzalo de Mena, after a vision of the Virgin over a local pottery, the tranquil monastery La Cartuja de Santa María was once a self-sufficient village, entirely cut off from the rest of the city. It was here that Columbus stayed before his visits to the Americas. The monastery suffered numerous indignities in the succeeding centuries: it was occupied by French troops in 1810-12 and, in a poor state, bought cheaply in 1839 by Charles Pickman, a British businessman, who set up a ceramics factory and lived there. Restored for the 1992 Expo, the huge brick kilns and chimneys that still dominate the site seem very surreal, although the effect is softened by pretty gardens of orange trees. From the stables and servants' quarters, a courtyard leads to the main cloister, which includes the Capilla de Santa Ana and a tomb, where Columbus's bones rested for 27 years. The church has the remains of a Mudéjar gallery and a beautiful stained-glass window, surrounded by tiles in blue and honey tones. Several rooms lead off the Mudéjar cloister, including the refectory, with its extraordinary *artesando* (coffered ceiling), used as a shooting gallery by French troops during the occupation. Also worth a look is the Capítulo de Monjes (chapter house), in which the patrons of the monastery are buried.

Centro Andaluz de Arte Contemporáneo

Avda Américo Vespucio 2 (955 03 70 70/ www.caac.es). **Open** as La Cartuja above. **Admission** *Collection & exhibition* €3. *Exhibition only* €1.80; free Tue with EU passport. **No credit cards. Map** p54 B6.

A separate building in the monastery complex, this is Andalucía's only contemporary art museum and holds a small permanent collection (not all of which is always on display), with some excellent pieces, mostly by Andalucian artists. Temporary exhibitions highlight little-known modern Andalucíans and there are also regular music concerts, cinema cycles and music recitals.

Outside the city

Itálica

Avda de Extremadura 2, Santiponce (955 99 65 83). **Open** *Apr-Sept* 8.30am-8.30pm Tue-Sat; 9am-3pm Sun. *Oct-Mar* 9am-5.30pm Tue-Sat; 10am-4pm Sun. **Admission** €1.50; free with EU passport. **No credit cards.**

Nine kilometres (five miles) north of Seville, near the village of Santiponce, are the ruins of what was once the third largest city in the Roman Empire. Founded in 206 BC, Itálica rose to prominence during the reign of Hadrian in the second century AD and boasted a population of almost half a million. Hadrian was one of three Roman Emperors born in the city, the others being Trajan and Theodosius. The Visigothic invasion signaled the end for Itálica, and subsequent centuries saw it despoiled and looted for much of its stone.

Today, it's a rather forlorn and barren spot, although the amphitheatre, with seating for at least 40,000 people, is undeniably impressive. Various of its streets, with the ruins of villas, temples and bath houses, are also clearly visible, and there are some beautiful mosaics in the Casa Neptune and the Casa de los Pájaros. The fascinating monastic complex of San Isidro del Campo (at the Seville entrance to Itálica) has recently been opened to the public, and holds an exceptional collection of art, ranging from medieval frescoes to a superb late Renaissance high altar by Pablo de Rojas.

Restaurants, Bars & Cafés

Tapas, *jamones* and some triumphantly old-school establishments.

Corral del Agua.

The line between tapas bar and restaurant can sometimes be blurry; Seville's establishments tend to serve all functions and the same place will do a coffee and croissant in the morning, a set lunch menu, dinner, late-night drinks and more than likely serve tapas all day long too. Many places settle for the happy combination of a rowdy tapas bar upfront and a quieter sit-down restaurant at the back.

The days of tapas coming free with your drink are long gone in Seville and these days you'll be lucky to get a free saucer of peanuts. Watch out for overpriced tourist traps, which abound in the city centre. Instead, venture a few streets beyond the major monuments and you'll discover some hidden gems, where your bill is chalked up on the bar, *jamones* hang from the ceiling, and old men yack about politics.

Barrio de Santa Cruz & around the cathedral

Restaurants

Al Sur

Paseo de Catalina de Ribera s/n (954 56 04 75). **Open** 8am-1am daily. **Average** €-€€. **Credit** AmEx, DC, MC, V. **Map** p55 F2 ❶

The views over the Jardines de Murillo are the perfect complement to Fátima Romero's cooking. Tapas and *raciones* are served all day, but the food is really worth making a meal of with dishes that include foie gras with Pedro Ximénez and baked apples or monkfish with caramel. There are also plenty of vegetarian options available.

La Albahaca

Plaza Santa Cruz 12 (954 22 07 14/www.andalunet.com/la-albahaca). **Open** noon-4pm; 8pm-midnight Mon-Sat. **Average** €€. **Credit** AmEx, DC, MC, V. **Map** p55 F2 ❷

This dreamy place is located in a fine converted palace (by Juan Talavera) on a romantic square. Inside it's decorated with *azulejos*, antique furniture and chandeliers; a perfect setting for inventive dishes like sea bass with apple and almond sauce, and venison with mushrooms and almonds.

Altamira

C/Santa María la Blanca 4 (954 42 50 30). **Open** 9am-2am daily. **Average** €-€€. **Credit** AmEx, DC, MC, V. **Map** p55 F2 ❸

This lovely restaurant in a pretty square serves ice-cold *fino*, huge salads and a wide range of tapas, including *berenjenas rellenas* (stuffed aubergines) and *gambas al ajillo* (prawns with garlic).

Bar Modesto

C/Cano y Cueto 5 (954 41 68 11/www.grupomodesto.com). **Open** 8am-2am daily. **Average** €€. **Credit** AmEx, DC, MC, V. **Map** p55 F2 ❹

A tapas bar/restaurant, part of a large, slightly anodyne but respectable chain. Dishes include *ortiguillas* (deep fried sea anemones) and *centollo gratinada* (spider crab gratin) or black clams.

Casa Robles

C/Álvarez Quintero 58 (954 21 31 50/www.roblesrestaurantes.com). **Open** 1-6pm, 9pm-1am daily. **Average** €€€€. **Credit** AmEx, DC, MC, V. **Map** p55 E3 ❺

Supposedly one of the best restaurants in town, but resting on its laurels. The meat and fish can be fine, but they can also be overcooked and presented with a handful of limp vegetables. Saving graces include an extensive wine list and some superb desserts; the *tocino de cielo* (a rich custard) is particularly tasty.

Corral del Agua

Callejón del Agua 6 (954 22 48 41/www.andalunet.com/corral-agua). **Open** noon-4pm, 8pm-midnight Mon-Sat. Closed Jan. **Average** €€€. **Credit** AmEx, DC, MC, V. **Map** p55 F3 ❻

Casa Placido. *See p83.*

Corral del Agua is in a converted 18th-century palace with a plant-filled patio, a pretty fountain and a garden. It serves simple but good dishes, such as sea bass in sherry and *salmorejo*. **Photo** *p81*.

Egaña Oriza

C/San Fernando 41 (954 22 72 11/www.restauranteoriza.com). **Open** 1.30-3.30pm, 9-11.30pm Mon-Fri; 9-11.30pm Sat. Closed Aug. **Average** €€€€. **Credit** AmEx, DC, MC, V. **Map** p55 G3 ❼

Upmarket and expensive, this is where businessmen entertain their clients by day and well-heeled couples sup in the evening. The Basque food is imaginative and delicate, though somewhat overrated, while the setting, right beside the Jardines de Murillo, is perfect. It has an adjacent tapas bar, with good ham croquettes and stuffed mussels.

Hostería del Laurel

Plaza de los Venerables 5 (954 22 02 95/www.hosteriadellaurel.com). **Open** 11am-4pm, 8pm-midnight daily. **Average** €€. **Credit** AmEx, DC, MC, V. **Map** p55 F3 ❽

Beautiful tiles from Triana and a ceiling hanging with *jamones* add atmosphere to this place, which is mentioned in the first act of *Don Juan* and has retained its ambience against the odds. House specials include the *frito sevillano*; a huge fish fry-up.

Mesón Don Raimundo

C/Argote de Molina 26 (954 22 33 55/www.mesondonraimundo.com). **Open** 12.30-4pm, 7.30pm-midnight daily. **Average** €€-€€€. **Credit** DC, MC, V. **Map** p55 E3 ❾

This large, luxurious restaurant is a treasure trove of original Roman columns, tapestries, oils and ceramics. There's history on the plates too, with Andaluz and Mozarabic cuisine, including game and seafood from the Costa Gaditana and desserts such as 'Sueños de Sevilla'; pastry and fruit drenched in orange blossom syrup and served with sesame and cream.

Pizzeria San Marco

C/Mesón del Moro 6 (954 21 43 90). **Open** 1.15-4.30pm, 8.15pm-12.30am daily. **Average** €€. **Credit** AmEx, DC, MC, V. **Map** p55 F3 ❿

Excellent pizza and pasta in a stylishly converted old Arab bathhouse near the Hospital de los Venerables. Try the mixed plate of antipasti to start.

Restaurante Becerrita

C/Recaredo 9 (954 41 20 57/www.becerrita.com). **Open** 12.30-4.30pm, 8pm-12.30am Mon-Sat; 12.30-4.30pm Sun. **Average** €€€. **Credit** AmEx, DC, MC, V. **Map** p55 E1 ⓫

In the same family for five generations, this sprawling restaurant is picturesque but has a modern Seville feel that reflects imaginative ways with classic local dishes. Try bull's tail croquettes, Iberian pork stew or spicy lamb's brains roasted in garlic.

Salvador Rojo

C/San Fernando 23 (954 22 97 25). **Open** noon-4.30pm, 8.30pm-1am Mon-Sat. Closed Aug. **Average** €€€. **Credit** AmEx, DC, MC, V. **Map** p55 G3 ⓬

The design is warm and simple, the service is superb, and the dishes, though generously proportioned, are delicate and refined. Try the *salteado de langostinos* with Thai rice or the crayfish as a starter; for mains, the *carne de cordero* (slices of lamb with potato purée) is recommended.

Tapas

La Bodeguita

C/Hernando Colón 1-3 (954 22 25 61). **Open** 7.30am-10pm Mon-Fri; 10am-10pm Sat, Sun. **Average** €. **Credit** AmEx, DC, MC, V. **Map** p55 E3 ⓭

It may be tiny, but La Bodeguita has an enormous range of tasty and inventive tapas, including *berenjenas rellenas de jamón y gambas* (aubergines stuffed with ham and prawns).

La Cava del Europa

C/Santa María la Blanca 40 (954 53 16 52). **Open** 8am-1am daily. **Average** €-€€. **Credit** AmEx, DC, MC, V. **Map** p55 F2 ⓮

Next to the Murillo gardens, this bar is famous for its internationally inspired tapas. The menu changes four times a year to match the seasons and might include anything from 'liquid' croquettes with *jamón ibérico* to spinach salad.

Casa Placido

C/Mesón del Moro 5 & C/Ximénez Enciso 11 (954 56 39 71). **Open** noon-4pm, 8pm-midnight Mon-Fri; noon-midnight Sat, Sun. **Average** €. **Credit** DC, MC, V. **Map** p55 F2 ⓯

This traditional *fino* bar makes no concessions to tourists, despite being at the heart of tourist Seville. It hasn't changed in decades, with *jamones* hanging from the ceiling, sherries served from the barrel and ancient posters on the walls.

Casa Román

Plaza de los Venerables 1 (954 22 84 83). **Open** 9.30am-4pm, 7.30pm-midnight Mon-Fri; 11am-4pm, 7.30pm-midnight Sat, Sun. **Average** €. **Credit** MC, DC, V. **Map** p55 F3 ⓰

Despite being in a prime spot in one of the barrio's most popular squares, this excellent old bar manages to retain a traditional feel. The menu is in Spanish only, fag ends and napkins cover the floor, and the *jamón* is among the finest in the city.

Cervecería Giralda

C/Mateos Gago 1 (954 22 74 35). **Open** 9am-midnight Mon-Sat; 10am-midnight Sun. **Average** €. **Credit** AmEx, DC, MC, V. **Map** p55 F3 ⓱

With the Giralda as a backdrop, this place gets understandably mobbed. Neither the service nor the tapas seems to suffer though. Excellent house specials include *patatas importancia* (baked potatoes with ham and cheese).

Las Columnas

C/Rodrigo Caro 1 (954 21 32 46). **Open** 7am-midnight daily. Closed 2wks July/Aug. **Average** €. **No credit cards**. **Map** p55 F3 ⓲

Just up from the Giralda, Las Columnas is a classic, with orders chalked on the bar, wise-cracking barmen and little dishes of tasty chickpea broth, *riñones de jerez* and oxtail stew. The *pringá* is delicious.

La Fresquita

C/Mateos Gago 29 (954 22 60 10). **Open** noon-4pm, 8pm-1am Mon-Sat. **Average** €. **No credit cards.** **Map** p55 E3 19

This pocket-handkerchief bar is festooned with religious decoration and frequented by the local *costaleros* (carriers of the Semana Santa floats) and *cofradías* (brotherhoods). Perch on a child-sized stool outside and enjoy a beer and some of José's famous spicy snails stewing over the camp stove in the corner.

La Goleta

C/Mateos Gago 20 (954 21 89 66). **Open** 12.30-4pm, 8pm-1.30am daily. **Average** €. **No credit cards.** **Map** p55 F3 20

Álvaro Peregil has inherited the outsized personality of his father (Bar Quitapesares, *see p85*) and runs a similarly friendly bar. Due to its tiny size, La Goleta can't help but be packed and totally chaotic, but it's the perfect stop for a chat over a *manzanilla* from Huelva and some basic tapas. The toilet is a strong contender for the world's smallest.

La Sacristía

C/Mateos Gago 18 (954 21 92 07). **Open** 12.30pm-midnight daily. **Average** €. **Credit** AmEx, MC, V. **Map** p55 F3 21

Stylish but friendly, La Sacristía has a wide range of good-sized tapas, such as *flamenquín caseros* (croquettes with bacon and mushrooms) and *tortillas* laced with whisky or Roquefort, and a fine wine list.

Cafés & bars

Aire de Sevilla

C/Aire 15 (955 01 00 24/955 01 00 25). **Open** 10am-midnight daily. **Average** €. **Credit** DC, MC, V. **Map** p55 E3 22

Richly embroidered cushions and the sound of running water accompany a tea menu of over 50 varieties in this gorgeous Arab-style bathhouse. From the terrace clients can enjoy the Giralda views and occasional recitals of Arabic music while sipping their fresh juice and eating baklava.

Centro

Restaurants

La Alicantina

Plaza del Salvador 2 (954 22 61 22). **Open** *July, Aug* noon-midnight Mon-Sat. *Sept-June* noon-midnight Mon-Sat; noon-5pm Sun. **Average** €. **Credit** AmEx, DC, MC, V. **Map** p54 D3 23

A very popular place with a great *terraza* and set in the middle of a bustling square, La Alicantina specialises in seafood, particularly of the shellfish variety, at reasonable prices. Try the lobster crêpes or the award-winning Russian salad.

Barbiana

C/Albaredo 11 (954 21 12 39). **Open** noon-4.30pm Mon-Sat; 8pm-midnight Sun. Closed Aug. **Average** €€. **Credit** AmEx, DC, MC, V. **Map** p55 E4 24

Quiet at dinner time but packed to the rafters for lunch, with flip-flopping fresh fish and seafood at surprisingly reasonable prices as the speciality. Reliable favourites are flash-fried *ortiguillas* (sea anemones) with liquid centres, and *tortillitas de camarones*, fritters of chickpea flour, baby prawns and green onions with the texture of crunchy lace.

El Burladero

Hotel Meliá Colón, C/Canalejas 1 (954 50 55 99). **Open** 1.30-3.30pm, 9-11.30pm daily. Closed Aug. **Average** €€€. **Credit** AmEx, DC, MC, V. **Map** p55 D4 25

Named after the wooden refuges in the bullring and dripping with taurine memorabilia, this classic pre-and-post *corrida* meeting point is one of the city's best-known restaurants. The food sometimes fails to live up to the hype, so sticking with classics like the *rabo de toro* (oxtail) is probably the safest bet.

La Habanita

C/Golfo 3, off C/Pérez Galdos (954 22 02 02/ www.restaurantehabanita.com). **Open** 12.30-4.30pm, 8pm-12.30am Mon-Sat; 12.30-4.30pm Sun. **Average** €. **Credit** MC, V. **Map** p54 D3 26

A fab restaurant in a tiny square close to Plaza Alfalfa specialising in tasty Cuban dishes like *arepas* (cornmeal rolls), fried bananas and black beans, and chicken breast in coconut sauce. It's also one of the few places in the city offering vegan dishes.

San Marco. *See p85.*

Restaurante Cereceto
C/Pérez Galdós 20 (954 22 05 67). **Open** *Mid June-mid Sept* 1.30-4.30pm, 8.30pm-midnight Mon-Fri; 8.30pm-12.30am Sat. *Mid Sept-mid June* 1.30-4.30pm, 8.30pm-midnight Tue-Sat; 1.30-4.30pm Sun. Closed last 2wks Aug. **Average** €€. **Credit** AmEx, DC, MC, V. **Map** p54 D3 27
Zebra-print walls and plush black seating make this restaurant stand out, as do the home-made breads, fresh pastas, sauces and fine-crust pizzas. There are plenty of veggie options such as spinach ravioli along with a good selection of salads.

San Marco
C/Cuna 6 (954 21 24 40/www.restaurantesan marco.com). **Open** 1.15-4.30pm, 8.15pm-12.30am daily. **Average** €€. **Credit** AmEx, DC, MC, V. **Map** p54 D3 28
Stylish San Marco offers French and Italian dishes at reasonable prices. The main restaurant is in an 18th-century palace with Moorish features, while the other branch serves great pizza and pasta in an old Arabic bathhouse (*see p83*).

Al Solito Posto
C/Huelva 8 (954 22 09 17). **Open** 1-4pm, 8.30pm-midnight Mon-Sat: 1-4pm Sun. Closed 2wks in Aug. **Average** €€. **Credit** AmEx, DC, MC, V. **Map** p54 D3 29
A popular and good-value Italian restaurant just by the Plaza de Pan. The modern decor is entirely free of the red-checked tablecloth clichés and there's also a nice terrace where diners choose from classic salads, pizza and pasta dishes.

Tapas

La Alacena de San Eloy
C/San Eloy 31 (954 21 55 80/www.laalacenade saneloy.com). **Open** noon-4pm, 8pm-midnight daily. **Average** €€. **Credit** AmEx, MC, V. **Map** p54 D4 30
This slick modern space punctuated with splashes of bright orange is a shop specialising in Andalucían hams, wines and other products, though it doubles as an excellent wine bar with a huge selection of high-quality tipples matched to tapas. The atmosphere can get alarmingly *pijo* (Sloaney) at times.

Bar Europa
C/Siete Revueltas 35 (954 22 13 54/www.bareuropa.info). **Open** 8am-1am daily. **Average** €€. **Credit** AmEx, MC, V. **Map** p54 D3 31
A handsome bar with gleaming wooden counter and chequered floor, the Europa also turns out outstanding food: house specials include a delicious *crema de calabacín al aroma de curry* (a creamy curried courgette soup), chicken salad, partridge pâté, moussaka and Roquefort crêpe.

Bar Manolo
Plaza Alfalfa 3 (954 21 41 76). **Open** 7am-midnight daily. **Average** €-€€. **No credit cards.** **Map** p54 D3 32
Cheap, bright and cheerful, Bar Manolo is a good spot for a morning coffee or a lunchtime snack. Specialises in *pescado frito*, snails and gazpacho.

Bar Quitapesares
C/Padre Gerónimo de Córdoba 3 (no phone). **Open** 1-4pm, 8pm-3am daily. Closed July & Aug. **Average** €. **No credit cards.** **Map** p54 D2 33
Singer-songwriter 'El Peregil' is one of Seville's best-loved personalities and his hugely atmospheric bar is full of photos spanning his illustrious singing career. He'll still burst into song occasionally and late at night there's the odd flamenco jam, fuelled by *manzanilla* and *chacina* (cured meats).

La Bodega
C/Alfalfa 4 (954 21 42 52). **Open** noon-4pm, 8pm-midnight daily. **Average** €. **No credit cards.** **Map** p54 D3 34
Heralded by a colourful arch of tiles depicting a beach scene, this traditional stand-up bar has the odd barrel or shelf to rest your drink on, but most people are scrummed around the bar. Specialities are cured Iberian ham cut wafer-thin from the many hanging overhead, and Andalucían wines.

Bodega Amarillo Albero
Plaza de la Gavídia 5 (954 21 90 85). **Open** noon-5pm, 8pm-midnight daily. **Average** €. **Credit** MC, V. **Map** p54 C4 35
The walls of this bodega are lined with sherry bottles and old photos, wine barrels stand in for tables, and there is a good selection of tapas.

Entrecárceles
C/Faisanes 1 (954 22 38 90). **Open** noon-4pm, 8pm-midnight daily. **Average** €€. **Credit** MC, V. **Map** p55 E3 36
A Dickensian tavern opened in 1894, Entrecárceles ('Between jails') gets it name from the tunnel that ran under here between the courthouse opposite and the former prison next door. Its tapas are elaborate confections such as layered aubergine with salmon mousse, cod and langoustine, and its lace-lined shelves sport bottles of impossibly rare sherries.

Patio San Eloy
C/San Eloy 9 (954 22 11 48). **Open** 11.30am-5pm, 6.30-11.30pm Mon-Thur, Sun; 11.30am-midnight Fri, Sat. **Average** €. **Credit** MC, V. **Map** p54 D4 37
Big, noisy and chaotic, Patio San Eloy is also very atmospheric. Locals drop by for a quick snack after finishing the shopping, waiters shout out orders and there are mountains of simple tapas and sandwiches to munch on while sitting on the rows of *azulejo*-covered steps that serve as seats and tables.

El Rinconcillo
C/Gerona 40 (954 22 31 83/www.elrinconcillo.es). **Open** 1pm-1am daily. Closed 2wks July/Aug. **Average** €. **Credit** AmEx, DC, MC, V. **Map** p54 D2 38
The city's oldest bar-restaurant dates from 1670 and is an essential stop for a real slice of *sevillano* atmosphere, with tiles, ancient wood fittings, bills chalked

El Rinconcillo. See p85.

up on the bar, and a haze of smoke and noise from *fino-* and *vino*-fuelled conversations (the non-smoking section, naturally, belongs to tourists). The tapas, particularly *espinacas con garbanzos* (spinach with chickpeas) and *fabes con pringá* (beans with various meats), are excellent.

Taberna Colóniales

Plaza del Cristo de Burgos 19 (954 50 11 36/37). **Open** noon-midnight daily. Closed 3wks Aug. **Average** €. **Credit** AmEx, DC, MC, V. **Map** p54 D3 39

A cramped, old-style bar with tables spilling out on to a pleasant square and some seating in a tiny room out back. A list of tapas includes fried quails' eggs with *jamón*. For something more substantial, *lomo de buey* is succulent grilled tenderloin cubed and served on a wooden platter to share, as is the delicious *secreto ibérico* (pork flank).

Cafés & bars

Bar El Tremendo

C/San Felipe 15 (954 21 47 47). **Open** 11am-midnight Mon, Tue, Thur-Sun. Closed Aug. **Average** €. **No credit cards**. **Map** p54 D3 40

El Tremendo is one of the best-known bars in the area, although there's nothing tremendous about its proportions – it's more of a stainless-steel beer counter than a bar. Locals squeeze around or gather on the pavement for cheap cold beers and a quick bite of cod or *mojama* (cured tuna).

Confitería La Campaña

C/Sierpes 1 & 3 (954 22 35 70/www.confiteriala campana.com). **Open** 8am-10pm Mon-Fri; 8am-11pm Sat, Sun. **Average** €. **Credit** AmEx, MC, DC, V. **Map** p54 D3/4 41

This dusty, gorgeous, old-style city caff was founded in 1885 and specialises in home-made chocolate, nougats, *yemas* and all things unhealthy and sweet. It is good for coffee and cakes too.

El Arenal

Restaurants

La Isla

C/Arfe 25 (954 21 26 31/www.restaurantela isla.com). **Open** 1-4.30pm, 8pm-midnight daily. Closed Aug. **Average** €€-€€€. **Credit** AmEx, DC, MC, V. **Map** p55 F4 42

With an impressive window display of fresh fish, this airy, attractive restaurant is run by a Galician family and is a long-standing favourite with well-heeled fish and seafood lovers. There is everything from *percebes* (goose barnacles) to spider crab, lobster and baby eels, and a good selection of Spanish wines.

Las Piletas

C/Marqués de Paradas 28 (954 22 04 04/www.anda lunet.com/piletas). **Open** 7am-1am daily. **Average** €€. **Credit** AmEx, DC, MC, V. **Map** p55 E5 43

Bulls' heads and matador posters hang everywhere in this high-ceilinged temple to taurine culture, where excellent barbecued lamb, steaks and *rabo de toro* (oxtail) are served accompanied by heavy red wines. Solo men come to watch the football at the bar, while a partitioned section offers seclusion.

Porta Rossa

C/Pastor y Landero 20 (954 21 61 39). **Open** *July* 9pm-midnight Mon; 2-4pm, 9pm-midnight Tue-Sat. *Sept-June* 2-4pm, 9pm-midnight Tue-Sat; 2-4pm Sun. Closed Aug. **Average** €€-€€€. **Credit** AmEx, DC, MC, V. **Map** p55 E4 44

If you need a change from Spanish cuisine, and fancy a refined, friendly atmosphere and superlative Italian cooking (with a *sevillano* touch), then this is the place for you. The decor is upmarket, stylish and modern, and the menu offers delicate pastas and subtle sauces. Recommended.

Taberna del Alabardero

C/Zaragoza 20 (954 50 27 21/www.tabernadel alabardero.com). **Open** 1-4pm, 8pm-1am daily. Closed Aug. **Average** €€€. **Credit** AmEx, DC, MC, V. **Map** p55 E4 ㊺

The warren of small dining rooms are all dark woods, soft lights, starched tablecloths and chandeliers. The emphasis is on meat dishes, including cheeks of Iberian pork and venison stew, but there's also seafood (spiny lobsters are reared on site) and an extensive wine list.

Tapas

Antonio Romero

C/Antonia Díaz 19 (954 22 39 39). **Open** noon-1am Tue-Sun. Closed Aug. **Average** €-€€. **Credit** AmEx, DC, MC, V. **Map** p55 F4 ㊻

Antonio Romero is always crowded with a noisy upmarket crowd (expect many polo shirts and knotted V-necks). Its speciality is *montaditos* (small, hot *bocadillos*) – especially good are the *mojama* (wind-dried tuna) with tomato and the *pringá*.

Bodega San José

C/Adriano 10 (954 22 41 05). **Open** 8am-11.30pm Mon-Sat; 8am-3pm Sun. **Average** €. **No credit cards**. **Map** p55 E4 ㊼

Drinks are chalked up on the bar and sherry is served from the barrels behind. The walls are covered in Semana Santa posters and the floor is covered in napkins and olive stones. Noisy, friendly: a real taste of old Seville.

Café Bar Taquilla

C/Adriano 24 (954 21 11 26). **Open** *July & Aug* 8am-4pm, 8pm-midnight Mon-Fri. *Sept-June* 8am-4pm, 8pm-midnight Mon-Sat. **Average** €. **No credit cards**. **Map** p55 E5 ㊽

Another bar situated by the bullring, the plain and humble 'Ticket Office' is decorated with the obligatory bull's head and old photos of the Maestranza, and is generally full of men debating the *corrida*. Nibble on a tasty *montadito* of cured ham and pork or go for the excellent *chipirones*.

Casa Morales

C/García de Vinuesa 11 (954 22 12 42). **Open** *July, Aug* noon-4pm, 8pm-midnight Mon-Fri. *Sept-June* noon-4pm, 8pm-midnight Mon-Sat. **Average** €. **Credit** (over €30 only) MC, V. **Map** p55 E/F4 ㊾

Founded in 1850 and largely unchanged since, this is allegedly the second-oldest bar in town and has certainly kept its looks. The atmosphere is traditional and the tapas are good: *lomo amontillado* (pork in sherry); *chorizo de venao* (venison) and *fabes* (a butterbean stew) among them.

La Leyenda

C/Reyes Católicos 4 (954 22 89 00). **Open** 8am-11pm daily. **Average** €. **Credit** AmEx, DC, MC, V. **Map** p55 E5 ㊿

Attached to the Hotel Bécquer, this smart tapas bar is more popular with office workers than tourists. Those in the know come to feast on creative dishes of turkey pâté with port jelly; duck magret with courgette and peach and grape compote, and tuna carpaccio with shiitake mushrooms.

Meson de la Infanta

C/Dos de Mayo 26 (954 56 15 54). **Open** noon-5pm, 8pm-midnight daily. **Average** €-€€. **Credit** MC, V. **Map** p55 F4 51

It's hard to go wrong at this historic tapas bar and restaurant, where all the usual dishes are given an extra touch of class: *manzanilla* is poured from stainless steel pots kept on a bed of ice and the pale but intense *gazpacho* is served in a slender glass. The acorn-fed Iberian ham is some of the best in the city.

El Rincón Gallego

C/Harinas 21 (954 22 43 11). **Open** noon-4.30pm, 8pm-1am Tue-Sun. **Average** €. **Credit** AmEx, MC, V. **Map** p55 E4 52

A tiny spot that specialises in food from Galicia, in particular seafood from the Rías Baxas. Try the *pulpo gallego* (octopus with paprika).

La Macarena

Restaurants

Naranja

C/Relator 21 (954 91 50 80/www.cocinanaranja.com). **Open** 2-4pm, 9pm-12.30am Tue-Sun. Closed Aug. **Average** €€-€€€. **Credit** AmEx, DC, MC, V. **Map** p54 A/B3 53

A good place to go when fried-fish fatigue sets in, minimalist Naranja is kitted out in orange with an international staff and a globe-trotting menu that lists everything from sushi to curry and steak.

Tapas

Bar Yebra

C/Medalla Milagrosa 3 (954 35 10 07). **Open** noon-5pm, 8.15pm-midnight Tue-Sat; noon-5pm Sun. Closed Aug. **Average** €-€€. **Credit** AmEx, DC, MC, V. **Map** p54 A1 54

This is the place to go in La Macarena for new Andaluz tapas such as *jabalí* (boar) with raspberry sauce or cod in almond sauce, although Yebra is also well known for its superlative take on the classic dish of *revuelto de chorizo*. Pay close attention when the waiters sing out the list of daily specials.

Cervecería la Plazoleta

Plaza San Juan de la Palma s/n (mobile 627 260 067). **Open** *June-Sept* noon-4pm, 8pm-1am Mon-Sat. *Oct-May* noon-1am Tue-Sat; noon-4pm Sun. **Average** €. **No credit cards**. **Map** p54 C3 55

Backed up against the church of San Juan de la Palma, this yellow-painted bar is a friendly place to stop for a beer and a tapa of cod brandade or roast lamb with mint. There are some wooden chairs and tables outside on the quiet square, while the inside of the bar is enlivened by old marionettes and radios.

Colmado Los Escolapios

Plaza Ponce de León 5 (954 56 24 49). **Open** 8am-5pm, 8pm-midnight Mon-Fri; 8pm-midnight Sat; noon-5pm Sun. **Average** €. **No credit cards.** **Map** p54 C2 56

A jolly, narrow bar with buttercup-yellow walls and a long list of original tapas, from ratatouille with couscous to chicken balls with wild mushroom sauce. The real specialities, though, are locally sourced cheeses and hams, along with a good selection of wines by the glass.

Taberna de León de San Marcós

C/Vergara 3 (954 22 74 88). **Open** 8am-1am daily. Closed Aug. **Average** €. **No credit cards.** **Map** p54 C2 57

With tables in the shadow of San Marcós church, this tiny bar has a friendly neighbourhood vibe. Try the *montaditos* (mini panini) with *salmorejo y jamón*, or the delicious *queso blanco* with *palometa* (like smoked salmon). Small earthenware dishes of various stews are also excellent.

Cafés & bars

Bodega Vizcaino

C/Feria 27 (954 38 60 57). **Open** 8.30am-12.30am Mon-Sat. Closed 3wks Aug/Sept. **No credit cards.** **Map** p54 D3 58

There's not a tapa in sight at this high-ceilinged old-school bar, just plenty of sawdust on the floor and lots of vermouth, moscatel and beer. The turnover of locals coming in to wet their whistles is so high that the tabs scrawled in chalk on the bar barely have time to dry before being wiped off again.

La Alameda

Restaurants

Az-Zait

Plaza San Lorenzo 1 (954 90 64 75). **Open** noon-4pm, 8pm-midnight Mon-Sat. Closed Aug. **Average** €€-€€€. **Credit** AmEx, DC, MC, V. **Map** p54 B4 59

The name is the Arabic for the juice of the olive, an important component in this charming and very romantic restaurant's cuisine, which is a combination of classic Andaluz, modern and Mozarabic influences. The *bonbon de foie* is a real taste explosion, as is the sea bass in a cream sauce. To top it all off, the service is unusually friendly and efficient.

El Gallinero de Sandra

Pasaje Esperanza Elena Caro 2, between C/Amor de Dios & C/Trajano (954 90 99 31). **Open** *July & Aug* 1.30-3.30pm, 9-11.30pm Mon-Fri. *Sept-June* 1.30-3.30pm, 9-11.30pm Tue-Sat; 1.30-3.30pm Sun. **Average** €€-€€€. **Credit** AmEx, DC, MC, V. **Map** p54 C3 60

A *gallinero,* or chicken coop, is slang for a madhouse and this bright white restaurant certainly can get rowdy once the sun goes down. Along a quiet passage with a large shaded terrace, crowds flock here for fusion cuisine a step above the usual, with dishes such as tuna tataki, mango ravioli or a delicious fondue of Torta de Casar cheese.

La Ilustre Victima

C/Correduria 35 (954 38 94 90). **Open** 9am-2am daily. Closed Aug. **Average** €. **Credit** AmEx, DC, MC, V. **Map** p54 B3 61

A studenty café/bar/restaurant with a laid-back feel, warm, dark colours and low lighting. A decent selection of tapas is served, as well as couscous, kebabs and fajitas with plenty of vegetarian options.

La Mata 24

Plaza de la Mata 24 (954 37 05 86). **Open** 2-4pm, 9.30pm-midnight daily. Closed 2wks Aug. **Average** €€-€€€. **Credit** AmEx, DC, MC, V. **Map** p54 B3 62

There's not an *azulejo* in sight at this oh-so-cool little restaurant that comes decorated in the required minimalist tones of grey and white. Located just off the Alameda, it opened in 2006 and serves creative Mediterranean cuisine such as caramelised steak with sugar cane and strawberry sauce or shrimp carpaccio with sautéed *gulas* (baby eels).

Tapas

Alcoy 10

C/Teodosio 66 (954 90 57 02). **Open** 1.30-4pm, 8.30pm-midnight Tue-Sat; 1.30-4pm Sun. **Average** €. **Credit** DC, MC, V. **Map** p54 B4 63

A really excellent new tapas bar off the tourist track, turning out plates of pepper risotto with *jamón*; mini skewers of fresh fat prawns with couscous; pork with honey and creamed cabbage, and shellfish croquettes. Arrive early for a pavement table.

Café Bar Sardinero

Plaza de San Lorenzo 15 (954 38 94 24). **Open** 7am-midnight Mon, Tue, Thur-Sun. Closed Aug. **Average** €. **Credit** AmEx, DC, MC, V. **Map** p54 B4 64

On a balmy summer evening there is no better terrace in Seville for watching a neighbourhood at play, complete with hordes of children running riot amongst the trees. As a bonus, El Sardinero is there to serve up cold beer and seemingly endless dishes of *gambas al ajillo*, snails and *chipirones*.

Eslava

C/Eslava 3-5 (954 90 65 68). **Open** *Bar* noon-12.30am Tue-Sat; noon-4pm Sun. *Restaurant* 1.30-4pm, 9-11pm Tue-Sat; 1.30-4pm Sun. Closed 1st 3wks Aug. **Average** €-€€. **Credit** AmEx, DC, MC, V. **Map** p54 B4 65

One of Seville's most popular tapas bars, Eslava is, of course, permanently crowded. Specials include

La Antigua Abacería, deliciously old-fashioned. *See p90.*

courgette quiche, steak in blue cheese, spinach strudel and a deliciously creamy *salmorejo*. The excellent restaurant at the back has one of the best and cheapest set lunches in town.

Piola

Alameda de Hércules 57 (954 37 71 91). **Open** 9am-2am daily. **Average** €-€€. **No credit cards.** **Map** p54 B3 66

A noisy, fun and typically laid-back bar with a slightly more international range of tapas than the more traditional bars, such as generous portions of quiche and lasagne, along with cocktails.

Cafés & bars

Bahia Bar

C/Amor de Dios 62 (954 90 75 90). **Open** 8.30am-2am daily. **Average** €. **No credit cards.** **Map** p54 C3 67

This brightly painted café specialises in fresh fruit juices and milkshakes, along with light snacks of the pitta and nachos variety.

Café Sónoro

Alameda de Hércules 71 (mobile 618 89 18 52). **Open** *June & July, Sept* 8pm-2.30am Tue-Sun. *Oct-May* 6pm-2am Tue-Sun. Closed Aug. **No credit cards.** **Map** p54 B3 68

With a terrace in a newly pedestrianised side street, this tiny retro-style bar is all about music, playing everything from jazz and soul to bossa nova.

Di-Vino

C/Peral 2 (954 90 27 13). **Open** 1.30-4.30pm, 9pm-3am Tue-Sun. Closed 2wks Aug. **No credit cards.** **Map** p54 A/B3 69

At the north end of the Alameda, this small, newly opened wine bar is run by two friendly women and specialises in Spanish wines. There are also high-quality tapas such as pork confit with chestnut purée to enjoy on the terrace over the road.

Etnia Espacio Universal

C/Jesús del Gran Poder 28 (954 38 41 09). **Open** *June-Sept* 6pm-2am daily. *Oct-May* 5pm-midnight daily. **Average** €. **Credit** AmEx, DC, MC, V. **Map** p54 C4 70

Above the Espacio Azahar hotel (*see p66*), the Etnia Espacio Universal is a beautiful, climate-controlled rooftop conservatory and terrace. Decorated in a vagely ethnic style, with bizarre wooden seats carved into the shape of hands, it also has the occasional DJ or live performance.

Triana

Restaurants

La Albariza

C/Betis 6 (954 33 20 16). **Open** 1.30-6pm, 8pm-midnight Mon-Sat. Closed last 2wks July. **Average** €. **Credit** MC, V. **Map** p55 F5 71

An inexpensive tapas bar and restaurant whose modest *bodega*-style decor of barrels and hanging hams belies the excellent quality of the cooking that is on offer – we recommend trying the cured pork or *puntillitos*, tiny fried squid.

Bouquet

C/Castilla 36 (954 33 38 19). **Open** 2-4.30pm, 9pm-midnight Tue-Sat. Closed 1st 2wks Aug. **Average** €€-€€€. **Map** p55 E6 72

This modern and deliciously airy restaurant, which opened for business in 2006, enjoys river views from its large window and terrace. The Mediterranean cuisine on offer comes in carefully sculpted arrangements of roast sea bass stuffed with spider crab or roast vegetables with Baena oil.

El Faro de Triana

Puente de Isabel II s/n (954 33 61 92). **Open** *Restaurant* 11am-4.30pm, 7.30pm-12.30am daily. *Bar* 10am-1am daily. **Average** €-€€. **Credit** DC, MC, V. **Map** p55 F5 73

A great spot by the bridge means that wherever you sit – in the restaurant, tapas bar or on the *terraza* – you will get a fantastic view of the river and the city. Despite the setting, the food is simple; mostly fresh fish and meats, very reasonably priced.

La María

C/Betis 12 (954 33 84 61). **Open** noon-4pm, 8pm-midnight Mon, Wed-Sun. **Average** €€€. **Credit** DC, MC, V. **Map** p55 F5 74

Your *secreto ibérico* is safe at **Los Chorritos**. *See p91.*

La María bills itself as a *parilla argentina* and serves some fine cuts of meat. It also offers a good selection of fish and seafood, and South American desserts such as *dulce de leche* pancakes.

Poncio

C/Victoria 8 (954 34 00 10/www.ponciorestaurantes.com). **Open** 2-4pm Mon; 2-4pm, 9-11.30pm Tue-Sat. Closed Aug. **Average** €€€. **Credit** AmEx, DC, MC, V. **Map** p55 F5 ⑮

Chef Willy Moya's imaginative cooking has made this restaurant a great success. If you don't go for the dish of the day – and most of the well-heeled diners do – try artichokes and asparagus in bitter orange escabeche or a carpaccio of salmon and monkfish with celery and walnut foam.

Restaurante Casa Manolo

C/San Jorge 16 (954 33 32 08). **Open** 9am-6pm, 8pm-1am Tue-Sun. **Average** €. **Credit** MC, V. **Map** p55 F6 ⑯

A real locals' place with a traditional atmosphere. Casa Manolo attracts a diverse crowd, drawn by the good selection of fish and meat dishes.

Río Grande

C/Betis s/n (954 27 39 56/www.riogrande-sevilla.com). **Open** 1-4pm, 8pm-midnight daily. **Average** €€. **Credit** AmEx, DC, MC, V. **Map** p55 G4 ⑰

Río Grande is the best-known restaurant on this side of the river, due to the views of the Torre del Oro and the Giralda that it provides. The outlook is a perfect backdrop for some tasty dishes such as *langostinos* from Isla Cristina and *almejas de faro en salsa verde* (clams in green sauce).

Tapas

La Antigua Abacería

C/Pureza 12 (954 33 03 49). **Open** 12.30-4pm, 8pm-midnight daily. **Average** €. **No credit cards. Map** p55 G5 ⑱

A gorgeous old deli-tapas bar, complete with a low wooden ceiling, green gingham tablecloths, lace curtains and *sevillanos* on the stereo. The tapas that is on offer includes *migas* (breadcrumbs fried with chorizo), venison or wild boar stew, lamb with pine nuts and raisins, and duck mousse. **Photo** *p89.*

Bar Bistec

C/Pelay Correa 34 (954 27 47 59). **Open** 11.30-4pm, 7.30pm-1am Mon, Tue, Thur-Sun. **Average** €. **Credit** AmEx, DC, MC, V. **Map** p55 G5 ⑲

Big, bright and atmospheric, the Bistec is tiled in perky cornflower and white with wilting bullfighting posters and religious paintings lining its walls. It's famous for its fried fish, but the *carrillada de cerdo ibérico* (a pork stew) is excellent.

Bar Santa Ana

C/Pureza 82 (954 27 21 02). **Open** 7.30am-1am Mon-Sat; 7.30am-5pm Sun. **Average** €. **Credit** AmEx, DC, MC, V. **Map** p55 F5 ⑳

Simple but well-sourced tapas are dealt out swiftly at this delightful corner shrine to bullfighting, the Virgin (and her mother, the Santa Ana of the name) and the Crucifixion. The bar hums with local banter, or you can eat bites like the sizeable pork steak and snails at tables by the church.

Los Chorritos

C/Betis s/n (954 33 14 99). **Open** *Mid Mar-Oct* 11am-4pm Tue, Thur-Sun; 8pm-1am Tue-Sun. **Average** €. **Credit** AmEx, DC, MC, V. **Map** p55 F5 ⑧①

Popular with both tourists and locals, this summertime riverside shack serves up a tender pork flank (*secreto ibérico*) and good roasted peppers. Great views of El Arenal, especially at sunset.

Las Golondrinas

C/Antillano Campos 26 (954 33 16 26). **Open** 1-4.30pm, 8pm-12.30am daily. **Average** €€. **Credit** AmEx, DC, MC, V. **Map** p55 F6 ⑧②

A hidden Triana treasure, the snaking wooden bar is hung with little ceramic troughs for your screwed-up napkins and toothpicks, and every surface is covered in tiles, including the staircase that leads up to a tiny seating area with doll-sized painted wooden tables. Specialities include pickled beetroot, artichokes or mixed peppers, and chunks of ribeye.

Mariscos Emilio

C/Genova 1 (954 27 06 06). **Open** noon-midnight daily. **Average** €. **Credit** AmEx, DC, MC, V. **Map** p55 G4 ⑧③

Also known as Cerveceria del Mar (both names appear on the outside of the establishment), this big, bright and ugly bar is justly famed for its superbly fresh seafood. Oysters are a speciality, as is *salpicón de mariscos* – a shellfish salad.

O'Tapas Albahaca

C/Pagés del Corro 119 (954 274 163). **Open** 1-4pm, 9-11.30pm Mon-Sat. Closed 2wks Aug. **Average** €€. **Credit** AmEx, DC, MC, V. **Map** p55 F/G5 ⑧④

Choose between the tiny front bar or the back restaurant to try mouth-watering dishes such as chickpeas with five types of wild mushroom, spinach and Cabrales cheese, or asparagus with baby eels topped with a fried egg. Locals also come for the fantastic €10 set lunch, to be enjoyed amid a hectic jumble of tiles, wooden wine crates and oil paintings.

Sol y Sombra

C/Castilla 147, 149 & 151 (954 33 39 35/www.tabernasolysombra.com). **Open** 1-4pm, 9pm-midnight daily. **Average** €€-€€€. **Credit** AmEx, DC, MC, V. **Map** p55 off E6.

Named after the seating system in the bullring, where seats are purchased and priced according to whether they are in the sun (*sol*) or the shade (*sombra*), this very traditional trio of two small, dark tavern rooms and a restaurant is papered with original bullfighting posters, one of which dates back to 1840. The ceilings are dense with hanging *jamones* and a house speciality is, naturally, bull's tail stew.

Nervión

This suburb (east of the centre, near the train station) has recently become known for its tapas bars, concentrated around two areas: a grid of streets bordered by C/Pirineos and Avda de la Buhaira, and further east around the Gran Plaza.

Restaurants

Al-Mutamid

C/Alfonso XI 1, corner of Gran Plaza (954 92 55 04/www.grupomodesto.com). **Open** noon-5pm, 8pm-midnight daily. Closed 2wks late Aug. **Average** €-€€. **Credit** AmEx, DC, MC, V.

Part of the excellent Modesto chain and a cut above the other branches, Al-Mutamid offers excellent service, upmarket surroundings and fine cuisine, with an emphasis on seafood.

El Fogón de Leña

Avda Luis de Morales s/n, near Nervión Plaza (954 53 90 36). **Open** 1-4.30pm, 8pm-midnight daily. **Average** €€. **Credit** AmEx, DC, MC, V. **Map** p55 off E/F1.

This excellent restaurant mini-chain (there's another in Cádiz and a couple more in Seville) serves huge cuts of meat cooked on an open grill. It's simple, hearty Andalucían cooking at its best, served in a farmhouse-style atmosphere.

Tapas

Entrebarriles

C/Juan de Mata Carriazo 4 (954 419199/www.entrebarriles.com). **Open** 1-5pm, 8.30pm-midnight daily. **Average** €-€€. **Credit** AmEx, DC, MC, V. **Map** p55 F1 ⑧⑤

Each of the high tables at this bright, modern bar is equipped with its own beer pump, allowing the people of Seville to serve themselves unlimited Cruzcampo; it's not free, though, since the draughts are registered digitally at the bar. The gimmick has proved wildly popular among younger diners, but it is backed up by some seriously good tapas.

La Monumental

Edificio Corona 6-8, C/Diego Angulo Íñiguez (954 42 33 85/www.la-monumental.com). **Open** 8am-1am daily. Closed Aug. **Average** €. **Credit** AmEx, DC, MC, V. **Map** p55 off E/F1.

An up-and-coming venue whose profile was boosted after it won first prize at the Feria de Tapas for its smoked salmon and shellfish gratin.

La Taberna de Azafrán

Avda Luis Montoto 148 (954 57 66 97). **Open** 12.30-4.30pm, 8.30pm-12.30am Mon-Sat. Closed Aug. **Average** €. **Credit** AmEx, DC, MC, V. **Map** p55 off E1.

Probably the most popular bar in the area, it's big and smart, and attracts a friendly crowd. The extensive list of tapas includes baked fish.

Shopping

So much more than flamenco thermometers and personalised bullfighting posters.

Seville's enormous shopping area stretches from the bullring to Plaza Alfalfa, extending to Plaza del Duque in the north and the cathedral in the south. Slick boutiques and chain stores share the pedestrianised thoroughfares and backstreets with more traditional shops selling religious trinkets, embroidered shawls.

At its heart are pedestriansed C/Sierpes and the streets running parallel with it: Calles Velázquez, Tetuán and Cuna. Many of these are shaded with special white canopies in summer. Here you'll find primarily clothes and fashion shops, among them branches of **El Corte Inglés** (Plaza del Duque s/n, 954 57 14 40, map C3), Spain's perennially popular department store. C/Cuna is especially strong on wedding boutiques and childrenswear, while footwear fetishists should try nearby C/Córdoba. High-end boutiques cluster around Plaza Nueva, with the Alameda the place to look for more bohemian houseware and clothes. Antiques abound around Plaza Alfalfa and on C/Feria in the Macarena; the cheapest and most traditional area to look for ceramics is Triana, particularly around Plaza del Callao and C/San Jorge.

If you need the comfort of air-conditioning, Seville's two main shopping centres are the Nervión Plaza commercial and entertainment complex (Plaza Avda Luis de Morales s/n, 954 98 91 31, www.nervionplaza.com) and the neo-Mudéjar Centro Comercial Plaza de Armas, (Plaza de La Legión s/n, 954 908 282), built as Seville's pavilion for the 1929 Ibero American Fair and subsequently a train station. It holds over 60 shops, a supermarket and a cineplex.

The rate of sales tax (IVA) depends on the type of product: it's currently seven per cent on food and 16 per cent on most other items. Note that if you're paying by credit card, you usually have to show photographic ID, such as a passport or driving licence.

Clothes, shoes & accessories

Agua de Sevilla

C/San Fernando 3, Santa Cruz (954 50 15 38/ www.aguadesevilla.com). **Open** *July, Aug* 10am-2pm, 5-9pm Mon-Fri. *Sept-June* 10am-2pm, 5-9pm Mon-Sat. **Credit** AmEx, DC, MC, V. **Map** p55 G3.

A good range of upmarket fashion and now homeware has been added to what was once a perfume store, although you can still take home the fragrance of the city's 20,000 orange trees with a bottle of Agua de Sevilla. The men's Noir version has stronger sandalwood notes.

Albero Zapatos

C/San Eloy 26, Centro (954 22 60 78). **Open** 10am-2pm, 5.30-9pm Mon-Fri; 10.15am-2.15pm Sat. **Credit** MC, V. **Map** p54 D4.

A great selection of own-label espadrilles in all styles and colours, along with brands such as Belén Gonzalo or Faeton for men and women.

El Caballo

Plaza Nueva 12, El Arenal (954 50 08 42). **Open** *July, Aug* 10am-8.30pm Mon-Fri. *Sept-June* 10am-8pm Mon-Fri; 10am-2pm Sat. **Credit** AmEx, DC, MC, V. **Map** p55 E4.

The best stop for high-quality, beautifully finished leather goods made in Seville. The classic range spans everything from wallets and toiletry bags to handbags, suitcases, belts and shoes.

Mango

C/Velazquez 7-9, Centro (954 22 33 89/www. mango.es). **Open** *Aug* 10am-2pm, 5.30-9pm Mon-Sat. *Sept-July* 10am-9pm Mon-Fri. **Credit** AmEx, DC, MC, V. **Map** p54 D4.

Spain's bastion of high-street womenswear has up-to-the-minute copies of catwalk fashion, and various branches throughout the city.

Pilar Burgos

C/Tetuán 16, Centro (954 56 21 17/www.pilar burgos.com). **Open** 10am-9pm Mon-Sat. **Credit** MC, V. **Map** p54 D4.

This hugely successful *sevillano* designer specialises in sharp, sexy, killer heels that are perfect for parties and complement the Andalucían taste for brightly coloured clothes.

Victorio y Lucchino

Plaza Nueva 10, Centro (954 22 79 51/www.victorio ylucchino.com). **Open** 10am-8.30pm Mon-Sat. **Credit** AmEx, MC, DC, V. **Map** p55 E4.

Seville's most famous design duo have a glossy showroom – complete with a waterfall in the back patio – filled with their trademark frills and polka dots: sexy, flirty, high-end fashion that's tastefully but unmistakeably *sevillano*. Upstairs there's a small men's collection, which is markedly more sober. The lovely junior range for girls aged two to 14 can be found at C/Sierpes 87 (954 22 79 51).

How to be a flamenco fashionista

Polka dots on poplin or psychedelic designs on silk? Elbow-length ruffled sleeves or simple shoulder straps? Calf-length or full-length skirts? If you want to dress to impress at Andalucía's foremost fiesta, Seville's Feria de Abril, you have to know what is *de moda* this season. Even at village fiestas, it's a definite no-no to wear the same dress two years running or even season to season, and the dress that was perfect for the Seville Feria just won't do for the famous Rocío pilgrimage. So-called *rociera* dresses have to be more practical: skirts are shorter and have fewer ruffles, making it easier to walk long distances or ride on horseback. New touches to the Rocío garb spotted in 2006 were flowers asymmetrically placed to one side of the forehead (instead of the conventional central position on top of the head), and gone were the flamboyant, oversized shoulder ruffles.

So how has the flamenco dress changed over the years? The basics involve a figure-hugging bodice and a flounced skirt, but anything goes for the rest of the outfit: from calico to crêpe fabrics, bright colours to floral designs. This year, stylish bullfighter jackets were in vogue, along with printed designs subtly influenced by 1960s psychedelic patterns. Features that never go out of fashion are the ubiquitous polka dots and the use of certain fabrics, such as poplin, piqué and gauzy fabrics.

Designs have varied enormously from decade to decade. Mirroring street fashion, hemlines rose in the 1960s to expose calves and (shock, horror) even knees. From the voluminous dresses of the 1950s – not the most practical of outfits, given the furnace-like heat of Andalucían summers – dresses are now less weighty, due to fewer flounces and lighter fabrics. Accessories are indispensable, so you'll need to get earrings, necklaces, bracelets, ornamental combs and embroidered silk shawls, not forgetting a large flower artfully placed in your hair.

Joining ranks with those parading some of the region's most elaborate flamenco creations at Seville's Feria doesn't come cheap. At El Corte Inglés prices for a dress start at €250, while a top-of-the-range *traje* will set you back over €1,000 – so you just can't afford to be ignorant of this season's trends.

Guitarras Cayuela.

Zara

Plaza Duque 1, Centro (954 21 48 75/www.zara.com). **Open** 10am-9pm Mon-Fri; 10am-2pm Sat. **Credit** AmEx, DC, MC, V. **Map** p54 C/D4.

Cheaper on its home turf, the well-executed and affordable copies of catwalk fashion appear on the rails in a heartbeat. There is also a decent selection of men's and children's fashion, and there are various branches throughout the city.

Children

Marco y Ana

C/Cuna 24, Centro (954 21 30 38). **Open** *July-mid Sept* 10am-1.30pm, 5-8.30pm Mon-Fri; 10am-1.30pm Sat. *Mid Sept-June* 10am-1.30pm, 5.30-8.30pm Mon-Sat. **Credit** AmEx, MC, DC, V. **Map** p54 D3.

The appropriately named Cradle Street has many children's shops but this one stands out for its locally produced, handmade clothes in sizes ranging from newborns to older toddlers. Choose from exquisite lace sun bonnets, microscopic crotcheted bootees and full *canastillas* (layettes).

Flamenco

Juan Foronda

C/Tetuán 28, Centro (954 22 60 60/www.juanforonda.com). **Open** *June-Sept* 9.45am-1.30pm, 4.30-8.30pm Mon-Fri; 10.15am-2pm Sat. *Oct-May* 9.45am-1.30pm, 4.30-8.30pm Mon-Fri; 10.15am-2pm, 5-8.30pm Sat. **Credit** AmEx, DC, MC, V. **Map** p54 D4.

Juan Foronda has sold *mantones* (shawls) and lace mantillas to the upper echelons of *sevillano* society since 1926. There's also a wide selection of bridal veils and tiaras. Prices range from around €80 to several thousand euros, and there are various outlets throughout the city.

María Rosa

C/Cuna 13, Centro (954 22 21 43/www.mariarosa-sevilla.com). **Open** *Jan-May* 10am-1.30pm, 5-8.30pm Mon-Sat. *June-Dec* 10am-1.30pm, 5-8.30pm Mon-Fri; 10am-1.30pm Sat. **Credit** AmEx, DC, MC, V. **Map** p54 D3.

Another of the city's superior flamenco outfitters. As well as dresses, there are men's suits and children's flamenco garb, along with accessories ranging from shoes to the huge plastic earrings that are de rigueur for the *feria*. There is another branch at C/Lineros 6 (954 21 64 65).

Raquel Urbano

C/Cuna 51, Centro (954 21 72 93). **Open** 10am-1.30pm, 5-8pm Mon-Fri; 10am-1.30pm Sat. **Credit** AmEx, DC, MC, V. **Map** p54 D3.

This small but well-stuffed flamenco outfitters has oodles of frills and flounces for women in some unusual colour combinations. Dresses can be altered to fit and range from €120 to well over €1,000.

Music

El Corte Inglés (*see p92*) has a decent selection of music CDs and instruments.

Compás Sur

C/Cuesta del Rosario 7E, Centro (954 21 56 62/www.compas-sur.com). **Open** *July, Aug* 10.30am-2.30pm, 5.30-10pm Mon-Fri; 10.30am-2.30pm Sat. *Sept-June* 10.30am-2.30pm, 5.30-10pm Mon-Sat. **Credit** AmEx, DC, MC, V. **Map** p55 E3.

An independent music shop packed with CDs, DVDs, books and sheet music, and percussion instruments, particularly the flamenco *cajón*. The speciality is flamenco and other Andalucían music of all stripes, including *coplas*, *rumbas*, *sevillanas*, *rock andaluz* and even the processional music played at Semana Santa.

Guitarras Cayuela
C/Zaragoza 4, El Arenal (954 22 45 57/www.juanluiscayuela.com). **Open** *July, Aug* 10am-1.30pm, 6-8.30pm Mon-Fri. *Sept-June* 10am-1.30pm, 5-8pm Mon-Fri. **Credit** AmEx, DC, MC, V. **Map** p55 E4.
Coming from a dynasty of guitarists and luthiers, Señor Cayuela has sold his immaculate handiwork to many of the flamenco greats. The collection comprises mainly classical and flamenco guitars and prices range from €108 to €2,700.

Ceramics

Cerámica Santa Ana
C/San Jorge 31, Triana (954 33 39 90). **Open** *Aug* 9.30am-2pm Mon-Fri; 10am-2pm Sat. *Sept-July* 9.30am-1.30pm, 5-8.30pm Mon-Sat. **Credit** MC, V. **Map** p55 F5/6.
The best of a cluster of ceramics shops, this stunning tile-covered building is an excellent source for the multi-coloured pottery that is the neighbourhood speciality, along with tiles, fountains and altarpieces.

Martian
C/Sierpes 74, Centro (954 21 34 13). **Open** 10am-2pm, 5pm-8.30pm Mon-Sat. **Credit** AmEx, DC, MC, V. **Map** p54 D4.
Vases, bowls, plates and jugs in three styles: *patio sevillano* (floral), *ceramica clásica* and *montería* (painted in a rustic style with hunting scenes).

El Postigo Lonja Municipal de Artesanía
C/Arfe s/n, El Arenal (954 56 00 13). **Open** 10am-7pm Mon-Fri; 10am-2pm Sat. **Credit** AmEx, DC, MC, V. **Map** p55 F4.
Cut out the middlemen by buying at this council-run arts and crafts market near the cathedral. It specialises in ceramics and jewellery entirely produced by local artisans.

Sevillarte
C/Sierpes 66, Centro (954 21 28 36/www.sevillarte.com). **Open** 10am-1.30pm, 5-8.30pm Mon-Fri; 10am-1.30pm Sat. **Credit** AmEx, DC, MC, V. **Map** p54 D4.
A good general artisan store with ceramics, bronze statuary, fans and silk shawls, many of them produced by local artists.

Speciality shops

Baco
C/Zaragoza 7, El Arenal (954 21 11 93/www.baco.es). **Open** 10am-2.30pm, 5.30-9pm Mon-Fri; 10am-2.30pm Sat. Closed Aug. **Credit** MC, V. **Map** p55 E4.
Small chain of six local delicatessens, well stocked with sherry, olive oils, pickles, hams, cheeses and local wines, along with their speciality product of dried bacalao (salt cod).
Other locations: throughout the city.

Rafael Ortíz
C/Mármoles 12, Santa Cruz (954 21 48 74/www.galeriarafaelortiz.com). **Open** 7-9pm Mon; 10am-1.30pm, 7-9pm Tue-Fri; 10am-1.30pm Sat. Closed Aug. **Credit** AmEx, DC, MC, V. **Map** p55 E3.
Founded in 1984, this is one of Seville's most respected art galleries, specialising in contemporary paintings. Artists are usually young Spaniards but there are also some international names. Exhibitions change every month or so.

Sevilla Futbol Club
C/Francos 25, Santa Cruz (954 22 12 22/www.sevillafc.es). **Open** 10am-10pm Mon-Sat. **Credit** MC, V. **Map** p55 E3.
Sevilla FC's official shop is a brightly lit barn stuffed with everything you'd expect, from strips, tracksuits, leisurewear and balls to ties and other accessories, all embossed with the team's shield.

Arts & Entertainment

Funfairs, flamenco and football for when sightseeing palls.

Children

The open space along the bank of the Guadalquivir river is a good place to run off steam, as is the lovely Parque de María Luisa – where you can feed the ducks at the Isla de los Patos or the photogenic flocks of friendly white doves. In Plaza de España you can rent a rowing boat and punt about the small moat; beyond is La Noria Panorámica (*see p78*), a big wheel that offers 360° views over the city.

There are several fun ways to tour the city: try an open-topped double-decker bus or a horse-drawn carriage (from Plaza Virgen de los Reyes, outside the cathedral), or hop aboard a cruise boat. For teens there's a party cruise at night with games and dance contests.

Aquópolis Sevilla

Avda del Deporte s/n (954 40 66 22/www.aquopolis.es). **Open** *June-Sept* noon-8pm Mon-Fri; 11am-8pm Sat, Sun. Closed Oct-May. **Admission** €15.50; €10.90 concessions. **Credit** AmEx, DC, MC, V.

Set in the Barrio las Delicias in the east of the city, this giant waterpark has the usual array of kamikaze chutes, foam slides, wave pools and white water rides. There is plenty for smaller children too.

Camelot Park

Avda Luis Montoto 132-134, Nervión (954 57 65 40/635 48 70 26/www.camelot-park.com). **Open** 5-8pm Mon-Fri; noon-8pm Sat, Sun. **Admission** €3-€6. **No credit cards**.

Open all year, this well-maintained fun park is full of attractions for children, from slides and swings to tunnels and bouncy castles.

Isla Mágica

Pabellón España, Isla de Cartuja (902 16 17 16/www.islamagica.es). **Open** *Apr-mid July* 11am-7pm Tue-Fri; 11am-10pm Sat, Sun. *Mid-end July* 11am-10pm Tue-Fri; 11am-midnight Sat, Sun. *Aug* 11am-midnight daily. *Sept, Oct* 11am-9pm Sat, Sun. Closed Nov-Mar. **Admission** €21-€23.50; €15-€16.50 concs. *Evening* €15-€16.50; €11-€12 concs. **Credit** AmEx, MC, V. **Map** p54 off A4/5.

This amusement park re-creates the glory days of the 16th-century Spanish empire. Across seven themed areas, such as El Dorado, the Amazon or the Port of America, visitors can enjoy white-knuckle rides or explore galleons, rainforests and Mayan temples. Little kids will enjoy the carousel and Fountain of Youth play area, while older kids go for the rollercoaster, free falls and water rides.

Pabellón de la Energía Viva

C/Marie Curie s/n, Isla de la Cartuja (902 43 22 22/www.pabellondelaenergiaviva.com). **Open** 10am-2pm, 4-7.30pm Mon-Sat. **Admission** €5.60; €4.95 concessions. **No credit cards**. **Map** p54 off A6.

One of the prettiest of the 1992 Expo pavilions, the Hungarian building has recently been transformed into an interactive environmental museum. The towers represent the world's principal religions and activities include a photovoltaic Scalextric, an 'intelligent house' that can be programmed by computer and a bicycle that measures your 'body battery'.

Film

Nearly all foreign cinema is dubbed into Spanish and it's hard to find anything but the most commercial Hollywood fare and Spanish

Isla Mágica.

releases; the art-house scene in Seville amounts to occasional screenings at bars and cultural centres. The **Seville Film Festival** (www.festivaldesevilla.com) in November offers subtitled contemporary European cinema.

Cine Avenida

C/Marqués de Paradas 15 (954 29 30 25/www.cineciudad.com). **Admission** *Mon-Thur* €3.80. *Fri-Sun* €5, €3.80 concessions. **Map** p54 D5.
The only reliable place in town for undubbed films. The five screens here show all the biggest releases, most of them in English.

Flamenco

Although Seville may claim to be the home of flamenco, most of what's touted here is pre-packaged stuff. The dinner-and-flamenco *tablaos* or anywhere you get a free glass of diluted sangria with your ticket is likely to be a travesty of the art, living off coach parties. Far better is the flamenco performed in *peñas* (flamenco social clubs), theatres and cultural centres. The tourist office has information about the **Bienal de Flamenco** and other flamenco events. Look out for the free bimonthly magazine *alma100*; it is good for tips on gigs and new records.

Flamenco bars offer a more intimate experience with greater audience participation and the drunken, slighty unhinged atmosphere that gives flamenco its magic. Some bars have set schedules, others are just places where the regulars jam together; seeing some spontaneous flamenco depends on luck and how long you are willing to hang about for.

In addition to the places listed below, good options include the excellent **Bar Quitapesares** (*see p85*) and the cultural space **El Imperdible** (*see p101*). **Teatro Central** (*see p101*) also runs flamenco cycles and the new **Museo del Baile Flamenco** (*see p71*) puts on occasional public performances and allows the public to observe dance classes and workshops. On Thursdays from October to May the **El Monte Cultural Foundation** (Ronda de Capuchinos 38, 954 417 811, 954 508 200, www.fundelmonte.es) runs excellent performances in its Joaquín Turina theatre.

Santa Cruz & Centro

La Carbonería

C/Levíes 18 (954 22 99 45/954 21 44 60). **Open** 8pm-3.30am daily. **Admission** free. **Map** p55 E2.
This old coal merchant's is a classic with a relaxed atmosphere and an eclectic mix of people. It's not solely dedicated to flamenco – there's also blues, ethnic music and rock – but there are often spontaneous performances if the right people come in.

Casa de la Memoría de al-Andalus

C/Ximénez Enciso 28 (954 56 06 70/www.casadelamemoria.com). **Open** 9am-2pm, 6-8pm daily. **Shows** 9pm daily. **Admission** *Cultural centre* €1. *Flamenco shows* €12; €10 concessions. . **Credit** MC, V. **Map** p55 F2.
This is the closest you'll get to anything authentic without walking the backstreets all night. Traditional flamenco dominates, but there are also concerts of medieval and Sefardí Judeo-Spanish music, all performed on an exquisite patio. Call in advance to reserve a place.

El Chiringuito

C/Huelva 36 (no phone). **Open** 8pm-1am Mon-Sat. Closed 2wks Aug. **Admission** free. **No credit cards**. **Map** p54 D3.
The only seats at this hole-in-the-wall place are wooden benches on the narrow backstreet. If you're lucky, some informal flamenco might come your way: over the last 25 years, Camarón, Emilio Maya and Potito have all performed here. On Tuesdays people flock for ribs at the free barbecue.

Los Gallos

Plaza Santa Cruz 11 (954 21 69 81/www.tablaolosgallos.com). **Shows** 8pm, 10.30pm daily. Closed Jan. **Admission** €27 incl drink. **Credit** AmEx, DC, MC, V. **Map** p55 F2.
One of the best choices for a high-quality formal performance with a good local reputation, this two-hour show is held in a small room on two levels. It can get quite intense on a good night; get there early for a seat on the lower floor.

El Tamboril

Plaza Santa Cruz s/n (954 56 15 90). **Open** *July, Aug* 6.30pm-3am Mon-Sat. *Sept-June* 6.30pm-3am daily. **Shows** *July, Aug* midnight Mon-Thur. *Sept-June* midnight daily. **Admission** free. **Map** p55 F2.
El Tamboril is famous for its large statue of the Virgin of Rocío, which inspires many an emotionally sung prayer between 11pm and midnight. If the mood is right, this is followed by spontaneous singing, guitar-playing and hand-clapping. You're as likely to hear salsa as flamenco, though.

El Arenal

El Arenal

C/Rodo 7 (954 21 64 92/www.tablaoelarenal.com). **Shows** 8.30pm, 10.30pm daily. **Admission** €33 incl drink; €64 incl dinner. **Credit** MC, V. **Map** p55 F4.
Between the bullring and the theatre, this aggressively advertised *tablao* is tourist-oriented, but the beamed 17th-century building is an attractive space and the performers are very slick.

Casa del Carmen

C/Marqués de Paradas 30 (954 21 28 89/www.casacarmenarteflamenco.com). **Open** 8.30pm-around 11pm daily. *Shows* 9.30pm daily. **Admission** €14; €9 concessions. **Credit** AmEx, DC, MC, V. **Map** p54 D5.

Los Gallos. See p97.

A new *tablao*, with shows in the patio of a 19th-century *palacio*, and high-quality artists rotating each night so that performances stay fresh and lively.

El Patio Sevillano

Paseo Cristóbal Colón 11A (954 21 41 20/www.elpatiosevillano.com). **Shows** 7.30pm, 10pm daily. **Admission** €32 incl drink. **Credit** AmEx, DC, MC, V. **Map** p55 F4/5.
With two shows a night on two different stages, this theatre packs 'em in. A lot of business comes from the tour buses, but the show is lively and the dancers accomplished. Like the Palacio Andaluz (*see right*), it aims to provide an entertaining spectacle rather than anything authentic.

Triana

This area has many flamenco bars with irregular opening hours and decidedly eclectic offerings. If you don't mind a gamble, wait until after midnight and try **El Mantoncillo** (C/Alfarería 104, map p55 E6) , **La Puerta de Triana** (C/Castilla 137, map p55 E6) or **La Sonanta** (C/San Jacinto 31, map p55 F6).

Casa Anselma

C/Pagés del Corro 49, with C/Antillano Campos (no phone). **Open** 8pm-2am Tue-Sun. **Shows** from midnight. Closed July & Aug. **Admission** free. **No credit cards**. **Map** p55 F6.
This iconic flamenco bar is always packed with locals and stamped indelibly with the huge personality of Anselma. She stalks the bar searching for anyone who has not bought a drink and at midnight turns off the lights to sing the Salve Rociera, a prayer to the Virgin of Rocío. Then the show begins, with much audience participation.

Lo Nuestro

C/Betis 31A (no phone). **Open** 11pm-5am daily. **Shows** midnight daily. **Admission** free. **No credit cards**. **Map** p55 F5.
One of the hardest-working flamenco bars in town, this plainly decorated but extremely popular riverfront space gets the crowd dancing with live *sevillanas* and rumbas every night.

La Taberna de Triana

C/Duarte 3 (mobile 647 647 730). **Open** 10pm-3am Tue-Sun. **Shows** from midnight Fri. Closed Aug. **Admission** free. **No credit cards**. **Map** p55 F5.
In a tavern decorated with *azulejos* and countless knick-knacks, join the rambunctious locals for a drink and live flamenco – mostly *sevillanas*.

La Macarena

El Palacio del Embrujo Andaluz

C/María Auxiliadora 18B (954 53 47 20/www.elpalacioandaluz.com). **Open** *Dinner* 9.30pm daily. *Shows* 10pm daily. **Admission** €32 incl drink; €50 incl tapas dinner; €66 incl dinner from *carta*. **Credit** AmEx, MC, V. **Map** p54 C1.
In the north of the city, opposite the Jardines del Valle, this is a huge show with a large cast and plenty of costume changes. A great spectacle, covering everything from *Carmen* to a 'La Macarena' finale, but miles away from true flamenco.

Peña Flamenca Torres Macarena

C/Torrijiano 29 (954 37 23 84). **Open** 9pm-3am Mon-Sat; noon-4pm Sun. Closed Aug. **Admission** *Shows* €6. **No credit cards**. **Map** p54 A3.
One of the most important *peñas* in all of Andalucía, the Macarena was founded in 1974 and now has over 130 members and a long waiting list. Their shows tend to be somewhat impromptu, but the place has a great reputation for high-quality, old-school music.

Gay

The key area in Seville's emerging gay scene is the Alameda de Hércules, an area that has gone from sleazy to slick in the last few years and now has plenty of mixed and gay bars. For cruising hit Plaza España and the fringes of Parque María Luisa or cross the river to Isla Cartuja to troll the Zona Estacionamiento Expo 92. There is a cluster of gay bars just north of the Puente de Triana along the Paseo de Colón, and many of the bars on and around the Alameda de Hércules are, if not gay, at least mixed. New lounge and restaurant clubs like **Buddha del Mar** and **Bauhaus** have a big gay presence, as does **El Capote** (for all, *see p99*). For each of the clubs listed below, admission varies according to the night.

Bars & clubs

El Barón Rampante

Arias Montano 3, La Alameda (no phone). **Open** 6pm-3am Mon-Thur, Sun; 6pm-4am Fri, Sat. **Admission** free. **No credit cards**. **Map** p54 B3.

This friendly and informal place is painted white and named after the Italo Calvino story. Playing electronica and house, it's relatively quiet until around midnight when beautiful gay boys flock here to knock back *chupitos* of honeyed rum.

Hércules Mítico

Alameda de Hércules 93 (no phone). **Open** 4pm-4am daily. **No credit cards**. **Map** p54 B3.
A small disco-bar that's a popular warm-up for clubbing later on. The terrace is mixed, but inside the atmosphere is a little spicier. Monthly parties feature strippers, go-go dancers and drag shows.

El Hombre y el Oso

C/Amor de Dios 32, La Alameda (954 56 30 29/ www.elhombreyeloso.net). **Open** 10.30pm-2.30am Mon-Thur, Sun; 10.30pm-3.30am Fri, Sat. **Admission** free. **No credit cards**. **Map** p54 C3/4.
'The Man and the Bear' opened in 1999 and has three floors, a cruising area and dark rooms. The video room plays a wide selection of bear videos, as well as falcon and colt classics. Check out the owner's collection of teddies behind the bar.

Isibilyya

Paseo de Colón 2, El Arenal (954 21 04 60). **Open** 8pm-4am Mon-Thur; 8pm-5am Sat; 10am-5am Sun. **Admission** free. **No credit cards**. **Map** p55 F4/5.
This very popular café-bar has the energy of a club. As the night progresses the lively terrace gets packed out with a young and up-for-it crowd that's mixed but predominantly gay and lesbian. Come on Thursdays and Sundays for the transvestite shows.

Ítaca

C/Amor de Dios 31, La Alameda (954 90 77 33). **Open** midnight-7am Wed-Sat. **No credit cards**. **Map** p54 C3/4.
Things get going after 3am at Seville's main gay club, with good dance music and a lively crowd. There's a large men-only area at the back, complete with a very cruisy darkroom loft full of private cabins. There are shows from Wednesday to Saturday.

Men to Men

C/Trajano 38, La Alameda (no phone, www.m2mbar.com). **Open** 10.30pm-5am Thur-Sun. **Admission** free. **No credit cards**. **Map** p54 C4.
M2M is where bears and mature or larger men go for no-nonsense copping off.

Noveccento

C/Julio César 10, El Arenal (954 22 91 02/www.noveccento.com). **Open** *June-Sept* 8pm-4am daily. *Oct-May* 5pm-2am daily. **Admission** free. **Credit** MC, V. **Map** p54/55 D/E5
A small and friendly bar-café that attracts a mixed crowd with a significant lesbian element. There are frequent art exhibitions, shows and special parties.

Sacha

C/Torneo 64, La Alameda (no phone, www.discotecasacha.net). **Open** *Oct-May* midnight-7.30am Thur-Sat. Closed June-Sept. **No credit cards**. **Map** p54 B5.
Latin house, kitschy disco and Spanish pop predominate in this intimate bar-club with a crazy array of go-go boys and ultra-flamboyant drag shows.

Why Not

C/Federico Sánchez s/n, El Arenal (954 22 26 36). **Open** 11pm-5am Thur-Sat. **No credit cards**. **Map** p55 F4.
A gloriously cheesy, gay male-dominated disco with pumping commercial chart music filling two dancefloors. In the summer months, there's an outdoor venue behind the bus station on Plaza de Armas.

Saunas

Nordik

C/Resolana 38, La Alameda (954 37 13 21/ www.saunanordik.com). **Open** noon-11pm Mon-Thur, Sun; noon-7am Fri, Sat. **Admission** *Mon, Wed, Fri-Sun* €12. *Tue, Thur* €10. **No credit cards**. **Map** p54 A3.
Nordik has a pool, video cabins, a labyrinth, jacuzzis and Finnish saunas.

Sauna Termas Hispalis

C/Céfiro 3, Santa Justa (954 58 02 20/www.grupopases.com). **Open** 8am-11pm Mon-Thur; 8am-midnight Fri-Sun. **Admission** *Mon-Sat* €9.50 8am-2pm; €11.50 2-8pm; €8.50 8-11pm. *Sun* €11.50. **Credit** AmEx, DC, MC, V. **Map** p55 off F1
Steam baths and dry saunas, along with a 16-man jacuzzi, video room, cruising area, labyrinth, cabins and a dark room. Near the train station.

Nightlife

Seville's best nightspots vary by season. In winter the focus is more on packed-out bars around **Plaza Alfalfa** and the **Alameda de Hércules** than anywhere else in town and weekends see the sheer number of people gridlock the traffic; the *marcha* goes on until

El Barón Rampante. See p98.

sunrise. When the weather starts to heat up, the action shifts to the so-called 'Costa de Guadalquivir' on **C/Torneo** (map p54 A4/B5), where the riverbank is packed with late-opening bars and discos. Opposite, on the **Isla de Cartuja**, the crowd is young and the emphasis is on rave-style clubs quaintly known as *discotecas*. Along the river in Triana, **C/Betis** (map p55 F6) is where all the bars and pubs spill out into the street in summer. Between May and October on La Cartuja and along the river, look out for the *terrazas de verano* – open-air, late-night bars.

Santa Cruz & Centro

Bauhaus

C/Marqués de Paradas 53 (954 22 42 10/www.bauhauscafe.com). **Open** noon-4am daily. Closed Aug. **Admission** free. **Credit** AmEx, DC, MC, V. **Map** p54 D5.

If you don't mind your crêpes having names like Nu jazz or Downtempo then this slick and ultra-modern place with Philippe Starck furniture might be for you. Some of the city's best DJs play after midnight, when Bauhaus becomes a very popular house club.

Catedral

Cuesta del Rosario 12 (954 21 90 29). **Open** *Mid Sept-mid July* midnight-5am Wed-Sat. Closed mid July-mid Sept. **Admission** €7-€10 incl drink. **Credit** AmEx, DC, MC, V. **Map** p55 E3.

A small and energetic disco bar playing all the latest chart hits to international students.

Flaherty's

C/Alemanes 7 (954 21 04 51/www.pflaherty.com). **Open** 11am-3am daily. **Admission** free. **Credit** AmEx, DC, MC, V. **Map** p55 D3.

The first Irish bar in Seville, this friendly theme bar has pub food and drink during the day. It gets going relatively early in the evening, making it a good spot for that first drink. There's live music on Thursdays from September to May.

El Garlochí

C/Boteros 26 (no phone). **Open** 5pm-3am Tue-Sun. Closed Aug. **Admission** free. **No credit cards**. **Map** p54 D3.

A blizzard of kitschy Semana Santa memorabilia, crucifixions and virgins covers every surface. There's even a small chapel by the entrance, incense and processional music on the stereo. The house drink is Sangre de Cristo (Blood of Christ), a sample of which sits on a small altar under a large golden crown.

La Rebótica

C/Pérez Galdós 11 (679 11 17 03). **Open** 10pm-2am Tue-Sat. Closed 2wks Aug. **Admission** free. **No credit cards**. **Map** p54 D3.

Wallpapered entirely in comics, from manga to Marvel, this tiny music-less bar is all about cheap *chupitos*: there are over 50 to choose from. One of the most popular shots is the Coscorrón – a corrosive blend of tequila, whisky, vodka and beer that is slammed on the bar before drinking.

El Arenal

Antigüedades

C/Argote de Molina 40 (no phone). **Open** 10pm-3am Tue-Sun. **No credit cards**. **Map** p55 E3.

A kooky bar that could be festooned with anything from papier-mâché body parts to dolls – the bizarre theme changes regularly. It's always packed, but a slightly older crowd ensures things stay mellow.

Bestiario

C/Zaragoza 33 (954 213 475). **Open** 4pm-3am daily. Closed Aug. **Admission** free. **Credit** DC, MC, V. **Map** p55 E4.

With deep, black sofas and lots of sharp-edged furniture, Bestiario fancies itself more of a lounge club than a bar. There's a DJ spinning house and Spanish pop and hipsters getting down on a small dancefloor.

Buddha del Mar

Plaza de la Legión s/n, Centro Comercial Plaza de Armas (954 08 90 95/www.buddhadelmar.com). **Open** 3.30pm-3am Mon-Thur, Sun; 3.30pm-6am Fri, Sat. **Admission** *Mon-Thur, Sun* free. *Fri, Sat* €20. **Credit** AmEx, DC, MC, V. **Map** p54 D5.

The new hangout for Seville's beautiful people and metrosexuals, Buddha occupies three floors of this old train station with candles, sandalwood incense and exotic decor. Following the model of the Madrid branch, it's a multitasking space: there's the pan-Asian Kudetá restaurant, along with a café, chill-out lounge, Balinese terrace and nightclub.

Capote

Puente Isabel II (680 18 22 25/www.terrazacapote.com). **Open** *Apr-Oct* 1pm-3am daily. Closed Nov-Mar. **Credit** AmEx, DC, MC, V. **Map** p55 E5.

Hidden down on the eastern riverbank, this glamorous summer terrace attracts a mixed crowd. There's chill-out music all day but things get going at around midnight, with the atmosphere often helped along by DJs and special party events.

Elefunk

Adriano 10 (954 22 25 81). **Open** 11pm-5am Tue-Sun. Closed July & Aug. **Admission** free. **No credit cards**. **Map** p55 E4.

The graffiti on the walls may signal hip hop, but this is in fact Seville's premier temple to funk. The fish-tanks on the bar also vibrate to a good dose of tribal house, 1980s electronica and even the Beatles.

Nuyor Café

C/Marqués de Paradas 30 (954 21 28 89). **Open** *Sept-Apr* 11pm-3am Wed-Sat. Closed May-Aug. **Admission** free. **No credit cards**. **Map** p54 D5.

The colonial-style 'New York' is a stylish spot for cocktails, Cuban coffee and cigars. Live Cuban bands play salsa from Thursday to Saturday, with flamenco gigs starting earlier in the evening.

El Garlochí. See p100.

La Alameda & La Macarena

Café del Latte
Jesús del Gran Poder 83 (954 90 46 07). **Open** 4pm-3am daily. Closed 2wks Aug. **Admission** free. **No credit cards. Map** p54 B3/4.
Once the Café del Mar, this so-called 'tea dance club' is still settling into its new skin. It's very chilled both night and day, though, with projections, ambient music and a varied following.

Ciudad Condal
Alameda de Hércules 94 (mobile 697 327 889). **Open** 8am-2pm, 5pm-1am daily. Closed 1wk Aug. **Admission** free. **No credit cards. Map** p54 B3.
Owned by a Barcelona native, this tiny bar is a little slice of design heaven, resplendent in black, white and red. Light electronica supplies a backdrop against which the young and beautiful sip cocktails.

Fun Club
Alameda de Hércules 86 (650 489 858/www.salafunclub.com). **Open** *Concerts* 9.30pm. *Club* midnight-7am Thur-Sat. Closed Aug. **Admission** *Concerts* €5-€12. *Club* €5. **No credit cards. Map** p54 B3.
A classic on the live music scene, this small club has bands at weekends. The bar is open till dawn. Music covers anything from *latina* to rock or electronica, and the place gets sweaty when it reaches capacity.

Malandar
C/Torneo 43 (954 22 14 17/954 37 88 73). **Open** midnight-6am Wed; 10pm-7am Thur-Sat; 8pm-2am Sun. **Admission** varies. **No credit cards. Map** p54 B5.
A musical lucky dip, this smart designer space by the river might be putting on a homage to Pink Floyd, a live performance from Senegalese musicians or a flamenco group like Almansur.

Naima Café Jazz
C/Trajano 47 (954 38 24 85/www.naimacafejazz.com). **Open** 3pm-3am daily. **Admission** free. **Credit** AmEx, DC, MC, V. **Map** p54 C4.
A relaxed and very cool little bar named after John Coltrane's first wife, and peppered with photos of various jazz luminaries.

Utopia
C/Barco 1 (no phone). **Open** 6pm-1.30am Mon-Thur, Sun; 5pm-4am Fri, Sat. **Admission** free. **Credit** MC, V. **Map** p54 B3.
Opened in 2006, this loft-style space is scattered with bean bags and low-slung sofas where student types chug cheap beer and listen to electronica.

Other districts

Al Alba
C/Betis 41A, Triana (www.alalbasevilla.com). **Open** 6.30pm-3am daily. Closed Aug. **Admission** free. **No credit cards. Map** p55 F5.
Owned by Vicky Berrocal, ex-wife of bullfighter Manuel Díaz 'El Cordobés', and named after their daughter, this bar has seen more local celebrities than most. The decor is modern monochrome and at night it becomes a flamenco disco packed with writhing young bodies dancing *sevillanas*.

Antique Theatro
Matemáticos Rey Pastor y Castro s/n, Isla de la Cartuja (954 46 22 07/www.antiquetheatro.com). **Open** *June-Sept* 11.30pm-3am Mon-Wed; 11.30pm-7am Thur-Sun. *Oct-May* 11.30pm-7am Thur-Sun. **Admission** *June-Sept* free. *Oct-May* €10. **Credit** AmEx, MC, DC, V. **Map** p54 off A5.
You'll have to dress up to get past the velvet rope and door muscle, but the reward is a sophisticated crowd, models, footballers, some vanguard decor and excellent DJs. In winter the place resembles a glamorous old dancehall; in summer the split-level space opens into a terrace known as Aqua.

Arena Sevilla/Kool
Avda María Luisa 1, Parque de María Luisa (954 62 42 90/www.arenasevilla.es). **Open** midnight-4.30am Tue-Thur; midnight-7am Fri-Sun. **Admission** €10 incl drink. **Credit** AmEx, DC, MC, V. **Map** p55 H3.
Ibiza finally lands in Seville: Arena, the football-pitch-sized terrace, opens from June to mid September, while the lavishly decorated club Kool is open all year. The place has its own microclimate with sand dunes, fire torches and water features. Burlesque acts and top DJs complete the transplant.

Sport

Bullfighting is halfway between sport and art; for the famous La Maestranza bullring, *see p75*. More popular locally is football. The city's two first division teams are **Sevilla FC** (Estadio Sánchez Pizjuán, Avda Eduardo Dato s/n, 954 53 53 53, www.sevillafc.es), who won their first European trophy when they became the 2006 UEFA Cup champions, and **Real Betis Balompié** (Estadio Ruiz de Lopera, Avda de Heliópolis s/n, 954 61 03 40, www.realbetisbalompie.es), which celebrates its centenary in 2007. Matches are played from September to May on Sunday afternoons.

Gimnasio Adonis

C/Alfonso el Sabio 7, Centro (954 21 54 74). **Open** *Aug* 8am-11pm Mon-Fri. *Sept-July* 8am-11pm Mon-Fri; 10am-2pm Sat. **Rates** €4.20. **No credit cards.** **Map** p54 D3.
In the Alfalfa area, this small but handy gym counts aerobics, spinning and step among its classes. The sauna is open to men on Mondays and Thursdays and women on Tuesdays and Fridays.

Real Club de Golf de Sevilla

Autovia Sevilla–Utrera, km 3.2 (954 12 43 01/ www.sevillagolf.com). **Open** 8am-11pm daily. **Rates** *Non-members* €90 Mon-Fri; €120 Sat, Sun. *Club hire* €45. **Credit** AmEx, DC, MC, V.
Seville's best course is the recently opened Royal Golf Club. It was the site for the World Cup and the facilities, which also include tennis courts and swimming pools, are some of the finest in the province.

Sato Sport Santa Justa

C/José Laguillo s/n, Santa Justa (954 54 62 90/ www.satosport.com). **Open** *Aug* 7am-11pm Mon-Fri. *Sept-July* 7am-11pm Mon-Fri; 9am-8pm Sat; 9am-2pm Sun. **Rates** *Non-members* €12/day. *Membership* €30-€50/mth, plus €76.60 joining fee. **No credit cards.** **Map** p54 off D1
This brand new fitness centre is one of the largest in Europe with five floors of pools, cardio equipment, and paddle and squash courts. Classes cover everything from ballroom dancing to tae kwon do.

Sevilla Gym

C/Amor de Dios 35, La Alameda (954 90 10 20/www.sevillagym.com). **Open** *Aug* 8am-11pm Mon-Fri. *Sept-July* 8am-11pm Mon-Fri; noon-3pm Sat. **Rates** *Non-members* €6/day. *Membership* €37/mth. **Credit** MC, V. **Map** p54 C3/4.
Great for the budget-conscious, this centre by the Alameda has a small gym, spinning, pilates, aerobics, and a jacuzzi and steam bath.

Theatre & music

In early June, the **Territorios Sevilla** series of gigs (954 59 08 67, www.territoriossevilla.com) attracts Spanish stars such as Bebe, as well as international artists like Nitin Sawhney and Cuba's Bebo Valdés Quartet; tickets (€12-€45) are available from **Palenque** and the **Teatro Lope de Vega**. For event information, www.elgiraldillo.es is always a good bet.

La Imperdible

Plaza San Antonio de Padua 9, off C/Alcoy, La Alameda (box office 954 90 54 58/www.imperdible.org). **Open** *Box office* 7-11pm Thur-Sat; 6-8pm Sun. Closed July, Aug. **Tickets** €10-€15; €8-€12 concessions. **Credit** MC, V. **Map** p54 B4.
Seville's leading venue for alternative theatre, the small independent 'Safety Pin' stages music, comedy and drama, as well as art exhibitions.

El Palenque

C/Blas Pascal s/n, Isla Cartuja (954 46 71 70/www.palenque.org). **Open/tickets** call for details. Closed Aug. **Credit** AmEx, DC, MC, V. **Map** p54 off A5/6.
Built for the 1992 Expo, the entrances, seating and stage are surrounded by water canals and fountain effects. It is primarily a concert venue.

Sala Endanza

C/San Luis 40, La Macarena (box office 954 56 26 16/www.endanza.org). **Open** call for details. Closed July, Aug. **No credit cards.** **Map** p54 B2.
Primarily devoted to dance, theatre and flamenco performances, this cosy space also puts on film screenings and exhibitions.

Teatro Central

C/José de Gálvez s/n, Isla de Cartuja (box office 955 03 72 00/www.teatrocentral.com). **Open** *Box office* 7-9pm Tue-Sun. Closed July, Aug. **Tickets** €10-€20; €8-€15 concessions. **Credit** AmEx, DC, MC, V. **Map** p54 off A5/6.
A diverse venue, this theatre hosts pop concerts, flamenco, plays, theatre, dance and classical music. Each year performances are arranged into themed seasons, concentrating on such subjects as contemporary theatre and dance, flamenco or jazz.

Teatro de la Maestranza

Paseo de Colón 22, El Arenal (information 954 22 33 44/tickets 954 22 65 73/www.teatromaestranza.com). **Open** *Box office* 10am-2pm, 6-9pm daily. **Tickets** €15-€84. **Credit** AmEx, DC, MC, V. **Map** p55 F4/5.
One of the most spacious modern theatres in Europe, and known for opera and operettas, the theatre tends to focus on classics with local appeal like *The Barber of Seville* and *The Marriage of Figaro*.

Teatro Lope de Vega

Avda de María Luisa s/n, Parque de María Luisa (954 59 08 67). **Open** *Box office* 11am-2pm, 6-9pm Tue-Fri; 2hrs before show Sat, Sun. Closed July, Aug. **Tickets** €6-€24. **Credit** MC, V. **Map** p55 H3.
Once part of the City of Seville pavilion for the 1929 Ibero American Fair and designed with baroque architectural elements inside and out. As well as a good range of drama, it also hosts concerts that run from classical and flamenco to jazz.

Resources

Getting around

Seville has a chronic traffic problem. The first line of a four-line metro system is now due to open by 2007 after myriad setbacks. For now, walking is the best way of getting around.

By bus

The city bus service (902 45 99 54, www.tussam.es) doesn't pass through the centre. Routes C3 and C4 loop the old city on the Ronda; C1 and C2 take in Triana, Isla de Cartuja and Santa Justa. 'Bonobús' tickets, available from newsstands and *estancos* (government-run cigarette and stamp shops) range from ten journeys (€4.20) to unlimited travel for one (€3) or three (€7) days.

Getting there

By air

For Aeropuerto de San Pablo, *see p310.*

By bus

Buses leave from Plaza de Armas (C/Cristo de la Expiración s/n, 954 90 80 40, map p54 D6) hourly on the hour to Huelva (Damas); hourly to Madrid (Socibus, www.socibus.es), and twice daily to Lisbon (Eurolines 954 90 78 44, www.eurolines.es). Buses to Cádiz, Córdoba, Málaga, Granada and Almería leave from El Prado de San Sebastián (Plaza de San Sebastián s/n, 954 41 71 18, map p55 G2).

By train

Estación Santa Justa is on Avda Kansas City (902 24 02 02), a 20-minute walk east of the centre. The super-fast AVE gets you from Seville via Córdoba to Madrid in 2hrs 30mins – or your money back; the Altaria train takes a more sedate 3hrs 30mins. Each day there are 15 trains to Cádiz (1hr 45mins), 15 to Jerez (1hr), 30 to Córdoba (40mins-1hr 10mins), six to Málaga (2hrs 25mins), four to Granada (3hrs), four to Almería (5hrs 20mins) and one to Jaén (3hrs).

Accident & emergency

Hospital Universitario Virgen de Macarena
C/Dr Marañon s/n (954 50 75 00). **Open** *A&E* 24hrs daily.

Internet

The tourist office at Plaza de San Francisco (*see below*) has free internet access. Otherwise, try **Amazonas Cyber** (Conde de Barajas 6, off Alameda de Hercules, 954 37 24 91, www.amazonascyber.com, map p54 B4), **Seville Internet Centre** (C/Almirantazgo 2, 1E, 954 50 02 75, www.sevilleinternetcenter.com, map p55 F4) or **WorldConnect** (C/Álvarez Quintero s/n, no phone, map p55 E3).

Police

Police station
Pabellón de Brasil, Isla de la Cartuja (092).

Post

Post office
Avenida de la Constitución 32 (954 21 11 81/www.correos.es). **Open** 10am-11pm Mon-Fri; 11am-midnight Sat; noon-11pm Sun. **Map** p55 F3.

Tickets

Sevillacard
www.sevillacard.es/902 088 908/91 524 13 70.
Price €27-€39.
Various Sevillacard packages give reduced entrance to major monuments and museums, tourist buses and attractions, and discounts on car hire and at various shops and restaurants.

Tourist information

Tourist offices
Edificio Laredo, Plaza de San Francisco 19 (954 59 52 88/www.turismo.sevilla.org). **Open** 8.30am-8.30pm Mon-Fri; 8.30am-3pm Sat, Sun. **Map** p55 E3.
Plaza del Triunfo 1-3 (954 50 10 01/www.turismo sevilla.org). **Open** 10.30am-2.30pm, 3.30-8pm Mon-Fri. **Map** p55 F3.
C/Arjona 28 (954 22 17 14/www.turismo.sevilla.org). **Open** 8.15am-8.45pm Mon-Fri; 9am-2pm Sat, Sun. **Map** p55 E5.
There are also tourist offices at the airport (954 44 91 28) and the train station (954 53 76 26).

What's on

For listings, get a copy of the excellent *El Giraldillo* or the monthly magazines *Guía de Ocio de Andalucía*, *¿Que Hacer?/What's On?*, *Welcome* and *Olé*. Online, check www.sevillainfo.com and www.lanetro.com.

Seville Province

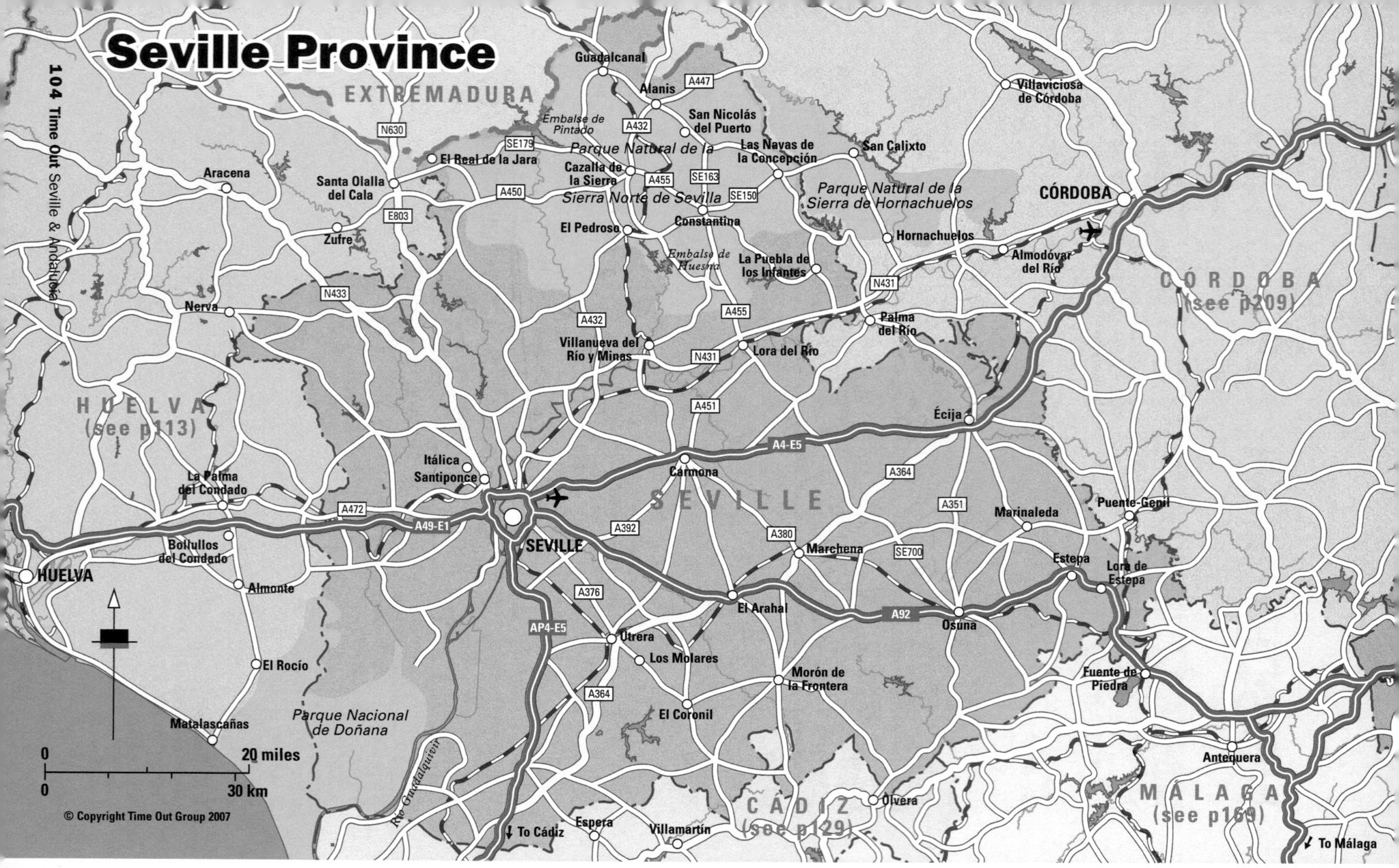

Seville Province

Beautiful historic towns and the natural beauty of the Sierra Norte.

Carmona.

The city of Seville features on most visitors' itineraries, yet the rest of the province is all but ignored by tourists. That's their loss, for the vast undulating plains to the east towards Córdoba contain some of the best-preserved historic towns in southern Spain, while the wilds to the north offer endless possibilities for nature boys and girls.

The area east of Seville, bounded by the Guadalquivir river to the north and the hills of the Sierra del Sur to the south, is known as **La Campiña**. This gently rolling countryside is an important agricultural area, patchworked with olive groves and cereals rippling in the breeze. At their best, La Campiña's towns – **Carmona**, **Écija** and **Osuna** are the pick – are beautifully preserved architectural history lessons, where you'll find Iberian sculptures, Roman walls, Visigothic churches, Moorish fortresses and palatial baroque townhouses.

The northern reaches of Seville province are dominated by the most dramatic portion of the vast Sierra Morena range – the **Sierra Norte**. Hair-raising mountain roads offer stunning views of verdant valleys below and swirling vultures above. This is one of the lesser-known areas of Andalucía, with few large towns, and wonderful hiking opportunities.

East of Seville

Carmona

The beautifully preserved town of **Carmona** (38 kilometres/24 miles east of Seville) is one of the oldest settlements in Spain, the site of human habitation for over half a million years. Its attraction for settlers is obvious: perched on a terraced escarpment, it enjoys a defensively perfect outlook across the *vega*. Today it's a prosperous, refined place, replete with classy boutiques, chic hotels and first-rate restaurants.

The efficient, friendly tourist office is a good place to start a tour of Carmona. It's located on the ground floor of the **Alcázar de la Puerta de Sevilla**. The Carthaginians set the template for this fortress, which was subsequently altered and developed by Roman and medieval rulers; climb the tower for a view of the town and surrounding plain. Carmona's other surviving gate, the **Puerta de Córdoba** (an elegant composite of Roman, Moorish and Renaissance elements), is at the opposite end of town on C/Dolores Quintanilla. Approaching it from the direction of Córdoba, you get a view of the remains of the city walls, the **Alcázar del Rey Don Pedro** (originally an Almohad fortress, now a *parador*; *see below*) and the Roman bridge.

From the tourist office, C/Prim leads east to the town's main square, Plaza San Fernando, around which are a number of good places to eat and drink. Off the south-eastern side of the *plaza* is Carmona's **Ayuntamiento** (C/El Salvador 2, 954 14 00 11), housed in a converted monastery; check out the Roman mosaic discovered in its courtyard in the 1920s.

Just to the north-east, on C/San Ildefonso, is the cathedral-like **Prioral de Santa María**, which has a beautiful orange tree patio (the only surviving part of the original mosque) with a unique Visigothic liturgical calendar from the sixth century inscribed on one of its pillars. The church itself is a soaring treasure trove of gold-plated altarpieces. Don't miss the statue of the Virgin of Grace (from c1300) – it's as ornate as a Fabergé egg. Among the crucifixes and chasubles you'll also find a sword owned by the founder of the Jesuits, Ignatius Loyola.

Next door, the town museum, the **Museo de la Ciudad**, is housed in the Casa Palacio Marqués de las Torres, one of Carmona's many ornately fronted baroque townhouses. This old-fashioned museum is gradually being modernised with more audio-visual exhibits. Highlights include vivid descriptions of Moorish kitchens and markets (with a shelf of spices to sniff), as well as recordings of typical folk songs.

The highlight of Roman Carmona is the **Necropolis**, which is around a kilometre (half a mile) south-west of the centre. It was used from the second century BC to the fourth century AD. The Tomb of Servilia and the Tomb of the Elephant can only be visited on a guided tour; call in advance to book. Both tombs contain the remains of chambers, courtyards and sarcophagi. You can also climb down into a typical family burial vault containing the original cremation urns stored in niches in the curved chamber wall. The site also has an informative and well-presented museum.

Alcázar de la Puerta de Sevilla

Arco de la Puerta de Sevilla s/n (tourist office 954 19 09 55). **Open** 10am-6pm Mon-Sat; 10am-3pm Sun. **Admission** €2; €1 concessions. **No credit cards**.

Museo de la Ciudad

Casa Palacio Marqués de las Torres, C/San Ildefonso 1 (954 14 01 28/www.museociudad.carmona.org). **Open** *Mid June-Aug* 10am-2pm, 6.30-8.30pm Mon-Fri; 9.30am-2pm Sat, Sun. *Sept-mid June* 11am-7pm Tue-Sun; 11am-2pm Mon. **Admission** €2; €1 concessions. **Credit** AmEx, DC, MC,V.

Necropolis

Avda Jorge Bonsor 9 (954 14 08 11/www.juntaandalucia.es/cultura). **Open** *Mid June-mid Sept* 8.30am-2pm Tue-Fri; 10am-2pm Sat. *Mid Sept-mid June* 9am-6pm Tue-Fri; 10am-2pm Sat, Sun. **Admission** €2; free with EUpassport. **No credit cards**.

Prioral de Santa María

Plaza Marqués de las Torres s/n (954 14 13 30). **Open** *Apr-Sept* 9am-2pm, 5.30-7.30pm Mon-Fri; 9am-2pm Sat. *Oct-Mar* 9am-2pm, 5-7pm Mon-Fri; 9am-2pm Sat. Closed 20 Aug-20 Sept. **Admission** €3; €1.80 concessions. **No credit cards**.

Where to eat & drink

For high-class international cuisine try Carmona's top hotels, especially **La Ferrara** restaurant (€€) of the Alcázar de la Reina (*see p107*), which has a vegetarian menu, and the sumptuous restaurant (€€€) in **Casa de Carmona** (*see below*), which has exquisite food (including Andalucían specialities) and service. A non-hotel alternative is the genteel, slightly snooty **San Fernando** (C/Sacramento 3, 954 14 35 56, closed dinner Sun, all Mon and all Aug, €€-€€€).

The tapas bar-restaurant in the town museum, **Mesón Sierra Mayor** (C/San Ildefonso 1, 954 14 44 04, €), is a converted stable with the horses' nameplates still on the wall above their stalls. **Bar Plaza** (Plaza San Fernando 2, 954 19 00 67, closed dinner Mon and 1st 2wks August, €-€€), on the main square, has terrace tables and does a good-value *menú* for €9. A stone's throw from the *parador* is **Meson Molino de la Romera** (C/Pedro I s/n, 954 14 20 00, closed dinner Sun and all Sept, €€), specialising in regional dishes and roast meats. Set within a restored 15th-century olive oil mill it also serves superbly fresh vegetarian dishes, including spinach with chick peas. In 2006 **La Alacena de Carmona** (Plaza de Lasso 2, 954 19 62 00, €€) – a modern tapas and wine bar – opened, serving excellent dishes such as *carrillada* (pork cheek) and *revuelto do alboronia* (scrambled egg with vegetables).

Where to stay

Carmona has three first-rate hotels. At the luxurious five-star **Hotel Casa de Carmona** (Plaza de Lasso 1, 954 19 10 00, www.casadecarmona.com, double €90-€200) you feel as if you're staying in a private, if palatial, home. Sumptuous rooms are hung with thick chintz drapes and adorned with four-posters, and you can help yourself from the drinks trolley in the library. There is a small pool. The **Parador Alcázar del Rey Don Pedro** (C/Alcázar s/n, 954 14 10 10, www.parador.es, double €150-

€160.50) is built on the ruins of a 14th-century fortified palace and has a beautiful pool with a view. Feel free to wander around inside and along the walls or have a drink in the bar. In a similar vein, but with a more homely, cosy feel, is the **Alcázar de la Reina** (Plaza de Lasso 2, 954 19 62 00, www.alcazar-reina.es, double €103.50-€200), which has fantastic views over the plain. The facilities, restaurant and staff are wonderful. Budget choice is very limited. The best is **Hostal Comercio** (C/Torre del Oro 56, 954 14 00 18, double €45-€65), part of which dates from the 15th century. It has 14 spacious, tastefully kept rooms and a lovely central patio.

Resources

Tourist information

Alcázar de la Puerta de Sevilla s/n (954 19 09 55/ www.turismo.carmona.org). **Open** 10am-6pm Mon-Sat; 10am-3pm Sun.

Écija

Écija, 53 kilometres (33 miles) east of Carmona, is sometimes known as the City of Towers, referring to the 11 distinctive tiled towers that adorn the town's churches and convents. From afar they provide an enchanting, twinkling welcome to the town. However, the sun that illuminates these towers has also been known to raise temperatures in the town to a vicious 52°C (126°F) in summer. At such times, the best thing to do is to slink from shade to shade, discovering Écija's crumbling, evocative Gothic-Mudéjar churches and grand baroque *palacios*.

Note: the recent tourism surge has inspired a fever of long-overdue restoration work in an attempt to reverse the decay of many of Écija's monuments (enquire at the tourist office to find out which are open). The town's main square, Plaza de España, should be a glorious open promenade surrounded by grand palaces and churches, but has been boarded up for years while the authorities build an underground car park and restore the square's buildings.

On the west side of the plaza is the tall **Ayuntamiento**, on the top floor of which is a camera obscura, with great views over the town (visits 12.30pm daily, €2.50, €2 concessions). Next door is the church of **Santa María** (Plaza de Santa María s/n, 954 83 04 30, open 10am-1pm, 6-9pm Mon-Sat, 10am-noon Sun), of interest chiefly for the archaeological artefacts within its patio. C/Canovas del Castillo leads south-west from the *plaza* to the superb 18th-century **Palacio de Benamejí**, the fancy floral marble portals of which belie its former status as an army barracks.

The building contains the tourist office, a good restaurant and the **Museo Histórico Municipal**. From here, C/Emilio Castellar runs east to another grand *palacio*, with a gracious patio and an ornate plasterwork stairwell, the **Palacio de Peñaflor**, currently being converted into a hotel. A little north of here, on Plaza San Juan, stands the church of **San Juan Bautista** (open noon-2pm daily), with perhaps the most outstanding and ornate baroque tower in town.

A few minutes' walk north of the Plaza de España is one of the most attractive of Écija's churches, the **Iglesia Mayor de Santa Cruz** (Plaza Nuestra Señora del Valle, open 9am-1pm; 5pm-9pm Mon-Sat, 10am-1pm, 6-8pm Sun). Its grounds contain the remains of a Muslim archway, a grand Renaissance arch and beautiful leafy gardens. The church's tower echoes details of Seville's Giralda. The patron saint of the city, Nuestra Señora del Valle, is housed here except on her feast day – on 8 September each year she is carried through the streets.

Museo Histórico Municipal

C/Canovas del Castillo 4 (954 83 04 31/http:// museo.ecija.org). **Open** *June-Sept* 9am-2pm Tue-Sun. *Oct-May* 9.30am-1.30pm, 4.30-6.30pm Mon-Fri; 9am-2pm Sat, Sun. **Admission** free.

Where to stay & eat

If you want to overnight, you can do no better than the **Palacio de los Granados** (C/Emilio Castelar 42, 955 90 53 44, www. palaciogranados.com, doubles €144.45-€173.35), a superbly restored and stylish 18th-century *palacio* hotel. **Hotel Platería** (C/Platería 4, 955 90 27 54, double €63.70-€80.80, restaurant €€) is the cheaper option, and comfortable enough, with a decent restaurant serving a set *menú* for a rock-bottom price (€6.60).

Restaurant Las Ninfas in the Palacio de Benamejí (C/Elvira 1, 955 90 45 92, closed Mon, €-€€) serves Italian dishes in stylish and historical surroundings, while the **Casa Machin Restaurante** (C/Galindo 4, 95 590 12 95, www.casamachin.com, €€) specialises in local produce.

The cosy **Bar La Reja** (C/Garcilópez 1, 954 83 30 12, closed Sun) is a favourite with locals for a leisurely drink, gossip and delicious snacks. To experience one of of Spain's best regional cuisines, visit the popular Galician restaurant **Bodegón de Gallego** (C/Arcipreste Aparicio 3, 954 83 26 18, www.bodegonde gallego.com, closed Aug, €€): if the *percebes* (goose-neck barnacles) are in season (winter), you won't regret trying them.

Palacio del Marqués de la Gomera.
See p109.

Resources

Tourist information

Ayuntamiento, Plaza de España 1 (955 90 29 33/ www.turismoecija.com). **Open** 9.30am-3pm Mon-Fri; 10.30am-1.30pm Sat-Sun.

Osuna

Residents of **Osuna** (34 kilometres/21 miles south of Écija) will proudly tell you that it lies at the geographical heart of Andalucía. Certainly, Osuna's location explains its importance since Iberian times (it thrived particularly, as Urso, under the Romans), and today it is one of the most beautifully preserved little towns in the whole of Andalucía.

Evidence of Osuna's ancient inhabitants can be seen in the tiny **Museo Arqueológico**, housed in a 12th-century tower (and one-time prison). A few of the most important finds, including bronze inscriptions of the laws of the Roman settlement, are now held in the national museum in Madrid, although copies are displayed here.

Up the hill from here, overlooking the town, is the 16th-century **Colegiata de Santa María de la Asunción**. It's an impressive, sturdy piece of Spanish Renaissance architecture, containing a hoard of sacred art including key works by José Ribera and important pieces by Juan de Mesa. The eccentric woman who has been showing visitors around the building for nearly a quarter of a century will happily play a Renaissance portable organ for you (it is kept in one of the chapels); she will also lead you into an exquisite classical plateresque courtyard that recently re-opened after renovation. The guided tour continues down to the funerary chapel of the Dukes of Osuna, a Renaissance jewel encrusted with magnificent carvings, and taking the form of a miniature church, complete with central choir. The Dukes of Osuna are buried in the wood and stone sarcophagi that lie beyond this.

The local ducal families were responsible for the town's ornate *casas señoriales* and convents, built to show off the family's wealth. Stroll down beautiful C/Sevilla, with its intricate façades, to get a good overview of Osuna's architecture. One of its highlights is the **Palacio del Marqués de la Gomera** (now a wonderful hotel, *see below*), which has one of the finest examples of a grand Osuna portico (one of the most original baroque porticoes in Spain). The front of the **Palacio del Cabildo Colegial** at No.16 displays a copy of Seville's Giralda, flanked by the *sevillana* martyrs Santa Justa and Santa Rufina.

While in the area, it's worth visiting the town of **Estepa** (24 kilometres/15 miles east of Osuna), which also contains some lovely baroque *palacios* and churches, and is famed within Spain for its lard-based almond biscuits known as *polverones*.

Colegiata de Santa María de la Asunción

Plaza de la Encarnación s/n (954 81 04 44). **Open** *May, June, Sept* 10am-1.30pm, 4-7pm daily. *July, Aug* 10am-1.30pm, 4-7pm Mon-Sat; 10am-1.30pm Sun. *Oct-Apr* 10am-1.30pm, 3.30-6.30pm daily. **Admission** €2. **No credit cards**.

Museo Arqueológico

Plaza de la Duquesa s/n (954 81 12 07). **Open** *June* 10am-1.30pm, 4-7pm daily. *July, Aug* 10am-1.30pm, 4-7pm Mon-Sat; 10am-1.30pm Sun. *Sept-May* 10am-1.30pm, 3.30-6.30pm daily. **Admission** €1.60. **No credit cards**.

Where to stay & eat

The four-star **Hotel Palacio del Marqués de la Gomera** (C/San Pedro 20, 954 81 22 23, www.hotelpalaciodelmarques.com, double €102.70-€143.40, restaurant €€) is reason enough to visit Osuna. A stunning *casa palacio* with its own baroque chapel, it has been tastefully and imaginatively restored, with 20 characterful, individually decorated rooms (the tower room, with its 180-degree views, is impossibly romantic). The hotel restaurant serves imaginative interpretations of traditional dishes in a refined atmosphere. **Hostal-Restaurante El Caballo Blanco** (C/Granada 1, 954 81 01 84, www.ursoweb.com, double €50) is a well-maintained, smart-looking pensión, but its en suite, air-conditioned rooms are rather poky. There's parking and a restaurant serving traditional dishes (closed Sun, €-€€).

For solidly traditional, fresh and lovingly prepared food, try **Restaurante Doña Guadalupe** (Plaza Guadalupe 6-8, 954 81 05 58, closed Tue and first 2wks Aug, €-€€), in a courtyard between C/Guadalupe and C/Quijada. It specialises in egg dishes and soups such as *ardoría* (a heavier, spicier version of *gazpacho*), as well as local game and home-made desserts.

The town's outstanding tapas bar is the **Casa Curro** (Plaza Salitre 5, 955 82 07 58, closed Mon and first 2wks Sept, €), south-west of the Plaza Mayor. Also recommended is the very pleasant, good-value bar-restaurant **El Mesón del Duque** (Plaza de la Duquesa 2, 954 81 28 45, closed Wed, €-€€). Recommended for a relaxed drink and snack at any time of the day is **Casino de Osuna** (Plaza Mayor s/n, 954 81 05 19, €), which has 1920s Mudéjar-style decor and views across the square.

Parque Natural de la Sierra.

Resources

Tourist information

Ayuntamiento, Plaza Mayor (954 81 58 51/www.ayto-osuna.es). **Open** 9am-2pm, 4-6pm Mon-Fri.

Getting there

By bus

Buses stop on Paseo del Estatuto in Carmona, with frequent services to Seville by Alsina (954 41 88 11), Casal (954 90 69 77) and Sevibús (954 90 11 60); there are also 2 buses daily to Córdoba. Écija is served by Linesur (954 98 82 22) to Seville, and Graells (957 25 81 00) to Córdoba. There are 11 buses daily between Seville and Osuna. Osuna's bus station (954 81 01 46) is on Avda de la Constitución.

By train

Osuna train station (954 81 03 08) is on Avenida de la Estación – it's a 20min uphill walk into the centre of town. There are 5 daily trains to Málaga (1hr 30mins), 8 to Seville (1hr), 3 to Granada (2hrs 20mins) and 3 to Almería (4hrs 50mins).

North of Seville

The attractions of the wild **Sierra Norte** mountains of northern Seville province may be well known to *sevillanos*, but few foreign tourists venture into this sparsely populated corner. A chunk of the vast Sierra Morena range forms the border with Extremadura, and largely falls within the protected 1,674 square kilometre (646 square mile) **Parque Natural de la Sierra Norte de Sevilla**.

None of the villages stands out in terms of sights. Indeed, they can seem bewilderingly similar, each with its castle on a hill, bar-lined *paseo* and Mudéjar church. Here, untamed nature is the draw. This is a resolutely rural area, and the best way to get to know it is by staying in a remote converted *finca* and taking part in outdoor pursuits, such as fishing, riding, climbing and hiking; contact the tourist offices for further details.

One of the two main settlements in northern Seville province, **Cazalla de la Sierra** (around 90 kilometres/56 miles north of Seville city), is a small town of typically steep cobbled streets lined with whitewashed houses. It's a bustling (often traffic-jammed) town, with a *paseo* – Paseo del Carmen – for summer drinking alfresco, and plenty of shops, banks and bars. The main sight is the large church of **Nuestra Señora de la Consolación** (open hours of services) on Plaza Mayor. Started in the 14th century, it's an architectural hotchpotch of Gothic-Mudéjar, Renaissance and baroque styles. There's a ruined castle on top of the hill behind the village.

Four kilometres (two-and-a-half miles) from Cazalla along the A455 towards Constantina is **La Cartuja de Cazalla**, a 15th-century charterhouse that has been slowly restored over many years and is now part hotel (*see p111*), part arts centre and gallery (954 88 45 16, www.cartujadecazalla.com, open 8am-2pm, 4-8pm daily, €3).

North of Cazalla, the A432 becomes the A447 and winds through stunning, lonely scenery towards the remote north of Córdoba province – it's a marvellous drive, during which you're unlikely to pass more than a couple of other cars.

For true wilderness, head west from Cazalla on the SE179 towards El Real de la Jara on the outer reaches of the Sierra. The 46-kilometre (29-mile) journey takes you through green,

Cazalla de la Sierra. *See p110.*

densely wooded valleys, over high passes and along the side of the **Embalse del Pintado** reservoir, a wild and beautiful spot. Non-motorised watersports are allowed on the lake, and there's a picnic area and jetty at the water's edge.

El Real de la Jara is a small, squat collection of whitewashed buildings, nestled beneath a recently renovated castle. Its now intact ramparts offer views north to the edge of Extremadura. In the town, the **Museo de Ciencas Naturales** (Torre de Reloj, C/Cervantes 44 s/n, contact the tourist office on 954 73 34 54, www.sierranortedesevilla.com for details) has two rooms full of stuffed animals – birds of prey, a lynx, a frog riding a tortoise and a selection of mammals having a grimacing competition. This weird collection is complemented by strange, oversized animal sculptures scattered about the village's streets.

Taking the A455 east from Cazalla towards Constantina, you drive alongside a pretty burbling stream and eventually come to the pretty **Isla Margarita** picnic area, just off the A455, where footpaths flank a rushing stream with small cascades. Picnic tables and barbecues are scattered under firs and willows. Nearby, you'll find the train station serving both Cazalla and Constantina.

Constantina (20 kilometres/12.5 miles south-west of Cazalla) is the most populated town in the Sierra Norte. Its genteel air is intensified by a number of *casas señoriales* with wrought-iron covered windows, tiled walls and old wooden doors. Among the town's sights is the 16th-century church of **Santa María de la Encarnación** (open hours of services). The church's ornately carved portal (Puerta de Perdón) is attributed to Hernán Ruíz (the architect of Córdoba cathedral and the belfry of Seville's Giralda). You can climb the Mudéjar tower as long as there are no storks nesting on the top. Looking down on the church from a hilltop position are the ruins of the **Castillo de la Armada**. Climb steep, stepped streets to reach the terraces of flowers, shrubs and cherry trees that gather at the castle's foot. The castle was the scene of countless squabbles between local nobles, but served as a fortress against the French in 1810.

The SE150 winds east from Constantina for 22 kilometres (14 miles) to **Las Navas de la Concepción**. This small town marks the eastern end of the Sierra, and its tourist office enthusiastically promotes Sierra activities. Many are organised by the **Hostal Los Monteros** (SE150, km0.2, 955 88 50 62), including cheesemaking, honey-collecting, mushroom-picking, and *matanza* – the traditional slaughtering and butchering of the valuable *cerdo ibérico* pig, with the chance to make your own *embutidos* (sausages). The tourist office has a leaflet detailing local walks.

Where to stay, eat & drink

Cazalla has the biggest concentration of accommodation in the Sierra (the area is very popular with weekenders from Seville). The **Posada del Moro** (Paseo del Moro 46, 954 88 48 58, www.laposadadelmoro.com, double €70-€100, restaurant €, closed Mon) is a relaxed, family-run restaurant. There's a terrace and a pool, and all rooms have a TV and faux-rustic frills. The restaurant serves simple but ample local dishes.

Grander lodgings can be found at the ten-room **Palacio de San Benito** (C/San Benito s/n, 954 88 33 36, www.palaciodesanbenito.com, double €144-€235.50), which was restored to its

17th-century glory by the present owners in 1997. The decor is ornate and the rooms are luxurious. There's also the additional draw of a lovely swimming pool in the garden.

Just outside town, the **Villa Turística de Cazalla** (A455, km3, 954 88 33 10) is a modern development of three bedrooms (double €61-€67.50) and 26 self-catering apartments (€70.60-€78.10 for 2 people, €106-€117.70 for 4) with wonderful views over a wooded valley. There's a pool, tennis court and a restaurant (try the superb wild boar with thyme), and activities such as 4x4 excursions, horse-riding and mushroom gathering can be arranged.

Some of the most interesting lodgings can be found next door at the **Hospedería La Cartuja de Cazalla** (A455, km2.5, 954 88 45 16, www.cartujadecazalla.com, double €96.30). This former Carthusian monastery (1476), which sits on a plateau near a natural spring, has been restored and converted to a hotel with cosy suites and rooms (a little pricey for the standard) in the monastery cloister, and a self-catering house in the grounds. Part of the complex is a centre for contemporary art and culture. The restaurant uses home-grown organic produce for its no-choice *menú* (which is rather expensive at €20); there's a charming swimming pool, and horse-riding excursions can be arranged.

Trasierra (Cazalla de la Sierra, 954 88 43 24, www.trasierra.co.uk) is a stunning 16th-century farmhouse overlooking the wooded Sierra Morena mountains. Stay in the cool and peaceful main house or rent a cottage, all beautifully decorated by the owner, Charlotte, who is an interior designer. Outside, there's a large pool and tennis court. Horse-riding, walking, painting and yoga weeks available.

Las Navezuelas (A432, km43.5, 954 88 47 64, www.lasnavezuelas.com, double €64.20-€67.40, closed early Jan-late Feb), on the road south towards El Pedroso, is a converted 16th-century olive mill and *finca*, surrounded by huge grounds. The garden has leafy archways, old whitewashed patios and a pool. There are also self-catering apartments for two (€91-€94.20), four (€118-€139) or six (€149.80, weekly rentals only Apr-Sept, €870) in the grounds. The lovely owner Luca Cicerella prepares one menu a day (lunch in August, dinner rest of year) from his own produce.

For food in Cazalla, try the great tapas at **Bar Los Mellis** (C/La Plazuela 3, 954 88 42 95, closed Mon, €), next to the Casino.

King Juan Carlos is an occasional visitor to tapas bar/restaurant **Cambio de Tercio** in Constantina (C/Virgen del Robledo 51 bajo, 955 88 10 80, closed Tue and last wk Sept, €€). The front tapas bar is small and overcrowded at lunch, while the more formal restaurant at the back specialises in local game, such as wild boar and partridge. The town's other local specialities are aniseed hooch and olive oil.

Casa María Pepe in Constantina (C/José de la Bastida 25, 955 88 02 82, double €50-€55) has nicely decorated rooms (with or without bath) in a lovingly converted mansion. From the town centre, a steep climb leads you to the three-star **Hotel San Blas** (C/Miraflores 4, 955 88 00 77, www.fp/hoteles.com, double €46-€64.20), a welcoming place with light, cool, well-equipped rooms and a pool. The hotel can help with excursions and activities. **El Martinete** (SE168, km12, 955 88 65 33, closed Mon, dinner Oct-June and all Sept, €) is a dinky bar-restaurant attached to a campsite, just outside San Nicolás. From the restaurant, a path leads alongside a stream to an open barbecue area and on to waterfalls, woods and the campsite reception.

Resources

Tourist information

Cazalla de la Sierra *Plaza Mayor s/n (954 88 35 62/www.cazalladelasierra.es).* **Open** 10am-2pm Tue, Wed; 10am-2pm, 6-8pm Thur; 10am-2pm, 6-9pm Fri, Sat; 11am-1pm Sun.

Constantina *Avda de Andalucía s/n (955 88 12 97/ www.constantina.org).* **Open** *June-Sept* 10am-2pm Tue-Sat; 11am-2pm Sun. *Oct-May* 10am-2pm, 5-7pm Tue-Sat; 11am-2pm Sun.

Las Navas de la Concepción *Plaza España 6 (955 88 51 12).* **Open** *July, Aug* 9am-2pm, 6-8pm Mon-Fri; 9am-2pm Sat. *Sept-June* 9am-2pm, 6-8pm Mon-Fri.

Parque Natural de la Sierra Norte de Sevilla *Centro de Visitantes 'El Robledo', A452, km1 (955 88 15 97/www,sierranortedesevilla.com).* **Open** *July-Sept* 10am-2pm Tue-Thur 6-8pm Fri; 10am-2pm, 6-8pm Sat, Sun. *Oct-Jun* 10am-2pm Tue-Thur; 10am-2pm, 4-6pm Sat, Sun.

Getting there

By bus

Linesur/Betica (954 98 82 20, www.linesur.com) runs several buses a day between Seville and most towns in the Sierra Norte. However, the services between towns are erratic, and there are no buses to either Huelva or Córdoba provinces. For further information and tickets, ask at Bar Gregorio in Constantina (C/Alférez Cabrera 11, 955 88 10 43).

By train

There are 2 trains daily from Seville to El Pedroso (1hr 30mins), Cazalla-Constantina (1hr 45mins) and Guadalcanal (2hrs 20mins). Another 2 trains travel in the opposite direction from Mérida. Be aware that Cazalla-Constantina station is several kilometres from both places.

Huelva Province

Features

Map

Huelva Province

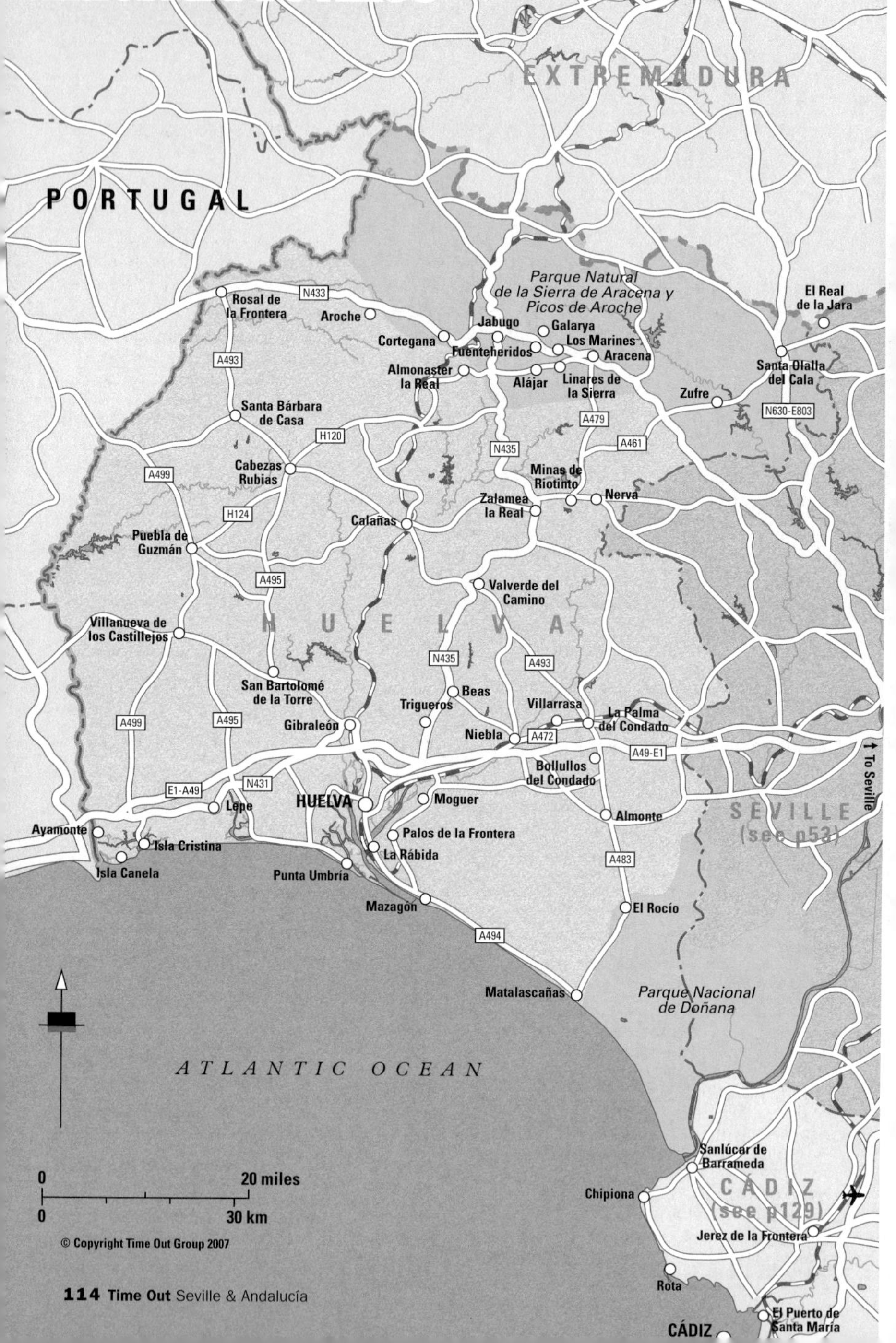

Introduction

Despite splendid beaches and beguiling northern hills, most tourists are just passing through Huelva.

Andalucía's westernmost province features on relatively few foreign tourists' itineraries. Part of this is understandable, part is just ignorance. With Portugal on its western flank, Extremadura to the north, Seville to the east and the Atlantic to the south, Huelva has long been thought of as little more than a region to pass through in order to get somewhere else. Apart from the many wonderful beaches, much of the southern part of the province is scenically dreary, yet the hilly north is hugely beguiling, and the town of El Rocío is unlike any in Andalucía.

HUELVA CITY AND THE COAST

Visually, Huelva is the least appealing of Andalucía's provincial capitals, with its small but attractive historic centre surrounded by modern apartment blocks and an ugly industrial fringe. However, the area immediately south of the city is rich in maritime heritage, particularly in relation to the pioneering voyages of Christopher Columbus. And much of the coastline is blessed with superb (though often windswept) white sand beaches, and resorts that boast some of Spain's best seafood restaurants. Although somewhat dull out of season, the resorts burst into life from Easter onwards, with mainly Spanish visitors. The most significant attraction on the coast is the immense expanse of the Parque Nacional de Doñana, a rigorously protected haven for bird- and wildlife and one of Europe's most important wetlands. The curious Wild West-style El Rocío, on the park's western edge, is the most interesting settlement in the area.

NORTH OF HUELVA

Without doubt, the most alluring region of Huelva province is the mountainous Sierra de Aracena in the north. Part of the huge Sierra Morena range that defines the northern boundary of Andalucía, the Sierra de Aracena is a rewarding and relatively compact area of modest peaks and wooded valleys, of friendly, pretty villages and memorable walking. This is the home, too, of the internationally salivated-over Jabugo ham. Tourism in these parts is low-key, though attractions such as Aracena's Gruta de las Maravillas (Cave of Marvels) are the equal of any in southern Spain.

The best...

Beaches

Mazagón (*p120*); **Punta Umbría** (*p119*).

Birds

Parque Nacional de Coto Doñana (*p118*).

Castles

Aracena (*p124*); **Aroche** (*p122*); **Cortegana** (*p123*).

Caves

Gruta de las Maravillas (*p125*).

Cowboys

El Rocío (*p121*).

Ham

Jabugo (*p123 & p126*).

Mariners

The Columbus Trail (*p117*).

Mines

Minas de Riotinto (*p125*).

Villages

Alájar (*p124*); **Almonaster La Real** (*p123*); **Aracena** (*p124*); **Zufre** (*p125*).

Huelva City & the Coast

Whence Columbus set forth.

Extending from the Portuguese coast in the west to the Doñana National Park in the east, the Huelvan coast is essentially one endless stretch of beach, punctuated by modern, Spanish resorts. Apart from tourism, the area relies on fishing and strawberry growing, and there's also evidence of declining mining and thriving petrochemical industries to blight some of the best views.

Huelva City

The city of Huelva offers little to attract tourists, though, if you're using public transport, it makes a handy base from which to explore the area. You may find it easier and cheaper to get accommodation here (or in Moguer, *see p117*) than in the resorts.

Huelva is a historically important city: its port supplied the Roman Empire with silver and copper, and Christopher Columbus set off on his historic voyages from the coast nearby (*see p117*). Remains of its former glory can be seen in the curious **Barrio Reina Victoria**, an estate of mock-Tudor villas built in the early 1900s by the British Río Tinto Mining Company to house its British workers. The town's **Museo Provincial** has remains from the Phoenician, Greek and Roman eras.

In the centre there are some pleasant pedestrianised shopping streets, or you can knock elbows with the locals at the no-nonsense market, **Mercado del Carmen** (C/Carmen), where marble slabs display an impressive array of glistening fish, or pick up some *mojama* (wind-dried tuna) from Cádiz. For a good view, climb up to **Parque Moret** and the **Santuario de Nuestra Señora de la Cinta** (a couple of kilometres north of the centre), where Columbus prayed before one of his voyages.

Another Columbus-related sight is the **Monumento a Colón** (Columbus Monument), sculpted by Gertrude V Whitney and donated by the US in 1929, standing huge, square and forlorn at the **Punta del Sebo**, the point where the rivers Odiel and Tinto meet. Back towards the city, curving gracefully out from the harbourside, is the massive **Muelle Río Tinto** (Río Tinto Pier), an impressive 19th-century iron structure from which the British used to ship out minerals from the Río Tinto Mines in the north of the province (*see p125*).

Huelva is on the edge of the **Paraje Natural Marismas del Odiel**, 71 square kilometres (27 square miles) of marshland that's home to herons, spoonbills and flamingoes. The Centro Visitantes de Calatilla (*see p117*) has exhibitions, information on footpaths, and a café. **Onubaland** (contact via tourist office, 959 50 90 11) organises excursions into the park on foot, by boat or with a 4x4.

Museo Provincial

Alameda Sundheim 13 (959 25 93 00). **Open** 2.30-8.30pm Tue; 9am-8.30pm Wed-Sat; 9am-2.30pm Sun. **Admission** free.

Where to eat & drink

Next to the Barrio Reina Victoria is the Galician/Basque restaurant **Las Meigas** (Avda de Guatemala 44, 959 27 19 58, closed Sun, €€), a mecca for fish fans. There are two good restaurants serving regional food near the Gran Teatro; **Azabache** (C/Vázquez López 22, 959 257 528, www.restauranteazabache.com, €€, closed Sat dinner, all day Sun and Aug) and the slightly pricier **El Portichuelo** (C/Vázquez López 15, 959 245 768, €€€, closed Sun & Mon) serving traditional regional dishes using local fish, seafood and cured ham. The old-school, flamenco atmosphere of **El Rinconcito** near the market is more local (C/Marina 4, no phone, €); try the Huelvan speciality *adobo de mero* (fried marinated fish). For tapas, try **Taberna del Condado** (Sor Angela de la Cruz 3, 959 261 123), which has great cured ham and local wines from the Condado region east of the city.

The best-known restaurant in the area is located eight kilometres (five miles) west of the city in Aljaraque – **Las Candelas** on the Punta Umbría road (959 31 83 01, closed Sun, €€); it serves up superb seafood at keen prices.

Where to stay

Most people stay at the **Hotel NH Luz Huelva** (Alameda Sundheim 26, 959 25 00 11, www.nh-hotels.com, double €104.85), a large, smart but bland member of the reliable NH chain. For something a bit more unusual, the two-star **Hotel Costa de la Luz** (C/José María Amo 8-10, 959 25 64 22, double €50-€55), near the market, is a weird and wonderful timewarp of 1970s kitsch.

Resources

Police station

Paseo de la Glorieta s/n (959 21 02 21).

Post office

Avda Tomás Dominguez s/n (902 19 71 97).

Tourist information

Plaza Alcalde Coto Mora 2 (959 65 02 00/959 65 02 02). **Open** 9am-7.30pm Mon-Fri; 10am-2pm Sat, Sun.

Plaza de las Monjas s/n (959 25 12 18). **Open** 10am-2.30pm, 3.30-8.30pm Mon-Fri; 10am-2.30pm, 4.30-7.30pm Sat.

Centro Visitantes de Calatilla, Ctra de Duque Juan Carlos I, km3 (959 50 90 11). **Open** *Apr-Sept* 10am-2pm, 6-8pm Tue-Sun. *Oct-Mar* 10am-2pm, 4-6pm Tue-Sun.

The Columbus Trail

Apart from its world-beating Jabugo ham, the province of Huelva is chiefly famed as the starting point of Christopher Columbus's first historic voyage to the New World. **La Rábida** (seven kilometres/four miles south of Huelva) is the main site for Columbus-related sightseeing. Take a monk-led tour through the simple, whitewashed **Monasterio de Santa María de la Rábida**, where Columbus (known in Spanish as Cristóbal Colón) spent time waiting for the go-ahead for his epic voyage. The monastery's church holds the tomb of local hero Captain Martín Alonso Pinzón (who accompanied Columbus across the Atlantic), as well as the only image of the Virgin Mary in Spain to have been blessed by the Pope. The flag room contains the flags of Latin American countries and coffers of sand from each land. At the waterfront you'll find the **Muelle de las Carabelas** (Pier of the Caravels), where full-scale replicas of Columbus's ships – the *Niña*, the *Pinta* and the *Santa María* – are moored, alongside a mock 15th-century European village. There's also a bar with a terrace.

Those keen to complete the Columbus tour can visit neighbouring **Palos de la Frontera**, which supplied Columbus with much of his crew, including the captains of the *Niña* and *Pinta*: Vincente Yañez Pinzón and Martín Alonso Pinzón. Columbus performed a vigil in the interesting **Convento de Santa Clara** in **Moguer**, eight kilometres (five miles) north of Palos. Moguer – a pretty town of low whitewashed houses and buzzing squares – is also worth visiting in its own right.

Convento de Santa Clara

Plaza de las Monjas s/n, Moguer (959 37 01 07). **Open** (*Tours hourly*) 11am-1pm, 5-7pm Tue-Thur. **Admission** €2. **No credit cards**.

Isla Cristina. *See p119.*

Monasterio de Santa María de la Rábida

La Rábida (959 35 04 11). **Open** 10am-1pm, 4-7pm Tue-Sat. **Admission** *Guided tour* €2.50. *Audio guide* €3. **No credit cards**.

Muelle de las Carabelas

Paraje de La Rábida (959 53 05 97). **Open** *June-Sept* 10am-2pm, 5-9pm Tue-Fri; 11am-8pm Sat, Sun. *Oct-May* 10am-7pm Tue-Sun. Phone for details of guided tours. **Admission** €3.20; €1.35 concessions. **No credit cards**.

Where to stay, eat & drink

In Moguer, the **Hostal Platero** (C/Aceña 4, 959 37 21 59, double €30) has simple but good-value en suite rooms with TV and air-con. The town has a host of good tapas bar such as the **Bar Eusebio** (Plaza Marqués 3, 959 37 03 52, €) or the wonderful **Mesón El Lobito** (C/Rábida 31, 959 37 06 60, €, closed Wed), a high-ceilinged barn festooned with farming implements, stuffed animals and wooden barrels. Its charms include dirt-cheap tapas and house Rioja, and meat and seafood grilled on an open fire.

Resources

Tourist information

Moguer *C/Castillo s/n (959 37 18 98/www.aytomoguer.es).* **Open** 9am-2pm, 4.30-7pm Mon-Sat; 10am-3pm Sun.

Coto Doñana

Protected since the 1960s as the **Parque Nacional de Doñana** and declared a UNESCO Biospheric Reserve, the vast floodplains of the Guadalquivir river, east of Huelva, incorporate some of the most important natural ecosystems in Europe. It consists of 507 square kilometres (196 square miles – surrounded by a further 265 square kilometres/102 square miles of protected buffer zone) of virgin beach, pine-covered sand dunes, marshland, riverbank, thickets of heather and gorse, and forests of cork and pine. This diversity attracts huge numbers of birds – over six million stop here on their annual migration – and shelters some highly endangered species. Among them is one of the only remaining populations (about 30-35 animals) of the world's most endangered feline, the Iberian lynx, and six or seven pairs of the extremely rare Spanish imperial eagle.

If you want to get beyond the limited number of marked footpaths on the park's periphery, you will have to join a guided tour in an all-terrain vehicle. There are two main points of entry to the park from the Huelva side – El Rocío (generally better for birdlife) and Matalascañas (better for a variety of landscapes and of animal species).

At the beach you can see hordes of seabirds: sanderlings, cormorants and

La Rábida *Paraje de la Rábida s/n (959 53 05 35).* **Open** *June-Sept* 10am-2pm, 5-9pm Tue-Fri; 11am-8pm Sat, Sun. *Oct-May* 10am-7pm Tue-Sun.

West of Huelva

Between the mouth of the Río de Huelva and the Portuguese border lies a string of beach resorts, ports and marshes. The roads here skirt around estuaries and streams, making driving a round-the-houses affair. In recent years large stretches of the coast west of Huelva (particularly around El Rompido and Ayamonte) have been given over to intensive farming of oysters, clams and prawns; seafood production now forms a major pillar of the Huelvan economy.

Ayamonte has few sights, but its pedestrianised shopping streets and agreeable squares are pleasant enough for a stroll. Situated on the Guadiana river, facing Portugal, this is Andalucía's westernmost town. The border is crossed by an elegant suspension bridge that can be seen straddling the skyline from some distance. The construction of the bridge (which opened in 1991) led to a huge slump in the local economy, as car drivers no longer needed to take the ferry from Ayamonte to Portugal. You can, though, still take a ferry across the river with **Transporte Fluvial del Guadiana** (959 47 06 17, €1.20). Ferries leave from the Muelle de Ayamonte every half hour daily from July to September, and every 40 minutes on weekdays from October to June; there are hourly services on Sundays.

Grupa Guiamundo (959 64 10 02/www.crucerosdelguadiana.com) offers pleasure trips up the Guadiana (€42 incl lunch, €19 children aged 9-11, free under-5s), also leaving from the Muelle de Ayamonte.

Isla Canela is the closest beach to Ayamonte (seven kilometres/four miles to the south-east), but is a soulless, purpose-built

the rare Audouin's gull, as well as peregrine falcons nesting in the ruins of the coastal defensive towers. In the forest of juniper, olive, pine and eucalyptus you'll spot deer and wild boar. The dunes are immense (parts of *Lawrence of Arabia* were filmed here) and move three to six metres (10-20 feet) a year, swallowing up swathes of pine trees on their way. The juniper bushes 'ride' the dunes, moving up and down on the sand. A major part of the park is marshland, whose unsuitability for agricultural exploitation has been the saving grace for nature in this area. The marsh is best in spring, when thousands of breeding birds can be seen.

A tour of the Doñana is an opportunity to experience a wilderness, but it also offers the chance to support the important conservation work that goes on here. The park continues to be under threat, however, by hotel developments (most notably at Matalascañas) that are nibbling at its edges, and agricultural activities, which cause pollution and put pressure on the park's water supply. With all the tours below, book well in advance in peak season.

Centro de Visitantes 'El Acebuche'

A483, km26 (959 43 04 32/www.donanavisitas.com). **Open** *June-Sept* 8.30am-9pm Mon-Sat; 8.30am-6pm Sun. *Oct-May* 8.30am-6pm Tue-Sun. **Rates** €23 for 4hr tour. **No credit cards.**

Offers four-hour tours, twice daily in all-terrain vehicles holding about 20 people. A 1.5km (one mile) footpath, 'Laguna del Acebuche' runs to eight observation points around the lake.

Club Hipico El Pasodoble

Parque Dunar, Matalascañas (959 44 82 41/www.marismadedonana.com). **Rates** *Horse treks* €24. *4x4 tours* €25. **No credit cards.**

El Pasodoble offers trips on horseback (two hours, twice daily) or in a 4x4 (four hours, twice daily) for all levels and ages through the park, mostly over the beach and dunes.

Discovering Doñana

C/Aguila Imperial 150, El Rocío (959 44 24 66/mobile 620 96 43 69/www.discoveringdonana.com). **Rates** *Group of 2-3* €110 half day; €140 whole day. *Extra person* €28 half day; €42 whole day. **No credit cards.**

Enjoyable half-day or full-day excursions in all-terrain vehicles for groups of up to six, with binoculars and an ornithologist guide supplied. Also organises airport transfers and accommodation.

Doñana Nature

C/Carretas 10, El Rocío (959 44 21 60/www.donana-nature.com). **Rates** €23 half day. **No credit cards.**

Specialists in Landrover tours for twitchers and photographers. Ask for enthusiastic and knowledgeable guide Antonio Rodríguez.

resort with a long, wide, rather exposed strand. Across the marshy inlet of the Marismas de Isla Cristina is the preferable **Isla Cristina** (**photo** *p117*), which has a spacious beach backed by pine trees. The fishing boats in the harbour create a lovely scene at sunset, and you can buy some of their catch – fresh, canned or salted – from the harbourside factories.

Heading along the coast east from here, you cross a peninsula of pine trees and dunes to reach **Punta Umbría**. This fishing port and holiday resort (the liveliest in the province) was first developed in 1880 by the British managers of the Río Tinto Mining Company (*see p125*). The town still has a certain British salt-and-vinegary feel to it – it's certainly tatty, but it also has a down-to-earth charm. The 13-kilometre (eight-mile) long blue flag-standard beach is a stretch of soft sand with a good scattering of beach bars, as well as a string, inevitably, of high-rise hotels.

Where to eat & drink

At weekends the Ayamonte locals head for the bars and cafés lining the main square, Plaza Laguna, and the long promenade of the Plaza Ribera, opposite the marina. On the Plaza Laguna is the **Passage Café** (No.11, 959 47 09 78, closed 2wks late Sept, €), a good spot for coffee and cake. Try the famous Huelvan charcuterie at **Mesones Juan Macías** (Paseo de la Ribera 2, 959 47 16 95, closed 2wks late Oct, €€), or, for fish straight from the boat, visit the cheerful **El Cocedero de Ayamonte** (Plaza de la Coronación s/n, no phone, €). Choose your seafood from the chalkboard menus or from the trays on the bar inside.

Opposite the beach in Isla Canela, the **Espuma del Mar** bar-restaurant (Paseo de los Gavilanes s/n, 959 47 72 85, €€) specialises in fresh local fish and shellfish and has outdoor tables. There are also *chiringuitos*, or beach-bar

El Rocío. *See p121.*

barbecues, serving food on the sand during the summer. Isla Cristina is famous for its *raya con tomate* (skate with tomato) and *mechado con atún* (tuna minced with bacon, garlic and parsley and cooked in the oven with an onion and wine sauce). Try them in any of the bars in town, or go for something flashier at the prizewinning **Casa Rufino** (Avda Playa Central s/n, 959 33 08 10, closed dinner Mon-Thur, Sun mid Sept-June and all Jan, €€€), which is possibly the best restaurant on the coast. You can sample seafood fresh off the boats in Punta Umbría at the bars opposite the port or along the nearby pedestrianised Calle Ancha. Try the locally caught *chirlas* (clams) at **El Marinero** (C/Ancha 61, no phone, €).

Where to stay

Ayamonte's accommodation options include the good-value **Parador de Ayamonte** (C/El Castillito s/n, 959 32 07 00, www.parador.es, double €96.30-€128.40, restaurant €€€); its restaurant offers classily presented local dishes. Isla Canela has the neo-Moorish splendour of the **Hotel Barceló Isla Canela** (Paseo de los Gavilanes s/n, 959 47 71 24, www.barcelo.com, closed Nov-Feb, double €80-€210 incl breakfast), which features the usual four-star facilities among lovely tiled patios and terraced pools. In Isla Cristina try the friendly, characterful **Hotel Los Geranios** (Avda de la Playa s/n, 959 33 18 00, double €81-€214), which has a swimming pool. Ten minutes' walk from the beach in El Rompido (16 kilometres west of Punta Umbría, on the Piedras river estuary) is the **Hotel Fuerte El Rompido** (Ctra H4111 km8, 959 39 99 29, www.fuerte hoteles.com, double €101-€289, closed Nov-mid Feb), a self-proclaimed 'eco hotel'. It provides free boat trips to a nearby stretch of virgin beach, and has pools indoors and outdoors.

In Punta Umbría, an attractive option is the traditional Andalucían-style **Barceló Punta Umbría** (Avda del Océano s/n, 959 49 54 00, www.barcelo.com, double €97-€219). Near C/Ancha, the friendly **Hostal Casa Manuela** (C/Carmen 8, 959 31 07 60, closed Oct-Mar, double €40-€65) has rooms with bath and TV.

Resources

Tourist information

Ayamonte *C/Huelva 27 (959 32 07 37)*. **Open** *July-Sept* 10am-2pm, 6-9pm Mon-Fri; 10am-2pm Sat *Oct-June* 10am-2pm, 5-7pm Mon-Fri; 10am-2pm Sat.

Isla Cristina *C/San Francisco 12, Edificio Casa Patio San Francisco, (959 33 26 94/www.islacristina.org)*. **Open** *Mar-Oct* 10am-2pm, 5.30-7.30pm Mon-Fri; 10am-2pm Sat, Sun. *Nov-Feb* 10am-2pm daily.

Punta Umbría *Avda Ciudad de Huelva s/n (959 49 51 60/www.puntaumbria.es)*. **Open** *June-Sept* 8am-3pm, 6-9pm Mon-Fri; 10am-1pm Sat. *Oct-May* 8am-3pm, 5-8pm Mon-Fri; 10am-1pm Sat.

El Rocío and east of Huelva

The beach resorts of Mazagón and Matalascañas mark either end of a long stretch of sandy coastline between Huelva city and the **Parque Nacional de Doñana** (*see p118* **Coto Doñana**). Neither offers much beyond sand, sea, dunes, pines and wind, and the usual seaside resort facilities. There's a nudist beach – the Cuesta de Maneli – at the 38 kilometre point on the C442 beach road.

Mazagón is a reasonable, low-rise resort. The best beach in the area, sheltered by steep cliffs, is six kilometres (four miles) east of town near the Parador de Mazagón (*see p121*). Further east, and right on the edge of the National Park, **Matalascañas** shocks with its unrelenting maze of tourist hotels and villas, and is best given a wide berth.

Heading inland through watery flatlands for 16 kilometres (ten miles) from Matalascañas brings you to one of the strangest and most wonderful little places in Andalucía: **El Rocío**. Looking for all the world like a Remember-the-Alamo Wild West town, its wide sand-strewn streets are lined with hitching posts for horses and Spanish colonial houses and churches. In fact, the resemblance is neither artifice nor coincidence. Many of the Spanish pioneers in North America originated from this corner of Andalucía, and took their style of domestic architecture with them. Horses remain the preferred mode of transport here, which explains the sandy streets (kinder on their hooves) – if you want to hire one, try **Doñana Ecuestre** (Avda Canariega s/n, 959 44 24 74, www.donanaecuestre.com, €17 for first hour, €6 per hour thereafter).

El Rocío is famous throughout Spain for the **Romería del Rocío**, a raucous pilgrimage held at Pentecost. The pilgrims are grouped into brotherhoods (*hermandades*), each with its own house in town, most of which sit empty for the rest of the year. The subject of all this attention, the statue of the Virgen del Rocío, can be seen in the **Ermita** (open summer 8am-10pm daily, winter 8.30am-8pm daily). The snowy-white Ermita was rebuilt in the '60s, but is still striking, especially reflected in the water of the **Marisma del Rocío**, the marshy lake fronting the town and home to flamingoes, herons, red kites and countless other species of birds.

Where to stay, eat & drink

The Parador de Mazagón (A494, km30, 959 53 63 00, www.parador.es, double €139-€150), six kilometres (four miles) south-east of Mazagón, built in the '60s, has a large garden with pool and clifftop views over the sea. A good, basic, cheap option nearby is the **Albergue-Campamento Juvenil Mazagón** (C/Cuesta de la Barca s/n, 959 52 45 29, 902 51 00 00, www.inturjoven.com, open summer only), which has four-person cabins (€14.50-€19 per person) and a campsite.

Don't even try to find accommodation in El Rocío during the Romería. At other times of year, the most luxurious option is the boutique **Hotel La Malvasia** (C/Sanlúcar 38, 959 44 38 70, www.lamalvasiahotel.com, double €139-€203 incl breakfast, restaurant €€€). Opened in 2005, it has elegant, plushly furnished rooms ('Cigüeña', at the top, has the best views), a small pool and an excellent restaurant. More straightforward, but comfortable, is the **Hotel Toruño** (Plaza de Acebuchal 22, 959 44 23 23, www.toruno.com, double €80-€353, restaurant €€). Most rooms have balconies overlooking the *marisma* and a minibar and TV, and the restaurant serves good, cheap local dishes. Just outside town is **El Cortijo de los Mimbrales** (A483, km30, 959 44 22 37, www.cortijo mimbrales.com, double €128-€172, cottage for 4 €289-€407 per night), with pretty, self-catering suites and rooms dotting lovely sprawling grounds with a small pool. El Rocío's real culinary surprise is the excellent **Aires de Doñana** restaurant (Avda de la Canariega 1, 959 44 27 19, closed Mon and first 2wks July, €€), overlooking the *marisma*. The indefatigable Manolo is a great host and cook and serves up imaginative dishes such as seaweed and shellfish croquettes or *arroz caldoso* (a broth-like paella) with langoustines. His home-made puddings are scrumptious. **Bar El Pocito** (C/Ermita 9, 959 44 25 55, closed Wed and 2wks Sept, €) is a cheaper option for tapas, conveniently located next to the Ermita with a view of the *marisma* from its terrace.

Resources

Tourist information

Matalascañas *Parque Dunar s/n (959 43 00 86)*. **Open** 10am-2pm Mon-Sun.

Mazagón *Avda de los Conquistadores s/n (959 37 60 44/63 00)*. **Open** 10am-2pm Mon-Fri.

El Rocío *Avda Canaliega s/n (959 44 38 08/www.turismodedonana.com)*. **Open** 10am-2pm, 5-7pm Mon-Sat; 9am-2pm Sun.

Getting there

By bus

Most services are run by Damas (959 25 69 00, www.damas-sa.es). Huelva bus station (C/Doctor Rubio) has frequent buses to Seville and along the coast (with connections at Almonte for El Rocío). There are also a few buses a day to the Sierra de Aracena and Portugal, and a daily service to Cádiz and Málaga. Ayamonte bus station is at Avda de Andalucía (959 32 11 71). From here there are 2 buses to Faro in Portugal (except Sunday), plus services to Isla Canela and Isla Cristina. Isla Cristina bus station is at C/Manuel Siurot s/n (959 33 16 52); the bus station in Punta Umbría is at Avda Ciudad de Huelva s/n (no telephone). El Rocío is served by regular buses to and from Huelva (via Almonte) and Seville.

By train

Huelva station is at Avda Italia, opposite C/Alfonso (902 24 02 02). There are 3 trains daily to and from Seville (1hr 30mins), 1 to Córdoba (2hrs 30mins) and Madrid (4hrs 50mins), and 2 services north to Almonaster-Cortegana (1hr 20mins-2hrs 40mins).

Sierra de Aracena

Solitude, scenery and lots of top-quality ham.

Aroche.

The northern part of Huelva province was popular almost exclusively with weekend and summer visitors from Seville up until the 1980s. Greatly improved access has now made the area almost as anglicised as Granada's Alpujarras. Its charm is certainly easy to understand. Most of it falls within the boundaries of the densely forested 1,870 square kilometre (722 square mile) **Parque Natural de la Sierra de Aracena y Picos de Aroche**, where small whitewashed villages cling to steep cliffs or nestle, half hidden, in wooded valleys. The economy is rural, producing world-renowned ham, as well as cheese and honey. It's gently pretty in parts, spectacularly beautiful in others, and its locals are as yet unjaded by too many tourists. There's a distinctive culture to be discovered here, and the best way to do this may be as part of an organised tour, on foot, horse or bicycle. If you prefer to travel solo, your own transport is a must; unless, of course, you choose to strike out and explore some of the many hiking paths that have been marked out throughout the area.

West Sierra de Aracena

Due to its proximity to the Portuguese border (28 kilometres/17 miles away), **Aroche** has been the subject of territorial disputes since the 13th century. Today, it is one of the best preserved and least touristy villages in the area. The **Castillo de Aroche**, at the top of its steep cobbled streets, bears witness to its contentious position. It was originally built in the 11th and 12th centuries but has been renovated almost continually ever since; it's now used as offices and a bullring.

On the road into Aroche is the weird **Museo del Santo Rosario**, which displays rosary beads fingered by such saintly figures as General Franco and President Nixon. More religious relics can be seen in the 15th- to 17th-century church of **Nuestra Señora de la Asunción** (open times of services), another much-renovated Aroche monument. It's an intriguing church, with Giralda-like tiers on its outer walls, a jumble of ancient doors and an incredibly ornate altar. In the fascinating **Museo Arqueológico** are artefacts that have been found around Aroche, including some Roman remains.

The well-restored 13th-century castle in **Cortegana**, 14 kilometres (nine miles) east of Aroche on the N433, also bears witness to border disputes with Portugal. Today, you can enjoy one of the finest 360-degree views of the Sierra from its battlements. Be transported back to the Middle Ages during the four-day **Jornadas Medievales** *feria*, usually held over the first weekend of August, when the locals display their archery and falconry skills, as well as indulging in medieval music, theatre, drinking and dancing. Cortegana's decayed casino is a wonderful (and, in Andalucía, rare) art nouveau building.

Seven kilometres (four-and-a-half miles) south-east of Cortegana is the lovely village of **Almonaster La Real** (**photo** *p124*), built around a stunning tenth-century mosque and citadel (usually open; if not, ask at the *ayuntamiento* for the key), which overlooks the village. The mosque shares the site with some Roman and Visigothic remains and a 19th-century bullring. Inside the crumbling, atmospheric walls you'll find archways, columns with Arabic inscriptions, a Muslim fountain for washing, a prayer niche, and faded murals. Climb the tower (carefully) for views across Almonaster and into the bullring. A good time to visit is during the colourful **Las Cruces de Mayo** festival on the first Sunday in May.

Ten kilometres (six miles) east of Cortegana is the village of **Jabugo**, home of Huelva's world-famous export– *jamón ibérico*, ham made from pampered black Iberian pigs that are fed exclusively on acorns (*see p126* **Jamón, jamón**). A couple of kilometres further east, **Galaroza** is a craft centre, with a number of workshops producing ceramics and rush-backed furniture. It's worth a visit on 6 September for the **Fiesta de los Jarritos**, when everyone runs around throwing water at each other (originally a pottery festival, now an excuse to get wet). Galaroza is also the starting point for a number of superb marked walks to neighbouring villages, including Jabugo, Fuenteheridos, Castaño del Robledo and Valdelarco. The latter is worth a visit for its superb restaurant, **La Maja** (*see below*).

Castillo de Aroche

Aroche (info Ayuntamiento 959 14 02 01). **Open** 10am-7pm Fri-Sun. **Admission** free.

Castillo de Cortegana

Cortegana (info Ayuntamiento 959 13 12 60). **Open** *Apr-Sept* 10am-1.30pm, 4.30-8pm Mon, Wed-Sun. *Oct-Mar* 11am-2pm, 4-6pm Mon, Wed-Sun. **Admission** €1.50; free under-8s.

Museo Arqueológico

Cilla de los Jerónimos, Aroche (no phone). **Open** 10am-2pm Fri-Sun. **Admission** free.

Museo del Santo Rosario

Paseo Ordóñez Valdés s/n, Aroche (no phone). Contact Manuel Amigo (959 14 02 61), the local authorised guide, who holds the keys for the Museo and will give you a tour (in Spanish only) for a voluntary contribution. He can be found at his house: C/Cilla 2, signposted from the main square, or ring in advance to arrange a time.

Where to stay, eat & drink

In Aroche's Plaza Juan Carlos, check out **Cafetería Las Peñas** (959 14 04 15, €), which serves great tapas and, at weekends, seafood caught off Isla Cristina. Climb the steps next to it to reach **Bar Lalo** (no phone) through the first door on the right. It's a small, smartish bar with cute balconies overlooking the *plaza*. Opposite Las Peñas, **La Caja** (no phone) is a male-oriented bar with a good selection of local firewater made from acorns (*bellotas*) or anis.

Two kilometres (about one mile) from Cortegana towards Almonaster, you pass the delightful **Casas Rurales Los Gallos** (Finca Los Gallos, Estación de Almonaster, 959 50 11 67, mobile 687 36 57 54, www.alojamientolos gallos.com, cottage for 2 €53-€65, for 4 €100-€112, for 6 €141-€160, with reductions on weekly rates). Several whitewashed self-catering cottages are scattered around beautiful leafy gardens with patios, arches, wells and a swimming pool.

Just outside Almonaster, **El Rincón de Curro** (Carretera Almonaster–Cortegana, km1, 959 14 31 49, €€) dishes up tasty traditional local cuisine. Curro himself will talk you through his specialities, including a delicious *sopa de olores* (fragrant soup).

A good place to stay in Almonaster is the smart and popular **Hotel-Restaurante Casa García** (Avenida San Martín 2, 959 14 31 09, www.hotelcasagarcia.com, double €53), which has lovely views. The restaurant (€€) offers local specialities using seasonal ingredients.

The village of Valdelarco is home to the wonderful restaurant **La Maja** (C/Doctor Rodiño 27, 959 12 49 15, closed Mon-Fri, €€, which serves up some original dishes, like *pimientos rellenos de jabalí* (peppers stuffed with wild boar), and has a terrace with lovely views of the surrounding countryside. In Galaroza the **Casa Castulo** (Plaza de la Libertad 2, 959 12 32 02, www.casacastulo.com, closed dinner Tue-Thur, all day Mon and June, €€-€€€) showcases some of the Sierra's most creative cooking using good-quality local ingredients. Try the squid and ham croquettes and aubergines and honey. Paintings by local artists adorn the walls.

Resources

Tourist information

Aroche *Centro de Visitantes, Antiguo Convento de la Cilla (no phone)*. **Open** 11am-2pm, 4-6pm Fri-Sun.

East Sierra de Aracena

One of the Sierra's most picturesque villages, and an excellent base for exploring the area, **Alájar** (15 kilometres/nine miles east of Almonaster) is a tight knot of mossy, uneven cobbled streets and rickety old stone buildings, dotted with better-preserved examples of baroque churches and fine houses (**photo** *p127*). The cobbles are often arranged in patterns, a common custom in the Sierra villages. Alájar shelters under the **Peña de Arias Montano**, a steep, leafy cliff, with caves at its foot and religious sites at its summit. This has been a spiritual area for centuries: ancient Iberian shamans are said to have had mushroom-induced visions here. This tradition was continued by Benito Arias Montano, Felipe II's confessor, who came here to meditate – on one occasion with his monarch. On the summit is a 16th-century church, Nuestra Señora de los Angeles (usually open), filled with pilgrims' offerings. The hallowed atmosphere is spoilt somewhat by the hordes that arrive on weekends and the tacky stalls outside selling local produce. Visit during the week and stroll in the woods for solitude and peace. To find out more about Arias Montano, visit the Centro de Visitantes (open 9am-2pm Mon-Fri). The exuberant **Romería de Nuestra Señora de los Angeles**, the Sierra's patron saint, takes place on 7-8 September, when processions from the surrounding villages congregate at the Peña for a day of eating, drinking and singing.

A few kilometres north of Alájar is the pretty village of **Fuenteheridos**. The lovely central square here has a 12-spring fountain surrounded by dark, ham-hung bars that are great for rubbing shoulders with gossiping locals. There's also the best *artesanía* shop in the Sierra, selling fine, locally made handicrafts.

Almonaster La Real. *See p123.*

Heading west from Alájar for four kilometres (two-and-a-half miles) brings you to **Linares de la Sierra**, where houses have their own personalised cobblestone thresholds. Narrow streets converge on an open sandy square that doubles as a bullring. It's worth stopping off at the **Restaurante Arrieros** (*see p126*).

A further six kilometres (four miles) east is the Sierra's main town, **Aracena**. There's an air of cool confidence about its well-preserved streets, pleasant squares and whitewashed houses with casement windows. At the top of the picturesque, cobbled C/Pozo de la Nieve, with its water features, souvenir shops, bars and restaurants, is the entrance to Aracena's main draw – the truly wonderful **Gruta de las Maravillas** (Cave of Marvels), where much of *Journey to the Centre of the Earth* and *Tarzan in King Solomon's Mines* were filmed. Visits to the caves are by guided tour only and numbers are limited. The tour takes an hour and leads you past spectacular rock formations and underground lakes that are reminiscent of *The Lord of the Rings*. There's a sign at the entrance warning visitors about the 95 to 98 per cent humidity and potential claustrophobia, though perhaps it would be better to prepare them for the eye-wateringly massive phallic shapes formed by some of the stalactites. The tour is in clear Spanish and the pleasant guides will usually help out any foreign tourists. Unlike many of Spain's caves, the Gruta de las Maravillas has been left almost untouched, which means you can really appreciate this incredible feat of nature.

The tourist office is opposite the cave entrance, with maps of Aracena and the Sierra, and walking guides. The Centro de Visitantes, housed in the Cabildo Viejo on Plaza Alta, has maps and information about the town, but is mainly the central information point for the Parque Natural de la Sierra de Aracena y Picos de Aroche. It has some interesting displays on the Sierra's history, geology, flora and fauna. Climb further up the hill to reach the ruins of the Templar castle, with a 13th-century Gothic-Mudéjar church within its walls. There are fine views of the town from here.

Towards the eastern reaches of the province, about 23 kilometres (14 miles) south-east of Aracena, the curious, vertiginous village of **Zufre** perches on the edge of a cliff, with terraced *huertas* (allotments) below. Look down across the plain to the Embalse de Zufre reservoir from the *mirador* of the elegant Paseo de los Alcaldes (C/Nuestra Señora del Puerto). The tranquillity of this small park of rose trees, lime trees and hedges is disturbed only by old gents engaged in fierce debates, swifts diving to and fro, and nesting storks clacking their beaks. On the first Saturday of every month there is a small but bustling *artesanía* market, where you can buy locally produced organic fruit, vegetables and cheeses, as well as leather and ceramic handicrafts.

As you walk Zufre's cobbled streets, you'll pass fountains and water features that have been used to irrigate the *huertas* for about half a century. On Plaza de la Iglesia are Zufre's monuments: the *ayuntamiento*, with old stone, throne-like seats that were used by the Inquisition, and the 16th-century church of La Purísima de Concepción (open times of services), attributed to Hernán Ruíz, who was also responsible for Seville's Giralda.

Gruta de las Maravillas

C/Pozo de la Nieve s/n (959 12 83 55). **Open** 10am-1.30pm, 3-6pm daily. **Admission** €7.70; €5.50 concessions. **No credit cards**. Numbers are limited so book ahead if possible.

The Río Tinto Mines

Just south of the Sierra de Aracena, you come to mining country. This area has been exploited for its mineral wealth for over 5,000 years; the **Minas de Riotinto** (Río Tinto Mines) are the world's oldest, and allegedly the original King Solomon's mines. The Phoenicians extracted copper, followed by the Romans, who mined silver extensively using slaves. The mines were then forgotten until the 18th century, when the Spanish government sold them to the British Rio Tinto Mining Company for a bargain price. The Brits ran the mines in typical efficient colonial style, building an English-style estate of Victorian villas to house British management and engineers, complete with a village green, and church. They also built the first golf course and football pitch in Spain.

The mines returned to Spanish control in 1954, and today the area is more tourist attraction than industrial site. The landscape is a sight in itself, with the Río Tinto tracing a rust-red line through the multicoloured earth. Despite its lunar appearance, Río Tinto may prove to have more in common with Mars than the moon, according to NASA, which believes that the area has a mineral and bacterial composition similar to the Red Planet. In 2003 it began drilling in the area to simulate a future mission to Mars.

The **Museo Minero** displays mining artefacts, a reconstruction of a Roman mine and Queen Victoria's sumptuous train carriage. From the museum you can go on a tour (in Spanish only) to one of the largest opencast mines in the world, the jaw-droppingly vast **Corta Atalaya**. Probably the best attraction is the 22-kilometre (15-mile) **Ferrocarril Turístico Minero**, with its restored steam train from the 1900s, which runs along the Río Tinto and through a spectacular mining landscape.

Museo Minero

Plaza Ernest Lluch s/n, Minas de Riotinto (959 59 00 25/www.parquemineroderiotinto.com). **Open** 10.30am-3pm, 4-7pm daily. Steam train runs daily Mar-Sept, weekend afternoons only Oct-Feb. **Admission** *Museum* €4. *Museum & Corte Atalaya* €9. *Museum, Corte Atalaya & Ferrocarril Turístico Minero* €17. **Credit** DC, MC, V.

Where to stay, eat & drink

Alájar has a great choice of places to eat. One of the best is **Mesón El Corcho** (Plaza España s/n, 959 12 57 79, closed Thur and last 2wks June, €€), a bar-restaurant with a decor based on the eponymous cork; treat yourself to its *gambones a la plancha* (grilled king-sized prawns). The Basque-run **La Peña** (Peña de Arias Montana, 959 501 340, closed dinner and Mon, €€-€€€) has views of the whitewashed hermitage from the balcony tables. Choose from flavoursome tapas such as aubergine and cured ham salad or full meals such as venison ragout, but save room for the home-made chocolate cake made with locally produced walnuts. The nearby **Hotel La Posada** (C/Médico Emilio

Jamón, jamón

Throughout the Sierra de Aracena, black Iberian pigs (*cerdos ibéricos*) snuffling in the ground for acorns *(bellotas)* are a common sight. The animal's meat is a ubiquitous feature on tapas menus in the Sierra, so much so that vegetarian visitors will suffer in this predominantly pig-rearing area. Traditionally, most families kept a pig or two, which provided a year-round supply of pork products. The whole family and their friends helped at the *matanza* (pig slaughter), with the men doing the butchering while the women made the sausages. Not for the squeamish, a *matanza* is a celebratory occasion where a pig is killed for all to see. Every part of the beast is used, from its distinctive black trotter – or *pata negra*, another name for *jamón ibérico* – to its tail and its snout. Today, the custom of the *matanza* is in decline, mainly because of stringent EU regulations.

However, with the increasing popularity of *jamón ibérico* from Jabugo, the pork industry still contributes significantly to the local economy, employing many locals during the winter, the *matanza* season. *Jamón de Jabugo* is regarded as the best in Spain, partly because the Sierra's air is ideal for drying hams. Other factors that contribute to the ham's quality are the breed of pig and its diet, consisting primarily of acorns. The free-ranging Iberian pig has a better distribution of fat than its more inactive counterparts, and deposits distinctive finely marbled fat in its muscles. It is significantly high in oleaic acid, like olive oil, and so helps to reduce cholesterol, as well as being lower in calories than other types of ham.

There are three types of *jamón ibérico*: *jamón de bellota* is the most expensive and comes from pigs that feed almost exclusively on acorns; *jamón de recebo* is from pigs that feed on acorns and cereals, mainly maize; *jamón de pienso* is the cheapest and is from pigs fed only cereals and *pienso* (processed animal feed). To prepare the hams, they are first buried in sea salt for up to a month and then hung up to be dried in fresh air. The third stage of curing lasts 18 to 24 months, when hams are hung in a *bodega* (cellar).

The top producer is Sánchez Romero Carvajal, which has created grades of *cinco jotas* ('five Js', the 'J' standing for 'Jabugo') to classify *jamón* quality. You can visit **Mesón Sánchez Romero Carvajal** (C/San Juan del Puerto, 959 12 10 71, €€) in Jabugo; the prices can be a little steep, but it's certainly worth a splurge. You can also buy its ham in local supermarkets; a *jamón* is the back leg, and a *paleta* is the front. Expect to pay around €27/kg for *jamón de bellota* and €15/kg for *jamón de recebo.*

You can see *jamón* being sliced at bars throughout the Sierra, which parade an endless variety of pig-derived dishes. Apart from another cured delicacy, *caña de lomo* (cured pork loin sausage), there are various cuts of pork – *lomo, solomillo, presa, pluma, secreto*; and different parts of the pig – *lengua* (tongue), *hígado* (liver), *orejas* (ears), *riñones* (kidneys), *carrillera* (cheek), *costillas* (ribs) and *castañuelas* (saliva glands).

González 2, 959 12 57 12, www.laposadadealajar.com, closed last 3wks Jan, 1st wk Feb, double €60) boasts green credentials like solar-powered hot water and organic locally produced food (book in advance). A short walk away is the Dutch-run **Molino Río Alájar** (Finca Cabeza del Molino s/n, 959 50 12 82, www.molinorioalajar.com, cottage for 2 €241 per weekend, €615 per week, cottage for 4 €294 per weekend, €824 per week). Beautifully furnished self-catering stone cottages are set in a leafy valley, and there's a swimming pool.

In Linares de la Sierra, reserve a table in advance at **Restaurante Arrieros** (C/Arrieros 2, 959 46 37 17, closed Mon and 4wks July-Aug, €€). This smart but cosy restaurant serves delicious local specialities.

Near the little village of Los Marines, between Fuenteheridos and Aracena, you can hire a self-catering cottage in the British-run **Finca Buen Vino** (N433, km95, 959 12 40 34, www.fincabuenvino.com, double €137-€158, cottage for 4 with pool €500-€1,000 per week). Surrounded by chestnut woods, orchards and grazing sheep, the cottages have private swimming pools and barbecue areas, or you can stay and eat handsomely in the main house. This gorgeously peaceful and relaxing oasis is perhaps the best accommodation in the area.

In Fuenteheridos, visit **Restaurante Biarritz** (C/Virgen de la Fuente s/n, 959 12 50 88, closed dinner Mon-Thur and 2wks June-July, €), a popular restaurant/tapas bar serving melt-in-the-mouth *caña de lomo* (cured pork sausage) and *solomillo con crema de jamón* (pork fillet with ham and cream sauce).

Despite being more on the tourist drag than its neighbours, rooms are limited in Aracena. The main hotel, **Los Castaños** (Avenida Huelva 5, www.loscastanos.com, 959 12 63 00, double €58.85), is a spruce two-star, with rooms decorated in rather depressing pinks and beiges. A cheaper, simpler option is **Casa Manolo** (C/Barberos 6, 959 12 80 14, double €23.55) for basic doubles without a bath. Situated in a beautiful wooded valley a kilometre out of Aracena is the lovely **Finca Valbono** (Ctra Aracena–Carboneras, km1, 959 12 77 11, www.fincavalbono.com, double €89, cottage for 2 €92, cottage for 4 €150). Hotel rooms and cottages are furnished in rustic style and there is a swimming pool, as well as horse riding and walks. On Aracena's main square, Plaza del Marqués de Aracena, is **Café-Bar Manzano** (959 12 63 37, closed Tue and last wk Sept, €), with one of the best and most extensive tapas menus in the Sierra.

For dessert, try some devilish cakes from the nearby **Confitería Casa Rufino** (C/Constitución 3, 959 12 81 21), an ornately tiled, 100-year-old cake and pastry shop – the best known in this part of Andalucía. Near the Gruta is the swish **Restaurante Montecruz** (C/San Pedro 39, www.restaurantemontecruz.com, 959 12 60 13, closed 2wks July, €€), serving some tasty game and typical Sierra fare such as wild mushrooms and the ubiquitous pork. If you've pigged out, then head to the nearby **La Tetería Andalusí** (Avda Reina Isabel de los Angeles, no phone, closed Mon, €) where you can sink into comfy floor cushions, sip mint tea and enjoy sumptuous Moroccan-style tagines and couscous dishes.

Resources

Tourist information

Parque Natural de la Sierra de Aracena y Picos de Aroche *Centro de Visitantes, Cabildo Viejo, Plaza Alta s/n, Aracena (959 12 88 25).* **Open** *July, Aug* 10am-2pm, 6-8pm Tue-Sun. *Sept-June* 10am-2pm, 4-6pm Tue-Sun.

Aracena *C/Pozo de la Nieve (959 12 82 06/www.aracena.es).* **Open** 10am-2pm, 4-7.30pm daily.

Getting there

By bus

Damas runs a limited service from Huelva (959 25 69 00, www.damas-sa.es); 2 on weekdays, 1 on weekends. Casal (954 99 92 90, www.autocarescasal.com) has 2 daily from Seville to Aracena. There's a twice-daily service between Aracena and the other towns and larger villages.

By train

One railway line runs north–south through Huelva province. The most convenient station for exploring the Sierra de Aracena is Estación de Almonaster-Cortegana, about 3km (1.5 miles) north of Almonaster on the way to Cortegana. It is served by a couple of trains a day to and from Huelva (2hrs 30mins).

Alájar. *See p124.*

Time Out
Travel Guides
Spain
Time Out
Barcelona
Time Out
Madrid
Time Out
Mallorca
Time Out
Seville
& Andalucía
FERIA DE SAN ISIDRO 2004
Del 8 de mayo al 5 de junio - A las 7 tarde
CCM
Caja
Castilla
La Mancha
www.las-ventas.com
Time Out
Guides
Available at all good bookshops
and at timeout.com/shop
PHOTO CREDIT: VENETIA DEARDEN

Cádiz Province & Gibraltar

Features

Maps

Cádiz Province

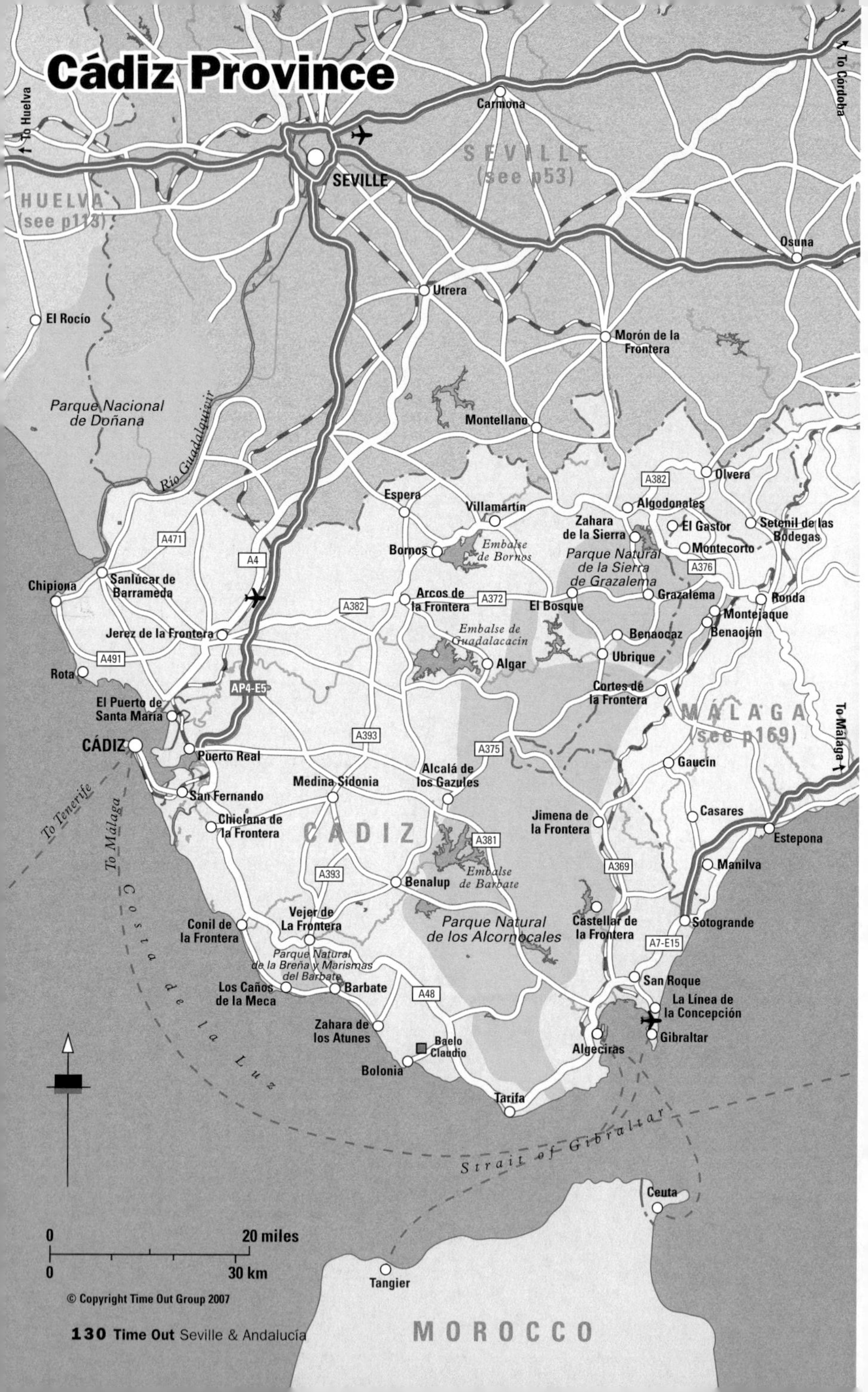

Introduction

Definitive Andalucía – with bit of Britain tacked on for good measure.

If you were to pick one province that represented the distillation of all things Andalucían, then it would have to be Cádiz. A distinctive and enjoyable provincial capital, a largely virgin coastline facing the untamed Atlantic, a dramatically hilly interior specked with white villages, vibrant towns, wonderful seafood, sherry, horses, flamenco and, on its doorstep, a political hot potato (or, rather, Rock).

CÁDIZ CITY

The provincial capital, dramatically isolated on a spit of land, and surrounded by the sea, is a singular place. Its old town, with long straight streets and projecting glazed balconies, is heavy with atmosphere and feels quite unlike any other Andalucían city. There are fine museums and churches plus, unsurprisingly, some of the best seafood in the region.

NORTH OF CÁDIZ

Just to the north of Cádiz lies the famous sherry triangle, made up of the towns of Jerez, El Puerto and Sanlúcar, all appealing places to visit in their own right. Apart from their *bodegas*, all three are famed for the excellence of their tapas. Jerez is also known for flamenco and horses, while Sanlúcar is a gateway to the wilderness of the Doñana National Park.

EAST OF CÁDIZ

The inland portion of Cádiz province is chiefly known for its collection of *pueblos blancos* (white villages), scattered like patches of pristine snow among the spectacular hills that merge into Málaga province. Arcos de la Frontera, one of the most impressively sited, makes an excellent base from which to explore some of the wild, lesser populated areas around.

COSTA DE LA LUZ

Running from Cádiz to Tarifa is the longest stretch of unspoiled coastline in Andalucía. Though development is proceeding at an alarming rate, there are still endless swathes of virgin golden sand to enjoy. The coast is at its most dramatic around the laid-back hippyish little resort of Los Caños de Meca, while Vejer de la Frontera, back from the coast, is the most perfect *pueblo blanco* in the area. The enjoyable town of Tarifa has a cool surf-dude vibe, and the constant winds around here draw in windsurfers from all over Europe.

GIBRALTAR

Geographically awe-inspiring, historically fascinating, aesthetically horrifying, Britain's controversial Mediterranean outpost raises strong emotions whether you're Gibraltarian, Spanish or just a visitor.

The best...

Architecture & history
Cádiz City (*pp132-8*).

Beaches
All along the **Costa de la Luz** (*pp156-65*).

Flamenco
Jerez (*p139*).

Low-key resorts
Los Caños de la Meca (*p156*); **Zahara de los Atunes** (*p158*).

Natural beauty
Doñana (*p146*); **Los Alcornocales** (*p152*); **Sierra de Grazalema** (*p153*).

Seafood & sherry
Jerez (*p139*); **El Puerto de Santa María** (*p148*); **Sanlúcar de Barrameda** (*p144*).

White villages
Arcos de la Frontera (*p150*); **Vejer de la Frontera** (*p158*); **Zahara de la Sierra** (*p154*).

Windsurfing
Tarifa (*p162*).

Cádiz City

Neglected by the hordes, Cádiz offers both history and a bouyant present.

Isolated at the end of a narrow strip of land, hammered by the sea on three sides, Cádiz is seemingly unchanged in more than 200 years. The city retains an air of faded grandeur; many of the buildings are in dire need of repair and, although a certain amount of restoration is taking place, the city authorities are not keen to prettify the place too much.

Cádiz today is made up of two distinct parts – the old city, crammed on to the fist-shaped headland, and the unappealing new town, stretching back from here to the mainland on either side of the Avda de Andalucía.

The city claims to be the oldest in western Europe and dates its history back to 1100 BC, when the Phoenicians knew it as Gadir – hence the name of its citizens, *gaditanos*. It was used as a base by the Carthaginians for military campaigns in the peninsula and prospered under Roman rule after Julius Caesar granted Gades, as it became known, the privileges of a Roman town.

After the Romans left, Cádiz declined, and it was only of minor importance under the Moors. Trade with the Americas helped revive its fortunes in the 16th century (though an English raid in 1596 destroyed a third of the city). The city's period of greatest prosperity began in 1717, when the silting up of the Guadalquivir led the Chamber of Commerce of the Americas to move here from Seville.

A century later, the town achieved its historical zenith when, in 1812, the short-lived Cortes (Spanish parliament) met here to declare the first Spanish constitution.

Today, Cádiz is a youthful, vibrant city of around 150,000, though the old town is haunted by an appealingly melancholic air. It remains undiscovered by mass foreign tourism and hosts what is indisputably the best carnival on mainland Spain (*see p137* **Party on**).

Sightseeing

The old part of Cádiz is compact and can be seen on foot in a day. The architecture of the old town dates mainly from the late 18th and early 19th centuries, and reflects a strong influence from France, with elegant neo-classical detailing and buildings arranged in long, straight rows. Another striking feature is the number of projecting glazed balconies.

A (now faded) red line through the town leads visitors from the Plaza San Juan de Dios, one of the town's prettiest squares, through the oldest part of town, the medieval **Barrio del Pópulo** (**photo** *p138*), via a number of other attractive streets and squares.

Plaza San Juan de Dios is a fine palm-fringed square fronted by the huge Ayuntamiento. Head west from here along C/Pelota and you will reach Plaza de la Catedral. Begun in 1722, when money from the Americas was pouring into Cádiz, the immense **Catedral Nueva** was designed by Vicente Acero and should have been one of the most architecturally memorable churches in Spain. However, money ran short and the project took far longer than expected, so that when it was finally completed (in 1853) it consisted of a mishmash of jarring styles. It is also fighting a losing battle against the elements and is visibly crumbling. Inside, there is a small museum with a collection of silver, the centrepiece of which is the so-called Millón, an over-the-top *custodia* encrusted with one million gems and precious stones. The tomb of locally born composer Manuel de Falla is in the crypt.

Just east of the current cathedral, in the Barrio del Pópulo, is Cádiz's former cathedral, now the church of **Santa Cruz** (open during services only). It was built in 1260 over a mosque, and was all but destroyed by the English in 1596; most of what you see today dates from the 17th century. The church is notable for its *retablos*.

Just beyond Santa Cruz lies the (currently closed) **Teatro Romano** (Roman theatre), dating from the first century BC. Ongoing excavations on the site have revealed much of the interior seating and galleries, as well as the remains of a Moorish fortress.

From Plaza de la Catedral, C/Compañía leads north-west to Plaza de las Flores, another attractive square that is home to the town's **Mercado Central** (Central Market), set mainly in a dilapidated 19th-century building, surrounded by bustling bars and cafés.

West of the square, just off C/Sacramento is the **Torre Tavira**, part of an 18th-century mansion and the tallest tower in the old city. It contains a camera obscura, giving stunning views over the city, and an exhibition on Cádiz's seafaring past.

A right turn on to C/Sagasta and first left on to C/Santa Inés bring you to two of Cádiz's most important and interesting buildings, the town's history museum, **Museo de las Cortes de Cádiz**, and the **Oratorio de San Felipe Neri** (Plaza San Felipe Neri, 956 21 16 12), closed for renovations until 2009. Historically one of the most significant buildings in Spain, the Oratorio is where a group of liberals assembled on 29 March 1812, in defiance of Napoleon, to draft the Cortes, a radical document that posited a Spanish constitution and declared Spain an independent republic with full religious and political freedom. The revolution was short-lived and it took another 163 years before Spain emerged as a fully fledged democracy, but the ideas of the Cádiz Cortes played a major part in shaping modern European politics.

The church itself has a pretty interior, with two sets of balconies and large windows in the dome illuminating the predominantly blue decor. The altar is decorated with an *Immaculate Conception* by Murillo. Next door, the centrepiece of the museum is an enormous scale model of the city as it was in 1777, which shows how little the old part of the city has changed in more than 200 years. The museum also contains numerous artefacts related to events in 1812.

A short walk west from here lies Cádiz's main theatre, the neo-Moorish **Gran Teatro Falla** (Plaza de Falla s/n, 956 22 02 28), named after one of the town's most famous sons, composer Manuel de Falla.

Another couple of minutes' walk west lies the delightful **Parque Genovés**, laid out along the seafront and home to a centuries-old dragon tree, imported from the Canary Islands. Follow the gardens round to the north-east to reach the **Baluarte de Candelaria**, a promontory that adjoins the Alameda de Marqués de Comillas, where you'll find more seafront gardens.

Inland from here, de Falla's birthplace is marked by a plaque in the garden-filled Plaza de Mina, also the site of the **Museo de Cádiz**. On the ground floor is a display of archaeological finds from the province covering the Roman, Phoenician and Greek periods – the two Phoenician tombs here are the equal of any in Spain. The fine art museum on the second floor contains some impressive paintings by Murillo, Zurbarán (an important series of panels from the charterhouse in Jerez) and Alonso Cano, and a Rubens, while the third floor concentrates on local ceramics and textiles as well as an antique puppet collection.

Just east of the Plaza de Mina is the church of **San Francisco** (open during services only) in the square of the same name and the nearby **Oratorio de Santa Cueva**, which contains the only Goya frescoes in Andalucía. These depict three key moments in Christ's life, including the Last Supper, at which Christ and the disciples are shown eating on the floor. Steps head down to a gloomy chapel.

The streets leading east from here – C/San Francisco, C/Rosario and, a few blocks south,

Catedral Nueva. *See p132.*

Cádiz Province

High-flying **Playa de la Victoria**.

C/Ancha, are some of the most attractive in the city, full of bars, restaurants and little shops. North-east of Plaza de San Francisco is the huge but rather soulless Plaza de España, with a monument to the Cortes at its centre. The *plaza* gives on to the bus station and the port area, from where boats depart for the Canary Islands.

At the opposite end of the old town, in the far south-western corner, is the old fishermen's quarter known as the **Barrio de la Viña**. The streets here are full of bars and restaurants as well as a number of *peñas de flamenco*. Just beyond it, fronting the old town's beach, Playa de la Caleta, are enormous, ancient dragon trees, which are particularly beautiful when floodlit. **Playa de la Caleta** is small, a bit dirty and beyond crowded in high season; **Playa de Santa María**, just outside the old town, suffers from a similar fate. If you're after some sun and sea, your best bet is to head to the enormous expanse of the **Playa de la Victoria**, further into the new town, which is huge, clean and hosts all the night-time action in summer.

Catedral Nueva

Plaza de la Catedral; entrance to museum on Plaza Fray Félix s/n (956 25 98 12). **Open** 10am-1.30pm, 4.30-7pm Tue-Fri; 10am-1pm Sat. **Admission** €4. **No credit cards**. **Map** p135 C2. **Photo** *p133.*

Museo de Cádiz

Plaza Mina s/n (956 21 22 81). **Open** 2.30-8pm Tue; 9am-8.30pm Wed-Sat; 9am-2.30pm Sun. **Admission** €1.50; free with EU passport. **No credit cards**. **Map** p135 B1.

Museo de las Cortes de Cádiz

C/Santa Inés 9 (956 22 17 88). **Open** 9am-1pm, 5-7pm Tue-Fri; 9am-1pm Sat, Sun. **Admission** free. **Map** p135 B2.

Oratorio de Santa Cueva

C/Rosario 10 (956 22 22 62). **Open** 10am-1pm, 5-8pm Tue-Fri; 10am-1pm Sat, Sun. **Admission** €2.50; €1.50 concessions. **No credit cards**. **Map** p135 B1.

Torre Tavira

C/Marqués del Real Tesoro 10 (956 21 29 10/ www.torretavira.com). **Open** *Mid June-mid Sept* 10am-7.30pm daily. *Mid Sept-mid June* 10am-5.30pm daily. **Admission** €3.50; €2.80 concessions. **No credit cards**. **Map** p135 B2.

Where to eat & drink

Old town

In addition to the places below, if you yearn for a taste of the real Cádiz (and aren't too fussy about decor) try the tapas bars **La Rambla** and **Noya** in C/Sopranis (which leads off Plaza San Juan de Dios, map C1).

Achuri

C/Plocia 15 (956 25 36 13). **Open** 1-4.30pm Mon-Wed, Sun; 1-4.30pm, 8.30pm-midnight Thur-Sat. Closed 2 wks Christmas. **Average** €€. **Credit** AmEx, V. **Map** p135 C1 ❶
This place is popular with *gaditanos* and specialises in Basque and Andalucían dishes, including *morros de cerdo* (pig snout, in spicy sauce).

El Aljibe

C/Plocia 25 (956 26 66 56). **Open** 12.30-4.30pm, 8pm-midnight daily. **Average** €€€. **Credit** DC, MC, V. **Map** p135 C1 ❷
Located in a historic house (and named after the old well in the basement), El Aljibe has superb tapas.

Balandro

Paseo Alameda de Apodaca 22 (956 22 09 92). **Open** noon-4.30pm, 8pm-1.30am Tue-Sat. **Average** €€€. **Credit** AmEx, DC, MC, V. **Map** p135 A1 ❸
Enjoying fine sea views, this stylish restaurant offers first-rate seafood and meat dishes, as well as tapas. The house special is *rollitos de dorado* (rolls of dorado fish).

Bar Terraza

Plaza de la Catedral 3 (956 26 53 91). **Open** *Mid June-mid Sept* 10am-midnight Mon-Sat. *Mid Sept-mid June* 10am-midnight Tue-Sun. **Average** €€€. **Credit** AmEx, DC, MC, V. **Map** p109 C2 ❹
In a superb spot by the cathedral, this 50-year-old institution serves high-quality regional dishes, but you do pay a premium for the location.

Cervecería-Marisquería Joselito

C/San Francisco 38 (956 26 65 48). **Open** 11am-4pm, 8pm-midnight Mon-Sat. **Average** €€. **Credit** AmEx, DC, MC, V. **Map** p135 B1 ❺

Owned by three friendly brothers, this much-loved twin-fronted institution occupies both a traditional spot on C/San Francisco and a trendy terrace overlooking the port. The house speciality *almejas joselito* (clams) and fried fish are excellent.

El Faro

C/San Felix 15 (956 21 10 68). **Open** 1-4.30pm, 8.30pm-midnight daily. **Average** €€€. **Credit** AmEx, DC, MC, V. **Map** p135 B3 ❻

Widely considered to be the number-one restaurant in town (and one of the best in the province), El Faro specialises in, of course, seafood. The menu has an extraordinary range and the quality of execution is sublime. House specialities include *lubina* (sea bass) and *cigalas* (crayfish). If you can't afford the restaurant, there is a first-class tapas bar too.

Gotinga

Plaza Mentidero 15 (856 07 05 80). **Open** *July-Sept* 1pm-1am Mon-Sat. *Oct-June* 9.30am-1am Mon-Sat. **Average** €€. **No credit cards.** **Map** p135 A2 ❼

This German-run place makes a refreshing change from traditional Spanish eateries: it does serve tapas, but they span a wide international range. It also offers some good salads, along with bottled beers and 12 types of tea.

Merodio

C/Libertad 4, Mercado Central, Plaza de Abastos (no phone). **Open** 9am-midnight daily. **Average** €. **No credit cards.** **Map** p135 B2 ❽

This Cádiz institution fronts the Mercado Central and is consequently always busy, especially at Carnaval, when it traditionally becomes a focal point for drunken revellers.

Pablito

Avda de Ramón de Carranza 29 (956 28 31 55). **Open** 8am-10pm Mon-Sat. **Average** €. **No credit cards.** **Map** p135 B1 ❾

Pablito is a well-established spot reliably offering simple but tasty fare, including *cazón en adobo* (fried fish). It's good-value *menú del día* is particularly worth a mention.

Taberna el Albero

C/San Félix 2 (956 22 08 38). **Open** noon-5pm, 8pm-1am daily. **Average** €. **Credit** AmEx, DC, MC, V. **Map** p135 B3 ⑩

Run by a one-time *torero*, this little bar, full of bull-fighting memorabilia of all kinds, is popular with local characters. Make sure you try the delicious *tortillitas de camarones* (prawn fritters).

New town

Arte Serrano

Paseo Marítimo 2 (956 27 72 58). **Open** 1-5pm, 8pm-midnight daily. **Average** €€. **Credit** AmEx, DC, V.

If you're tired of fish, then try this excellent meat restaurant, dedicated to porky products. All the *jamón*, *lomo* (pork loin) and *chorizo* is produced locally. It's not expensive and there is also an excellent selection of meaty tapas.

El Baro

Below Residencia Tiempo Libre, Paseo Marítimo s/n (956 25 79 57). **Open** noon-5pm, 7.30pm-midnight daily. **Average** €€. **Credit** DC, MC, V.

Serving fine fish and shellfish, El Baro is a cheaper alternative to La Marea just up the road (*see below*).

La Leyenda

Paseo Marítimo 20 (956 26 21 85). **Open** *July, Aug* 1-4pm, 9pm-midnight Mon-Sat. *Sept-June* 1-4pm, 9pm-midnight Tue-Sat; 1-4pm Sun. **Average** €€-€€€. **Credit** AmEx, DC, MC, V.

For a first-class three-course meal try this smart new town restaurant, which shares the same owner as Balandro (*see p134*). The food is excellent – try the chicken in Pedro Xímenez sauce.

La Marea

Paseo Marítimo 1 (956 28 03 47). **Open** 1.30-5pm, 8.30pm-1am daily. **Average** €€-€€€. **Credit** AmEx, DC, MC, V.

Regarded as the best seafood restaurant and tapas bar in this part of town, La Marea is not particularly classy, but prices are very reasonable and the menu is enormous: everything from the bay is here, including *lubina* (sea bass) and *langostinos*.

Nightlife

Apart from during the joyful chaos of Carnaval, and despite a large student population, Cádiz does not have a hugely exciting nightlife during the winter months. The **Punta de San Felipe** at the tip of the harbour is the most popular area for such after-dark revelry as there is: it's crammed with bars and discos, most of which get going after midnight. One of the best of these is **El Malecón** (Paseo Almirante Pascual Perry Junquera s/n, 956 22 45 19, closed Mon-Wed), which is a Latin dance venue popular with all ages.

Try also the streets around Plaza de Candelaria, Plaza de San Antonio and Plaza de Mina, which are popular with students. Plaza San Francisco gets packed on Friday and Saturday nights with students who buy spirits and mixers from nearby shops.

The **Barrio de la Viña** is a good area to find flamenco, although popular spots from the past like **Peña Juan Vilar** at C/Puerta la Caleta rarely put on shows these days. This area is also the heart of Carnaval preparations; the modern-day interpretation of Carnaval began in the Plaza del Tío de la Tiza (named after the man who revived the festivities), and many costumes and effigies are still made here.

Venues in the old town that put on regular flamenco shows include **La Cava** (C/Antonio Lopez, 956 21 18 66, www.flamencolacava.com, closed Mon-Wed, Fri & Sun in winter, shows 9pm, €22 with drink) and **Peña la Perla** (C/Carlos Ollero, 956 27 98 02, open Thur & Fri), next to the Cárcel Vieja.

Woodstock (C/Manuel Rances 13, 956 26 57 74) is an international bar that serves a decent pint and plays rock music. There are two other branches in Cádiz, on the Paseo Marítimo and on C/Canovas del Castillo. For varied live shows, try **Pay Pay** (no phone, closed Mon & Sun, free, map C1/2) on the corner of Calles Meson and Silencio, just behind the Teatro Romano. You can see anything here – flamenco, rock, tango and acoustic performances.

As soon as it starts to get warm, *gaditanos* decamp to the new town and the hundreds of bars and discos around the **Playa de la Victoria**. Most discos play a standard diet of dodgy Spanish techno called *bacalao*.

Where to stay

The old town is the place to stay, though accommodation is more luxurious in the new town, a good option if you want to be where the action is in the summer. Other than at Carnaval time, you will always be able to find a room: the old town, particularly off Plaza San Juan de Dios, is full of *hostales* and *pensiones*.

Old town

Hospederia Las Cortes de Cadiz

C/San Francisco 9 (956 22 04 89/www.hotellascortes.com). **Rates** (incl breakfast) €59-€96 single; €80-€134 double. **Credit** AmEx, DC, MC, V. **Map** p135 B1 ⑪

A comfortable three-star hotel, with a small gym and sauna, and a tower used to direct maritime traffic in the 18th and 19th centuries. Rates include an all-you-can-eat breakfast in the hotel's classy café. Rooms overlooking the central courtyard can get noisy.

Party on

Starting a couple of days before Shrove Tuesday, Cádiz's carnival is the biggest and best on mainland Spain (the one in Tenerife is its only rival), and signifies the start of the *fería* season in Andalucía. It's impossible to overestimate the importance of this ten-day orgy of excess to the average *gaditano*. Many locals spend all year designing costumes or rehearsing for a band. People come from all over the country and beyond to join in the festivities, so accommodation is at a premium.

Carnaval is about more than just drinking and dancing in the streets, though. Like Las Fallas in Valencia it has an overtly political message, with many people in satirical costumes lampooning local figures. It took its current form in the late 19th century thanks to a man called Antonio Rodríguez Martínez (El Tío de la Tiza), who is remembered by a plaque in the square of the same name. He organised bands of musicians to roam the streets of the old town. These (usually male) groups, in various stages of drunkenness, are still a major feature of Carnaval. Some are professional musicians or serious amateur singers, others are simply clueless and legless.

Throughout the ten days, floats, parades, competitions and concerts entertain revellers in many of the squares. If you stay for the whole time, you will find the festivities get progressively more chaotic; crowds of people throng the streets getting increasingly drunk and staggering around in outlandish costumes. There is also an almost continuous stream of revellers arriving on special Carnaval buses and trains from Jerez and Seville, and from the towns nearby, in particular from the US naval base at Rota.

Hostal Centro Sol

C/Manzanares 7 (956 28 31 03/www.hostal centrosolcadiz.com). **Rates** €37-€45 single; €44-€54 double. **Credit** AmEx, DC, MC, V. **Map** p135 B1 ⓬

This decent, clean guesthouse offers simple but adequate rooms around a central atrium, and a bar/café on the ground floor. It's spruce, light and attractive and also usefully central, near both the bus and train stations.

Hostal Marqués

C/Marqués de Cádiz 1 (956 28 58 54). **Rates** €20-€30 single; €35-€45 double. **No credit cards. Map** p135 C1 ⓭

This typical Cádiz house in the city centre is close to the town hall. As you might expect at these prices, rooms are a little spartan.

Hotel Francia y Paris

Plaza San Francisco 6 (956 22 23 48/www.hotel francia.com). **Rates** €60-€65 single; €74-€82 double. **Credit** AmEx, DC, MC, V. **Map** p135 B1 ⓮

A comfortable if slightly characterless three-star hotel on a pretty square, Hotel Francia y Paris is an excellent option if you want to soak up the old town atmosphere. Note that the square can get very noisy on weekend nights.

Parador de Cádiz

Avda Duque de Nájera 9 (956 22 69 05/www. parador.es). **Rates** (incl breakfast) €107-€116 single; €143-€154 double; €261-€282 suite. **Credit** AmEx, DC, MC, V. **Map** p135 B3 ⓯

This four-star *parador* is a modern building in an excellent position right on the seafront, near the town centre. It has a large swimming pool and a tiny spot of beach to call its own. The rooms are modern and comfortable; if you can, go for the suites with sea views. There's a good restaurant on site and plenty of parking.

Pensión Colón

C/Marqués de Cádiz 6 (956 28 53 51). **Rates** €40-€50 double. **No credit cards. Map** p135 C1 ⓰

Run by a friendly elderly couple, this simple *pensión* has good-value, clean rooms, some of them with en suite bathroom.

Pensión Fantoni

C/Flamenco 5 (956 28 27 04/www.hostalfantoni.net). **Rates** €30-€45 single; €40-€65 double; €60-€90 triple. **No credit cards. Map** p135 C1 ⓱

Budget accommodation in an 18th-century house decorated with tiles and marble, and with a pleasant terrace. Rooms overlook a central courtyard and can get noisy.

Barrio del Pópulo. *See p132.*

New town

Hotel Playa Victoria

Plaza Ingeniero la Cierva 4 (956 20 51 00/www. palafoxhoteles.com). **Rates** €133-€178 double; €324-€362 suite. **Credit** AmEx, DC, MC, V.

By far the most luxurious option, in a fantastic spot right on the beach and next to the best new town restaurants. Rooms are big, modern and comfortable, with balconies and sea views. The pool is virtually on the beach, and there's a good restaurant and bar.

Hotel Tryp La Caleta

Avda Amilcar Barca 47 (956 27 94 11/www. solmelia.com). **Rates** €60-€159 double **Credit** AmEx, DC, MC, V.

Despite the ugly exterior and characterless atmosphere, this new four-star has its advantages – right on the Playa de la Victoria, it has excellent facilities.

Resources

Internet

Red Net Center, Avda Cuesta de las Calesas 43 (956 28 09 49). **Open** 10am-11pm Mon-Thur; 11am-midnight Fri, Sat; 11am-11pm Sun.

Post office

Plaza Tapete s/n (956 21 05 11).

Police station

Plaza San Juan de Puerto Rico (956 24 11 00).

Tourist information

Avda Ramón de Carranza s/n (956 25 86 46/ www.cadizturismo.com). **Open** 9am-7pm Mon-Fri; 10am-2pm Sat, Sun. **Map** p135 B1.

Plaza San Juan de Dios 11 (956 24 10 01/ www.cadizayto.es/turismo). **Open** *June-Sept* 9am-2pm, 5-8pm daily. *Oct-May* 9am-2pm, 4-7pm daily. **Map** p135 C1.

The former covers the province, the second the city.

Getting there

By boat

Boat services run to Tenerife, Las Palmas de Gran Canaria and La Palma every Tuesday. Tickets and information are available from Transmediterránea (Avda Ramón de Carranza 26-8, 902 45 46 45, www. transmediterranea.es, map B/C1). El Vapor, the ferry across the bay to El Puerto, also departs from the port (mobile 629 46 80 14, www.vapordeelpuerto.com).

By bus

The Amarillos line, which runs from the bus station at Avda Ramón de Carranza 31 (956 29 08 00, map C1), has frequent services to the nearby resorts of El Puerto, Sanlúcar and Chipiona. Estación de Comes (Plaza de la Hispanidad, next to Plaza de España, 956 80 70 59) is used for long-distance services to Seville, points along the coast to Algeciras and beyond, and inland to Granada and Córdoba. There's also an El Puerto/Rota service from here. Secorbus runs 6 buses daily between Avda José Leon de Carranza 20 (902 22 92 92, www.socibus.es, map B1) and Madrid.

By train

The train station (Plaza de Sevilla, 902 24 02 02) is a few minutes' walk from the main square, Plaza San Juan de Dios. There are around 14 daily trains to Seville (2hrs), all of which call at El Puerto de Santa María (25mins from Cádiz) and Jerez (45mins from Cádiz). Four direct trains a day run to Córdoba (4hrs), and one a day to Jaén (5hrs).

North of Cádiz

A small area, rich in attractions – not least the top-notch restaurants.

The north-west corner of Cádiz province is sherry country, and it has the lively, likeable town of Jerez at its heart. The two other points of the 'sherry triangle' – Sanlúcar de Barrameda and El Puerto de Santa María – are also enjoyable places to visit. Both are famed for their seafood, and the former is one of the access points to the wild Parque Nacional de Doñana (*see p119* **Coto Doñana**).The stretch of coast here, which includes the resorts of Chipiona and Rota, is a favoured holiday spot for *sevillanos* and *gaditanos*, and in July and August you will be hard-pressed to find a room.

Jerez de la Frontera

The economy of the largest city in Cádiz province (36 kilometres/22 miles north-east of the provincial capital) is almost entirely dependent on the production and export – mainly to Britain – of sherry and brandy, but in recent years the famous brands have seen a fall in demand and profits, resulting in **Jerez de la Frontera** having one of the highest unemployment rates in Andalucía. Not that this is apparent as you wander around the well-maintained streets of the town, and it remains a relaxed and pleasant place to while away a day or two. As well as sherry and brandy in abundance, the town boasts superb tapas bars, some authentic flamenco venues and many outstanding buildings.

The name Jerez is an hispanicised version of the Phoenician 'Xeres' – the town formed part of the ancient empire of Tartessus. The Moors, who called the town 'Sherrish', ruled until 1264, and it is from around this time that the 'de la Frontera' was added – like so many Andalucían towns it was on the frontline of the constant skirmishes between Christians and Moors.

Aside from sherry, Jerez has two other main preoccupations: horses and flamenco. The Real Escuela Andaluz del Arte Ecuestre – the Royal Riding School – is based here (*see p145* **Bring on the dancing horses**), and, in the first half of May, the whole town dresses up for the **Feria del Caballo** (Horse Fair). Jerez also claims to be the home of flamenco (*see p142* **Finger-clickin' good**); the flamenco archive, the Centro Andaluz de Flamenco, is based here, and the city has one of the largest remaining gypsy populations in Andalucía.

Sightseeing

The heart of the city is C/Larga, which is also the main shopping drag. Its northern reaches are overlooked by the **Iglesia-Convento de Santo Domingo** (956 34 10 37, open hours of service), which has a masterful baroque altar – and the **Palacio Domecq**. This imposing late-baroque 18th-century pile is typical of the type of home the sherry barons built. Inside, the rooms are arranged around a beautiful marble-floored patio, which you can usually sneak a peek at from outside. Halfway down C/Larga is the **Gallo Azul**, a distinctive circular building from the late 19th century where *jerezanos* meet for a coffee or a *fino*. C/Larga leads south to Plaza del Arenal, scene of occasional horse races and the best area for tapas bars – not the square itself, but the streets leading off it.

North lies Plaza de la Asunción and the Renaissance/Plateresque **Cabildo Municipal** (old Town Hall). Opposite is the church of **San Dionisio** (closed until further notice), a Mudéjar building dedicated to Jerez's patron saint.

West along C/José Luis Diez stands the **Catedral de San Salvador**, also known as La Colegiata. Built on the site of an old mosque, with a free-standing bell tower (probably its minaret), it is a mix of Gothic, Renaissance and baroque styles. Begun in the 17th century, it is largely the work of Vicente Acero. Inside is Zurbarán's *La Virgen de Niña* and sculptures by Juan de Mesa. The first grapes of the harvest are pressed on the cathedral steps in early September.

Just south-west of the cathedral is the **Puerta del Arroyo**, a city gate dating from 1500. On either side of the gate are two of the town's largest sherry *bodegas*: **González-Byass** and **Domecq**. Another worth visiting is **Bodegas Sandeman**.

South of the cathedral is the 12th-century **Alcázar de Jerez**. The entrance has three sharp turnings to disorientate intruders, a characteristic it shares with many Islamic structures in Spain. Inside is a former mosque, later converted into the chapel of **Santa María la Real** (with a beautiful eight-sided cupola and *mihrab*), a bathhouse and a camera obscura, offering great views over the city.

North-west of the cathedral lies the gypsy district, the **Barrio de Santiago**. Consisting of a maze of winding streets lined by crumbling

Barrio de Santiago. See p139.

houses and churches, this is one of the most intact gypsy quarters in Andalucía and remains largely untouched by tourism. Within the *barrio*, located in two conjoined 16th-century palaces on Plaza del Mercado, is the **Museo Arqueológico** (956 33 33 16), closed indefinitely at the time of writing.

North-west of here, along C/Cordobeses, is a chunk of the old 12th-century Moorish walls (*murallas*) that once surrounded the town (other remnants are scattered around Jerez). C/Muro leads to Plaza de Santiago and its largely Gothic church.

South along C/Oliva is Plaza San Juan and the **Centro Andaluz de Flamenco**. This is Spain's central library and research centre for flamenco, and it puts on daily screenings of flamenco shows in a small cinema, and offers dance and guitar classes and study rooms.

A few minutes' walk north-west of Plaza de Santiago along C/Taxdirt is the **Parque Zoológico**, which is primarily a centre for the rehabilitation of injured and endangered animals. It is home to red panda, ibis and Iberian lynx, as well as two white tigers, a mother and daughter. The zoo is set in botanical gardens, where there are 33 pairs of nesting storks.

Heading north-east from Plaza de Santiago brings you to the **Centro Temático La Atalaya**. This area, once home to a worthy but dull clock museum and a few disused *bodegas*, was developed as a result of Jerez's high-profile hosting of the 2002 World Equestrian Games; the results are impressive. Within extensive grounds are two exhibitions, the **Palacio del Tiempo** (Palace of Time) and the **Misterio de Jerez** (Mystery of Sherry). Billed as a 'journey through time', the former consists of an enjoyable guided tour (introduced by a life-sized hologram of a person in 18th-century garb) through exquisitely designed rooms housing a collection of 302 antique working clocks. The latter is a multimedia show, using four enormous screens and a floor projection, which traces the origins, history, production and importance of sherry to the town.

North-east of La Atalaya is the **Real Escuela Andaluz del Arte Ecuestre** (Royal Riding School), the training and breeding centre of thoroughbred, or *pura raza*, Andalucían horses, whose lineage can be traced back to the 15th-century horses of La Cartuja (*see p145* **Bring on the dancing horses**).

Just outside Jerez is **La Cartuja** monastery (A381, km4, 956 15 64 65), founded in the 15th century, and one of the most architecturally and artistically important buildings in the province. Its highlight is a stunning baroque façade added two centuries later, with sculptures by Alonso Cano among others. The interior of the monastery is closed to the public, but it's worth a look at from the outside.

Alcázar de Jerez

C/Alameda Vieja s/n (956 32 69 23). **Open** *May-mid June* 10am-7.30pm Mon-Sat; 10am-2.30pm Sun. *Mid June-Apr* 10am-6pm Mon-Sat; 10am-2.30pm Sun. **Admission** *Alcázar* €3; €1.80 concessions. *Alcázar & camera obscura* €5.40; €4.20 concessions. **No credit cards. Map** p141 B3.

Bodegas González-Byass

C/Manuel María González 12 (956 35 70 16/www.gonzalezbyass.es). **Tours** (in English) *July, Aug* 11.30am, 12.30pm, 1.30pm, 4.30pm, 5.30pm, 6.30pm daily; tour with tapas 2pm daily. *Sept-June* 11.30am, 12.30pm, 1.30pm, 3.30pm, 4.30pm, 5.30pm daily; tour with tapas 2pm daily. **Admission** €9. *Tour with tapas* €14. **Credit** AmEx, DC, MC, V. **Map** p141 A/B3.

Bodegas Domecq

C/San Idelfonso 3 (956 15 15 00/www.domecq.es). **Tours** 11am, noon, 1pm Mon, Wed; 11am, noon, 1pm, 2pm Tue, Thur, Fri; noon, 2pm Sat. **Admission** €7-€11. **Credit** MC, V. **Map** p141 A3.

Bodegas Sandeman

C/Pizarro 10 (956 15 17 00/reservations 956 31 29 95/www.sandeman.com). **Open** *Mid Mar-Oct* 10am-5.30pm Mon-Fri. *Nov-mid Mar* 10am-3pm Mon-Fri. **Tours** *Mid Mar-Oct* 10.30am, noon, 1pm, 2pm, 3.30pm Mon-Fri; selected weekends (call to check). *Nov-mid Mar* 10.30am, noon, 1pm, 2pm Mon-Fri. **Admission** *Standard tour* €6; free under-12s. *Special tours* €16. **Credit** AmEx, DC, MC, V. **Map** p141 B1.

Catedral de San Salvador

Plaza de la Encarnación 3 (956 34 84 82). **Open** 11am-1pm Mon-Fri. **Admission** free. **Map** p141 B3.

Centro Andaluz de Flamenco

Plaza San Juan 1 (956 34 92 65/http://caf.cica.es). **Open** 9am-2pm Mon-Fri. **Admission** free. **Map** p141 B2.

Centro Temático La Atalaya

C/Cervantes 3 (956 18 21 00/www.elmisteriodejerez.org). **Open** *Mar-Oct* 10am-2pm, 6-7pm Tue-Sat; 10am-2pm Sun. *Nov-Feb* 10am-2pm Tue-Sat; 10am-2pm Sun. **Admission** *Palacio del Tiempo only* €6; €3 concessions. *Combined ticket* €9; €4.50 concessions. **Credit** MC, V. **Map** p141 B1.

Parque Zoológico

C/Taxdirt s/n (956 15 31 64). **Open** *June-Sept* 10am-8pm daily. *Oct-May* 10am-6pm Tue-Sun. **Admission** €6.30; €4.10 concessions. **Credit** MC, V. **Map** p141 off A1.

Where to eat & drink

The streets off Plaza del Arenal are home to some terrific tapas bars, particularly

Finger-clickin' good

Flamenco in Jerez is far less commercialised than elsewhere in Andalucía, and there are none of the big tourist flamenco shows you'll find in Seville and Córdoba. The best place to find flamenco is in the gypsy quarter, the Barrio de Santiago, which is full of *peñas* (semi-private flamenco clubs), some for *socios* (members) and some you can walk into off the street. The central section of the old quarter near Plaza Belén is earmarked to become a '*barrio de flamenco*', a move that will transform the town when completed.

The nature of the art is such that there are no set times or programmes: if someone is feeling particularly melancholic (or drunk), he (it is always he) may break into song. If someone else feels like dancing, he or she may get up and do a few turns. True flamenco is not about castanets and bright dresses, it's about smoky bars, a single guitar and tales of woe.

A full list of *peñas* and a map are available from the tourist office; some of the better-known ones are listed below. Authentic *peñas* don't have regular hours and often don't charge admission. Shows move between a district's different *peñas* on a monthly basis. Your best chance of catching a performance is at around 10pm on a Friday or Saturday night, but ring beforehand to check what's on. Another way to catch some quality flamenco is to visit during the month-long flamenco festival in September.

La Buena Gente

Plaza de San Lucas 9 (956 33 84 04). Closed July-Sept. **Map** p141 A2.

Don Antonio Chacón

C/Salas 12 (956 34 74 72). Closed July-Sept. **Map** p141 A2.

This is more of a cultural centre, which has weekly renditions on a Saturday.

El Garbanzo

C/Santa Clara 9 (no phone). Closed July-Sept. **Map** p141 off C3.

El Lagá de Tío Parrilla

Plaza del Mercado s/n (956 33 83 34). **Open** 8pm-late Mon-Sat. **Shows** 10.30pm. **Admission** (incl first drink) €15. **Credit** DC, MC, V. **Map** p141 A2.

Tourist venue next to the archaeological museum, with daily shows and a restaurant.

La Taberna Flamenca

C/Angostillo de Santiago 3 (956 32 36 93/mobile 649 38 39 78/www.latabernaflamenca.com). **Open** *June-Oct* 1.30-4pm, 8pm-midnight daily. *Nov-May* 1.30-4pm, 8pm-midnight Tue-Sat. Shows 2.30pm, 10.30pm Tue-Sat. **Admission** (incl 2 drinks) €15; (incl meal & drink) €35. **No credit cards**. **Map** p141 A1.

Perhaps the most touristy of the venues, with frequent shows and a restaurant attached.

Tío José de Paula

C/Merced 11 (956 32 01 96). Closed July-Sept. **Map** p141 A1/2.

C/Pescadería Vieja (a covered passageway, leading off to the north-west). For bars, try the streets around Avenida Domecq, particularly Calles Divina Pastora, Cádiz and Paul, and the area around the bullring. A hidden gem is **Bereber**, just off Plaza del Mercado in the Barrio de Santiago, a classy bar that boasts a beautiful courtyard setting, ideal for those hot summer nights (C/Cabezas 10, 956 34 42 46, open 4.30pm-late, map p141 A2 ❶).

Bar Juanito

C/Pescadería Vieja 8 & 10 (956 33 48 38). **Open** 1-5pm, 8.30-11.30pm daily. **Average** €€. **Credit** AmEx, DC, MC, V. **Map** p141 B3 ❷

The best tapas bar in town, Juanito has an enormous selection of tapas and *raciones*, including *alcachofas en salsa* (artichokes in sauce) and *costillas* (ribs).

Cafeteria Arenal 15

Plaza Arenal 15 (956 34 79 79/www.arenal15.com). **Open** 8am-midnight Mon-Fri; 8am-1am Sat.

Average €. **Credit** AmEx, DC, MC, V. **Map** p141 B/C3 ❸
This is a popular terrace restaurant offering award-winning tapas, including good seafood.

La Carboná

C/San Francisco de Paula 2 (956 34 74 75). **Open** 12.30-4.30pm, 8pm-12.30am Mon, Wed-Sun. **Average** €€. **Credit** AmEx, DC, MC, V. **Map** p141 off C3.
A barn of a place, set in an old *bodega*. Specialises in generous portions of barbecued fish and meat.

Gaitán

C/Gaitán 3 (956 34 58 59/www.restaurantegaitan.com). **Open** 1-4.30pm, 8.30-11.30pm Mon-Sat. **Average** €€. **Credit** AmEx, DC, MC, V. **Map** p141 B1 ❹
Popular with locals after Andalucian and Basque specialities at a decent price. It's chaotic but homely, and the waiters all seem to be over 100 years old.

El Marqués

Corner of C/Pizarro & Pozo del Olivar (956 03 15 00). **Open** 1.30-3.30pm, 8-11.30pm daily. **Average** €€€-€€€€. **Credit** AmEx, DC, MC, V. **Map** p141 B1 ❺
Close to the riding school and part of the Hotel Prestige-Palmera Plaza (*see below*), this suberb restaurant is housed in a grand restored *bodega*.

La Mesa Redonda

C/Manuel de Quintana 3 (956 34 00 69). **Open** 1.30-4pm, 9-11.30pm Mon-Sat. Closed mid July mid Aug. **Average** €€€-€€€€. **Credit** AmEx, DC, MC, V. **Map** p141 off C1.
Contender for best place in town. The interior is full of old furniture and paintings; you imagine youself in a private *palacio*. The constantly changing menu includes innovative dishes using shark, oxtail and stewed veal tongue. Press the buzzer to be let into the residential complex in which it's located.

Taberna Marinera

Plaza Rivero 2 (956 33 44 27). **Open** *Sept-mid June* noon-4pm, 8pm-midnight daily. *Mid June-Aug* 7.30pm-1.30am daily.**Average** €€. **Credit** AmEx, MC, V. **Map** p141 B2 ❻
A tiny place selling *embutidos* and good red wines in a pleasant square with several other decent bars. Try *bacalao ahumado* (smoked cod) with *salmorejo*.

Shopping

The main shopping area is pedestrianised C/Larga and the streets around it, including C/Honda and C/San Francisco, which fronts the main market. C/Porvera and the streets off it are better for smaller shops selling the likes of flamenco dresses and horse-related items.

The best place to buy sherry, *catavinos* (sherry glasses) and *venencias* (the long-handled things the pros use to pour), are the shops in the *bodegas*. There is a *rastro* (street market) in Plaza del Mercado on Sunday mornings.

Where to stay

Jerez is well served with hotels for all budgets, although rooms are scarce during the Horse Fair in May and the motorcycle championship. Many of the top hotels are located north-east of the town centre, around Avenida Alvaro Domecq. For the cheapest *hostales*, try Calles Morenos, Arcos and Higueras.

El Ancla

Plaza Mamelón s/n (956 32 12 97/www.helancla.com). **Rates** €30-€75 single; €45-€130 double. **Credit** MC, V. **Map** p141 C1 ❼
A good spot and good prices for simple, comfortable rooms. The pleasant café below has tables on the square and opens late.

Doña Blanca

C/Bodegas 11 (956 34 87 61/www.hoteldonablanca.com). **Rates** €63-€125 single; €80-€161 double. **Credit** AmEx, DC, MC, V. **Map** p141 C3 ❽
Probably the best hotel in the town centre, with 30 smart clean rooms, friendly service, a garage and satellite TV. The hotel was renovated in 2006.

Guadalete

Avda del Duque de Abrantes 50 (956 18 22 88/www.hotelguadalete.com). **Rates** €70 single; €83-€107 double; €242-€364 suite. **Credit** AmEx, DC, MC, V. **Map** p141 off B1.
The Guadalete's rooms are comfortable and of a decent size, and there's an outdoor pool and a decent restaurant. Good value for the quality, but a bit of a trek from the centre.

Hotel La Albarizuela

C/Honsario 6 (956 34 68 62/www.hotelalbarizuela.com). **Rates** €61-€106 single; €106-€150 double. **Credit** DC, MC, V. **Map** p141 off C2.
An ultra-modern three-star lacking in frills and furbelows, but clean and comfortable, with a café downstairs. The same people own the Hotel Trujillo (*see below*).

Hotel Prestige-Palmera Plaza

C/Pizarro 1 (956 03 15 00/www.palmeraplaza.com). **Rates** €112-€263 single; €128-€383 double; €197-€464 suite. **Credit** AmEx, MC, V. **Map** p141 off B1.
A five-star hotel north-east of the centre, with comfortable, understated rooms, most with balconies and large marble bathrooms, in a serene setting. Facilities include a pool, gym and sauna, as well as the 'Ask Me' information officers for all the latest and hippest things to do in the city.

Hotel Trujillo

C/Medina 36 (956 34 24 38/www.hoteltrujillo.com). **Rates** €25-€53.50 single; €51-€80 double. **Credit** DC, MC, V. **Map** p141 off C3.
Hotel Trujillo is the cheaper sister hotel of the Albarizuela (*see above*), and just as spick and span. Each of the 27 rooms are en suite and have TV and air-conditioning.

Hotel Villa Jerez

Avda de la Cruz Roja 7 (956 15 31 00/www.villa jerez.com). **Rates** €120-€190 single; €150-€240 double; €200-€360 junior suite; €540 suite. **Credit** AmEx, DC, MC, V. **Map** p141 off B1.

More luxurious than its five-star sister further out of town, this hotel has lush gardens, pool and gym.

Monte Castillo

A382, km9.6 (956 15 12 00/www.montecastillo. com). **Rates** (incl breakfast) €118-€315 single; €139-€330 double; €600-€1,065 suite. **Credit** AmEx, DC, MC, V.

With its own training ground inside the resort, this is where Manchester United choose to stay when they come to Jerez to train. If you are after unabashed luxury in an idyllic setting and you are a golf fan with very deep pockets, then this five-star joint is definitely the place for you. Well out of town.

Royal Sherry Park

Avda Alvaro Domecq 11 (956 31 76 14/www. hipotels.com). **Rates** €80-€268 single; €119-€268 double; €268-€352 suite. **Credit** AmEx, DC, MC, V. **Map** p141 off C1.

Modern and comfortable, this large and functional hotel has as its selling point wonderful indoor and outdoor pools. The buffet breakfast is also worth a mention.

San Andrés

C/Morenos 12-14 (956 34 09 83/www.hotelsan andres.com). **Rates** €18-€38 single; €25-€50 double. **Credit** DC, MC, V. **Map** p141 C2 ⑨

A pleasant, friendly place with a lovely leafy patio and clean simple rooms. The more expensive rooms have en suite facilities.

Serit

C/Higueras 7 (956 34 07 00/www.hotelserit.com). **Rates** €49-€96 single; €60-€128 double. **Credit** AmEx, DC, MC, V. **Map** p141 C3 ⑩

The Serit enjoys an excellent town-centre location, and offers quiet, comfortable and very reasonably priced rooms; those on the upper floors are lighter and roomier.

Resources

Internet

Conexion.net *Avda Lola Flores 6 (956 08 64 93).* **Open** 10am-2pm, 6-9pm Mon-Sat.

Police station

Avda de la Comedia s/n (956 35 99 00).

Post office

C/Cerrón 2 (956 32 67 29). **Map** p141 C3.

Tourist information

Edificio los Claustros, Alameda Cristina s/n (956 32 47 47/www.turismojerez.com). **Open** *Mid June-mid Sept* 10am-3pm, 5-7pm Mon-Fri; 10am-2.30pm Sat, Sun. *Mid Sept-mid June* 9.30am-2.30pm, 4.30-6.30pm Mon-Fri; 10am-2.30pm Sat, Sun. **Map** p141 B3.

Sanlúcar de Barrameda

In his book, *Inside Andalusia*, David Baird describes **Sanlúcar de Barrameda** as having the 'seedy demeanour of a colony in the tropics left behind by the *Conquistadores*' – and that's its appeal. This sizeable seaside town, 22 kilometres (14 miles) north-west of Jerez, is famed for its *manzanilla*, the lightest and driest of all sherries, which supposedly has a salty tang imparted by the sea breezes – it's a perfect accompaniment to the seafood for which the place is also known. Sanlúcar is agreeably sleepy outside high season, with a distinctive atmosphere and a crumbling charm, largely untouched by foreign tourism.

Sanlúcar has an illustrious history as one of the most important ports in the region, situated as it is on the mouth of the Guadalquivir. Magellan set sail from, and returned to, Sanlúcar on his round-the-world voyage; Columbus launched his second Indies voyage and third Americas trip from here in 1498; Francisco Pacheco, Velázquez's mentor and teacher, was born in Sanlúcar, and the town was the main base of the powerful Dukes of Medina Sidonia (the current Duchess still lives here).

Today, Sanlúcar is split into two main districts: the **Barrio Alto**, the old town on the hill, and the **Barrio Bajo** below it, leading down to the port area of the **Bajo de Guía**, a 15-minute walk from the Barrio Alto. All the sights are within the old town, the focus of which is the tapas bar-strewn Plaza Cabildo. C/Ancha, which crosses the top of the square and leads west into C/San Juan, is the town's main shopping street. At the end of the eastern end of C/Ancha are three churches: 16th-century **Santo Domingo**, **San Francisco**, built in the 17th century by the Dukes of Medina Sidonia, and **San Nicolás**.

South of here, up the hill, a flight of steps (Carril de Los Angeles) leads to the crumbling 15th-century **Castillo de Santiago**. Opposite the castle is the town's largest sherry maker, **Barbadillo** (founded in 1821). The company accounts for three quarters of all *manzanilla* production, and also makes Castillo de San Diego white wine from the same grape. You can visit the *bodega* (and several of the smaller producers, too – ask at the tourist office for a list), though reservations should be made in advance. Barbadillo recently opened a museum.

From the *bodega*, C/Sevilla leads into C/Luis Eguilaz and Sanlúcar's oldest church, **Nuestra Señora de la O** (open hours of services). Dating from the 14th century, it has an impressive Gothic façade and a 16th-century Mudéjar doorway. Beside it is the **Palacio de**

Bring on the dancing horses

Real Escuela Andaluz del Arte Ecuestre (Royal School of Equestrian Arts) is a town within a town; as important a cultural icon to the people of Jerez as the Giralda in Seville, or the Alhambra in Granada. Housed in a network of cathedral-like barns with vaulted ceilings, cobbles and the city's trademark buttercup-yellow paintwork, it has a theatrical air straight out of Dickens – entirely fitting for a school that teaches horses to dance and for a people with anglophile leanings.

You can visit the stables, saddlery and museum, but the world-famous dancing horses show is the focus. This is split into six or eight parts and lasts for an hour and a half, with a break. For some, it's sublime; for others, it is entirely unnatural.

Horses have poor memories and it takes them four years to learn the steps, skips and jumps they perform to classical music. While it's more cha-cha-cha than *Swan Lake*, the choreography of the show – called *Cómo Bailan Los Caballos Andaluces* (How the Horses of Andalucía Dance) – is still an astonishing spectacle that incorporates moves from the *doma vaquera* and *doma classica* (cowboy and classical dressage) styles, and a Puck-like equine leap whereby the horse throws its fore and hind legs out into mid-air and hovers momentarily before landing gracefully back on solid earth. All this performed by riders in 18th-century dress to the rhythmic clap of flamenco and moody piano music.

Of course this isn't the stuff of any old riding-school nag, and the *cartujano* horses in the lead roles have maintained 100 per cent of the characteristics that make them *pura raza española* (pure Spanish breed). Directly descended from a lineage established in the 15th century by monks at La Cartuja – a cross between the Andalucían horse, dating back to around 20 BC, and Arab and Berber horses brought over by the Moors – the resulting breed is a regal creature revered for its elegant gait, nimble hooves and apparent willingness to goose-step, head held high and tail aloft. The more famous Lippizaners of the Vienna Spanish Riding School are direct descendants of the *cartujano*.

Real Escuela Andaluz del Arte Ecuestre

Avda Duque de Abrantes s/n (956 31 96 35/ www.realescuela.org). **Open** *Guided tours* Mar-Oct 10am-1pm Mon, Wed, Fri; Nov-Feb 10am-1pm Mon-Wed, Fri. *Shows* Mar-July, Sept, Oct noon Tue, Thur; Aug noon Tue, Thur, Fri; Nov-Feb noon Thur. **Admission** *Tour* (see website for details) €3-€8; €2-€5 concs. *Show* €17-€23; €10.50-€14 concessions. **Credit** AmEx, MC, V. **Map** p141 off B1.

Chipiona. See p147.

los Duques de Medina Sidonia, a 16th-century pile that is still inhabited by the current bearer of the title, a duchess known locally as the Red Duchess for her campaigning on behalf of the very people her ancestors used to oppress. The building contains extensive archives (including a huge amount of documentation relating to the Spanish Armada) and is home to a number of valuable works of art, including some paintings by Goya.

Opposite the church is a very pretty square, Plaza de la Paz. Just west of here, on the corner of C/Caballeros and Cuesta de Belén, the Ayuntamiento (Town Hall) is in another palace, the **Palacio de Orleáns y Borbón**. This 19th-century neo-Moorish building with a curious Swiss-style chalet in the courtyard was the ducal home of the Montpensier family; you are free to wander around the public areas, which include a small park and patio (ask at the tourist office for details of more extensive tours).

The town market, off the Plaza del Roque, is one of the finest in the whole of Andalucía, with an enormous variety of local seafood and fresh vegetables on sale.

Sanlúcar is one of the main gateways into the wild and remote **Parque Nacional de Doñana**, just across the estuary. Four-hour tours can be arranged via the park visitors' centre (*see below*); they include a stop at an old village within the park, at a hide where you can spot birds (and if you're lucky, deer and wild boar), and at the salt flats where flamingoes congregate. For more information on the park, and for points of entry in Huelva province, *see p119* **Coto Doñana**.

Barbadillo

C/Luis Eguilaz 11 (956 38 55 00/www.barbadillo.com). **Open** *Museum* 11am-3pm Mon-Sat. *Tours* (in English) 11am. **Admission** €3. **Credit** AmEx, DC, MC, V.

Castillo de Santiago

C/Cava de Castillo s/n (no phone). **Open** 10am-3pm, 7-10pm daily. **Admission** €7. **No credit cards.**

Palacio de los Duques de Medina Sidonia

Plaza Condes de Niebla 1 (956 36 01 61). **Open** (guided tours only) 11am, noon Sun. **Admission** €3. **No credit cards.**

Palacio de Orleáns y Borbón

Cuesta de Belén s/n (956 38 80 00). **Open** 8am-2.30pm Mon-Fri. **Admission** free.

Where to eat & drink

The restaurants of Bajo de Guía, the old fishing district by the beach, which are widely regarded as some of the best in Andalucía, while the tapas bars on the central Plaza Cabildo and, indeed, throughout the town, are almost all first-rate. In the old fishing quarter, one of the most celebrated is **Casa Bigote** (Bajo de Guía s/n, 956 36 26 96, closed Sun and all Nov, €€€-€€€€), a shrine to squeakily fresh seafood, which is delivered daily from the nearby port of Bonanza. The same management runs a cheaper tapas bar next door. The other big name in the area is **Mirador de Doñana** (Bajo de Guía s/n, 956 36 42 05, closed mid Jan-mid Feb, €€€), where the speciality is known as *mi barca mirador*, a white fish in tomato sauce; wonderful *cigalas* (crayfish), *chocos* (cuttlefish) and *angulas* (eels) are also served, and there's a good tapas bar attached. Both places have fine views over the water to the Doñana.

Other worthwhile restaurants here are **Marisquería Poma** (Bajo de Guía 6, 956 36 51 53, closed Jan, €€€-€€€€) and **Joselito Huerta** (Bajo de Guía 30, 956 36 26 94, closed Mon & all Nov, €€), favoured by locals, with fine views from the upstairs dining room.

Around Plaza Cabildo, the star tapas bar is undoubtedly **Casa Balbino** (Plaza del Cabildo 14, 956 36 26 47, closed Jan, €€), which has a dauntingly long menu. House specials include *ortiguillas* (sea anemones) and *langostinos* (langoustines). There are plenty of other good places for sampling tapas in the immediate area – just follow your nose.

Where to stay

Sanlúcar has few hotels, and none over three stars. In summer it's almost impossible to find anywhere to stay, so book ahead. The nicest hotel is the three-star **Los Helechos** (Plaza Madre de Dios 9, 956 36 13 49, www.hotellos helechos.com, double €47-€67), with large, airy rooms and a delightful plant-filled patio. Also good is the atmospheric two-star **Posada del Palacio** (C/Caballero 11, 956 36 48 40, double €86-€107), opposite the town hall. The modern, comfortable **Hotel Doñana** (C/Orfeón Santa Cecilia s/n, 956 36 50 00, www.partner-hotels.com, double €66-€112) is well placed for the beach and restaurants by the old port. You can't miss the **Hotel Guadalquivir** (Calzada del Ejército 20, 956 36 07 42, double €55-€101, towering over the main square. The location's great, but it's rather characterless inside. Of the cheaper places, **Pensión La Bohemia** (C/Don Claudio 5, 956 36 95 99, double €35-€40) is in a quiet street in the old town; it's not well signed so you'll have to hunt it out. Even more basic, **Pensión Blanca Paloma** (Plaza de San Roque 15, 956 36 36 44, double €30) is in a good location, off lively Plaza Cabildo.

Resources

Internet

Cyber Guadalquivir, C/Infanta Beatriz 11 (956 36 74 03). **Open** 10am-12.30am Mon-Sat; noon-12.30am Sun. **Credit** MC, V.

Tourist information

Calzada del Ejército s/n (956 36 61 10/www.turismo sanlucar.com). **Open** *Mar-May, Oct, Nov* 10am-2pm, 5-7pm daily. *June-Sept* 10am-2pm, 6-8pm daily. *Dec-Feb* 10am-2pm, 4-6pm daily.

Centro de Visitantes de Doñana Fabrica de Hielo, Avda Bajo de Guía s/n (956 38 16 35/www.parque nacionaldonana.es). **Open** *Apr-Oct* 9am-8pm daily. *Nov-Mar* 9am-7pm daily. **Tickets** (for boat) €15.50; €7.50 concessions. **Credit** MC, V.

Chipiona & Rota

Nine kilometres (six miles) west of Sanlúcar is the pleasant seaside town of **Chipiona**, which makes a nice stop if you're after a few days lazing on the beach. Its 69-metre (226-foot) lighthouse (*faro*) is the tallest in Spain and the third highest in the world; on clear nights its beam can be seen from the coast of Portugal. If you're feeling fit you can climb the 344 steps (enquire at the tourist office about guided tours in English and for opening times).

There is little else to detain you in the way of sights, but the town does have a lovely old quarter of winding streets and shaded *plazas*. One such is Plaza de Juan Carlos, which is home to one of the prettiest buildings in town, the 16th-century **Parroquia de Nuestra Señora de la O** (Plaza San Carlos I s/n, 956 37 01 02, open hours of services). The 14th-century former monastery of **Nuestra Señora de Regla** (Paseo Costa de la Luz s/n, no phone, open 8am-noon, 5-7pm daily) is at the far end of the main beach, Playa de Regla. Chipiona's castle is undergoing long-term restoration work and is closed indefinitely.

Chipiona's real draw is its beaches – 12 kilometres (7.5 miles) of clean golden sand. The best is **Playa de Regla**, which gets very crowded in summer. For more peace, try **Playas Cruz del Mar** or **Las Canteras**. The once pristine stretch of coast between Chipiona and Rota has been dubbed the Costa Ballena (Whale Coast, despite there being none) and is currently disappearing under a sea of concrete and characterless five-star hotels and golf courses.

Rota's main claim to fame is as the site of one of the US's largest military bases in Spain. Franco, desperate for aid and keen to improve Spain's standing in the eyes of the rest of the world, gave the US a large chunk of land along this coast during the 1950s in return for financial help. The town (17 kilometres/11 miles south of Sanlúcar and Chipiona) has some lovely beaches, including an EU blue-flagged one, the **Playa de la Costilla**, and a large marina, but little charm. The main sight is the oft-restored Moorish **Castillo de Luna**, which houses the tourist office. The castle dates from the 12th century; its centrepiece is a very pretty patio with a fountain and a covered balcony. The 16th-century **Nuestra Señora de la O** (Plaza Bartolomé Pérez s/n, open hours of services) is a mix of architectural styles – Gothic, Plateresque and baroque.

Castillo de Luna

C/Cuna 2, Rota (956 84 63 45). **Open** *July-Sept* 9.30am-1.30pm, 5.30-8.30pm Mon-Fri; 10am-2pm, 6-9pm Sat, Sun. *Oct-June* 9.30am-1.30pm, 5-7.30pm Mon-Fri; 10am-2pm, 5-8pm Sat, Sun. **Admission** free.

Where to stay, eat & drink

Chipiona is bursting with *pensiones* and *hostales*. The only time you may find it difficult to find somewhere to stay is in summer. The best mid-priced option is the spotless, spacious **La Española** (C/Isaac Peral 4-6, 956 37 37 71, www.hotellaespanola.com, double €50-€60) – many of its rooms have sea views. The modest **Hostal Gran Capitán** (C/Fray Baldomero González 3-7, 956 37 09 29, closed Nov-Feb, double €36-€60) dates from the 1500s and was once the family home of El Gran Capitán, the Catholic monarchs' famed military commander.

Chipiona is not known for its restaurants. Perhaps the best is **Paco** (Puerto Deportivo, 956 37 46 64, closed Tue Oct-May and all Nov, €€), which draws customers – despite being badly signed and out of the way in the sailing marina – with seafood so fresh that a menu isn't deemed necessary or practical. **La Pañueleta** (C/Isaac Peral 4-6, 956 37 37 71, €) is another reasonable choice, offering a good selection of local fish in pleasant surroundings. **Peña Bética** (C/Larga 46, 956 37 43 44, €) is popular with local families and supporters of Real Betis, on which the decor is based. The food is simple, tasty and excellent value.

There are also numerous beach bars. Chipiona's nightlife takes place along Paseo Costa de la Luz and C/Tolosa Latour.

By far the best place to stay in Rota, in a prime location just off the beach, is the stylish four-star **Hotel Duque de Najera** (C/Gravina 2, 956 84 60 20, www.hotelduquedenajera.com, double €129-€185), which has a pool. Relatively new on the scene is the charming *hostal-restaurante* **Sixto** (Plaza Barroso 6, 956 84 63 10, double €65-€85, restaurant €), on a quiet square.

For food and drink in Rota, the best places are the restaurants on C/Mina. **Bodegon la Mina** (C/Mina 27, 956 81 62 97, €) is a friendly venue offering typical local dishes and occasionally hosting flamenco and jazz shows; try the *arrenque roteno* (a dry version of *gazpacho*). In high season, late-night drinking and dancing can be found along the Mirador de las Almenas, which flanks the Playa del Rompidillo.

Resources

Tourist information

Chipiona *C/Juan Carlos I 1-3 (956 37 72 63/www.chipiona.org).* **Open** *June-Sept* 8am-2pm, 6-8pm Mon-Fri; 11am-1.30pm Sat, Sun. *Oct-May* 8am-3pm, 5-7pm Mon-Fri; 11am-1.30pm Sat.

Rota *Castillo de la Luna, C/Cuna 2 (956 84 63 45/www.turismorota.com).* **Open** *July-Sept* 9.30am-1.30pm, 5.30-8.30pm Mon-Fri; 10am-2pm, 6-9pm Sat, Sun. *Oct-June* 9.30am-1.30pm, 5-7.30pm Mon-Fri; 10am-2pm, 5-8pm Sat, Sun.

El Puerto de Santa María

Midway between Cádiz and Jerez lies the third town in the 'sherry triangle'. **El Puerto de Santa María**, famed for its seafood, is something of a hidden gem, where foreign (though not Spanish) tourists are a rare sight. The town is set on the bay at the mouth of the Río Guadalete and surrounded by pretty beaches, and, though it has been marred by a lot of ugly modern development, its old quarter is an enchanting grid of streets running back from the waterfront, packed with restaurants, tapas bars and *bodegas*.

If you arrive by the *vapor* boat from Cádiz, you'll disembark by a riverside street, the Ribera del Marisco, directly opposite **El Fuente de las Galeras**, an 18th-century fountain with six spouts, which used to supply ships bound for the Americas with water. The old town stretches back from here. C/Luna leads west past the tourist office up to Plaza de España and the **Iglesia Mayor Prioral**. The church dates from the 15th century and was rebuilt in the 17th. Inside, it houses the effigy of the patron saint of the town, the Virgen de los Milagros.

On the other side of the square is the **Museo Municipal**, which contains a few archaeological remains, mainly dating from the palaeolithic era. C/Santa Lucía runs from Plaza de España to El Puerto's **Plaza de Toros**, the third-largest bullring in Spain after those of Madrid and Seville, and one revered by fans. From C/Santa Lucía, C/Federico Rubio leads towards the river, past the heavily restored 13th-century **Castillo de San Marcos**. Built on the site of a mosque and watchtower by Alfonso X (the Wise), the castle is well worth a look – particularly the pretty Mudéjar church inside.

The streets behind the castle contain a number of *palacios* left over from when the great sherry barons virtually ruled the town. Some are in a dreadful state of disrepair and are closed, others are being turned into hotels or smart apartments and some can be visited – the main ones being **Terry**, **501** and the biggest producer of Spanish brandy, **Osborne**.

Bodega Terry

C/Toneleros s/n (956 85 77 00). **Open** *Guided tour only* Apr-Sept 10am, noon Mon-Fri; noon Sat. Oct-Mar 10am, noon Mon-Fri. *Guided tour with tasting & show* (July-Sept only) 11am Wed, Fri, Sat. **Admission** *Guided tour* €6.50; free under-12s. **Credit** AmEx, DC, MC, V.

Bodega El Tiro

A4, km651 (956 85 42 28/www.osborne.es). **Open** 10.30am-1.30pm Mon-Fri. *Guided tours* (in English) 11.30am Mon-Fri. **Admission** €5; €1.50 concessions; free under-10s. **No credit cards**.

Bodegas 501 del Puerto

C/Valdés 9 (956 85 55 11/www.bodegas501.com). **Open** *Guided tour* noon Mon-Fri. **Admission** €4; free under-15s. **Credit** AmEx, MC, V.

Bodegas Osborne

Sherry Bodega de Mora, C/Los Moros s/n (956 86 91 00/www.osborne.es). **Open** *Guided tours* (in English) 10.30am Mon-Fri. **Admission** €5.50. **No credit cards**.

Castillo de San Marcos

C/Alfonso X el Sabio s/n (956 85 17 51). **Open** *July-Sept* 10am-2pm Tue-Sun. *Oct-June* 11am-2pm Tue, Thur, Sat. **Admission** €5; €2 concessions. **No credit cards**.

Museo Municipal

C/Pagador 1 (956 54 27 05). **Open** 10am-2pm Tue-Fri; 10.45am-2pm Sat, Sun. **Admission** free.

Plaza de Toros

956 54 15 78. **Open** 11am-1.30pm, 6-7.30pm Tue-Sun, except the day before & after a *corrida*. **Admission** *Corrida* phone for details; other times free.

Where to eat & drink

There are an enormous number of restaurants and tapas bars in El Puerto, most of them specialising in seafood that comes fresh from the bay. Most of them are superb. Many can be found along the riverside Ribera del Marisco and the lanes running off it. The king of them all, and quite possibly the finest seafood restaurant in Andalucía, is **El Faro del Puerto** (Ctra de Fuentebravía, km0.5, 956 87 09 52, www.elfarodelpuerto.com, closed dinner Sun, €€€€) – presentation is exquisite, preparation is innovative and the ingredients are of the highest quality. **Casa Flores** (C/Ribera del Río 9, 956 54 35 12, www.casaflores.com, €€€-€€€€) is another exemplary restaurant, again one of the best in the province, with a beautiful tiled interior and the freshest seafood. There is yet one more contender for El Puerto's culinary crown: **Los Portales** (C/Ribera del Río 13, 956 54 21 16, www.losportales.com, €€€-€€€€). Here you can expect more great seafood, with two *menús gastronomicos*. Far simpler, but equally famous, is **El Romerijo** (C/Jose Antonio Romero Zarazaga, 956 54 12 54, www.romerijo.com, €€-€€€). It serves fine, simple seafood at keen prices. Many locals buy their *gambas* (prawns) at the takeaway counter and then still eat at one of the restaurant's many tables.

For drinking, C/Micaela Aramburu is packed with pubs and bars, while for later-night action, head towards the bars and discos along the **Playa Santa Catalina** in the Vistahermosa district, west of the centre (take a cab), popular with a young, trendy Spanish crowd, and without a tourist in sight.

Where to stay

The beautiful five-star **Hotel Duques de Medinaceli** (Plaza de los Jazmines 2, 956 86 07 77, www.jale.com/dmedinaceli, double €166-€193) is a stunning 17th-century mansion that was once home to the Irish Terry family, famous for their sherry and brandy. It contains a botanical garden, a swimming pool and a first-class restaurant. Also recommended is the sumptuous four-star **Monasterio San Miguel** (C/Virgen de los Milagros 27, 956 54 04 40, www.jale.com/monasterio, double €151-€184), set in a 16th-century monastery, with a good restaurant and pool. Another fine place is the three-star **Los Cántaros** (C/Curva 6, 956 54 02 40, www.hotelloscantaros.com, double €75-€127). Located off pretty Ribera del Marisco, it has a bar and parking spaces.

Resources

Internet

Ciberbar, C/Aitana s/n (956 85 67 03). **Open** 10.30am-10.30pm daily.

Tourist information

C/Luna 22 (956 54 24 13/www.turismoelpuerto.com). **Open** *May-Sept* 10am-2pm, 6-8pm daily. *Oct-Mar* 10am-2pm, 5.30-7.30pm daily.

Getting there

By air

Jerez airport (information 956 15 00 00) is located 7km (4 miles) north-east of the town, off the A4 and AP4.

By boat

El Vapor (mobile 629 468 014) runs across from Cádiz to El Puerto several times daily. The journey takes around 45mins.

By bus

There are numerous daily bus services between Cádiz, El Puerto, Rota, Chipiona, Sanlúcar, Jerez, carrying on to Arcos and Seville. The major operating companies are Comes (956 80 70 59, 902 19 92 08), Linesur (also known as La Valenciana, 956 34 10 63, www.linesur.com) and Los Amarillos (956 38 50 60). The bus station in Jerez (956 33 96 66) is on Plaza de la Estación. In Sanlúcar, Linesur buses (to and from Jerez) leave from C/Herman Fermín, which is near the tourist office; Los Amarillos services go from Plaza de la Salle (they serve Chipiona, Cádiz and Seville). In El Puerto the buses stop at the bullring.

By train

Jerez and El Puerto are 10mins apart by train; services between Cádiz and Seville (around 15 per day) stop at both towns. It's about 30mins from El Puerto to Cádiz, and around 1hr 20mins from Jerez to Seville. Jerez's train station (956 33 48 13) is on the east side of the city on Plaza de la Estación, at the end of C/Cartuja. El Puerto's station is on the north side of town, a ten-minute walk from the old town.

East of Cádiz

Drive out among the white villages and into the wilds.

Arcos de la Frontera

Arrayed along a long, narrow strip of sheer cliff (*la peña*) overlooking the fertile Guadalete valley, 30 kilometres (19 miles) east of Jerez, Arcos de la Frontera is one of the most spectacular of the *pueblos blancos*.

There was an early Celtic settlement here, and during the Roman period a garrison post known as Arcos Briga was established on the easily defended plateau. During the Moorish period the town grew considerably and even briefly became an independent kingdom; all that remains from this time is the 11th-century castle. Arcos held out against the Christians until 1250 and, after its defeat, took the 'de la Frontera' appellation.

The historic part of the town, the *barrio antiguo*, stretches from the Cuesta de Belén to the Puerta de Matrera; it was declared a national monument in 1962. At its heart is the pretty **Plaza del Cabildo**, the cobbled main square that unpicturesquely doubles as a car park. To one side of the square stands the castle, rebuilt by the Christians in the 15th century (it is now privately owned and not open to the public). On its southern side is a *mirador* from where there are the best views along the cliff face. Look down and you'll see evidence of a recent rockfall that left the restaurant of the next-door *parador* hanging in space. The *parador* terrace (now safely underpinned) is a wonderful place for a sundowner and for watching the wheeling kestrels and choughs.

On the square's north-west side, the church of **Santa María** (956 70 00 06, closed Sun) is a real hotchpotch of architectural styles. Its main body dates from the late 18th century, although work began immediately following the Christian capture of Arcos in the 13th century, when a smaller church was built on the site of the old mosque. Most remarkable is its 15th-century Plateresque façade and the incomplete baroque bell tower that was built to replace the one destroyed by shocks from the Lisbon earthquake of 1755. Santa María was described in 1764 by the Holy Tribune in Rome as 'the oldest, most distinguished parish in Arcos', a declaration that put an end to its long-running rivalry with the 16th-century church of **San Pedro** (C/San Pedro 4, closed Sun), a few minutes' walk to the east, which perches precariously on the cliff's edge. From its tower there are wonderful views out across the town and eastwards towards the Grazalema massif.

If you're interested in local crafts, it's worth seeking out the **Galeria de Arte Arx-Arcis** (C/Marqués de Torresoto 11, 956 70 39 51), a labyrinthine building displaying handicrafts from the area, including blankets, paintings and ceramics. Or if you'd prefer local products of an edible nature, head for the **Convento de Mercedarias Descalzas** (C/de los Escribanos s/n), which is home to a closed order of nuns who raise funds by selling cakes and excellent biscuits. You'll see the convent entrance on the right-hand side in the narrow passageway leading from the *parador* to the Hotel El Convento. You ring a bell, make your order through a small grille and then have your goodies delivered on a revolving lantern, all without any face-to-face contact.

Other than the above, there isn't a vast amount of sightseeing to be done in Arcos. The best way to get a feel for the place is simply to wander through the backstreets of the old town and then to head for the new part of town to people-watch from one of its many terrace cafés. The town comes to life during its *feria* (at the end of September) and the 'Toro de Aleluya' on Easter Sunday, when bulls are run through the old town.

Where to eat & drink

The best tapas bars in the old town can be found on and around the Callejón de las Monjas, a continuation of Cuesta de Belén, which at its eastern end becomes Calle Botica. Check out **Don Fernando** (C/Botica 5, 956 71 73 26, €) for *raciones* of excellent ham and cheeses or, next door, the quieter **Mesón de Lola** (C/Botica 7, 956 70 22 11, €). One of the most atmospheric of the old town bars is **Alcaraván** (C/Nueva 1, 956 70 33 97, closed Mon, €), in a vaulted cellar just beneath the castle. There are great tapas as well as salad and steak, cooked on a small barbecue outside.

But there is far more action back down the Cuesta de Belén, beyond the Plaza de España, in the new part of town. There are several terrace bars (try **El Faro,** Debajo del Corral 14, 956 70

Location, location, location: **Arcos de la Frontera**.

00 14), tapas galore and a lighter mood than in the *barrio antiguo*, where some of the bar owners seem a mite world-weary.

For a full meal, try **El Convento** (C/Marqués de Torresoto 7, 956 70 32 22, closed 2wks July and 2wks Aug, €€-€€€), which is housed in a 17th-century palace and specialises in game. It is often closed one day a week, so call ahead. Or head for **Mesón El Patio** (Callejon de las Monjas 4, 956 70 23 02, www.mesonelpatio.com, closed Wed, €). Sawdust covers the floor of this down-to-earth tapas joint, where you can chow down on local dishes such as wild asparagus omelette and steamed snails. Antonio, the gregarious owner, also runs the barber's next door and the adjoining *pensión* (*see p152*). It's usually standing room only at 'Joselito's', as the **Taberna José de la Viuda** (Plaza Rafael Perez del Alamo 13, 956 70 12 09, €) is informally known. Goat's and sheep's cheeses and cured hams hang from the ceiling, and there's an impressive selection of 89 tapas and *raciones*. Resident DJ Joselito has a massive collection of flamenco tracks.

The town's flamenco club, **Peña Flamenca de Arcos** (Plaza de la Caridad s/n, 956 70 12 51) organises shows most Saturday nights during the summer and occasionally in winter. In July and August in various squares in the old town there are live flamenco concerts.

If you are looking for some action late into the night, head for the area close to the bus station: you'll be in lively company through to the early hours. Check out **Quo Vadis** or **Murga**. And if you fancy dancing until dawn in the summer months take a cab out to the lakeside disco-bar **Porto Alegre**, which doesn't really get going until past midnight.

Where to stay

La Casa Grande

C/Maldonado 10 (956 70 39 30/www.lacasagrande.net). Closed Jan. **Rates** €65-€75 double; €92-€95 suite. **Credit** AmEx, DC, MC, V.

Without doubt the top accommodation choice in Arcos. This 18th-century mansion was built at the very edge of the cliff and was the home of dancer Antonio Ruiz Soler before being bought by its present Catalan owners. They have converted the building into an elegant and intimate hotel. There are just four doubles and two suites, all tucked away at the top of the house and eclectically decorated, fusing Moroccan details with traditional local design. The Casa's most attractive feature is its rooftop terrace, which looks out across the rolling Cádiz plains.

Hotel El Convento

C/Maldonado 2 (956 70 23 33/www.webdearcos.com/elconvento). **Rates** €35-€55 single; €50-€80 double. Closed 2wks Jan. **Credit** AmEx, DC, MC, V.

The next-best option to La Casa Grande is just along the street. This former convent has 11 rooms, most with amazing views looking down on to the Guadalete river valley and the castle. The best rooms are in an annexe next door to the hotel. There's a rooftop terrace and the staff are on the ball.

Hotel Los Olivos

Paseo de Boliches 30 (956 70 08 11). **Rates** €40-€45 single; €60-€70 double. **Credit** AmEx, DC, MC, V.

Back down the hill towards the new town, Los Olivos is cheaper and less intimate than its sister hotel El Convento (*see above*) and the views are not nearly as spectacular. Still, it's bright, modern and cool and has a sunny, plant-filled courtyard where a buffet breakfast (€6) is served. Popular with tour groups.

Hotel Real de Veas

C/Corredera 12 (956 71 73 70). **Rates** (incl breakfast) €65-€75 double; €97-€107 suite. **Credit** AmEx, DC, MC, V.

This airy 19th-century townhouse has recently been converted to a small hotel by its friendly Spanish owners. Bedrooms are spotless and come with air-conditioning, TV, hydro-massage baths and mini-bars, yet still have a reasonable price tag.

Parador Arcos de la Frontera

Plaza del Cabildo s/n (956 70 05 00/www.parador.es). **Rates** €107-€116 single; €134 double; €145 double with terrace. **Credit** AmEx, DC, MC, V.

This elegant building in the centre of old Arcos is one of Andalucía's very best *paradores*. It was formerly 'La Casa del Corregidor' (a *corregidor* was the 16th-century equivalent of a mayor). The decor is a classy take on traditional Andalucian style: attractive tiles, oak furniture and earthy colours. The hotel's restaurant serves excellent food (set menu €27) and has stunning views. Both the central patio and poolside terrace bar are great places for a drink.

Pensión Callejón de las Monjas

C/Dean Espinosa 4 (956 70 23 02/www.mesonelpatio.com). **Rates** €20-€22 single; €33-€39 double. **Credit** AmEx, MC, V.

This family-run *pensión*, owned by the same family as the Mesón el Patio (*see p151*) is very handy for the old part of town and all the best tapas bars. The rooms are clean and bright but don't expect much of a view, and beware the noise coming from the bar next door.

Resources

Tourist information

Plaza del Cabildo s/n (956 70 22 64/www.ayuntamientoarcos.org). **Open** *Mid Mar-mid Oct* 10am-2pm, 4-8pm Mon-Sat; 10.30am-1.30pm Sun. *Mid Oct-mid Mar* 10am-2pm, 3.30-7.30pm Mon-Sat; 10am-2pm Sun.

Paseo de Andalucía (no phone). **Open** *Mid Feb-mid Nov* 10.30am-1.30pm, 5-7pm Mon-Fri; 10am-2pm Sat.Closed mid Nov-mid Feb.

The tourist offices offer tours of the old town from Monday to Friday. Call for details.

South & east of Arcos

The rolling countryside south of Arcos, heading towards the Costa de la Luz, is sparsely populated. The major settlement, **Medina Sidonia** (37 kilometres/23 miles south of Arcos) is perched on a hill, with views out over undulating wheat fields. It's a gorgeous, peaceful little town, well off the main *pueblos blancos* trail, with a number of fine buildings and churches, a ruined Moorish castle and Roman sewers. The ducal title of Medina Sidonia (awarded to the descendants of Gúzman 'El Bueno', who took the town from the Moors) has long been one of the most distinguished in Spain and, thanks to royal favours granted at the time of the *reconquista*, the family came to be one of the wealthiest in Andalucía, owning several vast estates. Famous family members have included the commander of the Spanish Armada, while the present 'red' Duchess lives in Sanlúcar (*see p144*) and is, puzzlingly, one of Andalucía's most outspoken socialists.

There are controversial plans afoot to change the face of the town for ever, with a huge housing project slated, at the foot of the hill.

East from here is the vast, rugged **Parque Natural los Alcornocales** (1,690 square kilometres/650 square miles), which extends along almost all of Cádiz province's eastern boundary. There are few roads and fewer people within the park, making for fine walking. In a forest glade on its northern edge are the ruins of the village of **La Sauceda**, which was destroyed by Franco for harbouring Republicans and criminals on the run; the surviving houses are now used as refuges for hikers. Technically, you need permission to visit the park from the park office in **Alcalá de los Gazules** (Plaza San Jorge 1, 956 42 02 77), a village with commanding views over the surrounding country located on the edge of the park (23 kilometres/14 miles east of Medina Sidonia).

On the other side of the park is **Jimena de la Frontera**, a large hill village beneath an extensive ruined Moorish castle. As in nearby

Medina Sidonia, conquest and fortune of Gúzman 'El Bueno'. *See p152.*

Gaucín, there's a strong expat (particularly British) influence here. Try to find time to hike along the spectacular Hozgarganta river valley beneath the village, where (weather permitting) there are some wonderful places to swim.

South of Jimena, off to one side of the A369 leading to Algeciras, is the uniquely beautiful but claustrophobic village of **Castellar de la Frontera**. The original inhabitants were obliged to leave the village in the late 1960s when it seemed that the rising waters from a new reservoir would cut off access. It never happened and a band of hippies, most of them German, moved in to squat the village. An uneasy stand-off between the newcomers and the locals ensued and continues to this day – even if most of the hippies have given up drug-dealing, bought their squatted houses, and embarked on new careers managing tea and souvenir shops.

While south-central Cádiz province is relatively neglected by visitors, the countryside east of Arcos is well-trodden tourist territory, with a string of picture-postcard white villages dotted among some of the most spectacular and varied mountain scenery in Spain.

The first place you reach heading east from Arcos along the A372 is **El Bosque** (32 kilometres/20 miles from Arcos), which makes a good base for exploring the **Parque Natural de la Sierra de Grazalema** (530 square kilometres/207 square miles). A UNESCO Biosphere Reserve since 1984, and one of the first Natural Parks established in Andalucía, the park contains some 1,300 plant species, as well as herds of red and roe deer, wild boar and ibex. Birds of prey, such as ospreys, Egyptian and griffon vultures, booted, short-toed and golden eagles are commonly seen. The park's botanical jewel is the hardy Abies pinsapo fir tree, which survived the last ice age and now only grows in three small areas in southern Spain and northern Morocco. Due to the rarity of these trees, and the risk of forest fires, you need to pick up a permit from the park's main visitor centre in El Bosque if you wish to walk through the pinsapo forest. You also require a permit to hike through the spectacular gorge of **Garganta Verde** (which lies close to the Zahara–Grazalema road; path at km3 – you'll need ropes and a high degree of fitness; the less athletic can just hike down to the canyon floor to the huge cave known as the **Ermita de la Garganta**) or if you wish to climb the park's highest peak, **El Torrejón** (1,640 metres/5,380 feet). A far easier path, with no permit required, follows the river between El Bosque and Benamahoma. It begins just behind Hotel Las Trucha and can be walked in little more than an hour.

The road east of El Bosque (A372) is one of the most scenic byways in Spain (and has featured in more than one car advert) and after 18 kilometres (11 miles) brings you to the village of **Grazalema**. This was a centre of the wool industry and became famous for its textiles during the 18th and 19th centuries. A number of grander-than-most village houses bear witness to an age when the village was so prosperous that it was known as 'Cádiz el Chico' (Little Cádiz). The **Artesanía Téxtil de Grazalema**, more commonly known as the museum of the 'Fábrica de Mantas' (A372, 956 13 20 08, closed Sat, Sun and Aug, free), is devoted to traditional methods of cloth-making and blanket-weaving. Fine blankets, as well as shawls and scarves, are still produced on industrial looms next door. The village was the subject of Pitt-Rivers' classic sociological study *People of the Sierra*.

Although Grazalema is undeniably pretty, it seems a little ill at ease with the huge seasonal influx of tourists, most of them day-trippers from Cádiz and Seville. At the weekend facilities are often overstretched and it is not unusual to have to queue for a table at one of the restaurants.

The best way to escape the hordes is to take to the hills: superb scenery, wildlife and amazing geology make the park a mecca for mountain-sports enthusiasts. If you want to get your adrenaline really pumping, try bungee-jumping, potholing or abseiling with **Horizon** (Corrales Terceros 29, 956 13 23 63, www.horizonaventura.com). For guided walks around Grazalema contact Jo Carter (956 13 23 97, www.grazalema.ws/eww1.html), who has lived in the village for several years, or, for longer, more remote rambles with great picnic lunches and 4x4 excursions call Guy Hunter-Watts (952 18 40 53).

Though it still gets its fair share of visitors, delightful little **Zahara de la Sierra** (17 kilometres/11 miles north of Grazalema by way of another stunning road that loops over the Paloma pass), seems to cope far better. Its hillside location, overlooking a reservoir, is wonderful. An 18th-century baroque church stands in the pretty main square, where there are a number of bars. Be sure to climb up to the restored Moorish castle for the most spectacular view of the village and lake. You'll often be treated to close encounters with soaring griffon vultures, which are part of the huge colony that nests in the nearby **Garganta Verde**. North-east of here, in the furthest tip of the province, is the curious village of **Setenil de las Bodegas**, many of whose streets are carved into the side of an overhanging gorge, such as C/Herreria, running down from the corner of Plaza Andalucía. It is worth visiting the castle and church at the top end of the village, but be warned that the driving can be a little hairy, with streets narrowing to virtually impassable.

Following the road south from Zahara along the southern side of the reservoir for five kilometres (three miles) you reach **Arroyomolinos**, where a river has been dammed to create a wonderful swimming area (but steer clear of it on busy summer weekends). Outside of the village, on the road to Grazalema, is the oldest olive oil mill in the Sierra, **El Vínculo** (956 12 30 02, mobile 696 40 43 68, www.zaharadelasierra.info/elvinculo, visits by appt only, €3-€6 per person); it makes for an interesting visit, especially when its gracious owner Juan Urruti is there to explain how his pure virgin olive oil is produced.

Half an hour's drive south-west of Grazalema, in the heart of the park, is **Ubrique**. Famous for leather (you'll see scores of handbag and shoe shops lining the streets), it's larger, more industrious and less picturesque than Grazalema and Zahara. It is also the home of bullfighter-megastar Jesulín de Ubrique, who owns a ritzy ranch just outside of town.

The main attraction in the area is the Roman city of **Ocuri**, which stands on the Benalfi crags, a kilometre from Ubrique. To reach it, take the mountain path leading to Benaocaz and La Manga de Villaluenga (ask at the tourist office). This path is, in fact, one of Spain's best preserved Roman roads, and the walk to loftily situated Benaocaz (where there are several bars with panoramic views). Only discovered during the last century, the Ocuri site contains incredibly well-preserved terraced walls (*oppidum*) and round houses comparable to those of Pompeii. Archaeological excavations began in the 1970s and unearthed a first-century crematorium, public baths, a necropolis and irrigation aquifers. Guided walks around the site can be arranged by the tourist office in Ubrique every Saturday and Sunday.

Where to stay & eat

In Medina Sidonia the **Casa La Loba** (C/La Loba 21, 956 41 20 51, www.casalaloba.com, double €95-€105) is a grand old townhouse with just three guest rooms and has been sympathetically decorated and restored by its Scottish owner, James Barr. There's a Moorish style patio and a small walled garden. An newer addition is the cool, clean **Hotel Medina Sidonia** (Plaza Llanete de Herederos 1, 956 41 23 17, www.tugasa.com, double €65), also in the heart of town. There are several tapas bars clustered around the main square, Plaza España, and it would a crime to miss Medina's speciality, *alfajores* (spiced pastries) – try them at the **Nuestra Señora de la Paz** bakery (C/San Juan 14, 956 41 01 61).

In Jimena **Hostal El Anon** (C/Consuelo 36, 956 64 01 13, www.andalucia.com/jimena/hostalanon, closed 2wks June and 2wks Nov, double €60 incl breakfast, apartments €70, restaurant €€-€€€, closed Wed) is run by Suzie Odell, who came to Jimena in the '70s. The *hostal* has become the main port of call for walkers in Jimena, while its reputation for good food brings day-trippers up from the coast. Rooms vary considerably – some are enormous and with views, others are smaller with dim lighting. There is a rooftop plunge pool, a little bar decked out like an English pub and a beamed restaurant offering international food. In Jimena you will also find friendly **Posada La Casa Grande** (C/Fuentenueva 42, 956 64 05 78, http://personal.iddeo.es/casagrande, double €30-€36, apartments €40-€72, restaurant €-€€, closed Tue) run by another expat, Tom Andresen, from Norway. Rooms are spacious, bright and there are self-catering apartments.

There are plenty of eating options in Jimena. **Restaurante-Bar España** (C/Sevilla 82, 956 64 00 49, closed Thur, €-€€) knocks out a decent range of regional dishes at low prices. Slightly more expensive is the **Restaurante-Bar Cuenca** (Avda los Deportes 21, 956 64 01 52, closed Tue, €€-€€€), one of the oldest restaurants in town, serving tapas as well as meat and fish. There is a good range of tapas bars in Jimena; the main meeting point for the local expat crowd is boisterous **Bar El Ventorrillero** (Plaza de la Constitución 2, 956 64 09 97, closed last 2wks Sept, €).

Just outside El Bosque is the attractive **Las Truchas** (Avda de la Diputación s/n, 956 71 60 61, www.tugasa.com, double €59-€86, restaurant €€), with a pool and an enormous, high-ceilinged restaurant specialising (as you might guess from the name) in trout from the fish farm just down the road, as well as lamb. Many of the rooms have large balconies.

On the outskirts of Grazalema, looking back across to the village, is the **Villa Turistica Grazalema** (Ctra Olivar s/n, 956 13 21 36, www.tugasa.com, double €59, apartment for 2 €70, apartment for 4 €123). In the village itself is the four-star **Hotel Puerta de la Villa** (Plaza Pequeña 8, 956 13 23 76, www.grazalemahotel.com, double €104-€129), a plush, slightly Forte-style place with a small pool, jacuzzi, gym and sauna. For budget travellers, **Casa de las Piedras** (C/Las Piedras 32, 956 13 20 14, www.casadelas piedras.net, double €45, restaurant €) is by far the best bet, and deservedly popular with walking groups. Some rooms are en suite and there's a lively patio restaurant offering hearty local dishes.

There are a number of good places to stay in Zahara. On the main drag, **Hotel Marqués de Zahara** (C/San Juan 3, 956 12 30 61, www. marquesdezahara.com, double €42-€48) offers simply furnished rooms around a cool, central patio. A cheaper option is family-run **Pensión Los Tadeos** (Paseo de la Fuente s/n, 956 12 30 86, double €43), which has excellent views and is next to the public swimming pool. There are stunning views and good food at the two-star, 17-room **Arco de la Villa** (Paseo Nazari s/n, 956 12 32 30, www.tugasa.com, double €59). The **Mesón los Estribos** (C/Fuerte 3, 956 12 31 45, closed Mon, €), opposite the main church, offers the best food in Zahara. Enjoy specialities such as (enormous) steaks, lamb stew and *perdíz encebollada* (roast partridge in an onion sauce) while enjoying wonderful views across the reservoir. Another good food option, back along the main street, is **Bar Los Naranjos** (C/San Juan 12, 956 12 33 14, €€). This is the best place for alfresco dining, with tables set out under the orange trees; the roast lamb is excellent, and there's a great selection of tapas.

The best of Setenil's bars is **Bar Frasquito** (C/Cuevas del Sol 75, 956 13 44 71, closed lunch and Mon, €), an atmospheric *bodega* bar with tables made from old sherry casks and a range of largely pork-based tapas. Restaurants are mainly clustered in the Plaza de Andalucía. Just above it, **El Mirador** (C/Callejón, 956 13 45 27, €€) has a great view over the houses set into the rock from a rather soulless dining room. Specialities include paella and other rice dishes.

Resources

Tourist information

Grazalema *Plaza de España 11 (956 13 20 73).* **Open** 10am-2pm, 4-9pm Mon-Fri; 10am-9pm Sat, Sun.

Medina Sidonia *Plaza Iglesia Mayor s/n (956 41 24 04/www.medinasidonia.com).* **Open** *Mar-June, Sept, Oct* 10am-2pm, 4-8pm daily. *July, Aug* 9.30am-2pm, 5-9.30pm daily. *Nov-Feb* 10.30am-2pm, 4-6.30pm daily.

Parque Natural de la Sierra de Grazalema *Avda de la Diputación, El Bosque (956 71 60 63).* **Open** 10am-2pm, 6-8pm Mon-Fri; 9am-2pm Sat, Sun.

Ubrique *C/Moreno de Mora 19A (956 46 49 00/ www.ayuntamientoubrique.es).* **Open** 10am-6.30pm Mon-Fri; 10am-3.30pm Sat; 10am-2.30pm Sun.

Zahara de la Sierra *Plaza del Rey 3 (956 12 31 14/www.zaharadelasierra.info).* **Open** 9am-2pm, 4-7pm daily.

Getting there

By bus

From Arcos (C/Corregidores, in the new town), Los Amarillos (956 70 49 77/956 32 93 47) runs up to 18 buses a day to Jerez (40mins), around 7 to El Bosque and a handful to other towns and villages in the region (it takes 2.5hrs to Ronda, 2hrs to Seville, 1.5hrs to Cádiz). Comes (902 19 92 08) also runs a number of services in the area.

Costa de la Luz

The jewel of southern Spain's coastline.

The Costa de la Luz has the most perfect beaches in Andalucía, the best views of Africa, the fieriest sunsets, the cleanest water, the best tube waves, the prettiest flowers and the greenest hills. In short, it's a small corner of paradise given a chilled-out ambience by the surfer's way of life, but with the good folk of the *campo* keeping its toes on the ground: a far cry from the jet set in Marbella, or the mad revellers of Torremolinos. And yet, there's still room for some of the best boutique accommodation in the land. Base yourself in Tarifa for beach parties and water sports, or Vejer for more genteel holidays of art, architecture and more upmarket dining, as well as quick access to pretty beaches and rolling countryside.

This is no longer a secret, however, and the extension of the AP7 motorway from Algeciras to Cádiz currently under way will undoubtedly affect the number of visitors to the area. However, the Costa de la Luz attracts a different breed of foreigner than the Costa del Sol: New Age travellers, surfers and rat-race refugees, most of whom want to see this spectacular, wind-lashed chunk of the world stay as it is. Much of the area is being granted protection, and building along the magnificent stretch of open ocean and flat alluvial plains from Conil to Caños de la Meca is strictly prohibited, while beautiful Parques Naturales already protect much of the area around Barbate and Tarifa.

Los Caños de la Meca.

Conil to Vejer

The immediate environs of Cádiz are not beguiling; heading south, the first resort with any appeal is **Conil de la Frontera**, 40 kilometres (25 miles) south of the provincial capital. Though it is not quite the 'Land of Delights' described by Arab colonisers, the quiet little town of Conil has a pretty, if tiny, historic quarter (it gets quite lively at the weekend) and huge expanses of beach. The town has several churches, all housing impressive religious artworks. Of particular note is the the 16th-century convent **La Parroquia de Santa Catalina** (open hours of services) on Plaza Constitución, with its kitschy gilded altar and piped music; while the town's icon, the dilapidated 15th-century watchtower, built by the famous soldier Guzmán el Bueno, is a good landmark for the 'tapas triangle' (*see p159*) should the straggly streets confuse you. Storks like to nest here in spring, filling the streets with the sound of clattering beaks.

The best beaches are west of the central **Playa de los Bateles**; here you'll find the reddish-coloured, cliff-hugging coves of **Calas de Roche**, **Fontanilla** and **Fuente del Gallo**. To reach them by car, follow signs to Puerto Pesquero and then hoof it over the rocks. If you fancy scuba diving in the area, contact **Marbella Diving Conil Adventure** (mobile 630 23 44 26, www.divetarifa.com), which is based at the Hotel Fuerte Conil (*see p159*).

From here, it's a 10-minute drive to **El Palmar**, an extensive stretch of windswept ocean and magnificent beach backed by low dunes. This is a top spot for traditional surfers (as opposed to kite- or windsurfers) and you won't find better waves until you hit Portugal. For now the flat plains are dotted only with a handful of low-rise houses, some basic accommodation and restaurants. However, plans to build a 1,400-bed hotel have been deeply controversial, with various environmental groups battling hard to get it stopped; a move supported by Conil council.

Around 16 kilometres (ten miles) further south is **Los Caños de la Meca**, once the coast's best-kept secret until, like many of the hippie colonies around the world, it got 'discovered'. With most of the true hippies gone, the scene at the summer campsites rivals that

Vejer de la Frontera. *See p158.*

of the infamous beach parties of Goa and Thailand in high season, though its chilled, alternative-lifestyle vibes endure.

Situated at the base of the **Parque Natural de la Breña y Marismas del Barbate**, Los Caños' beaches are backed by 30-metre (100-foot) cliffs, while the little town itself is overlooked by a giant pine-hooded sand dune, known locally as the 'magic mountain'; it's a calf-numbing hike to the top, but an exhilarating speed thrill coming down via the fire break. There are several great walks from here through the park (which has picnic and barbecue areas off the road) to Barbate along the cliffs and to the fresh waterfall of Las Cortinas in the same direction. West of Los Caños, a narrow lane leads to the **Faro de Trafalgar**, which continues to light the bay where Admiral Nelson met an untimely death during the Battle of Trafalgar in 1805. Below the lighthouse, in the direction of Conil, extends the beach of **Zahora** (not to be confused with Zahara de los Atunes; *see p158*), with mile on mile of white powder sand. It tends to be a little more sheltered from the persistent wind than most places along this coastline.

A further 12 kilometres (7.5 miles) along the coast, **Barbate** (sometimes referred to as Barbate de Franco; the dictator liked to spend summer here) has something of an insalubrious reputation for drugs and crime. The car parks for the Parque Natural, for example, have become notorious for break-ins. That said, if you're willing to brave the dodgy night-time characters, it is something of a hub for authentic flamenco, with a very active centre hosting regular performances (Peña Flamenca, Plaza Generalísimo Franco 14, 956 44 08 31). The unprepossessing town itself is dominated by the fishing industry and it has an excellent fish market that is worth a look (Mercado Abastos-OMIC, Avda de Andalucía, 956 43 46 27). Tuna is still caught using traditional trapnets or *almadrabas* during the season from February to May, as tuna reach the end of their long journey from the cold waters of Norway. The method dates back 3,000 years and involves vertical walls of netting, which funnel the fish into a central area from where they can easily be lifted on to boats. Considered to be home to the best tuna in the world for sushi, the port often hosts two or three Japanese fishing trawlers, who take around 85 per cent of all the tuna caught here.

A must-see for fans of modern art, the **Fundación NMAC (Montenmedio Arte Contemporáneo)** is a unique project in Spain that marries contemporary art and nature. Boasting an extraordinary collection of outdoor sculpture, installations, photography and paintings by contemporary artists from all over the world, and sitting pretty in the heart of Mediterranean forest and bush off the main A48, this site is one of the most daring and original contemporary art projects in Europe. The foundation plans to spend €5 million over the coming years expanding its existing facilities with three new exhibition spaces, a library, café, workshop and state-of-the-art auditorium. Dubbed the 'white stripe' project, the new building was designed by Alberto Campo Baeza, creating, quite literally, a wide 'white stripe across the Andalucían countryside'. He hopes the architecture will reflect the calibre of the art currently on display here, which is fast positioning the Fundación NMAC as one of the most important contemporary art spaces in Europe.

The incredibly preserved Roman ruins of **Baelo Claudia**.

Ten kilometres (six miles) on from Barbate, the once thriving tuna-fishing port of **Zahara de los Atunes** ('of the tuna') is now a popular and agreeably low-key summer resort (mainly for Spaniards) with a fine golden strand. The town now has two claims to fame. The first, according to locals, is that Cervantes was imprisoned here on charges of espionage, and mentions the town in his book *La Fregona Ilustre* ('The Illustrious Mop'). In it he says that no one deserves the name *pícaro* (lowlife) unless they've spent a couple of months fishing tuna out of Zahara. The second is that the wedding scene in Spanish director Pablo Carbonell's film, *Atún y Chocolate* was shot in Zahara's spectacular church, **Nuestra Señorita Carmen** (C/Gobernador Sanchez González). Sadly, the town's only other landmark building, the 15th-century **Castillo de las Almadrabas**, built by the Dukes of Medina Sidonia to protect the town against pirates, is in ruins.

This stretch of the coast has been colonised by Germans since the time of Franco, who offered sizeable plots of land belonging to the Spanish military to neo-Nazis.

Ten kilometres (six miles) inland from Barbate, **Vejer de la Frontera (photo** *p157*) is a delightful brilliant-white village that a few years ago was barely known to the outside world. Since then it's been 'discovered' and, intriguingly, attracts a curious array of rock dinosaurs and minor celebrities, but it's being respectfully developed with a steady increase of classy shops, restaurants and art galleries gradually filling up its lovely Moorish townhouses. Perched high on a hill, it was built to protect the fishing grounds and factories along the coast from marauders attacking from the north. Later it became an important Moorish agricultural centre and it retains a strongly Moorish atmosphere – the four gates of the original Moorish settlement survive.

Due north of the tourist office on C/Marqués de Tamarón, the 14th-century church of **Divino Salvador** is built on the site of a mosque in an intriguing mix of Mudéjar and Gothic styles. From here, follow C/Ramón y Cajal west to the **Convento de las Monjas Concepcionistas**, a restored 16th-century Renaissance building currently used as a venue for cultural events. This gives way to the **Arco de las Monjas**, a row of narrow arches framing a huddle of Vejer rooftops that lead into the Jewish quarter. Continue west along C/Judería to the **Arco de Puerta Cerrada** – the closed door. Also known as the Berber Gate, it was kept shut between the tenth and 12th centuries by Jewish residents fearful of attack by Barbary Coast pirates. The lovely little **Plazuela**, centred around an exuberant polychrome fountain, on the edge of the old Moorish village, has a number of good bars and restaurants.

Perhaps one of the most striking features of the Moors' presence here (until 1250) was *el cobijado*, a black garment somewhere between a burka and a nun's habit, which was worn by the women of the town until 1931. Today, the only place you're likely to see it is on a postcard or during the Fiesta Patronales in August. Other fun times to visit include the running of the bulls during **El Toro Embolao** on Easter Sunday and the **Eve of San Juan** (23 June), when effigies representing evil are burned in a fire in the main square. This is followed by a flaming effigy of a bull paraded around the town to the accompaniment of fireworks.

From Vejer, the main road runs south-east for 50 kilometres (31 miles) towards Tarifa. After 35 kilometres (22 miles), a right turn on to the CA9004 leads to the old Roman settlement of **Baelo Claudia**. Astonishingly complete, these romantically sited ruins are considered to be among the most important Roman sites on the Iberian peninsula. A two-kilometre walk (1.25

miles) around the site reveals the temples of Egyptian goddess Isis, and the Roman gods Juno, Jupiter and Minerva. From the remains of the basilica, marketplace, amphitheatre, hot baths, forum and fish-salting factories, visitors get a very real impression of what life in Roman times would have been like.

The nearby tiny village of **Bolonia** is somewhat overshadowed by its famous historical neighbour, but it's also worth a visit for its breathtaking position beneath craggy peaks and pasture that runs down to meet the sea. It's not a particularly pretty hamlet, and feels thrown together by accident rather than design, but the reason to come here is to go to its beauty of a beach and gaze across the water at the African coast. It is less windy than the beaches further south, and also attracts a number of camper vans. In high season the *chiringuitos* along the beach going into party mode providing such entertainment as there is. Out of season, it's pretty much a ghost town.

Baelo Claudia

Bolonia (956 68 85 30). **Open** *June-Oct* 10am-7.30pm Tue-Sat; 10am-1.30pm Sun. *Nov-Feb* 10am-5.30pm Mon-Sat; 10am-2pm Sun. *Mar-May* 10am-6.30pm Mon-Sat; 10am-2pm Sun. **Admission** €1.50; free with EU passport. **No credit cards**.

Fundación NMAC (Montenmedio Arte Contemporáneo)

A48, km42.5 (956 45 51 34/www.fundacion nmac.com). **Open** *July, Aug* 10am-2pm, 5-8.30pm Tue-Sun. *Sept-June* 10.30am-2.30pm, 4-6pm Tue-Sun. **Admission** €5; concessions €2.50. **No credit cards**.

Where to stay & eat

In Conil de la Frontera, the **Hostal Los Hermanos** (C/Virgen 2, 956 44 01 96, double €25-€50) was the birthplace of Conil's most famous poet and musician, Antonio Rodríguez Martínez. The building is 200 years old, with hefty wooden doors and a flower-filled courtyard. The old-fashioned, low-ceilinged rooms are clean and comfortable. **Hostal-Restaurante La Posada** (C/Quevedo s/n, 956 44 41 71, double €33-€72, restaurant €) offers more modern comforts, with the best of its eight rooms opening on to a roof terrace. It also has a handsome conservatory-style restaurant and a flower-filled garden for outdoor dining. The **Hotel Almadraba** (C/Señores Curas 4, 956 45 60 37, www.hotelalmadrabaconil.com, double €62-€110), in a restored Andalucían house built around a patio, has a fabulous roof terrace and tastefully decorated rooms. A little removed from the centre, **Hostal Lojo** (C/Canarias 2, 956 44 15 31, www.hostal-lojo.com, double €35-€80) is quiet and has a very pretty plant-filled patio, small diving school and snack bar.

A frightening number of four-star hotels are mushrooming up along the cliffs, north of the centre. The best is the ecologically run **Hotel Fuerte Conil** (Playa de la Fontanilla s/n, 956 44 33 44, www.fuertehoteles.com, closed mid Nov-mid Feb, double €101-€197). It has indoor and outdoor pools, a spa centre and a good international restaurant. For food, head for the so-called 'tapas triangle' between Plazas de España, Andalucía and Santa Catalina. On Santa Catalina, **El Resbalón** (No.7, 956 44 04 97, closed Oct-Feb, €) has a hefty tapas menu and weird decor: cuttlefish bones and other cadavers of the deep swing ominously from the ceiling. For picnic fodder, **Casa Manuela** (C/José Valarde) stocks excellent *charcuterie* and cheeses. The best seafood and fish are from either of the *chiringuitos* on the beach below Hotel Fuerte Conil. **Restaurante La Fontanilla** (Playa de la Fontanilla, 956 44 11 30, closed Nov & Dec, €€) serves excellent grilled fish and tender, juicy steaks from locally reared cattle; it also has a decent wine list.

El Palmar has several *hostales*, all pretty basic but they do the job. **Hostal La Ilusión** (956 23 23 98, closed Nov-Jan, double €50-€60)

Bolonia's beach.

has comfortable rooms, some with sea views, and a pleasant garden. At the southern end of the beach you'll find **La Chanca** (Carretera de la Playa, mobile 659 97 74 20, closed Jan & Feb, weekends Mar, June, Nov & Dec and Tue dinner Mar-June), situated in restored stone farm buildings. Fish is a better bet than meat here, and they do a superb version of the local dish, prawns and spinach.

In Los Caños de la Meca, few places give a taste of the good life quite so successfully as **Casas Karen** (C/Fuente del Madroño 6, 956 43 70 67, mobile 649 78 08 34, www.casaskaren.com, double cottage €124-€198 per night, €330-€627 per week) a rare piece of Eden if your idea of a proper holiday is to read and relax and take long walks on the beach. It's easily missed, so keep your eyes peeled for a sign reading '*apartamentos* and bungalows', about 500 metres after the turning for Faro de Trafalgar as you head into Los Caños. It's at the end of a sandy, pot-holed lane, and remains one of the best hideaways in Andalucía, with several lovingly converted, self-catering farmhouses, barns and traditional *chozas* (straw huts). Trafalgar beach is ten minutes' walk away and yoga sessions and massage can all be arranged.

Hostal Madreselva (Avda Trafalgar 112, 956 43 72 55, www.madreselvahotel.com/canos, double €59-€90) owned by the same people as the Hurricane (*see p164*), is a low-rise villa built around a courtyard, with a pool to the side. Rooms are comfortable and have walled terraces.

Due to Los Caños de la Meca's transient summer community, new bars and restaurants are constantly opening and closing. Most can be found along Los Caños's main street, Avda de Trafalgar, so you can't miss them; more often than not they're filled with disconsolate surfers waiting for their wave to come in. At No.96, **Trafalgar Restaurant Bar** (956 43 71 21, closed Oct-Apr, €) is a smart, salmon-pink villa, with an Andaluz-style patio dripping with flowers, and a focus on local produce, from tuna to Iberian pork. Try, too, aubergine flan with fresh cheese fondue, or the lobster paella.

About five kilometres (three miles) east of Los Caños, a tangle of sandy lanes leading to Playa de Zahora contains several isolated guesthouses and restaurants. Open year-round, the **Saboy Bar** (C/Mangeta 357, 699 323 089, €) is a cosy stone-and-thatch bar-restaurant with live music at the weekend, and occasional flamenco. It also rents out some two-up, two-

Into Africa

Once the jewel of the Mediterranean, **Tangier** was one of the most fashionable resorts frequented by Europeans in the first half of the 20th century, and by the 1950s half of her 120,000-strong population were expats. Among them was Barbara Hutton, the Woolworths heiress renowned for her parties and extravagance; she once had the narrow streets widened for her Rolls-Royce, and you can still occasionally hear the hawkers screeching 'Woolworths price' in the souks.

The town also became the adopted home of many of the 20th century's greatest writers and artists, who were mesmerised by its exoticism, its crystalline light, its Moorish architecture and its seemingly endless supply of vice. Tangier's period as an 'International Zone' exempted it from many laws and created a playground for hedonists. Immortalised by Paul Bowles in his novels *The Sheltering Sky* and *Let It Come Down*, both set in Fez and Tangier, the latter became a magnet for the beat generation: William Burroughs wrote *The Naked Lunch* from his room at the Hotel El Muniria on the rue Magellan, while Jack Kerouac followed later to help edit it. Ian Fleming gleaned inspiration for the 007 series at the Café de Paris on the Place du Faro, where spies traded secrets during World War II. Oscar Wilde, Francis Bacon and Joe Orton were all fans, drawn by its reputation as a city of sin.

Moroccan independence in 1956, however, soon put a stop to the partying – alcohol was banned in the *medina* (old town), brothels were cleared out and there was a general cleaning up. Ironically, and despite recent Draconian laws terrifying the populace into leaving tourists alone, it attracts hardly anyone today, much less the in-crowd. Dirty, run-down and impoverished, it's easier to loathe than love. There's only one way to deal with the city, and that is with an open mind and senses ready and willing to soak up every sight, smell and sound that it has to throw at you. Abandon yourself to it, and the Tangier that so inspired writers and artists less than a century ago may begin to reveal itself.

It is not a city of traditional sights, but there's more than enough to fill a day. The **Kasbah** is housed in a former 17th-century Sultan's palace – Dar el Makhzen – and has impressive carved wood ceilings and stunning views that take in both continents.

down cottages. Try **Venta Curro** (Playa de Zahora, 956 43 70 64, closed Tue in winter, €-€€) for hearty, home cooking. The ranch-like atmosphere of **Sajorami** (Playa de Zahora, 956 43 74 24, www.sajoramibeach.com, double €50-€80, restaurant €€) is a good base for outdoor holidays. Accommodation ranges from stone high-ceilinged rooms to wooden beachfront houses. The beachfront restaurant specialises in a Creole-style barbecue.

Another decent alternative-style guesthouse, **Casa Montecote** (La Muela 200, CA125, 956 44 84 89, www.casamontecote.com, apartment for 2 €50-€65 per night, €310-€420 per week) is tucked away in the hills, with large, unkempt gardens, a gym, sauna and swimming pool.

In Barbate, friendly **El Salao** (Avda Cabo Diego Pérez 37, 956 43 06 54, closed lunch Aug, all Mon & Tue Oct-Feb, €€) offers BBQ fish and meat in its small, ramshackle garden overlooking the river.

In Zahara, the nicest place to stay is the colonial-style **Hotel Gran Sol** (Avda de la Playa s/n, 956 43 93 09, www.gransolhotel.com, double €71-€110), whose walled gardens and swimming pool front the beach; ask for a room with a sea view and balcony over the pool.

Food-wise, you'll find a handful of beach bars in season. In town, the nautically themed **Casa Juanito** (C/Sagasta 7, 956 43 92 11, www.casajuanito.com, closed Nov-Jan, €-€€), established in 1948, is the oldest bar in town and good for locally caught tuna. Most of the night-time watering holes are on C/María Luisa.

Vejer boasts some of the most exceptional small hotels in the region. **Casa Cinco** (C/Sancho IV El Bravo 5, 956 45 50 29, www.hotelcasacinco.com, closed Jan, double €80-€128) has five individually decorated rooms, a cosy reading room strewn with leather sofas and stacked high with books, and a Moroccan-inspired roof terrace strewn with rugs, cushions and candles. **Escondrijo** (Callejon Oscuro 3, 956 44 74 38, www.escondrijo.com, double €80-€139) is another classy place, constructed from the remains of an old chapel. It has four stylish, characterful rooms, two with private terraces and all with stereos. There's a sun terrace, bar, movie lounge and internet access. The **Casablanca** (C/Canalejas 8, just behind Plaza de España, 956 44 75 69, www.andaluciacasablanca.com, closed late Dec-late Jan, double €45-€55) offers studio apartments, combining

Below, the **Grand Socco** (the Spanish word for souk) no longer has a market, but has become the town's hub, a meeting spot for tradesmen and a good place to breathe in the life of the town and watch Rif women in colourful garb drift by, before hurling yourself into the *medina* after them. Here the streets and passageways are filled with bright mountains of spices and colourful handicrafts – brightly embroidered shirts, *djellabas* and leather goods. If you speak a little French, all the better for bargain hunting.

The **Petit Socco** is at the heart of the *medina* and is the town's most attractive spot. No visit to Tangier is complete without passing time sipping hot, sugary mint tea in the *plaza* and watching the world go by. It's also the best place in town to feast on hearty tagines and couscous, before heading back to fortress Europe.

As Paul Bowles wrote in his 1958 essay 'The Worlds of Tangier': 'For the nine sight-seers who are mildly amused by the chaos and absurdity of the place, frankly repelled by its ugliness and squalor, or simply indifferent to whatever it may have to offer, there is a tenth one who straight away falls in love with it.'

GETTING THERE

FRS (956 68 18 30/43 25, www.frs.es) high-speed catamarans leave the Spanish coast every day from Tarifa (€29 one way, 35 minutes), from Algeciras (€36.50 one way, 70 minutes) in July only, and from Gibraltar (€27 one way, 80 minutes) on Fridays. The same company also offers day trips with an English-speaking guide, lunch and transfer included for €56, overnight trips staying in Tangier for €89, or two nights in the laid-back seaside resort of Asilah for €86. All travellers must carry a passport.

modern comforts with a colourful Moorish ambience. Its prize-winning interior patio, a large roof terrace and basement cave bar are added bonuses. Among the numerous communal areas at the labyrinthine **Hotel La Casa del Califa** (Plaza de España 16, 956 44 77 30, www.lacasadelcalifa.com, double €65-€85, restaurant €€) is a cushion-filled Arab-style lounge, a well-stocked library and a gorgeous secret garden and restaurant. The **Convento de San Francisco** (La Plazuela s/n, 956 45 10 01, double €77, restaurant €) dates back to the 17th century, with long, silent corridors and monastic features. A new addition is the boutiquey **Aqui Vejer** (C/Badillo 1-3, 956 45 07 90, www.aquivejer.com, double €80-€91). Built within the old walls of the village with interior courtyards, it has a designer feel.

Vejer is also gaining a well-deserved reputation as the dining room of the Costa de la Luz. For market-fresh tapas, **El Palenque** (C/Francisco 1, 956 45 17 04, closed Jan, €) occupies a fine sun trap in a patio behind the market. The food at **Restaurante Trafalgar** (Plaza de España 31, 956 44 76 38, closed Jan-mid Feb, €€-€€€) runs from Moroccan to Turkish to Greek, with pan-fried aubergines with tsatsiki, scrambled eggs with boquerones and coriander, tuna steaks and roast duck. For cutting-edge French cuisine in a restored 16th-century chapel, **La Vera Cruz** (C/Eduardo Shelly 1, 956 45 16 83, closed Jan & Wed Sept-July, €€€) is rapidly blazing a trail as one of the region's best restaurants; choose from home-made foie gras, local red mullet with leek compote, and duck breast with citrus glaze.

Bolonia is the place to be if you just want some quality seaside R&R. More places to stay are gradually springing up, but the best remains **La Posada de Lola** (C/El Lentiscal 26, 956 68 85 36, www.hostallola.com, double €37-€59), with a lush garden overlooking the hills, and fresh, cheerful rooms. **Hostal Rios** (Playa de Bolonia, 956 68 85 44, closed Nov, double €54-€75, apartment €54-€70) has basic, clean rooms and apartments overlooking the beach. **Hostal Los Jerezanos** (Playa de Bolonia, 956 68 85 45, double €80-€90 half-board) is a fairly simple place, and the communal spaces have more charm than the rooms themselves. All have small, closed-in terraces and there's a swimming pool.

The best place to eat in Bolonia is **Bar Las Rejas** (El Lentiscal 8, 956 68 85 46, €-€€, closed Wed from May to June and Mon-Fri from Oct to Apr). Aside from the roaring fire in the wintertime, little has been done to make this a welcoming place, but the home-made food can be wonderful and tends to offer more unusual treats, such as superb *croquetas* with squid ink. **Los Troncos** (Playa de Bolonia, 956 68 85 33, closed Dec-Feb, €-€€) has a lovely, grass garden leading down to the beach and a great *frito Bolonia* (the local fish fry), which includes baby squid, prawns, sardines, anchovies from the market in Barbate, all served in a great messy heap for €11. The *chiringuitos* in front of Baelo Claudia are also decent lunch stops. Or, at the opposite end of town, where the coast road peters out, **La Cabaña** is a lovely, thatched bar serving killer cocktails as the sun sets.

Resources

Internet

Barbate *Ciberplaya Lopez, Avda Atlántico 13 (956 43 04 34)* **Open** 10.30am-2.30pm, 4.30pm-11pm daily.

Conil de la Frontera *Café de la Habana, Plaza de Santa Catalina s/n (956 44 34 84).* **Open** 11.30am-midnight Mon-Thur, Sun; 11.30am-2am Fri, Sat.

Vejer de la Frontera *Por Ir Ya Estoy, Plaza San Francisco s/n (no phone).* **Open** varies.

Tourist information

Barbate *Avda/José Antonio 23 (956 43 39 62/www.barbate.es).* **Open** 8am-2.30pm Mon-Fri.

Conil de la Frontera *C/Carretera 1 (956 44 05 01/www.conil.org).* **Open** *June-Sept* 10.30am-2pm, 6-9pm daily. *Oct-Apr* 9am-2pm Mon-Sat.

Vejer de la Frontera *C/Los Remedios 2 (956 45 17 36/www.turismovejer.com).* **Open** *July-Sept* 10am-2pm, 4-9pm Mon-Sat; 10am-2pm Sun. *Oct-June* 10am-2pm, 4-6pm Mon-Sat.

Zahara de los Atunes *C/Doctor Sanchez Rodriguez s/n (956 44 95 25).* **Open** 11am-2pm, 6-9pm daily.

Tarifa

Welcome to the capital of the 'Costa del Windsurf' and the most happening town on the Costa de la Luz. With its lively, party atmosphere, brightly painted bars, sunny *plazas*, and warren-like, cobblestoned streets, **Tarifa** has a unique vibe that belongs more to the Caribbean, California or even nearby Africa than it does to Spain. It is one of the foremost windsurfing and kite-surfing destinations in the world, and the constant wind has led to hundreds of power-generating windmills being erected in the area. It's also the most southerly point of Europe – just 11 kilometres (seven miles) across the straits from Africa and a mere 35 minutes by boat (*see p160* **Into Africa**).

Tarifa's name derives from that of Tarif ibn Malik, the Moorish leader who took the town in 710 – the first Moorish possession in Spain – and made it the springboard for the Arab conquest. Castilian troops captured Tarifa

The church of **San Mateo**.

almost 600 years later (in 1292), and two thirds of the city walls that they built, plus the main gate, the **Puerta de Jerez**, are still standing. The 15th-century church of **San Mateo** (open hours of services) hides a beautiful late-Gothic interior behind a baroque exterior (added in the 18th century). It's also worth stopping in at the neo-Mudéjar market on C/Colón. The most impressive sight of all, however, is across the straits – the smoky-blue outline of Africa's Rif Mountains, best seen from atop the ramparts of the tenth-century Castillo de Guzmán el Bueno.

A tour of the **Castillo de Guzmán el Bueno** begins with the grisly account of how, during the Moorish siege of 1292, the enemies of Christian commander Alonso Pérez de Guzmán captured his nine-year-old son and demanded the keys to the castle in exchange for the boy's life. Refusing to give up his cause, Guzmán threw down his own knife from the ramparts in defiance, and was forced to watch as the Moors slit the boy's throat before him. He did, however, save Tarifa from the Moors, who returned to Africa empty-handed.

The majority of visitors, though, come to Tarifa for the sand, surf and summer beach parties along **Playa de los Lances**, due west of the town centre. However, conditions that make it a hot spot for windsurfers can make it sandblasting hell for anyone who just wants to lie in the sun. Tiny, scallop-shaped **Playa Chiquitita** is better for more sheltered bathing. Several miles west, a turn-off to Punta Paloma leads to a giant sand dune called **Playa de Valdevaqueros**, which is parked up with innumerable surfers' camper-vans in high season. But from here you can walk along the coast looking for more secluded coves and easily escape any crowds.

If you fancy taking advantage of the wealth of activities available in the area, try **Club Mistral** (Hurricane Hotel, A48, km78, 956 68 90 98, *see p164*) for kite- and windsurfing; **Aventura Marina** (€50 incl all equipment, with a second dive for just €28) at Club de Buceo Bahia (Avda Andalucía 1, www.aventuramarina.org, 956 05 46 26, mobile 609 59 40 20) for scuba diving; **FIRMM España** (C/Pedro Cortés 4, 956 62 70 08, tickets €30 for 2hr trip) or **Whale Watch España** (Avda de la Constitución 6, 956 68 22 47, www.whalewatchtarifa.net, tickets €30) are the places for whale- and dolphin-watching; and **Hurricane Hipica** (A48, km78, 956 68 90 92, www.tarifahip.com) is one for horse riding.

Castillo de Guzmán el Bueno

Open *June-mid Sept* 11am-2pm, 6-8pm Tue-Sat; 11am-2pm Sun. *Mid Sept-May* 11am-2pm, 5-7pm Tue-Sat; 11am-2pm Sun. **Admission** €1.80. **No credit cards**.

Where to eat & drink

Tarifa has an international restaurant scene, ranging from pizza and pasta to Mexican, Greek and North African. C/Sancho IV el Bravo is a good daytime grazing ground, with **Café Central** the prime spot for people-watching. You'll find most of the good dinner places around C/San Francisco, or the main drag, C/Batalla del Salado.

For more upmarket dining, the restaurant at the **Hotel Hurricane** (*see p164*, €€€) serves top-notch imaginative dishes using local produce on a verdant garden terrace. The A48 from Tarifa to Barbate also has an abundance of roadside eateries, ranging from *ventas* (country inn-style taverns) to theme bars.

Also check out **Venta El Juncal** (Ctra Santuario de la Luz, 956 68 11 22, closed Fri from Sept to June, €), which is almost iconic as a stop among travelling salesmen and surfers. It has heart-warming views across rolling countryside from its terrace. Best dishes include *pollo del campo* (local free-range chicken) and *potaje de garbanzos* (chickpea stew).

Where to stay

To get an idea of the kind of crowds to expect in high season, note that the campsites lining the shore provide space for around 4,000 tents. It's fiendishly difficult to get a room at this time, so booking is essential.

Out of season, take your pick from cheap and cheerful backpackers' *hostales* to chic boutique hotels. In the historic quarter just along from the church, the **Pensión Correo** (C/Coronel Moscardó 8, 956 68 02 06, www.pensioncorreo.

com, closed 2wks late Dec, double €50-€70) is a delightful, family-run *hostal* with eight brightly decorated rooms and a penthouse with private roof terrace. **Misiana** (C/San Joaquin 2, 956 62 70 83, www.misiana.com, double €61-€112) has gone a bit mad with the paintbox, but the penthouse is a treat, with lots of dark wood and leather. It also boasts the highest roof terrace in Tarifa, with stunning views over the town. Across the street, **La Sacristía** (C/San Donato 8, 956 68 17 59, www.lasacristia.net, double €115-€135) has become *the* boutique hotel of recent years, with its restaurant, café and clothing shop all crammed into a pint-sized patio. Rooms are cool and romantic, if a little on the small side, with four-poster beds and mosaic-tiled bathrooms.

Casa Amarilla (C/Sancho IV el Bravo 9, 956 68 19 93, www.lacasaamarilla.net, apartment for 2 €46-€70) is great for longer stays, offering 11 colourful Moorish-style apartments. **Hostal Africa** (C/María Antonia Toledo 12, 956 68 02 20, double €30-€60) is a snappily restored townhouse, popular with backpackers, with airy rooms, a roof terrace and storage space for bikes and boards. Just on the other side of the Puerta Jerez, **Hostal Asturiano** (C/Amador de los Rios 8, 956 68 06 19, double €45-€80) is tastefully furnished and a good bet if you can't find a room right in the centre.

Resort-type hotels face the beach a few kilometres out of town to the north. The **Arte Vida** (A48, km79.3, 956 68 52 46, www.hotelartevida.com, double €85-€130) is overrun with bronzed surfers. It has funky rooms with flowing white linen, hammocks and, of course, amazing views. Another place popular with the surfing fraternity, is **100% Fun** (A48, km76, 956 68 03 30, www.100x100fun.com, closed Nov-Feb, double €75-€115, restaurant €). It has a swimming pool, jungle-like garden, a Caribbean-feel beach-hut design and a good Tex-Mex restaurant. With its dramatic two-storey arches, Eastern-inspired bedrooms and palm-fringed views of the sea, the **Hotel Hurricane** (A48, km78, 956 68 49 19, www.hotelhurricane.com, double €89-€166) is down-to-earth and friendly despite its *Wallpaper** good looks.

Resources

Police station

Plaza Santa María 3 (956 68 21 74)

Post office

C/Coronel Moscardó 9 (956 68 42 37).

Tourist information

Paseo de la Alameda s/n (956 68 09 93/ www.aytotarifa.com). **Open** *July-mid Sept* 10.30am-2pm, 6-8pm Mon-Fri; 9am-2pm Sat & Sun. *Mid Sept-June* 10.30am-2pm, 4-6pm Mon-Fri; 9am-2pm Sat & Sun.

Algeciras & La Línea

As you cross the mountain range that separates Tarifa from **Algeciras** (stopping en route at the Mirador El Estrecho to take in the views), there is a sudden transformation in the scenery from the rolling hills, craggy mountaintops and blustery skies of the Costa de la Luz to the parched desert-like landscapes of the Costa del Sol. The greatest temptation on approaching Algeciras itself is to keep going. It's a polluted, industrial port, riddled with dodgy characters selling any illicit substance they can get their hands on. Most visitors today are here for one reason only: to catch the next ferry to Morocco.

If you are stuck here for a while, the San Isidro neighbourhood, around the leafy **Parque María Cristina**, is one of the oldest parts of the city and its narrow, cobblestoned streets and crooked houses are unexpectedly charming. Recent excavations of the Merinid town of **al-Binya**, discovered north of the Miel River and dating back to 1279, can be seen behind the fencing, and could finally put the town on the cultural map, at least for archaeology buffs.

The vibrant Andalucían flavour of the old town contrasts sharply with the heavy Arab influence elsewhere, particularly in July and August when the port bustles with Moroccan migrants returning home from their jobs in other parts of Spain and Europe. Around the port, the small bazaars and Moroccan tea shops are OK if you don't have time to head across the straits for the real thing. Be warned, this area is notorious for bag-snatchers and pickpockets.

Another town generally used as a transit point, this time for Gibraltar, is **La Línea de la Concepción**, across the Bay of Algeciras. Surrounded by eucalyptus groves, this low-rise, yellow-painted fishermen's village has been totally bypassed by the *costa* boom, which is both its curse and its blessing. Still relatively poor, the fisherman's quarter boasts fabulous views of the mighty Rock and some superb seafood restaurants, while the old town is a rather handsome affair with decent enough cafés. Make no mistake though, this is a gritty, *gitano* town with a deserved reputation for being a bit rough around the edges.

Where to stay & eat

In Algeciras, you'll find numerous cheap *hostales* in the streets behind Avda de la Marina and the port, and they vary considerably in quality. The **Hotel Marina Victoria** (Avda de la Marina 7, 956 65 01 11, double €45-€50) is a good bet if you're crossing the straits to Morocco early in the morning. The best rooms look directly over the port. The most upmarket place (and the first hotel to be built on the Andalucían coast) is the four-star **Reina Cristina** (Paseo de la Conferencia s/n, 956 60 26 22, www.reinacristina.com, double €83-€107), a beautiful colonial building set in verdant gardens that has welcomed the likes of Churchill, Roosevelt, Conan Doyle, Lorca, Orson Welles, Rock Hudson and Cole Porter. It was built by the British at the same time as they constructed the railway to Ronda.

More of a home than a hotel, the **Monte de la Torre** (Los Barrios, Cádiz, 956 66 00 00, www.andalucia.com/montedelatorre, closed mid Dec-mid Jan, double €120), five or so kilometres north of Algeciras in Los Barrios, is a good base for exploring the nearby Parque Natural de los Alcornocales. It's a fine 100-year-old house with period decor and vast gardens. Another good out-of-town option is the converted 15th-century convent of **La Almoraima** (A369, km22, 956 69 30 02, www.la-almoraima.com, double €102) with its original tower still intact. The convent has been sensitively remodelled, with tastefully furnished rooms arranged around a quiet courtyard.

In the town centre you'll find a number of decent restaurants around Plazas Alta and Palma serving good fish and seafood. **Restaurante Montes** (C/Juan Morrison 27, 956 65 42 07, €-€€€) is one of the more established places, offering a reasonable set menu. It specialises in *urta* (a succulent white fish, a member of the bream family). **Casa Castro** (Avda Blas Infante 5, no phone) is a classic, characterful drinking den, while the **Café Opera** (C/Alfonso XI 8, 956 66 48 50) attracts a well-heeled clientele; the pavement terrace is a choice locale for supping on a good cup of java and watching the world go by. The bazaars around the port offer Moroccan-style snacks. Otherwise, pack a picnic lunch from the market on Plaza Palma, and head for the leafy Parque de María Cristina.

If you are heading down to Tarifa from Málaga, it's well worth timing it so you can stop in La Línea around lunchtime. Check out **Bar Nuevo Hermanos Tomilleros** (Avda Menéndez Pelayo, 956 17 02 66, closed Mon and 2wks Sept, €). The bars on the windows and strip-lighting do little for the atmosphere, but the boat-fresh fish and seafood is superlative. It gets packed with locals so it's worth getting here for about 1.30pm. More upscale is the indigo-painted **Restaurante La Marina** (Paseo Marítimo s/n, La Atunara, 956 17 15 31, www.rest-lamarina.es, €€). There's a small terrace on to the sea, or a colonial-style dining room serving a full repertoire of the treasures of the deep as well as a good, authentic paella. Tapas are available at the bar and include more unusual delicacies such as sea urchins.

The best place to stay is probably the **Hotel La Línea de la Concepción** (C/Caireles 2, 956 17 55 66, www.ac-hoteles.es, double €73-€84), which is big, modern and efficient, with friendly staff and a pool. Gibraltar is a short cab ride or 25-minute walk away.

Resources

Internet

Info Net Algeciras, Av Virgen de la Palma 1 (956 66 52 74). **Open** 10am-2pm, 5-10pm Mon-Sat; 5-10pm Sun.

Tourist information

C/Juan de la Cierva s/n (956 57 26 36/www.ayto-algeciras.es). **Open** 9.30am-7.30pm Mon-Fri; 10am-2pm Sat & Sun.

Getting there

By boat

There are 2 daily sailings between Tarifa and Tangier by Ferries Rapidos de Sur (956 68 18 30, journey time 35mins). From Algeciras there are almost hourly ferry crossings every day to Ceuta and Tangier, taking around 1hr and 2hrs respectively. The fast ferry (*rápido*) to Ceuta takes 40mins, but is more expensive. Be sure to buy a ticket in advance during the summer months. Several companies operate out of Algeciras port. Euro Ferries (956 65 11 78) and Transmediterránea (902 45 46 45, www.transmediteranea.es) operate frequent daily passenger and car ferries to both destinations.

By bus

Tarifa bus station is at C/Batalla del Salado (956 68 40 38). There are daily buses to most major cities in Andalucía, and around 10 a day between Tarifa and Algeciras. Algeciras has two bus stations. The Comes station (C/San Bernardo, 956 65 34 56) runs daily buses to towns like La Línea, Tarifa and Cádiz. For other main Andalucían cities, Portillo (902 143 144, www.ctsa-portillo.com) and Comes (902 199 208, www.tgcomes.es) both run services from C/San Bernardo 15 (956 65 10 55). There are buses connecting the towns along the Costa de la Luz, although their schedules tend to be erratic. In Conil, buses stop on C/Carretera de Punto, in front of Hotel Don Pelayo (956 44 29 16); in Barbate the bus stop is at Avda Generalísimo 1 (956 43 05 94), and in Vejer it's at La Plazuela (956 44 71 46).

By train

There are no rail services on the Costa de la Luz. Algeciras train station (902 24 02 02) is at Ctra de Cádiz s/n, with 2 daily trains to Madrid (from 6hrs), 3 to Granada (4hrs 20mins) and 4 to Ronda (1hr 50mins), calling at stations along the Guadiaro valley.

Gibraltar

The Mediterranean's little bit of seaside Britain.

Something of a curio, Gibraltar sticks out of the bottom of Spain like a gigantic Roman nose. Viewed from afar, it is an undeniably impressive sight, rising from the sea to a height of 426 metres (1,398 feet). Up close, the town is nothing if not eccentric and, though you probably won't want to spend a huge amount of time here, it is certainly worth a day-trip – far better to stay, however, in the cheaper, better value hotels across the border in La Línea and further afield.

HISTORY

The gatekeeper of two continents, Europe and Africa, it is often said that Gibraltar has more history than it knows what to do with. To the ancients, Gibraltar was known as Monscalpe – one of the mythical pillars of Hercules, said to be a religious shrine and an entrance to Hades (the other is Jbel Musa, on the African side). More recently it has been a key military outpost, long fought over by the European powers.

The name Gibraltar comes from a corruption of the Arabic Jebel Tariq (literally 'Tariq's Mountain'). The Tariq in question was Tariq ibn Ziyad, the Governor of Tangier, who landed here in 711 and used it as a staging post for the Islamic conquest of Spain. Gibraltar remained under Moorish occupation for the next six centuries until it was reconquered by Spanish armies in 1462. In 1704 it fell to the British, and, by the 1713 Treaty of Utrecht, was ceded to Britain in perpetuity. Hankering after its lost appendage, Spain laid siege to the rock twice, in 1727 and 1779, but ultimately failed to regain it.

During the 18th and 19th centuries Britain developed Gibraltar as an important naval base. Miles of tunnels and chambers were dug out of the limestone, and a self-supporting underground city was constructed.

The Rock played a pivotal role in World War II, while the post-war years were marked by expansion, turning Gibraltar into a residential and commercial centre. In 1963 the question of Gibraltar's status came before the UN, and Spain seized the opportunity to revive its claim to the Rock. This coincided with increasing restrictions at the border between Gibraltar and Spain, which culminated in the complete closure of the border by Franco in 1969. It remained closed for the next 15 years, causing huge resentment among the locals, which is still very much alive today. Although Spain continues with determination to vie for the reintegration of Gibraltar into her territory, Gibraltarians continue to insist on their right to self-determination.

Interestingly, despite the trappings of Britishness – from the bobbies on the beat to the Gibraltar pound (you'll pay more using euros), the population is a complete stew. Gibraltarians – 75 per cent of the population – are a mix of Genoese, Jewish, Maltese, Spanish and British ancestry. About 14 per cent are really British, and about seven per cent are Moroccan. Yet, to many Gibraltarians, Spain seems as remote, hostile and alien as Mars.

With most of the garrison now gone, Gibraltar relies on tourism, banking and gambling to fuel its economy. It's also a tax haven for cheap booze, cigarettes, perfume and petrol. The town centre is an even grimmer version of run-down British seaside towns everywhere: chip shops, sweet rock and the smell of stale beer wafting out of grubby pubs.

Sightseeing

Despite covering a mere six square kilometres (two-and-a-half square miles), the Rock has no shortage of things to do. A cable car runs from Grand Parade at the far end of Main Street to the top of the Rock, with a stop at the **Apes' Den**, about halfway up. The famous Barbary apes (brought over from Morocco by the Moors) are Gibraltar's most popular attraction, but be warned, they have been known to bite, to steal and to pee on tourists while sitting on their heads. Don't feed them and keep your belongings clutched tightly to you. Traditionally it's been said that if the apes ever disappear from Gibraltar, so too will the British.

Gibraltar is riddled with caves and more than 140 have been discovered so far. The most famous is **St Michael's Cave**, to the south of the summit, which was long believed to be bottomless and a possible subterranean link to Africa. Summer concerts and recitals are often held inside its vast 'auditorium'. James Joyce fans take note: this was the site of Molly Bloom's deflowering in *Ulysses*.

Excavated by the British army in the late 18th century, the **Great Siege Tunnels** form part of may well be the most impressive defence system in the world. What you see today, including the office of General Eisenhower, is only a small part of what was once a 51-kilometre (32-mile) network that housed up to 18,000 Allied soldiers during World War II.

Further down the Rock, the **Moorish Castle** has a small museum showing two or three examples of intricately patterned Berber carpets from the High Atlas Mountains. In Moorish times, woven shapes within the fabric were used as code between the rulers of the day. The detailed intricacy of some carpets meant that the eyesight of the women making them deteriorated to such an extent that they could only make three in a lifetime.

In town, the **Gibraltar Museum** offers an interesting journey into Gibraltar's 200-million-year history, from the time when it was still geographically part of Africa. Highlights include the skull of a Neanderthal woman, discovered on the Rock in 1848, eight years before a similar skull was found in the Neander Valley, near Düsseldorf. Close by is the **Nefusot Yehuda Synagogue**. Dating from 1724, it is one of the oldest synagogues on the Iberian Peninsula. Tours are available with Holy Land Travel (75965) for a minimum donation of £3.

The **Shrine of Our Lady of Europe** (71230, closed Wed, Sat & Sun summer), originally a mosque, was converted into a chapel by the Spanish in 1462. This was the original Gibraltar lighthouse, sacked by the fearsome pirate Barbarossa. Miraculously, according to devotees, he missed the 15th-century statue of the Virgin and Child (still in place).

Gibraltar is probably the best spot in Andalucía for scuba diving, due to the nature of the Rock and the underwater life that dwells there. It's also among the cheapest. Try **Rock Marine Dive Gibraltar** (The Square, Marina Bay, 73147, www.divegibraltar.com). It's BSAC accredited and offers dives for £20 to £30.

Cable car

Lower station 77826/Upper station 78759.
Open *Departs from lower station* 9.30am-5.15pm daily. *Returns to lower station* 9.30am-5.45pm daily. Closed Sun Nov-Mar. **Tickets** *Return* £8; £16 incl entrance to nature reserve. **Credit** MC, V.

Gibraltar Museum

18-20 Bomb House Lane (74289/www.gib.gi/museum). **Open** 10am 6pm Mon-Fri; 10am-2pm Sat. **Admission** £2; £1 concessions. **Credit** MC, V.

Upper Rock Nature Reserve

Upper Rock. **Open** *June-Sept* 9.30am-6.45pm daily. *Oct-May* 9.30am-6pm daily **Admission** *Nature reserve only* 50p. *Nature reserve & attractions* £8; £4 concessions; £1.50 vehicles. **No credit cards**. The Apes' Den, the Moorish Castle, the Great Siege Tunnels and St Michael's Cave are all part of the Nature Reserve.

Where to eat & drink

If you've arrived from Spain, you'll need to revert to British eating hours and prices. You won't find any shortage of pub grub, fried breakfasts and fish-and-chip shops. However, with the recent smartening up of Gibraltar's image, the Rock's culinary efforts seem to be on the up too, and there's plenty of variety. For all-day English fry-ups, the **Star Bar** (12 Parliament Lane, 75924, £) is apparently one of the best, and is Gibraltar's oldest bar. **The Clipper** (78B Irish Town, 79791, £) offers hearty, home-cooked meals in a trad pub atmosphere. However, it could soon be outclassed by **Simon's** (44 Cornwall's Lane, 47515, closed Sun, ££-£££), a small, intimate bistro offering dishes like king prawn and spinach tart, and grilled swordfish.

Sacarello Coffee House (57 Irish Town, 70625, closed Sun, £) is a good bet for vegetarian snacks and home-made cakes, and **The Breadbin** (49 Main Street, 44558, closed Sun) makes a good range of tasty sandwiches, ideal for the beach or picnics. **Al Andalus** (3/2 College Lane, 49184, closed Sun, £) is good for Moroccan dishes, or try **Café Solo** (Unit 3, Casemates Square, 44449, £-££) for unfussy, well-prepared Italian dishes. **The Little Mermaid** (4/5 Admiral's Walk, Marina Bay, 77660, closed Sun, £-££) does Danish fare, such as marinated herring, and smoked eel and scrambled eggs. **Da Paolo** (Marina Bay, 76799, closed Sun, ££) is a great spot for fresh fish and has a fine wine list. **La Mamela** (Catalan Bay, 72373, £-££), meaning 'woman's breast', is named after the rock jutting out of the wash at the southern end of the beach. It's far and away the best fish restaurant in town, with specialities such as *caldereta del pescado y marisco* (a hearty seafood stew), though this must be booked a day in advance.

For truly world-class cooking there are two options: **Nuno's** Italian restaurant at the Caleta Hotel (Sir Herbert Miles Road, 76501, ££) is a highly sophisticated eaterie serving excellent pasta and breads made on the premises, and fine Italian wines, in a dramatic promontory location. On the other side of the Rock, **The Rib Room** at The Rock Hotel (3 Europa Road, 73000, www.rockhotelgibraltar.com, ££-£££) also has fine sea views and an interesting menu.

Nightlife

Although there are supposedly over 360 pubs here, Gib's nightlife is modest to say the least. The few more upmarket bars around Casemates Square attract a young, trendy crowd. **Corks Wine Bar** (79 Irish Town, 75566) gets busy mainly at weekends and has a touch more class than the local boozers, plus occasional live music. For dancing, there is **The Tunnel** (Casemates Square, 44878) or the **UnderGround** (8 West Place of Arms, 40651), with two dancefloors; however, more discerning clubbers hop across to Spain, where **Gabba** in La Línea is about the hottest thing around. Your only other option is to hit the tables of the **Casino** (7 Europa Road, 76666) next to The Rock hotel.

Resources

To phone Gibraltar from outside Spain, dial the international access number, then 350 and the local five-digit number. From within Spain, call 9567, and then the local number, unless you're within Cádiz province, where you dial 7 then the local number.

Patriotism, living and dead.

Internet

Café Cyberworld, Units 14-16, Ocean Heights Gallery (51416). **Open** noon-midnight daily.

Police station

New Mole House, Rosia Road (72500).

Post office

104 Main Street (75714).

Tourist information

Gibraltar Tourist Board, Duke of Kent House, Cathedral Square (74950/www.gibraltar.gi). **Open** 9am-5.30pm Mon-Fri.
Casemates Square office (74982). **Open** 10am-3pm Sat; 10am-1pm Sun.

Getting there

By air

There are direct flights from the UK to Gibraltar. For details on the airport, *see p308*.

By bus & car

Regular buses run from most of the major towns on the Costa to Gibraltar and/or, on the Spanish side, La Línea (the bus station is a 5min walk from the border). If you're visiting Gibraltar on a day trip, the easiest and quickest approach is to park your car at La Línea and walk or catch a bus (numbers 3 and 9) to the border. With the border now open 24 hours a day, the interminable queues of cars that once plagued the frontier are now reduced; average waiting time is around 20mins. You'll need a passport and, if you're travelling by car, insurance and rental documents, a certificate of registration, a nationality plate and a valid driving licence.

Málaga Province

Features

Maps

Málaga Province

Introduction

Forget the overdeveloped Costa del Sol and flee to the mountains and villages of the interior.

A third of all visitors to Andalucía don't get beyond Málaga province, and most of these don't go beyond the Costa del Sol, yet the ravaged coastline is by far the least appealing area of this beautiful and varied region. Travel inland for 20 minutes and you'll feel like you're in a different country of wildly picturesque mountains and too-perfect whitewashed villages. Tourism is far from unknown in the interior, but it's much more in balance with its environment than on the coast.

MÁLAGA CITY
Millions of package tourists may pass through its airport each year, but few of them trouble to visit the refreshingly Spanish provincial capital. There's history aplenty here, good shopping, a likeable, walkable centre, a new world-class Picasso museum and a varied and lively bar and restaurant scene that extends to the beaches east of the centre during summer.

COSTA DEL SOL
Spain's most infamous *costa* is not a pretty sight. Much of it is an endless agglomeration of concrete high-rises and heaving beaches, backed by monotonous *urbanizaciones* stretching ever further inland. Yet, if you're in the mood, it's not without appeal. Mad-for-it Torremolinos can be great fun, Marbella's prettified old town is genuinely lovely, and villages such as Benalmádena Pueblo and Casares retain much of their charm. And if it's crazy nightlife you're after, it's here in spades.

EAST OF MÁLAGA
Strictly speaking, the stretch of coastline east of Málaga is also part of the Costa del Sol, but it's generally less built-up. The resorts don't have much appeal until you reach Nerja – the most enjoyable town on the whole Costa. Stretching back from the coast is the relatively undiscovered and largely mountainous region known as the Axarquía, which contains any number of cute white-washed villages and offers fine walking.

NORTH OF MÁLAGA
Despite its proximity to the Costa del Sol, the country north of Málaga feels a world away. The major town here, Antequera, is a fascinating place, and there are compelling natural attractions nearby: the weird rock formations of El Torcal and the dramatic gorge of El Chorro.

WEST OF MÁLAGA
The wild scenery of the Serranía de Ronda, with its countless white villages, is a great draw. The spectacularly sited town of Ronda is a major tourist site, and in and around it are a wealth of stylish places to stay and eat.

The best...

Architecture
Antequera (*p194*).

Cool hotels, bars & restaurants
Ronda (*p200*).

Natural wonders
El Chorro (*p198*); **El Torcal** (*p197*).

Nightlife
Málaga City (*p172*); **Marbella** (*p181*); **Nerja** (*p191*); **Torremolinos** (*p178*).

Prehistory
Antequera (*p194*); **Cueva de la Pileta** (*p207*).

Towns
Antequera (*p194*); **Marbella** (*p181*); **Nerja** (*p191*); **Ronda** (*p200*).

Málaga City

Far more than just an airport: don't just pass through.

Málaga is the most genuine of all the towns on the Costa del Sol. With its vibrant old town, spit-and-sawdust tapas bars, pint-sized *plazas*, labyrinthine Jewish quarter and sunny, beach-side promenades, it has fiercely guarded its own special identity, refusing to become part of the resort frenzy further west. Add to that the enormous amount of money currently being thrown at it – pedestrianisation and beautification schemes, classy new hotels, the opening of the Picasso Museum – and this is clearly one city that is on the move.

Founded by the Phoenicians as Malaka in the eighth century BC, Málaga later became a prosperous Roman port, exporting iron, copper and lead from mines in the hills near Ronda. In the eighth century AD it was taken by the Moors and prospered under their rule until 1487. The city began attracting tourists in the 19th century, and since the 1960s it has been a hub for northern European sun-seekers – but is largely ignored as a destination in its own right. Thus it remains at heart a truly Spanish town, and, because of this, it's a great place to sample a real slice of Iberian life. The concrete blocks of its sprawling suburbs aren't prepossessing, but the lively, compact historic centre has retained its charm. The beaches (particularly El Pedregalejo) are good for long, lazy lunches, and the leafy Paseo del Parque is the place to head to stroll in the evenings with the locals.

Sightseeing

The most obvious place to begin is the **Catedral**, built on the site of the city's main mosque. Architecturally, it's a hotchpotch of styles: the heavy baroque façade was started in 1528, but not completed until the end of the 18th century, while the second bell tower was never built, earning the cathedral the nickname 'La Manquita' ('the one-armed one').

From here, C/San Agustín leads past the lovely **Museo Picasso Málaga**, which has brought the city new money, a new role and, above all, hope for a sparkling future. Thanks to the generosity of Picasso's heirs, the museum's permanent collection boasts 204 original works, which present a deeply personal retrospective of one of the most highly regarded artists of the 20th century. The collection traces the artist's development from his teenage years under the guidance of his father in A Coruña to his final piece *Man, Woman & Child*.

Beyond is the Plaza de la Merced and the **Casa Natal de Picasso**, where the artist was born in 1881. Today, the square is lined with pavement cafés, a lively place for drinks at night. (Be warned, though: it's also notorious for pickpockets and bag-snatchers.)

Art enthusiasts may also be interested in checking out the **CAC Málaga**, Málaga's contemporary art museum, which hosts an impressive line-up of international and home-grown artists.

Just north-west of Plaza Merced is the **Teatro Cervantes**, the most important theatre on the Costa del Sol, which hosts big-name music and theatre, as well as the annual **Festival de Málaga Cine Español** (Málaga Spanish Film Festival) in March.

South of the *plaza* is the most impressive of Málaga's sights: the Moorish **Alcazaba**. It was started in the 700s, but most of the current structure dates from the second half of the 11th century (though what you see now is largely a later rebuilding), when the break-up of the Western Caliphate allowed Málaga to declare its independence. Within the palace buildings is an archaeological museum. The grounds are an engaging series of rose gardens, interlaced with Moorish irrigation channels, stone fountains and brick archways. At the base of the Alcazaba, excavations of the impressive **Teatro Romano** (Roman Theatre) are just about complete after many years' work.

From here, a 20-minute climb up the hill brings you to the **Castillo de Gibralfaro**, commanding spectacular views over the city, and the **Jardines de Puerta Oscura** gardens, where the Moors are believed to have entered Málaga. The castle was built in the eighth century and later rebuilt in the 14th and 15th centuries. There's a shady café at the far end, a good spot to take in the views: you get a bird's-eye view of the **Plaza de Toros**, the Costa's most active bullring.

Five minutes' walk east of the bullring is the beautiful **Cementerio Inglés** (English Cemetery; open 10am-2pm daily, free, map p175 off F4), founded in 1829 to save non-Catholics the indignity of being buried on the beach in the middle of the night, it was the first of its kind in Spain. The brainchild and obsession

Architecturally confused, but gracious nonetheless: the **Catedral**. *See p172.*

of the British Consul William Mark, the lush cemetery, with its wonderful views down to the sea, inspired Hans Christian Andersen to write that he 'could well understand how a splenetic Englishman might take his own life in order to be buried in this place'.

On the west side of the centre, by the Guadalmedina river and housed within a 17th-century inn, is the **Museo de Artes y Costumbres Populares**, an enjoyably diverse museum dedicated to everyday life and social history over the past few centuries.

A few kilometres to the north lies the **Jardín Botánico La Concepción**, founded in the mid 19th century by an Englishwoman, Amalia Livermore, and her Spanish husband, and now an impressive and important botanic garden.

And there's no better way to finish a day of sightseeing than with a long, luxurious Turkish bath and massage in the beautiful, marble-lined steam rooms of **El Hammam**.

Alcazaba & the Castillo de Gibralfaro

C/Alcazabilla (952 22 72 30). **Open** *Apr-Sept* 9am-8pm daily. *Oct-Mar* 9am-6pm Tue-Sun. **Admission** €1.95; €3.20 for 2; 60¢ concessions; free after 2pm Sun. **No credit cards**. **Map** p175 D2/3.

CAC Málaga

C/Alemania s/n (952 12 00 55/www.cacmalaga.org). **Open** *Oct-mid June* 10am-8pm Tue-Sun. *Mid June-Sept* 10am-2pm, 5pm-9pm; times may change, so phone to check. **Admission** free. **Map** p175 off A4.

Casa Natal de Picasso

Plaza de la Merced 15 (952 06 02 15/www.fundacionpicasso.es). **Open** 10am-8pm Mon-Sat; 10am-2pm Sun. **Admission** €1. **No credit cards**. **Map** p175 E1.

Catedral & Museo Catedralicio

C/Molina Lario s/n (952 22 84 91). **Open** 10am-6pm Mon-Fri; 10am-5pm Sat. **Admission** €3.50; €1 concessions. **No credit cards**. **Map** p175 C3.

El Hammam

C/Tomás de Cózar 13 (952 21 23 27/www.elhammam.com). **Open** 10am-10pm daily. **Prices** *Bath* from €22. . **Credit** AmEx, DC, MC, V. **Map** p175 D2.

Jardín Botánico La Concepción

A45 Autopista Antequera–Madrid (952 25 21 48). **Open** 9.30am-5.30pm Tue-Sun; until 7pm Apr-Sept. Guided tours in English. **Admission** €3.15; €1.65 concessions. **No credit cards**.

Museo de Artes y Costumbres Populares

Pasillo de Santa Isabel 10 (952 21 71 37). **Open** 10am-1.30pm, 5-8pm Mon-Fri; 10am-1.30pm Sat. **Admission** €2; €1 concessions. **No credit cards**. **Map** p175 A1.

Museo Picasso Málaga

Palacio de los Condes de Buenavista, C/San Agustín 8 (902 44 33 77/www.museopicassomalaga.org). **Open** 10am-8pm Tue-Thur; 10am-9pm Fri, Sat; 10am-8pm Sun & hols. **Admission** *Collection* €6. *Exhibition* €4.50. *Combined* €8. Free under-10s. **No credit cards**. **Map** p175 D2.

Plaza de Toros

Paseo de Reding s/n (952 22 17 27/museum 952 22 62 92/www.plazalamalagueta.com). **Open** *Museum* 10am-1pm, 5-8pm Mon-Fri. **Admission** *Museum* €1.80. *Fights* €7-€111. **Credit** *Fights only* DC, MC, V. **Map** p175 F4.

Teatro Cervantes

C/Ramos Marín s/n (952 22 41 00/www.teatrocervantes.com). **Open** *Box office* 11am-2pm, 5.30-8.30pm Mon-Sat; 1hr before show on Sun. **Credit** DC, MC, V. **Map** p175 D1.

Where to eat & drink

You can tell it's time to *tapeo* in Málaga when the streets fill with the irresistible smells of frying fish, grilled seafood and lemon juice. Do as locals do and hop from one bar to another, grazing as you go on local wines, cured meats, cheeses and the famed *fritura malagueño* (a heap of golden fried fish). You should also check out the local-packed *marisquerías* (seafood joints) in the tiny alleyway of Calle Comisario, off the Alameda Principal.

No culinary tour of Málaga is complete without trying the local speciality, *sardinas ensartadas* (a string of grilled sardines), from the open-air cafés on El Pedregalejo beach.

For picnics, the wrought-iron **Mercado Central de Atarazanas** (map p175 A2) is fabulous for perky fresh fruit and vegetables, charcuterie, local cheeses and vats of olives.

Bar Orellana

C/Moreno Monroy 5 (952 223 012). **Open** 1.30-4pm, 8.30-11pm Tue-Sat; 1.30-4pm Sat. **Average** €. **No credit cards**. **Map** p175 C2 ❶

There's standing room only in this diminutive tapas bar, open since 1938. Free tapas given with drinks are excellent, but don't miss the *ligeras* (like tiny panini) of *palometa* (think thickly sliced smoked salmon), black pudding and so on.

Café de Paris

C/Vélez-Málaga 8 (952 22 50 43/www.rcafedeparis.com). **Open** 1.30-3.30pm, 8.30-10.30pm Tue-Sat. Closed last 2wks July. **Average** €€€€. **Credit** AmEx, DC, MC, V. **Map** p175 off F4.

One of the best restaurants in Andalucía, the Café de Paris boasts a Michelin star and a loyal following. Young chef José Carlos García dreams up dishes such as crayfish with creamed lettuce, and complements them with an extensive wine list.

La Casa del Angel

C/Madre de Dios 29 (952 60 87 50/www.lacasadelangel.com). **Open** 1-4pm, 8pm-midnight Tue-Sun. Closed 2wks June. **Average** €€€. **Credit** AmEx, DC, MC, V. **Map** p175 D1 ❷

This remarkable restaurant-museum is owned by the Spanish comedian Angel Garó. Its cuisine combines Grandma's home cooking with the region's Arabic heritage – with delicious results. The museum showcases an extraordinary collection of over 100 works from the 16th century to the present day, including pieces by Pablo Picasso, Joan Miró and Salvador Dalí. If you're not eating, it costs just €3 (including a drink) for a look around.

La Casa Guardia

Alameda Principal 18 (952 21 46 80). **Open** 9am-10pm Mon-Sat. **Average** €. **No credit cards**. **Map** p175 A3 ❸

The original and still the best; this is the oldest *taberna* in town (founded 1840). It serves Málaga wines, *manzanillas* and other sherries straight from the barrel, along with fresh grilled seafood tapas.

El Chinitas

C/Moreno Monroy 4-6 (952 21 09 72/952 22 64 40/www.chinitas.arrakis.es). **Open** 1-4pm, 8pm-midnight daily. **Average** €€€. **Credit** DC, MC, V. **Map** p175 B2 ❹

Once upon a time El Chinitas was frequented by bullfighters, artists and poets (including Lorca), and paraphernalia from those glory days abounds. It still offers an unarguably good feed, with dishes like rice and lobster, and acorn-fed pork loin topping the bill.

Clandestino

C/Niño de Guevara 3 (952 21 93 90/www.clandestino-resto.com). **Open** 1pm-1am daily. **Average** €-€€. **Credit** MC, V. **Map** p175 C2 ❺

Tucked away down a quiet side street in the heart of Malaga is this contemporary restaurant where black-clad and tattooed waiting staff serve imaginative world cuisine and Andalucían favourites.

El Marisquero

C/Olózaga 7 (mobile 670 064 804). **Open** 12.30-5pm daily. **Average** €. **No credit cards**. **Map** p175 A2 ❻

Fiercely popular with a local crowd, this no-nonsense seafood bar is the best place in town for fresh, excellent-value razor clams, spider crabs, crayfish, oysters and other treats from the deep.

Pepa y Pepe

C/Calderería 9 (mobile 615 656 984). **Open** 12.45-4pm, 8.15pm-midnight daily. **Average** €. **No credit cards**. **Map** p175 C1 ❼

A tiny neighbourhood bar with upended barrels providing outside seating. The Málaga wines here start at a dangerously low 70¢ a glass, while the super-fresh fried fish tapas will set you back a mere €2.50 for a generous half *ración*.

La Posada de Antonio

C/Granada 36 (952 21 70 69). **Open** 1pm-midnight Mon-Thur, Sun; 1pm-1am Fri, Sat. **Average** €€. **Credit** DC, MC, V. **Map** p175 C2 ❽

Antonio Banderas's barbecued meat barn packs in the punters for big juicy steaks, *chorizo*, chops, offal and chicken in all its guises, served on sizzling cast-iron platters.

El Refectorium

C/Cervantes 8 (952 21 89 90). **Open** 1-5pm Mon; 1-5pm, 8.30pm-midnight Tue-Sat. Closed 3wks June/July. **Average** €€-€€€. **Credit** DC, MC, V. **Map** p175 off F4.

A long-standing favourite with the bullfighting crowd (being situated just beyond the ring), El Refectorium is packed during *corridas*. At other times it's a great place for tapas or local dishes such as *ajo blanco* (garlic soup) and roast lamb.

La Tetería

C/San Agustín 9 (no phone). **Open** 3pm-midnight Mon; 9am-midnight Tue-Thur, Sun; 9am-2am Fri, Sat. **Average** €. **No credit cards**. **Map** p175 C2 ❾

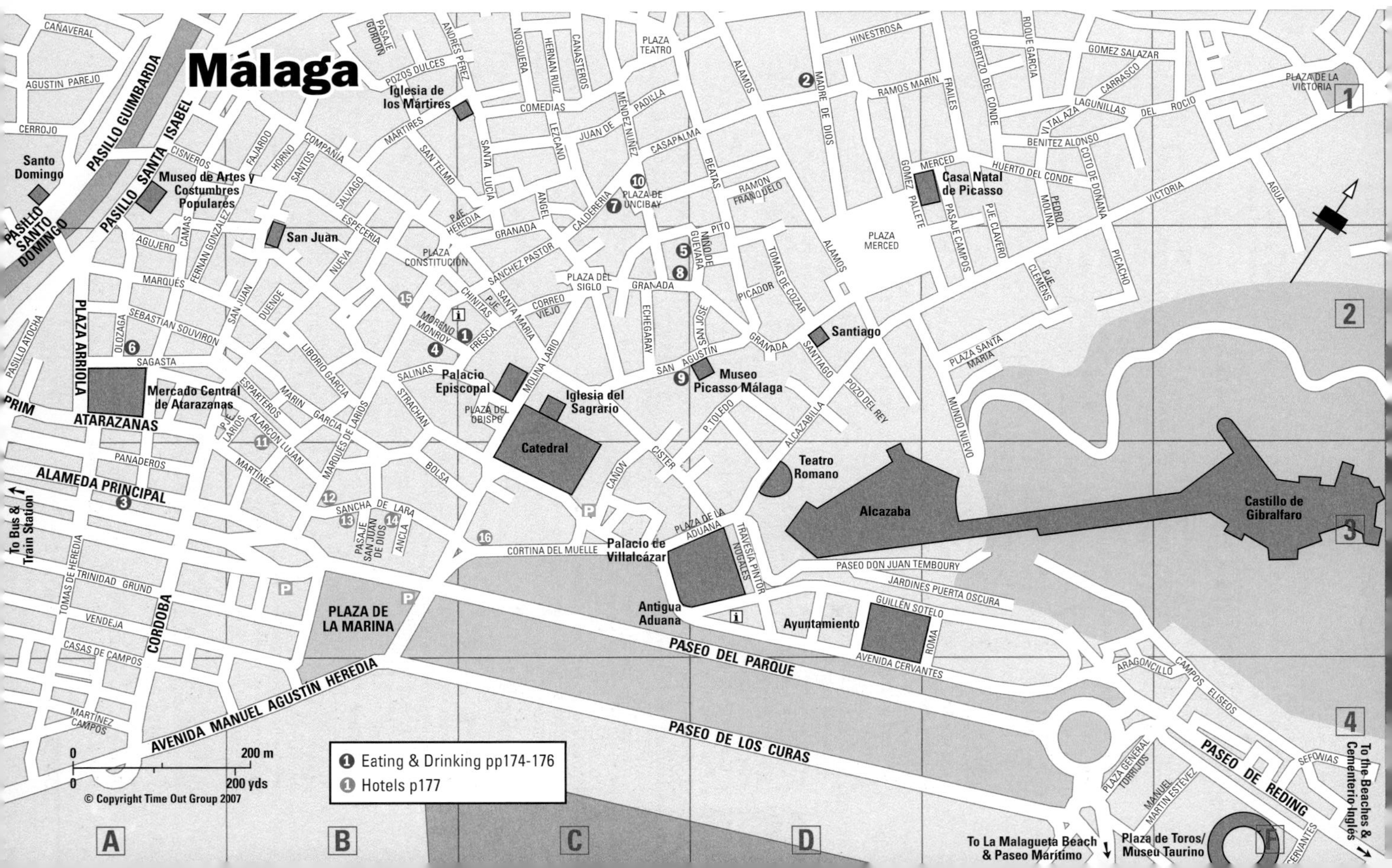
Málaga
Iglesia de los Mártires
Santo Domingo
Museo de Artes y Costumbres Populares
San Juan
Casa Natal de Picasso
Plaza Merced
Santiago
Museo Picasso Málaga
Palacio Episcopal
Iglesia del Sagrario
Catedral
Teatro Romano
Alcazaba
Castillo de Gibralfaro
Palacio de Villalcázar
Antigua Aduana
Ayuntamiento
Mercado Central de Atarazanas
Plaza de la Marina
Plaza Arriola
Alameda Principal
Paseo del Parque
Paseo de los Curas
Avenida Manuel Agustín Heredia
Paseo de Reding
Pasillo Guimbarda
Pasillo Santa Isabel
Pasillo Santo Domingo
Plaza de la Victoria
Plaza Teatro
Plaza Constitución
Plaza del Siglo
Plaza de Uncibay
Plaza del Obispo
Plaza de la Aduana
Plaza Santa María
Plaza General Torrijos
Cortina del Muelle
Paseo Don Juan Temboury
Jardines Puerta Oscura
Avenida Cervantes
Mundo Nuevo
Victoria
Alcazabilla
Granada
Álamos
Madre de Dios
Hinestrosa
Córdoba
Atarazanas
Prim
To Bus & Train Station
To La Malagueta Beach & Paseo Marítimo
Plaza de Toros/ Museu Taurino
To the Beaches & Cementerio Inglés
Eating & Drinking pp174-176
Hotels p177
200 m
200 yds
© Copyright Time Out Group 2007

All the fun of the *feria*

Even in Andalucía, no big city *feria* can compete with the wildness of Málaga's annual shindig. It all kicks off one Friday evening during the second or third week of August each year, when a Spanish celeb delivers the opening address – Julio Iglesias has had a turn, so too the revered young vocalist Estrella Morente – the fireworks go off and the party is on.

During the day you won't be able to avoid it. The old centre is taken up with people dancing the folkloric in the streets and squares, the bullring attracts a large and drunken crowd for its *corridas* and young girls in polka-dotted red, green and blue flamenco dresses are waltzed by dapper young boys in formal attire.

Back in 1498, when the *feria* began, it was a traditional religious event. It was only divided in response to the post-Civil War rise in tourism. Despite the loss of some traditions – children used to to ride horses through the city's main central squares during the day – what hasn't changed is the copious amount of *vino de málaga* (similar to sherry) dished out during the day. As with all proper festivals, the party is constantly evolving: these days you're likely to see the city's arterial road, C/Larios, jammed with young *malagueños* mixing it with foreigners to the bump of reggaeton. Following a crackdown after complaints about the noise, the day's fun is now all over by about 6pm and the action moves on to the night-time entertainments, held out in the Cortijo de Torres area. The night *feria* offers a funfair, a young people's area and lines of communal *casetas*. These 'small houses' are set up by neighbourhood associations, labour groups, political organisations and sports clubs. Unlike, say, the *feria* in Seville, these *casetas* are open to anyone, members and non-members alike, as a result of which you could find yourself drinking and dancing to Spanish diva Lola Flores at the Málaga scuba-diving association, bopping away to Ricky Martin with the Young Socialists' League of Málaga, twirling to *sevillanas* inside the Trinidad neighbourhood association or moshing to heavy-duty punk courtesy of the Málaga Squatters' League. It's all done with an unpretentiousness and openess that makes the *feria* damn good fun.

Gigs laid on in the evenings have featured everyone from Spain's first flamenco-blues legends Pata Negra to local hip hop star Mala Rodríguez. Afterwards, there's more dancing, usually until the sun comes up – and the next day's party starts.

Málaga Province

Situated right opposite the Museo Picasso, this charming Moroccan tearoom is a quiet place to start the day over a breakfast of muesli and yogurt.

El Tintero II

Ctra Almería 99 (952 20 44 64). **Open** 12.30pm-1.30am daily. **Average** €€. **No credit cards.**
On the seafront in El Palo, east of the centre, this popular, lively fish restaurant is a real experience – there's no menu, you just have to grab a waiter walking past with a plate of something you fancy.

Trayamar

Plaza Uncibay 9 (952 21 54 59). **Open** 2-4pm, 9pm-midnight Mon-Sat. **Average** €€€€. **Credit** AmEx, DC, MC, V. **Map** p175 C1 ⑩
A new addition to the city's hip-list, Trayamar is young, cool and minimalist, with surprisingly assured and sophisticated cooking.

Nightlife

Málaga is a city of many bars and few discos – most of the liveliest places can be found around Calles Granada, San Agustín and Méndez Núñez, north of the cathedral. The **Bodegas El Pimpi** (C/Granada 62, 952 22 89 90) is a classic drinking den, housed in a 200-year-old convent; it's where Antonio and Melanie drink when in town. **Onda Pasadena** (C/Gomez Pallete 5, no phone) has live music every night of the week, covering jazz, blues and flamenco. For cocktails and DJ grooves every night, check out **Mondo_Tike** (C/Méndez Núñez 3, no phone). But for grown-up drinks, head for the roof terrace at the **Hotel Larios** (*see p177*) – you can't beat a balmy night here under the stars with panoramic views. Increasingly popular with gay and straight crowds is the area around Plaza de la Merced. The **Café Calle de Bruselas** (No.16, 952 60 39 48) is reliable to start or end the night.

If Latin dancing is your thing, **Asúcar** (C/Juan de Padilla, no phone) gets steamy well into the early hours, and has free classes most nights. Málaga is not much of a flamenco city, but there is a **Museo Flamenco** at Peña de Juan Breva (Callejón Picador 2, 952 21 08 76), with shows from 11pm most Fridays. For live shows, try **Tablao Flamenco Vista Andalucía** (Avda Los Guindos 29, 952 23 11 57, www.vista andalucia.com, closed Sun & Mon).

Things really hot up during the *locos veranos* (or 'crazy summers') in the beach areas, with all-night music and dancing. **El Balneario** (C/Bolivia 40, 952 20 33 57, closed Mon Oct-May) is an outdoor bar, open all day. It may seem tatty and run-down, but the kids love it.

Where to stay

There's a handful of good hotels and *hostales* in the old centre, and another clutch in the streets just south of the Alameda Principal. An attractive alternative is the beachside neighbourhood of El Pedregalejo, which consists of low-rise, gingerbread houses and cute, two-storey cottages along the shore, a 30-minute walk from the centre.

Cohíba Hotel

Paseo Marítimo 64, El Pedregalejo (952 20 69 00/www.cohibahotel.com). **Rates** (incl breakfast) €57-€71 single; €89-€114 double; €113-€141 suite. **Credit** AmEx, DC, MC, V.
The best little beach hotel in Málaga, this three-star Cuban-owned place has cheerful rooms and a communal kitchen. It's also a happening nightspot.

Hostal Derby

Pasaje San Juan de Dios 1, 4° (952 22 13 01). **Rates** €30-36 single; €43-€48 double. **No credit cards.**
A friendly *hostal* with cheap, cheerful rooms. The best is number 15, with windows giving fine views over the port. There's also a communal balcony.

Hostal Juanita

4th floor, C/Alarcon Lujan 8 (952 21 35 86). **Rates** €25-€31 single; €35-€52 double; €48-€64 triple; €64-€86 quad. **No credit cards. Map** p175 B2/3 ⓫
A lift carries you to this fourth-floor *hostal* right in the centre of town. Rooms are simple but fresh, bright and airy.

Hostal Larios

3rd floor, C/Marqués de Larios 9 (952 22 54 90). **Rates** €29-€32 single; €47-€60 double. **Credit** MC, V. **Map** p175 B3 ⓬
Opened in 2004, this *hostal* is simple and neat with bright rooms (the best have balconies), all with their own bathroom, TV and air-conditioning.

Hostal Victoria

C/Sancha de Lara 3 (952 22 42 23). **Rates** €37-€72 single; €45-€90 double. **Credit** AmEx, DC, MC, V. **Map** p175 B3 ⓭
All rooms in this centrally located *hostal* have private bathroom and tub. Ask for one at the front; the rooms at the rear are a little poky.

Hotel Don Curro

C/Sancha de Lara 9 (952 22 72 00/www.hoteldoncurro.com). **Rates** €69-€76 single; €97-€100 double. **Credit** AmEx, DC, V. **Map** p175 B3 ⓮
This three-star hotel enjoys a central location and has modern, spacious rooms, a bar and a restaurant.

Hotel Larios

C/Marqués de Larios 2 (952 22 22 00/www.hotellarios.com). **Rates** €94-€123 single; €123-€164 double; €246-€278 suite. **Credit** AmEx, DC, MC, V. **Map** p175 B2 ⓯
The 40-room art deco Larios is Antonio Banderas's hotel of choice when revisiting the town of his youth. Dead central, it has a fabulous roof terrace and bar, stylish rooms and a bistro with live music or DJs most nights.

Málaga Palacio

Avenida Cortina del Muelle 1 (952 22 06 98/www.ac-hotels.com). **Rates** €137-€193. **Credit** AmEx, DC, MC, V. **Map** p175 C3 ⓰
Part of the chic AC chain, the 214-room Málaga Palacio is swish, ultra-modern and service oriented, with views over the leafy Paseo del Parque.

Parador del Gibralfaro

Camino de Gibralfaro s/n (952 22 19 02/www.parador.es). **Rates** €120-€150 single; €128-€205 superior double. **Credit** AmEx, DC, MC, V. **Map** p175 off F2.
This hilltop *parador* has luxurious, spacious rooms (all with terraces), a rooftop pool and a restaurant.

Resources

Internet

Ciber Teatro Romano, C/Alcazarilla s/n (952 60 45 22). **Open** 10am-2am daily. **Map** p175 D3.

Police station

Avenida de la Rosaleda 19 (952 12 65 00). **Map** p175 off A1.

Post office

Avenida Andalucía 33 (952 32 35 28).

Tourist information

Pasaje de Chinitas 4 (952 21 34 45/www.malagaturismo.com). **Open** 9am-7.30pm-Mon-Fri; 10am-7pm Sat; 10am-2pm Sun. **Map** p175 B/C2.
Casa del Jardinero, Avenida Cervantes 1 (952 12 20 20). **Open** 9am-6pm Mon-Fri; 10am-6pm Sat, Sun. **Map** p175 D3.
Plaza de la Marina (952 12 20 20). **Open** 9am-6pm Mon-Fri; 10am-6pm Sat, Sun. **Map** p175 B3.

Getting there

By bus

The bus station is next to the train station on Paseo de los Tilos (952 35 00 61, www.movelia.es). There are 10 daily buses to Granada (2hrs), 8 to Seville (2hrs 30 mins) and Almería (3hrs 30mins), 5 to Córdoba (3hrs), 3 to Cádiz (4hrs) and Jaén (4hrs 30mins), 10 to Nerja (1hr 30mins) and one every 15mins along the Costa. There are also hourly (or so) services to the airport.

By train

The train station is at Explanada de la Estación (952 36 02 02). There are 5 daily direct trains to Seville (2hrs 30mins) and 9 daily to Córdoba (2hrs 20mins).

Costa del Sol

We're all off to sunny Spain.

Wish you were here? **Torremolinos**.

Though it's already overflowing with tourists and built up beyond any hope of redemption, Spain's most notorious *costa* still pulls in the crowds (though numbers are dropping, *see p26*). On first impressions it might seem like an immense sprawl of monotonous development, but there is some entertainment to be had. Torremolinos (Torrie for short) is as wacky and kitsch as they come; so bad, you've got to love it. Marbella, the pearl of the south, is a shopping mecca, the playground of royalty and celebs, and a yachties' and golfers' paradise, while Estepona offers a relatively quiet, family atmosphere and plenty of theme parks for the kids. It's all the result of Franco's ill-advised plan to turn Spain's Mediterranean coast into the 'Florida of Europe' – not just a holiday mecca, but home to huge numbers of British, German and Scandinavian expats.

Just a few minutes' drive inland, life slows to a far more relaxed pace in some of the region's delightful white villages, such as Benahavis, Mijas and Casares. Meanwhile, rural tourism is flourishing in the nearby mountain reserves. With impressively cheap air fares to Málaga and bargain-price package deals, the appeal of the Costa del Sol isn't hard to fathom.

When driving along the Costa be warned that the A7 coastal road (the old N340) is often horribly jammed and is notoriously dangerous; it is well worth paying a few euros to use the newer AP7 toll road (the former A7-E15).

Torremolinos

Full to bursting with bucket-and-spade shops, British pubs and greasy caffs serving egg and chips, Torrie nevertheless has legions of fans who return to enjoy its screeching, plastic madness year after year. It's a particularly fun gay destination, with beach, bars and nightlife all on hand to help make it happen.

How times have changed. Five hundred years ago, this was a spa town, revered for the quality of its springs, which filled the baths and spas of nearby Roman settlements. By the 15th century the water supply was fuelling numerous coastal watchtowers (*torres*) and mills (*molinos*), whence the town takes its name.

The only real evidence of the town's past is the crumbling **Torre Vigia**, an Arab watchtower that pinpoints the heart of the old town. The steep streets that run down to the sea from here are more charming than you might expect. Though much of Torrie is still rather down at heel, the seafront has been smartened up, and you can now walk along it all the way to Benalmádena Costa (*see p179*), passing the quieter village and beach of **La Carihuela** on the way. The latter is a good place to stay if the centre seems like hard work. For kids, the primary attraction (apart from the beach) is **Crocodile Park**, starring Europe's largest croc, a monster 4.6 metres (15 feet) long.

Crocodile Park

C/Cuba 14 (952 05 17 82). **Open** 10am-6pm daily. **Admission** €9; €6.50 concessions. **Credit** MC, V.

Where to eat & drink

You'll find no shortage of pub grub and fry-ups along the old town's frenzied central vein, C/Miguel. Laying your hands on solid Spanish fare may prove more of a challenge. On the main drag, right opposite the Centro Comercial San Miguel, **La Chacha** (no phone) is little more than a hole-in-the-wall, but serves an extraordinary array of fresh, grilled seafood by weight. In the *barrio*, **Bodegas Quitapeñas** (C/Cuesta del Tajo 3, 952 38 62 44, €) is reliably excellent, offering fresh fish tapas and Málaga wine from the barrel. **La Mancha** (Avda Los Manantiales, Plaza Goya, 952 38 01 46, closed Mon, €€-€€€) serves traditional Spanish game.

Playa de la Carihuela is great for fish: the local favourite, **Casa Paco** (Paseo Marítimo La Carihuela s/n, 952 05 13 81, closed dinner Sun, all Mon, Dec & Jan, €€), does a huge skewer of freshly grilled sardines for around €5.

Nightlife

Salsa fans head for **Atrevete** (Avda Salvador Allende), a hot 'n' steamy joint near the beach in La Carihuela. Most of the superclubs and discos can be found on Avda Carlota Alessandri and around Avda Palma de Mallorca, west of the Plaza Costa del Sol. There's also quite a big, if obviously touristy, flamenco scene. **Pepe Lopez** (Plaza de la Gamba Alegre, 952 38 12 84, closed Sun all year and Mon-Thur Nov-Mar) puts on a decent show.

Torrie's thriving gay scene centres mostly around the La Nogalera area, a hotbed of bars, discos and saunas for a mostly male clientele. The **Palladium** (Avda Palma de Mallorca, 952 38 42 89, open Fri & Sat only) these days is more mixed these days, and has a swimming pool, balloons, and smoke and fake snow billowing from every corner. An annual gay rave in August features big stars and international DJs.

Where to stay

In the centre of town, the buttercup-yellow **Hotel Adriano** (Avda de los Manantiales 1, 952 05 08 38, www.hoteladriano.info, double €65-€98) has a roof terrace with sea views, high above the chaos below, and fresh, clean rooms. Ask about special deals here, as the suites with private terraces and sun loungers often go for the same price as a double. The same family also own the cheery **Hostal Doña Lola** (C/Cruz 10, 952 38 20 84, double €30-€45). In the so-called *'barri tipica'*, pretty **Hostal Micaela** (C/Bajondillo 4, 952 38 33 10, double €40-€50) is recognisable by its colourful Andalucían planters spilling over with geraniums; it's been here since 1972 and remains a hugely popular budget option.

In La Carihuela, the whimsical (and still resolutely Spanish) **Hotel Miami** (C/Aladino 14, 952 38 52 55, www.residencia-miami.com, double €36-€59) was built in the 1960s by one of Picasso's cousins and still has some of its original features, including a public area built in the style of the Sacramonte caves in the province of Granada. The lush garden and swimming pool provide a blissful retreat. The new and unlikely **La Luna Blanca** (Pasaje Cerrillo 2, 952 05 37 11, www.la-luna-blanca.com, double €88-€131 restaurant €€€) is Japanese-run and boasts clean, minimal lines and decent sushi.

Resources

Internet

Cyber Café Caracas, C/La Nogalera, by C/San Miguel (952 38 72 37). **Open** 10.30am-2pm, 4.30pm-midnight daily.

Police station

C/Rafael Quintana Rosado s/n (952 37 60 00).

Post office

C/Danza Invisible s/n (952 38 45 18).

Tourist information

Playa Bajondillo (952 37 19 09) & Plaza del Remo (952 37 29 56). **Open** *July* 10am-2pm, 5-8pm Mon-Fri. *Aug* 10am-2pm, 5-8pm daily. *Sept-June* 9.30am-2.30pm Mon-Fri.
There are additional offices in the Ayuntamiento (Plaza Blas Infante, 952 37 95 12, open 8.30am-1.30pm Mon-Fri) and on Plaza de la Independencia (952 37 42 31, open 10am-1.30pm Mon-Fri).

Benalmádena, Mijas & Fuengirola

Merging into Torremolinos, its eastern neighbour, is the equally brash **Benalmádena Costa**. The main attraction is the **Puerto Deportivo**, the Costa's most happening nightspot, which is particularly popular among young *malagueños*. Above the conurbation is **Benalmádena Pueblo**, an unexpectedly pretty village that gets two thumbs up for having escaped the overdevelopment all around. There's not much to do other than wander the streets, but it's a good place to stay if you must be close to the coast.

High up in the **Sierra de Mijas**, around six kilometres (four miles) behind Benalmádena, is **Mijas**, which became a popular haven for new bohemians keen to escape the burgeoning coast during the 1960s. They were surprised to find in their midst the town's former mayor Manuel Cortes, who had gone into hiding in the village after the Civil War, and only emerged in 1968. Mijas was the subject of Ronald Fraser's anthropological classic *The Pueblo*.

Today, the village has grown to become the second-largest *pueblo* on the Costa del Sol; more than 40 per cent of residents are foreigners. In season the town is overrun with day trippers, though in the evening it becomes the locals' own once more. *Burro* (donkey) taxis are available for hire. Take one up the rocky path to the **Sanctuario del Calvario**, a 16th-century shrine of the barefooted Carmelite brothers. The **Carromato de Max** – a museum of the world's tiniest things, including a copy of the *Last Supper* painted on a grain of rice and some fully clothed fleas – is the town's most preposterous attraction. The pretty, diminutive **Plaza de Toros** (952 48 52 48) is worth a visit, and if you feel so inclined there are *corridas* (bullfights) most Sundays.

Whatever it is that **Fuengirola** has in mind for its regeneration – it is the coast's number-one resort for Spanish tourists – it has been at it for several years now. Relentless drilling, cordoned-off roads and tarpaulin-wrapped buildings have long been the norm. Its beach is heinously crowded, and rather than staggering through the sprawl of the old town you could kill an hour on the ramparts of the tenth-century **Castillo de Sohail**, at the south-western end of the beach. The town's best features are Andalucía's largest street market, held on Tuesdays on Avda Jesús Santos Rein, and the night-time horse races held at the Hipódromo Costa del Sol on Saturdays throughout the summer. For kids, **Fuengirola Zoo** was voted best zoo in Spain by *National Geographic*, and boasts everything from lemurs to orangutans and gorillas to crocs, and is active in various conservation projects for saving endangered species.

Carromato de Max

Avda del Compás s/n, Mijas (no phone). **Open** *July-Sept* 10am-10pm daily. *Oct-June* 9.30am-7.30pm daily. **Admission** €3. **No credit cards.**

Fuengirola Zoo

C/Camilo José Cela 6 (952 66 63 01/www.zoofuengirola.com). **Open** *July-Aug* 10am-midnight daily. *Sept-June* 10am-7pm Mon-Fri; 10am-8pm Sat, Sun. **Admission** €13.10; €9 under-10s. **Credit** MC, V.

Hipódromo Costa del Sol

Urbanización El Chaparral s/n, Mijas Costa (952 59 27 00/www.carreraentertainment.com). **Open** *Races* 8pm Sat; 10am Sun. **Admission** €5. **Credit** MC, V.

Where to stay, eat & drink

The best places to stay along this stretch are Benalmádena and Mijas Pueblos. Fuengirola is best avoided. In Benalmádena Pueblo, **Hotel La Fonda** (Santo Domingo 7, 952 56 83 24, double €67-€99) was designed by César Manrique. It's a beautiful colonial-style building constructed around a network of Moorish-style, cobbled patios, with a large pool and a balcony terrace with fine views. **La Perla** (C/Ibiza 12, 952 56 81 66, closed Mon, €€€€) is an upmarket restaurant with a classy Mediterranean menu, specialising in game in winter, and is worth the trip up the hill.

On the Mijas Costa it seems nothing short of miraculous that a place like **The Beach House** (Urbanización El Chaparral, A7, km203, 95 249 45 40, www.beachhouse.nu, €125-€140) exists. Imagine waking up to the sound of waves crashing on the shore, and dazzling white archways surrounding a pretty tiled swimming pool with jaw-dropping views over the blue horizon – and you begin to get some idea of what it's like to stay here. Cool white walls and minimal Scandinavian furnishings ensure a blissful retreat from real life. There's no restaurant, but four minutes' walk down the beach will bring you to **Sheriff** (A7, km202, Mijas Costa, 952 49 37 22, €€€), which serves decent steaks and fresh fish on tables on the beach.

In Mijas Pueblo, the family-run **Hostal La Posada** (C/Coin 47, 952 48 53 10, double €35) has rooms and apartments and is deservedly popular with everyone from backpackers to middle-aged ramblers. The four-star **Hotel Mijas** (Urbanización Tamisa 2, 952 48 58 00, www.trhhoteles.es, double €82-€125) lets you kick back in style. For food, you have many options, not all of them good. **El Mirlo Blanco** (Plaza de la Constitución, 952 48 57 00, closed 2wks Jan, €€-€€€), however, is truly superb, and, unusually in the male-dominated world of restaurants, is run by three generations of women from the Basque country. They specialise in the delicacies of home: *angulas* (mind-bogglingly expensive baby eels), *txangurro* (spider crab) and *kokotxas de bacalao* (the throat membranes of cod). If you fancy something a little more down-to-earth, **Fiesta** (Avda de Mexico, 952 48 57 67, closed Sun and Nov, €€) does a great barbecue, while **Bar La Gamba** (C/San Sebastián 11, 952 48 57 22, closed Sun, €€), hidden away on a quiet side street, offers typical *casera* (home-style Spanish cooking) and – as you might guess from its name – prawns, on a pretty, vine-shaded roof terrace.

Resources

Internet

Benalmádena Costa *Cafés Cibernéticos, Dársena de Levante, Local A5 (952 57 65 83).* **Open** 11am-11pm daily.

Marbella.

Tourist information

Benalmádena Costa *Avda Antonio Machado 10, (952 44 12 95/24 94/www.benalmadena.com).* **Open** 9am-8.30pm Mon-Fri; 10am-4.30pm Sat.

Fuengirola *Avda Jesús Santos Rein 6 (952 46 74 57).* **Open** 9.30am-2pm, 5-7pm Mon-Fri; 10am-1pm Sat.

Mijas *Plaza Virgen de la Peña s/n (952 58 90 34/www.mijas.es).* **Open** *May-Sept* 9am-8pm Mon-Fri; 10am-3pm Sat. *Oct-Apr* 9am-7pm Mon-Fri; 10am-3pm Sat.

Marbella

The most expensive resort in Spain, Marbella promotes a particular brand of luxury tourism conceived largely by the town's larger-than-life former mayor Jesús Gil y Gil. After 11 years in office, Gil finally stood down in 2002, and was given a three-year prison sentence for financial irregularities concerning his Atlético de Madrid football club. He died in May 2004. Despite his dubious practices, Gil's property dealings have played no small part in Marbella's success.

From the top-quality restaurants and glitzy hotels of the Golden Mile to the luxury yachts and exclusive nightclubs of nearby **Puerto Banús** (even the Saudi king has a palace here), Marbella is a playground for royalty, celebrities and mafiosi.

Marbella's **Casco Antiguo** (old quarter) comes as a welcome relief after the high-rise horrors further east. It's a lovely tangle of narrow alleyways and twisted streets, free of lager louts and fish-and-chip shops, and filled with flowers; an annual prize is awarded to the town's prettiest street garden. Among the most attractive lanes is Calle Ortiz de Molinillos (just east of Plaza de los Naranjos), where creepers and vines choke wrought-iron balconies and a magnificent statue of the Virgin perches above it all in a turquoise-covered sentry box.

You can't miss the intimate central **Plaza de los Naranjos**, site of the old marketplace and orange orchard, now jammed with café tables. The scent of blossom in the evenings can be quite intoxicating. Also worth seeing is the **Museo del Grabado Español Contemporáneo**, an engraving museum housing works by Dalí, Miró and Picasso. It occupies a striking Renaissance building, formerly a poor hospital and children's home. Nearby, the church of **Nuestra Señora de la Encarnación** (open hours of services) was built in the 16th century, but like many Andalucían churches, was later remodelled in baroque style. One of the more curious of Marbella's sights is the **Museo de Bonsai**, the showcase of an obsessive collector.

Airline flights are one of the biggest producers of the global warming gas CO_2. But with **The CarbonNeutral Company** you can make your travel a little greener.
Go to **www.carbonneutral.com** to calculate your flight emissions then 'neutralise' them through international projects which save exactly the same amount of carbon dioxide.
Contact us at **shop@carbonneutral.com** or call into the office on **0870 199 99 88** for more details.
CarbonNeutral® flights

During the summer, the Paseo Marítimo springs to life as cafés and bars open their doors to face the sea. At the easternmost end you'll find the **Puerto Deportivo**. Once better known as the place to score drugs and women, it has begun to clean up its act, with some of the more salubrious business owners doing their best to promote it as a hip alternative to Puerto Banús.

Cabo Pino (between Marbella and Fuengirola) is a delightful little port with a number of decent eateries and the area's main nudist beach, while in high season a string of beaches west of town are the scene of all-night beach parties ruled by Europe's top DJs.

Museo de Bonsai

Parque Arroyo de la Represa, Avda Doctor Mais Viñal (952 86 29 26). **Open** *July, Aug* 10.30am-1.30pm, 4-7pm daily. *Sept-June* 10am-1.30pm, 4-7.30pm daily. **Admission** €4; €2 concessions. **No credit cards**.

Museo del Grabado Español Contemporáneo

C/Hospital Bazán s/n (952 76 57 41/www.museodelgrabado.com). **Open** *June-Sept* 10am-2pm, 7-9pm Tue-Sat. *Oct-May* 10am-2pm, 5.30-8.30pm Tue-Sat. **Admission** €3. **No credit cards**.

Where to eat & drink

With more than 600 restaurants to choose from, Marbella offers just about anything from anywhere in every price bracket. The Paseo Marítimo is good for funky bars and beachfront dining; head for the Golden Mile and Puerto Banús for posh dinners and world-class cuisine; but for sheer atmosphere, you can't beat the Casco Antiguo.

The hottest new restaurant in Andalucia, and one of the hottest in Spain, is Dani García's **Calima** (Hotel Gran Meliá Don Pepe, Avda José Meliá s/n, 952 76 42 52, closed Sun & Mon, €€€€), where floor-to-ceiling windows look over an artfully arranged terrace. The tasting menu is a sturdy €80, not including wine, but it's a memorable feast. Using all the latest razzle-dazzle cooking techniques, it might include a live oyster dotted with crystalised lemon and served with Bloody Mary sorbet – whipped up at the table with liquid nitrogen. There are pork cheeks in won ton, poached eggs like eyeballs, squid frills can-canning across seafood reductions, gilthead bream crackling, pineapple meringue on gingerbread croutons and more.

Other new hotspots include **Goizeko & Dalli's** (Urb. Mansión Club, Avda Buchinger s/n, 952 76 48 03, closed Sun, €€€€), which offers Basque-Italian fusion from Marbella's legendary Dalli family: the kings of pasta, they have several different restaurants scattered around the region.

Bar Altamirano (Plaza Altamirano 4, 952 82 49 32, closed Wed and mid Jan-mid Feb, €) remains one of the old town's best-kept secrets, serving some of the freshest fish and seafood tapas on the coast, including giant *carabineros* (red king prawns, crab claws and lobster). Also good are heaped plates of clams in garlic and oil and *gambas pil-pil.* It's always lively with locals, and doubles as a shrine to Spanish football.

In the Casco Antiguo it's worth hunting out C/San Lázaro – an alleyway off Plaza Victoria – which has a range of eateries from expensive but seductively romantic to dirt cheap and basic. Wander along C/Ortiz de Molinillo for local eats. **El Balcón de la Virgen** (C/Remedios 2, 952 77 60 92, closed Sun and mid Dec-mid Jan, €€) seems stuck in another time and place, with hearty, country fare to match. Try **La Querencía** (C/Tetuán 9, no phone, €) for cheap and tasty North African dishes. **ZoZoi** (Plaza Altamirano 1, 952 85 88 68, closed Sun and mid Jan-mid Feb, €€€€) is the darling of Marbella's hip young things for its adventurous fusion cooking and romantic terrace and dining rooms.

Visitors are spoiled for choice when it comes to eating out in the village of **Benahavis**, a pint-sized place just ten minutes' drive inland from Marbella. Standards are high, with prices to match, but it is *the* place to go on the Costa for foodies, offering a good range of cooking styles and regional dishes. Reserving is nearly always advisable, and be sure to check on opening hours; many places are open for dinner only. **Los Abanicos** (C/Málaga 15, 952 85 50 22, closed Tue, €€€-€€€€) is one of the old hands and remains a favourite among locals and expats for well-executed Mediterranean and international fare. For giant portions of tender, juicy chargrilled meat try **Rufinos** (C/Montemayor 5, 952 85 52 62, closed Wed, €€-€€€). For a truly special evening of fine food and wine, a fabulously detailed menu and splendid surrounds, the hotel **Amanhavis** (*see p185*) is well worth fitting into your itinerary.

Nightlife

Things don't get going until after midnight in Marbella, so eat late, before heading out to enjoy the flashiest club scene on the Costa. The superclubs are clustered at the Puerto Banús end of the Golden Mile. **Dreamers** (A7, km175, 952 81 20 80, www.dreamers-disco.com, €20-30 incl 1 drink) is a great-looking venue and plays a good variety of music, including sounds from the Berlin underground, while

Sign language

No way, José

The most common gesture simply expresses 'no'. In its rudimentary and most frequent form, your head shakes left to right and a 'tsk-tsk-tsk' sound is made by creating suction between your tongue and clamped front teeth. For emphasis, wave index finger left to right a few times. If you use your elbow as the pivot and move your whole forearm, you are saying 'Uh uh' or 'Absolutely not' – depending on the range of the motion.

Talk to the hand

If an argument surpasses a mere disagreement, you will eventually see either 'screw you' – made by taking a fist held sideways and moving it directly in front of you, stopping bluntly, as if knocking hard once on a door with the butt of your fist – or 'you're going to get it'. This is accentuated by karate-chopping the air once or twice at a 45º angle directly in front of you, and can also be called the if-you-keep-talking-like-that-I'm-going-to-kick-your-ass gesture.

¡Vamos!

Ready to go? No need to express this with words, just make your left forearm and hand rigid like a board. Take your right palm and smack it over your left hand. It means that within a few moments you'll be leaving.

Waxen faced

When someone is left with nothing – be it with no money or an unrequited sexual pursuit – they are left '*a dos velas*' (with two candles burning). Two fingers in the universal 'peace' sign are turned toward one's face and brought down over the eyes as far as the mouth, leaving the hand as a fist.

Achtung (maybe)

The '*ojo*' gesture means 'look out', 'be careful' or 'check out that fine human specimen over there'. Simply pull a lower eyelid down and look in the direction of whoever you wish to comment upon. In strangers this can indicate danger of pickpocketing or imminent flirtation.

Saving face

Whenever you get something for free, be it a blagged ticket, accommodation or a lunch, you get it '*por la cara/patilla*' ('by the face/sideburn'). To show this, a person will use their middle finger paired with their index finger and drag it down their cheek slowly, as if it were a razor.

Water off a duck's back

This sign demonstrates that you are unaffected by something that should perturb. Throw your hand outward (palm down) and up one time and say, 'Bah!' nonchalantly.

Dios mío

To create the opposite meaning, just shake your hand sideways (wrist bent, palm down and fingers towards you) several times, as if it's on fire or you just hit it with a hammer. This means any and all equivalent exclamations between 'Oh my God!' and 'Holy shit!'

Suite Restaurant & Lounge at the Hotel Puente Romano, A7, km177, 952 82 09 00, closed Sun-Thur) is good for R&B, soul and Latin house. Things get steadily more glam at **La Notte** (Camino de la Cruz, 952 86 69 96), but for sheer class you can't beat **Olivia Valere** (Ctra de Istán, km0.8, 952 82 88 61/45, www.oliviavalere.com). The playground of royalty and celebrities, and housed in a hybrid replica of the Alhambra and the Mezquita, this is one of the most beautiful nightclubs in the world. **Nikki Beach** (Hotel Don Carlos, Ctra de Cádiz km192, 952 83 62 39, www.nikkibeach.com) is another hip hangout that sizzles in the sun, attracting jet-setters and the local glitterati to its all-white lounge lizard and champagne parties. The truly cool arrive and leave by yacht. Another good choice for lounging with the jet set, **Liquid Lounge** (Marina Banús, 952 90 88 31, €€€) is fun and funky, with good cocktails and decent risottos, steaks and salads.

Famed veteran flamenco artist Ana María's **Tablao Ana María** offers evenings of foot-stamping action (Plaza Santo Cristo 4/5, 952 82 31 07, closed Mon, €20 incl drink).

Where to stay

Budget accommodation is mostly in the Casco Antiguo and ranges from fun, friendly backpackers' hostels to simple hotels in restored townhouses. **Hostal del Pilar** (C/Mesoncillo 4, off C/Peral, 952 82 99 36, www.hostel-marbella.com, double €40-€50) was built in 1635 to accommodate monks travelling from Madrid. These days you'll find like-minded folk from all over the world swapping travel stories while basking on the roof terrace with a beer. Nearby, **Hostal Paco** (C/Peral 16, 952 77 12 00, double €45-€55) is a fresh, clean, no-frills *hostal* with friendly staff.

There are also a couple of classy boutique hotels, both of them less expensive than you might imagine. **La Morada Mas Hermosa Hotel** (C/Montenebros 16A, 952 92 44 67, www.lamoradamashermosa.com, double €66-€92) is tucked down a leafy mews and has just five simply but elegantly decorated rooms. The best room (twin beds) has a spiral staircase leading up to a private terrace. **The Town House** (C/Alderete 7, Plaza Tetuán, www.townhouse.nu, 952 90 17 91, double €110-€130), owned by the same people as the Beach House (*see p180*), is elegance personified, with carved wood ceilings, sumptuous fabrics, chandeliers, glittering tiles and lots of marble. All rooms are individually decorated (a four-poster bed in No.6, a private terrace for No.9) and there's a rooftop terrace with views over the city's skyline, and tables and chairs in the *plaza*.

Sandwiched between the sea and the centre of town, the big four-star **El Fuerte** (Avda El Fuerte, 952 92 00 00, www.fuerte hoteles.com, double €143-€264) does a splendid job of managing to offer a personal service despite its size, and has all the facilities you'd expect, plus spa treatments at its sister hotel just down the road.

Located in the hills perhaps 20 minutes' drive north-west of Marbella, the **Amanhavis Hotel and Restaurant** (C/del Pilar 3, Benahavis, 952 85 60 26, www.amanhavis.com, closed 8 Jan-12 Feb, double €106-€170, restaurant €€€€) is a wonderful, intriguing place to stay. Surrounding an intimate garden and plunge pool, nine unique rooms each tell a different story: the Astronomer's Observatory provides stargazers with a skylight and brass telescope, while Sultan Boabdil's chamber is a sumptuous silken retreat, ideal for honeymooners. The dining room is housed in part of the original 350-year-old building, and the excellent food shows amazing attention to detail.

Resources

Police station

C/Juan de la Cierva s/n (952 89 99 00).

Post office

C/Jacinto Benavente 14 (952 77 28 98).

Tourist information

Plaza de los Naranjos 1 (952 82 35 50/www.marbella.es). **Open** 9am-9pm Mon-Fri; 10am-2pm Sat.

There are other offices at Glorietas de la Fontanilla s/n (952 77 14 42) and at Arco de Marbella (952 82 28 18), tucked beneath the pearly concrete arch as you drive into town on the A7.

Sierra Blanca

Towering behind Marbella are the hills of the **Sierra Blanca**, offering a much-needed escape route when all that partying gets too much. Eight kilometres (five miles) north of Marbella on the A355, the small sugar-cube village of **Ojén** clings to a valley wall at the base of the Sierra, sprouting a good many orange orchards. It makes an ideal base for exploring the area. The village's main attraction is the **Museo del Vino Málaga**, which does wine tastings and sells a large selection of Málaga province's most revered bottles, including the 'Viejo Abuelo 10-años'. The museum is housed in an 18th-century building, which was founded as Andalucía's first *aguardiente* distillery in 1830. It became so famous that for a long time it was common in Spain to ask simply for a 'copa de Ojén'. In the 1930s the abandoned distillery became the headquarters of the CNT – the syndicate of Spanish anarchists.

From here, a 15-minute drive will take you up to the **Refugio de Juanar**, at 760 metres (2,500 feet). The hotel (*see p186*) provides a good map of the area, with hiking routes and photographs of the flora and fauna you may encounter.

Should you happen to be in the town of **Monda** (11 kilometres/7 miles beyond Ojén) on a particular Sunday in March, you can join in celebrations for the 'world's biggest soup' – a dubious-looking gloop of bread, peppers, tomatoes, garlic, oil and eggs, served to anyone who wants it from a gigantic wooden bowl. If that doesn't take your fancy, you can always have lunch at the **Hotel El Castillo** (*see p186*).

A number of local companies offer tours and specialist activities in the Sierra Blanca: among them are **Guías Daidín** in Marbella (C/Ancha 7, 952 82 05 79, www.daidin.com) for trekking and archaeological digs; **Monte Aventura** (Plaza de Andalucía 1, Ojén, 952 88 15 19 Mon-Fri, mobile 656 96 04 78 Sat, Sun) for guided tours; and the **Safari Shop** in Puerto Banús (Centro Comercial Cristamar B61, Avda Naciónes Unidas, 952 90 50 82 Mon-Fri, mobile 609 51 75 17 Sat, Sun, www.spain4fun.com) for canoeing, caving and rock-climbing expeditions.

Museo del Vino Málaga

C/Carrera 39, Ojén (952 88 14 53). **Open** *July, Aug* 10am-3pm, 6-9.30pm daily. *Sept-June* 11am-3pm, 4-8pm daily. **Admission** free.

Where to stay, eat & drink

In Ojén, **La Posada del Ángel** (C/Mesones 21, 952 88 18 08, www.laposadadelangel.com, double €75-€99) is a beautifully restored village house built around a wood-columned courtyard and furnished with country antiques. Some rooms have balconies; all have cable TV and internet access. A cheaper, more basic option with great views is the **Hostal El Solar** (C/Córdoba 2, 952 88 11 49, double €30-€40).

High in the mountains, the **Refugio de Juanar** (Sierra Blanca s/n, 952 88 10 00, www.juanar.com, double €91-€105) is where Charles de Gaulle chose to finish his memoirs in 1970. The best rooms have open fireplaces and jacuzzis, while the restaurant, housed in a converted hunting lodge, specialises in locally caught game.

For an unusual treat, stay at **Hotel El Castillo de Monda** (Avda de Castillo s/n, 952 45 71 42, www.mondacastle.es, double €120-€213) on its perch above the town of the same name. It's the epitome of Moorish splendour, and has preserved some macabre artefacts, including a few human skulls, which glint from darkened corners. The **Santa Fe Hotel Restaurante** (Carretera de Monda, km3, 952 45 29 16, www.santafe-hotel.com, closed 2wks Nov & 2wks Jan-Feb, double €66, restaurant €€€) is another gem, with just five rustic bedrooms above a great little pub. Facilities include a swimming pool, conservatory and a roaring fire in winter.

Estepona & around

Estepona, Roman in origin, is a pretty if somewhat jaded place, and the most genuinely Spanish town between here and Málaga. Development has been kept on a fairly strict leash and the town has been spruced up considerably in the last couple of years. Estepona's beaches boast the cleanest water on the coast and are flanked not by high-rises but by a handful of palm-thatched *chiringuitos*. Though it doesn't possess the good looks of Marbella's Casco Antiguo, its old town, around **Plaza Las Flores** and **Plaza Arce**, is worth exploring.

Around 16 kilometres (ten miles) west of Estepona, up in the **Sierra Bermeja**, the road to Casares resembles Tolkien's Shire, with lush green hillsides and wild flowers blooming everywhere in spring. Locally known as the 'hanging village', **Casares** is one of the most spectacular of the *pueblos blancos*. Presided over by an 18th-century church and a Moorish castle, the upper reaches appear dangerously fragile when viewed from the road spiralling out of town towards **Manilva**. The surrounding countryside is virtually untouched and great for rambling.

Casares takes its name from Julius Caesar, who was fighting Gaius Pompey for control of Spain in these parts around 45 BC. The battle took place near where present-day Monda stands, but, according to local legend, Caesar stopped en route to bathe in Manilva's sulphurous springs, known as **La Hedionda** (the foul-smelling woman), where he reputedly rid himself of a nasty skin infection. If you want to share his bathwater, follow signs from the main road to the **Roman Oasis Restaurant** (Camino Sabanias Alcazares s/n, 952 89 23 80, www.insanctum.com, closed Oct-May, €€-€€€), then take a dirt road upstream until you spy a small white dome on the riverbank. Beneath these arches, the eerie blue sulphurous water lapping against the ancient stone produces a magical effect. Six kilometres (four miles) out of the town, on the private estate of Alechipe, are the remains of the Roman town of **Lacipo**, itself built over an Iberian settlement. Ask at the tourist office for more information about visiting this extraordinary site.

Where to stay, eat & drink

In Estepona, if you're on a budget, **Hostal El Pilar** (Plaza Las Flores 10, 952 80 00 18, www.ainte.net/hostalelpilar, double €39-€50) is charming and has been in the same family since 1870; the best rooms have balconies opening on to the *plaza*. At the other end of the scale is the new **Kempinski** (Ctra de Cádiz, km 159, Playa El Padrón, 952 80 95 00, www.kempinski-spain.com, double €251-€310), a faux-adobe palace on the edge of town. Vast bedrooms have sea views, and there are acres of grounds, several swimming pools, a spa and three decent restaurants.

In the last few years nearly all of the hotels on the seafront have been refurbished. Many of the rooms at the freshly painted **Hotel Mediterráneo** (Avda de España 68, 952 79 38 93, double €47-€55) have sea views.

Eating options in Estepona are numerous. **Los Rosales** (C/Damas 12, 952 79 29 45, www.infhos.com/losrosales, closed Sun and

Casares, a classic *pueblo blanco. See p186.*

Nov, €€€), does excellent seafood at its simplest and freshest, but if you're looking for the ultimate fisherman's lunch, **La Escollera** (Puerto Pesquero de Estepona, 952 80 63 54, closed Mon, €€) will not disappoint. Portions are huge and the *navajas* (razor clams) are peerless. (To reach it, walk past the marina towards the docks and you'll find it by the beach entrance.) **La Casa de Mi Abuela** (C/Caridad 54, 952 79 19 67, closed Tue and May, €€) serves prime, Argentinian steaks, while at the Marbella end of the street, the ceilings of **Sabor Andaluz** (C/Caridad 44, 952 79 52 93, €€) are dripping with acorn-fed *jamones, salchichones* and other pig delicacies. Most of the town's night-time action is centred around Calles Real and Caridad.

Hikers will find Casares a good base, but bear in mind that many of its streets are too steep and narrow to be reached by car. The **Hotel Rural Casares** (C/Copera 52, 952 89 52 11, www.hotelcasares.com, double €60) has pleasant rooms featuring brick archways and exposed beams. There are a couple of cheaper *pensiones* around Plaza de España, where the **Bar Nuevo Antiguo** (Plaza de España 19, 952 89 44 31, closed Sun, €) offers good meals and tapas. The roof terrace at **La Bodeguita de Medio** (Plaza de España 15,952 89 40 36, closed Mon, €) is lovely for drinks. Or head up to one of the restaurants tucked under the crumbling ramparts of the castle for panoramic vistas.

The best place in the area for food, **The Forge** (Finca el Forjador, Carretera de Casares, km10, 952 89 51 20, www.forgerestaurant.netfirms.com, closed Mon & Tue and Feb, €€-€€€) is largely hidden by thick cork and oak woods, olive trees and wild blooms. The two- and three-course menus combine Middle Eastern-, African- and Greek-inspired dishes. Book several weeks in advance for lunch on Sundays.

Resources

Police station

Estepona *Avda Los Frutales 1 (952 80 02 43).*

Post office

Estepona *C/Martínez Castro 1 (952 80 05 37).*

Tourist information

Casares *C/Carreras 51 (952 89 55 21).* **Open** 11am-2.30pm, 4-6.30pm Mon-Fri; 11am-4pm Sat.

Estepona *Avda San Lorenzo 1 (952 80 20 02/09 13/www.estepona.es).* **Open** 9am-8pm Mon-Fri; 10am-1.30pm Sat.

Getting there

By bus

Buses run from Málaga to Marbella (Avda Trapiche, 952 76 44 00) via Torremolinos (C/Hoyos, 952 38 24 19) and Fuengirola (Avda Matias Saez de Tejada, 952 47 40 88) every 15mins daily. From Marbella, hourly buses serve the main towns along the rest of the coast, and there are also less frequent buses on to Algeciras and Cádiz. Buses also run inland from Marbella to Ronda, and from Estepona to Algeciras, Torremolinos and Benalmadena. All are run by Portilla (902 14 31 44).

By train

From Málaga (via the airport) trains run every 30mins to Torremolinos (15mins from the airport), Benalmádena Costa and Fuengirola (30mins from the airport).

East of Málaga

If a beach party in Nerja doesn't appeal, hie thee to the lovely hinterland.

Vélez-Málaga, capital of the Axarquía. *See p189.*

The eastern Costa is markedly less developed than the Costa del Sol (largely because its beaches are less appealing), meaning its towns retain much of their Spanish flavour, though none is wildly interesting. The best is the relaxed, Brit-dominated resort of **Nerja**, which has a charming old town, pretty sculpted coves and plenty of bars and restaurants. Inland, the **Axarquía** (literally, 'land to the east') is great for walkers. This is where you'll find *pueblos blancos* where, despite the expat resident count rising, life goes on much as it has for decades.

The Montes de Málaga

Local people often talk of Málaga's two lungs: one is the Mediterranean, the other is the deep green, pine-forested **Parque Natural de los Montes de Málaga**, reaching up to 1,031 metres (3,383 feet) above the city to the north-east. Rarely visited by tourists, the park covers nearly 50 square miles (19 square miles) of deep gorges, sun-dappled forests of pine trees, holm oaks and olives, and lush valleys. Just 30 or so minutes' drive from the city centre, it's a quick and convenient retreat from the bustle of the town and is exhilarating hiking and mountain-biking territory.

Where to stay & eat

Many *ventas* (country inns) line the mountain road through the Montes de Málaga, and their menus have changed little since the days when bandits sheltered here. There are also two exceptional places to stay. If total solitude is what you seek, the **Hotel Humaina** (Ctra Colmenar s/n, 952 64 10 25, www.hotelhumaina.es, double €76-€82, restaurant €€) is a family-run retreat in the heart of the park, nestling halfway down a verdant valley. The restaurant specialises in hearty mountain fare.

Alternatively, **Hotel Cortijo La Reina** (Ctra Málaga–Comenar, km548.5, 951 01 40 00, www.hotelcortijolareina.com, double €116-€150, restaurant €€-€€€) offers luxury accommodation in a converted mansion. There's an in-house *bodega* for tasting the local wines, and individually decorated bedrooms, all with either a fireplace or a pot-bellied stove.

The Axarquía

Far more appealing than the built-up coast is the rolling interior, known as the Axarquía, which stretches back from the sea towards the hills that mark the border with Granada province. This white village-specked region is easily accessible from Málaga, and is slowly being discovered by tourists in search of an alternative holiday. It's a good winter destination, when cooler temperatures are kinder to walkers, and the hotels, restaurants and bars that stay open are real travellers' rests, warmed by wood-burning fires and serving hearty home cooking. Despite attempts to preserve the area for rural tourism, development, mainly in the form of faux-white village *urbanizaciones*, is slowly creeping its way into the hills, and there is a real danger that more intensive exploitation of the Axarquía might be on the way.

The capital of the Axarquía is the busy town of **Vélez-Málaga** (**photo** *p188*), four kilometres (2.5 miles) inland from Torre del Mar. In 1487 this was one of the last Moorish strongholds to fall to Christian forces. The (restored) tower of the Moorish castle still looks out over the largely modern town, which is a pleasant place for a wander, containing a handful of interesting *palacios* and churches. The best day to visit is Wednesday, when a lively street market takes place; plans for a regular 'medieval' market on the Paseo Nuevo, at least one weekend a month, look set to go ahead – check with the tourist office for details.

It's worth exploring the more out-of-the-way villages, such as **Comares**, one of the highest settlements in Andalucía; **El Borge**, tucked into a hollow in a valley; **Sedella**, a Moorish village rarely visited by tourists; and **Periana**, which presides over the **Embalse de la Viñuela**, where you can rent pedalos to mess about on the glassy reservoir.

Marking the eastern boundary of the Axarquía and Málaga province is a *jamón*-shaped hunk of mountainous national reserve known as the **Sierra de Tejeda**. Less than an hour's drive from Málaga, and very handy from Nerja, it offers a convenient foray into the wilds, and superb hiking trails, horse-riding and wildlife-spotting opportunities.

For a long time this area was a notorious haunt of *bandoleros* (bandits), who preyed upon traders carrying produce from Granada to the coast. Later, guerrillas used the craggy outpost as a camp during the Civil War. Interested visitors can hike the Ruta del Acebuchal Puerto Blanquillo, following a marked trail from the roadside (the first left heading north from Frigiliana). It takes about an hour each way, and ends up in the village of Acebuchal, abandoned during the war. After being left to rot for decades, the last few of years have seen it spruced up by savvy developers and it's now possible to rent houses in the village if you want a tranquil base for a longer stay.

Just seven kilometres (four miles) north of Nerja, the whitewashed houses of **Frigiliana** cling to the flank of the Sierra de Tejeda like limpets to a rock. This is the most visited of the villages of the Axarquía, and it is incredibly pretty; so much so that it has become something of a theme park. If you have your own transport it is far more pleasant to visit in the early evening when most of the daytrippers have returned to the coast. Frigiliana is developing at a shocking rate, with multi-storeyed apartment blocks springing up all around the pretty centre. The old town, however, is picture-perfect, with ornately cobbled streets, and flowers and ferns tumbling from every available windowsill, wheelbarrow and watering can in town. It's also not a bad place for stocking up on local ceramics, olive-wood bowls and the local sweet wines, the once-revered 'Málaga-sack'. For good historical tours contact 952 53 42 40, www.frigiliana.com (€5).

The conical hill, **El Fuerte**, that rises up behind Frigiliana makes a decent early evening hike. Just climb the steep streets out of the old town and follow your nose until the cobblestones turn to dusty goat tracks and the whitewashed homes are replaced by fig trees and views of the Mediterranean. It was here that the 1569 rebellion of the Moriscos was finally defeated.

Heading north of the town, the valleys and ridges become less populated, save for the odd itinerant goat grazing on the steps and terraces where farmers grow their citrus and avocado crops. As the road to the village of **Cómpeta** reaches higher ground, these are replaced with olive groves and vines. Originally a Moorish settlement, there's not a great deal to see or do here except enjoy the tranquillity of the place, and sample Cómpeta's most prized product: *jaral*. All the bars here serve it. If you happen to be in the village on 15 August, the annual festival – Noche del Vino – celebrates the grape and its harvest by doling out as much free wine as revellers can handle.

Where to stay & eat

The Axarquía is full of small, out-of-the-way places to stay and eat, and nearly all of them are blessed with spectacular settings and superb views. Just 30 minutes' drive from the coast in El Borge, the stone cottage of **Posada del Bandolero** (C/Cristo 1, El Borge, 952 51

94 50, double €40-€45, restaurant €€, closed Wed) is a treat. Andalucía's answer to Dick Turpin, Luis Muñoz García, was born here, and the inn, with its crooked beams and cobbled floors, oozes old-fashioned warmth and character; it also has a good regional restaurant.

In the northern Axarquía, where the olive terraces finally give way to bald-headed peaks of navy granite, the **Venta de Alfarnate** (Antigua Ctra de Málaga–Granada, km513, 952 75 93 88, closed June & July, €€-€€€) stands on the outskirts of Alfarnate. Believed to be the oldest functioning inn in Andalucía, dating back to the early 1800s, it was once notorious for harbouring the bandits and highwaymen who terrorised travellers on the old road from Málaga to Granada, while at the same time providing shelter for such dignitaries as King Alfonso XIII. Dig into meaty dishes in a jumble of different dining rooms, most with crackling fires. Should you wish to stay and explore the area on foot, **Cortijo Pulgarín Bajo** (Alfarnatejo, 952 46 23 05, mobile 620 05 97 87, €130 for a 2-bed house for a weekend, €330 for a week) gives a taste of *finca* living. Old-fashioned and basic, it sits amid bracing mountain scenery and has a good-sized pool.

On the edge of the Sierra de Tejeda in Sedella, **La Casa Pinta** (952 50 89 55, double €43) is the only place to stay, commanding a spectacular position on a ridge above town. The rooms are cool and spacious, and have tea- and coffee-making facilities. The restaurant serves Spanish dishes made with local produce.

For a retreat-style holiday, **Montaña Palmera** (El Cañuelo, Periana, 952 53 65 07, www.montanapalmera.com, closed Nov, double €59 incl breakfast) offers week-long yoga courses, trips to local hot springs and massage. A great hideout for people travelling alone and peace-loving couples (no kids allowed), it also has a pretty swimming pool overlooking the rolling hills.

Above Frigiliana, the mountain-top **Hotel Los Caracoles** (Crta Frigiliana–Torrox, km4.6, 952 03 06 80, www.hotelloscaracoles.com, double €64-€77, caracol room €96-€110), inspired by Gaudí's creations in Barcelona, is the most unusual hotel in the area. The spiral-shaped cottages (*caracol* means 'snail') have living areas and private terraces, ideal for a romantic getaway. There's a good Moorish-influenced restaurant too (€€, closed Mon). Another good bet is the 12-room **Hotel Rural La Posada Morisca** (Loma de la Cruz, Carretera Montaña Frigiliana–Torrox, 952 53 41 51, www.laposadamorisca.com, closed Jan, double €72-90, restaurant €€-€€€, closed lunch and all Sun) built along a ridge just above Frigiliana. All rooms have terraces and wood-burning stoves, making it especially snug out of season, and the views are magnificent. The restaurant offers interesting salads, such as watercress and eel, and unfussy mains.

In Frigiliana, the **Hotel Villa Frigiliana** (C/San Sebastián, 952 53 33 93, www.villafrigiliana.com, double €72-€102 breakfast incl) is closer in quality to a four-star than its three-star badge suggests. Rooms are spacious and pleasant – the best, which are on the fourth floor, have their own terraces. There's a swimming pool too.

Frigiliana has numerous places to eat, but the best is the atmospheric **La Bodeguilla** (C/Chorruelo 7, 952 53 41 16, €), consisting of a series of heavily planted, interconnecting cobbled *plazitas* off a tiny street. Rosario started the restaurant from her living room 20 years ago, and now, with the help of her four daughters, she knocks out exemplary regional cooking. Alternatively, the **Garden Restaurant** (C/Cubos, 952 53 31 85, closed Tue, €€) has changed hands and had some much-needed TLC poured into it. Set in an elegant, lush garden, tucked into the side of the mountain, with wonderful views and a chilled-out bar area for tapas and drinks, it has only outdoor seating. The food is wonderful, with imaginative salads and local meats, cheeses and wines. Owner Rob Grimmonds also rents out smart two-bedroom apartments with shared pool for around €650 a week (less in low season).

In Cómpeta, very pleasant self-catering accommodation is available at **Casa La Piedra** (Plazoleta 17, 952 51 63 29, www.2sandra.com, double €70). **Las Tres Abejas** (C/Panaderos 43/45, 952 55 33 75, www.lastresabejas.com, double €48) is a cosy, pint-sized B&B, with friendly British owners and plenty of cute features, such as a plunge pool on the upper roof terrace. The village's wonderful wood-stove bakery is opposite. Alternatively, the three-star **El Balcón de Cómpeta** (C/San Antonio 75, 952 55 35 35, double €67-€82) has the usual mod cons, plus tennis courts and a good swimming pool – ask for a room with a balcony.

The **Museo del Vino** (Avenida Constitución 6, 952 55 33 14, closed Mon, €) is a fun, atmospheric place for wine and tapas, while the tiny *finca* **Bodegas Almijara**, a couple of kilometres out of town (Ctra Canillas de Albaida, 952 55 32 85) does free tastings for potential customers. For eats, the long-established **El Pilón** (C/Laberinto, 952 55 35 12, €-€€) is a firm favourite for grills, and also does an excellent pot-roasted rabbit dish. For top-quality Spanish nosh, head uptown to **Cortijo Paco** (Avda Canillas 6, 952 55 36 47, closed Mon and June-Aug, €€).

Resources

Internet

Vélez-Málaga *Ciber-Café Intern@te, C/Doctor Laureano Casquero, Bajo 5 (952 50 44 54).* **Open** 10am-midnight Mon-Sat; 4pm-midnight Sun.

Police station

Frigiliana *Pl del Ingenio (mobile 658 79 27 51).*
Vélez-Málaga *Pl de San Roque s/n (952 54 92 38).*

Post office

Frigiliana *C/Den Imán 1 (no phone).*
Vélez-Málaga *Plaza San Roque 12 (952 50 01 43).*

Tourist information

Cómpeta *Plaza Almijara s/n (952 55 33 18/952 55 36 85).* **Open** *July-Aug* 10am-2pm Wed-Sat; *Sept-June* 9am-2pm, 3-6pm Wed-Sat; 10am-3pm Sun.
Frigiliana *Cuesta del Apero 10 (952 53 42 61).* **Open** 9am-8pm Mon-Fri; 10am-1.30pm, 4-8pm Sat, Sun.

The coast to Nerja

Travelling east from Málaga takes you along one of the most banal stretches of coastline in Spain. A wall of nondescript concrete high-rises, it has neither the madness of Torrie nor the glamour of Marbella's golden mile, and is barely worth a glance until you arrive at Nerja.

The first sizeable resort you come to is unappealing **Rincón de la Victoria**, which warrants a stop only to explore the nearby grottoes of the **Cueva del Tesoro**. According to legend, this is where the Moorish emirs hid their treasure, though the loot has never been found. The next major settlement along the coast is **Torre del Mar**, less gloomy than it might first appear. The Paseo de Larios has become the new heart of the city and is relatively leafy and graceful, with numerous pavement cafés, tapas bars and fish restaurants.

Around 50 kilometres (30 miles) east of Málaga, **Nerja** is one of the very few towns on the Costa del Sol that has not had its charms submerged under a sea of concrete. Since the 1960s boom in tourism, this once tiny fishing village has grown to a population of around 16,000, of whom a fifth are foreign residents (75 per cent of these are British) – you are more likely to hear English spoken than any other language. Wedged between the Mediterranean and the umber, ice-cream-cone peaks of the Sierra de Tejeda, it's a useful base for exploring the Axarquía.

Its focal point is the **Balcón de Europa**, a handsome promenade. Built on the site of a Moorish castle, it juts out towards the sea, flanked by towering palms and lined with ice-cream vendors, cafés, dried fruit and nut stands, and the odd touristy horse and carriage. But if you really want to get a taste of how things were before the boom, follow the town wall west of the Balcón to **El Salón** beach. Its scrubby cliffs made development impossible and the only buildings you'll see are two or three small fishing cottages. Sadly, cliff erosion is occurring at such an alarming rate that the old cliff path that connected all the town's beaches is unlikely to open again. The horseshoe-shaped *playas* of **Carabeo** and **Calahonda**, however, are still easily accessed via steps from the old town.

Nerja really comes alive in the summer, particularly during the wild festival of San Isidro, which takes place in the caves in mid May, and on the eve of San Juan in June, which features the best beach party of the year. Young and old gather on the strand at midnight and stagger backwards into the sea, before dancing until dawn breaks.

By far the biggest attraction in the area is the **Cueva de Nerja** (**photo** *p192*), which dates back five million years. This spectacular series of caves resembles something from Tolkien.

Balcón de Europa.

The grand central column in Cataclysm Hall, at 32 metres (105 feet) high, is the tallest in the world and took a trillion drops of water to form. It is possible to take spelunking tours of the caves by prior arrangement, and if you happen to be in town at the end of July, do check out the **International Festival of Music and Dance**, which takes place here.

If you want to escape the crowds (other than on summer weekends and throughout August), head for the beautiful – naturist-friendly – beach of **Cantarijján**, ten kilometres (six miles) east of Nerja, which has a couple of excellent *chiringuitos* that can rustle up a mean paella.

There's no shortage of adventure sports and activities available in the area. **Scuba Nerja** (Playa Burriana, 952 52 72 51, www.scubanerja.com) runs one- and two-tank dives, and offers day trips aboard its catamaran along the coast, stopping at one of the area's best beaches for a paella lunch. **Cortijo Hidalgo** (Castillo Alto, Casa 73E, 630 28 62 39, €17/hr) organises horseback tours of the Sierra Tejeda.

Cueva de Nerja

Ctra de Maro (952 52 95 20). **Open** *July, Aug* 10am-2pm, 4-8pm daily. *Sept-June* 10am-2pm, 4-6.30pm daily. **Admission** €7; €3.50 concessions. **No credit cards**.

Cueva del Tesoro

A7-E15, Rincón de la Victoria (952 40 61 62/ www.sopde.es/naturaleza). **Guided tours** 10.45am, 11.30am, 12.15pm, 1pm, 3.45pm, 4.30pm, 5.15pm daily. **Admission** (incl guided tour in English) €4.25, €2.50 concessions. **No credit cards**.

Where to eat

There are about 300 bars and restaurants in Nerja, some of them excellent, others way south of mediocre. Among the stars is **Scarletta's** (C/Cristo 38, 952 52 00 11, closed lunch, closed Sun and mid Nov-mid Feb, €€-€€€), a trendy eaterie with bags of style, killer cocktails and friendly staff. The menu offers a range of classics from around the world, from Thai curries and barbecue ribs to Irish fillet steaks. It has two enticing rooftop terraces.

For mammoth portions of home-made pasta and 28 different sauces, try **El Gato Negro** (C/Carabeo 19, 952 52 50 92, €€), an intimate little Italian bistro decorated with baroque drapes, stone statues and a painted ceiling. It doubles as a shrine to Pavarotti, whose hits will serenade you through dinner, except on Saturdays when you can expect live flamenco.

For traditional tapas, Nerja has a handful of options. **Bar El Pulguilla** (C/Almirante Ferrandiz 26, 952 52 13 84, closed Mon, €)

Cueva de Nerja. *See p191.*

has strip lighting and stainless steel bar tops in classic style. The tapas are superlative and often come free. Cold beer and *manzanilla* (dry sherry) are best accompanied by tapas of octopus salad, steamed clams, grilled prawns and skewers of spice-rubbed chicken. **Marisqueria La Marina** (C/Castilla Pérez 28, 952 52 12 99, closed 2wks Oct, €-€€) is just slightly more formal than either of the above. The specials are *pulpo a la resaca* (roast octopus), *coquiñas* (small, sweet purple-lipped clams), *vitorias* (small anchovies) and a beautifully simple tomato salad.

On the international front, **Lan Sang** (C/Málaga 12, Edificio Cuatro Caminos, 952 52 80 53, www.lansang.com, closed lunch Mon, €€) an excellent Thai-Laotian place offering lip-smackingly authentic dishes such as *sai kok lao* (pork sausages with Lao spices), larb salad (shredded chicken with chilli and lemongrass) and *pa neung king* (steamed sea bass with ginger and spring onion). You might also enjoy checking out the cave-like interior and colourful decor of Mexican restaurant **El Cielito Lindo** (C/El Barrio 26, 952 52 74 95, €€). Specials include a gargantuan spear of char-grilled meats.

A once quiet fishing beach, Playa Burriana is now chock-full of eateries, bars and *chiringuitos* barbecuing fish out of old Nerja fishing boats. Favourites remain **Merendero Ayo** (Playa Burriana s/n, 952 52 22 89, €) for paella cooked in a giant pan over an open flame, and the Belgian-owned **Nerja de Nerja** (Playa Burriana, 952 52 09 28, closed Wed, €-€€) for mussels and seriously stiff drinks.

Where to drink/nightlife

One of Nerja's prettiest bars, the **Mirador del Bendito Café** (no phone), is hacked into the cliff just beneath Plaza Cueva del Bendito, offering shade beneath lovely palm-thatched umbrellas in a luxuriant subtropical garden.

Most dancing and late-night drinking places (open until 4 or 5am) are around C/Antonio Millón and Plaza Tutti-Frutti (both north-west of the Balcón). **La Iguana** (C/Antonio Millón C/1, Edificio Jábega II, no phone) and **Casbah** are two of the most popular hangouts. **Cayma** (C/Cristo 56, no phone) is good for 1960s, '70s and '80s disco music. For a boogie, try the small, intimate **Bogey Bar** (C/Pintada 22, no phone), **Jimmy's** (C/Antonio Millón C/6, Edificio Venus, 952 52 19 15, closed mid Sept-May) or **Castillo** (C/Diputación 12, no phone), perhaps the best disco in town.

Playa Burriana has seen increasing numbers of trendy bars opening up in the last few years. Among them are **Copacabana** (C/Filipinas 3, 952 52 71 14) run by a young, friendly French couple, and **H20** (Playa Burriana, 952 52 59 71), the closest thing Nerja has to a designer cocktail and wine bar.

There are innumerable places offering flamenco *espectáculos* (shows) at varying prices and with varying degrees of talent. **El Colono** (C/Granada 6, 952 52 18 26, dinner shows Wed, Fri) claims to stage *flamenco puro*. Reservations are recommended for this twice-weekly dinner-dance extravaganza; tickets cost from €32. **El Burro Blanco** (C/Gloria 3, no phone) is more casual and has raucous singing and dancing every night from 10pm.

Where to stay

There is no shortage of high-quality options. C/Pintada is home to several budget *hostales*, all similar in price and quality. One of the best cheap places is the centrally located **Hostal Miguel** (C/Almirante Ferrandiz 31, 952 52 15 23, www.hostalmiguel.com, double €33-€49), run by a young, enthusiastic English couple. This popular nine-room *hostal* has a sunshiney feel. The roof terrace and lounge are bonuses, as is its dead central location. Book early.

On the seafront, the **Hostal Marazul** (Avda del Mediterráneo, 952 52 41 91, double €32-€51) is another good deal; all rooms are sea-facing and the best have private sun terraces. On the other side of the Balcón, **Hostal Tres Soles** (C/Carabeo 40, 952 52 51 57, double €30-€45) is clean and simple, with all mod cons, and is very kid friendly. If you want to stay on the Balcón, the four-star **Hotel Balcón de Europa** (Paseo Balcón de Europa 1, 952 52 08 00, www.hotelbalconeuropa.com, double €94-€164) is the best-known option, but for a fraction of the cost, the **Hostal Marissal** (Paseo Balcón de Europa 3, 952 52 01 99, www.hostalmarissal.com, double €40-€60, restaurant €€) next door is highly recommended. Above a good bar-restaurant, its immaculate rooms are superb value. Nearby, the three-star **Hotel Cavana** (Plaza Cavana 10, 952 52 40 00, double €75-€117) is modern, if a little clinical. Its main selling points are indoor and rooftop pools, a sauna and a jacuzzi.

The most luxurious place to stay in town is the **Parador de Nerja** (C/Almuñécar 8, 952 52 00 50, www.parador.es, double €139-€149), despite an exterior that resembles a multi-storey car park. It has spacious, elegant bedrooms (most are sea-facing), manicured lawns, swimming pool, tennis courts, a restaurant and piano bar. If you're after boutique-style accommodation, two places stand out. The **Hotel Paraíso del Mar** (C/Prolongación de Carabeo 22, 952 52 16 21, double €82-€120) has wonderful terraced gardens carved out of the cliff leading down to Burriana beach. Alternatively, in the neighbouring village of Maro (about three kilometres/two miles east of Nerja), **Hotel Romantico Casa Maro** (952 52 95 52, www.hotel-casa-maro.com, double €60-€104) offers cliff-top views, cute bedrooms and an intimate covered terrace. It's also a good place for fish and seafood.

Resources

Internet

Europaweb, C/Málaga s/n (952 52 61 47).
Open *June-Sept* 10am-midnight daily. *Sept-May* 10am-10pm daily.

Police station

C/Virgen de Pilar 1 (952 52 15 45).

Post office

C/Almirante Ferrandiz 6 (952 52 17 49).

Tourist information

Puerta del Mar 2 (952 52 15 31/www.nerja.org).
Open 10am-2pm, 4.30-7pm Mon-Fri; 10am-1.30pm Sat.

Getting there

There's no public transport in the Montes de Málaga, and very little in the Axarquía, so renting a car is advisable.

By bus

Alsina Graells (952 52 15 04) runs hourly buses from Málaga to Nerja (via major coastal towns). Loymerbus (952 54 11 13) run 3 a day to Cómpeta. An hourly bus runs daily from Nerja to Frigiliana. Frequent buses run from Torre del Mar to Vélez-Málaga.

North of Málaga

Prehistoric dolmens, Roman ruins and great tapas.

Antequera

Nestled among steep, rugged mountain peaks, Antequera is a thriving settlement of around 40,000, with a well-preserved old centre and some fascinating sights, from neolithic dolmens to a ninth-century Moorish castle and some of Andalucía's finest baroque interiors.

It was probably a significant settlement as far back as 2500 BC; the size and sophistication of the town's three dolmens, suggest the presence of a large, well-organised prehistoric community of nobles and workers with powerful leaders and strong religious beliefs. With the arrival of the Romans in the first century AD came great wealth and magnificent villas. One such mansion has been excavated near the station, an effort that has revealed an outstanding set of mosaics and priceless artefacts (now on show at the town's Museo Municipal). Recognising Antequera's strategic importance (and, therefore, it's vulnerability), the Moors, who took control of the area in the ninth century, endowed it with an imposing Alcazaba (hilltop castle). Under Spanish Christian rule, the town expanded both literally and culturally, emerging as a prestigious centre of literature and learning during the 16th century.

Sightseeing

Start your tour at the **Arco de los Gigantes**. Located in the oldest part of town on Calle Colegio, this imposing triumphal arch was erected in 1585 by Felipe II, who decorated it with Roman sculptures, tableaux and fragments. Known as Spain's oldest (and smallest) open-air museum, the arch can be climbed via a stone stairway.

The same stairway leads to the medieval **Alcazaba**, which occupies the highest point in the town. Once a great defensive fortress, it is now reduced to a collection of expertly restored exterior walls that have been incorporated into a simple but lovely formal garden of cypresses and yews. The most complete structures within the Alcazaba are two keeps, one of which, the **Torre del Homenaje**, can normally be visited (closed Mon, free). Before leaving the castle, take a moment to admire the distant view of **La Peña de los Enamorados** (Lovers' Rock), known colloquially as 'Franco's Nose'. Shaped like the head of a sleeping giant, this huge natural formation is located halfway between Antequera and neighbouring Archidona. Its official name comes from a touching local legend about a Moorish girl and a Christian boy who fell in love shortly before the conquest of Granada in 1492. Realising they could never be together, the young couple hurled themselves from the top of the rock, choosing togetherness in death over life apart.

Just beyond the triumphal arch and castle stands the **Real Colegiata de Santa María la Mayor**. Constructed between 1514 and 1550, the church is the principal feature of the beautifully proportioned Plaza de los Escribanos. The exterior, set against dramatic mountain scenery, is notable for its elegant early Renaissance façade. Beyond the imposing, Arab-style door is an elegant interior, with a fine Mudéjar *artesanado* ceiling. Notice the small side chapel (on the left as you enter), which contains Roman remains. Just before you reach the altar there is another, larger side chapel with a lovely Moorish-style wooden ceiling and some delicate stucco work around the paintings. Before leaving the square, take a moment to admire the excavated Roman baths to one side of Santa María.

If Santa María is arresting thanks to its austerity, the nearby church of **El Carmen** is precisely the opposite. Located just below Plaza de los Escribanos on Plaza El Carmen, it boasts a stunningly elaborate late-baroque interior hidden away behind a deceptively simple façade. Its *retablo* is one of the most intricate in all Andalucía, and an excellent example of the churrigueresque style. Carved in unpainted red pine, it is littered with delicately sculpted biblical figures, saints, bishops and angels.

From Plaza El Carmen, descend Cuesta de los Rojas to reach the **Museo Conventual de las Descalzas**, the first of the town's two small but interesting museums. Housed in a 17th-century convent built for the Barefoot (*descalzas*) Carmelites, it contains a substantial collection of religious art, including a painting by Lucas Giordano of St Teresa of Avila, the 16th-century founder of the religious order.

Around the corner, on Plaza del Coso Viejo, Antequera's excellent **Museo Municipal** occupies a beautiful 18th-century palace with

Capilla Tribuna del Portichuelo.

a fine Mudéjar-baroque bell tower. Once the private residence of the aristocratic Nájera family, the *palacio* has an interior courtyard now used to display Roman artefacts, and several exhibition rooms containing – among other things – a collection of 17th-century paintings by the Mexican artist Juan Correa and a lifelike portrait of St Francis by Pedro de Mena. The museum's prize exhibit, however, is a complete Roman bronze of a nude boy known as 'Ephebus of Antequera'. The statue, which stands 1.4 metres (4.6 feet) high, is one of only six such figures in the world and is probably the finest piece of Roman sculpture in Spain. A superb example of the sensual nature of imperial art at that time; it was found at the Roman villa located near the station. The villa is still being excavated, but when it does open to the public it will be a world-class site, thanks to its spectacular mosaics, a large proportion of which remain intact.

Antequera's historical wealth means that it possesses a disproportionately large number of architecturally significant churches. One of the most striking is **San Sebastián (photo** *p196*; open hours of services), a 16th-century building on Plaza San Sebastián, which succeeded Santa María as the town's principal centre of learning in the late 17th century. Located next to a fin-de-siècle palace, the church has on its exterior two outstanding and somewhat contradictory features: a Renaissance-style façade adorned with statues of saints Paul, Peter and Sebastian, plus Carlos V's coat of arms; and a graceful Mudéjar-baroque tower, constructed in the early 18th century with intricate brickwork and a glazed ceramic spire crowned by a weathercock.

From Plaza San Sebastián, take C/Cuesta de la Paz and follow it all the way to Plaza El Portichuelo, an enchanting square containing the pretty church of **Jesús** (open 10am-12.30pm daily). It was constructed in the 18th century in baroque-Mudéjar style using pink and white bricks, and incorporates the **Capilla Tribuna del Portichuelo**, which houses the Virgen del Socorro, a key focus in the town's Semana Santa celebrations. Further north, the simple 18th-century church of **Santiago** (open hours of services) stands practically side-by-side at the junction of Cuesta de Archidona and Calle de Belén with the ornate 17th-century baroque **Convento de Belén** (open 8am-5.30pm daily).

What distinguishes Antequera most clearly from other southern Spanish towns, however, are its three Neolithic dolmens (burial chambers), located on the north-eastern outskirts of town, which rate as some of the most important prehistoric remains in the country. The largest and oldest, **Dólmen de Viera** and **Dólmen de Menga**, are only a short distance from the centre on the Archidona–Granada road (turn right down C/Belén by the church of Santiago, following the 'Dólmenes' sign for ten minutes). The Menga dolmen (roughly 4,500 years old and probably the tomb of an important nobleman) consists of a huge underground gallery lined with 32 vertical stone slabs, the largest of which weighs 180 tonnes. Don't miss the engraved symbols and human figures at the entrance. Thought to be slightly more recent, the Viera dolmen has a long, narrow tunnel leading to a small burial chamber. To reach **El Romeral** dolmen, continue on the same road for three kilometres (two miles). Turn left after the industrial estate, following signs for Córdoba and Seville. After 500 metres, turn left at a roundabout and follow the signs for 'Dólmen El Romeral'. This is the most recent (at 3,800 years old) and most sophisticated of the three sites, with two domed brick chambers – the smallest would have been used for offerings to the dead.

San Sebastián church. *See p195.*

El Carmen
Plaza del Carmen (952 84 29 22). **Open** *June-Sept* 10am-2pm, 5-8pm Mon-Sat; 10am-2pm Sun. *Oct-May* 10am-2pm, 4-7pm Mon-Sat; 10am-2pm Sun. **Admission** €1.50; 60¢ concessions.

Dólmen el Romeral
Cerro Romeral s/n (no phone). **Open** 9am-6pm Tue-Sat; 9.30am-2.30pm Sun. **Admission** free.

Dólmenes de Viera & Menga
Ctra Antequera–Archidona (no phone). **Open** 9am-6pm Tue-Sat; 9.30am-2.30pm Sun. **Admission** free.

Museo Conventual de las Descalzas
Plaza de las Descalzas 3 (952 84 19 77). Closed until late 2007.

Museo Municipal
Palacio de Nájera, Plaza de Coso Viejo s/n (952 70 40 51). **Open** *Mid June-Sept* 8.30pm-10.30pm Tue-Fri; 10am-1.30pm Sat, Sun. *Oct-mid June* 10am-1.30pm, 4.30-6.30pm Tue-Fri; 10am-1.30pm Sat, Sun. **Admission** €3; free under-18s. Obligatory guided tours every 30mins. **No credit cards**. Opening hours are subject to change, so call ahead.

Real Colegiata de Santa María la Mayor
Plaza de los Escribanos (952 84 61 43). **Open** *June* 9am-3pm Tue-Fri; 10.30am-2pm Sat; 11.30am-2pm Sun. *July-mid Sept* 10.30am-2pm, 8.30-10.30pm Tue-Fri; 10.30am-2pm Sat; 11.30am-2pm Sun. *Mid Sept-May* 10.30am-2pm, 4.30-6.30pm Tue-Fri; 10.30am -2pm Sat; 11.30am-2pm Sun. **Admission** free.

Where to eat & drink

El Angelote
Plaza Coso Viejo (952 70 34 65). **Open** noon-5pm, 7pm-2am Tue-Sun. Closed 2wks Aug. **Average** €€. **Credit** MC, V.
Next to the Museo Municipal is one of Antequera's best-known eateries. Local specialities such as *porra antequerana* (a dip like thick gazpacho) are served in a pleasant, rustic-style dining room.

Bar-Restaurante Plaza San Sebastián
Plaza San Sebastián 4 (952 84 42 39). **Open** 7am-2.30am daily. **Average** €. **Credit** MC, V.
This central bar-restaurant-hotel (€40-€55 double) draws tourists to its terrace and locals into its cavernous exterior for good simple tapas and *raciones*.

Caserío de San Benito
Ctra Córdoba–Málaga, km108 (952 11 11 03/ www.caseriodesanbenito.com). **Open** *Mid July-mid Sept* noon-5pm, 8pm-midnight Tue-Sun. *Mid Sept-June* 8pm-midnight Fri-Sun. Closed 2wks early July. **Average** €€€. **Credit** AmEx, MC, V.
One of the region's best restaurants, 20km (12-mile) from Antequera, in an old farmhouse. Try the *arroz con conejo* (rice with rabbit), and leave room for pud.

El Escribano
Plaza de los Escribanos 11 (952 70 65 33). **Open** *July-Sept* 11am-11.30pm Tue-Sun. *Oct-June* 11am-11.30pm Tue-Sat; 11am-4pm Sun. Closed 2wks Sept & Oct. **Average** €€. **Credit** MC, V.
A simple restaurant with tables spilling out on to the *plaza*, serving good, traditional Spanish dishes in a glorious location facing the church of Santa María la Mayor.

Where to stay

In addition to the places below, the following are decent central options: **Hotel Colón** (C/Infante Don Fernando 29, 952 84 00 10, www.castelcolon.com, double €40), **Pensión Reyes** (C/La Tercia 4, 952 84 10 28, double €30), the **Hotel Coso Viejo** (C/Encarnación 5, 952 70 50 45, double €64-€80) and the **Bar-Restaurante Plaza San Sebastián** (*see left*).

Hotel Antequera Golf
Urbanización Santa Catalina (952 70 45 31/www.hotel antequera.com). **Rates** €73-€84 single; €91-€105 double; €182-€209 suite. **Credit** AmEx, MC, V.
The town's parador is a comfortable, modern building, located just outside the centre. The rooms are spacious, and it has every modern convenience, including a bar, pool and ts own golf course.

Hotel Castilla
C/Infante Don Fernando 40 (952 84 30 90/ www.castillahotel.com). **Rates** €25-€36 single; €40-€50 double; €54-€60 triple. **Credit** MC, V.
A new building in the heart of the old town, the two-star Castilla has comfortable, if rather bland, rooms equipped with satellite television and air-con.

Pensión Madrona
C/Calzada 27-29 (952 84 00 14). **Rates** €22 single; €35 double; €54 triple. **Credit** MC, V.
Clean, basic accommodation located a five-minute walk north-east of Plaza San Sebastián. Don't miss out on the delicious *churros* and breakfasts.

Around Antequera

Located just to the south of the town is the **Paraje Natural Torcal de Antequera**, better known as **El Torcal**, a nature reserve containing some spectacularly weird rock formations. The park covers 2,000 hectares (eight square miles) and is dominated by a 1,369-metre (4,491-foot) mountain that has been splintered, gnarled, serrated and fractured over approximately 150 million years into bizarrely shaped calceous rocks (**photo** *p199*). The 1.4-kilometre (one-mile) Ruta Verde walk starts and ends near the visitors' centre and is marked by green posts. You will need a car to get to the park, whichi is signed from the C3310 between Antequera and Villanueva de la Concepción.

Don't miss Birdwatching spots

Andalucía is twitching heaven. Thanks to its unique geographical position, almost within touching distance of Africa and on major migration routes, and its huge ecological and climatic diversity, southern Spain supports a huge range of breeding and migrant species. Many, such as the red-knobbed coot and white-rumped swift, are found nowhere else on the continent, and even the uninitiated will get a kick from witnessing the exoticism of many of the passerines and wetland species and the majesty of the soaring raptors.

For more details, get hold of Ernest Garcia and Andrew Patterson's authoritative *Where to Watch Birds in Southern and Western Spain* and check the website of the Spanish Ornithological Society (Sociedad Española de Ornitología, www.seo.org).

COTO DONANA

This immense national park and its surrounding protected areas occupy more than 1,300 square kilometres (500 square miles) of the western Guadalquivir estuary at the boundary of Huelva and Sevilla provinces. The Doñana is one of the most important wetland sites in Europe, supporting huge concentrations of wildfowl in winter, as well as breeding populations of cattle and little egrets, grey, night, purple and squacco herons, and glossy ibises. There are raptors aplenty, including around 15 pairs of the ultra-rare Spanish imperial eagle. The interior of the park is accessible only by guided tour but there is a variety of good sites on the periphery, including El Rocío, where you may be able to spot up to 70 species. The park's information centre, El Acebuche (*see p119* **Coto Doñana**) can provide information.

GIBRALTAR, TARIFA AND AROUND

The southern tip of the continent is the place to head for the best views of migrating raptors and seabirds. Gibraltar allows up-close views of the former (it's possible to see more than a dozen species on a good day in spring or autumn). The area around Tarifa has the edge for watching stork and crane migrations, while Tarifa's beach (Playa de los Lances) is thronged in winter with waders and gulls (including Audouin's gulls). Punta Secreta, on the CA223 south from Algeciras, is another great spot for migration-watching. The steppe-like plain of La Janda (viewable from the minor road from Facinas to Benalup) offers the chance to see species such as little bustards and stone curlews. Up the Costa de la Luz at Sierra de la Plata (near Bolonia) is the first known breeding site in Europe of the white-rumped swift.

LAGUNA DE FUENTE DE PIEDRA

The chief draw of this large, shallow saline lake in Málaga province is the only regular breeding colony of greater flamingoes in Spain. The lagoon attracts as many as 16,000 pairs annually. It lies close to the village of Fuente de Piedra, just off the A92 motorway between Sevilla and Granada.

RIO GUADALQUIVIR, CÓRDOBA

Right in the heart of the city, in reed beds by the Puente Romano in front of the Mezquita, is a remarkable and highly visible egret colony. As well as cattle and little egrets, there's a wide variety of other species to be seen, including night and squacco herons, white storks, little bitterns and purple gallinules. On the Mezquita itself is a lesser kestrel colony. *See p212.*

West of El Torcal lies the area's other great natural wonder, the deep, rugged canyon of the Río Guadalhorce, known as the **Garganta del Chorro** (El Chorro Gorge). Here, breathtakingly steep limestone walls create some of the most dramatic scenery in Spain. To reach it, follow the signs for Camping El Chorro and continue past the campsite for a few minutes on a rough track until you reach a small car park, with a metal gate blocking the way just beyond it. Leave your car here and take the wide track heading upwards for around 15 minutes. You'll soon see the gorge and a green-painted railway bridge ahead of you. Although officially prohibited, many visitors then cross over the rail bridge and walk through the rail tunnel for more stunning views.

El Chorro's most famous (and frightening) sight is the crumbling concrete walkway, known as the **Caminito del Rey** (King's Pathway), that snakes along the walls of the gorge. It was constructed in 1901-05 to move workers and materials between El Chorro Falls and the Gaitanejo Falls on the other side of the gorge, but has been closed now for some years following its partial collapse and the deaths of a number of people who attempted to walk it. A €7 million restoration is in the pipeline.

Nearby is the ninth-century church and fortress remains of **Bobastro**, just west of El Chorro. Hidden behind a rocky hill (which you'll have to climb), the church is unusual for several reasons: it was built as a Christian place of worship when Andalucía was ruled by Muslims; it is cut entirely out of bare rock; and it is supposed to contain the tomb of Ibn Hafsun, a Christian emir who founded a short-lived independent state in the region in 880.

Heading north-west towards Seville from Antequera for about 20 kilometres (12 miles) brings you to one of the area's most unexpected natural features, the **Laguna de Fuente de Piedra** (*see p198* **Don't miss**), Andalucía's largest natural lake and an important breeding ground for the greater flamingo, vast numbers of which fly over from Senegal in winter, hatch their chicks in spring and then depart for Africa in August when the water dries up.

Eighteen kilometres (11 miles) north-east of Antequera, the town of **Archidona** is chiefly of note for its unique and largely unaltered octagonal main square, built in 1780-86 with stone from El Torcal.

Where to stay & eat

The outstanding place to stay near **El Torcal** is **La Posada del Torcal** (Villanueva de la Concepción, 952 03 11 77, www.laposadadeltorcal.com, double €134-€279, restaurant €€€€), a laid-back hilltop *cortijo* with ten luxurious rooms and a pool. If you want to stay near El Chorro, **La Garganta** (Barriada del Chorro, 952 49 51 19, apartments €60-€90) offers excellent apartments with views, a pool and a restaurant. Just east of El Chorro is **Cortijo Valverde** (Ctra de Alora, km35.5, Valle de Abdalajis, 952 11 29 79, www.cortijovalverde.com, double €103-€106), with seven rooms. From the pool and attractive gardens are great views over the surrounding countryside.

Resources

Police station

Antequera *Avda de la Legión (952 70 81 04).*

Post office

Antequera *C/Nájera 26 (952 84 20 83).*

Tourist information

Antequera *Plaza de San Sebastián 7 (952 70 25 05/www.antequera.es).* **Open** *Mid June-Sept* 11am-2pm, 5-8pm Mon-Sat; 11am-2pm Sun. *Oct-mid June* 10.30am-1.30pm, 4-7pm Mon-Sat; 11am-2pm Sun.

Reserva Natural Laguna de Fuente de Piedra *Cerro del Palo s/n, Fuente de Piedra (952 73 54 53).* **Open** *Apr-Sept* 10am-1pm, 6-8pm Tue; 10am-2pm, 6-8pm Wed-Sun. *Oct-Mar* 10am-1pm, 4-6pm Tue; 10am-2pm, 4-6pm Wed-Sun.

Getting there

By bus

From Antequera, Alsina Graells (952 84 13 65) and Casado (952 84 19 57) both run regular buses daily to Málaga (1hr 15mins), 6 to Seville (2hrs 40mins), 5 to Granada (1hr 45mins) and 2 to Córdoba (2hrs 15mins).

By train

Antequera's train station is on Avda de la Estación. There are 5 trains a day to Granada (1hr 30mins), 4 to Seville (1hr 30mins) and 3 to Algeciras (2hrs 50mins) via Ronda (1hr 10mins). For Málaga and Córdoba, change at Bobadilla. A couple of trains a day from Málaga stop at El Chorro (40mins).

Málaga Province

El Torcal. *See p197.*

West of Málaga

Find out why Ronda is the most-visited town in western Andalucía.

Ronda

Spread out along a high cliff that has been cleft in two by the mighty Guadalevín gorge, and surrounded on all sides by rumpled mountains, it is easy to see why **Ronda** has long captured the imagination of travellers. With the Costa del Sol little more than half an hour away by car (albeit via a heart-stopping road that cuts a series of dizzy loops up and up from San Pedro), the town sometimes struggles to cope with the huge influx of tourists who are disgorged by the coachload from mid-morning onwards. In order to avoid being swamped by the bumbag brigade, try to leave exploring the town until later in the day. Once the coaches are heading back down the hill, Ronda again becomes a magical place, the *ciudad soñada* (town of dreams) of artists and poets.

Ronda's reputation certainly isn't a recent phenomenon. When the 19th-century Romantic movement espoused Spain, the region became an obligatory stop on the Grand Tour. The likes of Victor Hugo, Théophile Gautier, David Roberts, George Borrow and Richard Ford all waxed lyrical about the town's extraordinary beauty, and later it was to beguile Rainer Maria Rilke, Ernest Hemingway and Orson Welles, among others. For Hemingway and Welles the town's central role in the history of bullfighting was a major draw; both coincided with the apogee of Ronda's most famous *torero*, Antonio Ordóñez. Hemingway quipped that this was the perfect place to spend a honeymoon 'because there's nothing to do' and Welles was so taken with the place he asked that his ashes be scattered in the patio of Ordóñez's farm, just north of town.

The classic postcard view of Ronda is looking up at the cliff-top buildings ranged on either side of the gorge of the Guadalevín, known by all locals simply as **El Tajo (photo** *p201*). The gorge is spanned by the late 18th-century **Puente Nuevo** (New Bridge), which was eventually completed, after works spanning more than four decades, in 1793, and which has become the town's neural centre as well as its adopted symbol. It links the old Moorish citadel in the south to the newer town, which could only develop once the gorge had been spanned. Most shops, bars and restaurants are in the newer town (the **Mercadillo** quarter), while the majority of the interesting buildings and boutique hotels are in the old town (known as **La Ciudad**). Beyond La Ciudad, the *barrio* of San Francisco is far less touristy and contains some of Ronda's best tapas bars.

In most guidebooks you'll find the tragicomic legend of the Puente Nuevo's architect, Martín de Aldehuela, who supposedly fell to his death during his final inspection of the bridge when he lunged to grab his hat, blown off by the wind. (The truth is disappointingly prosaic: he died in a hospital bed in Málaga.) During the Civil War both Nationalist and Republican prisoners were forced to jump to their deaths in the gorge, events that were to act as a touchstone for Hemingway's *For Whom the Bell Tolls*. Above the bridge's central arch was a tiny prison cell that later became a bar and now houses a small museum.

Crossing the bridge into the old town, take the first left to reach the fancifully named **Casa del Rey Moro** (House of the Moorish King). It actually dates from 1709, although beneath the house is a lengthy rock-cut stairway, **La Mina**, which dates back to Moorish times. If you're feeling fit you can descend the 365 steps to the bottom of the gorge, where you emerge beside the Guadalevín via a keyhole-arched doorway. There are wonderful views from the gardens, which were laid out by the French landscape gardener de Forestier.

Further down the hill is the 18th-century **Palacio del Marqués de Salvatierra**. The unusual figurines carved on its façade were inspired by Native American art. If you continue downhill – passing beneath the **Arco de Felipe V (photo** *p201*), then crossing over the **Puente de San Miguel**, Ronda's oldest bridge – you reach the **Baños Arabes** (Arab Baths). Although much of the marble and mosaic that once adorned the baths is gone, most of the main 13th-century structure remains intact, making this probably Andalucía's best-preserved *hammam*.

Back up in the old town, past the 14th-century **Minarete de San Sebastián** (a Nasrid-style minaret) and the **Museo del Bandolero**, devoted to the bandits who once dominated the surrounding country, is the lovely orange-tree-lined **Plaza Duquesa de Parcent**. Prior to the completion of the bullring, *corridas* were frequently held here.

The sights of **Ronda**.

To one side is the town hall and across the way stands the church of **Santa María la Mayor**. It has had many incarnations: first it was a Roman Temple dedicated to Julius Caesar, then a mosque and finally the town's main church. The construction of the present building began in the early 16th century after Ronda fell to the Christians following a protracted siege. You can see the remains of the ornate *mihrab* (the prayer niche where the Koran was kept) in the entrance hall, as well as the minaret, which, embellished with a lantern, became the Christian belfry. The church's most beautiful paintings and *retablos* (altarpieces) were destroyed during the Civil War and were replaced by an extraordinary series of paintings depicting strangely hermaphrodite saints and apostles.

Just west of the church is the most emblematic of Ronda's many fine buildings, the **Palacio de Mondragón** (**photo** *p201*). Home to a succession of Moorish governors until the Reconquista (King Fernando slept here after the siege of Ronda in 1485), it was converted into a Mudéjar-Renaissance mansion named after the knight Melchor de Mondragón, whose coat of arms is above the palace's main entrance. It now houses a museum of local archaeology and an offshoot of Málaga University, which organises intensive Spanish courses. But by far its most charming feature is its formal garden, which runs right to the edge of the cliff and provides a backdrop for photographs of newly-weds and children taking first communion. In the 1960s the palace became the home of the writer Alastair Boyd (Lord Kilmarnock), who opened a school for studying Spanish here. A number of well-heeled Brits passed through as well as a succession of writers, including Patrick Leigh Fermor and Martin Amis. Boyd's two books about the area, *In the Sierras of the South* and *The Road from Ronda*, are essential reading for anyone with more than a passing interest in the area.

From the nearby Plaza del Campillo, a path winds down the gorge below the Puente Nuevo to a rocky outcrop, from where you can take the classic gorge snap. Persevere to the bottom and, in spring, you'll find yourself wandering through a multi-hued ocean of wild flowers. From here you can loop back up to the Barrio de San Francisco. There's also a wonderful walk (much enjoyed by Rilke) from Ronda to the **Ermita de la Virgen de la Cabeza** (ask at the tourist office for details), passing the house where the painter David Bomberg lived during the last years of his life. Considered one of the greatest artists of the Spanish landscape, he died in 1957, largely ignored by the British art world, and an unknown figure in Spain.

Back across the Puente Nuevo in the new part of town is the **Plaza de España** and a stunningly sited *parador* (*see p206*) with views across the gorge to the old town.

Just beyond it is the **Plaza de Toros** (**photo** *p201*), built in 1785 by the Puente Nuevo's architect Martín de Aldehuela. It is one of the oldest, most beautiful bullrings in Spain. Here that local *torero* Pedro Romero (1754-1839) established the blueprint for modern bullfighting techniques and style. In his long career (he retired at 72), Romero killed 6,000 bulls and was never seriously injured.

The history of Ronda's bullring is the history of bullfighting itself and dates back to 1572, when Felipe II set up the Real Maestranza de Caballería, an exclusive academy in Ronda that aimed to teach young noblemen the art of horsemanship in battle at a time when the *morisco* rebellions threatened the established order. A century or so later, Pedro Romero's grandfather came to the rescue of a nobleman who had been unseated while testing his horsemanship against a wild bull by sweeping his wide-brimmed Andalucían hat in front of the bull to distract it. Thus was born the *corrida de toros*. In time the academy became a training school for young bullfighters. The pricey museum is a taxidermist's paradise, full of massive bulls' heads. There are also blood-stained matador costumes and photographs of the *corrida* spanning several decades.

Since 1957 Ronda has celebrated the **Fiestas de Pedro Romero** (on the Saturday of the September *feria*) with traditional Goya-esque bullfights (Goya was a friend of Romero), where fighters don the traditional costumes that were worn at the end of the 18th century. It remains one of the most important events on the bullfighting calendar and tickets change hands on the black market for huge sums.

Behind the bullring a walkway, the **Paseo de los Ingleses**, runs along the cliff edge, giving wonderful views towards the old town and out over open countryside. It takes its name from the many Brits who stayed in Ronda when it became a hill station for the Gibraltar garrison.

Baños Arabes

Barrio de Padre Jesús (mobile 656 95 09 37). **Open** *Mar-Oct* 10am-7pm daily. *Nov-Feb* 10am-6pm Mon-Fri; 10am-3pm Sat, Sun. **Admission** €2; €1 concessions; free under-14s. **No credit cards.** **Map** p203 B2.

Casa del Rey Moro

C/Santo Domingo 9 (952 18 72 00). **Open** *Mar-Oct* 10am-8pm daily. *Nov-Feb* 10am-7pm daily. **Admission** €4; €2 under-14s. **Credit** DC, MC, V. **Map** p203 B2.

Museo del Bandolero

C/Armiñán 65 (952 87 77 85/ www.museobandolero.com). **Open** *Mar-Oct* 10.30am-8.30pm daily. *Nov-Feb* 10.30am-6.30pm daily. **Admission** €3; €2.50 concessions. **No credit cards. Map** p203 B3.

Palacio de Mondragón

Plaza de Mondragón s/n (952 87 84 50/08 18). **Open** *Mar-Oct* 10am-7pm Mon-Fri. *Nov-Feb* 10am-6pm Sat; 10am-3pm Sun. **Admission** €2; €1 concessions. **No credit cards. Map** p203 A3.

Plaza de Toros/ Museo Taurino

C/Virgen de la Paz 15 (952 87 41 32). **Open** *Corridas* phone for details. *Museum* Apr-Sept 10am-8pm daily. Mar, Oct 10am-7pm daily. Nov-Feb 10am-6pm daily. **Admission** €5. **No credit cards. Map** p203 A1.

Santa María la Mayor

Plaza Duquesa de Parcent s/n (952 87 86 53/www.colegiata.com). **Open** *Apr-Oct* 10am-8pm daily. *Nov-Mar* 10am-6pm daily. **Admission** €2; €1.50 concessions. **No credit cards. Map** p203 B3.

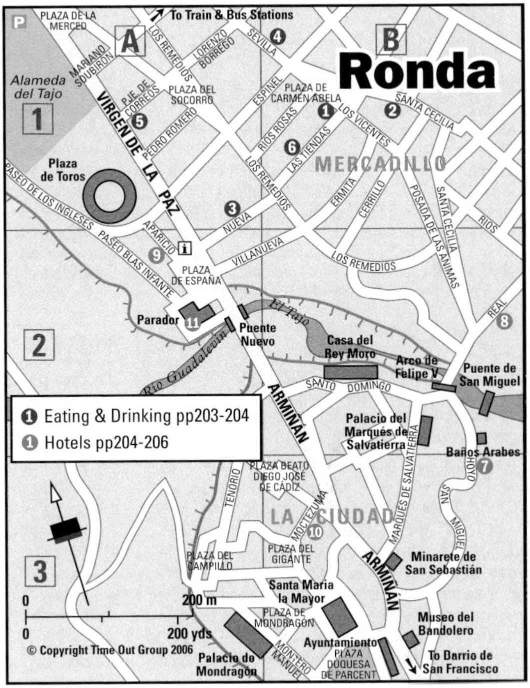

Where to eat & drink

You're best off avoiding the plentiful tourist traps around the Plaza de España, where world-weary waiters try to entice you in for the *menú del día*. Instead, head for the untouristy Barrio de San Francisco at the end of the old town, or to places further into the new town. Note that a number of Ronda's hotels (*see p204*) have excellent restaurants.

Almocábar

Plaza Ruedo Alameda 5 (952 87 59 77). **Open** 1-5pm, 7-11.30pm Mon, Wed-Sun. Closed mid Aug-mid Sept. **Average** €€-€€€. **Credit** AmEx, DC, MC, V. **Map** p203 off B3.

One of Ronda's best places for tapas or a full-blown meal. The front bar serves tasty *montaditos* of beef and avocado; salmon and curd cheese, and pork with grilled pepper. The attractive restaurant has interesting Arab-Andalus dishes, volcanic stone-grilled meat and exceptional roast lamb. Try too the excellent local red, Cortijo de las Monjas.

Bar Restaurante Moreno

Avda Ricardo Naverrete 4 (952 87 58 88). **Open** 12.30-4.30pm, 8pm-midnight Mon, Thur-Sun; 12.30-4.30pm Tue. Closed 2wks Feb & 2wks Aug. **Average** €€. **Credit** AmEx, DC, MC, V. **Map** p203 off B1.

Tucked behind the railway station, Moreno's is always buzzing and the food is excellent. There is no menu – choose from the fresh fish and seafood piled up on ice or order a char-grilled steak, and be sure to try the house specialities: stuffed trout and *cogollos con anchoas* (lettuce hearts draped in anchovies drizzled with hot olive oil and garlic). The owner will also reel off the tapas specials of the day.

Casa María

Plaza Ruedo Alameda 27 (952 87 62 12/mobile 670 79 24 38). **Open** 1-5pm, 7.30pm-12.30am Tue-Sun. Closed Christmas-mid Jan. **Average** €€. **Credit** MC, V. **Map** p203 off B3.

Casa María has a good range of fresh seafood, great steaks and some interesting salads; try the Basque cod or marinated goose liver. Its tables spill out on to the square, and it's nearly always packed, so be sure to book, especially in winter when dining space inside is limited. The wine list is one of the best in Ronda. Popular with the local expat crowd.

Los Cazadores

C/Rosal 1 (952 19 03 16). **Open** 1-4pm, 8pm-midnight Mon, Tue, Fri-Sun; 1-4pm Wed. Closed Sept. **Average** €-€€. **Credit** MC, V. **Map** p203 off B1.

Good, simple tapas and *raciones*, including superb shellfish, a pretty decent selection of fish dishes and fantastic *berenjenas* (fried aubergine slices). The place is very popular with locals, especially at lunch, so it's best to book.

La Farola

Plaza de Carmen Abela 9 (952 87 15 47). **Open** 9am-11pm Mon-Sat. **Average** €. **No credit cards. Map** p203 B1 ❶

One of the longest-established and best-loved tapas joints in town. Specialities include *chorizo* (paprika-spiced sausages), *berenjenas* (fried aubergine) and *chipirones* (baby squid).

Faustino

C/Santa Cecilia 4 (952 19 03 07). **Open** 11.30am-1am Tue-Sun. Closed 2wks Aug. **Average** €. **No credit cards. Map** p203 B1 ❷

Faustino is among the most popular tapas bars in town and draws in locals and visitors with its friendly, lively atmosphere and very reliable food. Try a *serranito* – a small sandwich of *jamón serrano*, green pepper and pork.

La Giralda

C/Nueva 19 (952 87 28 02). **Open** noon-4.30pm, 8pm-midnight Mon, Tue, Thur-Sun. Closed 2wks Jan. **Average** €. **No credit cards. Map** p203 A1 ❸

Named after Seville's famous tower, La Giralda's most delicious culinary treat is its *pinchito de gambas* (prawn kebab), spiked with the owner's secret seasoning. Be sure to order at least three or four per person. Other fresh seafood dishes include *mejillones* (mussels), or try the delicious grilled *setas* (wild mushrooms).

La Gota de Vino

C/Sevilla 13 (952 87 57 16). **Open** 7pm-1am Tue-Sat. **Average** €€. **Credit** AmEx, MC, V. **Map** p203 B1 ❹

Friendly owner Luigi Pignatelli refers to his bar as a *vinoteca* and offers a superb selection of his favourite wines, ranging from €7 to €40 per bottle. An excellent young chef magics up creative cuisine using Italian and Spanish ingredients as well as whatever is best in the local market.

El Patio

C/Espinel 100 (952 87 10 15). **Open** *May-Sept* noon-4pm, 8pm-midnight Mon-Fri; noon-4pm Sat. *Oct-Apr* noon-4pm, 8pm-midnight Mon, Tue, Fri-Sun; noon-4pm Wed. **Average** €-€€. **Credit** MC, V. **Map** p203 off B1.

A cheap and cheerful tapas bar with a local feel. Try the house *revuelto* (scrambled eggs) with asparagus, pancetta, mushrooms and prawns. At lunchtime there's a good-value set *menú* for €7.50-€8.50.

La Taberna de Rafael Espejo

Pasaje de Correos 2 (mobile 630 46 24 20). **Open** 2-5pm, 9pm-midnight Mon-Sat. **Average** €. **No credit cards. Map** p203 A1 ❺

A family-run, no-frills tapas bar, popular with locals and plastered with photos of flamenco artists (the owner Rafael included). If you are lucky you may see some impromptu flamenco. Regional cheeses, cured ham and superb grilled liver kebabs are among the dishes on offer, and there's a decent selection of casked sherries too. A great place for an aperitif.

Tetería Al-Zahra

C/Tiendas 19 (mobile 607 74 51 73). **Open** 4pm-midnight Mon, Wed-Sun. **Average** €. **No credit cards. Map** p203 B1 ❻

This atmospheric, traditional cushion-floored Moroccan tearoom is very popular with a young Ronda crowd. Join it and owner Daniel for mint tea, Moroccan pancakes and cakes. Part of a new vogue for all things Moroccan that has recently taken root in Andalucía.

Nightlife

Ronda's previously rather conservative nightlife scene has picked up somewhat in the last couple of years. Bars and clubs tend to spring up and disappear from year to year, but look out for places such as **Kopas** (C/Rios Rosas 9) and **Limbo** (Plaza Carmen de Abela, 956 87 68 70), which often feature DJs. In summer a huge *discoteca de verano* (summer disco) opens at the far end of Avenida de Málaga, just beyond the roundabout on the Campillos road, where the young and not-so-young rock on all the way through until dawn on Friday and Saturday nights.

Shopping

Ronda has some of the cheapest high-quality leather-goods stores in Spain, much of their merchandise produced in nearby Ubrique, leather capital of the south. And there are also masses of shops selling local ceramics, as well as lots of imported stuff from Morocco (which you may well be told is 'local'). Ronda is also famous for its rustic pine furniture (*mueble rondeño*), which more often than not is made from new pine planks that have been scraped and battered to give the patina of time.

Where to stay

In and around Ronda there is a huge range of characterful and often dashingly chic accommodation, but be sure to book as far in advance as possible.

Alavera de los Baños

Hoyo San Miguel s/n (952 87 91 43/www.andalucia.com/alavera). Closed Dec, Jan. **Rates** (incl breakfast) €60 single; €85-€100 double. **Average** €€. **Credit** MC, V. **Map** p203 B3 ❼

Next door to one of Spain's best-preserved Arab baths, this intimate hotel has great views across open country to the Real Maestranza riding school. The decor is a colourful mix of things rustic and

Jardín de la Muralla.

North African. Bedrooms have wrought-iron beds and oak furniture but are generally small: it is well worth shelling out extra for a room with a terrace. The restaurant offers organic Mediterranean, Spanish, and North African dishes with some interesting vegetarian options and excellent salads. Breakfast is superb and there is a pretty garden with masses of greenery and a small plunge pool.

EnFrenteArte

C/Real 40-42 (952 87 90 88/47 33/www.enfrente arte.com). **Rates** (incl breakfast) €71 single; €83-€106 double. **Credit** MC, V. **Map** p203 B2 8

Both owned and run by Belgian entrepreneur Filip Eyckmans, EnFrenteArte is far from your average hostelry. Wine, beer, coffee and freshly squeezed orange juices, and a buffet breakfast are laid on for no extra charge. Resident chef Encarni González prepares dishes like tortilla and grilled king prawn salad. The decor is stylish and most rooms are large, with four-poster beds and en suite bathrooms, the best with their own terrace. Use of the internet, swimming pool, sauna, jacuzzi, games and music room is included in the room price.

Hotel La Española

C/José Aparacio 3-5 (952 87 34 88). **Rates** €57-€67 single; €89-€100 double. **Credit** AmEx, MC, V. **Map** p203 A2 9

A good option if you're travelling on a tight budget, La Española is tucked away in the narrow pedestrian street leading from the bullring to the *parador*. Four of its 16 rooms have extraordinary views out across the cliff, so try to book room 205, 206, 207 or 208. The staff are friendly, and rooms have recently been refurbished.

Hotel La Fuente de la Higuera

Partido de los Frontones s/n (952 11 43 55/www.hotellafuente.com). **Rates** (incl breakfast) €144 double; €190-€278 suite. **Average** €€€€. **Credit** MC, V. **Map** p203 off A1.

This is the best expensive option in the Ronda area for those wishing to relax in a country setting in style and tranquillity. The hotel, run by Pom and Tina Piek, exudes the kind of cool chic that has glossy magazine editors drooling, with sleek wooden interiors imported from the Far East and contemporary art on the walls. From the hotel's terrace restaurant undulating farmland rolls up towards Ronda. Life centres around the poolside terrace in summer or the dining room in winter, where there is a huge CD collection including everything from flamenco to jazz to blues to chill-out. The hotel is located a few kilometres north of Ronda.

Hotel San Gabriel

C/Marqués de Moctezuma 19 (952 19 03 92/www.hotelsangabriel.com). Closed 2wks July. **Rates** €83-€96 double; €105-€108 suite. **Credit** AmEx, DC, MC, V. **Map** p203 B3 10

Run by an exceptionally friendly local family, this gem of a hotel in the old town has cool, beautifully restored wooden interiors (rescued from the old town hall) in the billiard room, a small poetry library (to which guests are encouraged to contribute) and a ten-seat mini-DVD cinema (salvaged from the town theatre). Bullfighting memorabilia and signed photos of celebrity guests such as Bob Hoskins and Isabella Rossellini adorn the walls.

Jardín de la Muralla

C/Espiritu Santo 13 (952 87 27 64/www.jardindelamuralla.com). **Rates** (incl breakfast) €85.60 single/double. **Credit** AmEx, MC, V. **Map** p203 off B3.

Jardín de la Muralla is a lovely converted townhouse with delightful gardens that tumble down between the Espiritu Santo church and the *muralla* (old city wall). There's a pool with views right across the valley and a cosy book-lined lounge complete with a log fire. Rooms are quirkily decorated but retain many original features. The hotel is located in the Barrio San Francisco.

Serranía de Ronda.

El Juncal

A366, km1 (952 16 11 70/www.eljuncal.com). **Rates** €126-€257 double. **Credit** AmEx, DC, MC, V.
Located just outside Ronda, in a converted 17th-century house, El Juncal has eight spacious rooms, each with a private terrace, plus two villa suites. Decor and ambience are Zen-meets-Alessi, and highlights include a swimming pool, jacuzzi, sauna and an adjacent *bodega*, where you can sample the hotel's wine, Pasos Largos (named after a local bandit). The stark minimalism is not to all tastes, however.

Parador de Ronda

Plaza de España s/n (952 87 75 00/www.parador.es). **Rates** €150-€187 double; €203-268 duplex. **Average** €€-€€€. **Credit** AmEx, DC, MC, V. **Map** p203 A2 ⓫
The position of Ronda's *parador* can't be bettered, perched right at the edge of the gorge with views across to the old town and to the mountain ridge beyond. The decor is a surprisingly innovative post-modern pot-pourri: most of it works well. Bedrooms are sleek and plush (many have stupendous views), bathrooms are up to the usual high *parador* standards, and there's an outdoor pool, which enjoys views across the gorge. But you need to book well ahead – the place has a near 100% occupancy rate, one of the highest of any hotel in Spain.

Resources

Internet

El Choque Ideal, C/Espíritu Santo 9 (952 16 19 18).

Police station

Ayuntamiento, Plaza Duquesa de Parcent 3 (952 87 32 40).

Post office

C/Virgen de la Paz 20 (952 87 25 57). **Map** p203 A1.

Tourist information

Paseo Blas Infante s/n (952 18 71 19/www.turismoderonda.es). **Open** 9.30am-7.30pm Mon-Fri; 10am-2pm, 3.30-6.30pm Sat, Sun. **Map** p203 B2.
Plaza de España 9 (952 87 12 72). **Open** 9am-7.30pm Mon-Fri; 10am-2pm Sat, Sun. **Map** p203 B2.

Serranía de Ronda & the *pueblos blancos*

The mountainous country around Ronda, the **Serranía de Ronda**, is some of the wildest and most beautiful in Andalucía, and you'll soon see why it has long captured the imagination of the Romantics and landscape artists. Depending on the season, it can appear mercilessly parched and raw or lushly green with a spectacular profusion of wild flowers and provides some superb walking. Tourist offices can supply details of local routes.

The area is famed for its *pueblos blancos* (white villages). Although you'll come across picture-postcard whitewashed hamlets throughout Andalucía, some of the very prettiest are to be found in the Serranía, and you could easily spend a fortnight's holiday driving (or walking) from one to the next. Tourism in this area has not reached anything like the scale of the coast, but for a decade or two the Serranía has figured large on the tourist map and increasing numbers of expats are

Setenil de las Bodegas.

setting up home in the region. There are those who feel that, as in the Alpujarras, this influx of foreigners is changing the character of the region and putting otherwise affordable village houses out of the range of young Andalucians. As a visitor you'll benefit from the fact that there is an ever-increasing number of excellent places to stay and eat, and you can hardly blame anyone for wanting to live in this uniquely beautiful part of Spain.

One of the most popular and interesting excursions from Ronda is to the prehistoric **Cueva de la Pileta**. Discovered in 1905 by local farmer José Bullón (or by a British officer collecting chough's eggs, as another version of the story has it), the cave remains in the Bullón family's possession, in spite of attempts by the local government to expropriate it. The hour-long tours, by the light of spluttering Davey lamps, are without doubt the most atmospheric and exciting in Andalucía. As well as stalactites and stalagmites, there are naturalistic cave paintings of animals and fish dating from the late palaeolithic period (around 25,000 BC). To reach the cave, take the MA505 (which becomes the MA501) towards Montejaque and Benaoján from the A376 Ronda–Seville main road and look for the signs. You can't pre-book a visit, but need to wait outside the cave entrance for the previous group to emerge or, if you are there first thing, for a member of the Bullón family to arrive from their farm in the valley below. Take warm clothes with you in the cooler months: the area outside the cave catches the winds that are funnelled along the Guadiaro valley.

A few kilometres north-west of Ronda are the hilltop Roman ruins of **Ronda La Vieja**. Site of the Roman town of Acinipo, whose heyday was in the first century AD, much remains to be excavated, but you can see the massive theatre hewn out of the hillside. A ten-minute drive north-west brings you to the pretty village of **Setenil de las Bodegas**.

The A369, heading south-west from Ronda, is a spectacular mountain road that passes several *pueblos blancos* before arriving in **Gaucín**, one of the area's best-known villages. British officers who served in Gibraltar during the 19th century used to ride through en route to Ronda; since then Gaucín has become hugely popular amongst wealthy expats, its property prices have rocketed and new restaurants, hotels and bars seem to open by the day. Yet its winding streets, thankfully unsuitable for coach parties, retain much charm and the locals remain friendly. Gaucín is perched more than 600 metres (1,970 feet) up in the Serranía; on a clear day you can see the mountains of Morocco and, at night, the twinkling lights of Tangier. It has long been a strategic stronghold, as is easy to imagine as you clamber around the ruined Moorish castle that overlooks the town. An old man usually hangs around by its entrance and will open up the gate and show you inside the chapel in return for a little loose change.

Just outside Gaucín, in **Estación de Cortes**, two young Brits, Melanie and Tristram Templar of **Unseen Andalucía** (952 15 33 30, melytigre@eresmas.com), have been organising walks for several years. They can take you on a full- or half-day hike with a picnic provided or can put together a longer, bespoke itinerary.

Cueva de la Pileta

MA501 (952 16 73 43). **Tours** hourly 10am-1pm, 4-6pm daily. **Admission** €6.50; €3 concessions. **No credit cards**.

Ronda La Vieja

MA449 (mobile 630 42 99 49). **Open** 10am-5pm Tue-Sat; 10am-2.30pm Sun. **Admission** free.

Where to stay & eat

In the sleepy village of Montecorto, a few kilometres south of the Roman theatre of Acinipo, is a great, friendly, laid-back B&B, **El Tejar** (952 18 40 53, double €64-€80, closed June-Aug). The house is the highest in the village and all the bedrooms have wonderful views out to the peaks of the Grazalema park. There's a spring-fed pool surrounded by tall bamboo and a great collection of music and books, as well as a well-stocked honesty bar. The owner has written walking guides and has masses of route descriptions and maps.

Gaucín. See p207.

On the road to Benaoján, seven kilometres (11 miles) south-west of Ronda, is the **Cueva del Gato** (Ctra Benaojan-Ronda km3, 952 16 72 96, www.hotelcuevadelgato.com, double €70), with seven individually decorated rooms named after caves within the famous Cueva del Gato, 100 metres away. Converted watermill **El Molino del Santo** (Estación de Benaoján, 952 16 71 51, www.elmolinodelsanto.com, closed mid Nov-mid Feb, double €80-€224, restaurant €€-€€€), set in the beautiful Guadiaro valley, attracts large numbers of mainly British guests of all ages; it's an ideal place for families with young children. The staff are friendly and efficient, and the restaurant has an interesting menu that mixes local dishes with some veggie options.

If you prefer the idea of cheap local tapas, walk down the road to the entrance of the village opposite the railway station to **Bar Stop** (Barriada, Estación de Benaoján, 952 16 71 42, closed Sat, €). The restaurant is packed at lunchtime on weekdays when local workers turn up for the excellent *menú del día*.

In Gaucín the best food in town can be found at the **Hotel Restaurante La Fructuosa** (C/Convento 67, 952 15 10 72, www.lafructuosa.com, double €85-98 incl breakfast, restaurant open dinner Wed-Sat May-Oct, €€), with Moroccan-style dishes; there are also five beautifully decorated rooms.

The luxurious and deservedly popular **Hotel Casablanca** (C/Teodoro de Molina 12, 952 15 10 19, www.casablanca-gaucin.com, closed late Nov-early Feb, double €140-€200 incl breakfast, restaurant €€€), under new management, has had a complete facelift and promises to be as good as ever. This surprisingly grand village house has bags of relaxed character, a small pool and a crow's nest of a terrace from which you can see Africa.

A good place to stay between Ronda and Gaucín is the **Hoopoe Yurt Hotel** in Cortes de la Frontera (952 11 70 55, www.yurthotel.com, double €115), where you can choose between an Afghani or Mongolian yurt in cork oak and olive groves at this utterly original eco-camp hotel. You can't fault the hotel's green credentials: electricity comes from solar energy and all organic waste is recycled.

Fifteen kilometres (24 miles) south of Ronda, the **Hotel Los Castaños** (C/Iglesia 40, Cartajima, 952 18 07 78, www.loscastanos.com, double €107) has six pretty, whitewashed rooms, some with mountain views, along with a rooftop terrace and plunge pool.

Resources

Tourist information

Parque Natural de la Sierra de las Nieves
Casa del Guarda, C/Alameda de Tajo s/n, Ronda (952 87 77 78). **Open** 8am-1.30pm Mon-Fri.

Getting there

By bus

Ronda's bus station (952 87 22 60) is on Plaza Concepción García, close to the train station and around 15mins on foot from the Puente Nuevo. For a timetable of buses to and from Ronda get hold of a copy of the local newspaper, *Ronda Semanal*. There's 1 daily bus to Benaoján and Montejaque, and 1 to Gaucín, 10 daily to Málaga, 5 to Arcos, 5 to Cádiz, 5 to Marbella, 5 to Seville, and 2 to Grazalema and Zahara de la Sierra.

By train

Ronda's rail station (902 24 02 02) is in the new town on Avda de Andalucía, about a 20min walk from the Puente Nuevo. Tickets can also be bought over the phone on 952 87 16 62. Ronda is on the line between Granada and Algeciras. There are 3 trains a day from Granada to Ronda (2hrs 30mins) and 6 daily from Ronda to Algeciras (1hr 40mins), 3 of which call at the stations in the Guadiaro valley and Jimena. For trains to and from Málaga, Córdoba, Seville and Cádiz, change at Bobadilla. Estación de Gaucín is 13km (8 miles) from Gaucín.

Córdoba Province

Features

Maps

Córdoba Province

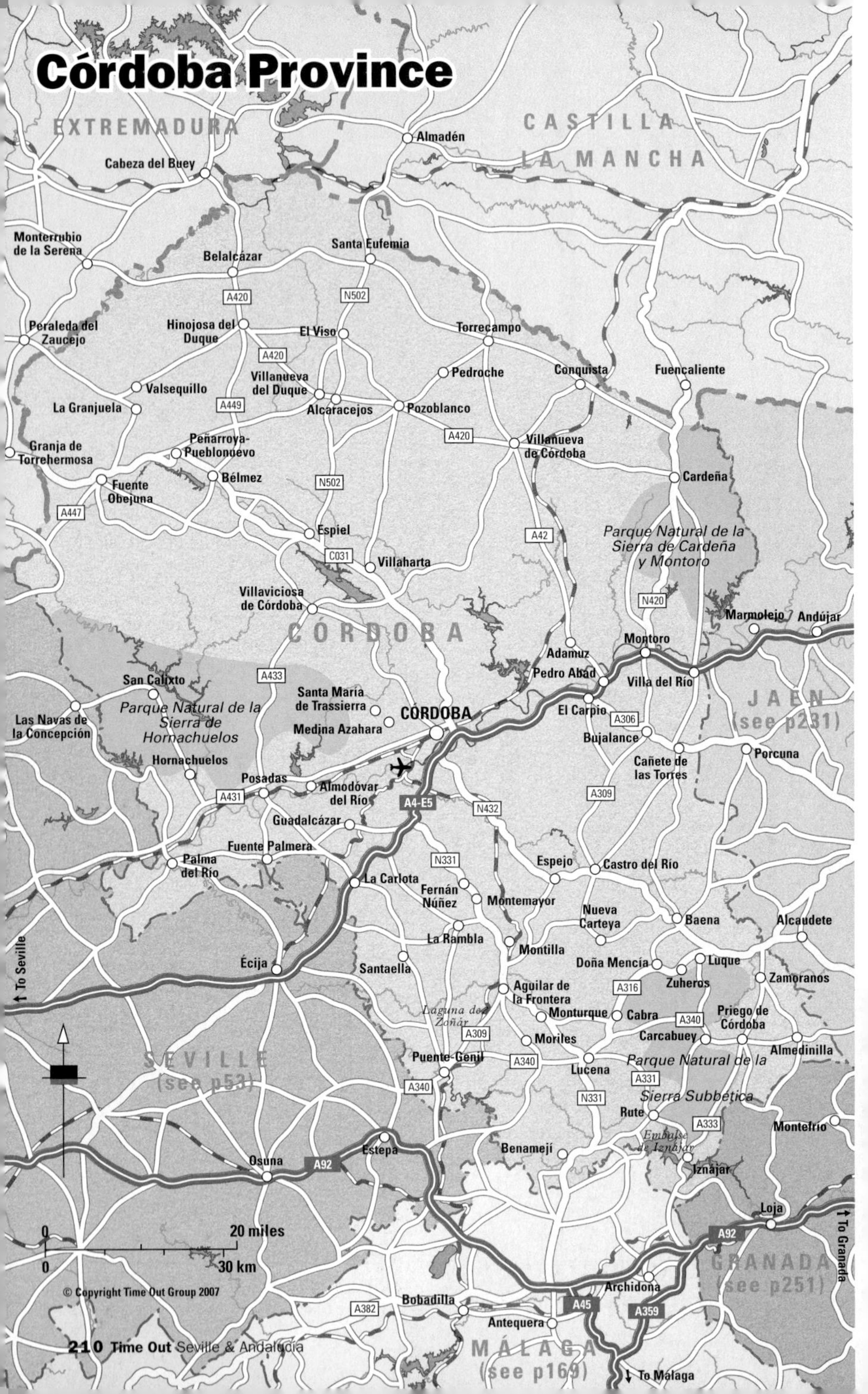

Introduction

Once the heart of Moorish al-Andalus, Córdoba is the place for foodies, fans of historical architecture and lovers of outdoor pleasures.

The city of Córdoba and, more specifically, its far-famed mosque, finds a place on most visitors' hit lists, but the huge and hugely varied province at the heart of which it sits is far less known to tourists. The Guadalquivir river valley has long nurtured agriculture and ancient towns; to the north, huge skies and vast empty plains predominate; to the south, wine and olive oil production fuels a series of likeable, industrious towns.

CÓRDOBA CITY

The regional capital is a compact, attractive city that is perfect for exploring on foot. Its premier draw is the magnificent Mezquita, the most ambitious mosque ever built and a potent symbol of the city's pre-eminence in the glory days of al-Andalus. Around the Mezquita, the city's Jewish quarter is a network of whitewashed alleys and patios, while to the north are a sprinkling of lovely Renaissance churches. Córdoba is also famed within Andalucía for its fine restaurants – probably the best in the region. Close to the city are the remains of Medina Azahara, a huge fairy-tale palace built by successive Caliphs.

THE GUADALQUIVIR VALLEY AND NORTH OF CÓRDOBA

The Guadalquivir valley, running east and west from Córdoba, is a gentle, fertile place with some attractive towns. Almodóvar del Río, to the west, stands out for miles for the cinematic splendour of its hilltop castle, while Montoro clings to steep cliffs that rise up from the river. There are two Natural Parks in this area, both with unmissable scenery, flora and fauna. North from the Guadalquivir valley, a wilder, harsher landscape emerges and towns take on a road-movie edge. Among the heights of the Sierra Morena, and far off the tourist trail, neglected castles and old mining towns wait to be explored.

SOUTH OF CÓRDOBA

The landscape and economy south of Córdoba are dominated by the twin liquid resources of wine and olive oil. Montilla is home to the sherry-like drink of the same name, while Baena produces some of the best olive oil in Europe. The olive tree is ubiquitous in this region, covering both the gentle swathes of fertile land known as the Campiña and the more dramatic heights of the Parque Natural de la Sierra Subbética. Roman and Moorish remains have been found in many of the towns in this area, and there are some spectacular baroque churches to discover, particularly in Priego de Córdoba.

The best...

Baroque architecture
Priego de Córdoba (*p229*).

Festivals
Cabra (*p227*); **Córdoba City** (*p212*).

Castle
Almodóvar del Río (*p224*).

Mosque
Córdoba City (*p212*).

Olive oil
Baena (*p229*).

Restaurants
Córdoba City (*p212*).

Wildernesses
Sierra de Cardeña y Montoro (*p224*); **Sierra de Hornachuelos** (*p224*); **Sierra Subbética** (*p229*).

Wines
Montilla (*p227*).

Córdoba City

Despite its compact dimensions, Córdoba City packs in history, modernity and a whole lot of charm.

The city of Córdoba wears many masks: living museum, sleepy Andalucían backwater and bustling modern city, all crammed into a relatively small area. At its heart is the resplendent **Mezquita** – one of the greatest of all Moorish monuments. This heart's arteries, the tiny whitewashed streets of the Judería, are clogged with tacky and twee establishments serving tourists' needs. Yet, away from the Mezquita, the whitewashed streets can sometimes feel like those of a somnolent country village, even though only a couple of minutes' walk away broad avenues roar with traffic and the peripheral parks are alive with the chatter of families.

Apart from the Mezquita and the impressive ruins nearby of Medina Azahara (*see p226* **Medina Azahara**), Córdoba has only a few sights: museums, galleries and pleasant botanical gardens. Gastronomy is, perhaps, a greater draw, for there's arguably better eating to be had in Córdoba than anywhere else in the region. The favourite time to visit is during the unique **Concurso de Patios** in May (the second or third weekend), when hundreds of flower-filled private patios are opened to the public.

HISTORY

Córdoba first came to prominence as a Roman port on the highest navigable stretch of the Guadalquivir river. It was then famed for its olive oil and its poetry – Roman wordsmiths Seneca and Lucan were both born here. With the decline of the Roman Empire, Córdoba fell to the Vandals and then the Visigoths, before being taken by the Moors in 755.

The next three centuries were Córdoba's Golden Age. The Umayyad prince Abd al-Rahman I established the independent state of al-Andalus with Córdoba as its capital, and started the building of the Mezquita. But it was Abd al-Rahman III (912-61) who really put Córdoba on the map, ushering in a period of major civic and cultural prosperity and building the large, dreamlike royal city of Medina Azahara. Though certainly exaggerated, the statistics quoted by the 17th-century Arab historian al-Maqqari give an idea of the splendour of the city at its peak. According to him, Córdoba boasted 3,000 mosques, 80,000 shops, 400,000 books in the library, 27 schools, 50 hospitals, 900 public baths, and public lighting in the streets.

Abd al-Rahman III's son, al-Hakam II (961-76), was a scholarly, peace-loving leader who built one of the great libraries of the age. In contrast was the warlike al-Mansur (977-1002), who used his position as regent to overthrow the child successor Hisham II, and famously stole the huge cathedral bells from Santiago de Compostela and had them melted down to make lamps for the Mezquita. (Two and a half centuries later, when Fernando III conquered Córdoba, his first action was to have the lamps carried back to Santiago and remade into bells.)

Al-Mansur was the last of the great Córdoban leaders. Eventually, his Berber army revolted against its master, and the puppet Caliphs that followed never regained the brilliance of their predecessors. However, Córdoba's reputation as a centre for culture and scholarship remained until the Christian conquest in 1236. Many of the period's greatest philosophers and scientists were born, lived or died here, such as the great astronomer and mathematician Maslama al-Mayriti, the 'father of surgery' al-Zahrawi (Abulcasis) and the multi-talented Jewish doctor, rabbi and scholar Maimonides.

Today, Córdoba flourishes modestly but happily, with an economy based around agriculture, tourism and light industry. The university was re-established in 1971, turning the city once again into a centre of learning, with a faculty devoted to the study of Muslim history and culture.

Sightseeing

The Mezquita

The Mezquita, the most ambitious mosque ever built by the Moors, was started by Abd al-Rahman I in 786 on the site of a former Visigoth cathedral, which had itself been built on top of a Roman temple dedicated to Janus. Subsequent Caliphs and Emirs all left their mark on the mosque, but the most surprising addition is the incongruous Renaissance cathedral constructed at its very heart.

The mosque is the origin of the Caliphal architectural style, combining Roman,

The **Mezquita**. *See p212.*

Visigothic, Byzantine, Syrian and Persian elements, and became the reference point for all Arab-Hispanic architecture until the Reconquista. It conforms to the Muslim tradition of creating buildings that have humble, plain exteriors with dog-legged entrances that serve as a tease before the opulence and splendour of their interiors. In contrast to narrow Christian churches, the Mezquita is broad, to allow as many worshippers as possible to the front of the mosque, where they are closest to Mecca.

Considering the alterations and additions to which it has been subjected, the Mezquita could easily have become a mess of conflicting styles and extensions. However, the building hangs together supremely well, helped by its predominantly uniform rectangular design.

Its imposing outer walls retain their original highly decorated entrances, although only one – the **Puerta del Perdón** (Gate of Forgiveness) – now opens. It leads into the **Patio de los Naranjos**, an immense courtyard of orange trees, palms and fountains, originally used for ablutions by Muslims before prayer. At the corner of the patio, Abd al-Rahman III's beautiful minaret has been replaced by a 16th-century bell tower (closed to the public).

From here, 19 doors originally opened into the mosque itself, flooding the interior with sunlight. Now only one (the Puerta de las Palmas, or Gate of Palms) opens into the original section of the mosque, built by Abd al-Rahman I. In the subdued half-light you can just pick out the astounding number of columns and the striking terracotta- and white-striped double arches. The impressive design is due to architectural improvisation. The Mezquita's architect was given a hotchpotch of old columns from Córdoba's Visigothic cathedral, the city's Roman buildings and others shipped in from Constantinople – making it difficult to achieve a uniform ceiling height. The solution was to use the tall columns as a base, on which were placed the smaller columns to create the ceiling arches. These evoke the shape of the date palm, much favoured in Moorish architecture, and may have been inspired by the designs of Roman aqueducts, which also used arcading.

The unity of the interior is broken by Abd al-Hakam II's tenth-century extension, which doubled the size of the mosque and created a magnificant *mihrab* (prayer-niche), meant to indicate the direction of Mecca and amplify the words of the Imam. (However, this mosque is, unusually, oriented towards Damascus rather than Mecca, perhaps due to Abd Al-Rahman I's nostalgia for his hometown.) The *mihrab* was constructed by Byzantine craftsmen. Its inner chamber has a shell-shaped ceiling carved from one piece of marble. To the side, chambers decorated with elaborate mosaics of gold, red, turquoise and green form the *maksura*, where the Caliph and his attendants would have prayed.

Opposite the *mihrab* is the **Capilla de Villaviciosa**, built in 1377 with convoluted Mudéjar arches, and the **Capilla Real**, constructed as a small funeral chapel for Fernando IV and Alfonso XI of Castilla. These relatively small-scale, sensitive Christian additions are in stark contrast to the Renaissance cathedral, built in 1523 with the support of Carlos V, that crouches in the centre of the Mezquita. Construction involved blocking up the mosque's open arches. It may be a blot on the Mezquita's original landscape, but the cathedral has some worthy architectural details, particularly its churrigueresque choir stalls. Carlos V failed to see its virtues, however, lamenting after it had been built that he had 'destroyed something that was unique in the world'. Yet, overall, the Christian elements of the Mezquita are eclipsed by the overwhelming Islamic architecture bearing down on all sides. Even today, when locals come to worship here, they say they are 'going to mass at the mosque'.

The Mezquita

C/Torrijos s/n (957 47 05 12). **Open** *Mar, July-Oct* 10am-6.30pm Mon-Sat; 8.30-9.45am, 2-6.30pm Sun. *Feb, Nov* 10am-5.30pm Mon-Sat; 8.30-9.45am, 2-5.30pm Sun. *Jan, Dec* 10am-5pm Mon-Sat; 8.30-9.45am, 2-5pm Sun. *Apr-June* 10am-7pm Mon-Sat; 8.30am-9.45am, 2-7pm Sun. **Admission** €8. **No credit cards. Map** p215 B4.

The Judería & around

A good place to start a tour of the old Jewish quarter, which radiates out from the Mezquita, is the tourist office at C/Torrijos, where you can pick up a map and the all-important, ever-changing monument and museum opening times. Next door is the **Museo Diocesano de Bellas Artes** in the former Palacio Episcopal, which can be visited with the Mezquita ticket (though is closed for renovations until the end of 2006). The palace was constructed on the site of the original Moorish Alcázar and has a beautiful, airy patio. Medieval wood sculpture, religious tapestries and a collection of psalm books, as well as works by local artists, are among the exhibits. Next to this is another *palacio*, the **Palacio de Congresos y Exposiciones**. If it's not closed for a function, visit the lovely patio where you can sit and have a drink and tapas, or browse the ceramics shop in its cloisters.

South of here stands the **Alcázar de los Reyes Cristianos**, a fortified palace beside the river built in 1328 by Alfonso XI. The

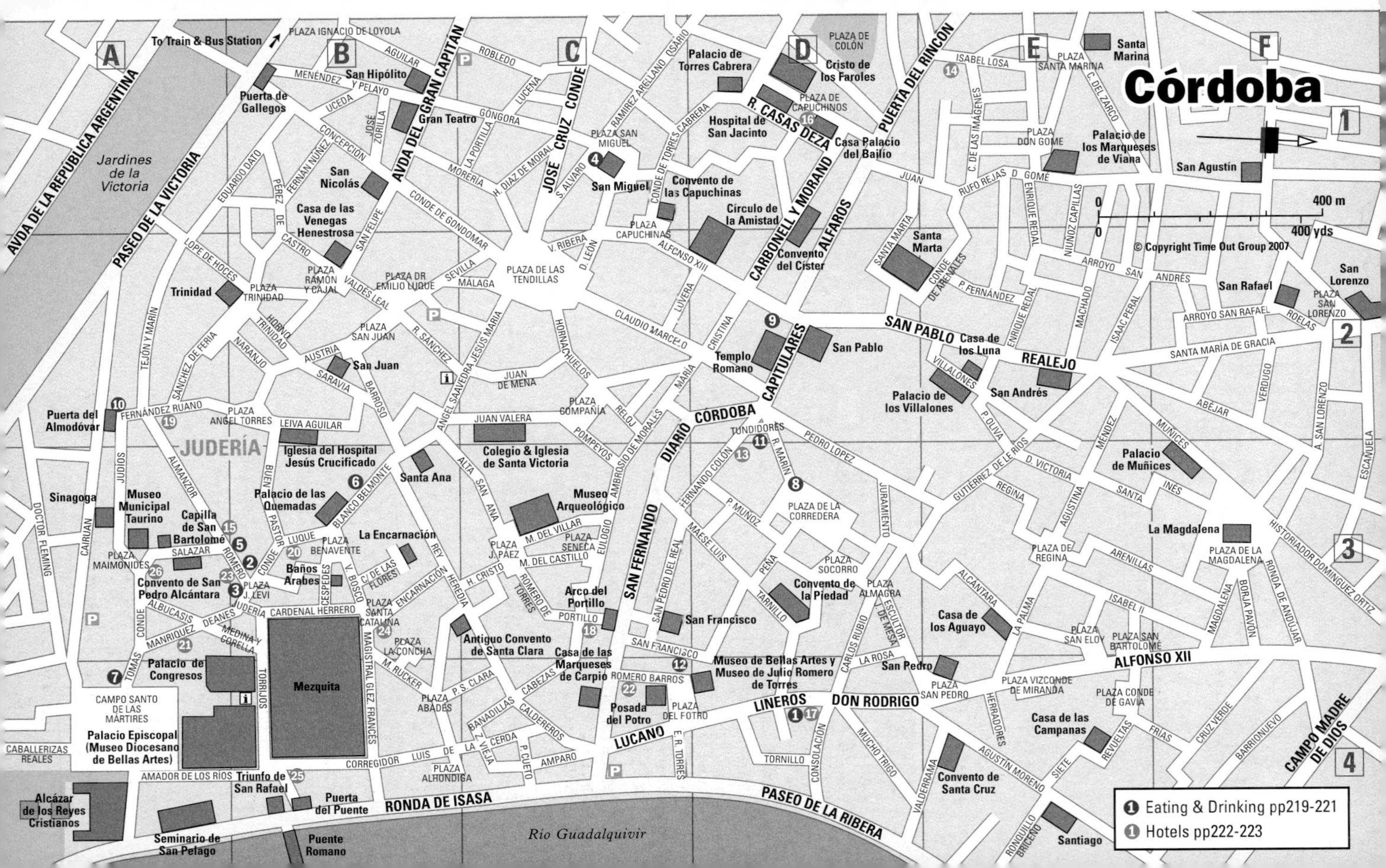
Córdoba
Eating & Drinking pp219-221
Hotels pp222-223
© Copyright Time Out Group 2007
0
400 m
0
400 yds
A
B
C
D
E
F
1
2
3
4
To Train & Bus Station
AVDA DE LA REPÚBLICA ARGENTINA
PASEO DE LA VICTORIA
Jardines de la Victoria
PLAZA IGNACIO DE LOYOLA
AVDA DEL GRAN CAPITÁN
JOSÉ CRUZ CONDE
PUERTA DEL RINCON
R. CASAS DEZA
CARBONELL Y MORAND
ALFAROS
CAPITULARES
SAN PABLO
REALEJO
DIARIO CÓRDOBA
SAN FERNANDO
LINEROS
DON RODRIGO
ALFONSO XII
LUCANO
RONDA DE ISASA
PASEO DE LA RIBERA
CAMPO MADRE DE DIOS
Río Guadalquivir
JUDERÍA
Puerta de Gallegos
San Hipólito
Gran Teatro
San Nicolás
Casa de las Venegas Henestrosa
Trinidad
San Juan
San Miguel
Palacio de Torres Cabrera
Hospital de San Jacinto
Cristo de los Faroles
Casa Palacio del Bailío
Convento de las Capuchinas
Círculo de la Amistad
Convento del Císter
Santa Marta
Templo Romano
San Pablo
Casa de los Luna
Palacio de los Villalones
San Andrés
San Agustín
Palacio de los Marqueses de Viana
Santa Marina
San Rafael
San Lorenzo
Palacio de Muñices
La Magdalena
Puerta del Almodóvar
Sinagoga
Museo Municipal Taurino
Capilla de San Bartolomé
Convento de San Pedro Alcántara
Palacio de Congresos
Palacio Episcopal (Museo Diocesano de Bellas Artes)
Alcázar de los Reyes Cristianos
Seminario de San Pelagio
Puente Romano
Triunfo de San Rafael
Puerta del Puente
Mezquita
Baños Árabes
Palacio de las Quemadas
Iglesia del Hospital Jesús Crucificado
Santa Ana
Colegio & Iglesia de Santa Victoria
Museo Arqueológico
La Encarnación
Antiguo Convento de Santa Clara
Arco del Portillo
Casa de las Marqueses de Carpio
Posada del Potro
San Francisco
Museo de Bellas Artes y Museo de Julio Romero de Torres
Convento de la Piedad
San Pedro
Casa de los Aguayo
Casa de las Campanas
Convento de Santa Cruz
Santiago
CAMPO SANTO DE LAS MÁRTIRES
CABALLERIZAS REALES
PLAZA DE COLÓN
PLAZA DE CAPUCHINOS
PLAZA SAN MIGUEL
PLAZA CAPUCHINAS
PLAZA DE LAS TENDILLAS
PLAZA DR EMILIO LUQUE
PLAZA RAMÓN Y CAJAL
PLAZA TRINIDAD
PLAZA SAN JUAN
PLAZA ANGEL TORRES
PLAZA COMPAÑÍA
PLAZA DE LA CORREDERA
PLAZA SOCORRO
PLAZA ALMAGRA
PLAZA DE REGINA
PLAZA DE LA MAGDALENA
PLAZA SAN ELOY
PLAZA SAN BARTOLOMÉ
PLAZA SAN PEDRO
PLAZA VIZCONDE DE MIRANDA
PLAZA CONDE DE GAVIA
PLAZA DEL POTRO
PLAZA ALHÓNDIGA
PLAZA ABADES
PLAZA LA CONCHA
PLAZA SANTA CATALINA
PLAZA BENAVENTE
PLAZA J. LEVI
PLAZA MAIMÓNIDES
PLAZA J. PÁEZ
PLAZA SENECA
PLAZA SANTA MARINA
PLAZA DON GOME
PLAZA SAN LORENZO
AGUILAR
MENÉNDEZ Y PELAYO
UCEDA
JOSÉ ZORILLA
ROBLEDO
GÓNGORA
LUCENA
LA PORTILLA
MORERÍA
H. DIAZ DE MORAL
CONCEPCIÓN
FERNAN NUÑEZ
EDUARDO DATO
PÉREZ DE CASTRO
SAN FELIPE
CONDE DE GONDOMAR
LOPE DE HOCES
S. ALVARO
RAMÍREZ ARELLANO OSARIO
CONDE DE TORRES CABRERA
V. RIBERA
D. LEÓN
ALFONSO XIII
SEVILLA
MÁLAGA
VALDÉS LEAL
HORNO TRINIDAD
NARANJO
SÁNCHEZ DE FERIA
TEJÓN Y MARÍN
AUSTRIA
SARAVIA
BARROSO
R. SÁNCHEZ
ANGEL SAAVEDRA JESÚS MARÍA
JUAN DE MENA
HORNACHUELOS
CLAUDIO MARCELO
LUVERA
CRISTINA
MARÍA
RELOJ
POMPEYOS
AMBROSIO DE MORALES
JUAN VALERA
FERNÁNDEZ RUANO
LEIVA AGUILAR
JUDÍOS
ALMANZOR
BUEN PASTOR
BLANCO BELMONTE
LUQUE
ALTA SAN ANA
REY HEREDIA
DOCTOR FLEMING
CAIRUAN
SALAZAR
ROMERO
CONDE
TOMAS CONDE
ALBUCASIS
DEANES
MANRIQUEZ
JUDERÍA
MEDINA Y CORELLA
CARDENAL HERRERO
TORRIJOS
CÉSPEDES
V. BOSCO
C/ DE LAS FLORES
ENCARNACIÓN
MAGISTRAL GLEZ. FRANCÉS
M. RUCKER
P. S. CLARA
CABEZAS
BANADILLAS
LA Z. VIEJA
CERDA
P. CUETO
CALDEREROS
AMPARO
CORREGIDOR LUIS DE LA CERDA
AMADOR DE LOS RÍOS
H. CRISTO
ROMERO DE TORRES
M. DEL VILLAR
M. DEL CASTILLO
EULOGIO
PORTILLO
SAN FRANCISCO
ROMERO BARROS
SAN PEDRO DEL REAL
MAESE LUIS
P. MUÑOZ
FERNANDO COLÓN
TUNDIDORES
R. MARÍN
PEDRO LÓPEZ
JURAMENTO
PEÑA
TARNILLO
CARLOS RUBIO
J. DE MESA
ESCULTOR
LA ROSA
E. R. TORRES
TORNILLO
CONSOLACIÓN
MUCHO TRIGO
VALDERRAMA
HERRADORES
AGUSTÍN MORENO
SIETE REVUELTAS
RONQUILLO BRICEÑO
FRÍAS
CRUZ VERDE
BARRIONUEVO
ALCÁNTARA
LA PALMA
ISABEL II
MAGDALENA
BORJA PAVÓN
RONDA DE ANDÚJAR
HISTORIADOR DOMÍNGUEZ ORTIZ
ARENILLAS
REGINA
AGUSTINA
SANTA INÉS
GUTIÉRREZ DE LE RÍOS
D. VICTORIA
P. OLIVA
MÉNDEZ
MUÑICES
ABÉJAR
VERDUGO
A. SAN LORENZO
ESCAÑUELA
SANTA MARÍA DE GRACIA
ARROYO SAN RAFAEL
ROELAS
ARROYO
SAN ANDRÉS
ISAAC PERAL
MACHADO
NIUÑOZ CAPILLAS
ENRIQUE REDAL
RUFO REJAS
D. GOMÉ
C. DE LAS IMÁGENES
ISABEL LOSA
C. DEL ZARCO
JUAN
SANTA MARTA
CONDE DE ARENALES
P. FERNÁNDEZ
VILLALONES
1
2
3
4
5
6
7
8
9
10
11
12
13
14
15
16
17
18
19
20
21
22
23
24
25
26

The atmospheric **Judería** quarter. *See p214.*

building was used by the Inquisition from the 1500s until 1820, and later became a prison until the 1950s, resulting in the loss of much of its original grandeur. However, it still incorporates remarkable Arabian baths, Roman mosaics, a marble sarcophagus from the third century and three of its original towers. The small on-site museum is worth a visit, and the gorgeous Moorish-style gardens are a real delight.

The tiny **Calleja de las Flores**, just west of the Mezquita, draws in a constant stream of camera-toting tourists for its neatly framed view of the mosque's bell tower. It's also home to some of the last remaining workshops where Córdoba's famous worked-leather goods are made and sold (*see p221*).

The nearby **Museo Arqueológico** is set inside the beautiful Renaissance **Casa Páez**. During its conversion, a Roman patio was discovered, which is now exhibited along with other Roman, Iberian and Moorish remains.

South-west of the Mezquita, heading towards the Puerta de Almodóvar, which is Córdoba's last standing old town gate, you'll find the 14th-century **Sinagoga** (synagogue) in C/Maimonides. This is one of only three surviving original synagogues from this period in Spain.

The **Puerta de Almodóvar** is the city's only surviving 14th-century gate. From here, a pleasant walk leads east along the old city walls towards the Guadalquivir river. Alternatively, head west to reach the **Jardines de la Victoria**, the city's main promenade park.

Alcázar de los Reyes Cristianos

Campo Santo de los Mártires s/n (957 42 01 51). **Open** *Mid June-mid Sept* 8.30am-2pm Tue-Sun. *Mid Sep-mid Oct* 10am-2pm, 5.30-7.30 Tue-Sat; 9.30am-2.30pm Sun. *Mid Oct-mid June* 10am-2pm, 4.30-6.30pm Tue-Sat; 9.30am-2.30pm Sun. **Admission** €4; €2 concessions; free under-14s & over-75s; free to all Fri. **No credit cards. Map** p215 A4.

Museo Arqueológico

Plaza Jerónimo Páez 7 (957 47 40 11). **Open** 2.30-8.30pm Tue; 9am-8.30pm Wed-Sat; 9am-2.30pm Sun. **Admission** €1.50; free with EU passport. **No credit cards. Map** p215 C3.

Museo Diocesano de Bellas Artes

Palacio Episcopal, C/Torrijos 12 (957 49 60 85). **Open** 9.30am-1.30pm, 4-6pm Mon-Fri; 9.30am-1.30pm Sat. **Admission** €1.50; free with Mezquita ticket. **No credit cards. Map** p215 A4.

Palacio de Congresos y Exposiciones de Córdoba

C/Torrijos 10 (957 48 31 12/www.cordoba congress.com). **Open** 9.30am-2.30pm, 5-8pm Mon-Fri, occasional weekends. **Admission** free. **Map** p215 A4.

Sinagoga

C/Judería 20 (957 20 29 28). **Open** 9.30am-2pm, 3.30-5.30pm Tue-Sat; 9.30am-1.30pm Sun. **Admission** 30¢; free with EU passport. **No credit cards. Map** p215 A3.

Along the Guadalquivir

Head towards the river from the Mezquita and you'll see the **Puente Romano**, the much altered Roman bridge. At its western end stands the **Triunfo de San Rafael** (Triumph of San Rafael monument) and the **Puerta del Puente** (Bridge Gate), built by Felipe II in 1572, replacing an original Roman structure. On the bridge's far side rises the **Torre de la Calahorra**. Built in 1369 as a lookout, it now contains a small museum of Córdoba's history, focusing on the 'three cultures' – Muslim, Jewish and Christian – in the 12th and 13th centuries. On the river are the remains of the **Molino de la Albolafía**, one of several Moorish mills along the Guadalquivir. The reed beds around the Puente Romano are home to a remarkable collection of birdlife.

Follow the river south along its western bank to Córdoba's **Jardín Botánico** (Botanical Garden), which offers a fragrant, leafy respite

The arcaded splendour of **Plaza de la Corredera**.

from the heat and noise. You can also visit the garden's paeleontology and ethnobotany museums, a café and a small gift shop.

Jardín Botánico

Avda de Linneo s/n (957 20 00 18/www.jardin botanicodecordoba.com). **Open** *Gardens* Apr-June 10am-9pm Tue-Sat; 10am-2.30pm Sun. July-Sept 10am-3pm, 7pm-midnight Tue-Sat; 10am-2.30pm Sun. Oct-Mar 10am-6.30pm Tue-Sat; 10am-2.30pm Sun. *Museo de Etnobotanica & Museo de Paleobotanico* Apr-June 10am-2pm, 4-9pm Tue-Sat; 10am-2.30pm Sun. July-Sept 10am-3pm, 7pm-10pm Tue-Sat; 10am-2.30pm Sun. Oct-Mar 10am-2pm, 4pm-6.30pm Tue-Sat; 10am-2.30pm Sun. **Admission** €2; €1.30 concessions. **No credit cards**. **Map** p215 off A4.

Torre de la Calahorra

Puente Romano (957 29 39 29/www.torre calahorra.com). **Open** *Museum* May-Sept 10am-2pm, 4.30-8.30pm daily. Oct-Apr 10am-6pm daily. **Admission** €4.50; €3 concessions. **No credit cards**. **Map**p215 off B4.

Plaza del Potro & Plaza de la Corredera

On the river side of the Mezquita, C/Corregidor Luis de la Cerda leads northwards to the **Medina Califal**, a Moorish-style modern bathhouse with hot and cold baths, massage and other treatments. Booking is essential.

Continuing in the same direction, you pass through a rabbit warren of alleys and streets to arrive at **Plaza del Potro**. The inn on its south side, the **Posada del Potro** (957 47 20 00, admission free), is mentioned in *Don Quixote* and almost certainly accommodated Cervantes on his visits to the city. It now hosts contemporary art exhibitions.

Opposite, the **Museo de Bellas Artes**, housed in the former 16th-century Hospital de la Caridad, has a collection of works by local artists. Across the hospital's pretty courtyard is the former home of the Córdoban artist **Julio Romero de Torres** (1885-1930), which is now a small museum.

West of here is the splendour of the **Plaza de la Corredera**. A huge arcaded square, it hosted horse races, bullfights and public executions in the Middle Ages; today it still holds cultural and sporting events, but its main draw is the indoor market on one side, and the bars and bric-a-brac stalls that line its cloisters.

A few minutes' walk north along C/Pedro Lopez brings you out at Plaza Luis Venegas, where the stark modern lines of the **Museo Regina** jewellery museum rise from ancient stone foundations. Visits of Museo Regina are by guided tour only (English available) and pre-booking is advisable.

Medina Califal

C/Corregidor Luis de la Cerda 51 (957 48 47 46/ www.hammamspain.com). **Open** 10am-midnight daily. **Rates** *Bath, massage & aromatherapy* €27; €21 concessions, 10am-4pm Mon-Fri only. *Bath only* €20. **Credit** AmEx, DC, MC, V. **Map** p215 C4.

Museo de Bellas Artes

Plaza del Potro 1 (957 47 13 14). **Open** 2.30-8.30pm Tue; 9am-8.30pm Wed-Sat; 9am-2.30pm Sun. **Admission** €2.50; free with EU passport. **No credit cards**. **Map** p215 D4.

Museo de Julio Romero de Torres

Plaza del Potro 1 (957 76 02 69). **Open** *May-mid June* 10am-2pm, 5.30-7.30pm Tue-Sat; 9.30am-2.30pm Sun. *Oct-Apr* 10am-2pm, 4.30-6.30pm Tue-Sat; 9.30am-2.30pm Sun. **Admission** €4; €2 concessions; free to all Fri. **No credit cards**. **Map** p215 D4.

Museo Regina

Plaza Luis Venegas 1, off C/Pedro Lopez (957 49 68 89/www.museoregina.com). **Open** *June-mid Sept* 9am-2pm, 5.30-9pm daily. *Mid Sept-May* 10am-3pm, 5-8pm daily. **Admission** €3; €1.50 concessions. **Credit** AmEx, DC, MC, V. **Map** p215 D3.

Plaza de las Tendillas & beyond

West of Plaza de la Corredera, the modern city starts to assert itself. Its focal point is **Plaza de las Tendillas**, from which Córdoba's main shopping streets radiate. The square is dominated by an old fountain and an equestrian statue of El Gran Capitán, a Córdoban general whose Italian campaigns in the late 15th century brought him international fame.

C/Claudio Marcelo leads from the *plaza* to the **Templo Romano** (reconstructed pillars from a first-century Roman temple) and the church of **San Pablo** (open hours of services). The architecture of the latter displays the transition between the Romanesque and the Gothic, with Mudéjar features. Further north-east is a trio of Reconquista churches: **San Andrés** on C/Realejo, the neo-classical **San Rafael** on C/Roelas and the stunning Gothic-Mudéjar **San Lorenzo** on C/María Auxiliadora (all open hours of services). The latter has a converted minaret tower and a beautiful rose window.

The twisting streets and small squares west of here shelter several more beautiful Gothic churches built soon after the Reconquista. **Santa Marina** (open hours of services) has a particularly attractive setting in a small *plaza* (Plaza Santa Marina) with a monument to the legendary local-born bullfighter Manolete.

Just south-east of here is the splendid **Palacio de Viana**. The compulsory guided tour takes you through the interior, which still contains the furnishings of the Viana family, but the highlight is the palace's 14 beautiful patios and gardens, constructed between the 14th and 18th centuries. The gardens and patios can be visited without a guided tour.

A little south of Santa Marina is the **Plaza de Capuchinos**, a raised, enclosed *plaza* dominated by the famous 18th-century statue of *El Cristo de los Faroles* (Christ of the Lanterns), which seems especially mystical when you see it lit up at night.

Just west of here are the ornate gardens of the **Plaza de Colón**, flanked on the western side by the very grand baroque **Palacio de la Diputación**. North-west of the *plaza* is the **Torre de la Malmuerta** ('bad death'), a 15th-century battlement tower, supposedly built in contrition by a nobleman who had murdered his adulterous wife – another story is that he bricked up his unfaithful wife in the walls.

There are several churches worth a visit on the route from here back towards the Judería, including **San Miguel** (open hours of services). It is located in a pretty *plaza* of the same name (which has some good café-bars) and houses a wonderful 18th-century *retablo* in red marble.

Palacio de Viana

Plaza Don Gome 2 (957 49 67 41). **Open** *June-Sept* 9am-2pm Mon-Sat; *Oct-May* 10am-1pm, 4-6pm Mon-Fri; 10am-1pm Sat. **Admission** *Patios only* €3. *Palace (guided tour only) & patios* €6. **No credit cards**. **Map** p215 E1.

Where to eat & drink

Córdoba is Andalucía's culinary capital. Spain's ongoing culinary revolution is taking a while to filter into the regional restaurant scene but Córdoba is in its vanguard down south. **Casa Pepe**, for instance, has become famed for its light variations on traditional dishes and for its El Bulli-inspired innovations, while **Bodegas Campos** is another haven of lightness of touch and culinary imagination. Near the train station, around Avda de la Libertad, there is a new cluster of designer bars, restaurants and clubs, which provide a cool alternative if you've overdosed on traditional taverns.

Bambuddha

Avda Gran Capitán 46 (no phone/www.bambuddha.es). **Open** 3pm-4am daily. **No credit cards**. **Map** p215 off C1.

As the name suggests, this is a place to sink into the plush low seating and chill out in the laid-back atmosphere. Unless it's comedy night, in which case the vibe is much more cheerful, brighter and louder.

Bodegas Campos

C/Lineros 32 (957 49 75 00/www.bodegascampos.com). **Open** 1-5pm, 8.30pm-midnight Mon-Sat; 1-5pm Sun. **Average** €€€€. **Credit** DC, MC, V. **Map** p215 D4 ❶

This elegant and sensationally beautiful restaurant (with its numerous patios) may not be cheap, but each dish is produced using top ingredients and great skill. Highlights include a superb salt cod and orange salad and four-chocolate tart. It's equally good as a place for a glass of Montilla and a tapa up at the bar if you're less hungry.

Cafeteria El Rincón de Carmen

C/Romero 4 (957 29 10 55). **Open** noon-4pm, 8-11pm Mon-Sat; noon-4pm Sun. **Average** €. **Credit** AmEx, MC, V. **Map** p215 B3 ❷

Settle into large wicker chairs to breakfast cheaply on *tostadas* and freshly squeezed OJ at this airy café.

Casa Pepe de la Judería

C/Romero 1 (957 20 07 44/www.casapepejuderia.com). **Open** 1-4pm, 8.30-11.30pm daily. **Average** *Tapas* €-€€. *Restaurant* €€-€€€. **Credit** AmEx, DC, MC, V. **Map** p215 B3 ❸

The tapas and talk are equally good at Córdoba classic **Taberna Salinas**. *See p221.*

This innovative restaurant has a tangle of dining rooms and a gorgeous roof terrace with views of the Mezquita. The menu is diverse, with delicacies such as the Morisco dish *mazamorra* (egg, garlic and oil soup). The restaurant prides itself on its desserts, which might include 'citrus soup' with pineapple foam. Tapas are served in the busy side bar. Touristy, but good all the same.

Casa El Pisto

Plaza San Miguel 1 (957 47 01 66). **Open** noon-4pm, 8pm-midnight Mon-Sat; noon-4pm Sun. Closed Aug. **Average** €. **Credit** AmEx, DC, MC, V. **Map** p215 C1 ❹

'The Barrel' is a legendary Córdoban bar in a delightful old house, with great Montilla and a busy, buzzy atmosphere. It's big with bullfighting aficionados and serves terrific tapas.

El Churrasco

C/Romero 16 (957 29 08 19/www.elchurrasco.com). **Open** 1-4pm, 8.30pm-midnight daily. Closed Aug. **Average** €€-€€€€. **Credit** AmEx, DC, MC, V. **Map** p215 B3 ❺

Loved by locals, tourists and Tony Blair, this is a safe bet for traditional Andalucían fare and old-style waiter service. Try El Churrasco's signature dish: *churrasco cordobés* (pork loin with 'Arabic' sweet-and-sour sauce) or crispy aubergine with *salmorejo*. Sure it's touristy, but get over it and enjoy eating under a lemon tree.

El Faro

C/Blanco Belmonte 6 (957 48 62 14). **Open** 1-4pm, 8.30pm-12.30am Tue-Sun. **Average** €€. **Credit** AmEx, DC, MC, V. **Map** p215 B3 ❻

A modest side entrance makes this quiet, unpretentious restaurant easy to miss (just west of the Mezquita). Splash out on a mixed seafood platter or try the simple but tasty fried red mullet. The restaurant also has an excellent sister seafood bar – look out for its cute lighthouse-themed exterior.

Other locations: El Faro, C/Sevilla 3 (957 47 83 51).

Los Marqueses

C/Tomás Conde 8 (957 20 20 94/www.restaurantelosmarqueses.com). **Open** *July, Aug* 1-4pm, 8-11.30pm Mon-Sat; *Sept-June* 1-4pm, 8-11.30pm Tue-Sun. **Average** €€€-€€€€. **Credit** AmEx, MC, V. **Map** p215 A4 ❼

The *marqueses* after whom this extremely smart restaurant is named gaze down imperiously from oil paintings that dominate the small, elegant dining room. Highlights of the menu include beetroot gazpacho with apple ravioli, lobster salad and shoulder of suckling lamb, but all the dishes are expertly executed with creative touches.

El Sotano

Plaza de la Corredera 1 (957 48 45 70). **Open** *Mid June-Oct* 9am-5pm, 8pm-2am daily. *Nov-mid June* 9am-2am daily. **Average** €. **Credit** AmEx, DC, MC, V. **Map** p215 D3 ❽

This funky little bar, run by two friendly young guys, is decorated in warm yellows and oranges. With plenty of of terrace tables, it's a chilled spot for a drink or reasonably priced snacks.

Soul

C/Alfonso XIII 3 (957 49 15 80). **Open** 9am-3am Mon-Fri; 5pm-3am Sat, Sun. Closed Aug. **Average** €. **No credit cards**. **Map** p215 D2 ❾

Soul puts its namesake into its breakfasts, with bread baked in a wood-burning oven (Omega3, raisin-and-walnut, and multicereal varieties), topped with honey or speciality jams. Later in the day and into the evening a young crowd lounges amid the funky decor.

Taberna Casa Bravo

C/Puerta de Almodóvar s/n (957 29 29 79). **Open** noon-4pm, 8pm-midnight Mon, Wed-Sat; noon-4pm Sun. **Average** €-€€. **Credit** AmEx, DC, MC, V. **Map** p215 A2 ❿

This extremely friendly tapas bar-restaurant is well patronised by locals, most of whom choose to linger in the small atmospheric bar area, laden with bullfighting photos and posters, rather than the larger dining room. Everything is excellent quality, from a simple dish of plump cracked green olives to the ominous-sounding, but delicious 'meat in sauce' (*carne en salsa*).

Taberna Salinas

C/Tundidores 3 (957 48 01 35). **Open** noon-4pm, 8pm-midnight Mon-Sat. Closed Aug. **Average** €. **Credit** AmEx, DC, MC, V. **Map** p215 D2 ⓫

This bustling bar and great patio restaurant with barrels of Montilla and antique olive-wood furniture has been around since 1879. Try the excellent tapas, including fried squid, pig's trotters and ewe's cheese. Located between Plaza de la Corredera and C/Fernando Colón.

Taberna Sociedad de Plateros

C/San Francisco 6 (957 47 00 42). **Open** noon-4pm, 8pm-midnight Tue-Sun. **Average** €€. **Credit** AmEx, DC, MC, V. **Map** p215 C4 ⓬

Many of Córdoba's old *bodegas* are run by the silversmiths' guild (Sociedad de Plateros). This airy, popular place is a great favourite of the guitarist Paco Peña, who lives around the corner. Service ranges from charming to indifferent, depending on the waiter, and you may have to be pushy to get a table. Low prices may tempt you to over-order the generous *raciones*. Food is basic but good, with heavy-duty highlights such as an enormous entrecôte.

Wenguè

Avda Gran Capitán 48 (957 81 05 90). **Open** 7am-2am daily. **Average** €€. **Credit** V. **Map** p215 off C1.

This colonial-style bar and restaurant is open for everything from breakfast to late-night drinks. The crowd is a mixed bag of local workers during the day, but gets markedly hipper as the evening wears on and the music volume rises. Dishes are Andalucían and vaguely oriental, with a good-value lunch.

Shopping

For general and high-street shops, head for the streets off Plaza de las Tendillas. Note: many of the smaller shops close on Saturday afternoon as well as all day Sunday.

Córdoba has a strong tradition in jewellery-making (especially silver) and leather-working, and the handcrafted results of these traditions make great gifts. **Plata Natura** (C/Cardenal González 53, 957 49 87 18) showcases stylish jewellery from contemporary designers in a small gallery-like showroom/shop near the river. Perhaps the only place where you can still buy genuine handcrafted leather goods in Córdoba is **Meryan** (Calleja de las Flores 2, 957 48 71 65, www.meryancor.com, map p215 B3), opened by Angel and Mercedes López-Obrero in the 1950s, and now run by their sons. Prices range from a few euros for a comb case to around a thousand for an embossed chair or trunk.

Córdoba is the gastronomic hub of Andalucía, and there are plenty of good delis. Try **Andalusí** (C/Rodriguez Marín 22, 957 48 89 61, map p215 D3) or the family-run **Bodegas Mezquita** (C/Corregidor Luis de la Cerda 73, 957 49 81 17, www.bodegasmezquita.com, map p215 B4). The produce market on Plaza de la Corredera (9am-1.30pm Mon-Sat) is also a good bet for picnic goodies. For something to drink, head for **La Bodega** (Calleja Herradores s/n, off C/Alfonso XII, no phone, map p215 E4), a tiny, well-hidden *bodega*. The friendly owner sits sewing in the window until locals come to fill their bottles with wines from the barrel.

Arts & entertainment

Film

The **Filmoteca de Andalucía** (C/Medina y Corella 5, 957 48 18 35, www.filmotecadeandalucia.com) is the centre for film in Andalucía. Housed in a wonderful patioed art-house cinema, it is worth seeking out to see classic, original-language, subtitled (in Spanish, of course) films. Note: there are no screenings during July and August.

Music, drama & dance

The **Gran Teatro** (Avda Gran Capitán 3, 957 48 02 37, www.teatrocordoba.com, map p215 B1) is the city's grandest performing-arts venue and hosts performances of drama, dance and music, including concerts by the Orquesta de Córdoba.

The **Festival de Córdoba-Guitarra** (www.guitarracordoba.com) in July attracts national and international stars to play in some of the city's iconic sites. Concerts by flamenco, jazz and classical guitarists (such as Paco Peña, Carlos Santana and BB King) are complemented by workshops, exhibitions and films.

Flamenco

Córdoba is the home of the modern flamenco star Paco Peña, and puts on good, reasonably authentic flamenco all year round. Look out for performances by internationally acclaimed stars at the **Gran Teatro** (*see above*), which also hosts (although only every three years, next due in 2007) the **Concurso Nacional de Arte Flamenco** competition. Next door to the tourist office, opposite the Mezquita, is **Tablao Flamenco Cardenal** (C/Torrijos 10, 957 49 33 20, www.tablaocardenal.com, shows 10.30pm Mon-Sat, tickets €19 incl drink, map p215 B4), where performances by an array of established artists are held in a high-ceilinged hall or on the patio. Book to reserve a table close to the stage.

Sport

If you're interested in seeing a *corrida*, details and tickets are available from the **Plaza de Toros** on Avda Gran Vía Parque (957 23 35 07, tickets from €25) to the north-west of the city. Guided tours of the bullring are also available. The city's capable football team, Córdoba, can be checked out at **El Nuevo Arcángel** stadium, east of the river (Avda del Arcángel s/n, 957 75 19 34, www.cordobacf.com).

Where to stay

Most beds in Córdoba are found in the Judería around the Mezquita. One of the pleasures of staying here is that even the meanest *hostal* is likely to have a cute flower-filled patio. Check if your hotel has parking if you need it. It's best not to drive in Córdoba at all, or else dump your car as soon as possible. Hotel rates can soar during Semana Santa and the May fiestas.

Casa de los Azulejos

C/Fernando Colón 5 (957 47 00 00/www.casadelosazulejos.com). **Rates** (incl breakfast) €80.25-€107 single; €91-€139 double; €123-€181.90 suite. **Credit** AmEx, MC, V. **Map** p215 D3 ⓭

Casa de los Azulejos is a stunningly converted *palacio* with eight individually decorated rooms overlooking leafy patios. Original features, including a majestic staircase, carved woodwork and Sevillian wall tiles, have been complemented with playful modern touches, such as colourful bathrooms. The hotel also has a South American-Andalucían restaurant (€€€) and a Mexican *cantina*.

Casa de los Naranjos

C/Isabel Losa 8 (957 47 05 87/www.casadelosnaranjos.com). **Rates** €64-€102 double. **Credit** MC, V. **Map** p215 E1 ⓮

A quiet converted mid-19th century townhouse near the Palacio de Viana. Although there is the usual calming courtyard, with stylish tables for breakfast and dinner, they have not gone overboard with the Andalucían décor; the 20 rooms are quite simple.

Hospedería de Churrasco

C/Romero 38 (957 29 48 08/www.elchurrasco.com). **Rates** €128.40-€181.90 double. **Credit** AmEx, DC, MC, V. **Map** p215 A/B3 ⓯

Alongside the famed restaurant of the same name, this new boutique hotel has no truck with minimalist trends. The nine rooms are plushly decorated with every sort of fancy adornment imaginable, but they have managed to get internet-connected computers in there too. Very comfy, great location and of course blowout meals just a stagger away.

Hospes Palacio del Bailío

C/Ramírez de las Casas Deza 10-12 (957 498 993/www.hospes.es). **Rates** €193-€267 double; €278-€642 suite. **Credit** AmEx, DC, MC, V. **Map** p215 D1 ⓰

A serene, five-star haven just off the tourist beat but centrally located. The whitewashed mansion dates back to the 16th century and conceals a series of courtyards planted with jasmine, orange and lemon trees. There tradition ends, however, as the building has been revamped in neutral tones, but with a few Roman remains and 16th-century murals thrown in. The Grand Suite Loft is a spectacular space with 16 windows along one side overlooking a patio.

Hostal Lineros

C/Lineros 38 (957 48 25 17/www.hostallineros38.com). **Rates** €32.10-€53.50 single; €51.40-€62 double; €64.20-€85.60 triple; €83.50-€101.65 quad; €96.30-€123.05 suite. **Credit** AmEx, MC, V. **Map** p215 D4 ⓱

This good-value *hostal* features lovely Moorish detailing. The two internal patios contain a *salon de té*, decorated with leather pouffes, deep-cushioned seating and a stained-glass ceiling. Splash out and stay in Room 8, an atmospheric suite with a wooden four-poster bed, two further beds and a jacuzzi.

Hostal El Portillo

C/Cabezas 2 (957 47 20 91/www.hostalelportillo.com). **Rates** €18-€20 single; €30-€35 double; €45-€50 triple. **No credit cards**. **Map** p215 C3 ⓲

A plain but homely *hostal*, with touches of character and a friendly atmosphere, tucked away in the warren of streets north of the Mezquita. Room 2 is a double with a small balcony. Other rooms face the small, flower-filled internal patio.

Hostal El Reposo de Bagdad

C/Fernández Ruano 11 (957 20 28 54/http://hostalbagdad.eresmas.com). **Rates** €20-€22 single; €36-€38 double. **Credit** MC, V. **Map** p215 A2 ⓳

This new *hostal* near the Puerta de Almodóvar, offers characterful, comfortable en suite rooms at a bargain price. The upper rooms are calm and comfy, with white walls and bed linen. The ground floor has beautiful (though dark) Moorish-style tiled bedrooms, a leafy patio and a tearoom.

Hostal Séneca

C/Conde y Luque 7 (957 47 32 34/hostalseneca@hotmail.com). **Rates** (incl breakfast) €19-€25 single; €35-€50 double. **Credit** V. **Map** p215 B3 ⓴

This friendly, old-fashioned *hostal* is a very popular and cheap place to stay, with gorgeous stained-glass windows on the first floor and a delightful patio at ground level. The cheaper rooms don't have en suite bathrooms. You may need to book well ahead.

Hotel González

C/Manriquez 3 (957 47 98 19/www.hotelgonzalez.com). **Rates** €27-€48 single; €43.90-€97.40 double. **Credit** AmEx, MC, V. **Map** p215 A3 ㉑

This popular hotel near the Mezquita is housed in a restored 16th-century *palacio*, once home to relations of Córdoban painter Julio Romero de Torres. The rooms are decorated with reproduction antique furniture and heavy curtains. Breakfast is served in a traditional, plant-filled patio.

Hotel, Hostal y Apartamentos Maestre

C/Romero Barros 4 & 6 (957 47 24 10/www.hotelmaestre.com). **Rates** *Hostal* €30-€38 double. *Hotel* €50-€54 double. *Apartments* €50-€74. **Credit** AmEx, DC, MC, V. **Map** p209 C4 ㉒

The Maestre is a bit of muddle – stark, modern marble-and-chrome reception rooms clash with pleasant leafy patios. But it does have some smart apartments fantastically situated on Plaza del Potro.

Hotel Lola

C/Romero 3 (957 20 03 05/www.hotelconencantolola.com). **Rates** (incl breakfast) €84.40-€121.55 double. **Credit** AmEx, DC, MC, V. **Map** p215 A/B3 ㉓

Located in the heart of the Judería, with a roof terrace that overlooks the Mezquita's bell tower, this traditional Córdoban house is a charming and unusual small hotel. The eight guest rooms have clusters of antiques and baroque touches.

Hotel Mezquita

Plaza Santa Catalina 1 (957 47 55 85/hotelmezquita@wanadoo.es). **Rates** €26.75-€51.35 single; €44-€100.60 double. **Credit** MC, V. **Map** p215 B3 ㉔

A superbly located two-star hotel in a restored 16th-century mansion right by the Mezquita. Room 4 is a nice, light corner room that overlooks the Mezquita walls, as does Room 5.

Hotel Posada de Vallina

C/Corregidor Luis de la Cerda 83 (957 49 87 50/www.hotelvallina.com). **Rates** (incl breakfast) €74.90-€96.30 single; €85.60-€107 double. **Credit** AmEx, DC, MC, V. **Map** p215 B4 ㉕

This historic inn on the east side of the Mezquita once housed labourers building the old mosque, and Columbus is rumoured to have stayed in room 104. Compared to its colourful history and the atmospheric breakfast patio, the rooms are a bit bland.

NH Amistad

Plaza de Maimonides 3 (957 42 03 35/www.nh-hotels.com). **Rates** €150-€178.60 double. **Credit** AmEx, DC, MC, V. **Map** p215 A3 ㉖

Built on the southern edge of the Judería into the old city walls, this is a quiet, cool and stylish hotel. The large patio is a calm, airy place in which to relax over a coffee, and, when it's too hot for sightseeing, there's a plunge pool and sun terrace on the third floor of the neighbouring building to enjoy. Bedrooms are a touch corporate but luxurious, and breakfast is a buffet feast, with a chef on hand to cook to order.

Resources

Internet

Odisea, Plaza Mármol de Bañuelos 1, off C/Diego de León (957 47 38 10). **Open** 10am-11pm Mon-Sat; 4-11pm Sun. **Map** p215 C2.

Police station

Avda Doctor Fleming 2 (957 59 45 00). **Map** p215 A3.

Post office

Correos Jefatura Provincial, C/José Cruz Conde 15 (957 49 63 42). **Open** 8.30am-8.30pm Mon-Fri; 9.30am-2pm Sat. **Map** p215 C1.

Tourist information

Palacio de Exposiciones y Congresos, C/Torrijos 10 (957 47 12 35/otcordoba@andalucia.org). **Open** 9am-7pm Mon-Fri, 10am-7.30pm Sat, 10am-2pm Sun. **Map** p215 B4.

Getting there

By bus

The main bus station (957 40 40 40) is at Plaza de las Tres Culturas, next to the AVE train station (map p215 off A1). Alsina Graells (957 27 81 00, www.alsinagraells.es) runs buses between Córdoba and Granada (3hrs), Málaga (3hrs) and Seville (2hrs), with less frequent connections and extensions to other destinations, including Cádiz, Algeciras and the Costa del Sol. Bacoma (957 27 98 60) runs 1 bus a day between Córdoba and Alicante and 3 a day to Barcelona and Valencia. Secorbús (957 40 24 76) runs about 5 buses a day between Madrid and Córdoba.

By train

Córdoba's station is at Avda de América, 30mins' walk west of the Mezquita; there's a ticket office in town at Ronda de los Tejares 10 near Plaza de Colón. The AVE high-speed train links Córdoba with Seville (45mins) and Madrid (2hrs), with frequent services. The Talgo train links Córdoba and Málaga (6 daily, 2hrs). There are also standard daily services to Cádiz (4 trains, 3hrs), Málaga (10 trains, 2hrs 15mins) and other Andalucían cities. For train information, contact RENFE (902 24 02 02, www.renfe.es).

Around Córdoba

Valleys and hills dotted with magnificent castles and churches.

The Guadalquivir valley

Twenty-five kilometres (16 miles) west of Córdoba city along the A431 lies **Almodóvar del Río**, dominated by its castle. Originally built in the eighth century, but much altered and restored since (most of it is now an ugly neo-Gothic pastiche), it was one of the most formidable fortresses in the region. There is a great view across the Guadalquivir valley from the precipitous battlements.

A further 30 kilometres (19 miles) west, **Palma del Río**, originally a strategic Roman settlement, lies on the border with Seville province. Some of the town's 12th-century walls survive, but the real attraction is the 15th-century monastery that has been converted into the **Hospedería de San Francisco**, a luxurious hotel (*see p225*). Heading north from Palma del Río, the CO140 passes through a beautiful slice of countryside, where prairie-like fields are interrupted by old wooden bridges and water towers. After 17 kilometres (11 miles), you reach **Hornachuelos**, a small, whitewashed village balanced on steep cliffs around the ruins of its old Moorish castle.

From here, the CO142 enters the **Parque Natural de la Sierra de Hornachuelos**, with a bumpy track leading to the gorgeous **Monasterio de Santa María de los Angeles**; it's privately owned but worth a look from the outside. Much of the park is made up of gentle hills covered in holm and gall oaks, pine and cork. It is home to Andalucía's second largest colony of black vultures, but more common spottings are of Imperial and Royal eagles. Continue on the CO142 to eventually reach **San Calixto**, a community of around 20 Carmelite nuns, who sell home-made cakes and biscuits through a revolving window.

Another scenic drive can be enjoyed by taking the rural A433, nine kilometres (six miles) west of Almodóvar del Río at Posadas, which curves north for 63 kilometres (39 miles) to join the main CO31 from Córdoba. The stunning journey takes you from the fertile lowlands to heights where cork gives way to fir.

The attractive town of **Montoro**, 42 kilometres (26 miles) east of Córdoba on the A4-E5 motorway, sits atop a hill overlooking the **Puente de la Doñadas**. It is said that the bridge, which took 50 years to build (it was finished in 1480), was only completed because the local women sold their jewellery to raise the necessary funds (hence its name, 'bridge of the lay sisters'). The prominent tower belongs to the 15th-century church of **San Bartolomé** (open hours of services) on the central Plaza de España. In the same square, the old ducal palace (now the town hall) houses the tourist office and the **Museo Arqueológico Municipal**. For a taste of big-time kitsch, seek out **Casa de las Conchas** (C/Grajas 17), a house decorated entirely in shells that have been collected by the owner Francisco del Río. He will proudly show off his home for a small fee. Montoro is also the site of one of the oldest churches in the province (on C/B Comacho, just north of the square), the 13th-century **Santa María de la Mota** (open hours of services).

From Montoro there is a delightful route through the Sierra Morena on the CO414 west to the laid-back town of **Adamuz**. Alternatively, the N420 north goes through the western edge of the **Parque Natural de la Sierra de Cardeña y Montoro**, with views to the peaks of the Sierra de Andújar. The **Presa de Martín Gonzalo**, 17 kilometres (11 miles) north-east of Montoro, is a good picnic spot by a lake. To overnight in the area, stop off in **Cardeña** (33 kilometres/20 miles north of Montoro), which has a fair selection of hotels.

A few kilometres south-west of Montoro in **Pedro Abad** you'll find the first mosque founded in Spain since the time of Moors. The foundation stone of the Ahmadiyya sect's Basharat Mosque was laid in 1980 (though Marbella's mosque was completed first).

Castillo de Almodóvar del Río

Almodóvar del Río (957 63 40 55/670 33 84 30/www.castillodealmodovar.com). **Open** *Apr-Sept* 11am-2.30pm, 4-8pm Mon-Fri; 11am-8pm Sat, Sun; *Oct-Mar* 11am-2.30pm, 4-7pm Mon-Fri; 11am-7pm Sat, Sun. **Admission** €5; €4 concessions. **Credit** AmEx, DC, MC, V.

Museo Arqueológico Municipal

Plaza Santa María de la Mota s/n, Montoro (957 16 00 89). **Open** 11am-1pm Sat, Sun. **Admission** free.

Where to stay, eat & drink

In Almodóvar del Río, the unfussy **La Taverna** (C/Antonio Machado 24, 957 71 36 84, closed Sun dinner, all Mon & all Aug, €€-€€€)

Castillo de Almodóvar del Río. See p224.

has a deserved reputation for posh home cooking. In Palma del Río stay at the stark but luxurious **Hospedería de San Francisco** (Avda Pio XII 35, 957 71 01 83, www.casasy palacios.com, double €101.65-€118.80). The hotel is a converted 15th-century monastery with an exquisite swimming pool and a good restaurant (€€-€€€). Budget travellers could try the good-value **El Alamo** (Ctra Comarcal 141, 957 64 04 76, www.hornaocio.com, double €50-€60), just outside Hornachuelos.

If you stop in Montoro, **Bar Yepez** (Plaza del Charco 4, 957 16 01 23, closed Tue and first 2wks in Aug, €-€€) is a good watering hole and tapas joint, and the attractive neo-Moorish **Casino** (off Plaza M Benitez) is a good place to try no-nonsense tapas like pigs' brains.

If you crave tranquillity and a remote rural setting, head for **Hacienda La Colora** (C0414, km16, 957 33 60 77, www.lacolora.com, double €100-€120), an 18th-century former olive oil-producing farm, now converted into a hotel. There are lovely walks around the estate, plus a pool and restaurant.

Resources

Tourist information

Montoro *Plaza de España 8 (957 16 00 89/www.montoro.es).* **Open** 9am-3pm Mon-Fri; 10am-1pm Sat; 10am-2pm Sun.

Palma del Río *C/Cardenal Potocarrerro s/n (957 64 43 70/www.palmadelrio.es).* **Open** 10am-2pm, 5-8pm Tue-Fri; 10am-2pm Sat.

North of Córdoba

The wild landscapes north of Córdoba – mountainous in the west and east, broad and gently rolling in the north – stand out from the rest of Andalucía. It's poor and starkly beautiful. Sparsely populated, it makes for good driving country; few of its towns merit much more than a glance from afar (generally at the ruins of their respective castles).

The main CO31 runs north-west from Córdoba into the high Sierra Morena and on to Extremadura. After 50 kilometres (31 miles), it's worth taking the N502 north on a lengthy detour towards the far north. There's not a lot to do up here, but the driving is magnificent.

A left turn at Alcaracejos on to the A420 leads you through a wide open landscape of olive groves, oaks and farmland, and, after 20 kilometres (12.5 miles), you arrive in **Hinojosa del Duque**, with views to the distant mountains. Hinojosa is a fly-blown workaday town, but its so-called 'Cathedral of the Sierra', **San Juan Bautista** (open hours of services) is well worth a look. Largely Gothic-Renaissance in style, it has a portal by Hernán Ruiz (who designed the cathedral within the Mezquita in Córdoba), a fine Mudéjar stuccoed ceiling, a baroque altar and some *trompe l'oeil* carving on the window to the left of the main door. There are a couple of tapas places in the same square.

From **Fuente Obejuna**, a poor neglected town south-west of here – and immortalised in the play by Lope de Vega after the villagers hacked their tyrannical lord to pieces – the wild, lonely and stunning A447 winds through the mountains into northern Seville province. Be warned, though, it's a slow 56 kilometres before you hit civilisation again.

Where to stay, eat & drink

Accommodation in this area tends to be cheap and simple. **La Paloma** (N502, km2, 957 15 82 42, double €26), in the pretty village of Santa

Medina Azahara

In AD 929, when the Emir of Córdoba, Abd al-Rahman III, became Caliph, he set about building a new palace and *medina* to firmly establish his authority and the magnificence of the fledgling Caliphate. The complex was named after his favourite wife, Az-Zahra (the Radiant), and has been described by the historian Felipe Fernández-Armesto as 'worldly and ostentatious... both a pleasure-dome and a power-house'.

Work on Medina Azahara began in 936 on a huge site west of Córdoba. In addition to palace buildings, the complex contained a zoo, aviary, four huge fish ponds, 300 baths, 400 houses, weapons factories and barracks for the royal guard, as well as numerous markets, workshops and mosques. The *medina* reputedly accommodated 4,000 slaves and a harem of over 6,000 women.

At the heart of the complex was the Alcázar, or palace. Chroniclers tell of its extraordinary beauty, in particular the splendid Throne Hall and the Golden Salon, both decorated with arches of ebony and ivory, and ornaments of marble, gold and precious stones. Another hall was built around a huge shallow bowl of mercury that would be rocked by a slave to send sunbeams skittering about the room.

After some stable years under al-Hakam II, who continued to endow the new royal city, greater opulence was to come under tough-guy al-Mansur. As a calculated snub to the dynasty he nominally served, the soldier-ruler built yet another palace, larger than Abd al-Rahman III's, and finished in just two years. Al-Mansur died in 1002 and his younger son failed to rise to the challenge of his father's legacy. In 1009 Medina Azahara was looted and sacked by Berber mutineers who ravaged the entire complex.

For the following centuries Medina Azahara existed only in history as 'old Córdoba', until excavations brought its stories back to life in 1910. The site is around ten kilometres (six miles) west of the provincial capital, on gentle fertile slopes, dotted with cypresses, below the Sierra Morena. Excavations are ongoing and only a tenth of the original walled city has been exposed, corresponding to the central section of the Alcázar. The directed route through the complex ends on the lower terraces at the Chamber of Abd al-Rahman III. This hall would have been used for majestic receptions, although a vivid imagination is needed to conjure up the gleaming white marble floors and jewelled walls. Although the ruins only hint at past grandeur, they offer a tantalising glimpse into this short-lived but fantastic city.

Medina Azahara

A431, km6 (957 32 91 30). **Open** *May-mid Sept* 10am-8.30pm Tue-Sat; 10am-2pm Sun. *Mid Sept-Apr* 10am-6pm Tue-Sat; 10am-2pm Sun. **Admission** €1.50; free with EU passport. **No credit cards**.

Eufemia at the northern edge of the province, with delicious home-cooked food and cheap tapas. Just down the road is the **Bar Las Catalanas** (N502, 957 15 82 69, €) for snacks.

Outside Pozoblanco is the delightful **Cortijo Palomar de la Morra** (Avda Argentina 8, C0421, km3, 957 77 15 85, mobile 678 42 89 23, www.palomardelamorra.com, from €260 for 4-6 people). Simple, traditional bedrooms share use of a homely communal lounge and a swimming pool – a luxury for these parts.

Resources

Tourist information

Fuente Obejuna *C/Luis Rodríguez 27 (957 58 49 00)*. **Open** 10am-2pm Mon-Fri.

Montilla & around

South of Córdoba, the N331 branches off the A4-E5 motorway to Seville on what has been dubbed the *Ruta del Vino* (Wine Route) by the tourist board. It passes through wide, rolling sweeps of wheat fields before reaching picturesque castle-topped **Montemayor**, perched on the highest hill in the area, with stunning views from the town's *mirador*. In Plaza de la Constitución is a miniature copy of the Alhambra's Fountain of the Lions, and a fascinating stash of local archaeological finds in the **Museo Arqueológico Ulía**. A five-minute drive south-west from here brings you to **La Rambla**, famed for its pottery. Plenty of shops sell the spouted drinking vessels known as *botijos*. Around here, olive trees and vines start to dominate the undulating landscape.

Twelve kilometres (7.5 miles) east of La Rambla is **Montilla**, site of the crucial Battle of Munda in 45 BC, where Julius Caesar beat the supporters of Pompey, bringing to an end the Roman civil war and giving Caesar authority, albeit briefly, over the entire Roman Empire. Apart from the obvious temptation of its superb wines, the town is not hugely appealing, though it does have a fascinating small museum, the **Casa Museo del Inca Garcilaso**, dedicated to the Hispano-Inca son of a *conquistador*, who chronicled Inca civilisation in the 16th century. Also in Montilla, the church of **Santa Clara** (open hours of services) has a fine late-Gothic façade and paintings by Alonso Cano.

If you want to visit a *bodega*, try **Bodegas Alvear**, one of the major producers. Montilla wine has long lived in the shadow of its more famous cousin, sherry. Unlike its coastal relation, Montilla (lacking an outlet to the sea and, thus, easy shipping abroad) is little-known internationally, yet many of its wines are superb and deserve to be better appreciated.

Ten kilometres (six miles) south of Montilla is **Aguilar de la Frontera**, an attractive town where the striking and unusual octagonal Plaza de San José (designed by Vicente Gutiérrez in 1806, and inspired by a similar square in Archidona) has managed to retain its dignity, despite being used as a car park. Check out the **Torre Civil del Reloj**, an impressive clock tower topped with a huge, teetering stork's nest or, for the best views, head for the **Peñon de Moro**, the site of the old castle. Close by is the church of **Santa María del Soterraño** (open hours of services), which dates originally from the Middle Ages, but was replaced in 1530 by a Gothic-Mudéjar building.

South-west of Aguilar, off the A309, is the tranquil **Laguna de Zóñar**, a protected area that's home to many migratory birds, including flamingoes, while another ten minutes' drive further on is the town of **Puente-Genil**, where you can sample the fine local quince jam.

Turning east off the N331 at Monturque on to the A342 takes you, after a fine drive through olive groves, to **Cabra**. This pleasant town was an important Roman colony, a Visigothic bishopric and a provincial capital under the Moors, as related in its **Museo Arqueológico Municipal**. The spectacular church of **La Asunción** (open hours of services) near the castle is converted from a mosque, and retains 44 red marble columns, reminiscent of the Mezquita. Today, Cabra is big on candle-making and festivals. It has a spectacular Easter Sunday extravaganza, followed by its own patio festival at the beginning of May. On 4 September the Virgen de la Sierra is brought into town for a week-long celebration, including cultural events, *corridas* and a flower fight. For the rest of the year, she rests in her sanctuary, off the A340 towards Priego de Córdoba. Off the same road is **La Fuente del Rio**, a natural spring with a series of swimming pools and a picnic area.

South from Cabra, on the main N331, is the sizeable town of **Lucena**, a furniture centre with American-style warehouse showrooms

Montemayor.

on its outskirts and a real baroque treat at its heart. Until the 12th century, Lucena was an independent Jewish republic within the Córdoban Caliphate, and, in 1483, the site of a battle that resulted in the capture of Boabdil, the last Moorish ruler of Granada. Today it is one of the wealthiest towns (per capita) in Spain. The church of **San Mateo** (open hours of services) on Plaza Nueva has a wonderfully over the top 18th-century octagonal *sagrario* chapel, whose central shrine is crammed with flying cherubs and exquisite plasterwork – it's one of the masterpieces of Andalucían baroque. Climb uphill to the **Sanctuario de la Virgen de Araceli**, where there is a bar selling excellent home-produced *charcuterie*, and wonderful views.

The A331 runs from Lucena south-east for 20 kilometres (12.5 miles) towards **Rute**. The appeal of the village's Moorish castle and baroque church is eclipsed by the attraction of the potent *anís* spirit that is distilled here. Many bodegas offer a taste, while the **Museo Anís** explains the manufacture and history of the spirit, followed by a chance to sample and buy the stuff at the end.

For energetic visitors there's a scenic 18-kilometre (11-mile) walk from Rute around the **Embalse de Iznájar** (the largest reservoir in Andalucía), and on to the lovely little town of Iznájar. **Iznájar** sits high above the reservoir, near the Granada province border, and has an attractive ruined **Alcazaba** dating from the eighth century, and the church of **Santiago** (open hours of services), built inside its walls in the 16th century; call at the Ayuntamiento to collect the key for both. Canoes and dinghies can be hired from the sailing club. A sleepy place today, Iznájar was the setting for an 1861 peasants' revolt against the landowners; inevitably, it was swiftly and brutally crushed.

Bodegas Alvear

Avda de María Auxiliadora 1, Montilla (957 66 40 14/www.alvear.es). **Open** *July, Aug, Jan, Feb* 10am-2pm Mon-Fri; (call in advance) 11am-2pm Sat. *Sept-Dec, Mar-June* 10am-2pm, 5-7pm Mon-Fri; 11am-2pm Sat. **Admission** *Mon-Fri* €2.95. *Sat* €3.95. **No credit cards.**

Casa Museo del Inca Garcilaso

C/Capitán Alonso de Varga 3, Montilla (957 65 24 62). **Open** *July, Aug* 10am-2pm Mon-Fri; 11am-2pm Sat, Sun. *Sept-June* 10am-2pm, 5-7pm Mon-Fri; 11am-2pm Sat, Sun. **Admission** free.

Museo Anís

Paseo del Fresno 2, Rute (957 53 81 43/54/www. museodelanis.com). **Open** *June-Aug* 8am-3pm Mon-Fri; (call in advance) 11am-2pm Sat, Sun. *Sept-May* 9am-2pm, 4-7pm Mon-Fri; 11am-2pm Sat, Sun. Ring bell if closed. **Admission** free.

Museo Arqueológico Municipal

C/Martín Belda 23, Cabra (957 52 01 10). **Open** 11am-2pm, 6-9pm Mon-Fri; 11am-2pm Sat. **Admission** free.

Museo Arqueológico Ulía

Plaza de la Constitución s/n, Montemayor (no phone). **Admission** free.

Where to stay & eat

In Aguilar de la Frontera, the basic but cheap **Hostal Queen III** (C/Pescaderías 6, off Plaza de San José, 957 66 02 22, double €40-€53, restaurant €) has a bar and a simple choice of food. For slightly more fancy Andalucían fare, try **Restaurante Guillermo** (C/Moralejo 47, 957 66 00 48, €). The popular **Gran Bar** (C/Andalucía 23, no phone, €) also serves tapas.

There are some cheap *hostales* in Montilla, but just outside town is the lovely eight-room **Finca Buytrón** (C/Gran Capitán 24, 957 65 01 52, www.fincabuytron.com, double €60), a homely, rural farmhouse dating back to 1567, which has an outdoor pool. For food, try the award-winning **Las Camachas** (Avda de Europa 3, 957 65 00 04, €€€), which serves fine local specialities and has a bargain *menú*.

In Lucena, the 28-room **Husa Santo Domingo** is housed in the converted convent of Santo Domingo (C/Juan Jiménez Cuenca 16, 957 51 11 00, www.husa.es, double €103). Much of the building's original character has been lost, but it's luxurious, in a predictable way.

The **María Luisa** (A331, km22, 957 53 80 96, www.zercahoteles.com, double €68.50-€74.90) is a good-value modern roadside hotel just south of Rute, with a small indoor pool.

Resources

Tourist information

Cabra *C/Santa Rosalía 2 (957 52 01 10/www. turismodecabra.es).* **Open** *June-Sept* 10am-1.30pm; 6-8.30pm Tue-Fri; 11am-2pm Sat, Sun. *Oct-May* 10am-1.30pm, 5-7pm Tue-Fri; 11am-2pm Sat, Sun.

Lucena *Castillo del Moral, Pasaje Cristo del Amor 1 (957 51 32 82/www.turlucena.com).* **Open** *Mid June-Sept* 9am-2pm, 6-10pm Tue-Fri; 11am-2pm, 7-9pm Sat, Sun. *Oct-mid June* 9am-2pm, 5-9pm Tue-Fri; 11am-2pm, 6-8pm Sat, Sun.

Montilla *C/Capitán Alonso de Vergas 3 (957 65 24 62/www.turismomontilla.com).* **Open** *July, Aug* 10am-2pm Mon-Fri; 11am-2pm Sat, Sun. *Sept-June* 10am-2pm, 5-7pm Mon-Fri; 11am-2pm Sat, Sun.

Priego de Córdoba & around

From Córdoba, the N432 leads south-east along what has been dubbed the *Ruta del Aceite* (Oil Route), towards the heights of the Sierra

Priego de Córdoba.

Subbética. After ten or so minutes' driving, the stunning fortress of **Torres Cabrera** lurches into view above the wheat plains and olive groves, setting the tone for further attractive Moorish-castle-topped towns.

Twenty kilometres (12.5 miles) south-east of Castro is **Baena**, famed for the quality of its olive oil. For those interested in ancient oil production, the **Museo del Olivar y el Aceite** is worth a visit, as is the **Museo Arqueológico** (also known as the Museo Histórico Municipal). The same building also houses the **Museo de Semana Santa** (currently closed for renovation), which explains Baena's unusual Easter ritual, in which hundreds of brightly dressed drummers in plumed helmets, divided into rival teams known as the *coliblancos* and the *colinegros*, try to outdo each other in volume and stamina. Elsewhere, check out the 18th-century arcaded *almacén* (warehouse) on Plaza de la Constitución, which houses a cultural centre and one of the best tapas bars in town.

Beyond Baena, the mountains of the **Parque Natural de la Sierra Subbética** (320 square kilometres/124 square miles) beckon, and the A316 climbs up to the most picturesque village in the region. **Zuheros** is a cluster of beautiful whitewashed houses clinging to the cliffs, topped by a Moorish castle with spectacular views. Nearby, **La Cueva de los Murciélagos** (Cave of the Bats) doesn't actually shelter any bats, but you'll see some incredible stalactites and stalagmites on the guided tour, which describes the neolithic paintings and human remains that were found here. The caves are approached via a hair-raisingly spectacular road up from Zuheros following the Canyon de Baillón to the rocky, wild scrub landscape that is a dominant feature of the Subbética.

Nearby **Luque** is also very pretty, with a castle dating back to the ninth century perched high above the town. Its lively central square is overlooked by the handsome honey-coloured Renaissance façade of its church, **La Asunción**. From here, wind your way south to Priego de Córdoba.

Priego de Córdoba is a fine town with a whiff of sophistication about it, and sits on a rocky outcrop looking south-west up to the highest mountain in the province, **La Tiñosa** (1,570 metres/5,150 feet). The town's glorious churches (all open 11am-1pm, 5-7pm daily) have earned Priego the soubriquet of capital of Córdoban baroque architecture. The main ones to check out are the church of **La Asunción** (on Plaza Abad Palomino), with its handsome sacristy and golden balcony, created in 1784, and the church of **La Aurora** (Carrera de Álvarez), which has a wedding-cake façade. The magnificence of Priego's churches was made possible by the boom in silk production in the town during the 18th century. The main monument to the industry is the **Fuente del Rey** on C/Río, a fountain with 139 water spouts surrounding a statue of Neptune.

Beyond the much-altered Moorish castle lies a maze of narrow winding alleys, bedecked with geraniums, that form the delightful **Barrio de la Villa**, dating back to Moorish times. The lanes are united by the Balcón de Aldarve, an elevated promenade with magnificent views. The Paseo de Colón, a quiet shady walkway and ornamental garden, shares the same view. For a better understanding of Priego's history, check out the local **Museo Histórico Municipal**, which displays local paleolithic, Roman and Moorish remains.

A few kilometres west from Priego is the small village of **Carcabuey** with its Gothic-Renaissance church of **La Asunción** (open times of services). Further south you'll pass through some of the prettiest scenery in the Subbética en route to the small village of **Los Villares**, where there are lots of signposted walks to suit all abilities.

To the east of Priego is the little town of **Almedinilla**, recently thrust into the limelight with the discovery of a large Roman villa, **El Ruedo** (Ctra A340, km84.7, 957 703 317, admission €2.20, closed Mon & Tue).

Cueva de los Murciélagos

Zuheros (957 69 45 45/www.cuevadelosmurcielagos.com). **Open** (guided tours only) *Apr-Sept* 12.30pm, 5.30pm Mon-Fri; 11am, 12.30pm, 2pm, 5pm, 6.30pm Sat, Sun. *Oct-Mar* 12.30pm, 4.30pm Mon-Fri; 11am, 12.30pm, 2pm, 4pm, 5.30pm Sat, Sun. **Admission** €4.80. **No credit cards.**

Call a week in advance to book.

Museo Arqueológico

Mirador, Zuheros (957 69 45 45). **Open** (tours on the hour) *Apr-Sept* 10am-2pm, 5-7pm daily. *Oct-May* 10am-2pm; 4-6pm daily. **Admission** €1.80 (includes guided tour of castle). **No credit cards.**

Museo Arqueológico

Casa de la Tercia, C/Santo Domingo de Henares 5, off Plaza de la Constitución, Baena (957 66 50 20). **Open** 11am-2pm, 6-8pm Tue-Sun. **Admission** free.

Museo del Olivar y el Aceite

C/Cañada 7, Baena (957 69 16 41/www.museoaceite.com). **Open** *Apr-Sept* 11am-2pm, 4-6pm Tue-Sat; 11am-2pm Sun. *Oct-Mar* 11am-2pm, 6pm-8pm Tue-Sat; 11am-2pm Sun. **Admission** €2. **No credit cards.**

Museo Histórico Municipal

Carrera de las Monjas 16, Priego de Córdoba (957 54 09 47). **Open** 10am-1.30pm, 6-8.30pm Tue-Fri; 10am-1.30pm, 5-7.30pm Sat; 10am-1.30pm Sun. **Admission** free.

Nuñez de Prado

Avda de Cervantes 15, Baena (957 67 01 41). **Open** *July-Sept* 8am-3pm Mon-Fri. *Oct-June* 9am-2pm, 4-6.30pm. **Admission** free.

Phone 3-4 days ahead to arrange a tour.

Where to stay & eat

The best hotel in Baena is **La Casa del Grande** (Avda de Cervantes 35, 957 67 19 05, double €83-€103, restaurant €€), a grand, faintly Gothic pile, with large, airy rooms and a very good restaurant. For a gastronomic treat, eat under the stone-vaulted ceiling at **Mesón Casa del Monte** (Plaza de la Constitución s/n, 957 67 16 75, closed Mon, €€). Try the *habas 'mata' con jamón* (beans, ham and eggs).

In Zuheros, the modern **Hotel Zuhaira** (C/Mirador 10, 957 69 46 93, www.zuheros.com, double €54-€68, restaurant €€) is well priced and situated, with a good restaurant.

Three kilometres (two miles) north-west of Priego is **Hotel Huerta de las Palomas** (CP99, km3, 957 72 03 05, www.zercahoteles.com, double €85.60-€98.40), a tranquil spot in the heart of the Sierra, with a pool, sauna and first-class restaurant (€€); it's an ideal base for hiking. In Priego itself there are some basic hotels, including the good-value **Hostal Rafi** (C/Isabel la Católica 4, 957 54 07 49, www.hostalrafi.net, double €38.50-€42.80), which has clean, air-conditioned rooms and a restaurant/bar. The best restaurant in town is **Restaurante Río** (C/Río 5, 957 54 00 74, closed dinner Tue and all Mon, €€), where the speciality is *collejas* (a type of chard) and an interesting English translation of the menu (numerous dishes feature 'scum'). Another top spot for food is **Balcón de Adarve** (Paseo de Colombia 36, 957 54 70 75, closed Mon, €€-€€€), which has a tapas bar and terrace restaurant with great views. Inside the Barrio de la Villa the quiet Plaza Santa Ana has a couple of tapas bars with tables outside.

South-west of Priego de Córdoba on the CV220 is the **Posada la Niña Margarita** (Aldea Los Villares, 5km from Carcabuey, 957 70 40 54, www.casasdelasubbetica.com, double €60), a delightful old house with a pool, surrounded by self-catering apartments; it makes another great base for walking.

Resources

Tourist information

Baena C/Virrey del Pino 8 *(957 67 17 57/www.ayto-baena.es).* **Open** 10am-2pm, 5-8pm Tue-Sun.

Parque Natural de la Sierra Subbética *Centro de Visitantes, A340, km57, Cabra (957 33 40 34).* **Open** *Apr-Sept* 10am-2pm Wed-Fri; 10am-2pm, 6-8pm Sat, Sun. *Oct-Mar* 10am-2pm Wed-Fri; 10am-2pm, 4-6pm Sat, Sun.

Priego de Córdoba *Carerra de Monjas 1 (957 70 06 25/www.turismodepriego.com).* **Open** 10am-1.30pm, 4.30-6.30pm Tue-Sat; 10am-3pm Sun.

Zuheros *C/Nueva 1 (957 69 45 45).* **Open** *Apr-Sept* 10am-2pm, 5-7pm daily. *Oct-May* 10am-2pm; 4-6pm daily.

Getting there

By bus

Buses run from Córdoba to the main towns in the region, but few head in to the north. For information, call 957 40 40 40.

By train

Six trains a day run from Córdoba to Seville via Palma del Río. Trains also run south from Córdoba twice a day via Montilla (40mins), Aguilar de la Frontera (45mins) and Puente-Genil (1hr). There are no rail services in the north of Córdoba province.

Jaén Province

Features

Maps

Jaén Province

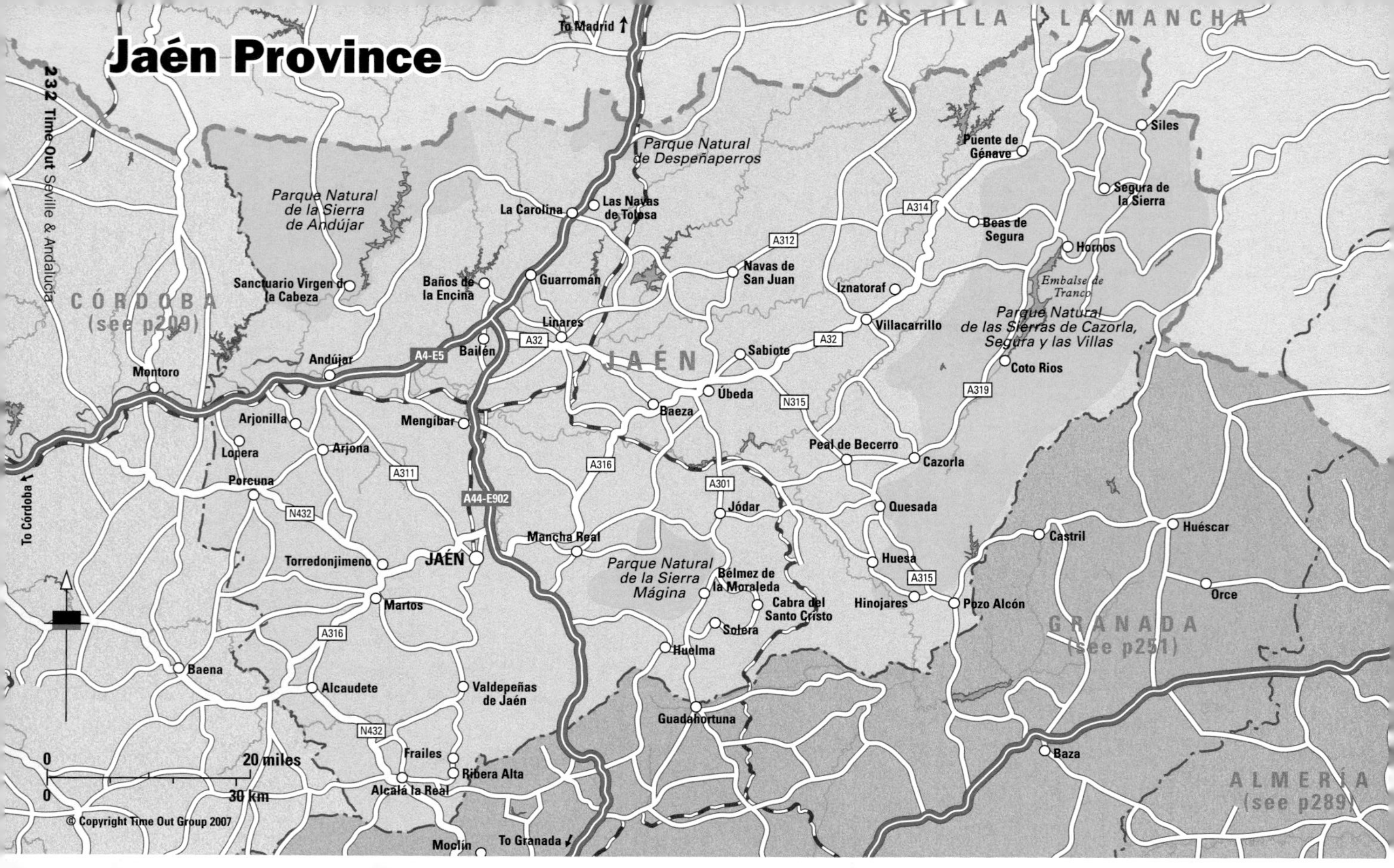

Introduction

Acres of olive groves and two evocative Renaissance towns distinguish this little-visited province.

Despite being the traditional entry point into Andalucía from Castilla (via the Despeñaperros pass), the north-eastern province of Jaén is one of the least known parts of the region. As its surfeit of castles testifies, this was the front line between Christian and Moorish forces for centuries. Defined to the north by the brooding Sierra Morena, and to the east by the more appealing Sierra de Segura, the majority of the province is a hypnotic rolling expanse of olive fields. The precariously monocultural economy depends almost solely on olive cultivation, and nowhere in Andalucía is the distinction between the wealthy minority and the poor majority so stark. Few tourists come to Jaén, and most of those who do stop only at the spectacular Renaissance towns of Úbeda and Baeza. Yet, for those who care to look, the province offers a wealth of historical, cultural and natural attractions.

JAÉN CITY

The provincial capital, though largely modern and not immediately engaging, is a lively town with a distinctive character. Backed by a dramatically sited castle, Jaén has a Moorish core of winding streets, classic tapas bars, and a couple of excellent museums.

The best...

Architecture
Baeza (*p242*); **Jaén City** (*pp234-36*); **Úbeda** (*p245*).

Castles
Alcalá La Real (*p237*); **Baños de la Encina** (*p241*); **Jaén City** (*p234*); **Segura de la Sierra** (*p249*).

Food & drink
Baeza (*p242*); **Úbeda** (*p245*).

Mountains
Sierras de Cazorla, Segura y las Villas (*p249*); **Sierra Mágina** (*p238*).

Villages
Cazorla (*p249*); **Hornos** (*p250*); **Iznatoraf** (*p249*); **Sabiote** (*p248*); **Segura de la Sierra** (*p249*).

SOUTH AND NORTH OF JAÉN

A monotonous yet weirdly intoxicating eternity of undulating olive fields stretches west into Córdoba province and north to the foothills of the Sierra Morena. Its uniform appearance belies the fact that this is a region of immense archaeological richness and diversity, and was a key battleground – both in the early stages of the Reconquista and in the Spanish Civil War. The southern part of Jaén province is a land of many olives and few visitors, with the hills of the Sierra Sur de Jaén and the Sierra Mágina providing the major scenic draws.

EAST OF JAÉN

The neighbouring frozen-in-time Renaissance towns of Baeza and Úbeda are the most popular draw in the province, and deservedly so. Their embarrassment of 16th-century architectural riches makes them two of the most charming and unique towns in the whole of Spain, and yet they have somehow escaped the coach parties. Not far away lies the huge extent of the mountainous Parque Natural de las Sierras de Cazorla, Segura y Las Villas, a wonderfully diverse natural playground.

Jaén City

Sleepy, dusty provincial city with a surprising wealth of sights.

The regional capital doesn't get much positive press from guidebooks. And, approaching through its tatty, depressed suburbs, it's not hard to see why. Unemployment here, as in much of the rest of the province, is high, and 20th-century development has done Jaén few aesthetic favours. Yet the city rewards those who aren't put off by first impressions, and has attractions enough to occupy a day.

The hulking mass of the outsize cathedral and the impressive form of the Castillo de Santa Catalina dominate Jaén, while all around stretches an endless ocean of olive trees. Jaén's economy has been intimately connected with *aceitunas* (olives) since Roman times. Under the Moors this was a key staging post between Castilla and the rest of Andalucía (the name derives from *Geen*, meaning 'caravan route'), but, when the city fell to Fernando III in 1246, its Moorish ruler was forced to flee to Granada (where he founded the Nasrid dynasty), and a long period of decline followed.

Jaén has yet to recover, and a faint air of desperation can be sensed in many parts of the city. Sadly, things are unlikely to improve in the near future now that the European Commission has slashed subsidies for olive oil production. At least the opening of a university in the 1990s has livened up the nightlife.

Sightseeing

In a nutshell, Jaén's must-see sights are the cathedral, the castle, the Arab baths and the Iberian sculptures in the Museo Provincial.

The **Catedral de Jaén** (**photo** *p236*), built on the site of the town mosque, dwarfs the surrounding buildings. Construction began in the mid 16th century under Andrés de Vandelvira, though it was not completed until the late 18th century. The exuberant west façade (incorporating superb statuary by *sevillano* Pedro Roldán) dates from the late 17th century, and contrasts with the dark and somewhat forbidding atmosphere within. Don't miss the fine late-baroque carvings in the choir.

The streets leading from the cathedral towards the church of **San Ildefonso** (953 19 03 46, open 8.30am-noon daily) are some of Jaén's liveliest at night. The church, founded in the 13th century, but rebuilt and altered many times since, is dedicated to Jaén's patron saint.

Just north-west of here is Jaén's main square, the unimpressive, incoherent Plaza de la Constitución, from which the wide Paseo de la Estación heads straight north towards the train station. On the Paseo's western side, just after a hideous monument to the battles of Las Navas de Tolosa and Bailén, is the **Museo Provincial**. Built in 1920 into the 16th-century remains of an old granary and the church of San Miguel, the museum's ground floor is devoted to archaeological finds from the surrounding area. Upstairs is the **Museo de Bellas Artes**, containing an amusing collection of 19th- and 20th-century works, which veer from the titillating to the ridiculous. In a separate room there's a Picasso drawing, surrounded by works by his near contemporary, Jaén-born Manuel Ángeles Ortiz. However, the real reason to visit the Museo Provincial is to admire the best collection of fifth-century BC Iberian sculptures in Spain. These luminous, vivacious, yet exquisitely controlled pieces were discovered in 1975 at Obulco, outside the town of Porcuna in the west of the province. The sculptures can be found in the basement of the Sala de Exposiciones Grabado, to the right of the main building.

North-west of the cathedral, the winding streets of the old Moorish town climb the lower slopes of Santa Catalina hill – this is the most pleasant area for strolling. Here you'll find the **Palacio de Villadompardo**, a late-16th-century building encompassing the superb 11th-century **Baños Árabes** (Arab Baths – the largest to survive in Spain), the enjoyable **Museo Internacional de Arte Naïf** (International Museum of Naïve Art) and the **Museo de Artes y Costumbres Populares** (Museum of Popular Arts and Customs).

A little further up the street is the **Real Monasterio de Santo Domingo** (953 23 85 00, closed Sat & Sun), a 14th-century monastery built over a Moorish palace, which has one of the loveliest cloisters in the city. The building has had a number of incarnations, and now houses the town's archives.

Just north-west, in the Plaza de la Magdalena, is the church of **La Magdalena** (953 19 03 09), again, built over a mosque and reputedly the oldest church in the city. The bell tower was the minaret and you can still see the courtyard where the faithful performed their ablutions.

You can climb from the old town up to the **Castillo de Santa Catalina**, but it's long and arduous. More realistic is to drive up to enjoy the views. There's been a castle here since the 13th century, though it has been remodelled many times since. Even when the castle is closed, you can park in the *parador* car park and walk beside the walls to the end of the ridge, which is dominated by a huge cross. Part of the castle is now Jaén's finest hotel – stop in for a drink.

Castillo de Santa Catalina

953 12 07 33. **Open** *May-Sept* 10am-2pm, 5-9pm Tue-Sun. *Oct-Apr* 10am-2pm, 3.30-7.30pm Tue-Sun. **Admission** €3; €1-€2 concessions. **No credit cards. Map** p235 A1.

Catedral de Jaén

Plaza Santa María (953 23 42 33/www.catedraldejaen.es). **Open** *Cathedral* Apr-June 8.30am-1pm, 5-8pm Mon-Sat; 9am-1pm, 6-8pm Sun. July-Sept 8.30am-1pm, 5-8pm Mon-Sat; 9am-1pm Sun. Oct-Mar 8.30am-1pm, 4-7pm Mon-Sat; 9am-1pm, 5-7pm Sun. *Museum* 10.30am-1pm, 5-8pm Tue-Sun. **Admission** €3. **No credit cards. Map** p235 A1/2.

Museo Provincial & Museo de Bellas Artes

Paseo de la Estación 27 (953 25 06 00). **Open** 2.30-8.30pm Tue; 9am-8.30pm Wed-Sat; 9am-2.30pm Sun. **Admission** €1.50; free with EU passport. **Map** p235 off B2.

Palacio de Villadompardo

Plaza Santa Luisa de Marillac s/n (953 24 80 68). **Open** 9am-8pm Tue-Fri; 9.30am-2.30pm Sat, Sun. **Admission** free. **Map** p235 B1.

Where to eat & drink

The main areas to head for are the streets north of the cathedral (particularly C/Arco de Consuelo) and the parallel streets running east from the cathedral to the church of San Ildefonso. The nicest spot for sitting outside in the centre is **Bar El Pósito** on the lively Plaza del Pósito.

Casa Vicente

C/Francisco Martín Mora s/n (953 23 28 16). **Open** 1pm-5pm, 8pm-midnight daily. **Average** €€. **No credit cards. Map** p235 A1 ❶

Located in a fine mansion close to the cathedral, this attractive old restaurant specialises in trad local dishes, such as *pastel de carne de caza* (game pie).

La Gamba de Oro

C/Nueva 5 (953 24 17 46). **Open** 11am-4pm, 8pm-midnight Mon, Tue, Thur-Sun. **Average** €€. **Credit** V. **Map** p235 A2 ❷

It's not much to look at, but the locals flock to this bar-restaurant for the best seafood in town, including spider crab, oysters and *quisquillas de Motril.*

El Gorrión

C/Arco de Consuelo 7 (953 23 20 00). **Open** noon-4pm, 8pm-2am Tue-Sun. Closed 4wks July-Aug. **No credit cards. Map** p235 A1 ❸

This famous old bar opened in 1888 and looks as though it hasn't changed since. If you ask the bartender, he'll be pleased to take you down to the cellar to view the splendidly gruesome remains of a leg of *jamón*, put into a glass case after World War I.

Taberna La Manchega

C/Bernardo López 8 (953 23 21 92). **Open** 10am-2pm, 8pm-midnight daily. Closed Aug. **No credit cards. Map** p235 A1 ❹

A lively tapas bar that's been around for over a century. The first-rate, ultra-cheap food includes great baked potatoes and a huge range of *bocadillos*.

Taberna Pepón

C/Doctor Eduardo Arroyo 12 (953 23 63 68). **Open** noon-4pm, 7.30pm-midnight Mon-Sat. Closed July. **No credit cards. Map** p235 A1 ❺

Another reliable old bar that's full of character, with the requisite *jamones* hanging from the ceiling beside the strip lighting.

La Viña

C/Maestra 8 (953 23 96 60). **Open** noon-4pm, 8.30pm-midnight Mon-Sat. **Credit** MC, V. **Map** p235 A1 ❻

A bustling bar-restaurant with all the tapas you'd expect and some slightly less so, such as crayfish sliced and layered with mango. Pavement tables attract a surcharge.

Where to stay

There's scant accommodation in Jaén, and what there is – with the notable exception of the *parador* – tends to be characterless. At the bottom end of the scale there are a number of *pensiones*, including **Hostal Renfe** (Paseo de la Estación s/n, 953 27 47 04, www.hostalrenfejaen.cjb.net, double €48.15, map p235 A/B2), which is in the train station, and **Carlos V** (Avda Madrid 4, 953 22 20 91, double €32, map B2), close to the bus station.

Hostal La Española

C/Bernardo López 9 (953 23 02 54). **Rates** €17-€22 single; €32-€42 double; €43-€54 triple. **No credit cards. Map** p235 A1 ❼

This creaky, crumbling but characterful *hostal* is the only place to stay in the old town. It's within staggering distance of some of Jaén's best tapas bars.

Hotel Condestable Iranzo

Paseo de la Estación 32 (953 22 28 00/www.condestable.com). **Rates** €72.70-€82.40 single; €92-€103.80 double; €147.65-€158.35 suite. **Credit** AmEx, MC, V. **Map** p235 B2 ❽

This three-star near the Museo Provincial has a big flashy lobby, comfortable rooms and, er, bingo.

Hotel Europa

Plaza de Belén 1 (953 22 27 00/www.gremiodehospedaje.com). **Rates** €45 single; €55 double; €68 triple. **Credit** AmEx, DC, MC, V. **Map** p235 B2 ❾

Part of the Husa chain, this three-star offers plenty of comfort and smart communal facilities.

Parador Castillo de Santa Catalina

953 23 00 00/www.parador.es. **Rates** €94.15-€101.85 single; €133.75-€144.45 double. **Credit** AmEx, DC, MC, V. **Map** p235 A1 ❿

By far the best place to stay in town, with stone corridors, massive vaulted ceilings, suits of armour, vast fireplaces and hanging tapestries in the public rooms. All the usual *parador* comfort, plus rooms with terraces and some of the most spectacular views you'll ever enjoy. A restaurant and pool too.

Catedral de Jaén. *See p234.*

Hotel Xauen

Plaza Deán Mazas 3 (953 24 07 89/www.hotelxauenjaen.com). **Rates** (incl breakfast) €53.50 single; €53.50-€85.60 double. **Credit** MC, V. **Map** p235 A2 ⓫

This three-star is the most central of Jaén's hotels (just off Plaza de la Constitución), though it has little else to recommend it. Rooms are smallish and no better than functional.

Resources

Internet

Cyber Cu@k, Adarves Bajos 24 (953 19 06 16). **Open** *Mid June-mid Sept* 6pm-midnight daily. *Mid Sept-mid June* 5.30-11.30pm Mon-Fri; 6pm-midnight Sat, Sun. **Map** p235 A2.

Police station

C/Arquitecto Berges 11 (953 29 51 17). **Map** p235 B2.

Post office

Plaza de los Jardinillos (953 24 78 00). **Open** 8.30am-8.30pm Mon-Fri; 9.30am-2pm Sat. **Map** p235 A/B1.

Tourist information

C/Maestra 13 bajo (953 24 26 24/19 04 55/www.aytojaen.es). **Open** 9am-7.30pm Mon-Fri; 10am-2pm Sat, Sun. **Map** p235 A1.

Getting there

By bus

The bus station is at Plaza Coca de la Piñera 6 (953 25 01 06, map B2). There are around 3 buses a day to Seville (5hrs), 2 to Almería (4hrs 30mins), 8 to Córdoba (2hrs), 14 to Granada (2hrs), 6 to Madrid (6hrs), 4 to Málaga (4hrs), 14 to Úbeda and Baeza (1hr 30mins/1hr) and 2 to Cazorla (2hrs).

By train

The railway station is on Plaza de Jaén de la Paz (also known as Paseo de la Estación, 902 24 02 02) on the northern side of the town (map off B2) – a couple of kilometres from the centre. There is 1 direct train a day to Córdoba (1hr 35mins), 1 to Seville (3hrs) and 2 to Madrid (4hrs 10mins).

South & North of Jaén

Obscure corners of Jaén province that are short on tourists but long on history.

Alcalá La Real.

South of Jaén

Few visitors stop in southern Jaén. At first glance it seems little more than one vast expanse of olive fields, cut through by a couple of speedy roads designed to take you somewhere more interesting. Yet it's an area that rewards the curious and offers plentiful insight into the real Andalucía, a world away from the *costas* and other tourist centres.

Its urban hub is **Alcalá La Real**, 50 kilometres (31 miles) north-west of Granada, and around 70 kilometres (44 miles) south of Jaén. The escarpment from which the modern town descends has been inhabited since prehistoric times and was a strategically key Moorish stronghold, protecting the northern approaches to Granada. Christian forces took the town in 1341 (from which time the 'Real' – Royal – of its name dates). The citadel, known as the **Fortaleza de la Mota**, is well worth a visit, and contains a mélange of ruins and structures dating from the 12th century to the 16th. At the highest level, the Moorish keep contains a museum of local archaeological finds. The Golden Age sculptor Juan Martínez Montañés was born in Alcalá in 1568, and is commemorated by a statue in the attractive old town square.

Around 28 kilometres (18 miles) north-west of here is **Alcaudete**, topped by another Moorish castle (closed for restoration). Like many places in Jaén, it's an uneasy mix of wealth (for the few) and poverty (for the many). During the winter olive harvest there's work for all; the rest of the year there's chronic unemployment, and flat-capped men hang around listlessly outside the shuttered mansions of the olive oil barons.

North of Alcaudete, and 24 kilometres (15 miles) west of Jaén city, **Martos** is another centre of olive oil production, backed by a ruined castle atop a huge outcrop of rock. In the first week of December, the olive harvest is celebrated here by the four-day **Fiesta de la Aceituna**.

Between Alcalá La Real and Jaén city lies the beautiful but little-visited **Sierra Sur de Jaén**, a wild yet intimate expanse of wooded hills and valleys (one containing an isolated hideaway used by superstar *matadores* such as Jesulín de Ubrique). In recent years, the pristine scenery has been marred somewhat by the erection of huge power-generating windmills.

The workaday, friendly village of **Frailes**, 15 kilometres (nine miles) east of Alcalá, is part-time home to the British writer Michael Jacobs, author of *Andalucía*, the best general book on the region. Jacobs' wonderful book, *The Factory of Light*, tells the story of Frailes, its inhabitants and a remarkable cinematic event that he masterminded here in 2001, when the village's abandoned but perfectly preserved cinema was reopened for one final performance, attracting the ageing Spanish film star Sara Montiel and the national press. It also became the subject of a short film entitled *Rewind: El último cuplé*.

North of Frailes a long, slow road winds through stunning virgin hills to Jaén city via the sizeable village of **Valdepeñas de Jaén**. At the latter, don't miss a wonderful short walk up the **Paraje de las Chorreras** – a cool, verdant rocky gorge through which a crystal stream descends. It's not much more than half-an-hour's stroll to the top and back again (look for the sign on the south side of Valdepeñas next to the Muebles Almendra furniture shop).

The Sierra Sur has a strong local tradition of mysticism and faith-healing (documented as far back as the 15th century), which continues today. The most distinctive of the area's healers are the so-called *santones* or 'saints', who are thought of as intermediaries between the earthly and supernatural realms. Unrecognised by the Catholic church, but famous locally for having worked countless miracles, they have powers that are said to be hereditary.

The most revered of all the local saints is the 'Santo Custodio', who, though he died in 1961, is still the object of a huge (if partially secretive) cult. He lived all his life in the now-prosperous hamlet of **La Hoya del Salobral** – to reach it turn right four kilometres (2.5 miles) north of Frailes on the Noalejo road. Follow the sign marked 'Ermita' to the top of a rocky outcrop that has spectacular views of the Sierra Nevada. In recent years the Catholic Church has built a sanctuary to the Virgen de la Cabeza here, which, on the last Sunday of April, attracts up to 10,000 pilgrims. The pilgrimage is really a disguised homage to the Santo Custodio, who came up here to pray in a small rock shelter. This shelter, marked by a cross garlanded with flowers, is reached by steps to the right of the sanctuary, and is filled with offerings. The Santo Custodio's house stands in the main square of La Hoya del Salobral, and is technically open to visitors every morning; it's a fascinating example of an almost unchanged rural dwelling from around 1900.

Just east of Jaén city is the rugged **Parque Natural de la Sierra Mágina**. Though easily accessible, this mountainous park sees few visitors, and 200 square kilometres (80 square miles) provide wonderful walking territory without much chance of bumping into anyone else. The town of **Huelma** is a possible base, and there are a number of other interesting places worthy of a visit, such as **Solera** (which offers fabulous views of the Sierra), **Bélmez de la Moraleda**, with a ruined Renaissance castle, and handsome **Cabra del Santo Cristo**, named after a much venerated image of Christ that was being transported from Burgos to Guadix when it was intercepted by the locals of Cabra, who decided they liked the image so much that they wouldn't let it go any further.

Fortaleza de la Mota

Alcalá La Real (953 58 20 77). **Open** *June-Sept* 10.30am-1.30pm, 5-8pm daily. *Oct-May* 10.30am-1.30pm, 3.30-6.30pm daily. **Admission** €1.50; €1 concessions; free under-12s. **No credit cards**.

Where to stay & eat

The area is so far off the tourist trail that accommodation options are few. In Alcalá, the best choice is the two-star **Hospedería Zacatin** (C/Pradillo 2, 953 58 05 68, www.hospederiazacatin.com, double €36-€40), which has a decent restaurant (€).

In Frailes, the somewhat eccentric **Hostal Ardales** (C/Avenida 18, 953 59 35 08, double €40) is above the Aztec-inspired village disco, so can get noisy at weekends. Wonderful, simple home cooking (particularly goat, as the name implies) is available in **El Choto** (C/Deán Mudarra 24, 953 59 32 85, closed Thur, €). The biggest culinary surprise hereabouts is the **Rey de Copas** in the village of Ribera Alta, next to Frailes (Ctra de Frailes 27, 953 59 33 05, closed Tue, €€-€€€). An unassuming frontage leads into an elegant dining room where chef Juan Matías del Moral Garrido serves up startlingly

World power

The small, conservative and still relatively little-visited town of Alcalá la Real is the most unlikely sounding venue for Andalucía's leading annual festival of world music, **Etnosur** (www.etnosur.com). Inspired by WOMAD, a charismatic local journalist, Pedro Melguizo, conceived the festival in 1996. Over the intervening years he has assembled a remarkable team of assistants whose idealism and passionate musical tastes are combined with a professionalism that is no less impressive. Unlike all other festivals of this stature, its concerts are entirely free of charge. It also prides itself on having no need for publicity: word of mouth alone has created a huge and loyal fan base.

For three days, usually coinciding with the penultimate weekend in July, Alcalá la Real is enlivened by the sounds of constant drumming, and by an invasion of hippies from all over Spain and beyond. During the early years of the festival, the town's staid, middle-class population regularly complained about so many New Age visitors, who camp throughout the town, bathe nude in local pools, and smoke so much pot that the festival has come to be known as 'Etnoporro' (*porro* being the Spanish word for 'joint'). However, an extraordinary tolerance has now built up between townspeople and hippies; one of the many noteworthy features of this easygoing festival is the broad mix of people and age groups.

During the day you and your children can sign up for free workshops devoted to activities as diverse as yoga or flamenco rhythm, or you can join the strolling crowds in Alcalá's shaded *paseo* to be entertained by musicians, story-tellers, clowns, magicians and other street performers. After a siesta come the first of the day's serious concerts, which take place within the keep of the town's dominating and magnificent citadel. By the time the sun is setting, most people will be making their way down to the site of the town's Tuesday market, which serves as the festival's main enclosure, and contains two stages facing each other across a vast and generally packed area.

Groups from places as far apart as New Zealand, Brazil, Poland, Colombia, India, Turkey and Ghana have all been persuaded to perform here, and have included some of the major names in the field of world music, including the Indian percussionist Trilok Gurtu, the Sami singer Mari Boine, Polish klezmer group Kroke, Cameroonian bassist and singer Richard Bona, the avant-garde flamenco artist Diego Carrasco, and the pioneering keyboard player and composer Joe Zawinul. Should you ever tire of the music, you can always wander off into the section devoted to stalls selling ethnic food, or else hang out at one of the many animated open-air bars, drinking from one of the provocatively inscribed Etnosur cups that have now become collectors' items. The show goes on until dawn.

innovative cuisine using top-quality local ingredients. Opening hours aren't reliable; phone to check.

In Huelma, the **Angel** (Ctra La Cerradura-Huelma s/n, 953 39 08 70, double €30) has 27 decent rooms. In Cabra del Santo Cristo, **Casa Herminia** (C/Moya 12, 953 39 75 06, closed 1st 2wks Sept, €), located in a converted cinema, does an excellent home-made partridge pâté and a good lunch menu.

Resources

Tourist information

Parque Natural de la Sierra Mágina *Centro de Visitantes 'Castillo de Jódar', A301, km24, Jódar (953 78 76 56).* **Open** *May-Sept* 10am-2pm Thur, Fri; 10am-2pm, 6-8pm Sat, Sun. *Oct-Mar* 10am-2pm Thur, Fri; 10am-2pm, 4-6pm Sat, Sun.

Getting there

By bus

Alsina Graells (www.alsinagraells.es) runs 10 buses a day (fewer at weekends) between Granada and Alcalá (45mins-1hr), 2 a day to Alcaudete (1hr) and 1 a day to Cabra (1hr). There are 4 a day Mon-Fri and 1 on Sat & Sun (Autocares Contreras, www.autocarescontreras.com) between Jaén and Alcalá.

North of Jaén

At first glance it doesn't look much, but the friendly little town of **Porcuna**, close to the border with Córdoba province (just off the A306) has hidden depths. In Iberian times it was known as Obulco, and just north of the town at Cerrillo Blanco a funeral site was uncovered that contained possibly the finest Iberian-era sculptures yet found in Spain; it is now open as the **Parque Arqueológico de Cerrillo Blanco**. Although the original sculptures are housed in the Museo Provincial in Jaén (*see p234*), a couple of replicas can be seen in a small museum (www.museodeobulco.com) in Porcuna's *ayuntamiento*, and there are further interesting archaeological finds in the recently restored 15th-century **Torre de Boabdil**. The tower was once part of Porcuna's all-but-vanished fortifications, and, in 1485, acted as prison for the last Moorish king of Granada, Boabdil, following his capture after the Battle of Lucena.

Porcuna's other points of interest include the late 19th-century church of **Nuestra Señora de la Asunción** (open hours of services), which contains paintings by the much-loved Córdoban peddler of kitsch, Julio Romero de Torres, and what is probably the region's oddest attraction, the **Casa de Piedra** (House of Stone), designed and built entirely by hand in self-quarried stone between 1931 and 1960 by the frankly unhinged Antonio Aguilera, who embodied the Francoist ideals of iron will and unbending hard work.

Ten kilometres (six miles) north of Porcuna is the smaller town of **Lopera**, centred around a Moorish castle (closed to the public) and enjoying fine views over olive groves. At one time there were ten *bodegas* in Lopera – only one remains: the atmospherically cobwebby **Bodega Herruzo** (C/Doctor Fleming), which does tastings of the local sweet wines. The town is chiefly of interest, however, as a key Civil War site – it was here that the English writers John Cornford and Ralph Fox were killed; bunkers and trenches still scar the surrounding countryside.

The largest settlement in this north-western corner of Jaén is **Andújar**, 45 kilometres (28 miles) from the provincial capital. It's a busy, likeable, if not particularly picturesque town of Roman origin, sitting at the foot of the Sierra Morena. A much-restored bridge over the Guadalquivir river dates back to the time of Trajan. On the Plaza Santa María a medieval bell tower now houses the tourist office, while opposite is the 13th-century church of **Santa María**. Inside is an outstanding painting by El Greco, *Christ on the Mount of Olives*, as well as an *Immaculate Conception* by Pacheco, Velázquez's teacher.

North of Andújar, the remote and little-visited **Parque Natural de la Sierra de Andújar** (740 square kilometres/285 square miles) stretches into the Sierra Morena mountains. Hunting, cattle farming, bee-keeping and the production of cork are the area's traditional activities, while its inaccessibility provides sanctuary for the likes of Imperial eagles. Once a year (in April) the peace is broken by the **Romería de la Virgen de la Cabeza** (*see p49*), one of Andalucía's largest pilgrimages, when

Baños de la Encina. *See p241.*

thousands travel to the Sanctuario Virgen de la Cabeza, 31 kilometres (19 miles) north of Andújar. The mountain setting is superb, though the original shrine (founded in the 13th century) is long gone and the current sanctuary is a bleak Franco-era structure. This was the site of a famous siege during the Civil War, when 250 Nationalist Guardia Civil held out for nine months in 1936-37 against a Republican army that eventually numbered 20,000.

From Andújar, the motorway to Madrid skirts the foothills of the Sierra Morena, passing the charming town of **Baños de la Encina**, just to the north, which is dominated by one of the best preserved Moorish castles in Andalucía, the elliptical **Castillo de Burgalimar**. Completed in AD 968 (though the large keep was added in the 13th and 14th centuries), the castle is entered through a double-horseshoe arch, and the battlements that link its 14 square towers can be climbed. The village itself is an appealing spot for a night's stay, and contains a number of fine *palacios* and churches, including the **Ermita de Jesús de Llano**, which has a wonderfully over-the-top baroque shrine. Knock and ask one of the nuns to show you in.

Casa de Piedra

Paseo de Jesús s/n, Porcuna (953 54 41 77). **Open** *Mid June-mid Sept* 9am-2pm, 4-9pm daily. *Mid Sept-mid June* 9am-2pm, 3-6pm daily. **Admission** €2. **No credit cards**.

Castillo de Burgalimar

Baños de la Encina (953 61 32 00).
Call at C/Santa María 10 at a reasonable hour, and Don Antonio will escort you with the key.

Parque Arqueológico de Cerrillo Blanco

Porcuna. **Open** (by appointment with Ayuntamiento on 953 54 40 04) *July-Sept* 9am-noon daily. *Oct-June* 10am-noon daily.

Torre de Boabdil

C/José Moreno Torres s/n, Porcuna (www.museodeobulco.com). **Open** *June-Aug* noon-2pm, 7-9pm Sat. *Sept-May* noon-1pm Tue-Thur; noon-2pm Fri, Sun; noon-2pm, 4-7pm Sat.

Where to stay & eat

In Porcuna, squeeze yourself into **Epi** (C/Ramón y Cajal 5, no phone), one of the smallest bars in Andalucía and in the same family for more than a century (there's no sign outside). The only place to stay here is **El Triunfo** (C/Carrera de Jesús 19, 953 54 47 71, www.restauranteeltriunfo.com, double €40), which also has a good restaurant (€-€€).

In Andújar, the two-star **Don Pedro** (C/Gabriel Zamora 5, 953 50 12 74, double €43-€58) is the one of the best places to stay in the centre. The best-known restaurant in town is **Restaurante Madrid–Sevilla** (Plaza del Sol 4, 953 50 05 94, closed dinner Mon-Wed and last 2wks Sept, €€), named after its position on the old road between the two cities, and purveyor of some classic meaty dishes (the game is particularly good); it has an enormous wine cellar. For cheaper but equally hearty fare, try **Las Perolas** (C/Serpiente 6, 953 50 67 26, closed Mon and July, €).

In Baños de la Encina, the three-star **Hotel Restaurante Baños** (C/Cerro La Llana s/n, 953 61 40 68, www.hotelbanos.com, double €62-€68, restaurant €-€€) has a big terrace and many rooms enjoying fine views of the castle, but a faintly institutional air. More charming is the **Hospederia Rural Palacio Guzmanes** (C/Trinidad 4, 953 61 30 75, www.palacioguzmanes.com, double €75-€140, restaurant €€), a lovely old country house incorporating some of the 13th-century city walls. Rooms vary – some have hydromassage baths, others have wood-burning stoves and so on (check website) and there is a small pool and good-value restaurant on the terrace overlooking the plains. The sweet **Posá La Cestería** (C/Conquista 25, mobile 697 953 318, whole house €80 per night) is excellent value, with two double bedrooms.

Resources

Tourist information

Andújar *Torre de Reloj, Plaza de Santa María (953 50 49 59/www.andujar.es).* **Open** *July-Sept* 8am-2pm Tue-Sat. *Oct-June* 10am-2pm, 5-8pm Mon-Sat.

Parque Natural de la Sierra de Andújar *Centro de Visitantes, J5010, km12 (953 54 90 30).* **Open** *May-Sept* 9am-1pm Thur, Sun; 9am-1pm, 6-8pm Fri, Sat. *Oct-Apr* 9am-1pm Thur; 9am-1pm, 6-8pm Fri-Sun.

Porcuna *Ayuntamiento, Plaza de Andalucía s/n (953 54 40 04).* **Open** 8am-3pm Mon-Fri.

Getting there

By bus

Andújar bus station (953 51 30 72/www.infonegocio.com/estacionbusandujar) is at Sector Seville 27. Around 18 buses (fewer at weekends) run daily from Andújar to Jaén, 3 go to Écija, Carmona and on to Seville, 6 to Córdoba (3 on weekends), 2 to Baeza and Úbeda, and 2 on weekdays to Lopera and Porcuna.

By train

There is 1 daily direct train from Andújar station (902 24 02 02) to Jaén (45mins), 4 to Linares-Baeza (30mins), 5 to Córdoba (50mins), 2 to Seville (2hrs 15mins) and 1 to Cádiz (4hrs).

East of Jaén

Home to Renaissance gems aplenty.

Baeza

Although Jaén province is one of the lesser-known corners of Andalucía, it contains what are undoubtedly two of the region's (and the country's) Renaissance jewels – the glorious neighbouring towns of Baeza and Úbeda. **Baeza**, the smaller of the two (and the less affected by unsympathetic 20th-century development), lies 48 kilometres (30 miles) north-east of Jaén city. It was a significant centre in Roman and Visigothic times, and the capital of a sizeable city state under the Moors. When it fell to Christian forces in 1227 the incoming nobles proceeded to indulge in centuries of violent bickering with each other before the town enjoyed its golden age (like Úbeda) in the 16th century. It was during this brief time that Baeza's nobles commissioned the wealth of buildings that distinguish this compact, sleepy town today.

Tourism is not novel in Baeza, but the coach parties rarely stay the night, and evenings are often the loveliest times to wander the streets and look out over the surrounding countryside, echoing the words of one-time resident, the poet Antonio Machado: 'Fields of Baeza, I shall dream of you when I can no longer see you.'

Sightseeing

The town's focal point is the coffin-shaped, bar-specked Paseo de la Constitución, which joins the smaller Plaza de España at its northern end. The outstanding building on the *paseo*'s eastern side is the 16th-century **La Alhóndiga**, an elegant arcaded corn exchange, while the 17th-century **Casas Consistoriales Bajas** (Lower Town Hall) is the pick of the buildings on the opposite side. Overlooking Plaza de España is the **Torre de los Aliatares**, one of the few remnants of Baeza's Moorish fortifications.

The southern end of the Paseo de la Constitución leads into the tiny, exquisite Plaza del Pópulo, with the Fuente de los Leones (Fountain of the Lions) at its centre. Here you can pick up a town map from the tourist office, which is housed within the **Casa del Pópulo**. The other building of note on the square is the **Antigua Carnicería** (Old Slaughterhouse), bearing the two-headed eagle of Emperor Carlos V. On the square's southern side are two arches: the **Puerta de Jaén** (Jaén Gate), and the **Arco de Villalar**, erected by Carlos to commemorate the crushing of the Castilian revolt of the Comuneros (1520-21).

Uphill, east of the *plaza*, lies the peaceful heart of Renaissance Baeza. From behind the tourist office, follow Cuesta San Gil and turn left up C/Obispo Mengibar to reach stunning Plaza Santa María. Its eastern side is formed by conjoined buildings: the **Casas Consistoriales Altas** (Upper Town Hall; currently being renovated) and the **Santa Iglesia Catedral** (**photo** *p244*). The latter was built on the site of a mosque in the 13th century and given a fine nave in the mid 16th century by Andrés de Vandelvira, though the late-Gothic chancel

Plaza del Pópulo.

remains. The greatest surprise within the airy interior comes if you put a €1 coin in a box marked 'Custodia' at the end of the aisle (on the side of the main door). A painting slides back to reveal an astonishingly ornate revolving 18th-century silver custodia (by Córdoban Nuñez de Castro). The church tower can be climbed, though the views are disappointing; the bells are fenced off, meaning you can't get to the edge of the tower overlooking the town. On the opposite side of the *plaza* is the rather severe 17th-century **Seminario Conciliar de San Felipe Neri**, now home to the International University of Andalucía.

From here, C/San Felipe Neri leads to the arresting **Palacio de Jabalquinto** (currently being renovated), the most unusually decorated building in Baeza. Built for the Benavides family in the 15th century, its façade is a riot of Isabelline-plateresque ornamentation. In stark contrast, the *palacio* is faced by the engagingly simple 13th-century church of **Santa Cruz**.

Continuing along the street brings you to the huge **Universidad**, the former university, where poet Antonio Machado (*see p32*) taught French for eight years until 1919 (after it had been converted into a school). The interior patio is open to the public, as is Machado's classroom (953 74 01 50, closed Wed, Machado's classroom by appointment only), which has been kept much as it was in his day and contains various artefacts related to his time in Baeza.

There is a further clutch of fine buildings west of the Paseo de la Constitución. Taking C/Gaspar Becerra, you soon reach the **Ayuntamiento** (Town Hall; originally the law courts and a prison), a stunning exercise in plateresque exuberance, completed in 1569. Opposite, at the corner of the street, is the house where Machado resided during most of his stay in the town. At the other end of Pasaje Cardenal Benavides is the church of **La Purísima Concepción**, while just south of here on C/de San Francisco are the partially restored remains of Vandelvira's **Convento de San Francisco**, which was badly damaged by an earthquake and then by marauding French troops in the early 19th century.

From Plaza de España, C/de San Pablo leads northwards past a series of fine 16th-century Renaissance mansions, the star of which is **Casa Cabrera**. A little further up is the 15th-century Gothic church of **San Pablo**.

Where to eat & drink

The **Hotel Palacete Santa Ana** (*see p244*) also has a good restaurant, located close to the hotel at C/Escopeteros 12.

Cafeteria Mercantil

Plaza de España s/n (953 74 09 71). **Open** 7am-midnight daily. **Average** €. **No credit cards. Map** p243 A1 ❶

Machado was a regular at this atmospheric place with a large terrace. It's the most popular spot in town and features a huge menu of tapas and *raciones*, including shellfish, various *tortillas* and good ice-cream to finish.

Casa Juanito

Paseo Arca de Agua s/n (953 74 00 40/www.juanitobaeza.com). **Open** 1.15-3.30pm Mon, Sun; 1.15pm-3.30pm, 8.30pm-11pm Tue-Sat. Closed 1st 3wks July. **Average** €€. **Credit** MC, V.

Hugely celebrated – despite its location next to a petrol station on the road to Úbeda – but overrated.

Santa Iglesia Catedral. See p242.

Restaurante Sali

Pasaje Cardenal Benavides 15 (953 74 13 65/www.restaurantesali.com). **Open** 1-5pm, 8pm-midnight Mon, Tue, Thur-Sun. Closed 2wks Sept. **Average** €€. **Credit** AmEx, MC, V. **Map** p243 A2 ❷

The Sali's sprawling terrace is a peaceful place to sit with a *caña* and a selection of tapas from a long list. Alternatively, gutsier dishes include oxtail stew and the speciality, roast kid, along with some wonderfully fresh shellfish.

El Sarmiento

Plaza del Arcediano 10 (953 74 03 23). **Open** *June-Aug* 1.30-4pm, 8.30-11.30pm Tue-Sun; *Sept-May* 1.30-4pm, 8.30-11.30pm Tue-Sat, 1.30-4pm Sun. Closed 1st 2wks July. **Average** €€€. **Credit** MC, V. **Map** p243 B2 ❸

Tucked into the streets behind the cathedral, this upmarket eaterie is famed for its local fare, with game dishes such as *perdiz* (partridge) in season. It has a pleasant *terraza*.

Vandelvira

C/San Francisco 14 (953 74 81 72/www.vandelvira.es). **Open** 1.30-4pm, 8.30-11pm Tue-Sat; 1.30-4pm Sun. **Average** €€. **Credit** AmEx, DC, MC, V. **Map** p243 A2 ❹

The finest dining choice in town, located within a restored part of Vandelvira's beautiful 16th-century Convento de San Francisco. Dishes are mostly local with a twist: salad of wind-dried tuna with orange and spring onions; pork jowl with apple purée, or *torrijas* (like bread and butter pudding) with black olive ice-cream and baked peach.

Where to stay

La Casona del Arco

C/Sacramento 3 (953 74 72 08/www.lacasonadelarco.com). **Rates** (incl breakfast) €65-€86 single; €86-€107 double; €105-€128 suite. **Credit** AmEx, MC, V. **Map** p243 B1 ❺

Opened in spring 2006 and converted from an 18th-century mansion, La Casona has tastefully decked-out rooms, an elegant, antique-filled lounge and small pool. Downstairs is a sauna and jacuzzi. Check the website for special offers.

Hotel Palacete Santa Ana

C/Santa Ana Vieja 9 (953 74 16 57/www.palacetesantaana.com). **Rates** €44.95-€53.50 single; €57.80-€77.05 double; €128.40 suite. **Credit** AmEx, MC, DC, V. **Map** p243 A2 ❻

This beautifully restored 16th-century *palacio* has 30 exquisite bedrooms filled with antiques and paintings, plus patios for guests to enjoy, a restaurant, roof terrace and wine bar with over 1,200 bottles and flamenco at weekends.

Hotel Puerta de la Luna

C/Canónigo Melgares Raya s/n (953 74 70 19/www.hotelpuertadelaluna.es). **Rates** €78.10-€123.05 single/double; €155.15-€224.70 suite. **Credit** AmEx, DC, MC, V. **Map** p243 B2 ❼

A former home for the canons of the cathedral, the original 16th-century building has been lovingly restored, with 44 boutique-style rooms, some with *terrazas*, ranged round a pretty courtyard with a small pool in the centre. There is also a spa, Turkish baths, garage and an excellent restaurant. Ask about special offers on rates.

Hotel TRH Baeza

C/Concepción 3 (953 74 81 30/www.trhhoteles.com). **Rates** €64.20-€79.70 single; €77.05-€92.55 double; €128.40-€143.90 suite. **Credit** AmEx, MC, V. **Map** p243 A1 ❽

This hotel, within the unsympathetically modernised 16th-century Renaissance Hospital de la Inmaculad Concepción, has 84 functional rooms in a peaceful location.

Pensión El Patio

C/Conde Romanones 13 (953 74 02 00). **Rates** €15-€17 single; €25-€34 double. **No credit cards.** **Map** p243 B2 ❾

A very cheap *pensión* in a wonderfully crumbling 17th-century *palacio*. Cheaper rooms share a communal bathroom.

Resources

Internet

Speed Informática, Plaza de la Constitución 2 (953 74 70 05/www.speed.com.es). **Open** *Mid June-mid Sept* 10am-2pm, 5.30-9.30pm Mon-Fri; 10am-2pm Sat. *Mid Sept-mid June* 10am-2pm, 5-9pm Mon-Fri; 10am-2pm Sat. **Map** p243 A/B2.

Tourist information

Plaza del Pópulo s/n (953 74 04 44). **Open** *June-Aug* 9am-8pm Mon-Fri; 10am-2pm Sat, Sun. *Sept-May* 9am-7pm Mon-Fri; 10am-2pm Sat, Sun. **Map** p237 B2.

Úbeda

Úbeda, nine kilometres (six miles) east of Baeza and 57 kilometres (36 miles) north-east of Jaén, is one of the most extraordinary towns in Andalucía, and Spain – not that you'd know it from its scruffy outskirts. Cradled within an arc of unappealing modern development lies a historical centre of remarkable coherence and architectural richness.

Úbeda's origins are ancient, but it only developed into a centre of importance after the arrival of the Moors. When the town fell to Fernando III in 1234, the king established a number of noble families to oversee the area, who, following generations of infighting, had settled most of their differences by the time of Úbeda's greatest period of prosperity in the 16th century. The most significant figures of the time were Francisco de los Cobos y Molina – who, as secretary to Emperor Carlos V, amassed phenomenal wealth and power – and his nephew, Juan Vázquez de Molina, who replaced his uncle when Carlos decided that Francisco's ambitions were getting out of hand, and later served Felipe II. Between them they commissioned many of the Renaissance mansions and churches that grace Úbeda today, a large number of which are the work of the city's greatest architect, Andrés de Vandelvira.

The fortunes of the town's nobility and textile trade declined rapidly in the early 17th century, and few significant building projects were undertaken after this time, which is what gives the old centre its unique, preserved-in-amber Renaissance cast.

Sightseeing

The centrepiece of Úbeda's Zona Monumental is undoubtedly the astonishing, elongated **Plaza de Vázquez de Molina**, lined on every side by remarkable buildings. At its eastern end stands the **Sacra Capilla del Salvador del Mundo (photo** *p247*), loosely based on designs by Diego de Siloé but built by Vandelvira. The chapel, commissioned by Francisco de los Cobos y Molina (who is buried within) is a masterpiece of the Spanish Renaissance; it was completed in just over 20 years (1536-59),

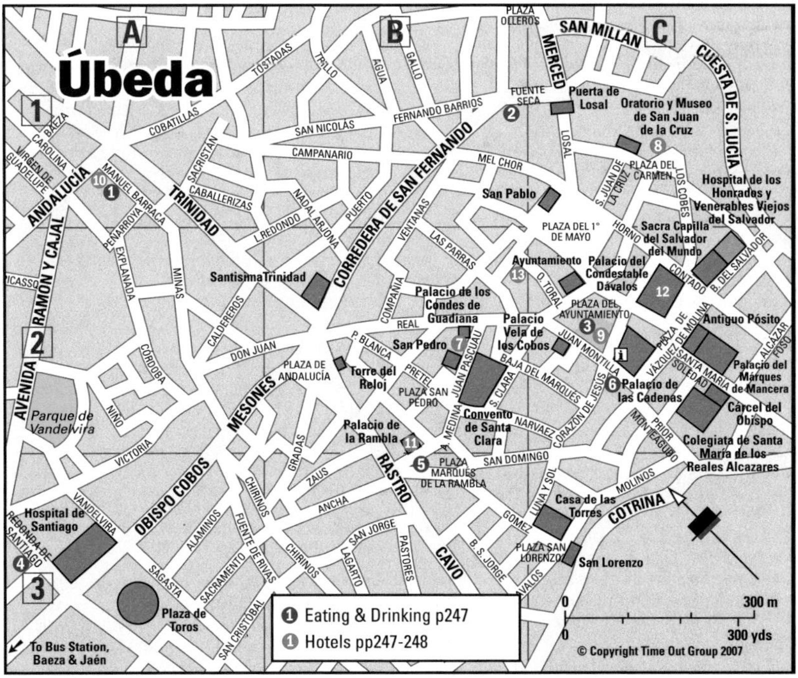

and has been little altered since. Inside, the church is dominated by a glittering polychrome *retablo* of the Transfiguration over the high altar. The figure of Christ is by Alonso Berruguete; the rest of the scene is a modern restoration following Civil War damage.

Immediately east of the chapel is the former old-folks' home, the **Hospital de los Honrados y Venerables Viejos del Salvador**, with a Vandelvira façade. It marks the abrupt edge of town, with fine views over olive fields towards the mountains.

Back on the *plaza*, to the west of the church, is the **Palacio del Condestable Dávalos**, now home to one of the most elegant hotels in the state-owned *parador* chain (*see p248*). Opposite is the **Antiguo Pósito**, the old granary, attached to the **Palacio del Marqués de Mancera**, a solid structure, somewhat retro when it was built at the turn of the 16th century.

At right angles to the *palacio*, and fronting a statue to Vandelvira and a tourist information booth, is the **Cárcel del Obispo** (Bishop's Prison; now a police station), which adjoins the **Colegiata de Santa María de los Reales Alacazares**. This church, consecrated in the 1230s, stands on the site of Úbeda's main mosque. It displays a range of Gothic, Mudéjar, Renaissance, baroque and neo-Gothic styles.

Across the square is the vast yet neatly proportioned **Palacio de Juan Vázquez de Molina**, popularly known at the **Palacio de las Cadenas** (after the chains that once decorated its façade). Construction was started by Vandelvira in 1540, but Vázquez de Molina never lived here, deciding even before its completion that the building should be used as a Dominican convent (953 75 04 40, open 9am-2pm, 5-9pm daily, free).

Wandering the narrow streets north and west of the Plaza de Vázquez de Molina reveals countless other examples of superb Renaissance architecture. Heading west along Calles Afán de Rivera and Ventanas brings you to Plaza San Lorenzo, where the church of **San Lorenzo** is built into the old city wall (its ivy-clad bell tower provides a picturesque photo opportunity). On the same square is the **Casa de las Torres** (953 75 05 18, open 8am-2.15pm Mon-Fri, free, closed Aug; **photo** *p247*), named after its two hefty towers. Built in the first two decades of the 16th century, this was the first plateresque mansion in Úbeda, and contains one of the town's first Renaissance patios; it now houses a school of arts and crafts.

North of here, the 16th-century **Palacio del Marqués de la Rambla**, on Plaza del Marqués, is now an upmarket hotel (*see p248*). Just to the east, facing each other across C/Juan Pascuau, are the church of **San Pedro** (built at the end of the 14th century, with a façade dating from 1605) and the **Convento de Santa Clara**, founded in 1290 as the first Franciscan convent in Andalucía, then altered many times up until the 18th century and currently undergoing more restoration work. The nuns sell a range of baked goodies to the public. Further along the street is the **Palacio de los Condes de Guadiana**.

From here, C/Real – the main shopping street of the old town – leads down to Plaza del Ayuntamiento, flanked to the south by one side of the Palacio de las Cadenas, and with the fine **Palacio Vela de los Cobos** by Vandelvira at its north-west corner.

North-east of the square is Plaza Primero de Mayo, home to the vast late-Gothic church of **San Pablo** (13th-14th centuries) and, at its south-west corner, the graceful, arcaded 16th-century **Ayuntamiento** (the old Town Hall).

C/Juan de la Cruz is where the saint-poet John of the Cross died of gangrene in 1591. Little of the 16th-century building remains, though a small museum dedicated to the saint – the **Museo Biblioteca San Juan de la Cruz** – includes the cell in which he died and artefacts relating to his life. A chapel, the **Oratorio de San Juan de la Cruz**, was built in 1627 to house his tomb, but his remains were subsequently moved to Segovia.

North of here is a superb double horseshoe-arched 14th-century Mudéjar gate, the **Puerta de Losal**, from which C/de la Merced runs to C/de Valencia and into the heart of Úbeda's pottery quarter. The town's traditional green-glazed ceramics make great souvenirs.

At the north-west edge of the old town, the partially arcaded Plaza de Andalucía is overlooked by the (unusually for Úbeda) largely baroque 18th-century church and convent of **Santisima Trinidad** and the **Torre del Reloj**, a 16th-century clock tower atop a hunk of 13th-century city wall. Shopping streets stretch out from the square; C/Mesones leads into Carrera del Obispo Cobos and down to the bullring, bus station and Vandelvira's austere **Hospital de Santiago**, sometimes known as the 'Andalucían Escorial'.

Museo Biblioteca San Juan de la Cruz

C/Carmen 13 (953 75 06 15). **Open** 11am-1pm, 5-7pm Tue-Sun. **Admission** €1.50; €1 concessions. **No credit cards. Map** p241 C1.

Sacra Capilla del Salvador del Mundo

C/Baja del Salvador s/n (953 75 81 50). **Open** *Mid June-mid Sept* 10am-2pm, 5-7.30pm Mon-Sat; 11am-2pm, 4.30-7.30pm Sun. *Mid Sept-mid June* 10am-2pm,

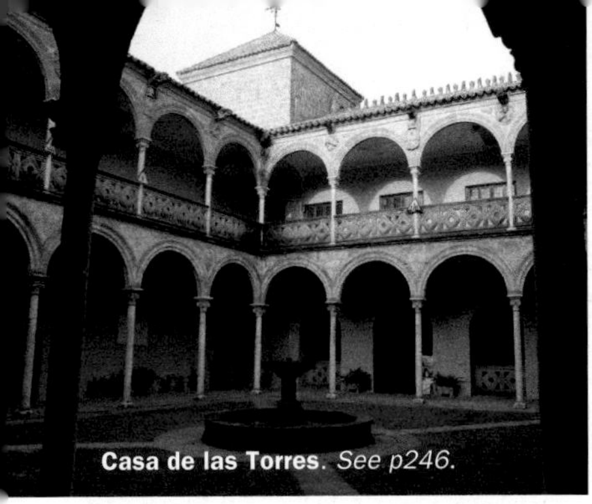
Casa de las Torres. *See p246.*

Sacra Capilla del Salvador. *See p245.*

4-6.30pm Mon-Sat; 11am-2pm, 4-7pm Sun. **Admission** €3; €1.50 concessions. **No credit cards**. **Map** p245 C2.

Where to eat & drink

The old town can be deathly quiet after dark, with only a scattering of eating and drinking options. There's more choice around Avda Ramón y Cajal in the new town, particularly at the lower end of C/Virgen de Guadalupe.

El Gallo Rojo

Plaza Manuel Baraca 3 (953 75 20 38). **Open** 9am-4pm, 7.30-11pm daily. Closed 2wks Oct. **Average** €. **Credit** MC, V. **Map** p245 A1 ❶

At the new town end of C/Trinidad, this lively bar-restaurant has outside tables and good, solid food.

Mesón Gabino

C/Fuente Seca 2 (953 75 75 53). **Open** noon-4.30pm Mon; noon-4.30pm, 8.30pm-midnight Tue-Sun. **Average** €€. **Credit** MC, V. **Map** p245 B1 ❷

Raciones and plates of roast *choto* (kid) and baked fish are available on the pavement terrace or in a cosy dining room. Do like the locals and start with a shot glass of snails.

Mesón Navarro

Plaza del Ayuntamiento 2 (953 79 06 38). **Open** 1-4pm, 8.30-11pm daily. **Average** €. **Credit** MC, V. **Map** p245 C2 ❸

Still firmly in the hands of the locals despite its prime old town location, this is easily the best place for a tapa and a tipple in the area. Though it has a dining room at the back, most of Navarro's lively clientele stand at the bar or take one of the tables at the front (or out on the *plaza* during the summer months). Try the local speciality *andrajos* (pasta soup), or the partridge salad.

El Porche

Redondo de Santiago 7 (953 75 72 87/www.restauranteelporche.com). **Open** 1-4pm, 8.30-11.30pm daily. **Average** €€. **Credit** AmEx, DC, MC, V. **Map** p245 A3 ❹

A classy place on the edge of the new town, close to the Hospital de Santiago, serving superior versions of the Spanish classics in a refined setting. Part of the roof is open to the sky on temperate days.

Restaurante Marqués

Plaza Marqués de la Rambla 2 (953 75 72 55/www.hotel-maria-de-molina.com). **Open** 1.30-4pm Tue-Fri; 1.30-4pm, 8.30-11pm Sat, Sun. **Average** €-€€. **Credit** MC, V. **Map** p245 B2/3 ❺

Located on a tiny *plaza*, this excellent restaurant is owned by the Hotel María de Molina (*see p248*). Its traditional Spanish dishes include venison, *kokotxas* (cod or hake cheeks) and partridge stew.

Restaurante El Seco

C/Corazón de Jesús 8 (953 79 14 52). **Open** 1-4pm Mon-Thur, Sun; 1-4pm, 8-11.30pm Fri, Sat. **Average** €€. **Credit** AmEx, MC, V. **Map** p245 C2 ❻

Cheap but imaginative dishes served up in a simply decorated dining room. Try the meatballs with almond sauce, sole in cava with prawns or the Cazorla trout with capers.

Where to stay

All the classiest accommodation is in the old town, which is by far the nicest area to stay (although it does tend to be largely lifeless at night). All the budget places are in the new town, mostly along busy Avda Ramón y Cajal, a ten-minute walk from the centre. There's little to choose between the hostels – try **Hostal Sevilla** (Avda Ramón y Cajal 7, 953 75 06 12, closed Aug, double €36-€40). Closer to the old town is the **Hostal Victoria** (C/Alaminos 5, 953 75 29 52, double €36-€37).

Álvar Fáñez

C/Juan Pasquau 5 (953 79 60 43/www.alvarfanez.com). **Rates** (incl breakfast) €53.50-€94.15 single; €70.60-€141.25 double; €100.60-€201.15 triple; €188.30-€250.40 quad. **Credit** AmEx, MC, V. **Map** p245 B2 ❼

Álvar Fáñez was a Christian knight who (according to a sadly apocryphal story) strayed off into the nearby hills in pursuit of a Moorish girl, thereby missing a key battle against the Moors. His peregrinations gave rise to the popular expression 'to wander off on the hills of Úbeda', meaning 'to be distracted'. The 12-room hotel that bears his name is a classy, stylish affair, arrayed around a courtyard and well located in the old town. Its restaurant is situated in a 16th-century *bodega*.

Parque Natural de Cazorla. *See p249.*

Hospedería El Blanquillo

Plaza del Carmen 1 (953 79 54 05/www.el blanquillo.com). **Rates** (incl breakfast) €43-€53 single; €64-€77 double. **Credit** AmEx, DC, MC, V. **Map** p245 C1 ⑧

Another hotel housed in a Renaissance mansion. Rooms ranged around a central patio are slightly disappointing considering the grandeur of the surroundings, but they are at least comfortable enough and cheap at the price. The rooftop terrace is a good place for a sundowner, with an incredible view.

Hotel María de Molina

Plaza del Ayuntamiento s/n (953 79 53 56/ www.hotel-maria-de-molina.com). **Rates** €53.50-€73.85 single; €82.40-€105.95 double. **Credit** AmEx, DC, MC, V. **Map** p245 C2 ⑨

This delightful hotel, arrayed around an elegant courtyard, is excellent value for money and occupies a prime position, just a minute's walk from the glorious Plaza de Vázquez de Molina. Its 27 rooms are kitted out with rustic repro furniture and the bathrooms are first rate.

Hotel La Paz

C/Andalucía 1 (953 75 08 48/www.hotel-lapaz.com). **Rates** €45 single; €60 double; €81 triple; €100 4-person apartment. **Credit** MC, V. **Map** p245 A1 ⑩

This two-star hotel is the most upmarket option in the new town. It looks a bit grim from the outside, but some of its 40 rooms (all with air-con and TV) are a good size and unexpectedly stylish. A number of those looking over the street have balconies, but the traffic noise can be a problem.

Palacio de la Rambla

Plaza del Marqués 1 (953 75 01 96/www.palacio delarambla.com). Closed mid July-mid Aug. **Rates** (incl breakfast) €85.60 single; €115.55-€139 double; €128.40-€149.80 suite. **Credit** AmEx, DC, MC, V. **Map** p245 B2/3 ⑪

Live like a marquis in the Marquesa de la Rambla's 16th-century *palacio*. The eight wonderful rooms, many of them decorated with antiques, surround an atmosphere-rich courtyard.

Parador Condestable Dávalos

Plaza Vázquez de Molina s/n (953 75 03 45/ www.parador.es). **Rates** €119.85-€128.40 single; €149.80-€187.25 double; €224.70-€240.75 suite. **Credit** AmEx, DC, MC, V. **Map** p245 C2 ⑫

One of the loveliest of all the hotels in the *parador* chain, this 16th-century mansion, formerly home to the chaplain of the neighbouring church of San Salvador, is on Úbeda's grandest square. It's been sensitively modernised, and has all the usual *parador* luxury touches. Non-guests can enjoy the courtyard for the price of a drink.

Rosaleda de Don Pedro

C/Obispo Toral 2 (953 79 61 11/www. rosaledadedonpedro.com). **Rates** €64.20-€90.95 single; €80.25-€112.35 double. **Credit** DC, MC, V. **Map** p245 C2 ⑬

This newish hotel in the old town is comfortable for a three star, and boasts the only hotel pool in Úbeda. The rooms overlooking the street are slightly quieter, as those facing the patio are subjected to a peculiar selection of piped '80s hits.

Resources

Internet

Cyberworld, C/Picasso 8 (953 75 75 29). **Open** 11am-2pm, 5-10pm daily. **Map** p245 A2.

Tourist information

Palacio de Marqués de Contadero, C/Baja del Marqués 4 (953 75 08 97). **Open** *June-Sept* 9am-8pm Mon-Fri; 10am-2pm Sat, Sun. *Oct-May* 9am-7pm Mon-Fri; 10am-2pm Sat, Sun. **Map** p245 C2.

Cazorla & around

If you are heading towards the Cazorla Natural Park from Úbeda, it's worth making brief detours to see a couple of fine villages. **Sabiote** (nine kilometres/five-and-a-half miles north-east of Úbeda) is a tranquil, little-visited place with handsome Renaissance buildings, extensively preserved medieval walls, a Renaissance castle (one of the most impressive in Andalucía; a policeman from the town hall will accompany you there) and wonderful views. Its heyday was the 16th century, when Carlos V's secretary Francisco de los Cobos y Molina made it the capital of his fiefdom. The 16th-century architect Vandelvira was born in the village.

Iznatoraf, a further 30 kilometres (19 miles) north-east towards Albacete, is a delightful village of narrow, whitewashed streets ablaze with different blooms. On the stately Plaza San Fernando check out the Renaissance church, Nuestra Señora de la Asunción, built over the Moorish mezquita. The village enjoys an eyrie of a location, with remarkable 360-degree views of the surrounding countryside.

The one natural draw in eastern Jaén is the huge and varied **Parque Natural de las Sierras de Cazorla, Segura y las Villas** (**photo** *p248*). Covering 2,094 square kilometres (809 square miles), it is one of Spain's largest Natural Parks and encompasses vast expanses of wooded mountains (a number of peaks top 2,000 metres/6,560 feet), flatlands, a 20-kilometre (12.5-mile) reservoir and a wide variety of flora and fauna. The vegetation is some of the richest to be found in the Mediterranean basin, with 1,300 catalogued species (24 of which are exclusive to the area, including the Cazorla violet), and provides a home to Spanish ibex, wild boar and otters, golden eagles and Egyptian vultures, and such exclusive species as the wall lizard of Valverde.

The one major centre for the park is the town of Cazorla in the south; the northern part is far less touristed. Despite its size, the park can get very busy in summer and at weekends (only a few roads cross it). Out of season you'll have the roads and trails to yourself.

Located 45 kilometres east of Úbeda, and 900 metres (3,000 feet) up on the edge of the Sierra de Cazorla, the heavily touristed town of **Cazorla** is the main jumping-off point for the park. C/Doctor Muñoz leads from the lively Plaza de la Constitución up to Plaza de la Corredera, the oval-shaped focus of this part of Cazorla, and then, through narrow streets to the Plaza de Santa María. Here stand the remains of the ruined 16th-century church of **Santa María**, built by Andrés de Vandelvira and trashed by Napoleon's soldiers.

A short, steep walk up from the Plaza brings you to the **Castillo de la Yedra**, which was largely built by the Moors on the site of a Roman fortification, and was restored in the 15th century. A kilometre outside town at the village of La Iruela there's an even more spectacularly sited ruined Moorish castle – you can scramble up to it.

The A315 runs through the southernmost tip of the park, crossing the Sierra and descending into the desert landscapes of Granada province. It's a fine drive, and passes the small town of **Quesada**. The works contained within the town's **Museo Rafael Zabaleta**, dedicated to the local painter, are of no great merit, but Zabaleta knew many of the great artistic names of his day, and there are lithographs dedicated to him by the likes of Picasso and Miró. Further on is the **Sanctuario de Tíscar**, a commandingly situated shrine (built over a Moorish fortress) containing an image of the Virgin and a painting by Zabaleta of the annual pilgrimage here.

The main road into the park from Cazorla goes past La Iruela, snakes over the Sierra de Cazorla and then heads north-east through the spectacular wooded Guadalquivir valley towards the long reservoir, the Embalse de Tranco. Just off this stretch of road are most of the park's hotels, campsites, picnic sites and visitor facilities. The Torre del Vinagre Centro de Visitantes (around 30 kilometres/19 miles from Cazorla) has information on all aspects of the park, including accommodation, and details of the many wonderful walks in the area.

Castillo de la Yedra

Cazorla (653 71 00 39). **Open** 3-8pm Tue; 9am-8pm Wed-Sat; 9am-2pm Sun. **Admission** €1.50; free with EU passport.

Museo Rafael Zabaleta

C/Arco de los Santos s/n, Quesada (info 953 73 31 33). **Open** *May-Sept* 10am-2pm, 5-9pm Wed-Sun. *Oct-Apr* 10am-2pm, 4-8pm Wed-Sun. **Admission** €2. **No credit cards**.

The museum was due to move to Plaza Cesario Rodríguez Aguilera in spring/summer 2006. The website www.turismoencazorla.com has up-to-date information.

Segura de la Sierra & around

Far fewer visitors come to the northern part of the park than the more easily accessible southern reaches, yet it's worth the journey just to see the most stunningly sited village in the area: **Segura de la Sierra**. Clinging to the slopes of a hill beneath a (much restored) Moorish castle, this tiny place has just as commanding a position – and yet it was one of the earliest fortresses in Andalucía to fall to the Christians (in 1214). The village's other main attraction is the mid 12th-century **Baño Moro** (Moorish bath), just off the Plaza Mayor. Both castle and bath house are usually open all day every day. It's also worth taking a look at the strange, tiny, rectangular bullring on the way up to the castle.

Around 20 kilometres (12.5 miles) south-west of Segura is **Hornos**, another pretty castle-topped village in a spectacular setting, with wonderful views out over the waters of the **Embalse de Tranco** – a lookout point is signposted from the passageway next to the church. From here, it's a lovely meandering drive alongside the reservoir towards **Coto Rios**, an agreeable little village with plenty of accommodation options nearby.

Where to stay, eat & drink

In Sabiote the snowy-white interiors at the **Palacio Las Manillas** (C/Castillo 1, 953 77 43 46, www.palaciolasmanillas.com, double €75-€86) belie its Renaissance façade. It has a decent restaurant (€) and can arrange trekking.

There's plenty of accommodation in Cazorla. Of the cheaper options, the **Pensión Taxi** (Travesía de San Antón 7, 953 72 05 25, mobile 606 58 76 57, double €36) is handily located just off Plaza de la Constitución; **Pensión Betis** (Plaza Corredera 19, 953 72 05 40, double €24-€26) is another possibility.

The **Villa Turistica de Cazorla** (Ladera San Isicio s/n, 953 71 01 00, www.villacazorla.com, €47.95-€92.60 for 2 people) on the edge of town offers immaculate rooms, plus a pool and restaurant. In La Iruela, just outside Cazorla, the classy but good-value **Hotel Sierra de Cazorla** (Carretera de la Sierra s/n, 953 72 00 15, www.hotelsierradecazorla.com, double €55.40-€72.20) also has a pool and restaurant – be sure to ask for a room enjoying the spectacular view of the castle. The luxury **Parador El Adelantado** (953 72 70 75, www.parador.es, closed Jan, 2wks end Dec, double €96.30-€128.40) is 25 kilometres (16 miles) from Cazorla in a beautiful, isolated position within the park – be warned, though, that most rooms do not have views. There's a pool in the grounds.

There is no shortage of friendly tapas bars in Iznatoraf, including the **Bar Yedra** (C/Alcalde Juan Martínez 5, mobile 628 494 944), which has tables out on the Plaza San Fernando.

Cazorla is also well equipped with good tapas bars, particularly around the main squares. Try **Bar Las Vegas** (Plaza de la Corredera 17, 953 72 02 77, closed Mon & dinner Sun, 2wks Jan & 2wks June, €) or **Bar Sola** (C/Doctor Muñoz 30, 953 72 00 58, closed Sun & 2wks July, €). For a quarter of a century the most upmarket dining option in town has been José and Rosa's outstanding, inventive **La Sarga** (Plaza del Mercado s/n, 953 72 15 07, closed Tue & Sept, €€€), where specialities include a supreme of pheasant with grape sauce, and artichokes with a rosemary sauce.

In Segura, **La Mesa Segureña** (C/Postigo 2, 953 48 21 01, www.lamesadesegura.com, closed Wed & dinner Sun, €) is an eating option and rents out apartments (€55 for 2 people).

If you want to stay in Hornos, try **Bar El Cruce** (Puerta Nueva 27, 953 49 50 03, closed some Mons Oct-Apr, double €30), or **El Mirador** (Puerta Nueva 11, 953 49 50 19, double €30, restaurant €) – the latter, as the name implies, has rooms with lovely views.

If you want to stay out in the wilds, try the self-catering cottages at **El Mesoncillo** in La Platera, not far from Hornos (mobile 646 81 02 52, www.mesoncillo.com, €42-€48 for 2 or 3, €66-€72 for 4-6, cheaper weekly rates) or, for a bit more luxury (and a swimming pool), the **Hotel La Hortizuela** (Carretera del Tranco, km50.5, 953 71 31 50, www.lahortizuela.com, closed early Jan-late Feb, double €55-€60).

Resources

Internet

Cazorla *Parra Multistore, Plaza de la Constitución 12 (953 72 08 75).* **Open** 10am-2pm, 4.30-9.30pm daily.

Tourist information

Cazorla *Paseo del Santo Cristo 17 (953 71 01 02/www.ayto-cazorla.es).* **Open** *Mid June-mid Oct* 10am-1pm, 5.30-8pm daily. *Oct-mid June* 10am-1pm, 5-7.30pm daily.

Parque Natural de las Sierras de Cazorla, Segura y las Villas *Centro de Visitantes 'Torre del Vinagre', Carretera del Tranco, km46, Santiago-Pontones (953 71 30 17/www.ayto-cazorla.es).* **Open** *Mid June-Sept* 11am-2pm, 5-8pm daily. *Oct-mid June* 11am-2pm, 4-7pm Tue-Sun.

Getting there

By bus

There are plentiful buses each day to Jaén and Úbeda. Úbeda's bus station is at C/San José s/n (953 75 21 57, on the western side of town (close to the Hospital de Santiago), from where there are frequent services to Jaén, Córdoba, Granada, Málaga and Seville. Cazorla buses stop at Plaza del Pueblo (Alsina Graells 953 75 21 57, www.alsinagraells.com). There are several Alsina Graells services a day to/from Baeza and Úbeda (approx 25mins). Baeza bus station is at C/Alcalde Puche Pardo (953 74 04 68).

By train

The nearest train station to Baeza and Úbeda is Linares-Baeza (902 24 02 02), 15km/9 miles from Baeza and 19km/12 miles from Úbeda. Buses to both towns connect with most trains. There are 3 direct daily trains from Jaén (40 mins), 4 from Córdoba (1hr 20mins), 1 from Seville (3hrs), 3 from Málaga (3hrs 30mins), 3 from Almería (3hrs 45mins), 4 from Granada (2hrs 15mins) and 7 from Madrid (3hrs 10mins).

Granada Province

Features

Maps

Granada Province

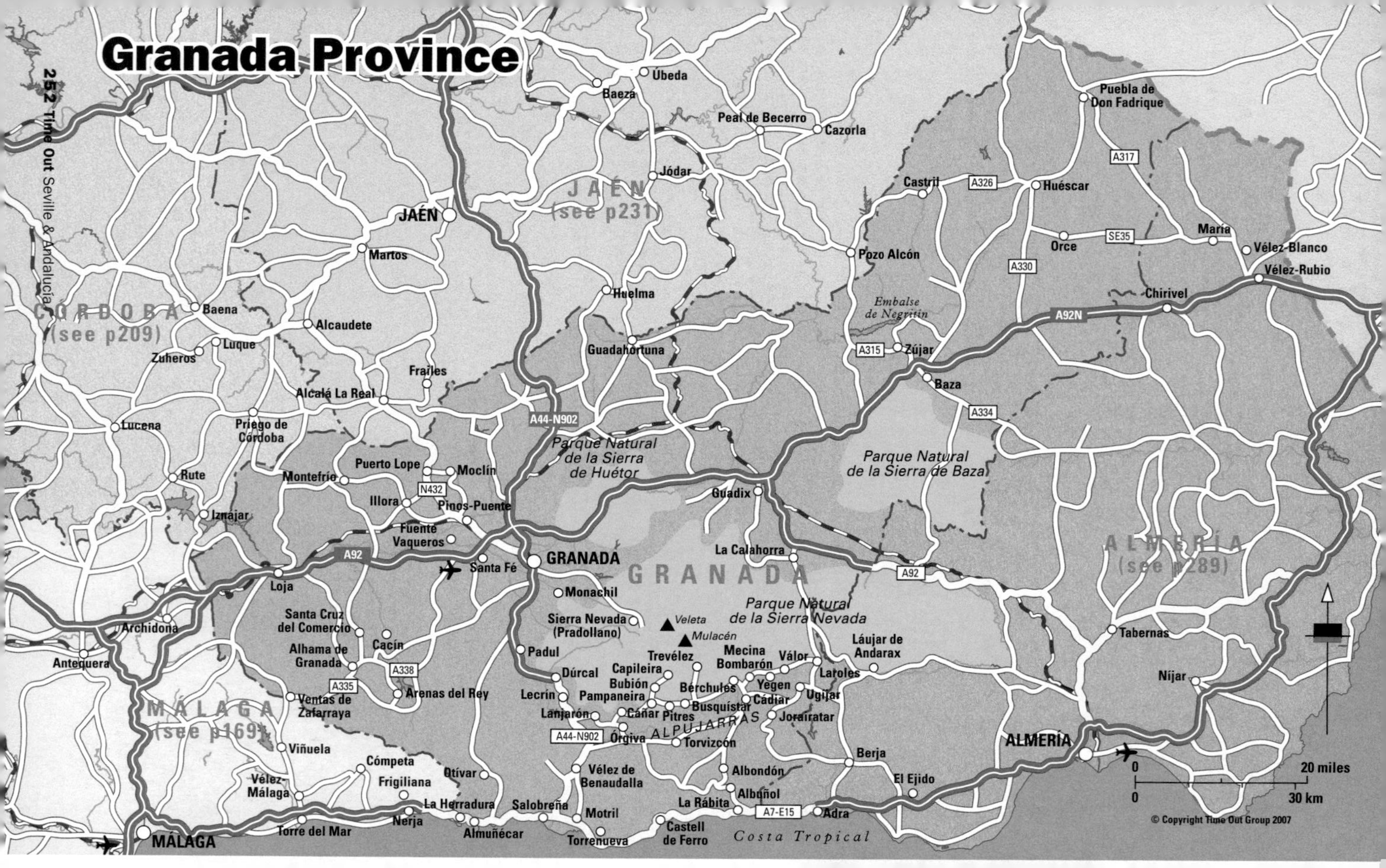

Introduction

The Alhambra alone is reason enough to visit, but the delights of this varied province stretch right back to the birth of European man.

Whatever you seek, you shall find it somewhere in this most varied of provinces – an outstanding palace overlooking a fascinating city, the tallest mountains in Spain, the solitude of wild desert landscapes, the bustle of lively seaside resorts; the list goes on...

GRANADA CITY
The glorious, fêted Alhambra remains Granada's (and Andalucía's) prize attraction. But the mystique of this extraordinary palace should not detract from the city's many other draws: a fine Renaissance cathedral; an atmospheric Moorish quarter; gypsy cave dwellings; and an over-the-top baroque monastery – not to mention free tapas and a lively nightlife scene.

AROUND GRANADA
Beyond the flat expanse of the *vega* to the west of Granada City is a region of rolling hills and olive groves that formed a buffer zone between the Nasrid kingdom and advancing Christian forces from the 13th to 15th centuries. The events of the *reconquista* are writ large in its numerous castles and churches. Highlights include the spectacularly sited small towns of Moclín, Montefrío and Alhama de Granada.

Head east from the city and raw, arid, bleached landscapes open up. Amid the desert-like fastnesses are a handful of unique destinations – the town of Guadix with its extensive cave quarter and impressive cathedral, the remarkable Renaissance castle of La Calahorra, and even – perhaps – the cradle of European man in Orce.

THE SIERRA NEVADA AND THE ALPUJARRAS
South-east of Granada City rises the Sierra Nevada, with Spain's highest peaks and Europe's most southerly ski resort. On the southern slopes, the Alpujarras once sheltered Moorish exiles from Granada, and now attract increasing numbers of expat northern Europeans. This enclave of river valleys and villages is one of the most picturesque in Andalucía, perfect for walking and hiking.

COSTA TROPICAL
The coast of Granada province has been dubbed the Costa Tropical due to its balmy climate, which allows tropical fruits and sugar cane to thrive. It's less developed than the Costa del Sol and less intensively farmed than the Costa de Almería. The main resorts of Almuñécar and Salobreña, although developed, are the most attractive places to stay.

The best...

Architecture, Moorish heritage, tapas & nightlife
Granada City (*pp254-74*).

Castle
La Calahorra (*p279*).

Cave dwellings
Guadix (*p277*); **Sacromonte** in Granada City (*p264*).

Mountains
Sierra Nevada (*p281*).

Towns & villages
Alhama de Granada (*p276*); **Castril** (*p279*); **Montefrío** (*p275*) and the **Alpujarras** generally (*pp281-5*).

Views
The **Alhambra** from the **Mirador de San Nicolás** (*p264*); the **Valle de Poqueira** from **Capileira** (*p283*); the **Sierra Nevada** from **Moclín** (*p275*); the **Axarquía** from the **Zafarraya Pass** (*p276*).

Granada City

Site of one of Europe's most breathtaking palaces.

During his stay at the Alhambra in 1829, Washington Irving was startled one evening by a 'turbaned Moor' sitting in the Patio of the Lions. To the romantically minded American diplomat, it seemed as if 'some ancient inhabitant of the Alhambra had broken the spell of the centuries and become visible', but the Moor assured him that he was merely a trinket seller who liked to visit the Alhambra because it reminded him of the old Muslim palaces of his homeland.

Nearly two centuries later, nowhere else in Spain can evoke past Islamic glories with such force; the Alhambra is, quite simply, a medieval Moor's idea of paradise, and the most complete surviving example of its kind in the world.

The Alhambra is the main draw to Granada still; indeed, many visitors stay near the monument, visit it and leave without even venturing into the centre of town, and certainly Granada doesn't have Seville's obvious grandeur, or Córdoba's chocolate-box quaintness. Yet what it does have is the vibrancy and colour of a bustling town with a young population (the thousands of students at its university joined by an equal number of party-hungry backpackers), and its roughness, gruffness and edge will appeal to some – just as it will repel others. Its nightlife is probably the best and hippest in Andalucía. And despite the *granadinos*' dour, unfriendly reputation, the city remains one of the few places in Andalucía to maintain the generous tradition of free tapas with every drink in most bars.

Apart from the cathedral and some glorious baroque churches, the heart of the modern city isn't that pretty, but it is crowned by two jewels – the Alhambra and the Albaicín district, facing each other over the gorge of the Darro valley, with the (almost always) snow-capped peaks of the Sierra Nevada as a breathtaking backdrop. Both are important markers of the Moorish influence on Granada – an influence that can still be sensed in the Albaicín's whitewashed *carmen* villas, and which is undergoing something of a rebirth. A fashion for North African and Eastern exoticism means there are almost as many couscous houses and *teterías* as tapas bars on the main *tapeo* drags, and gaudily tiled 'Arabian' bathhouses offer to indulge visitors like a sultan. A more authentic reflection of the renewed appreciation of Granada's Muslim past can be seen in the building of the major new mosque and Islamic studies centre in the Albaicín, the workshops and conferences promoted by the Legado Andalusi cultural education foundation and the 'Science in El Andalus' exhibition at the Parque de las Ciencias.

One tip: the city is a nightmare to negotiate by car (and has been deliberately made so). Finding a parking space in the centre is all but impossible, so head straight for a car park.

HISTORY

The present city of Granada was the site of small Iberian, Roman and Visigothic settlements, but did not achieve any significance until well after its initial takeover by Muslim invaders from Africa in 711. It was during the 11th century that the Berber tribe known as the Zirids established themselves in nearby Illiberis (Elvira), and then decided to move to the more easily defensible Garnatha. (The name eventually became Granada; it is mere coincidence that this means 'pomegranate' in Spanish, although this fruit has become a much-loved symbol of the city.) The Zirids made their headquarters in the Albaicín (a pre-existing Jewish settlement, about which virtually nothing is known, was on the future Alhambra hill).

By the 13th century, as the Castilians began to reclaim the *taifas* of Córdoba, Jaén and Seville, the population of Granada swelled with refugee Muslims, mostly concentrated in the Albaicín. The Nasrid chieftain known as Mohammed I entered Granada in 1237 and soon annexed Almería and Málaga to form the last independent emirate, with Granada as the capital. He was a canny politician, maintaining this last bastion of al-Andalus with the aid of North African Berber princes, while simultaneously paying tributes to Castilla. He even provided the Christian armies with military aid in campaigns against other Moorish *taifas*, most famously in the siege of Seville.

Over the next 250 years, Granada enjoyed relative peace and prosperity, which provided fertile ground for artistic and scientific progress. However, the Nasrids were always living on borrowed time and, by the 15th century, relations had become strained with the kingdoms of Aragón and Castilla, now powerfully united through the marriage of

The Alhambra's **Palacios Nazaríes**. *See p261.*

Fernando and Isabel. In 1481 Sultan Muley Hasen could no longer keep up with the escalating payments demanded by the Catholics and threw down the gauntlet to Fernando's messenger: 'Tell your king that Granada no longer mints coins to pay Christians. Now it forges swords and lances to fight them.' Legend has bestowed Fernando with an equally pithy reply: 'I'll pluck the seeds from this pomegranate one by one.'

His strategy was simply to sit back and let the internal feuds that plagued the Sultanate do their work. Harem quarrels over the accession had divided Granada into factions, one side backing Muley Hasen's wife and her son 'Boabdil' (a Spanish corruption of Abu-Abdullah), another side supporting the sons of the Sultan's Christian concubine, Zoraya, and still others in favour of his brother, El Zagal. The bloody soap opera finally concluded with Boabdil taking possession of Granada – although his rule was to be a short one. In 1491 over 150,000 Catholic troops sealed the city with a heavy blockade.

Boabdil, last Sultan of the Nasrid dynasty, finally surrendered on 2 January 1492 on the condition that Spanish Muslims be allowed to retain their religion, language, traditions and judicial system. Fernando and Isabel soon reneged on this promise; their brutal treatment of Granada's Jewish and Muslim citizenry resulted in rebellion and mass emigration. Drained of artisans and trade, the city fell into economic decline (though major monuments, such as the cathedral, were built in the Renaissance and baroque periods), which was further compounded by the later destruction and looting by Napoleon's troops.

The 1898 Baedeker guide described Granada as 'a living ruin'. Modernisation in the 20th century has not necessarily improved matters. The poet Ángel Ganivet decried the new 'love of the straight line' as contrary to Granada's dreamy, tranquil spirit, and many (including Lorca) mourned the covering over of the Río Darro; the waters that once irrigated the gardens of sultans now trickle under the traffic-choked boulevards of the city centre.

The Alhambra

Since Washington Irving's 'rediscovery' of the Alhambra in the early 19th century, and the subsequent flood of panegyrics celebrating its wonders that issued from the pens of Romantic travellers, this remarkable palace has been one of the major tourist destinations not just in Andalucía, or Spain, but in the whole of Europe.

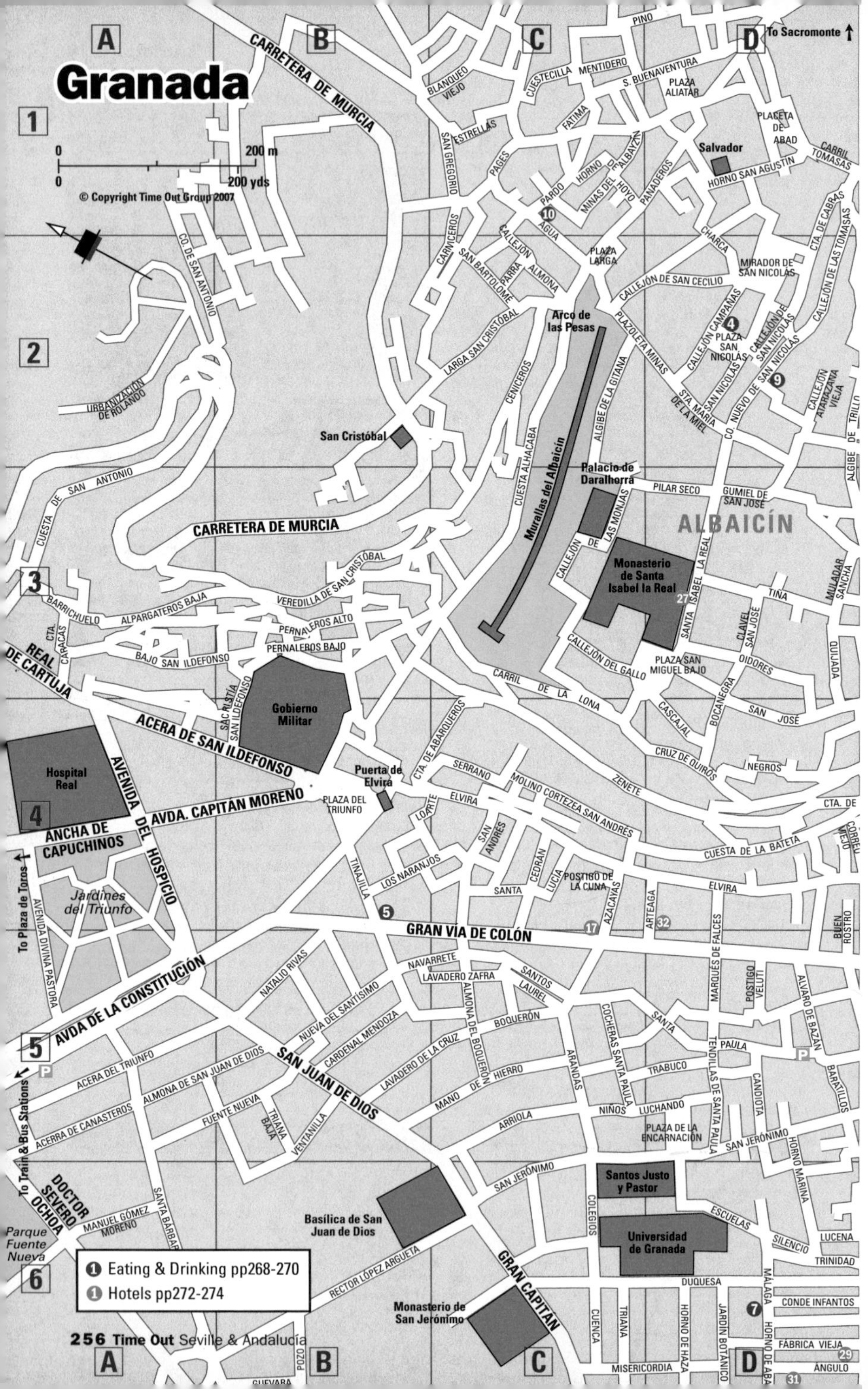
Granada
A
B
C
D
1
2
3
4
5
6
To Sacromonte
0
200 m
0
200 yds
© Copyright Time Out Group 2007
CARRETERA DE MURCIA
PINO
BLANQUEO VIEJO
CUESTECILLA
MENTIDERO
S. BUENAVENTURA
PLAZA ALIATAR
ESTRELLAS
SAN GREGORIO
FATIMA
PAGES
HORNO DE
ALBAYZIN
PANADEROS
Salvador
PLACETA DE ABAD
CARRIL TOMASAS
HORNO SAN AGUSTIN
PARDO
MINAS DEL
HOYO
AGUA
CARNICEROS
CALLEJÓN
SAN BARTOLOMÉ
PARRA
ALMONA
PLAZA LARGA
CHARCA
MIRADOR DE SAN NICOLÁS
CTA. DE CABRAS
CTA. DE LAS TOMASAS
CALLEJÓN DE LAS TOMASAS
CALLEJÓN DE SAN CECILIO
CO. DE SAN ANTONIO
Arco de las Pesas
PLAZOLETA MINAS
CALLEJÓN CAMPANAS
PLAZA SAN NICOLÁS
CALLEJÓN DE SAN NICOLÁS
SAN NICOLÁS
CO. NUEVO DE SAN NICOLÁS
STA. MARÍA DE LA MIEL
CALLEJÓN ATARAZANA VIEJA
TRILLO
ALGIBE DE TRILLO
LARGA SAN CRISTÓBAL
CENICEROS
ALGIBE DE LA GITANA
URBANIZACIÓN DE ROLANDO
San Cristóbal
CUESTA ALHACABA
Murallas del Albaicín
Palacio de Daralhorra
PILAR SECO
GUMIEL DE SAN JOSÉ
ALBAICÍN
CUESTA DE SAN ANTONIO
CARRETERA DE MURCIA
LAS MONJAS
CALLEJÓN DE
Monasterio de Santa Isabel la Real
SANTA ISABEL LA REAL
MULADAR SANCHA
TINA
CLAVEL SAN JOSÉ
VEREDILLA DE SAN CRISTÓBAL
BARRICHUELO
ALPARGATEROS BAJA
CTA. CARACAS
PERNALEROS ALTO
PERNALEROS BAJO
BAJO SAN ILDEFONSO
CALLEJÓN DEL GALLO
PLAZA SAN MIGUEL BAJO
OIDORES
QUIJADA
REAL DE CARTUJA
SACRISTÍA SAN ILDEFONSO
Gobierno Militar
CARRIL DE LA LONA
CASCAJAL
BOCANEGRA
SAN JOSÉ
ACERA DE SAN ILDEFONSO
Hospital Real
AVENIDA DEL HOSPICIO
CTA. DE ABARQUEROS
SERRANO
CRUZ DE QUIRÓS
NEGROS
Puerta de Elvira
MOLINO CORTEZEA SAN ANDRÉS
ZENETE
CTA. DE
AVDA. CAPITÁN MORENO
PLAZA DEL TRIUNFO
ELVIRA
LOARTE
SAN ANDRÉS
CORREO VIEJO
ANCHA DE CAPUCHINOS
CUESTA DE LA BATETA
Jardines del Triunfo
To Plaza de Toros
TINAJILLA
LOS NARANJOS
SANTA
CEDRÁN
LUCÍA
POSTIGO DE LA CUNA
AZACAYAS
ARTEAGA
ELVIRA
BUEN ROSTRO
AVENIDA DIVINA PASTORA
GRAN VÍA DE COLÓN
NAVARRETE
LAVADERO ZAFRA
SANTOS
LAUREL
MARQUÉS DE FALCES
POSTIGO VELUTI
ALVARO DE BAZÁN
AVDA DE LA CONSTITUCIÓN
NATALIO RIVAS
NUEVA DEL SANTÍSIMO
ALMONA DEL BOQUERÓN
COCHERAS SANTA PAULA
BOQUERÓN
SANTA PAULA
CARDENAL MENDOZA
LAVADERO DE LA CRUZ
SAN JUAN DE DIOS
ACERA DEL TRIUNFO
ALMONA DE SAN JUAN DE DIOS
ARANDAS
TRABUCO
TENDILLAS DE SANTA PAULA
CANDIOTA
BARATILLOS
MANO DE HIERRO
NIÑOS
LUCHANDO
To Train & Bus Stations
ACERRA DE CANASTEROS
FUENTE NUEVA
TRIANA BAJA
VENTANILLA
ARRIOLA
PLAZA DE LA ENCARNACIÓN
SAN JERÓNIMO
HORNO MARINA
SAN JERÓNIMO
Santos Justo y Pastor
To Train & Bus Stations
DOCTOR SEVERO OCHOA
SANTA BÁRBARA
MANUEL GÓMEZ MORENO
Basílica de San Juan de Dios
COLEGIOS
ESCUELAS
Universidad de Granada
SILENCIO
LUCENA
TRINIDAD
Parque Fuente Nueva
RECTOR LÓPEZ ARGUETA
GRAN CAPITÁN
DUQUESA
Monasterio de San Jerónimo
CUENCA
TRIANA
HORNO DE HAZA
JARDÍN BOTÁNICO
MÁLAGA
HORNO DE ABAD
CONDE INFANTOS
FÁBRICA VIEJA
ÁNGULO
MISERICORDIA
POZO
GUEVARA
❶ Eating & Drinking pp268-270
① Hotels pp272-274

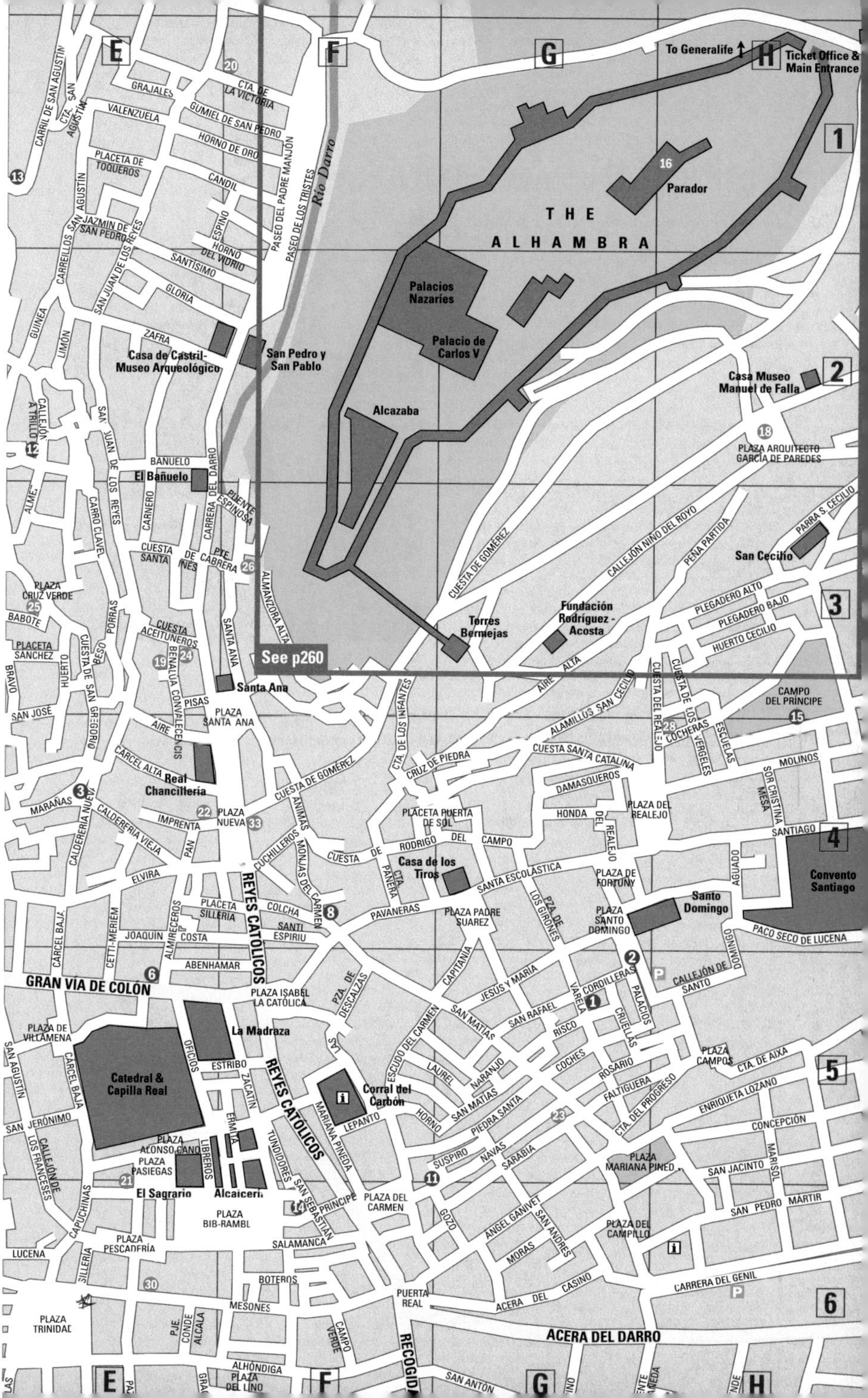

E
F
G
H
1
2
3
4
5
6
To Generalife
Ticket Office & Main Entrance
THE ALHAMBRA
Parador
16
Palacios Nazaríes
Palacio de Carlos V
Alcazaba
Torres Bermejas
Fundación Rodríguez-Acosta
Casa Museo Manuel de Falla
18
PLAZA ARQUITECTO GARCÍA DE PAREDES
San Cecilio
PARRA S. CECILIO
CALLEJÓN NIÑO DEL ROYO
PEÑA PARTIDA
PLEGADERO ALTO
PLEGADERO BAJO
HUERTO CECILIO
CUESTA DE GOMÉREZ
AIRE ALTA
See p260
Río Darro
PASEO DEL PADRE MANJÓN
PASEO DE LOS TRISTES
San Pedro y San Pablo
Casa de Castril-Museo Arqueológico
20
CTA. DE LA VICTORIA
GRAJALES
VALENZUELA
GUMIEL DE SAN PEDRO
HORNO DE ORO
CANDIL
ESPINO
HORNO DEL VIDRIO
SANTÍSIMO
GLORIA
ZAFRA
PLACETA DE TOQUEROS
JAZMÍN DE SAN PEDRO
SAN JUAN DE LOS REYES
CARREILLOS SAN AGUSTÍN
CARRIL DE SAN AGUSTÍN
CTA. SAN AGUSTÍN
13
GUINEA
LIMÓN
CALLEJÓN A TRILLO
12
SAN JUAN DE LOS REYES
BAÑUELO
El Bañuelo
CARRERA DEL DARRO
PUENTE ESPINOSA
CARNERO
CARRO CLAVEL
ALMEZ
CUESTA SANTA INÉS
PTE. DE CABRERA
26
ALMANZORA ALTA
PLAZA CRUZ VERDE
25
BABOTE
PLACETA SÁNCHEZ
BRAVO
HUERTO
CUESTA DE SAN GREGORIO
BESO
PORRAS
CUESTA ACEITUNEROS
19
24
BENALÚA CONVALECENCIA
SANTA ANA
Santa Ana
PISAS
PLAZA SANTA ANA
SAN JOSÉ
AIRE
CÁRCEL ALTA
Real Chancillería
3
MARAÑAS
CALDERERÍA NUEVA
CALDERERÍA VIEJA
22
PLAZA NUEVA
33
IMPRENTA
PAN
ELVIRA
CUESTA DE GOMÉREZ
ÁNIMAS
CUCHILLEROS
MONJAS DEL CARMEN
CTA. DE LOS INFANTES
CRUZ DE PIEDRA
ALAMILLOS SAN CECILIO
CUESTA SANTA CATALINA
CUESTA DEL REALEJO
CUESTA DE LOS VERGELES
28
COCHERAS
ESCUELAS
CAMPO DEL PRÍNCIPE
15
MOLINOS
SOR CRISTINA MESA
DAMASQUEROS
PLAZA DEL REALEJO
HONDA
DEL REALEJO
PLACETA PUERTA DE SOL
CUESTA DE RODRIGO DEL CAMPO
SANTIAGO
Convento Santiago
AGUADO
Casa de los Tiros
CTA. PANERA
SANTA ESCOLÁSTICA
PLAZA DE FORTUNY
Santo Domingo
PLAZA SANTO DOMINGO
PZA. DE LOS GIRONES
PACO SECO DE LUCENA
DOMINGO
CALLEJÓN DE SANTO
2
P
PLACETA SILLERÍA
COLCHA
SANTI ESPIRIU
8
PAVANERAS
PLAZA PADRE SUÁREZ
REYES CATÓLICOS
ALMIRECEROS
CÁRCEL BAJA
CETTI-MERIEM
JOAQUÍN COSTA
ABENHAMAR
6
GRAN VÍA DE COLÓN
PLAZA ISABEL LA CATÓLICA
PZA. DE DESCALZAS
CAPITANÍA
JESÚS Y MARÍA
CORDILLERAS
VARELA
1
PALACIOS
SAN MATÍAS
SAN RAFAEL
RISCO
CRUELLAS
PLAZA DE VILLAMENA
SAN AGUSTÍN
CÁRCEL BAJA
Catedral & Capilla Real
OFICIOS
La Madraza
ESTRIBO
ZACATÍN
LAS
ESCUDO DEL CARMEN
LAUREL
NARANJO
COCHES
ROSARIO
PLAZA CAMPOS
CTA. DE AIXA
FALTIGUERA
CTA. DEL PROGRESO
ENRIQUETA LOZANO
Corral del Carbón
SAN MATÍAS
PIEDRA SANTA
23
CONCEPCIÓN
SAN JERÓNIMO
CALLEJÓN DE LOS FRANCESES
PLAZA ALONSO CANO
PLAZA PASIEGAS
21
El Sagrario
ERMITA
LIBREROS
Alcaicería
TUNDIDORES
SAN SEBASTIÁN
MARIANA PINEDA
LEPANTO
HORNO
SUSPIRO
NAVAS
SARABIA
PLAZA MARIANA PINEDA
SAN JACINTO
MARISOL
11
14
PRÍNCIPE
PLAZA DEL CARMEN
GOZO
ÁNGEL GANIVET
SAN ANDRÉS
SAN PEDRO MÁRTIR
CAPUCHINAS
PLAZA BIB-RAMBL
LUCENA
PLAZA PESCADERÍA
SILLERÍA
SALAMANCA
MORAS
PLAZA DEL CAMPILLO
30
BOTEROS
PUERTA REAL
ACERA DEL CASINO
CARRERA DEL GENIL
MESONES
PLAZA TRINIDAD
PJE. CONDE ALCALÁ
CAMPO VERDE
RECOGIDAS
ACERA DEL DARRO
ALHÓNDIGA
PLAZA DEL LINO
SAN ANTÓN

Visiting the Alhambra

The Alhambra's immense popularity (it is the most visited monument in Spain) has resulted in an admission policy that limits the daily number of visitors. This means that, effectively, tickets must be bought in advance (although it is possible to turn up on the day, it's not advised). The prime attraction, the Palacios Nazaríes, are easily log-jammed by crowds of tourists, and each visitor is subject to a strictly observed entrance system of half-hourly time slots, which are printed on the tickets. You must enter the Palacios during your allocated time, but, once inside, you are free to stay as long as you like. It's essential to arrive well before your appointed slot to give yourself time to pick up your ticket from the ticket office and make your way to the entrance of the Palacios.

Alternatively, you can visit just the gardens with a special ticket. For this, you buy either a morning (8.30am-2pm) or afternoon (Mar-Oct 2-8pm; Nov-Feb 2-6pm) ticket and can enter at any time during these periods.

WHERE TO BUY TICKETS

Buy your tickets as far in advance as possible. You can do this for a 88¢ commission through the BBVA bank, either in branches or at cash machines; on the phone (902 22 44 60 within Spain/+34 91 537 91 78 from outside Spain); or online at www.alhambratickets.com. You pick up the tickets at the Alhambra ticket office on the day of your visit; you'll need your reference number, passport and the card used to buy the tickets.The only place to buy tickets for entry the same day is at the Alhambra ticket office. But this can involve extremely lengthy queues and there may be no tickets left when you get to the front. If you have no alternative, arrive at the ticket office as early in the day as possible. Otherwise, your hotel can usually book Alhambra tickets for you.

If you buy the Granada City Pass (Bono Turístico) (*see p274*), then your Alhambra entry slot and ticket are part of the package.

THE BEST TIME AND WAY TO VISIT

If possible, try to visit out of peak season. For the best, least crowded experience, we can't emphasise strongly enough that it's worth forcing yourself out of bed and pre-booking a ticket for the first slot of the day (8.30-9am). If you manage this, head straight for the Palacios Nazaríes on entering the complex, and then, when the doors open, zip through the first couple of rooms (you can always backtrack later) so that you can enjoy the later chambers and patios in solitude – an unforgettable experience.

Be sure to frequently sit on the ground when contemplating your surroundings – the Nasrids would have viewed their palaces from cushions and carpets on the floor. It has also been suggested that the rulers were largely absent during the day and that the architecture and decoration of the Alhambra was specifically designed to be appreciated by candle- and moonlight. Book for one of the magical night-time visits and you'll soon find yourself subscribing to the theory. The Junta de Andalucía's website on the Alhambra can be found at www.alhambra-patronato.es.

Note: The details below may change without notice; be sure to check the Alhambra's website or call the phone numbers above beforehand.

The Alhambra & Generalife

Information 958 22 95 75. **Open** *Mar-Oct* 8.30am-8pm daily (ticket office 8am-7pm). Night-time visit 10-11.30pm Tue-Sat (ticket office 9.30-10.30pm). *Nov-Feb* 8.30am-6pm daily (ticket office 8am-5pm). Night-time visit 8-9.30pm Fri, Sat (ticket office 7.30-8.30pm). **Admission** €10; €7 concessions; under-8s free. *Gardens only* €5. **No credit cards** (at ticket office). **Map** p257 G1 & p260.

The Alhambra complex of buildings and gardens started life in the 11th century as a basic structure of blush-coloured walls and fortified towers, which gave the site its name: *qa'lat al-Hamra* or the 'Red Castle'. Its strategic location on the inaccessible hill of al-Sabikah attracted Mohammed I, the founder of the Nasrid dynasty (1237-1492), who set up a hydraulic system of aqueducts and cisterns to support an independent township. The most spectacular period of Nasrid architecture came in the mid to late 14th century during the reigns of his successors, Yusuf I and Mohammed V, who built the Palacio de los Leones and the Palacio de Comares; 'Granada in those days was as a silver vase filled with emeralds and jacinths,' sighed one Moorish poet. The subsequent additions of Christian monarchs rankle with many visitors and certainly disrupt the aesthetic unity of the Alhambra, yet the Palacio de Carlos V and the Convento de San Francisco are undeniably beautiful in their own right and heighten the Alhambra's sense of history.

After Carlos V left in the mid 16th century, the whole site gradually fell into ruin and went on to suffer terrible abuse at the hands of Napoleon's troops, who were stationed here in 1812. Twenty years later Washington Irving's bestselling book, *Tales of the Alhambra*, put Granada firmly on the tourist map and the Spanish government finally allotted funds to the site's restoration; it remains an ongoing project (though the recent directorship of Mateo Revilla was highly controversial, with more and more of the complex being closed to tourists).

The recommended route through the site allows a slow immersion in the historical contexts. It begins at the **Alcazaba** military fortress to the west, followed by the **Palacio de Carlos V**, the **Palacios Nazaríes** (the highlight of any visit), with a stroll through the **Generalife** gardens forming a sensual coda.

The tour of the entire complex takes at least three hours, and involves quite a lot of walking, so wear comfy shoes and bring something to drink, particularly in summer. The detailed audio guide is a good investment and is available in various languages on deposit of a passport or credit card.

Entering the complex

To protect the monument, vehicular access is restricted to taxis and the **Alhambrabus** (numbers 30 and 32, every 10mins from the Plaza Nueva, 90¢). Cars follow a circuitous route to the car park just above the ticket offices. On foot, the standard ascent is up Cuesta de Gomérez from Plaza Nueva: a steep 20-minute walk to the ticket offices. This narrow street, lined with *hostales* and souvenir shops, opens out into a shady avenue once you reach the **Puerta de las Granadas** (Gate of the Pomegranates), an imposing Renaissance arch built by Carlos V, with the eighth-century **Torres Bermejas** (Vermillion Towers) to the south. From here, the left-hand path takes you to a king-sized drinking fountain added by Carlos V and overlooked by the most impressive of the four Alhambra gateways, the **Puerta de la Justicia** (Gate of Justice), built by Yusuf I in 1348. As is the custom in defensive Arab gateways, the steep road makes four right-angled turns to slow down invading armies and make them sitting ducks for the defending forces. The marble keystone is decorated with a sculpted hand thought to represent the five precepts of Islam, while on an inner arch is a sculpture of the famous Nasrid key, only found on gateways in the kingdom of Granada. The key symbolises the opening to paradise and, more prosaically, indicated the entrance to a township or *medina*.

Beyond the ticket barriers, follow signs for the Palacios Nazaríes along a cypress-lined walk past the ruins of the old **medina**. This was once a thriving city, complete with houses, schools, baths, a tannery, a mosque and kilns. Cypress trees were planted here as symbols of mourning and eternity during the Alhambra's reconstruction to simulate fallen walls and trace the lines of the original buildings.

At the end of the walk is the **Convento de San Francisco** (now a luxury *parador*; *see p272*), where Isabel and Fernando were temporarily interred during the construction of the Capilla Real (*see p266*); a marble floor-slab by the tiny chapel commemorates their stay. From here, C/Real runs west down the hill, past a strip of tacky tourist shops and the bulky Palacio de Carlos V to the **Puerta del Vino** (Wine Gate; this ruddy-coloured arch formed the toll-gate and principal access to the *medina*) and the Alcazaba.

The Alcazaba

Through the Puerta del Vino is the **Plaza de los Aljibes**, where giant underground cisterns (*aljibes*) were built immediately after the Christian conquest. Look out for the small plaque on the left, just inside the gate, which commemorates the invalid soldier, José García, who risked his life to stay behind and defuse the explosives planted by Napoleon's troops when they left Granada in 1812.

Though much of the Moorish Alcazaba is ruined, its towers and walls are well preserved, and you can trace the foundations of what was

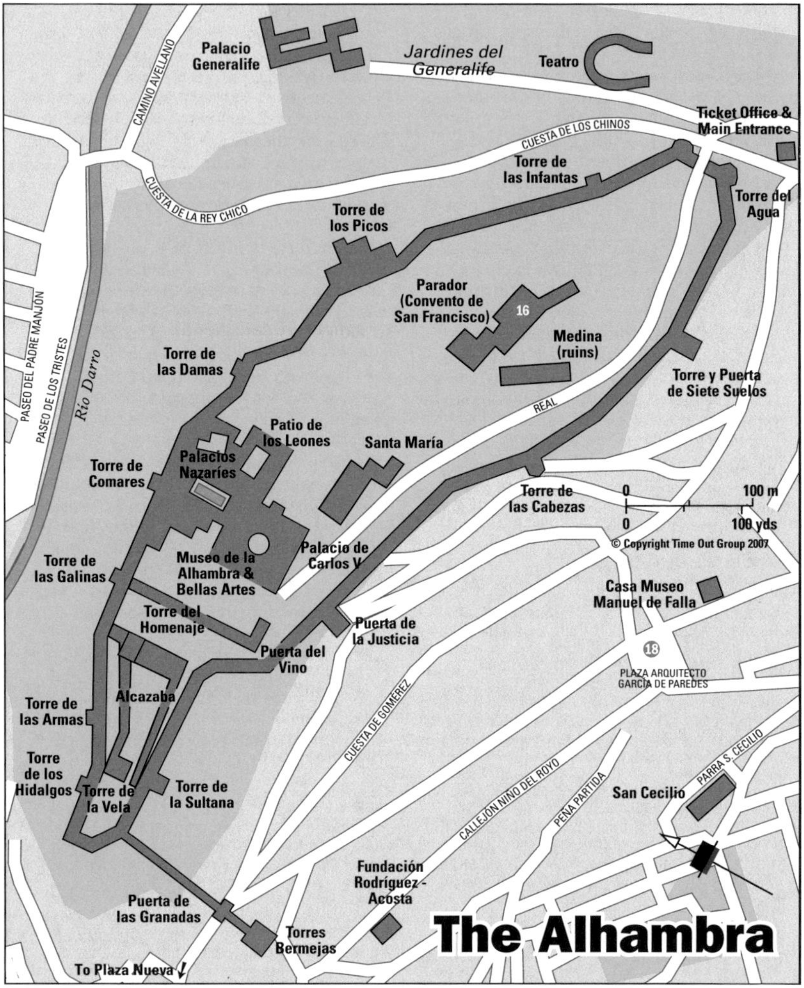

once a fortified military zone, complete with barracks, dungeons, a mosque, a communal bath and the Plaza de Armas parade ground. Of the four towers, the best known is the **Torre de la Vela**, an imposing landmark and watchtower that has featured in the city's official coat of arms since 1843. The tower is also a potent symbol of the Catholic victory over the Moors, as it was from here that Fernando and Isabel flew the victorious Christian flags on 2 January 1492; the event is still celebrated locally on the same date each year as **El Día de la Toma** (though to increasing protests).

Palacio de Carlos V

East of the Alcazaba is the huge bulk of the Renaissance Palacio de Carlos V. The chance to build a palace in the very heart of the last Muslim stronghold in Europe was too loaded with symbolism for a Christian warlord like Emperor Carlos V to resist. It may hardly blend with the Palacios Nazaríes next door, but is nevertheless one of the finest expressions of Tuscan Renaissance architecture outside Italy. Designed by Pedro Machuca, a student of Michelangelo, the centrepiece is a two-tiered circular courtyard, set inside a perfect square, with an octagonal chapel in the north-eastern corner. The carved reliefs show bloody battle scenes on the western side and mythological scenes to the south, representing the Emperor and the Empress respectively.

On the ground floor of the Palacio is the **Museo de la Alhambra**, home to the world's finest collection of Nasrid art, largely made up of findings from the Alhambra itself. The star exhibits are the huge carved door taken from the Sala de las dos Hermanas, the 132-centimetre-high (51-inch) 'Gazelle Jar', with lacy blue and gold decoration depicting oriental-style gazelles (which have since become the symbol of the Alhambra Foundation) and a magnificent fountain from the Caliphate period depicting lions attacking gazelles.

In various parts of the Alhambra complex you'll see carved the words 'Plus Ultra'. This was Carlos V's megalomaniacal family motto (literally, 'there is more'; an immodest riposte to Alexander the Great's supposed utterance of 'ne plus ultra', 'there is no more', implying he'd conquered all there was to conquer).

Museo de la Alhambra

Ground floor, Palacio de Carlos V (958 02 79 00). **Open** 9am-2.30pm Tue-Sat. **Admission** free.

Palacios Nazaríes

The Alhambra's star attraction is undoubtedly the **Palacios Nazaríes** (Nasrid Palaces; **photo** *p255*). Built in brick, wood and adobe, it's remarkable that this beautiful and fragile collection of stunningly decorated buildings and courtyards survives. It is easily the finest surviving example of Nasrid art and architecture.

The purpose of the art of this period was, by rhythmic symmetries and endless sequences of repetition, to express the infinite glory of Allah in finite terms. Linear mazes of cursive and Kufic script feature heavily in the decoration; mostly as poems eulogising the sultans and their palace or as repeated verses from the Koran, most frequently the Nasrid motto and war cry: '*Wa la ghalib ila Allah*' ('There is no conqueror but Allah').

The eight-pointed star is also a key feature, expressing the convergence of heaven and earth. Just when it seems that a pattern is sealed in perfection, there is a gap or irregularity. Builders and decorators included these on purpose – to aspire to create something perfect was forbidden as blasphemous by the Koran. The same humility (and, moreover, the Nasrids' straitened circumstances) is implied in the choice of cheap and perishable materials, such as plaster, wood and clay.

The palace complex consists of three major sections, each set around a courtyard and each with its own function: the **Palacio de Mexuar**, where the sultans conducted their official business and saw to judicial matters; the **Palacio de Comares** (or Serallo), where they would receive emissaries and important guests, and the **Palacio de Leones** (or Harem), the private living quarters of the sultan and his family.

PALACIO DE MEXUAR

The **Mexuar** is the first area of the palaces that visitors enter. Completed in 1365 (though greatly altered on many occasions since), it's thought to pre-date the other two surviving palace complexes. Its name possibly derives from the Arabic word *mashawari*, meaning 'place of counsel', and it seems to have been dedicated to judicial and bureaucratic business. The strange mixture of Islamic and Catholic decoration in the main chamber comes from the 16th-century conversion of the room into a chapel, complete with a choir in the upper balustrade. The adjoining **Cuarto Dorado** (Golden Room) was probably used as an antechamber to the Palacio de Comares, and was where the ruler, seated on a throne, held public audiences.

PALACIO DE COMARES

The breathtaking stucco work, glazed tiles and carved wood of the Palacio de Comares (or Serallo) were largely created for Mohammed V in 1370. This area separated the administrative zone of the palace from the private royal quarters (though it should be noted that it's almost impossible to determine the function of many of the rooms in the Alhambra as this was likely to have been fluid). The Cuarto Dorado leads into the delicate stucco arcades of the **Patio de los Arrayanes** (Patio of the Myrtles), originally built during the reign of Yusuf I (1333-54). For all its splendour it still adheres to the basic blueprint of Islamic domestic design: an enclosed space looking on to a patio with a central pool and perfumed plants. The four dwellings along the sides may possibly have housed the four wives allowed to each Muslim male.

Linking the patio to the 45-metre (148-foot) **Torre de Comares** (Comares Tower) is the **Sala de la Barca** (Hall of the Boat), which served as the antechamber to the throne room. Its name might derive from the hull-shaped wooden ceiling (a copy of the original that burned down in 1890), but is more likely to be a corruption of the Arabic phrase 'al-Baraka' (benediction or blessing), which is endlessly carved on the walls.

The throne room itself, also known as the **Sala de Comares** or the **Salón de Embajadores** (Hall of the Ambassadors), is one of the most spectacular and intimidating chambers in the Nasrid palaces. The inclined planes of the inlaid cedarwood ceiling create a dizzying three-dimensional effect and represent the seven heavens of Koranic paradise with Allah residing at its peak. Emblems of Fernando and Isabel were later worked into the dome and into the flooring beneath.

BANOS REALES

From the Palacio de Comares, a passage leads to the **Baños Reales** (Royal Baths), probably built during the reign of Ismail I (1314-25). The first chamber you come to is the rest room, the **Sala de las Camas** (Hall of the Beds), with benches separated by horseshoe arches. There's a gallery from where it is said the Sultan would watch his naked wives, then throw an apple to the one with whom he'd chosen to spend the night. This room was subject to a much-criticised reconstruction in the 19th century. From here another passage leads to the other bathing rooms: the cold room, the warm room and then the hot room, which would have contained two large hot water basins in which to submerge oneself.

PALACIO DE LEONES

Adjoining the Palacio de Comares, the Palacio de Leones was built during the reign of Mohammed V (1362-91) as private quarters for the ruler and his family. (In Nasrid times, the two palaces were separate, with no access between them.) At its heart is the arcaded **Patio de los Leones**, a breathtaking structure which centres on a fountain surrounded by 12 lions; it's become the archetypal image of Moorish Granada. The original, not-very-realistic lions are now gradually being replaced by copies. The channels, which begin and end in the central fountain, are a representation of the four rivers of paradise, while the po-faced beasts may represent the 12 signs of the zodiac, the 12 hours of the clock or may be a gift from a Jewish tribe representing the 12 tribes of Israel. The marble fountain is wreathed in verses by Ibn Zamrak that poetically describe its complicated hydraulic system. Although there's an ascetic beauty to the patio's warm-hued stone and stucco, this isn't what you would have seen in the 14th century; it was originally painted in vibrant tones and – like most of the rest of the complex – hung with colourful textiles. At the east end of the patio is the **Sala de los Reyes** (Hall of the Kings), named after the painted sheepskin ceiling panels that some claim depict the Nasrid emirs.

On the patio's south side is the **Sala de los Abencerrajes**, which has a stunning stalactite ceiling arranged within an eight-pointed star, and 16 windows that flood light over the milky stucco. It is reflected back on itself by the marble pool beneath, but this serenity belies the violent story that gives the room its name. It was here that Sultan Muley Hasen slaughtered the males of the Abencerraje family after one of them was suspected of having a fling with Zoraya, his favourite concubine; the rust stains on the floor are popularly supposed to be the victims' indelible blood. The lateral staircases led up to the harem, where the concubines were waited on by blind eunuchs and kept from view behind trellised wooden screens.

The **Sala de las dos Hermanas** (Hall of the Two Sisters) at the north end of the patio takes its name from twin marble floor-slabs. The *muqarnas* ceiling incorporates a cupola of over 5,000 tiny, hanging prisms refracting light from one central star, and the walls are decorated with a lengthy poem by Ibn Zamrak celebrating the circumcision of the Sultan's son.

The Sala leads through to the **Sala de los Ajimeces** or **Mirador de Daraxa** (a corruption of the Arabic '*ayn dar Aixa*' or 'eyes of the house of Aixa'), whose mullioned windows were low-slung to allow inhabitants to enjoy the view from a lounging position. The richness of the colourful stucco, the stained-glass ceiling and the elaborate tiling have led many to claim it as the perfect example of the Nasrid baroque style. A small passage from here takes you to the chambers built to accommodate Carlos V in 1528 while his nearby palace was under construction, and which were later inhabited by Washington Irving.

To the east lies the area known as the **Partal**, made up of gardens grouped around the five porticoed arches (today known as the **Torre de las Damas**) that remain from an older palace, constructed by Mohammed III (1302-09). From this area you can explore the towers and fortress walls, some of which retain their battlements and defensive trenches.

The Generalife

An inspired pattern of walkways, fountains and garden patios covers the adjoining **Cerro del Sol** (Hill of the Sun) like a living Persian carpet. These are the pleasure gardens of the sultans, known as the Generalife (*yannat al-arif* or Garden of the Architect), where the imagination of the Islamic gardeners pushed the potential of their natural materials to new heights. In the **Patio de la Acequia** (Patio of the Conduit) water spouts in a jaunty criss-cross pattern down the length of two long pools, while in the upper gardens the **Escalera de Agua** (Water Staircase) has balustrades topped by a gushing stream of water. The steps may have originally led to an oratory and were designed for the ablutions required before Muslim prayer. Just beneath is the high-walled **Patio de la Sultana**, where Zoraya used to meet her Abencerraje lover in the secret shade of a massive cypress tree. The gardens are a wonderful place to rest after trekking around the rest of the Alhambra. They enjoy stunning views over the complex and towards the Albaicín, and are impossibly romantic at night.

While on the Alhambra hill, art- and music-lovers might want to check out two small museums. Between 1916 and 1930 the painter José María Rodríguez-Acosta built for himself one of Andalucía's most notable 20th-century buildings, fusing modernist and historical styles. It is now home to the **Fundación Rodríguez-Acosta** and features a regularly changing programme of art exhibitions and events. The Cádiz-born composer Manuel de Falla lived in Granada between 1919 and 1939, and his home in the city has been restored as the **Casa Museo Manuel de Falla**.

Casa Museo Manuel de Falla

C/Antequeruela Alta 11 (958 22 21 88/www.museomanueldefalla.com). **Open** 10am-2pm Tue-Sun. **Admission** €3; €1 concessions. **No credit cards**. **Map** p257 H2 & p260.

Fundación Rodriguez-Acosta

Callejón Niños del Rollo 8 (958 22 74 97/www.fundacionrodriguezacosta.com). **Open** 10am-2pm Wed-Sun; open by prior arrangement Tue. **Admission** €4; €2 concessions; free under-8s. **No credit cards**. **Map** p257 G3 & p260.

The Albaicín

The hillside facing the Alhambra was one of the most densely populated and wealthy areas of Moorish Granada. Its typical *carmenes* (villas with terraced gardens and patios) and narrow cobbled streets are beautifully preserved. The name Albaicín derives from the name of the Muslims of Baeza who were expelled by the Christians and resettled here in 1227; at its zenith there were over 30 mosques in the district, most of which were converted to Christian churches after the Reconquista. Today, the Muslim population of Granada is again increasing. A large mosque (the **Mezquita de Granada**) has been built next to the Mirador de San Nicolás, along with an Islamic studies centre. The mosque's small, peaceful garden (with the same view as the Mirador) can be visited, and there's usually someone there to offer mint tea and information.

The Albaicín.

The best approach to the Albaicín is from the Carrera del Darro, a narrow, cobbled road that flanks the Río Darro. At No.43 is the ornate **Casa de Castril**, once owned by the secretary to Fernando and Isabel. It was purposely built in the Islamic quarter as part of the attempt to Christianise the area after the *reconquista*. Since 1879 the mansion has served as the province's **Museo Arqueológico y Etnológico** (Archaeological and Ethnological Museum). Seven rooms display Granadan artefacts from the palaeolithic period up until 1492.

Over the water, opposite the church of **San Pedro y San Pablo** (open hours of services), is the crumbling tower and amputated arch of **La Puerta de los Tableros**, a bridge and gateway connecting the Alhambra with the Albaicín.

Following the river under the Alhambra's battlements, the road opens out into the tree-shaded **Paseo de los Tristes**. Bullfights and tournaments used to be held here, but it is now full of restaurants and bars. At the end of the road, take the left turning along Cuesta del Chapiz to reach the heart of the Albaicín. Keep following this road as it bends to the left. Pass the church of **El Salvador** (Plaza de Abad 2, no phone, closed Sun), which was built over a mosque and retains its original patio, to reach C/Panaderos. This leads to the lively produce markets on Plaza Larga.

The Lorca trail

Federico García Lorca, the most widely translated Spanish author of all time, was born in 1898 in the village of Fuente Vaqueros, west of Granada; his birthplace now houses a small, but beautifully laid-out museum. Although the family moved to the city when Lorca was 11, the rural surroundings and folklore of his early childhood retained a strong hold on his adult imagination. Through his mother's influence, Lorca became a highly accomplished pianist, and his love of traditional music and flamenco lay at the very heart of his poetic vision. (Much to his father's irritation, it also distracted him from his law degree at the University of Granada.)

After some modest success with his play *Mariana Pineda*, he finally achieved major renown in 1928 with *El Romancero Gitano*, a poetic blend of gypsy ballads, mythology and surrealism. Overnight, he became seen as a champion of Andalucían subculture and Spain's 'Gypsy Poet' – a title he detested. He then began, however, a highly prolific period that established his reputation as a playwright. The 'rural' trilogy of *Bodas de Sangre* (*Blood Wedding*), *Yerma* and *La Casa de Bernada Alba* (*The House of Bernada Alba*) gained massive popularity both at home in Spain and in Latin America.

In July 1936, with the country on the brink of civil war, Lorca made a fatal decision to postpone a trip to Mexico and spend the summer in Granada. The city quickly fell to the Falangists, who launched a crusade to hunt down and execute all Republican sympathisers. Although Lorca was not politically active, he was associated with the liberal left by dint of his homosexuality, the 'inflammatory' nature of his plays, and the fact that his sister, Concha, was married to Granada's newly elected socialist mayor. Lorca sought refuge at the house of Luis Rosales (now the Hotel Reina Cristina), but was dragged out of hiding on 16 August and murdered three days later in the nearby village of Viznar. As Lorca eerily predicted in a poem, his body was never found.

The other major landmark in the Albaicín is the large rectangular **Mirador de San Nicolás**. If you head up the slope from either C/Elvira or Carrera del Darro you're likely to hit it eventually; the lookout offers the quintessential Alhambra view, especially at sunset when the opaline Sierra Nevada glows in the background.

Note: the Albaicín has an ongoing petty crime problem and you should be careful to keep to main routes and make sure your valuables are out of sight, particularly after dark. Don't be scared, but do be careful.

Mezquita de Granada

Plaza San Nicolás (958 20 19 03/www.mezquitadegranada.com). **Open** *Garden* Apr-Sept 11am-2pm, 6-9.30pm daily. Oct-Mar 11am-2pm, 5-7pm daily. **Admission** free. **Map** p256 D2.

Museo Arqueológico y Etnológico

Casa de Castril, Carrera del Darro 43 (958 22 56 40). **Open** 2.30-8.30pm Tue; 9am-8.30pm Wed-Sat; 9am-2.30pm Sun. **Admission** €1.50; free with EU passport. **No credit cards**. **Map** p257 E2.

Sacromonte

Bordering the Albaicín to the north-east is **Sacromonte**, the heart of the gypsy (*gitano*) quarter. The *gitanos* originated from India and had appeared in Spain by the mid 15th century, with their own dress, customs and language (*caló*). They were deemed a threat to public order and their civil rights were severely restricted in the following centuries, leaving them marginalised on the edges of society. Today, the strongest residue of their ancient traditions – not to mention a crucially important source of income – is the *zambra* (a generic name for *gitano* dances and music); indeed many of Spain's finest flamenco artists have come from gypsy families.

The gypsy cave quarters on Sacromonte hill were initially segregated from the Albaicín by a 14th-century Moorish rampart, but the influx of a poor, rural population at the end of the 19th century rapidly increased the need for cheap cave dwellings, and by 1950 there were over 3,500 inhabited caves in the district. Although

Under the Franco administration any mention of Lorca's name was prohibited, but the city has finally given Lorca the recognition he deserves; one of the family properties in Granada has been converted into a memorial park and museum (the **Huerta de San Vicente**), though, alas, the architects have also succeeded in almost entirely destroying the atmosphere of the place – the characterless modern park replaced a wonderful old orchard.

The other major Lorca sites are the **Museo-Casa Natal Federico García Lorca** Fuente Vaqueros and **Parque Federico García Lorca** in the village of Viznar, where he was shot.

Huerta de San Vicente

C/Virgen Blanca s/n (958 25 84 66/ www.huertadesanvicente.com). **Open** (guided tours every 45mins) *Jan-Mar, Oct-Dec* 10am-1pm, 4-7pm Tue-Sun. *Apr-June, Sept* 10am-1pm, 5-8pm Tue-Sun. *July, Aug* 10am-3pm Tue-Sun. **Admission** €3; concessions €1; free to all Wed. **No credit cards.**

Named after Lorca's mother, Vicenta, this house was the summer residence of the Lorca family from 1926 to 1936. It is now surrounded by a manicured park flanked by the Neptuno shopping mall, but when Lorca lived here it sat amid orchards, with views of the Sierra that filled Lorca with inspiration: 'It is there, in my Huerta de San Vicente, that I write my most tranquil theatre.' The downstairs rooms hold some original furniture, portraits and photographs. Upstairs memorabilia includes a hand-painted poster for 'La Barraca', Lorca's travelling theatre troupe, which took popular farces and tragedies to rural Spanish communities. To reach Huerta de San Vicente, take bus No.4 heading west from Gran Vía or Plaza del Carmen towards the Palacio de Deportes.

Museo-Casa Natal Federico García Lorca

C/Poeta García Lorca 4, Fuente Vaqueros (958 51 64 53/www.museogarcialorca.org). **Open** (guided tour only) *July, Aug* hourly 10am-2pm. *Sept-June* hourly 10am-2pm & 5-7pm. **Admission** €1.80. **No credit cards.**

Although Lorca's simple birthplace has been extensively altered, the well-cared-for museum remains evocative. Downstairs, the family's living quarters have been re-created, while the top-floor granary has an extensive display of memorabilia, including costumes, posters and drafts of Lorca's plays. Buses leave Granada for Fuente Vaqueros between 9am and 9pm hourly Monday to Friday, and every two hours at weekends.

many were abandoned after heavy floods in 1963, about 80 per cent of the Sacromonte population continues to live in converted caves nowadays, and some of these dwellings are surprisingly luxurious.

For a better understanding of the Sacromonte cave community, it's worth visiting the **Centro de Interpretación del Sacromonte**. This fascinating open-air centre, incorporating seven reconstructed cave dwellings, aims to explain the environmental and socio-cultural genesis of Sacromonte, and to preserve some of its dying local traditions. Call for information about occasional live performances.

Also to be found on the hill is the **Abadía del Sacromonte**, a little-visited abbey that contains a superb collection of religious art and treasures. It was founded in the 17th century after 25 leaden tablets inscribed in Arabic and other items concerning the martyrdom of Saint Cecilio (the city's patron saint) were discovered on the site. Unfortunately, later evidence suggested that the tablets were fakes. To reach the abbey, take the number 31 bus.

Abadía del Sacromonte

Camino Abadía del Sacromonte s/n (958 22 14 45). **Open** (guided tours every 30mins) 11am-1pm, 4-6pm Tue-Sat; 11am-noon, 1-2pm Sun. **Admission** €3; €2 concessions. **No credit cards. Map** p256 off D1.

Centro de Interpretación del Sacromonte

Barranco de los Negros (958 21 51 20/www. sacromontegranada.com). **Open** *Apr-Oct* 10am-2pm, 5-9pm Tue-Fri; 11am-9pm Sat, Sun. *Nov-May* 10am-2pm, 4-7pm Tue-Fri; 11am-7pm Sat, Sun. **Admission** *Museum* €4; free under-4s. *Mirador & botanical route* €1; free under-4s. **No credit cards. Map** p256 off C1.

The cathedral & around

West of the Alhambra hill and the Albaicín, modern Granada sprawls out across the plain. The backbone of the city is the traffic-choked Gran Vía, which stretches from the Jardines del Triunfo to Plaza Isabel la Católica. The major sightseeing focus in this part of town is immediately west of Plaza Isabel la Católica: the **cathedral** and the **Capilla Real**.

Santa Iglesia cathedral.

A few months before her death in 1504, Isabel commissioned Enrique de Egas to build the **Capilla Real** (Royal Chapel) as a mausoleum for herself and her husband, who wished to be buried in Granada, the scene of their most important victory. The late-Gothic chapel was completed in the following decades and is Granada's finest Christian building.

The royal coffins rest in the crypt; they are simple, plain lead boxes, but sit beneath elaborate Renaissance sepulchres. The lower of the two sepulchres is by the Florentine sculptor Domenico Fancelli, and is covered in myriad symbols of Isabel and Fernando's reign: corpulent lions denoting royal status; griffons representing paganism; and a pelican ripping open its own chest as a symbol of Christian sacrifice. The split pomegranate, a metaphor for defeated Granada, is depicted underneath the Reyes Católicos' unifying emblems of the yoke and sheaf of arrows. Isabel and Fernando themselves look peaceful, if a little jowly; the fact that Isabel wielded greater power is perhaps suggested by her head sinking more deeply into the pillow than her husband's.

Next to Fancelli's sepulchre is the tomb of Isabel and Fernando's daughter, Juana la Loca ('the Mad'), and her faithless husband, Felipe el Hermoso ('the Handsome'). This second tomb, carved by Bartolomé Ordóñez, is grander in dimension but lacks the fine expression of Fancelli's work.

In front of the tombs, the stunning altarpiece depicts the life of Christ and the tortures of John the Baptist and John the Evangelist in lingering detail, while, to the right, two massive carved wooden doors lead to the **Sacristía**. This houses a priceless collection of crown jewels, including Isabel's crown and sceptre and Fernando's sword, which were traditionally paraded though Granada in the annual celebration of the conquest. There are also 15th-century Flemish paintings, including works by Rogier van der Weyden, Hans Memling and Dieric Bouts.

Almost immediately opposite the entrance to the Capilla Real, is **La Madraza** (C/Oficios 14), with a stunning original *mihrab* (prayer niche). This building is all that remains of the richly decorated Moorish university (*medressa* in Arabic) constructed on the orders of Yusuf I in 1349. It's now part of the modern university.

Built on to the Capilla Real is the **Santa Iglesia Catedral Metropolitana de Granada**, which was to replace Granada's mosque as a final expression of the Catholic rehabilitation of the city. It was started in the 1520s by the Gothicist Enrique de Egas, and then taken over five years later by Renaissance-inclined Diego de Siloé. Though it wasn't finished until the 18th century, the interior was constructed much as de Siloé had intended and is one of the most sensational and original examples of Spanish Renaissance architecture. Highlights are the bright, lofty curves of Siloé's central chapel and Alonso Cano's melancholy Immaculate Virgin in the sacristy.

The cathedral's vertiginous main façade by Cano is designed to resemble a Roman triumphal arch – an allusion to the Christian victory over Islam – and is best viewed from the Plaza Alonso Cano, which also contains a statue of the architect (bearing an uncanny resemblance to the young Charlton Heston).

From here, the Alcaicería runs towards C/Reyes Católicos. Once a bustling bazaar, which had existed since the days of the old *medina*, it's now a rather tacky tourist arcade. The original structures burned down in a fire in 1843 and were replaced with the gaudy stucco you see today.

Directly opposite the main arcade as it emerges on to C/Reyes Católicos is the graceful brick archway that forms the entrance to the **Corral del Carbón**. Built at the beginning of the 14th century and situated in the streets that led from the city gates to the *medina*, this is the best surviving example of a typical eastern *caravanserai* in Spain. Merchants lodged and stored their goods on the upper floors while their animals were safely tethered in the courtyard below. Its present name derives from the coal merchants who used it 200 years later. It has recently been restored and now houses shops and galleries.

Capilla Real

C/Oficios 3 (958 22 92 39/www.capillarealgranada.com). **Open** *Apr-Oct* 10.30am-1pm, 4-7pm Mon-Sat; 11am-1pm, 4-7pm Sun. *Nov-Mar* 10.30am-1pm, 3.30-6.30pm Mon-Sat; 11am-1pm, 3.30-6.30pm Sun. **Admission** €3; free under-10s. **No credit cards**. **Map** p257 E5.

Santa Iglesia Catedral Metropolitana de Granada

C/Gran Vía 5 (958 22 29 59). **Open** *Apr-Oct* 10.45am-1.30pm, 4-8pm Mon-Sat; 4-8pm Sun. *Nov-Mar* 10.45am-1.30pm, 4-7pm Mon-Sat; 4-7pm Sun. **Admission** €3; free under-10s. **No credit cards**. **Map** p257 E5.

The University & the north

Five minutes' walk west of the cathedral is the **Universidad de Granada**, founded by Carlos V in 1531 in order to propagate the teaching of Christian doctrine, and now home to 60,000 students (a good number of whom are foreigners). The old university building (now the law faculty) has a baroque portal.

Also in Plaza de la Universidad, the sumptuous 18th-century church of **Santos Justo y Pastor** (open hours of services) stands on the site of the old mosque and Majadalbecy cistern; it's worth having a peek inside for its frescoes and sacristy treasures.

The quarter's real gem, however, is the **Monasterio de San Jerónimo** (**photo** *p268*), which lies at the very end of C/Duquesa. The monastery, founded by Fernando and Isabel, was originally sited in Santa Fé to the west of the city, but a plague of insects forced the Hieronymite order to move to Granada in 1521. One of the graceful courtyards is filled with fragrant orange trees and portals by Diego de Siloé, the other – only glimpsed through a grille – has Gothic gargoyles and Mudéjar wooden ceilings, and served as lodgings for Empress Isabel on her honeymoon. (Carlos V, her new husband, rather unromantically stayed at the Alhambra.) The stunning frescoed church is a masterpiece of the Spanish Renaissance and the burial place of 'El Gran Capitán' Gonzalo Fernández de Córdoba, the swashbuckling commander of Isabel and Fernando's troops. His many victories are depicted in some of the church's frescoes, and his jewelled sword originally slotted into the painting to the left of the magnificent altarpiece, but was stolen in the 17th century and replaced with a wooden copy.

Gonzalo also provided the land for the **Monasterio de la Cartuja**, located on the northern outskirts of the city. This is Spain's most lavishly decorated 16th-century Carthusian monastery and houses some show-stopping examples of Spanish baroque. After rooms full of grisly paintings depicting the torture of English monks under Henry VIII, the visitor is rewarded with the glorious splendours of the church itself, especially the blinding effect of the Virgin of the Assumption surrounded by mirror-encrusted golden pillars. Behind the presbytery is a tabernacle of polychrome marble, jasper and rare woods, which sits under a frescoed cupola by Palomino depicting Saint Bruno, the monastery's founding father. The whole extravaganza is topped off by the single-nave sacristy, where cataracts of white pillars, foaming with geometrical mouldings, shoot down from another frescoed cupola and an impossibly ornate vaulted ceiling. To reach the monastery, catch bus number 8 or letter 'C' from Gran Vía, heading away from Plaza Isabel la Católica.

Monasterio de la Cartuja

Paseo de la Cartuja s/n (958 16 19 32). **Open** *Apr-Oct* 10am-1pm, 4-8pm daily. *Nov-Mar* 10am-1pm, 3.30-6pm daily. **Admission** €3; free under-8s. **No credit cards**.

Monasterio de San Jerónimo

C/Rector López Argueta 9 (958 27 93 37). **Open** *Apr-Oct* 10am-1.30pm, 4-7.30pm daily. *Nov-Mar* 10am-1.30pm, 3-6.30pm daily. **Admission** €3. **No credit cards**. **Map** p256 C6.

Parque de las Ciencias

In a city with so much history and art, it may seem strange to visit something as futuristic as a science park, but it's entirely appropriate. A fascinating exhibition here celebrates the philosophers, thinkers, engineers and artists of al-Andalus who made invaluable contributions

Monasterio San Jerónimo. See p267.

to modern science in all its forms. The park extends over a huge site, with lots of outdoor installations – an astronomy garden, hydraulics exhibits, a maze, a 'mental gymnasium' (oversize puzzles), and lots of toys and gadgets demonstrating scientific principles, as well as a butterfly house. It is located on the south-western edge of the city. To reach it, take bus 4, 5, 10 or 11; if travelling by car, you'll see it from the A338 heading towards Alhama de Granada, or come off the A44-E902 Jaén–Motril motorway at 'Salida 131' (for Palacio de Congresos).

Parque de las Ciencias

Avda del Mediterráneo (958 13 19 00/www.parqueciencias.com). **Open** 10am-7pm Tue-Sat; 10am-3pm Sun. **Admission** *Museum* €4; €3 concessions. *Planetarium* €1.80; €1.50 concessions. **Credit** V.

Where to eat & drink

The tourist breakfast hotspots are terrace tables on neighbouring Plazas Bib-Rambla, Pescaderia and Pasiegas, behind the cathedral. For a cheaper *desayuno* with the locals, try **Cafe Opera** (C/Alvaró de Bazan, map p260 D5), by the *mercado municipal*, **Cafeteria Carlos** (C/Molinos 2), near Campo del Príncipe, or the slick new **Cafe Bar Sancho** (C/Tablas 16, map p257 E6), off Plaza Trinidad. This square also has a great little bread stall, **Kiosco Enriqueta**, with golden brioches and sugar-dusted *ensaimadas* (doughy pastries) for breakfast on the go.

Granada is one of the few places left in Spain where the free tapas tradition still thrives. Order a drink at a bar and, if the server shouts '*Un primero*' ('One first'), you know your first free tapas is on its way. Usually, the level of gastro delight rises with each drink (eg olives with the *primero*, ham with *segundo*, paella with *tercero*) but it varies from bar to bar (and hour to hour). The bars listed below generally give good *primero*. Top tapas-hunting grounds are on and around Plaza Campo del Príncipe (map p257 H3), C/Navas (map p257 G5) and C/Elvira (map p256 D4).

C/Elvira and its environs are also home to the reverse *reconquista* of Granada's gastro landscape – with kebab shops and *teterías* (tea rooms) jostling for space. The *teterías* are popular with backpackers and young locals and are becoming vital stops on the nightlife trail, some offering live music along with infusions and hookahs. The best and most tranquil *tetería*, though, is **La Tetería del Bañuelo** (Plazeta de la Concepcíon, 958 22 41 97, map p257 H5), which has a peaceful leafy terrace and lush, ornate interior. Another with good sticky cakes, a long list of teas and occasional live world music is **Dar Ziryab** (C/Calderería Nueva 11, mobile 607 920 931).

A new interest in Granada's Moorish past is also enlivening the normally staid offerings in the city's restaurants – especially in the **Albaicín**. Here you'll find a slew of *carmen* restaurants with beautiful terraces and gardens. Beware, though, that many are trading on their views, rather than the food and service.

It's easy to avoid the tourist traps – steer clear of laminated menus and touting waiters – which are predictably clustered around the Alhambra, Plaza Nueva and Plaza Bib-Rambla. To dine with the locals, head for the area above the Camino del Ronda around Plaza de Gracia (map p257 off E5) or to the *pijo* (posh) bars and restaurants within the Plaza de Toros (map p256 off A5), such as restaurant **La Ermita** (Plaza de Toros 25, 958 29 02 57) and tapas bar **Tendido Uno** (Plaza de Toros, 958 27 23 02, www.tendido1.com).

Albahaca

C/Varela 17 (958 22 49 23). **Open** 1.30-3.30pm, 8.30-11pm Tue-Sat; 1.30-3.30pm Sun. Closed Aug. **Average** €€. **Credit** MC, V. **Map** p257 G5 ❶

Near Santo Domingo church, this good-value restaurant has a slightly genteel tearoom feel. The simple, strangely Brit-like dishes include roast lamb with duchesse potatoes and salmon in hazelnut sauce.

Ajo Blanco

C/Palacios 17 (958 22 81 28). **Open** 1-3.30pm, 8pm-1am Mon-Sat. **Average** €. **No credit cards**. **Map** p257 G5 ❷

Tucked away down some steps opposite Santo Domingo, this tiny wine bar is a real find. The charming owner, Nicolás Fernández Única, has a superb *bodega*, including some fantastic cavas that you won't find anywhere else in Granada. His small range of (free) tapas are gastronomic delights.

Arrayanes

Cuesta Marañas 4 (958 22 84 01/www.rest-arrayanes.com). **Open** 1.30-4.30pm, 7.30-11.30pm Mon, Wed-Sun. **Average** €€. **Credit** MC, V. **Map** p257 E4 ❸

Just off Caldereria Nueva, this is far and away the best Moroccan restaurant in town. Specialities such as tagines, *pasteles*, brochettes and couscous are served up in ornate and convivial surroundings, although the new dining room upstairs lacks the atmosphere of downstairs. The friendly owner speaks seven languages. Unlicensed.

Bar Kiki

Plaza de San Nicolás 9 (958 27 67 15/mobile 639 02 16 87). **Open** 8am-midnight Mon, Tue, Thur-Sun; 8am-6pm Wed. Closed 2wks July. **Average** €€. **No credit cards**. **Map** p256 D2 ❹

Considering its location, this should be a tourist trap, but it's actually wonderful: sunny terrace tables (the locals eat inside), amazing tapas and *platos*, and an outstanding *bodega* of quality wines.

Bodega Espadafor

C/Tinajilla s/n (958 20 21 38). **Open** *June-Sept* noon-4pm, 8pm-midnight Mon-Sat. *Oct-May* noon-4pm, 8pm-midnight Tue-Sun. **Average** €. **No credit cards**. **Map** p256 B4 ❺

A rough diamond, this historic (opened 1910) barn-like tapas bar doesn't need its beautiful old tiles, distinctive mural and old *feria* posters to attract attention – its delicious tapas and good service are more than enough reason to linger. If you're not given the wonderful *jamón asado* (roast pork) as your first tapas, don't wait – just buy some.

Bodegas Castañeda

C/Almireceros 1-3 (958 21 54 64). **Open** 11.30am-4.30pm, 7.30pm-1am Mon-Thur; 11.30am-1am Fri-Sun. **Average** €-€€. **Credit** MC, V. **Map** p257 E5 ❻

This traditional stand-up bar (divided into two following a family dispute) is packed out at weekends with a mix of locals and tourists taking advantage of good free tapas. The *verbena* (selection) of canapés is big enough for sharing as is the *tabla caliente* (a selection of hot tapas).

Botánico

C/Málaga 3 (958 27 15 98). **Open** 1pm-1am Mon-Thur, Sun; 1pm-2am Fri-Sat. **Average** €€. **Credit** MC, V. **Map** p256 D6 ❼

With terrace tables alongside the botanical gardens, this minimalist cream and orange joint has lounge-style sounds, light simple dishes of the day and a creative, fusion menu, including veggie options and a range of huge salads. At lunchtime, there's a good-sized set *menú* (€11).

La Brujidera – Casa del Vino

C/Monjas del Carmen 2 (958 22 25 95). **Open** 12.30-4pm, 8.30pm-1am Mon-Thur, Sun; 12.30-4pm, 8.30pm-2am Fri, Sat. **Average** €€. **No credit cards**. **Map** p257 F4 ❽

This small, smoky wine bar stocks an impressive array of Spanish wines, and serves up interesting tapas, such as *mollejas* (duck gizards) in orange sauce or marinaded *lomo de orza* (pork loin).

Carmen de Verde Luna

Camino Nuevo de San Nicolás 16 (958 29 17 94). **Open** *Mar-Dec* 8.30-11pm Wed-Sun. Closed Jan, Feb & 1wk July-Aug. **Average** €€€. **Credit** MC, V. **Map** p257 D2 ❾

A young team runs this *carmen* terrace restaurant – one of the more affordable dining-with-a-view options to be found in the Albaicín. The monthly-changing menu is based on seasonal produce, featuring dishes such as artichokes with bean mousse, prawns and crisped ham.

Casa Torcuato

C/Agua 20 (958 20 28 18/www.casatorcuato.es). **Open** *June-Sept* noon-4pm, 8pm-midnight Mon, Wed-Sun. *Oct-May* noon-4pm, 8pm-midnight Mon-Sat; 11am-4pm Sun. **Average** €-€€. **Credit** DC, MC, V. **Map** p256 C1 ❿

It seems the whole of the Albaicín, locals and tourists, descends on this famed bar-restaurant for the excellent fried fish tapas or dishes such as *solomillo* with foie gras and mushrooms, and pork loin with grapes. Terrace tables offer a more tranquil experience at the weekend.

Los Diamantes

C/Navas 28 (no phone). **Open** 1-4pm, 8-10.30pm Mon-Fri. Closed Sept. **Average** €. **No credit cards**. **Map** p257 F/G4/5 ⓫

This tiny, bustling seafood tapas bar would be easy to miss were it not for the crowds of locals jostling for wonderfully sweet prawns and so on, yours for the price of a beer. Its tiled walls and long zinc counter give it a trad feel but don't help the noise levels. Some of the best free tapas in Granada.

Mesón El Trillo

Callejón de Aljibe de Trillo 3 (958 22 51 82/www.granadainfo.com/trillo). **Open** 1.30-4pm, 8pm-midnight Mon, Wed-Sun. **Average** €€. **Credit** DC, MC, V. **Map** p257 E2 ⓬

To gain admission, ring the bell at the gate of this tranquil, friendly garden restaurant deep in the Albaicín. The Basque chef/owner blends elements of the superb cuisine of her homeland with distinctly Granadan touches in the large-portioned, large-flavoured dishes. Highlights include *bacalao al pil pil* (salt cod with garlic and chilli) and a creamy cheesecake-style raspberry tart. The set lunch-time *menú* is a steal.

Mirador de Aixa

Carril San Agustín 2 (958 22 36 16/www.miradordeaixa.com). **Open** *July-Sept* 9pm-midnight Mon; 1.30-3.30pm, 9pm-midnight Tue-Sat; 1.30-3.30pm Sun. *Oct-June* 1.30-3.30pm, 9pm-midnight Mon-Sat; 1.30-3.30pm Sun. Closed 2wks Jan/Feb & 2wks Nov. **Average** €€€€. **Credit** MC, V. **Map** p257 E1 13

One of the best 'mirador' *carmen* restaurants looking across at the Alhambra from the Albaicín, Mirador de Aixa is a family concern. There's a small dining room and outside terrace, as well as terraced gardens dotted with fruit trees, jasmine and fragrant herbs. The cod poached in oil with prawns and peppers, and the chocolate dessert *lagrimas de Boabdil* ('tears of Boabdil'), are recommended.

La Ninfa

Campo del Príncipe 14 (958 22 96 30). **Open** 1.30-4.30pm, 8.30pm-12.30am daily. **Average** €€. **Credit** MC, V. **Map** p257 off H4.

Owned by the same people as the *hostal* of the same name across the square (*see p273*), La Ninfa turns out good, fresh seafood, and fairly functional pizza and pasta dishes. The real reason to come is to sit on the lovely plant-filled rooftop terrace.

El Rincón de Michael Landon

C/Rector García Duarte 2 (no phone). **Open** noon-4pm, 8pm-1am Mon-Sat; 8pm-1am Sun. **Average** €. **No credit cards. Map** p256 off C5.

In the heart of the student nightlife quarter, this grungy-but-fun little bar is a friendly spot for a snack and a beer and for finding out where the best late-night clubs of the moment are. The friendly couple that run it know all about the local night scene and are retro kitsch fans; even the tapas sport names such as Falcon Crest and Starsky & Hutch.

La Sabanilla

C/San Sebastián 14 (mobile 659 11 85 83). **Open** 8.45pm-2am Tue-Sun. Closed 2wks late Aug. **Average** €. **No credit cards. Map** p257 F6 14

One of the oldest, smallest and hardest-to-find bars in the city barrels out excellent local wines and sherries to a friendly crowd.

Taberna La Opipara

Campo del Príncipe 15 (958 22 70 83). **Open** 12.30-4.30pm, 8pm-1am Tue-Sun; 8.30pm-1am Mon. **Average** €€. **No credit cards. Map** p257 H3 15

Among the sprawl of bars on this square, the warm colours, candlelight and chilled tunes make this a welcoming space – an atmosphere reinforced by its enthusiastic owner Manuel, who serves salads, *tostadas* and *raciones*, such as French farmhouse cheeses and *mojama* (air-dried tuna) from Barbate.

Las Tinajas

C/Martínez Campos 17 (958 25 43 93). **Open** noon-5pm, 8pm-midnight daily. Closed mid July-mid Aug. **Average** €€€€. **Credit** V. **Map** p257 off G6.

Always crowded, this reassuringly staid, traditionally decorated tapas bar and restaurant is roundly regarded as one of the best places to eat in town. The menu features a range of classic dishes with an Arabic hint, such as suckling lamb with honey and Mozarabe-style ham.

Tragaluz

C/Nevot 26 (958 22 29 24/mobile 687 32 27 04). **Open** 1.30-4pm, 8.30pm-midnight Tue-Sat; 1.30-4pm Sun. Closed Aug. **Average** €€-€€€. **Credit** V. **Map** p257 off F2/3.

Named for its skylight (*tragaluz*), this friendly restaurant, just east of the Campo del Príncipe, is a well-known meeting place for artists, writers and others fond of a hearty discussion over the excellent tagines, houmous and other dishes with a Moorish flavour. The owner, writer and academic Mustafa Akalay Nasser, is a local celeb. The restaurant does not always open midweek if there are no bookings.

Flamenco

There's plenty of flamenco to be found in Granada, but if someone tells you where to see real flamenco, chances are it won't, in fact, be very real; flamenco is by nature a spontaneous phenomenon. If you hang out in an Albaicín or Sacromonte bar and you're very lucky, you may get to eavesdrop on a *gitano* knees-up. If you want something scheduled, however, you'll have to compromise.

The *zambras* at the flamenco caves in the Sacromonte are expensive and very touristy. Although the performers are usually fine, they're normally pretty bored, and the uninitiated audience can't give them the feedback they need for a special performance. Also, most hotels push pricey packages where you're ferried to and from the cave, given a walking tour and a free drink as well as the show. You may save a few quid just turning up and seeing what's on offer, but ask about prices before going in or ordering anything.

One place in the Albaicín that offers a better experience for the more knowledgeable flamenco fan (at a decent price) is the **Peña**

Las Tinajas.

La Plateria (Placeta de Toqueros 7, 958 21 06 50), the oldest flamenco *peña* (a kind of flamenco social/fan club) in Granada, which has shows open to the general public on Thursdays at 10pm (€6 incl drink, no shows Aug & Sept). An even cheaper option is a performance in one of the tearooms and bars around C/Elvira, where a renewed interest in the possible Arabic roots of flamenco takes the form of 'flamenco-fusion' performances by young local musicians. Entry is normally free, though drinks prices may go up when there's live music. A good bet is the bar **Eshavira** (*see below*).

But if you really want to see top-class flamenco, time your visit to coincide with a performance by touring professional artists at venues like the Centro Internacional de Estudios Gitanos, more commonly known as **La Chumbera** (Camino del Monte s/n, 958 21 56 47, www.centroflamenco.org) or, better still, come during the international music and dance festival (**Festival Internacional de Música y Danza de Granada**) in June and July, which often attracts top national flamenco stars, and also offers lots of free shows.

Nightlife

With a large student population augmented by waves of young travellers, Granada has plenty of life in its nightlife. The heart of Granada clubland is split by the Gran Vía – the university area below it features mostly small, fashion-conscious music venues and cheap-beer pubs. The lower reaches of the Albaicín (around C/Elvira) generally hosts a grungier dope-led scene, where your politics (sexual as well as social) are more important than your labels. To mix with the beautiful people, head out to the Plaza de Toros (map p256 off A5), or try along C/Pedro Antonio de Alarcón (map p257 off G5). The disco-caves in Sacromonte fill up in the summer with sweaty youth and cheesy hits.

To get the low-down on the gay/lesbian/mixed scene, start with tapas (great tortilla) at friendly, lesbian-leaning **La Tortuga** (C/Elvira 46, map p256 D4) or **La Sal** (C/Santa Paula 11, no phone, map p256 D5) the oldest *ambiente* bar in town. The pick-up parlour **Tic-Tac** (C/Horno de Haza 19, 958 29 63 66, map p256 D6), with its busy dark room, is one for the boys. There are normally more guys than gals at swish disco **Six Colours** (C/Tendillas de Santa Paula 6, 958 20 39 95, open from 9pm daily, free, map p256 D5) too – though straight women may be attracted by the claim that it pulls in the best-looking men in town. For information on the web about the city's gay scene, see http://granadainfo.com/pamela/gaygranada.htm.

Afrodisia (C/Almona del Boquerón, corner of C/Zafra, no phone, open from 11pm daily, free, map p256 C5) is where Granada's b-boys and smokers come for 'underground blacksounds' – hip hop (Tuesday), ska and reggae (Wednesday), funk and afro-latino sounds (Thursday), jazz (Sunday) and any of the above on Fridays and Saturdays.

Enano Rojo (C/Elvira 91, 958 20 30 84, open from 10pm daily, free, map p256 C4) is a hot and sweaty bar that's always spilling out into the street; there's funk, soul and hip hop on the decks, with live music on Wednesday and Thursday nights.

Down the most unlikely looking alleyway off C/Azacayas lurks **Eshavira** (C/Postigo de la Cuna 2, 958 25 84 49, admission varies, map p256 C4) a low-ceilinged, smoky bar, which serves up great live jazz on Wednesday and Thursday and flamenco on Sunday nights; veteran guitarist Emilio Maya is a regular.

Not far away is **Granada Diez** (C/Cárcel Baja 10, 958 22 40 01, €8 incl one drink, map p257 E5), a super-kitschy converted cinema that becomes a club after midnight (though it doesn't really kick off until around 3am); the squidgy gold sofas hold dressed-up behinds when they're not shaking to Spanish Top 40 and cheesy tunes. No trainers.

Granada's anglophile indie kids crowd into the city's top power pop stop **Sugarpop** (C/Gran Capitán 25, mobile 615 592 416, map p256 C6) for friendly vibes, Radiohead and reasonably priced drinks.

Shopping

Granada's main shopping area is centred on the streets south of the cathedral. Department store **El Corte Inglés** (Carrera del Genil 22, 958 22 32 40, map p257 H6) is a good one-stop shop. For food shopping, try the **mercado municipal** on C/San Agustín (map p257 E5), off the Gran Vía, and the street stalls that run from here to Plaza Pescadería. For bric-a-brac and antiques head for the C/Elvira and its surrounding streets.

Specialist food shops worth seeking out include **La Alacena** (C/San Jerónimo 3, 958 20 68 90, www.alacena.net, closed last 2wks Jan, map p257 E5), run by a Spanish-British couple, which sells olive oils, hams and other regional produce; and **La Oliva** (C/Rosario 9, 958 22 57 54, map p257 G5), whose warm, knowledgeable owner Francisco offers tastings of his superb artisanal wines, cheeses, oils, preserves, honeys, chocolates and hams. For sweet Moroccan delights, such as *briwat* with lemon and honey, try **Nujaila** (C/Calderería Nueva, 958 21 00 20, map p257 E4).

Other interesting specialist shops are **Cerámica Fabre** (Plaza Pescadería s/n, 958 28 81 92, map p257 E6), with its typical local handmade blue-and-green-painted ceramics; the classical and flamenco guitar workshop **Guitarreria Germán Pérez Barranco** (C/Reyes Católicos 47, 958 22 70 33, www.guitarreria.com, map p257 F5) is also a reliable place for non-aficionados to make their first flamenco CD purchase; **Manuel Morillo Castillo** (Ánimas 1, 958 22 57 15, map p257 F4) for Arab-style furniture and boxes from an on-site *taracea* workshop; and the city's only international book shop, **Metro Bookshop** (C/Gracia 31, 958 26 15 65, map p257 E6).

Where to stay

Hotel rooms fill quickly in Granada; always book ahead if possible, particularly in high season. If you turn up without a reservation, head for the streets around Plaza de la Trinidad (map p257 E6), which are crammed with *hostales*, or contact the tourist office (*see p274*).

Hotels around Plaza Nueva are central but the streets are noisy; old buildings converted into boutique hotels in the Albaícin are more atmospheric but harder to find; places near the Alhambra are quieter at night and obviously benefit from easy access to the monument, but are isolated from the rest of the city at the top of a steep hill. If you're driving, check if your hotel is reachable by car, and where you should park – parking generally in the city is a nightmare.

Note: the hotels and *hostales* below are listed by price, with the most expensive places first.

Parador San Francisco

C/Real de la Alhambra s/n (958 22 14 40/www.parador.es). **Rates** €268 single/double; €270-€361 triple; €401 suite. **Credit** AmEx, DC, MC, V. **Map** p257 H1 & p260 ⓰

If you can book far enough in advance, then an Albaicín-view room in this converted monastery in the grounds of the Alhambra is an unforgettable place to lay your head. Even if you don't stay here, you can still soak up the atmosphere by coming for a drink or the set-price lunch *menú* in the terrace bar-restaurant (smart-casual dress).

Palacio de los Patos

Solarillo de Gracia 1 (958 53 65 16/www.hospes.es). **Rates** €172-€268 single; €193-€355 double; €301-€752 suite. **Credit** AmEx, DC, MC, V. **Map** p257 off F6.

Granada's latest and hippest hotel is this study in marble and snowy-white minimalism from the Hospes chain. The 'Palace of the Ducks' (oddly heralded by two swans at the entrance) opened in 2006 and needs a while for its gardens to take root, but in the meantime is more than comfortable, with generous Korres toiletries, Hotel Costes-style music wafting through its public spaces and a basement spa.

Hotel AC Palacio de Santa Paula

Gran Vía de Colon 31 (958 80 57 40/www.ac-hotels.com). **Rates** €193-€249 single/double; €300-€387 suite. **Credit** AmEx, MC, V. **Map** p256 C4 ⓱

The modern, business-like façade of Granada's only five-star hotel hides an enchanting historic interior. The luxurious rooms also mix sleek modern design and technology with antique charm. Nice touches include free newspapers, coffee in the 'library' and minibar (beer and soft drinks). There's a small sauna, steam room and gym, and a smart fusion restaurant in the beautiful cloisters. Ask about off-season and weekend deals.

Alhambra Palace

Plaza Arquitecto García de Paredes 1 (958 22 14 68/www.h-alhambrapalace.es). **Rates** €150 single; €203 double; €287 junior suite. **Credit** AmEx, DC, MC, V. **Map** p257 H2 & p260 ⓲

Perfectly positioned for the Alhambra, this neo-Moorish four-star hotel was built in 1910. Almost all of its 126 gracious, if slightly worn, rooms (and the terrace bar) boast breathtaking views of the Sierra Nevada, Granada itself and the *vega*. Be warned that eating and drinking in the hotel can work out very expensive, however.

Casa de los Migueletes

C/Benalúa 11 (958 21 07 00/www.casamigueletes.com). **Rates** €138 single/double; €245-€373 suite. **Credit** AmEx, DC, MC, V. **Map** p257 E3 ⓳

Follow the signs from Plaza Nueva down winding cobbled alleys to this 17th-century mansion, beautifully converted into a boutique hotel. It's an oasis of calm, reserved elegance – an ambience reflected by the helpful staff (who can offer great restaurant recommendations). You don't get the full benefit of your historical surroundings in the lower-end rooms, so be prepared to fork out for an Alhambra view (at least €192) or the luxury Alhambra suite with a fabulous view, four-poster bed and jacuzzi.

Hotel Casa Morisca

Cuesta de la Victoria 9 (958 22 11 00/www.hotelcasamorisca.com). **Rates** €154 single/double; €210 suite. **Credit** AmEx, MC, V. **Map** p257 F1 ⓴

This restored 15th-century mansion preserves the patio, barrel-vaulted stable (now the breakfast room) and painted wooden ceilings of the original structure. Friendly staff, smart (if not always spacious) rooms and antique-filled corridors create an ambience of blissful luxury.

Catedral Suites

Plaza de las Pasiegas s/n (958 53 51 30/www.catedral-suites.com). **Rates** €141 single/double; €166 triple. **Credit** AmEx, DC, MC, V. **Map** p257 E5 ㉑

The recently opened Catedral Suites are elegant self-catering apartments in an enviable position overlooking the *plaza* and the cathedral (No.12 has windows overlooking the plaza on two sides). The kitchenettes and bathrooms are well equipped and the decor is crisp and understated, with white walls, parquet floors and a muted colour scheme.

Hotel Plaza Nueva

C/Imprenta 2 (958 21 52 73/www.hotelplaza nueva.com). **Rates** €118 single; €139 double; €187 suite. **Credit** MC, V. **Map** p257 E4 ㉒

This four-star hotel offers 25 bright, comfortable (if a possibly a bit staid) rooms in a great location. It's worth paying extra for views over the Alhambra and Plaza Nueva, especially during the Semana Santa processions. Staff are very polite and helpful.

Palacio de los Navas

C/Navas 1 (958 21 57 80/www.palaciodelasnavas. com). **Rates** €97 single; €129-€150 double; €188-€213 suite. **Credit** MC, V. **Map** p257 G5 ㉓

A new and 21st-century boutique hotel housed in a 16th-century former palace, the Palacio de las Navas. It has had modern additions such as flat-screen TVs in the bedrooms, while respecting many of its original features.

Hotel Casa del Capitel Nazarí

C/Cuesta Aceituneros 6 (958 21 52 60/www.hotel casacapitel.com). **Rates** €60-€102 single; €75-€102 double. **Credit** MC, V. **Map** p257 E3 ㉔

Seventeen rooms clad in wood beams and white linen (and with internet connections) cluster around galleries and cloisters chock-a-block with historic features. There's a cosy TV room and an ornate patio where changing art exhibitions are displayed. Plaza Nueva is seconds away.

Hotel Alixares

Paseo de la Sabica 40 (958 22 55 75/www.hoteles porcel.com). **Rates** €77 single; €102 double; €120 triple; €140 suite. **Credit** AmEx, DC, MC, V. **Map** p257 off H1.

If you want to stay near the Alhambra you could do a lot worse than the package-tour-style, 171-room, three-star Alixares. Better value than both its luxury and budget neighbours, it has good facilities (including an outdoor pool) and views at a reasonable (and often negotiable) price. Some rooms have a small terrace and suite 510 has a corner jacuzzi bath and terrace with views over the *vega*.

Casa del Aljarife

Placeta de la Cruz Verde 2 (958 22 24 25/www.casa delaljarife.com). **Rates** €79 single; €97 double; €124 triple. **Credit** MC, V. **Map** p257 E3 ㉕

Christian Most has converted this 17th-century Albaicín house into a beautiful, warm, luxury B&B. Through the leafy patio you reach the four charming, individually decorated rooms through low-ceilinged, wood-beamed corridors and up wonky staircases. Room 4 is our favourite; it's the smallest but has incredible views and a wonderful bathroom. There's no better place to stay in Granada, so be sure to book ahead.

Santa Ana Apartamentos Turísticos

Cabrera 9 (958 22 81 30/mobile 647 77 41 73/ www.apartamentos-santaana.com). **Rates** (min stay 2 nights) €70 2 people; €100 3-4 people. **Credit** MC, V. **Map** p257 F3 ㉖

Casa de los Migueletes

Overlooking the Darro river, these five apartments are light, modern and extremely spacious, with TV, bathroom, fully equipped kitchen and some great views over the Albaicín. There's also a cave apartment set into the rock face under the Alhambra.

Hospedería del Convento

C/Santa Isabel la Real 11 (958 27 50 15/ www.hospederiadelconvento.com). **Rates** €60-€80 single/double. **No credit cards. Map** p256 D3 ㉗

A delightful converted convent tucked away in the Albaicín. Functioning predominantly as a Spanish language school, it also has a handful of small, charming rooms to rent, one with its own terrace. A roof terrace looks out at the Alhambra and there is a communal kitchen.

Cuevas El Abanico

Verea de Enmedio 89 (958 22 61 99/mobile 608 84 84 97/www.el-abanico.com). **Rates** (min stay 2 nights) €60 cave for 1-2 people; €80 cave for 3 people; €90 2-bedroom cave for 1-4 people; €100 2-bedroom cave for 5 people. **Credit** MC, V. **Map** p257 off D1.

Express your inner troglodyte by staying in one of these cave houses at the edge of the Sacromonte district, equipped with simple kitchens (a couple of electric rings and a sink), fireplaces and modern bathrooms. The five caves open on to a shared terrace with far-reaching views.

Hostal Restaurante La Ninfa

Cocheras de San Cecilio 9 (958 22 79 85/ www.hostallaninfa.net). **Rates** €45 single; €52 double; €65 twin. **Credit** MC, V. **Map** p257 H4 ㉘

The façade of this friendly *hostal* is almost too cute to be true, with hundreds of painted ceramic stars and plant pots covering the exterior. Inside, the kitsch factor goes through the roof, but fortunately the 11 bedrooms are somewhat more restrained, with exposed beams, comfortable furnishings and en suite bathrooms.

Hostal Márquez

C/Fábrica Vieja 8 (958 27 50 13). **Rates** €19 single; €32-€38 double; €54 triple. **Credit** MC, V. **Map** p256 D6 ㉙

A well-cared-for and great-value *hostal* in the university area. Small but clean rooms have iron bedsteads, TVs and good bathrooms (get an en suite; the communal facilities are shared by up to three rooms). Those facing the interior can be quite dark; exterior rooms are brighter but a little noisier.

Hostal Mesones

C/Mesones 44 (958 26 32 44). **Rates** €20 single; €30-€38 double; €45 triple. **Credit** MC, V. **Map** p257 E6 ㉚

Trinket-filled stairways lead to sparkling, well-furnished and -equipped rooms, with balconies overlooking the street. All rooms have private bathrooms, whether en suite or in the corridor. Corridors can be locked off to form 'apartments' for groups. Top marks for location, vibe and value.

Hostal Meridiano

C/Angulo 9 (958 25 05 44/www.hostalmeridiano.com). **Rates** €18 single; €32-€38 double; €45-€55 triple. **Credit** AmEx, MC, V. **Map** p256 D6 ㉛

An extremely friendly, peaceful and bargain-priced *hostal* near Plaza Trinidad. All the rooms are clean and appealing, but the best are on the first floor. Only four have double beds and some share a bathroom (at most between four people). There's also internet access and a drinks machine in reception. The multilingual owners can shower you with information about Granada, should you need it.

Hostal Arteaga

C/Arteaga 3 (958 20 88 41). **Rates** €25 single; €38 double; €55 triple; €65 quad. **Credit** DC, MC, V. **Map** p256 D4 ㉜

This basic but homely *hostal* just off the Gran Vía, at the bottom of the Albaicín, has a really friendly, relaxed vibe thanks to owner María Angeles. Rooms tend to be smallish and darkish but are jollied up with sunny bedlinen.

Hostal Venecia

2nd floor, Cuesta de Gomérez 2 (958 22 39 87). **Rates** €15-€18 single; €30-€42 double. **Credit** MC, V. **Map** p257 F4 ㉝

A basic but characterful *hostal.* The well-turned-out Marí Carmen is as particular about the appearance of her place as she is about her own. A good choice for backpacking groups of friends who want a quiet family atmosphere – scented candles burn in the kitsch corridors and guests are offered a herbal infusion in the morning. Room 1 is a bargain considering its view over Plaza Nueva.

Resources

The **Granada City Pass (Bono Turístico)** costs €22.50 (from the Alhambra and Capilla Real ticket offices) or €24.50 (from Caja General de Ahorros de Granada bank in Plaza Isabel La Católica) and is valid for seven days. It can be used for nine rides on bus or minibus services in the city, one day's free pass on the tourist bus (www.granadatur.com), and admission to the Alhambra (pre-programmed entry has to be agreed at time of booking), the Parque de las Ciencias, Monasterio de la Cartuja, Monasterio de San Jerónimo, the cathedral and Capilla Real. It may also entitle you to hotel and restaurant discounts. For details go to the website http://caja.caja-granada.es and click on '*entradas*' and then '*bono turístico*'.

Internet

Uninet, Plaza de la Encarnación 2 (958 20 83 82). **Open** 9.30am-11pm daily. **Map** p256 D5.

Mundo Latino, C/Panaderos 26 (958 270 526). **Open** 11-2pm, 4.30-9.30pm Mon-Fri. **Map** p256 D1.

Police station

C/Duquesa s/n (958 80 80 00). **Map** p256 D6.

Post office

Puerta Real 2 (958 21 55 98). **Map** p257 F6.

Tourist information

Turismo de Granada, Plaza Mariana Pineda 10 (958 24 71 28/www.turismodegranada.org). **Open** 9am-8pm Mon-Fri; 10am-7pm Sat; 10am-3pm Sun. **Map** p257 F5.

The main tourist information centre. Other smaller offices are at C/Santa Ana 4 (958 22 59 90) and the Alhambra ticket office (958 22 95 75, *see p258*).

Getting there

By air

Granada's airport, with an increasing number of flights from the UK, is located 17km (11 miles) west of the city. *See p308.*

By bus

Except for local buses to nearby towns, all services operate from the bus station on Carretera de Jaén (3km/2 miles north-west of the city centre, 958 18 54 80). To get to the station from the city centre, take bus numbers 3 and 33, which stop along Gran Vía. The largest company is Alsina Graells (958 18 54 80, www.alsinagraells.es), which has 9 daily services to Córdoba (2hrs 30mins), 9 to Seville (3-4hrs), 17 to Málaga (2hrs), 6 to the Alpujarras (1-3hrs) and 10 to Madrid (5hrs). Autedía (958 70 00 90) covers the north and east of the province of Granada, while Bonal (958 46 50 22) runs one bus daily to the Sierra Nevada (1hr) in summer and about four in winter.

By train

Granada's railway station is at Avda Andaluces s/n (902 24 02 02), a couple of kilometres west of the city centre. From here there are 4 trains every day to Seville (2hrs 30mins-3hrs), 4 daily to Almería (2hrs 30mins), 3 daily to Ronda (3hrs) and 2 daily to Madrid (6hrs).

Around Granada

Where magnificent desert and parched mountains shade into rural tranquillity.

Alhama de Granada. See p276.

West of Granada

The rolling landscapes of western Granada province, polka-dotted with countless olive trees, have more in common with south-eastern Córdoba than the Granadan *vega* or mountains to the east. Fortified Moorish castles and fine Renaissance churches speak of the importance of this region in the final years of the Nasrid kingdom, when it formed a frontier between Granada and the encroaching Christian forces.

The village of **Moclín**, 35 kilometres/22 miles north-west of Granada, clusters below a craggy hill topped by an extensive castle, in fine walking country. After the fall of Alcalá La Real in 1341, it became a key stronghold in the defence of Granada, before finally succumbing to the Christians in 1486. The lower part of the castle consists of a tower gateway, fortified wall, Renaissance granary and the church of **El Cristo del Paño** (open hours of services), donated to the town by Fernando and Isabel. The church houses a 16th-century canvas of Christ that is said to heal cataracts – a condition popularly known as *el paño*, or 'the cloth', because it veils the sight – and to improve female fertility. The *romería* to the church on 5 October is one of the most popular events in the province and is described in Lorca's tragedy *Yerma*. A steep, rocky climb upwards leads to the Moorish citadel, offering sublime views across olive-clad hills towards the Granadan *vega* and the Sierra Nevada.

Around Moclín are a number of watchtowers that provided a defensive network for the Nasrid state. There are also prehistoric remains in the area, including notable neolithic cave paintings and megalithic dolmens; ask at the *ayuntamiento* for details of walking routes.

Thirty-two kilometres (20 miles) west of Moclín by road, and close to the Córdoban border, **Montefrío** enjoys a stunning setting between rocky hills and olive groves. A vast ledge of rock juts out of the earth at a jaunty angle above the town, topped by the 16th-century church of **La Villa** and the remains of the walled Moorish **Alcazaba**. The church, by Diego de Siloé, has a lovely vaulted interior. It is no longer used for services, because of the heart-stoppingly steep climb to reach it, but instead houses an interactive museum on the history of the region (opening times are erratic). At the centre of the town, the sloping Plaza de España is dominated by the bulging dome of the Pantheon-like church of **La Encarnación** (open hours of services), built to the designs of Spain's leading neo-classical architect, Ventura Rodríguez; venture inside to admire its vast, womb-like cupola and peculiar acoustics. On the other side of the square is the 17th-century **Ayuntamiento** and the 16th-century **Casa de los Oficios**, which houses the tourist office.

Signposted off the GR222, a few kilometres east of Montefrío, is the extraordinary archaeological site of **Las Peñas de los Gitanos**. This extensive area flanked by limestone cliffs was occupied from the third millennium BC until the Middle Ages and incorporates cave dwellings, neolithic dolmens, a ruined Roman fort, a Visigothic burial ground and a medieval citadel. In the gorge below are the remains of six Roman watermills. Ask at the tourist office for directions to the site.

Alhama de Granada (53 kilometres/33 miles south-west of Granada; **photo** *p275*) was an important spa town under the Moors, and its conquest by Christian forces in 1482 was one of the defining moments in the *reconquista*, as it blocked one of the Nasrid kingdom's routes to the coast. On the outskirts, a minor road leads past a Roman bridge to the spa that gives the town its name – *al hamma* means 'hot springs' in Arabic. Any illusions of finding a luxurious health resort are disabused by the sanatorium-style hotel building and the sight of elderly clients in towels. However, the setting in a wooded gorge is idyllic, and the naturally hot bathing pools (closed Nov-May) are enticing. The original Moorish baths no longer exist, but a magnificent cistern from around 1100, resembling a submerged mosque, does survive.

The town itself is situated on a rocky shelf above a cliff-lined *tajo* (ravine) formed by the Río Alhama. Winding streets lead to the sleepy Plaza de la Constitución in the old town, where swifts swoop amid pleasant terrace cafés. At the far end is a private Moorish castle with some unfortunate 19th-century embellishments. Past the tourist office on the east side of the square is the charming **El Carmen** church (open hours of services), behind which is a *mirador* over the gorge. Beyond the Plaza de la Constitución, narrow medieval streets twist around the Plaza de los Presos and its granary. Fronting the square is the 16th-century church of **La Encarnación** (open hours of services), whose Renaissance bell tower by Diego de Siloé dominates the skyline. Fernando and Isabel donated the church to Alhama shortly after the *reconquista*; the vestments in the sacristy may have been embroidered by the Queen herself.

South of Alhama, the A355 emerges on to a wide fertile valley, backed to the west by the bare, elephant-hide bulk of the **Sierra de Loja**. From here it climbs to the edge of the **Sierra de Tejeda**, where the road drops away with a lurch through the **Zafarraya Pass** and a view across the Axarquía to the Med.

Where to stay & eat

El Rincón de Marcelo (C/San José 25, 958 41 76 95, www.rincondemarcelo.com, double €45, restaurant €, hotel and restaurant closed 1wk July & 1wk Sept, restaurant closed Mon) is a comfortable rural *hostal* and restaurant in the village of Tózar, close to Moclín.

On the outskirts of Montefrío, the three-star **Hotel Enrea** (Paraje de la Enrea s/n, 958 33 66 62, www.hotel-laenrea.com, double €64-€75) has 19 spacious bedrooms in a converted olive mill, plus a bar and pleasant courtyard. In Montefrío, the friendly **Mesón Pregonero** (Plaza de España 3, 958 33 61 17, closed Tue and 2wks early July, €), next to the tourist office, offers generous tapas and a good lunch menu; try the house special, roast ham. The tourist office can provide details of delightful *casas rurales* in the vicinity, including **El Castillo** (958 20 88 92, www.granadainfo.com/castillo, sleeps up to nine people for €300 for two nights), below La Villa church, and **Casa Paquita** (958 31 05 32, www.casasdepaquita.com, from €60 a day for two people), close to the Peñas de los Gitanos site.

On the outskirts of Alhama, the **Hotel Balneario de Alhama** (958 35 00 11, www.balnearioalhamadegranada.com, closed mid Nov-mid Mar, double €93-€102) offers spa facilities and all mod cons combined with a faintly institutional atmosphere. In the town itself there's the pleasant **Pensión San José** (Plaza de la Constitución 27, 958 35 01 56, double €31-€36) and **La Seguiriya** (C/Las Peñas 12, 958 36 08 01, www.laseguiriya.com, double €60, restaurant €€), owned by a flamenco singer who has named its characterful rooms after flamenco styles. The restaurant serves local specialities such as salt cod and orange salad, or baked sea bream. Just outside Alhama, the **Hotel-Restaurante El Ventorro** (Carretera de Jatar, km2, 958 35 04 38, closed 2wks Jan, double €50, restaurant €, closed Mon), offers rooms, trad cuisine and walking and riding excursions.

Right by the western border with Málaga province, a little off the motorway, is the flashy five-star **Finca La Bobadilla** (exit 175 from A92, 958 32 18 61, www.la-bobadilla.com, closed last 3wks Jan, double €288-€355, restaurant €€€€), a favourite with Tom Cruise and his sort. Set within a 400-hectare (1,000-acre) estate, the hotel has a lovely main courtyard, a chapel and a labyrinth of pathways. All rooms are splendidly kitted out and have views of the pretty gardens or the estate. There are also two restaurants, an outdoor and an indoor pool, a jacuzzi and beauty treatments.

Resources

Tourist information

Alhama de Granada *Ayuntamiento, Paseo Montes Jovellar s/n (958 36 06 86/www.turismodealhama.org).* **Open** *Late June-mid Sept* 9.30am-2pm Mon-Fri; 10am-2pm Sat, Sun. *Mid Sept-late June* 9.30am-3pm Mon-Fri; 10am-2pm Sat, Sun.

Moclín *Ayuntamiento, Plaza de España 1 (958 40 30 51).* **Open** 8am-2pm Mon-Fri.

Montefrío *Plaza de España 1 (958 33 60 04/www.montefrio.org).* **Open** 10am-2pm, 4.30-6pm Mon-Fri; 10.30am-1.30pm Sat, Sun.

Getting there

By bus

Alsina-Graells (958 18 54 80, www.alsinagraells.es) runs 2 daily buses from Granada to Montefrío Mon-Sat, and 1 service on Sun (1hr 15mins). Autobuses Ronabus has 2 daily services to Moclín from outside the University of Granada. There are also daily services from Granada to Alhama.

East of Granada

Tourists may pour into the city of Granada by their thousands, but only a tiny fraction of these visitors venture into the vast open spaces to the east. It's their loss. Between the *sierras* that define the province's boundaries is a majestic landscape redolent of the American West, a tough land of parched, multihued soil and scrubby vegetation, punctuated by a couple of silvery reservoirs, its plains ripped and corrugated by countless twisting ravines.

Just east of Granada, the motorway passes through the small but spectacular **Parque Natural de la Sierra de Huétor** before skirting the largest, most interesting and strangest settlement in the eastern half of the province, **Guadix**. Located 55 kilometres (34 miles) east of Granada, this town is one of the oldest in Spain – it was an important Roman colony and one of the first Visigothic bishoprics in the country. Today, Guadix is chiefly famed for its cave dwellings. Wind-whipped pinnacles of tufa give the town a surreal backdrop and for centuries have provided an easily worked material for the construction of cave houses, which protect their occupants from the savage heat of summer. The caves were first inhabited during the Moorish period, and 2,000 are still in use, making up the largest inhabited cave complex in Europe. Wandering around the cave district, the **Barrio Santiago**, is a surreal and voyeuristic experience; you half expect a hobbit to come scuttling out of every round door. Be warned: any offer to see inside a cave will likely be followed by a demand for money. If you want to know more about the troglodyte life, visit the **Cueva-Museo**.

The old quarter of Guadix, extending south from Plaza de las Américas and the cathedral, makes for enjoyable wandering. Started in 1510, and not completed until 1796, the impressive **Catedral** is a melding of the original Gothic design, remodelling by Diego de Siloé and later baroque additions (including possibly Andalucía's most spectacular baroque façade). There is a small religious museum attached. An arch in front of the cathedral leads to the arcaded Renaissance Plaza de la Constitución (aka Plaza Mayor), which was badly damaged in the Civil War but has been restored. South of here, the Renaissance **Palacio de Peñaflor**

The **Catedral** in Guadix.

Keeping cavey

Apartment to rent. Sleeps six, with bathroom, parking space, fireplace, central heating, fully equipped kitchen, including fridge, cooker, toaster, cafetière, crockery, washing machine and iron. Oh, and it's a cave.

Andalucians have been enjoying the delights of cave life for thousands of years, as shown by cave paintings in Nerja and the Cueva de los Murciélagos and the Sierra Subbética. Today, living in a cave is anything but primitive, however. The 1960s tourist boom led to many being abandoned or used as hippie squats. But now property prices are soaring, local architects specialise in carving something beautiful out of the rock to your specific design, and you can even spend your holiday in one. The village of Guadix is the centre of this activity, with several thousand variously sized caves, but there are similar homes across the entire Altiplano area. The village of Galera is another of the current hot spots, while the Sacromonte hills on the outskirts of Granada have also been historically popular with the *gitano* population.

So why should you choose limestone over brick? Well, for a start, caves are dry and warm, hovering around a comfortable 18° to 20° all year round. There are no roofing problems nor rising damp. It's nice and quiet. And if you want to extend your property, you basically hack back into the mountain with your pick. Fancy a new bookcase? Get out your chisel.

All your basics are there too – hot and cold running water, electricity and that most modern of must-haves, ADSL. And, of course, there's the pure strangeness of it all, odd passageways, round walls and ceilings, a great address.

In terms of prices, you should be able to pick up a basic cave from €20,000 as long as you don't mind doing refurbishments. For something along more conventional three-bedroom lines, expect to shell out €100,00 but, as you'd expect, it all comes down to location, location, location.

MORE INFORMATION

Various estate agents based in Andalucía specialise in cave properties. One of the leaders is **Spanish Inland Properties** (958 73 90 32, www.spanish-inland-properties.com), or try **Kite & Co** (958 744000, www.kiteandco.com).

stands next to the Gothic-Mudéjar church of **Santiago** and the originally 11th-century Moorish **Alcazaba** (closed for restoration).

Impressive though this castle is, it can't compare with that of **La Calahorra**, located on a small hill at the foot of the Sierra Nevada, around 20 kilometres (12 miles) south-east of Guadix. One of only a handful of new castles built by Christian forces after the fall of Granada in 1492, its austere rectangular plan with cylindrical, domed towers is in contrast to the elegant Italianate interior set around a two-storey arcaded marble courtyard.

The motorway from Guadix heads east through increasingly wild, desert-like scenery to the bustling but not especially interesting town of **Baza**. South are the mountainous 522 square kilometres (202 square mile) **Parque Natural de la Sierra de Baza**, an extension of Almería's Sierra de los Filabres.

It's a tremendous drive north from Baza on the A315 and A326, past the vast **Embalse de Negratín** reservoir and up into the hills via the hugely appealing village of **Castril**. Situated at the entrance to a mountainous nature reserve, and with panoramic views towards Baza and the Sierra Nevada, Castril is a well-preserved village built around a massive rock pinnacle. At its highest end is a homely Renaissance church, while far below is a spectacular modern footpath jutting above a mountain torrent.

The A326 continues to the town of **Huescar**, which was on the turbulent Arab–Christian frontline and, due to a bizarre anomaly, at war with Denmark from 1809 until 1981. Today it's a busy modern town, though not without interest – for instance, the decaying façade of the **Casa de los Peñalva** (on Paseo del Santo Cristo, just off the main square) is one of the very few examples of art nouveau in Andalucía.

Castillo de la Calahorra

La Calahorra (958 67 70 98). **Open** 10am-1pm, 4-6pm Wed. **Admission** free. **No credit cards**.

Catedral de Guadix & Museo

Guadix (958 66 50 89). **Open** 10.30am-1pm, 4-6pm Mon-Sat. **Admission** €3; €2 concessions. **No credit cards**.

Cueva-Museo

Plaza de la Ermita Nueva, off Plaza del Padre Poveda, Guadix (958 66 93 00). **Open** *June-Aug* 10am-2pm, 5-7pm daily. *Sept-May* 10am-2pm, 4-6pm Mon-Sat; 10am-2pm Sun. **Admission** €1.35; 70¢ concessions. **No credit cards**.

Where to stay, eat & drink

Tourism is rare in this part of the province, and accommodation scarce. In Guadix, the most central place to stay is the somewhat faded three-star **Hotel Comercio** (C/Mira de Amezcua 3, 958 66 05 00, www.hotelcomercio.com, double €64), which has a good restaurant (€€). If you fancy kipping in a cave, try **Cuevas Pedro Antonio de Alarcón** (Barriada San Torcuato s/n, 958 66 49 86, www.andalucia.com/cavehotel, cave for two €59-€73), with all mod cons and pool, or, a few kilometres north of Guadix near Benalúa, **Cuevas La Granja** (Camino de la Granja s/n, 958 67 60 00, mobile 666 55 80 30, www.cuevas.org, cave for 2 €63-€68), which are equally luxuriously appointed and can sleep up to 6 people; the complex also has a restaurant and pool. For eating in Guadix, try Plaza de la Constitución or the area around the Plaza de los Naranjos.

A fine spot to eat in La Calahorra is **Manjon** (C/Los Caños 20, 958 67 70 81, €), just off the main square, which specialises in fish and roast lamb; it also has an attached *hostal* (double €35).

In Castril, the 21-room two-star **La Fuente** (Avenida del Portillo s/n, 958 72 00 30, double €44) is a pleasant place to lay your head, while **El Café de Emilio** (C/Carmen 10, 958 72 00 05, €) is an endearing old bar and the best place in the area to try local specialities like *maimones* (a tomato and red pepper stew), though you'll need to order in advance.

There are also cave dwellings around Orce. Facilities at the **Cuevas de Orce** (A317, 958 74 62 81, www.cuevasdeorce.com, cave for two €64-€80) include cable TV, bathroom and kitchen.

Resources

Tourist information

Guadix *Avda Mariana Pineda s/n (958 66 26 65).* **Open** 8.30am-3.30pm Mon-Fri.
Parque Natural de la Sierra de Baza *Centro de Visitantes 'Narváez', Monte Narváez, A92, km324 (958 00 20 18).* **Open** *Easter-Sept* 10am-2pm, 6-8pm Fri-Sun. *Oct-Easter* 10am-2pm, 4-6pm Fri-Sun.

Getting there

By bus

Maestra Autedia (958 40 06 01, www.maestra-autedia.com) runs most buses in the area. From Granada there are 11 daily to Guadix (1hr); 8 go on to Baza (45mins from Guadix), 4 continue to La Calahorra (55mins from Guadix) and 2 go on to Orce (55mins from Baza). There's 1 daily between Baza and Castril (1hr 40mins).

By train

There are around 7 daily trains between Almería and Guadix (1hr 15mins), 4 daily from Guadix to Almería (1hr) and 3 daily to Linares-Baeza (1hr 50mins).

Sierra Nevada & the Alpujarras

Beautiful sweeping valleys and the majesty of Spain's tallest mountains.

Sierra Nevada ski area.

Much of the visual appeal of the Alhambra is provided by its awesome backdrop – the snow-crowned peaks of the mighty Sierra Nevada, the highest mountain range in Spain. The two highest peaks **Mulhacén** (3,482 metres/11,424 feet) and **Veleta** (3,392 metres/11,128 feet) wear a white mantle almost year round, yet are barely an hour's drive from the coast, allowing *granadinos* to ski in the morning and hit the beach in the afternoon.

For centuries, the only people to labour up the Sierra Nevada's peaks were the *neveros* (icemen), who carried blocks of ice down from the high mountains to sell in the city. Today, though, the mountains draw ever-increasing numbers of visitors for a huge range of outdoor activities, from skiing (the season runs from November to May) and hiking to mountain-biking and paragliding.

Between the Sierra Nevada and the lower hills of the coastal ranges to the south lie the Alpujarras, described by British writer Gerald Brenan as 'a little country, shut in by its almost impassable mountains'. Access is considerably easier today, but the Alpujarras retains a distinctive feel. This fertile but traditionally poor region, dotted with distinctive mountain villages, was first inhabited by the Visigoths and later by the Moors, who developed a unique system of irrigation and planted mulberry trees for the silk trade, which flourished here during the 13th century. After the Christian conquest of Granada, the Alpujarras became a final enclave of Moorish resistance. Boabdil, the last Nasrid Sultan, was initially exiled here, and the area remained beyond effective Catholic control until 1568. Even when Felipe III ordered the expulsion of Muslims from Spain, two Moorish families were told to remain in each Alpujarran village to educate relocated peasants from the north about methods of irrigation. In the following centuries, the Alpujarras remained poor, isolated and forgotten. It's only in recent years, with the influx of tourists and northern European expats, that this beautiful region has regained some prosperity and self-confidence.

There are around 70 villages in the Alpujarras today, distinguished by a style of architecture that's otherwise found only in the Moroccan Rif mountains. The low-lying dwellings have thick walls covered in local grey clay known as *launa* and are linked together by little bridge-like passageways known as *tinaos*. Their flat roofs double as terraces, and sport tall, distinctive chimneys; in silhouette they look like people wearing wide-brimmed hats.

Sierra Nevada

The Sierra Nevada's environmental status vies for supremacy with its burgeoning ski industry. Around the resort of **Sierra Nevada** (aka **Solynieve** – 'sun and snow', aka **Pradollano**), on the western flank of Veleta, are 62 kilometres (39 miles) of slopes and 19 ski lifts. For more details, contact the **Sierra Nevada Club** (Plaza de Andalucía, 958 24 91 11, 902 70 80 90, www.sierranevada.es). The resort, although well equipped, is a crass blot on the landscape, and spookily empty out of season, though activities such as mountain biking, hiking and horse-trekking are being made available to entice summer visitors. On the A395, north-west of the resort, the park information centre gives details on environmental issues and outdoor activities, and has a terrace café with spectacular views. Note that the road over the Sierra is closed to traffic above the Borreguiles ski station, but walkers can continue through the barren landscape up to the peak of Veleta (a reasonable three-hour hike) or even on to the village of Capileira, 30 kilometres (19 miles) to the south (*see p283*), passing the summit of Mulhacén.

Where to stay & eat

Many of the resort's hotels close at the end of the ski season, so always call ahead to check. One of the more attractive options is the **Hotel Rumaykiyya** (Urbanización Solynieve, 958 48 14 00, closed May-Nov, double €250-€377), where you can relax with a post-piste sauna, jacuzzi or massage. It also has a buffet restaurant, **La Alquería** (dinner €€€€). A cheaper choice is **Hotel Monte Sol** (Edificio Acongra s/n, 958 48 10 00, www.hotelmontesolarttyco.com, (half-board) double €83-€128, closed May-late Nov), which offers en suite rooms and buffet-style meals. Or there's the great-value youth hostel: **Albergue Juvenil** (C/Peñones 22, 958 48 03 05, www.inturjoven.com, closed Aug, dorm bed €13-€19).

Resources

Tourist information

Parque Nacional de la Sierra Nevada *A395, km23, Güéjar Sierra (958 34 06 25).* **Open** *July-Sept* 10am-2pm, 4.30-7pm daily. *Oct-June* 10am-2pm, 4-6pm daily.

West Alpujarras

South of Granada the N323 climbs towards the **Puerto del Suspiro del Moro** (Pass of the Moor's Sigh). According to legend, this is where the banished Boabdil turned for one last look at his beloved Granada in 1492. His mother was not sympathetic: 'Weep like a woman, you, who have not defended your kingdom like a man.'

From the pass, the road descends into the **Valle de Lecrín**, a sweeping landscape of olive groves and citrus trees. To the east, where the valley meets the mass of the Sierra Nevada, is the spa town of **Lanjarón**, famed throughout Spain for its mineral water. The spa itself (Avenida de Constitución s/n, 958 77 01 37, www.balneariodelanjaron.com, closed Jan) is in an unprepossessing, institutional building at the west end of town, and attracts elderly clients for hydrotherapy and other treatments. Below the long main street is a ruined Moorish castle on a striking promontory – there's not much left of the original structure, but the views across the gorge to the mountains are extraordinary. You can explore the area on horseback with Sarah at **Caballo Blanco** (958 34 71 75, mobile 627 79 48 91, 2hr trek €30).

Nine kilometres (six miles) east of Lanjarón is **Órgiva**, a gently sprawling market town set in a wide river basin at the foot of the mountains. During the Civil War it was evacuated and remained a no-go zone until the war ended in 1939. Fully recovered from those bloody days, today it is the commercial hub of the area, though it is most notable for its large New Age and mostly British hippie colony, which occupies camper vans and teepees on the edge of town. The New Agers are most conspicuous during the Thursday market, where their crystals and tambourines provide a curious counterpoint to the local produce and cheap clothing. The area has seen a huge increase in British residents in the last few years, partially as a result of Chris Stewart's bestseller *Driving Over Lemons*, which is set in these parts.

Above Órgiva the road twists and turns towards the 'high' Alpujarras. The villages of **Cañar**, **Carataunas** and **Soportújar** have spectacular views south towards the bulk of the Sierra Lújar, and offer a first taste of the region's distinctive architecture. A couple of kilometres further on (opposite the **Ermita del Padre Eterno** chapel), a rough gravel track leads up to the blissfully tranquil **O Sel Ling Buddhist Centre** (958 34 31 34, open 3-6pm daily, admission free). This high mountain retreat, consists of a scattered group of dwellings, a library, temple and *stupa*.

Where to stay & eat

In the Valle de Lecrín there's comfortable accommodation and delicious breakfasts on offer at the British-run **Cortijo del Pino** (C/Fernán Nuñez 2, La Loma, 958 77 62 57, double €83) in Albuñuelas.

Hippies in Órgiva.

There are plenty of places to stay on the main drag in Lanjarón, none of them terribly inspiring. The most upmarket is the **Hotel Castillo Alcadima** (C/Francisco Tarrega 3, 958 77 08 09, www.alcadima.com, double €64), which is built around a series of gardens, patios and terraces. and has swimming pools and tennis courts. On a smaller scale, the **Hotel Albergue de Mecina** (C/La Fuente s/n, 958 76 62 54, double €80, restaurant €€) has spacious, comfortable rooms and a rustic restaurant. A cheaper option is to head for the super-friendly **Hotel Lanjarón** (C/Pérez Chaves 7, 958 77 00 94, www.h-lanjaron.com, double €36). It's basic but clean and comfortable. By far the most pleasant option, and ideal if you want to use the area as a base for hiking, is to head two kilometres out of town to either **Cortijo El Arao** or **Cortijo La Fuente** (958 77 20 18, mobile 658 11 35 85, €18 per person), rural cottages that sleep four or six , with pool, fireplaces and lots of privacy. Restaurants and cafés abound along Lanjarón's long main street.

Órgiva's best place to stay is the friendly **Hotel Taray** (A348, km18, 958 78 45 25, double €77, restaurant €€), surrounded by lush, secluded gardens, turtle ponds and an enormous swimming pool; its restaurant utilises home-grown produce and local trout. For unexpected seclusion in the heart of town, try the lovely **Casa Rural El Molíno** (C/González Robles 16, mobile 646 61 66 28, www.casarura lelmolino.com, double €50-€54), a former olive mill that's now a five-bedroomed hotel with a bath-jacuzzi on the patio. There are plenty of reasonable tapas bars and cafés in the town centre. The **Hostal Alma Alpujarreña** (C/González Robles 49, 958 78 40 85, double €40, restaurant €), with its pretty bougainvillea covered terrace, is hugely popular for home-cooked meals, while **Mesón Casa Santiago** (Plaza García Moreno 13, 958 78 42 29, closed Wed, €) is recommended for getting tanked up on local wines and cider.

A kilometre outside Órgiva, the **Puerta de la Alpujarra** (Las Barreras, 958 78 44 50, www.campings.net/puertadelaalpujarra, €) does a good-value menu, offering soups, salads, roast chicken and fresh fish; it also has live flamenco, jazz and blues bands every weekend. The restaurant is part of a well-equipped campsite.

In keeping with Órgiva's reputation as a mecca for northern Europeans seeking an alternative lifestyle in the sun, **Cortijo Romero** (01494 765775 in the UK, www. cortijo-romero.co.uk) offers residential courses in yoga, shiatsu and other therapies.

Resources

Internet

Lanjarón *Cyberplay Internet, next to the Ermita de San Roque (no phone).* **Open** 10am-1.30pm, 5.30-10pm Mon-Sat.

Órgiva *Ciber Ocio, Avda González Robles 26, next to the Mirasol Hotel (958 78 42 79).* **Open** 10.30am-2pm, 5.30-9pm Mon-Fri; 10.30am-2pm Sat.

Tourist information

Central de Reservas de Valle de Lecrín *C/Barrio Bajo 21, Dúrcal (958 78 15 71/mobile 619 94 30 63/www.elvalledelecrin.com).* **Open** 10am-1.30pm, 5.30-8.30pm Mon-Fri; 10.30am-1.30pm Sat.

Lanjarón *Avenida de la Constitución s/n, opposite the Balneario (958 77 04 62).* **Open** 10am-2pm, 5-9pm Mon, Tue, Thur-Sat; 10am-2pm Sun.

Central Alpujarras

Generally regarded as the most beautiful of the Alpujarran valleys (and the most touristed as a result), the **Valle de Poqueira** is a steep-sided, verdant river gorge, flanked by

Pampaneira.

cultivated terraces and backed by snowy peaks. In a picture-perfect location on its eastern side are the villages of Pampaneira, Bubión and Capileira; there are well-signposted walking routes connecting all three.

The lowest of the three, **Pampaneira** has a beautiful little central square in front of its ochre-coloured 16th-century church. Here you'll find crafts shops, with traditional rugs and ceramics on display, plus a couple of bars and the Nevadensis information centre (*see p284*). Above the square, typical Alpujarran dwellings tumble down the hillside, interlinked by a network of *tinaos* and steep narrow streets. The *matanzas* (pig-slaughter festivities), held from 5-8 December, are among the best in Spain.

Higher up the valley, **Bubión** is more sprawling than its neighbours, its houses spilling down towards Plaza Iglesia. In Moorish times, the church was both mosque and watchtower, and offers a superb view of the valley. Also on the square is the **Casa Alpujarreña** folk museum, while nearby is the **Taller del Telar** (C/Trinidad s/n, 958 76 31 71), where rugs, blankets and shawls are woven on a hand-operated loom.

Capileira is the highest of the villages and a good base for mountain walking and climbing. Beyond here, the road (now permanently closed to traffic) continues upwards close to the peaks of Mulhacén and Veleta, before descending to the Sierra Nevada ski resort (*see p281*). The **Museo de Capileira** has displays of local crafts, plus artefacts associated with the Guadix-born writer, Pedro Antonio de Alarcón, who wrote about the Alpujarras in the 19th century.

Elsewhere, seek out **El Horno de Luisa**, a bakery that still uses its 500-year-old Moorish oven. There are myriad walks from the villages, including trails through the Poqueira gorge, and east towards Pitres and Trevélez. For serious and well-equipped climbers, the ascent of Mulhacén takes two days from Capileira. Horse treks (Cabalgar Rutas Alternativas, 958 76 31 35, www.ridingandalucia.com) and paragliding (Horizonte Vertical, 958 30 82 91) are also available.

Under the Moors, the settlements of **Pitres**, **Pórtugos**, **Mecina Fondales**, **Ferreirola** and **Busquístar** formed a league of villages known as the 'Tahá', from the Arabic *tá* meaning 'obedience'. Situated to the east of Pampaneira, they are more tranquil than their Poqueira neighbours, offering a taste of mountain life little affected by tourism. The surrounding landscape is characterised by orchards and streams and provides plenty of opportunities for walking and exploring.

Beyond Buquístar, the road turns north into a dramatic, rugged valley towards **Trevélez** (meaning 'three villages'). Even today, the *barrios bajo*, *medio* and *alto* each retain a distinctive flavour, and it's worth hiking to the higher parts to get a taste of old Trevélez (the *barrio bajo* is the most touristy, with innumerable shops hawking local artisans' wares). At 1,476 metres (4,842 feet) above sea level, this is the highest permanently occupied village in Spain, and is a starting point for ascents of the Sierra Nevada peaks. On 5 August each year, the villagers climb Mulhacén themselves to celebrate the festival of the **Virgen de los Nieves**. Trevélez is famed for its snow-cured *jamón serrano*; you'll see huge haunches of it hanging from every available inch of ceiling in the village's shops and restaurants.

Casa Alpujarreña

Plaza Iglesia 5, Bubión (958 76 30 32/www.bubion.org). **Open** 11am-2pm Mon, Wed, Thur, Sun; 11am-2pm, 5-7pm Fri, Sat. **Admission** €1.80. **No credit cards**.

Museo de Capileira
C/Mentidero 15, Capileira (958 76 30 51).
Open 11.30am-2.30pm Tue-Sun. **Admission** €1.
No credit cards.

Where to stay & eat

In Pampaneira, **Hostal Ruta del Mulhacén** (Avenida de la Alpujarra 6, 958 76 30 10, www.rutadelmulhacen.com, early Jan-early Feb, double €36-€45) has en suite rooms strewn with colourful woven blankets and *jarapas* (rugs). Just below the village, the terrace at **Bar-Restaurante Guillermo** (Carretera Pampaneira, km46, 958 76 30 23, €-€€) is one of the most popular haunts, and great for drinks and complimentary tapas.

In Bubión, **Las Terrazas** (Placeta del Sol 7, 958 76 30 34, closed Jan, double from €31) is a friendly *pensión* with an extraordinary view; many rooms have terraces. For food, the best options are **La Artesa** (C/Carretera 2, 958 76 34 37, closed 2wks early Jan & 2wks early July, €-€€) and **Restaurant Teide** (C/Carretera s/n, 958 76 30 84, closed mid June-early Jul, €-€€), on either side of the main road.

In Capileira, **Casa Ibero** (C/Parra 1, 958 76 32 56, €-€€) serves international food, including vegetarian dishes. In winter there's lively flamenco every Thursday at the **Cortijo Catifalarga** (800 metres up into the Sierra, 958 34 33 57, www.catifalarga.com, double €62-€74, restaurant €), which has apartments, rooms, a restaurant and pool. For self-catering chalet-style accommodation try the **Cortijo Los Molinillos** (Carretera Bubión–Capileira, Km1, 958 34 30 79, 2-4 people €60 a day, €400 a week), which is solar-powered and has views across to Morocco; book well in advance. The excellent campsite **Balcón de Pitres** (958 76 61 11, €5 per person, €5 per tent, €6 caravan) nestles among trees just west of Pitres; it has self-catering cabins, a pool and a restaurant.

Book well in advance for a chance to stay at **Sierra y Mar** in Ferreirola (C/Albaycín 3, 958 76 61 71, double €52), a beautiful B&B with a heavenly walled garden. Another good option is the modern but cosy **Hotel de Mecina** in Mecina Fondales (C/La Fuente s/n, 958 76 62 54, double €75, restaurant €-€€).

There are numerous restaurants and hotels in Trevélez's *barrio bajo*. In the *barrio alto*, **La Sala Baja** (C/Cuesta Principal 44, 958 85 85 28, €-€€) has a sweet terrace overlooking the town and a delightfully cosy dining room. **La Fragua I & II** (C/San Antonio 4, Barrio Alto, 958 85 86 26, 958 85 85 12, www.hotellafragua.com, closed mid Jan-mid Feb, double €39-€48, restaurant €) are the nicest places to stay, with fabulous views and a lovely restaurant.

The most upmarket place to stay in the area is the **Hotel Alcazaba de Busquístar** (GR421, km37, 958 85 86 87, www.alcazabadebusquistar.com, double €82-€93), five kilometres (three miles) south of Trevélez, not to be confused with the more rustic **Alcazar de Busquístar** (Paraje los Álamos 1, 958 48 67 94, double €51), which is in the village. Rooms are very old-fashioned but the surrounds are stunning and it has a delightful restaurant with gingham tablecloths and corn dollies, and a pool. For super-cheap, basic and out-of-the-way accommodation, head down the mountain to **Posada María** (Cástaras, 958 85 55 31, http://es.geocities.com/castarasposada, double €21).

For local rental accommodation, contact the rural tourist agency **Rustic Blue** (Barrio La Ermita, Bubión, 958 76 33 81).

Resources

Tourist information

Pampaneira *Nevadensis, Plaza de la Libertad (958 76 31 27/www.nevadensis.com).* **Open** 10am-3pm Mon, Sun; 10am-2pm, 4-7pm Tue-Sat.

East Alpujarras

Heading out of the Trevélez valley and east towards **Juviles** – famed for its silk in Moorish times – the landscape begins to open out, changing from the steep, wooded inclines of the western Alpujarras to drier, rockier terrain. **Bérchules** and **Alcútar** are surrounded by chestnut trees and offer splendid views over the Cádiar valley to the green and brown folds of the Sierra de la Contraviesa.

Continue through the increasingly arid sandstone landscape to reach the characteristic villages of **Mecina Bombarón** and **Yegen**. The latter is famous as the one-time home of the English writer Gerald Brenan, who moved here in 1920. During eight years' residence Brenan did some prodigious walking (including trekking from Granada to Yegen in one day) and became intimately acquainted with his new home. He recorded his experiences in *South from Granada*, which remains the best account of life in the region and a must-read for any visitor to the Alpujarras. A plaque in the *barrio alto* marks the house where he lived. Many aspects of Brenan's description of Yegen in 1920 still hold true today: 'It was a poor village, standing high above the sea, with an immense view in front of it. With its grey box-shaped houses of a battered Corbusier style, all running down the hill and fusing into one another, and its flat clay roofs and small smoking chimneys, it suggested something that had been made out of the earth by insects.'

Yegen.

The larger village of **Válor**, a couple of kilometres to the east, is incredibly pretty, and has its own soap and cheese factories. Here, the houses with pitched roofs mark a significant change from the dominant Alpujarran architecture. Válor's **Fiesta Patronales** in September is the best of the region's 'Moors and Christians' pageants (*see p51*), and celebrates the resistance of local-born *morisco* Aben Humaya to 16th-century Catholic persecution.

Beyond here the road splits, south to **Ugíjar** – the main town of the eastern Alpujarras, which years ago attracted innumerable fortune hunters seeking gold in its river, but is lacking in any real attractions today – and east to **Mairena** and **Laroles**, at the extremity of the Granadan Alpujarras. From the latter, you can enjoy the superb drive over the Sierra Nevada, via the **Puerto de la Ragua** pass, to reach the stunning castle of **La Calahorra** (*see p279*), or continue east to Laujar de Andarax and the Almerían Alpujarras.

Where to stay & eat

In Bérchules, **El Paraje** (GR421, km6, mobile 626 18 60 35, www.elparaje.com, double €35-€45) is run by a Dutch couple. All rooms retain their original features but have been updated with the odd designer flourish. There's also a pleasant living and dinifng area for home-cooked meals. Alternatively, you'll find good rooms, fine food and a warm welcome at **Hotel Los Bérchules** (Ctra de Bérchules 20, 958 85 25 30, www.hotelberchules.com, double €44-€49, restaurant €€).

For eats in Valór, the **Restaurante Aben Humeya** (C/Los Bolos s/n, 958 85 18 10, €-€€) serves free tapas with drinks and has a superb restaurant specialising in typical *alpujarreño* cuisine, particularly game birds.

Just up the road in Mairena, **Casa Las Chimeneas** (C/Amargua 6, 958 76 03 52, www.alpujarra-tours.com, double €60) specialises in walking tours. Accommodation is in a lovingly restored *cortijo* with astonishing views; all seven spacious bedrooms have en suite bathrooms and a balcony or terrace. Homey communal areas have crackling fires and rocking chairs, and the terrace is a top spot for evening barbecues and a dip in the pool as the sun goes down.

The rooms at **El Rincón de Yegen** (Camino de Gerald Brenan, 958 85 12 70, closed 1st 2wks Feb, double €40, restaurant €€, closed Tue) are cosily decked out with woven rugs and blankets; the hotel also has a small pool. The restaurant is first-rate, set in pretty gardens, and offers interesting dishes such as onion and basil tart, stuffed pork loin and local partridge.

Another super place to stay is the **Alquería de Morayma** (A348 Cádiar, 958 34 32 21, www.alqueriamorayma.com, double €59, restaurant €€), based around an organic farm and vineyard. The farmhouse has a lovely dining room where you can feast on excellent local cuisine, while the outbuildings – including a converted chapel – house rooms and self-contained suites, stylishly decorated with Alpujarran and Moorish furnishings. There's a pool for use in high season.

Getting there

By bus

Alsina Graells (958 18 54 80) runs 2 buses daily between Granada and Alcútar, calling at Lanjarón (1hr), Órgiva (1hr 30mins), the Poqueira villages (2hrs 5mins) and Pitres (2hrs 45mins), with 2 services continuing to Trevélez (3hrs 15mins) and Alcútar (3hrs 50mins). Other buses travel from Granada to Ugíjar via Torvizcón (2hrs 20mins), Cádiar (3hrs), Yegen (3hrs 30mins) and Válor (3hrs 45mins). Ugíjar and Bérchules are also served by buses from Almería. There are less frequent bus services between Lanjarón and Motril/Málaga. Autocares Bonal (958 46 50 22) runs 1 bus daily in summer from Granada to the Sierra Nevada ski resort (1hr); in winter there are 3 buses Mon-Fri and 4 on Sat, Sun.

Costa Tropical

Tropical, no, but not without its charms.

Almuñécar.

Granada province's stretch of coastline has been dubbed, optimistically, the Costa Tropical. West of La Herradura lies a beautiful and little-explored coast of sandstone cliffs, herb-scented hills and tiny, secluded beaches. East of here, however, monstrous plastic greenhouses are gobbling up the plains, though there are still a couple of towns worth a stop; in particular Salobreña and the quiet, thoroughly Spanish resorts of Castell de Ferro and Calahonda.

Almuñécar & around

Just over the Málaga–Granada border, the sleepy resort of **La Herradura** is situated on a wide bay. Clear waters have made the village a hub for watersports, particularly scuba-diving: try **Windsurf La Herradura** (Paseo Marítimo 34, 958 64 01 43, www.windsurflaherradura.com) for sailing and windsurfing lessons and hire. A little east is the **Marina del Este** yacht marina (958 64 08 01, www.marinasmediterraneo.com), the naturist **Playa del Muerte** and a small bay at **Cotobro**, with a seafront *paseo* leading into the main resort of Almuñécar. The nicest beaches, however, are back towards Nerja, such as the nudist beach of **Cantariján**, just beyond the Cerro Gordo tunnel.

From afar **Almuñécar** doesn't look like it has much to recommend it. The urban centre is a jumble of one-way streets and pile-'em-high, sell-'em-cheap apartment blocks; parking is nightmarish. But the lively Friday market attracts folks from miles around, there's a decent strand, and the old town of **Sexitano** is a delight, with whitewashed houses and cobbled streets crammed with top-notch tapas.

The two main beaches, the **Playa San Cristóbal** and the **Playa Puerto del Mar**, are separated by the rocky **Peñón del Santo** headland. The shaley beaches are packed in high season, but at other times you'll find acres of space. The town's tourist office is in a lovely 19th-century, neo-Moorish mansion, a block inland from the Playa San Cristóbal. Opposite is a small botanic garden, **Parque El Majuelo**, incorporating the curious remains of a Roman fish-curing factory (Factoría de Salzones).

From here it's a steep climb to the **Castillo de San Miguel**, crowning the old town. The original Phoenician fort was taken over by the Romans and later by the Moors. Surrendered to the Christians in 1489, it gained its current name and underwent extensive remodelling. There are fine views from here, and a small museum showing the development of Almuñécar. The whitewashed houses and narrow streets between the castle and the museum transport you a long way from the tourist-thronged modernity of the coastal strip. Continue downhill from the museum to reach café-lined Plaza Ayuntamiento, the 17th-century church of **La Encarnación** (Puerta de Granada 1, 958 63 06 46, open hours of service), and the busy Plaza Mayor, where excavation work has revealed remains of the Roman water system.

A prestigious **International Jazz Festival** is held in Almuñécar in July, and it's also a good place to join in the revelry honouring the Virgin of El Carmen on 16 July, when fishermen adorn their boats with flowers and ribbons.

The tourist office can direct you to several impressive Roman aqueducts around the village of **Torrecuevas**. From here there is also access to the **Peña Escrita** ecological park, four square kilometres (1.5 square miles) of mountain reserve. Beyond Torrecuevas the road snakes north by the Río Verde, to the pleasant mountain villages of **Jete**, **Otívar** and **Lentegí** and into the eastern Alpujarras (*see p284*).

Castillo de San Miguel

Open *Apr-June* 10.30am-1.30pm, 5-7.30pm Tue-Sat; 10.30am-1.30pm Sun. *July-mid Sept* 10.30am-1.30pm, 6.30-9pm Tue-Sat; 10.30am-1.30pm Sun. *Mid Sept-Mar* 10.30am-1.30pm, 4-6.30pm Tue-Sat; 10.30am-2.30pm Sun. **Admission** (with Museo Arqueológico) €2.20; €1.50 concessions. **No credit cards**.

Where to eat & drink

There are plenty of seafront restaurants and bars in Almuñécar, but the old town is a better bet. Try the impressive **Horno de Candida**, the catering school's restaurant (C/Orovia 3, 958 63 46 07, closed lunch Sun, €), with its pleasant rooftop terrace. **Bodega Francisco** (C/Real 7, 958 63 01 68, closed Nov & Feb, €) is authentic as they come, with barrels of *fino* behind the bar and *jamón* hanging from the ceiling. In La Herradura, the **Hotel La Tartana** restaurant (*see below*; closed lunch & all Sun July-Sept, Mon Oct-June, €€-€€€) is becoming one of the region's best, with American-International fusion dishes (Asian fish cakes and stuffed *jalapeños*, baby back ribs and meat loaf), in beautiful, romantic surrounds. Booking is crucial. Back on the beach, the **Restaurante El Chamboa de Joaquin** (Playa de la Herradura, Paseo Andrés Segovia s/n, 958 64 00 44, €€) is a bit hit-or-miss, but is famed for its giant *paella* served every Saturday and Sunday from 2.30pm throughout the summer. The west end of the beach has several lively beach bars.

On the old coast road, turning off at the La Herradura ceramics sign is the **Mirador de Cerro Gordo** (Ctra Vieja Granada-Malaga, 958 34 90 99, closed lunch July & Aug, €€€). The network of shady patios, terraces and stone turrets perched on a promontory looking over La Herradura and Nerja make this one of the prettiest places on the Costa Tropical. The Moroccan-inflected food is good; try chicken in orange and mint with saffron couscous.

Inland, a number of roadside restaurants in Otívar offer mountain views to accompany the local delicacy, *pollo a la manzana* (chicken with apples). Order this in advance at **El Capricho** (Ctra Otívar, 958 64 50 75, €€) a raucous, outdoor cafeteria-style place which is justly famous for its roasts; touristy but still good fun. Towards Nerja, **La Barraca** (Cantarijan Playa, 958 34 92 87, €€) does decent food and has live Cuban music and dancing on Wednesday nights from July to September.

Where to stay

Among the hotels along Playa San Cristóbal in Almuñécar is the **Hotel Casablanca** (Plaza San Cristóbal 4, 958 63 55 75, www.almunecar.info/casablanca, double €50-€70), a friendly two-star. In Sexitano, the **Hostal Altamar** (C/Alta del Mar 13, 958 63 03 46, www.hostalaltamar.com, closed Oct-Mar, double €36-€50) is a steal, with bright rooms and a cosy lounge.

In La Herradura, the **Hotel Tartana** (A7-E15, exit 14, Urbanización San Nicolás, 958 64 05 35, www.hotellatartana.com, double €61-€74) can't be beat for boutique chic. Its six Moorish-accented rooms around a central courtyard have 16th-century fittings and huge double beds. Several pretty terraces have sea views, but suffer the rumble of traffic, and there's a candlelit bar and restaurant (*see above*). A block from the beach, the recently opened **Hotel Almijara** (C/Acera del Pilar 6, 958 61 80 53, www.hotelalmijara.com, double €63-€110) has comfortable, Laura Ashley-esque rooms. The roof terrace bar and restaurant is great on a moonlit night. On the beach, **Hostal La Caleta** (Paseo Andrés Segovia 11, 958 82 70 07, double €40-€50) is friendly, clean and has a cheap, decent restaurant beneath it.

Inland, you'll find log cabins (€37-€59 for 2 people), simple *casas* (€51-€89 for 4 people), a campsite (€10-€13 per tent) and a restaurant (€-€€) in the **Peña Escrita** ecological park (mobile 615 32 14 62, www.pescrita.com; *see above*).

Resources

Internet

Almuñécar *Mundo Digital, C/Alta del Mar 8 (958 63 40 07)*. **Open** 10am-2pm, 5-10pm Mon-Sat; 7-10pm Sun.

La Herradura *Panoramix Informática, C/Unidad 9 (958 64 01 49)*. **Open** 10am-2pm, 5-9pm Mon-Sat.

Tourist information

Almuñécar *Palacete de la Najarra, Avda de Europa s/n (958 63 11 25/www.almunecar.info)*. **Open** *Apr-June, mid Sept-Oct* 10am-2pm, 5-8pm daily. *July-mid Sept* 10am-2pm, 6-9pm daily. *Nov-Mar* 10am-2pm, 4.30-7pm daily.

La Herradura *Paseo Andrés Segovia (629 069 467)*. **Open** *Apr-June, mid Sept-Oct* 10am-1.30pm, 5-7pm Mon-Fri; 10am-1.30pm Sat, Sun. *July-mid Sept* 11am-1.30pm, 6-8.30pm Mon-Sat; 10am-2pm Sun. *Nov-Mar* 10am-1.30pm, 4-6pm Mon-Fri; 10am-1.30pm Sat, Sun.

Salobreña & further east

From Almuñécar the A7-E15 continues east on to a wide coastal plain, backed by the hills of the **Sierra de las Guájares**. There's a great view of **Salobreña** (**photo** *p288*) from the

Salobreña. *See p287.*

road: perched on a steep hill, surrounded by a sea of sugar cane, its whitewashed houses tumble down from the Moorish Alcazaba. Sadly, the impact of its location has been dulled in recent years by development and an encroaching tide of growers' plastic. Two pebbly beaches are separated by rocky **El Peñón** headland, and backed by an increasing number of apartments and holiday complexes.

The old town is a pretty tangle of crooked streets and not too touristy; you can easily spend a morning getting pleasantly lost. The ruined **Castillo Árabe** offers panoramic views of the plains, the snowy Sierra Nevada and the coast. From here, follow a steep, flower-adorned *paseo* down to the 16th-century church of **Nuestra Señora del Rosario** (Plaza de la Iglesia, no phone, open hours of services), built in Múdejar style on the site of the town's former mosque. Just below it is La Boveda, a medieval passageway into the fortified town. Close by in the Plaza Antigua Ayuntamiento, the old town hall houses the **Museo Histórico**, with artefacts from Salobreña's 6,000-year history. A flower-filled promenade, Paseo de las Flores, circumnavigates the hill's northern flank below the castle, with views of the town's 19th-century sugar-processing plant.

From here things slide downhill. **Motril**, inland to the east, is an unappealing industrial centre, while the nearby resort of **Torrenueva** veers from hot and heaving in high summer to drab and deserted out of season. Towards Almería, as the plastic greenhouses get more prevalent, so too the resorts, such as **La Rábita**, become less appealing.

Castillo Árabe

Salobreña (958 61 27 33). **Open** *July-mid Sept* 10.30am-1.30pm, 6-9pm daily. *Mid Sept-June* 10.30am-1.30pm, 5-9pm daily. **Admission** *Castillo Árabe only* €2.15. *Combined with Museo Histórico* €2.85. **No credit cards**.

Museo Histórico

Plaza Antigua Ayuntamiento, Salobreña (958 61 27 33). **Open** as Castillo Árabe above. **Admission** *Museo Historico only* €2.15. *Combined with Castillo Árabe* €2.85. **No credit cards**.

Where to stay, eat & drink

The most luxurious place to stay in the area is the Italianate **Casa de los Bates** (A7-E15, km329.5, 958 34 94 95, www.casadelosbates.com, double €142) between Salobreña and Motril. Built in the late 19th century, it has been beautifully restored with period details, and is surrounded by a luscious tropical garden with pool. Budget options in Salobreña include **Pensión Marí Carmen** (C/Nueva 32, 958 61 09 06, double €24-€32) and **Pensión San José** (C/Cristo 68, 958 61 03 54, double €24), with simple rooms round a charming, bougainvillea-filled courtyard; bathrooms are communal.

For food, **Bar Restaurante Pesetas** (C/Bóveda 11, 958 61 01 82, closed Mon Oct-June, €€) sticks to the basics with an excellent and extensive range of fish and shellfish tapas; it has a pleasant roof terrace. Otherwise, there are plenty of restaurants serving seafood and steaks along the beach.

Resources

Tourist information

Salobreña *Plaza Goya s/n (958 61 03 14/www.ayto-salobrena.org).* **Open** *July-mid Sept* 9.30am-1.30pm, 4-7pm daily. *Mid Sept-June* 9.30am-1.30pm, 4-7pm Mon-Sat.

Getting there

By bus

Málaga–Almería buses connect regularly with local services. Almuñécar bus station (Avda Juan Carlos I/Avda Fenicia) has frequent buses to/from Granada.

Almería Province

Features

Maps

Almería Province

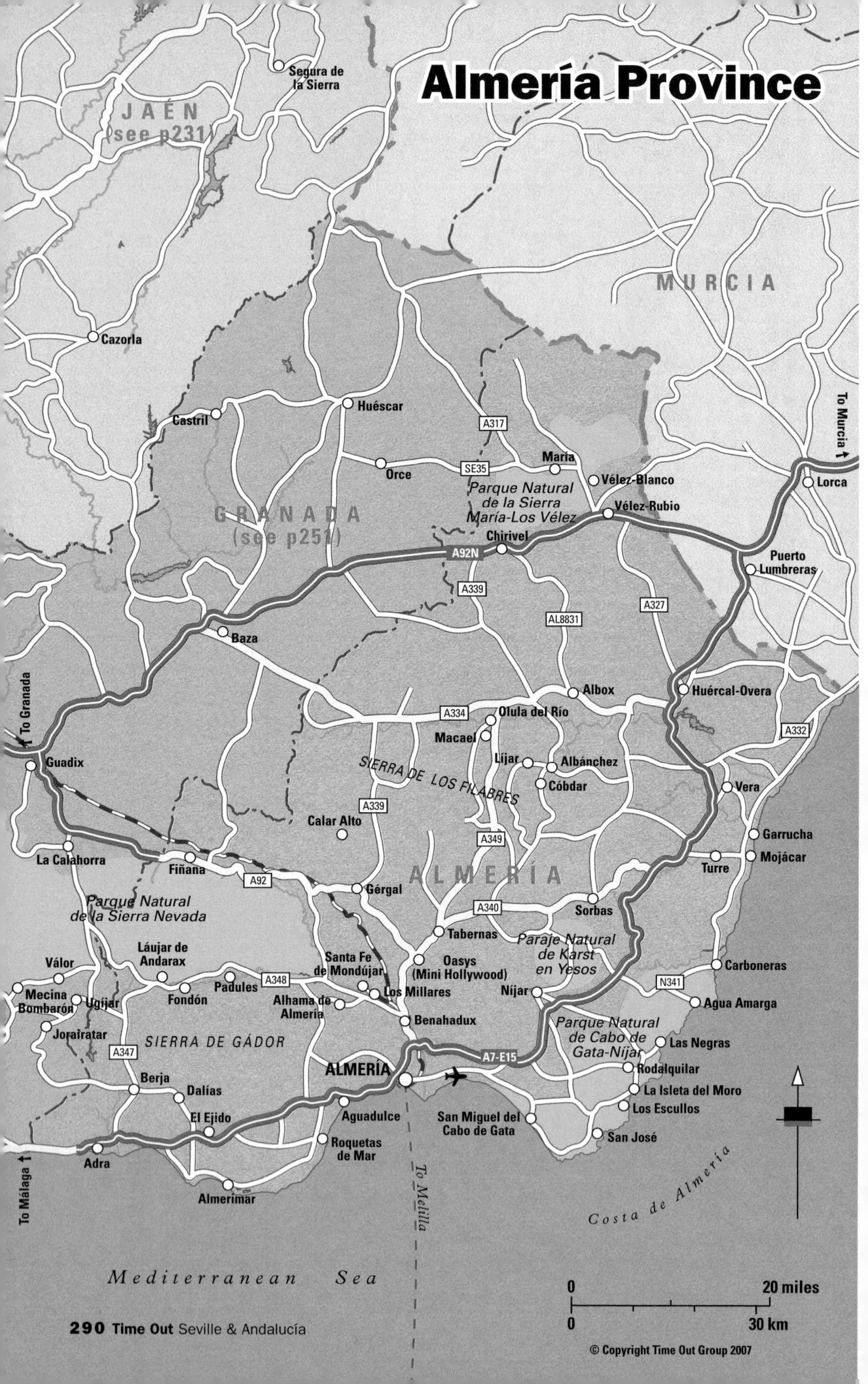

Introduction

Beware package tourists – strike out instead for the wild interior or the fine beaches of Cabo de Gata.

As the hottest, driest and sunniest corner of Europe, Almería province may seem to have long had it made as a holiday destination. Yet, prior to the development of intensive fruit- and vegetable-growing under plastic, this was one of the poorest corners of Spain. But, as the supermarket orders and package tourists have poured in over the last couple of decades, so has the economy of Almería turned around, and, alas, so has much of the coast become blighted by seas of plastic and holiday complexes. However, oases remain, and once you leave the coast, the wilderness of the interior comes as a surprising and welcome tonic.

ALMERÍA CITY

The provincial capital is a city on the move. A key port in Moorish times, but something of a backwater ever since, Almería is finally starting to assert itself as the *plasticultura* wealth rolls in. It's a relaxed and eminently enjoyable little city, with enough attractions and distractions to take up a leisurely couple of days. The magnificent Moorish Alcazaba is the major draw, but there's also plenty of good wandering to be done in the old town, and no shortage of first-rate tapas bars in which to shelter from the sun.

COSTA DE ALMERÍA

The coastline of Almería province splits neatly into three distinct segments. Closest to Granada province, and stretching all the way to Almería city, is the almost entirely unappealing stretch of plastic-tent-covered land, punctuated by the odd antiseptic resort. East of the capital, in utter contrast, is the magnificent and unspoiled Cabo de Gata – a wild and raw expanse of hills, tiny fishing villages and superb beaches. North of here is the wannabe Costa del Sol, centred around Mojácar – touristville, for sure, but good relaxed fun if you're in the mood.

ALMERÍA INTERIOR

Few tourists venture away from Almería's coast, other than to visit the bizarre Western theme park of Mini Hollywood, which leaves the sparsely populated, vivid red desert landscapes and the obscure mountains of the Sierra de la Filabres to the adventuresome few. This is tremendous driving country, and in the far north there is more little-visited hill country in the area around the appealing town of Vélez Blanco.

The best...

Beaches
Cabo de Gata (*p297*).

Castles
Almería City (*p292*); **Gérgal** (*p305*); **Tabernas** (*p305*); **Vélez Blanco** (*p303*).

Cowboys
Oasys (*p304*); **Texas Hollywood** (*p305*).

Deserts
Around **Tabernas** (*p305*).

Moorish heritage
Almería City (*pp292-6*).

Mountains
Almerían Alpujarras (*p305*); **Sierra de los Filabres** (*p304*).

Nightlife
Mojácar Playa (*p301*).

Prehistory
Cueva de los Letreros (*p303*); **Los Millares** (*p305*).

Resorts
Agua Amarga (*p299*); **Mojácar Playa** (*p301*); **San José** (*p298*).

Almería City

Ancient forts and forward thinking.

When you've got the likes of Seville, Granada, and Cádiz for rivals, it's perhaps no surprise that the city of Almería isn't on many tourists' itineraries, but it is laid-back, local and low on tourists, despite its bustling international airport. Today, the city is largely a bustling modern affair, yet it has a long and – at one distant point at least – important history. Its peak of influence came a thousand years ago, when the Caliph of Córdoba decided to build an arsenal and fort (Alcazaba) here, transforming the town into the foremost port in al-Andalus. Almerians will proudly recite to you the old saying that 'When Almería was Almería, Granada was but its farm'. Silk and ceramics, poetry and philosophy flourished, but not for long. By the mid 12th century, the city had started to decline, helped on its way by a series of earthquakes. Recently, however, it has started to shake off its centuries-old feeling of decay and neglect. As agri-business and tourism euros flow in, the future of Almería is looking brighter than it has for 800 years.

Sightseeing

The main area of interest for visitors is the old town, sandwiched between the Alcazaba in the west and the Rambla de Belén in the east (also known as the Avda de Federico García Lorca – once a dry riverbed, now a pleasant, wide, tree-lined boulevard). The port marks the southern boundary of the old city, while the Puerta de Purchena (the original gate is long gone) is as far north as most visitors venture.

Almería is dominated by one sight above all: the mighty **Alcazaba** – one of the greatest surviving examples of Almohad military architecture. Its crenellated walls (1,430 metres/4,692 feet long), commanding the hill on the west side of the city and overlooking the harbour, still impress today; their impact, when first erected on the orders of the Caliph of Córdoba, Abd al-Rahman III in 995, can only be imagined. The fortress was later altered and extended by Fernando and Isabel.

The Alcazaba, which is reached via a zigzagging path from C/Almanzor, is divided into three distinct sections – two of Moorish origin, one of later Christian construction. The entrance, via the **Puerta de la Justicia** (Gate of Justice), brings you into the first Moorish section, now filled with gardens. Originally, a small town occupied the site, complete with houses, public baths, water cisterns and other civic facilities.

Dividing this area from the second Moorish section of the Alcazaba is a wall that continues down into the valley to the north and up to the **Cerro de San Cristóbal** (St Christopher's Hill, complete with an oversize statue of Christ) in a great and highly photogenic sweep. The wall was an extension of the original fortifications, ordered by the *taifa* king Jayran in 1014-28. (It can be reached along C/Antonio Vico from the Puerta de Purchena.) Behind the wall, surprisingly, are pens of gazelles, antelopes and other endangered Saharan species – this is the **Instituto de Aclimatación de Fauna Sahariana**, a research and rescue centre.

The second compound of the Alcazaba once contained a range of buildings, including a palace said to rival the Alhambra. Alas, all that remains are the remains, though they make for fascinating archaeology. A Moorish house has been re-created here, and it is possible to make out the ground plan of a bathhouse.

Another wall divides this area from the smallest of the three sections, the castle constructed by Fernando and Isabel on the taking of the city in 1489. Massive walls and circular towers – which were needed following the invention of effective artillery – distinguish this area. The **Torre de Homenaje** (Tower of Homage) contains a small photographic exhibition organised by the Centro Andaluz de la Fotografía, which also has a gallery in town (*see p294*). From the western **Torre de Pólvora** (Gunpowder Tower) there are fine views to the former cave dwellings of the poor Barrio Chanca district.

After the obligatory visit to the Alcazaba, the best way to get to know Almería is simply to wander the streets of the old town. Start, perhaps, at the tourist office close to the port on Parque Nicolás Salmerón, pick up a city map, and then head north-west towards the 16th-century **Catedral** (**photo** *p295*). Its formidably rugged construction was never intended to be a style statement; rather, it was designed to be part church, part stronghold, since the city at this time was constantly being harassed by pirates and disaffected *moriscos*.

The **Alcazaba**. *See p292.*

The cathedral was founded in 1524 on the site of Almería's main mosque, which had been converted into a church but destroyed in an earthquake two years earlier. The initially Isabelline-Gothic style employed was modified to a Renaissance model when Juan de Orea took over its construction in 1550. Inside, the church has three naves with Gothic vaulting, and is surprisingly graceful and unadorned. The best paintings hang in the **Capilla de la Piedad** (behind the altar), and include three works by Alonso Cano and an *Immaculate Conception* by Murillo. The unusually spacious cloister was added in the 18th century in neo-classical style.

On the cathedral's east side is Plaza Bendicho, which contains, in its south-west corner, the city's oldest house, known as the **Casa de los Puche**. It dates from the 18th century – and looks like it hasn't been maintained since – and now belongs to the brotherhood of the Cofradía del Prendimiento. North-west of the cathedral, and closed to traffic, is the 17th-century arcaded Plaza de la Constitución (also known as the Plaza Vieja), containing the pastel-shaded *ayuntamiento* (town hall) and a gleaming white marble memorial to 24 liberals who landed at Almería in 1831 to proclaim liberty from the rule of Ferdinand VII, only to be captured and shot.

Further north, the ancient C/de las Tiendas contains one of Almería's most interesting churches, **Santiago** (open hours of services), designed (like the cathedral) by Juan de Orea, and erected in the 1550s. The streets around here contain many of the city's best bars, restaurants and shops. C/Real is one such street: here you'll find the minor charms of the new **Museo del Aceite de Oliva** (Olive Oil Museum), where you can stop in for excellent tapas. Close by, on C/Tenor Iribarne, are the Moorish water cisterns, the **Aljibes Arabes**.

Further south is the headquarters of the first-rate **Centro Andaluz de la Fotografía** (Andalucían Centre for Photography), which regularly puts on interesting exhibitions. Close by is the long Paseo de Almería, the city's principal artery. Here, at No.56, stands the grand, late 19th-century **Círculo Mercantil e Industrial y Teatro Cervantes**, which now contains the incongruously named but agreeable Molly Malone bar (*see p296*).

West of here you may come across crowds of North and sub-Saharan Africans queuing outside government agencies – Almería is one of the main ports of entry for migrant workers, most of whom are destined for the stifling *plasticultura* tents that scar the coastline west of the city (*see p300* **Plastic fantastic**).

Imagine

Not a lot of people know it, but **John Lennon** wrote *Strawberry Fields Forever* in Almería. During 1966 the Beatle was staying in the city for six weeks during the filming of Richard Lester's anti-war black comedy *How I Won the War*, about a group of British soldiers dropped behind enemy lines to create a cricket pitch to impress a visiting VIP.

Lennon starred as Private Digweed, lining up alongside a distinguished cast that included Michael Crawford, Michael Hordern, Sheila Hancock, Roy Kinnear and Robert Hardy. The wild arid landscapes around Carboneras, Tabernas and Cabo de Gata stood in for Egypt in the film.

Initially, John stayed in a small apartment called El Delfín Verde near the city beach of El Zapillo. It was here that he started strumming the initial chords of *Strawberry Fields*. Later, his wife Cynthia and Ringo came out to celebrate John's 26th birthday at the nearby La Manzanilla restaurant (alas, La Manzanilla is no longer in existence).

At Cynthia's request John then moved to a bigger house, Santa Isabel (on Camino de Romero, on the north-eastern edge of the city), where he completed the song and recorded a number of demo versions of it. The house had been abandoned for 30 years before local journalist and Beatles fan Adolfo Iglesias uncovered its story (www.upv.es/~ecabrera/letme/almeria.html). It is now being converted into a cultural centre by the city council, though, sadly, there are no plans to acknowledge the Lennon connection, or the fact that Sam Spiegel used the building as his production centre for *Lawrence of Arabia*.

Information on John's sojourn in Almería is frustratingly scant. Iglesias has uncovered what he can: this includes such facts as that like many English visitors Lennon got sunburned, that few Spaniards asked for his autograph (though one group of children did it four times, with Ringo as mediator) and that John's Rolls-Royce broke down, forcing him and Cynthia to travel around by taxi. Years later the relevant cab driver 'had no memories whatsoever' of his famous passengers.

Across the Paseo, and further north, is the two-level covered **mercado** (market), built in the 1890s, while east of the Rambla is the **Centro de Arte** (Arts Centre), which puts on art exhibitions. Not far away is the **Museo de Almería**, the city's most impressive museum. Highlights from its holdings include those from the Chalcolithic site of Los Millares (*see p305*).

Alcazaba

C/Almanzor s/n (950 27 16 17). **Open** *Apr-Sept* 9am-8.30pm Tue-Sun. *Oct-Mar* 9am-6.30pm Tue-Sun. **Admission** €1.50; free with EU passport. **No credit cards**.

Alijbes Arabes

C/Tenor Iribarne (950 27 30 39). **Open** 9am-2pm Mon-Fri. **Admission** free.

Biblioteca Pública Francisco Villaespesa

C/Hermanos Machado s/n (950 23 03 75). **Open** *July-Sept* 9am-9pm Mon-Fri. *Oct-June* 9am-9pm Mon-Fri, 9am-2pm Sat. **Admission** free.

Catedral de Almería

Entrance on C/Velasquez (mobile 650 23 19 26). **Open** 10am-4.30pm Mon-Fri; 10am-1pm Sat. **Admission** €2. **No credit cards**.

Centro Andaluz de la Fotografía

C/Martínez Campos 20, 1st Floor; exhibition entrance on C/Pablo Cazard 1 (950 00 27 00/ caf.ccul@juntadeandalucia.es). **Open** 8pm-3pm Mon-Fri. **Admission** free.

Centro de Arte

Plaza Carlos Cano s/n (950 26 96 80). **Open** 6-9pm Mon; 11am-2pm, 6-9pm Tue-Sat; 11am-2pm Sun. **Admission** free.

Museo del Aceite de Oliva

C/Real 15 (950 62 00 02/www.castillodetabernas.com). **Open** 10am-2pm, 5-8.30pm Mon-Sat. **Admission** free.

Museo de Almería

Ctra de Ronda 91, Plaza Luis Siret s/n (950 64 98 00/www.juntadeandalucia.es/cultura/museos). **Open** 2.30-8.30pm Tue; 9am-8.30pm Wed-Sat; 9am-2.30pm Sun. **Admission** €1.50, free with EU passport.

Almería's **Catedral**. *See p292.*

Where to eat & drink

The streets immediately south of the Puerta de Purchena and those between the cathedral and the Paseo de Almería are the best places to head for a drink or meal. The quality of the tapas bars is generally higher than that of the restaurants. One of the city's classics is the **Casa Puga** (C/Jovellanos 7, 950 23 15 30, www.barcasapuga.es, closed Sun & Sept, €), with an astonishing wine list. It's been in the same family since 1870. For designer tapas, try the superb **El Quinto Toro** (C/Juan Leal 6, 950 23 91 35, €€) on the street leading south from the market. The **Restaurante Sol de Almería** (C/Ulpiano Díaz 7, 950 26 29 60, €) offers the twin charms of a cheap *menú* (€9.50) and a pleasant patio at the back, while the **Restaurante Valentín** (C/Tenor Iribarne 19, 950 26 44 75, €€€€) is classier but correspondingly pricey, and specialises in seafood. For something different, try the **Tetería Almedina** (C/La Paz 2, mobile 629 27 78 27, closed Mon, €€). At the foot of the Alcazaba, this Moroccan-style teahouse serves traditional teas, sweet cakes, and more substantial dishes such as couscous with lamb.

Nightlife

The city doesn't have many nightclubs or late-night bars – those that exist can be found within a few streets of each other, west of the Paseo de Almería, just south of C/Padre Luque, or along the Parque Nicolás Salmerón, where the city youth congregates outside with shop-bought bottles of spirits and cola on Friday and Saturday nights.

Most of Almería's summer nightlife is in the beach resorts west of the city. Almería's top flamenco club, located in the atmospheric Aljibes Árabes, is the thoroughly authentic **Peña El Taranto** (C/Tenor Iribarne 20, 950 23 50 57, bar closed last 2wks Sept and no shows July-mid Oct, admission €14), which has shows every couple of weeks between October and July. Though, strictly speaking, you need to be a member here, sometimes you can walk in off the street. Outside show times it's a bar with a pleasant roof terrace.

Almería has a bit of an Irish vibe at nights; pick from the **Mae West** (Parque Nicolás Salmerón 9, 950 25 35 20, closed Sun), the **Molly Malone** (Teatro Cervantes, Paseo de Almería 56, 950 24 62 83) or the **Irish Tavern** (C/González Egea 4, no phone).

Shopping

The city isn't particularly notable for its shops. Most of its commercial activity is concentrated on the streets radiating out from the Puerta de Purchena, and particularly in those between here and Plaza San Pedro to the south. For guides, maps and English-language books, try **Libreria Cajal** (C/Navarro Rodrigo 14, 950 23 61 48) or **Picasso** (C/Reyes Católicos 18, 950 23 56 00), both just south of the market. For clothes and shoes try Paseo de Almería; staples **Zara** (950 27 44 20) and **Mango** (950 23 00 60) are at numbers 83 and 47 respectively.

Where to stay

Almería is not blessed with a huge range of characterful accommodation; set your sights on clean and adequate. The **AM Torreluz** (Plaza Flores 5, 950 23 49 99, www.amhoteles.com, double €157-€171) is a fairly characterless four-star with a gym and small rooftop pool. The **Gran Hotel Almería** (Avda Reina Regente 8, 950 23 80 11, www.citymar.com, double €155) is the flashest option in town, with a pool and a private garage (a definite boon – parking in the centre is very limited), and a location close to the port. **Hostal Nixar** (C/Antonio Vico 24, 950 23 72 55, double €40-€48) is an unremarkable but adequate hostal, well located just west of the Puerta de Purchena. Nearby, and better value, is the **Hotel Seville** (C/Granada 25, 950 23 02 09, double €45-€53). The **Hotel Costasol** (Paseo de Almería 58, 950 23 40 11, www.hotelcostasol.com, double €81-€92) is old-fashioned, but not offensively so, and it's good value for the central location. Out near the train station, the **NH Ciudad de Almería** (Jardín de Medina s/n, 950 18 25 00, www.nh-hotels.com, double €70-€155) offers plenty of creature comforts and a decent helping of style.

Resources

Police station

C/Santos Zarate 15 (950 62 12 05).

Post office

Plaza Casanello 1 (950 28 15 01).

Tourist information

Parque Nicolás Salmerón s/n, corner of C/Martínez Campos (950 27 43 55/www.andalucia.org). **Open** 9am-7.30pm Mon-Fri; 10am-2pm Sat, Sun.

Getting there

By air

Almería's airport is 10km (6 miles) east of the city. *See p308.*

By boat

Trasmediterranea (902 45 46 45/950 23 61 55, www.trasmediterranea.es) has 1 sailing most days (more in summer) to the Melilla in Morocco (6hrs by standard boat, 3hrs 30mins by the summer fast boat). Ferrimaroc (950 27 48 00) runs a similar service to the Moroccan town of Nador, south of Melilla (7hrs).

By bus

A number of companies serve Almería's bus station (950 26 20 98), just north of the train station on Plaza Barcelona. Each day, Alsina Graells (950 23 81 97, www.alsinagraells.es) operates to and from Adra (1hr 15mins; hourly), 2 buses to Cádiz (9hrs), 1 to Córdoba (5hrs 15mins), 5 to Granada (2hrs 15mins), 4 to Málaga (3hrs 30mins) and 3 to Seville (5hrs 30mins). Bernardo (950 25 04 22, www.autocaresbernardo.com) has 2-3 daily buses to San José (1hr).

By train

Almería's railway station is located a kilometre east of the centre at Plaza de la Estación. For ticket sales/reservations, call 902 24 02 02; for international info, phone 902 24 34 02. Almería is at the end of the line that runs to Seville via Granada. There are 3 daily trains to Seville (just over 5hrs), all of which call at Granada (2hr 15mins) and Antequera (3hrs 30mins), and 1 additional daily service between Almería and Granada. Before it reaches Granada, a fork from this line heads north towards Madrid (2 trains daily, 6hrs 45mins). To reach Almería from Cádiz or Huelva you'll need to change at Seville.

Costa de Almería

Volcanic landscapes, unspoilt beaches and an awful lot of tomato plants.

Cabo de Gata.

Adra to Aguadulce

Heading into Almería province along the coast road from Granada's optimistically named 'Costa Tropical' (*see pp286-88*), you'll already have become familiar with the huge, hideous plastic tents that are squeezed on to whatever level land is available. Yet nothing will have prepared you for what awaits along the stretch of coast from Adra to Almería city. From the foot of the Sierra de Gádor mountains to the coastline, an overwhelming sea of pale green and grey plastic shimmers beneath a blast-furnace sun. Under here grows much of the fruit and vegetables bought in supermarkets across northern Europe. This is *plasticultura*, the Almerían miracle – an economic gold mine, a social time bomb and an aesthetic nightmare (*see p300* **Plastic fantastic**). This dispiriting sight does nothing to encourage the visitor to linger in the area, and the local towns and resorts are largely characterless, dull and overdeveloped. **Aguadulce**, ten kilometres (six miles) from Almería city, is the oldest resort on this part of the coast and probably the most attractive (but this isn't saying much), with a long, inviting beach.

Almería province has far better to offer, however. If you crave sand and sea, but want to avoid the usual Costa atmosphere, overdevelopment and crowds, head straight onwards to the Cabo de Gata.

Cabo de Gata

After you've butted your way through the sea of plastic west of Almería city, nothing could come as a more delightful contrast than the Cabo de Gata. This wild, mountainous stretch of coast has been largely protected from encroaching *plasticultura* by its designation since 1987 as a Parque Natural. It's a unique environment, with the lowest annual rainfall in Europe (around 200 millimetres/eight inches), whose dramatic topography encompasses basalt and gypsum formations, towering cliffs and undulating red plains, reefs and islands and scores of secluded coves and sandy beaches. More than 1,000 plant species and over 50 types of vertebrate can be found in the semi-desert landscape, including the natterjack toad, the troglodyte bat, the hoopoe and the flamingo.

Unlike the wildlife, humans have found it less easy to survive on the Cabo de Gata. The high temperatures, sparse rainfall and scarcity of spring water made agriculture difficult. What's more, following the expulsion of the Moors from Spain, this coast was under constant threat of harassment from North African pirates. Over the centuries a series of defensive fortifications was constructed – 14 survive today within the boundaries of the park.

Times are changing, although, and not all the development is positive. The march of the plastic tents has reached the very edges of the park and even encroached into it in certain areas. The biggest threat to the Cabo de Gata's protected status is a new development strategy that has allowed the growth of urban centres within the park, abolished height and size restrictions for new buildings and approved 80 new plastic tent sites within the park itself.

Coming from Almería city, a suitable place to begin a tour of the Cabo de Gata is the **Centro de Visitantes de las Amoladeros**, just off the road from Retamar to the cape itself. This is a good spot to pick up maps and guides, before continuing on to the village properly known as **San Miguel del Cabo de Gata** (though more usually called simply Cabo de Gata). There has been a settlement on this site for several hundred years, though, beyond the 18th-century watchtower at the southern edge of the village and the 19th-century parish church, you wouldn't know it. It does, however, have

Agua Amarga.

a long and surprisingly – given the proximity to Almería – tranquil beach, and there are a handful of bars and cafés along the front.

The road continues along the coast towards the haunting silhouette of the **Iglesia de las Salinas** – an isolated, weirdly ravaged church built in 1907, and looking like a relic from one of the westerns filmed around Tabernas. The church stands sentinel over the economically and ecologically significant salt pans (*salinas*). These are rich in halophilous plants, providing food for more than 80 types of bird that pass through, and reed beds for nesting. The most famous residents and visitors are pink flamingoes. A hide is provided for twitchers.

The road continues on past a couple of tiny villages, then starts to climb and wind (and becomes perilously narrow in parts), past a small, quiet beach (**Playa de Corralete**) before arriving at a dead end at a lighthouse – the **Faro de Cabo de Gata**. The first lighthouse on this site was built in 1863, warning ships of the treacherous rocks of the **Arrecife de la Sirenas** (Reef of the Sirens), located just below. The sirens in question were, in fact, a colony of seals which lived here until recently. The views from here are superb, and there's a tapas bar (**El Faro**, 950 16 00 54) just before you reach the lighthouse. Boat trips ply these treacherous waters from April to September (up to eight a day); call ahead to make a reservation (mobile 637 44 91 69, www.elcaboafondo.com, €15, €12 children).

Around eight kilometres (five miles) east along the coast is the Cabo de Gata's main resort, **San José**. There's no through road for cars here, but there is a well-marked trail for walkers, which passes through some stunning scenery and by a number of pristine beaches, such as the **Playa del Mónsul** (which featured in *Indiana Jones and the Last Crusade*).

Drivers need to backtrack to around four kilometres (2.5 miles) before the village of Cabo de Gata and take the road to San José from there. The resort is a relaxed place to hang out, with a reasonable beach (though a better one, the **Playa de Genoveses**, is just around the headland to the south-west). However, holiday developments are breaking out all over San José at an alarming rate and their number and architectural banality threaten to swamp the character of the town. There is good diving to be had here: try **Isub San José** (C/Babor 3, 950 38 00 04, www.isubsanjose.com) and **Alpha** (Puerto, 950 38 03 21, www.alphabuceo.com, closed Jan & Feb).

One of the most attractive features of the Cabo de Gata is that roads run along very little of its coastline, allowing for undisturbed walks and swimming in isolated coves. Just such a peaceful trek of seven kilometres (four miles) from San José northwards brings you to the next coastal settlement, tiny **Los Escullos** (drivers need to head inland from San José and take the first road on the right). There's little to detain you here bar a couple of places to stay and eat, some ruined buildings and the largely reconstructed **Castillo de San Felipe**, which sits atop a curious outcrop of fossilised sand dune. The fort dates from 1765 – one of nine four-cannon batteries built at the time along the coast of the Kingdom of Granada.

A kilometre further on lies the town of **La Isleta del Moro**. Some fishing still takes place here, but the cranes have descended, and the holiday flats are rising. For the moment, though, it retains a quirky low-key charm and has a good beach immediately to the north.

From Isleta, the road runs to the palm-fringed beach **Cala de los Toros**, before turning inland towards **Rodalquilar**. Just before it turns inland you can make your way down. The sizeable village of Rodalquilar has a strangely disconcerting atmosphere, due largely to the number of derelict and crumbling houses on its outskirts and the abandoned mine workings above it. Mining has been big in the area for centuries and probably dates back to before Roman times, but the mines were finally closed in 1966, devastating the economy and population of the village.

The main road continues north. A kilometre further on, a rough road leads down to the long, quiet, if slightly grubby, sweep of sand at **El Playazo**. The road to the beach passes a decrepit, squat little tower that is actually the oldest fortification on the coast, the **Torre de los Alumbres**, built around 1510.

The next settlement along the coast is **Las Negras**, which, like La Isleta, is changing character rapidly as it is developed for tourism. The beach is not very appealing, but there are a couple of decent places to eat and drink. An hour's pleasant walk from here (unless you can persuade a fisherman to take you in a boat) lies the famous nudist colony of **San Pedro**, home to hippies of various nationalities, living in caves and tents around the pretty bay. Take plenty of water for both legs of the journey, and, as frequent hand-painted, multilingual signs beseech you, take your rubbish with you.

The next resort along (from Las Negras drive back to the motorway or take the ten-kilometre/six-mile road from Fernán Pérez) – is the delightful **Agua Amarga** (meaning 'bitter water'), which marks the northernmost reaches of the park. This thoroughly chilled-out place is possibly the most appealing spot to stay on the peninsula, with a few excellent accommodation and eating and drinking options. North of here, halfway to Carboneras, is an attractive and quiet beach with fine shingle and turquoise waters, the **Playa de los Muertos**.

A few kilometres inland from the Cabo de Gata, across the motorway, is the pretty town of **Níjar**. Despite being geographically separate, it is also, somewhat inexplicably, part of the Natural Park (the official name of which is the Parque Natural de Cabo de Gata-Níjar). Níjar's main claim to fame, however, is its pottery, which is bold, bright and colourful. The long, steep main street is lined with shops displaying pottery and *jarapas* (rag-made bedspreads and rugs), for which Níjar is also known. Be warned that the town is very much on the tourist trail, and there's a fair amount of tat on display, though pickings are richer on C/Eras in the Barrio Alfarero, which forks off the main street. The most charming part of Níjar is the area above the church, a maze of whitewashed alleys, many of which are decorated with plants in home-thrown pots.

Lovers of deserts should take the AL102 north from Níjar, through the eroded canyonland of the **Paraje Natural de Karst en Yesos**, and continue on to **Sorbas**, which hangs on the edge of a gorge. It lends its name to the magnificent caves, the **Cuevas de Sorbas**, in the Paraje Natural, which can be visited on guided tours (950 36 47 04, www.cuevasdesorbas.com, tours €11-€20, €7-€14 concessions, call ahead to book).

Where to stay, eat & drink

Along the beachfront in the village of Cabo de Gata, pretty **La Goleta** (950 37 02 15, www.lagoletacabodegata.com, closed Mon Oct-June and all Nov, €€) is the best bet for a meal, though the more basic **Bar Playa** (C/Barrio Nuevo 78, mobile 659 08 49 64, €) does good tapas and *raciones*. For en suite rooms try the **Hostal Las Dunas** (Barrio Nuevo 58, 950 37 00 72, closed Dec, double €48.15-€54.60), a couple of minutes' walk from the beach.

In San José the best high-end choice is the **Cortijo El Sotillo** (950 61 11 00, www.el sortillo.org, double €96.30-€132.70), on the edge of town. This sympathetically designed ranch-like complex (horse riding can be arranged) has spacious rooms, each with its own little terrace, and a pool. The same management have an upmarket place in town, **Doña Pakyta** (C/Correos s/n, 950 61 11 75, www.hotelpakyta.com, double €110-€161), which has wonderful views of the bay from its *terrazas*, but no pool. Cheaper places include the highly recommended 25-room **Hotel Atalaya** (C/Correos s/n, 950 38 00 85, www.atalayadelsur.com, double €45-€96), a keenly priced, tasteful place where the good-sized rooms all have little terraces. There's also the **Hostal Costa Rica** (C/Correos s/n, 950 38 01 03, double €53.50-€74.90) and the **Hostal Bahía** (C/Correos 16, 950 38 03 07, double €36.40-€74.90). Both are in the centre of the village, near the beach.

There are a number of places to eat on the main road into San José, but by far the most attractive spot is the strip of restaurant-bars between the beach and the harbour. There's also a more upmarket restaurant in the **Cortijo**

El Sotillo (*see above,* 950 38 02 16, €€€), while **La Gallineta** (Ctra San José s/n, 950 38 05 01, www.lagallineta.net, closed Tue and Nov-Feb, €€€), in the little village of Pozo de los Frailes just outside San José, is the most refined choice in the area. For later drinking, there are a clutch of places off the main square, where you'll also find the excellent Italian restaurant **Bistro La Plaza** (C/Plaza 3, 950 38 04 22, €), which offers generous salads, excellent crispy pizzas and carafes of good house red.

The place to stay and eat in La Isleta del Moro is the superbly located beachside **Hostal Isleta del Moro** (C/Areiz s/n, 950 38 97 13, double €25.50-€52.50), with excellent seafood.

In Rodalquilar, the **Hotel Rodalquilar** (Paraje de los Albacetes s/n, 902 99 59 78, www.hotelrodalquilar.com, double €81-€148 is a stylish four-star hotel with a courtyard pool shaded by palm trees, as well as a gym, sauna, jacuzzi and restaurant.

In Agua Amarga, several boutique hotels have sprung up in recent years, among the best of which is the stylish **El Tío Kiko** (C/Embarque s/n, 950 13 80 80, www.eltiokiko.com, closed Dec, double incl breakfast €160-€235), at the top of town; the whitewashed rooms have terraces and jacuzzis, and are arranged round a pool area. The breakfasts are superb. Just outside the town are several other good choices: at **Joya de Cabo de Gata** (Charo's Houses, Paraje de la Joya, mobile 619 15 95 87, www.lajoyadecabodegata.com, double cottage €120-€190, tent €80-€140) you can hire a cottage or a bedouin tent, while for cooling off outdoors, there's an open-air jacuzzi, a pool and an Arabian summerhouse. Its impressive eco-friendly credentials include recycling water, solar energy and organic breakfasts. **Hotel MiKasa** (Ctra de Carboneras s/n, 950 13 80 73/www.mikasasuites.com, double incl breakfast €128.40-€246.10, closed Jan & Feb) is a whitewashed low-rise hotel, with a spa, gym, two pools (one heated) and an outdoor jacuzzi. Many rooms have a terrace or sea view and some have jacuzzis.

The **Hostal Restaurante La Palmera** (C/Aguada s/n, 950 13 82 08, double €60-€90), at the northern end of the beach (ask for a room with a sea view), has a good restaurant attached (€€). Other options are the friendly French-owned **Hotel Family** (C/La Lomilla s/n, 950 13 80 14, closed Nov & first 2wks Dec, double €45-€120) and the two-star **Hotel Las Calas** (C/Desagüe s/n, 950 13 80 16, www.hotellascalas.com, closed Dec, double €66-€97) at the other end of the beach. The beachfront **Bar Restaurante Playa** (Playa Agua Amarga, 950 13 81 67, closed Dec-Feb, €€) serves up enormous plates of *calamares a la plancha*,

Plastic fantastic

Almería has always had the sun (320 days a year of it); what it's lacked is the water. The invention of drip-feed irrigation and the tapping of deep water sources, however, has transformed what was once parched wilderness into some of the most valuable agricultural land in the world. With additional advances in biological engineering, Almería's *plasticultura* bigwigs became able to force-grow fruit and veg to order – any size, any shape, any colour, any time of year.

Quite apart from fears about the depletion of water reserves, the thoroughly unorganic nature of the business and objections about the emphasis on appearance over taste, the meteoric expansion of *plasticultura* has brought with it a variety of social problems. A shortage of local labour meant that large numbers of workers from all over Spain and from North and sub-Saharan Africa were drawn to the region to work in the usually stifling, back-breaking environments inside the tents (known as *invernaderos*). The conditions they lived in were frequently

appalling, and local resentment of the newcomers simmered away before exploding into a major riot in 2000.

Since then, the government has taken some measures to improve the lot of the workers, and put in place a better health nd social infrastructure. Their lives, however, remain unenviably tough, and the spectre of racism still haunts the coast.

Mojácar Pueblo.

while just beyond is another good restaurant, **Costamarga** (Playa Agua Amarga, 950 13 80 35, closed Wed Apr-Jun and all Oct-Mar, €€), with a wide selection of fresh fish. Behind the front, **Café Bar La Plaza** (C/Ferrocarril Minero s/n, 950 13 82 14, closed Thur Jan-Mar and all Nov & Dec, €) is a locals' favourite. There are a number of campsites in the area. Contact the tourist office in San José for details.

Resources

Internet

San José *Blablabla, Pasaje del Curry s/n (950 61 10 44/www.parquenatural.com/blablabla).* **Open** 9am-3pm, 8pm-midnight Mon, Tue, Thur-Sat; 8pm-midnight Wed; 9am-3pm Sun.

Tourist information

Parque Natural de Cabo de Gata-Níjar *Centro de Visitantes de las Amoladeros, Ctra Cabo de Gata–Almería, km7 (950 16 04 35/www.cabodegata-nijar.com).* **Open** *July-Sept* 10am-2pm, 5.30-9pm daily. *Oct-June* 10am-3pm daily.

San José/Níjar *C/Correos s/n, San José (950 38 02 99/www.cabodegata-nijar.com).* **Open** *Easter-Oct* 10am-2pm, 5-9.30pm daily. *Nov-Easter* 10am-2pm, 5-8pm Mon-Sat; 10am-2pm Sun.

Mojácar & around

While the stretch of the Almería coast from Agra to Aguadulce is largely given over to agriculture, and the Cabo de Gata is chiefly left to nature, the most easterly part of the Andalucían coastline is rapidly becoming the province of hardcore tourism. When the Costa del Sol was being pumped with development money and concrete in the 1960s, a community of writers and artists settled in the lhilltop village of **Mojácar**, in what was in those days a sparsely populated and impoverished part of the coastline. In the last fifteen years or so Mojácar has certainly made up for lost time, developing at an ever-increasing rate; it's now Almería's major resort.

There are, in fact, two Mojácars. The original *pueblo* – enjoying an eagle's nest of a location a kilometre inland – and the newer *playa* (beach), essentially a six-kilometre (four-mile) strip of hotels, restaurants and bars lining a beachside road. It's still easy to see what drew all those artistic types to the *pueblo* 40 years ago: its setting is impossibly picturesque, its flower-clad white houses and labyrinthine alleys remain irresistibly photogenic. Yet there's no location in the world that can't be ruined by one coach party too many. It's at its most appealing in the evening when the daytime crowds have left and you can watch the sun set over the hills from one of the cafés in the town square.

While the *pueblo* might still make some pretence of being a 'traditional' Almerían village, the *playa* knows exactly what it is – a sun, sea and sand service station. As intensive holiday development goes, it's actually not too tacky, and the beach is certainly attractive.

The sprawl of Mojácar ends abruptly in the south, and the road winds along some lovely coastline, with the odd decent (and usually not too crowded) beach, before arriving at the unprepossessing town of **Carboneras**.

The same road heading north passes by endless holiday complexes before arriving at the nondescript fishing town of **Garrucha**. There's little incentive to stay here, but it is worth stopping to sample the excellent fresh fish.

If you're travelling with kids, you may wish to head inland for ten kilometres (six miles) to cool off at the **Parque Acuático Vera**.

Parque Acuático Vera

C3327 (902 36 12 94/www.aquavera.com). **Open** *Mid May-June, 2wks Sept* 11am-6pm daily. *July, Aug* 11am-7.30pm daily. **Admission** €14.50; €9.50 under-12s. **Credit** AmEx, MC, V.

Mojácar Playa.

Where to stay, eat & drink

The best of the places to stay and eat in Mojácar Pueblo are the long-established **Mamabel's** (C/Embajadores 5, 950 47 24 48, www.mamabels.com, double €68.50-€92), which has eight individually decorated rooms and a terrace with stunning views, and the charming **Mirador del Castillo** (950 47 30 22, www.elcastillomojacar.com, double €48-€75, restaurant €€, closed Nov-May). Opened in 2006, it is perched at the very top of the village, with magnificent views and a lovely, secluded garden with swimming pool. Other options include the big, ugly three-star **Hotel El Moresco** (Avda de Camp s/n, 950 47 80 25, closed mid Sept-mid Oct, double €54.25-€95.80), which does have the advantage of a rooftop pool and great views from most rooms, and the British-run **Pensión El Torreón** (C/Jazmín 4-6, 950 47 52 59, double incl breakfast €40-€60), which has a beautiful patio-reception and flower-filled balcony with stunning views. Some of the rooms have showers, but share a toilet.

There are a lot of overpriced restaurants in Mójacar Pueblo, but you won't go far wrong with **Palacio** (Plaza del Caño 3, 950 47 28 46, €€€) and **Mamabel's** (*see above*; €€, closed lunch, all Sun and all Jan & Feb), or at one of the tapas bars around the main square. It's worth climbing to the top of the village to admire the views and sip a drink in one of the bars on the **Mirador del Castillo** square, while contemplating the (alas, now disproved) legend that Walt Disney was born in Mojácar, subsequently orphaned and adopted. If you are after a late-night drink in the *pueblo*, your best bet is **Budú** (C/Estación Nueva, no phone, closed Oct-Apr), right at the top of town.

There are countless hotels and *hostales* in Mojácar Playa. The top option is the large, modern **Parador de Mojácar** (Paseo del Mediterráneo 339, 950 47 82 50, www.parador.es, double €117-€128), though many of its rooms are closed for refurbishment until May 2008. The **Hotel Virgen del Mar** (Paseo del Mediterráneo 245, 950 47 22 22, www.hotelvirgendelmar.com, double €40-€80, restaurant €€) is a good option, with a decent restaurant.

Food in Mojácar Playa is generally of a pretty low standard, though there's no shortage of choice (particularly at the southern end of the beach, where you'll also find most of the bars). Your best bet is probably **Tito's** (Mojácar Playa, 950 61 50 30, closed Dec-late Mar, €), which serves an eclectic range of dishes (such as Thai beef salad and tuna sashimi) in a relaxed beachside atmosphere. The restaurant in the *parador* (*see above*) is about as upmarket as you'll get round these parts.

Resources

Internet

Mojácar Playa *Indaltur, Paseo Mediterráneo 293 (950 61 51 56).* **Open** 10am-2pm, 5-8pm Mon-Fri; 10am-2pm Sat.

Tourist information

Mojácar Pueblo *C/Glorieta 1 (950 61 50 25/ www.mojacar.es).* **Open** *Apr-Oct* 10am-2pm, 5-8pm Mon-Fri; 10.30am-1.30pm, 5-8pm Sat. *Nov-Mar* 10am-2pm, 5-7.30pm Mon-Fri; 10.30am-1.30pm Sat.

There's also an info point on the beach in Mojácar Playa, in front of the shopping centre.

Getting there

By bus

Alsina Graells (950 23 81 97) runs hourly daily services between Adra and Almería, all of which call at Aguadulce, and there are also half-hourly buses between Almería and Roquetas de Mar. Alsa Enatcar (info 913 27 05 40, www.alsa.es, tickets 950 61 70 25/71 36) runs about 3 buses daily from Almería to Mojácar, and hourly buses run between Mojácar Playa and Pueblo. Public transport is scarce in the Cabo de Gata. Autocares Bernardo (954 25 04 22/www.autocaresbernardo.com) runs 3 buses daily to San José from Almería, and 4 from San José to Almería, except Sundays when there are 2 either way. One bus runs between Isleta del Moro and Almería on Mondays and Saturdays.

Almería Interior

Just deserts.

Most visitors to Almería province stick closely to the coastline, losing sight of the sea only for such standard tourist forays as trips to Oasys (previously known as Mini Hollywood) and Níjar. Yet this is all to the benefit of those with a little more initiative. It's true that much of the province's interior is desert wilderness, but it's a magnificent wilderness, veering from mountain peaks to lunar canyonscapes.

Vélez Blanco & around

In the north of Almería province lies the **Parque Natural de la Sierra María-Los Vélez** (226 square kilometres/87 square miles), a mountainous, multi-hued expanse of trees, rock and dust. There's plenty of rugged walking in the area – for details, ask at the park visitors' centre.

There are two main towns in the area: **Vélez Rubio**, the larger of the two, which is chiefly of note for its superb, outsize, mid 18th-century church; and the more appealing **Vélez Blanco**. The latter is a close-knit, relaxed place, clustered under one of the most striking castles in Andalucía. This was originally a simple Moorish structure, but was embellished and extended in the early 16th century, with a superb Renaissance bronze door and the courtyard fitted out entirely in marble. To appreciate this, alas, you will need to visit the Metropolitan Museum of Art in New York, for the castle's impoverished owner sold off almost all the internal decoration in the early 19th century; the courtyard was eventually acquired and reconstructed by the US museum. Still, although it may be a shell, the castle is still atmospheric, and the views from its towers are quite superb. Part of the castle is currently closed for restoration.

A kilometre south of Vélez Blanco on the road to Vélez Rubio is a sign (close to a petrol station) to the **Cueva de los Letreros**. The cave is actually more of a shallow depression in a wall of rock, but it contains the faint remains of 6,000-year-old cave paintings depicting animals, birds, symbols and human figures. It was here that the '*indalo*' (a stick figure holding an arc over its head) was first seen – it's since been adopted as the symbol of Almería province. To see the cave, go first to the Natural Park visitors' centre in Vélez Blanco (*see below*) to get the key to the gate (the *cueva* is fenced off); you'll need to leave your passport as a deposit. You can take your car a certain distance along the rough road towards the cave, but there's still a steep 15-minute walk up to the cave itself.

Castillo de Vélez Blanco

Mobile 607 41 51 55. **Open** 10am-2pm Wed-Sun. **Admission** free.

Where to stay & eat

The best place to stay in Vélez Blanco is undoubtedly the **Casa de los Arcos** (C/San Francisco 2, 950 61 48 05, www.casadelosarcos.net, closed June, double €53.50-€70),

Vélez Blanco.

Oasys.

a beautifully converted 18th/19th-century mansion, and surprisingly good value. Second choice would be the newer **Hotel Velad Al-Abyadh** (C/Balsa Parra 28, 950 41 51 09, www.hotelvelad.com, double €58-€67), where many of the bedrooms have magnificent views (ask for an exterior room). If you're on a tighter budget, try the **Hostal Restaurante La Sociedad** (C/Corredera 14, 950 41 50 27, double €30-€40), which has decent rooms. Its bar is a focus of local life, and serves good tapas and *raciones*. Among the few more upmarket places to eat is **El Molino** (C/Curtidores s/n, 950 41 50 70, closed 3 wks July, dinner Thur & Sun) with its lovely terrace.

Resources

Tourist information

Parque Natural de la Sierra de María-Los Vélez *Centro de Visitantes 'Almacén del Trigo', Avda del Marqués de los Vélez s/n, Vélez Blanco (950 41 53 54).* **Open** 10am-2pm Mon-Thur, Sun; 10am-2pm, 6-8pm Sat.

The Sierra de los Filabres to the Almerían Alpujarras

The centre of Almería province is dominated by the mountains of the **Sierra de los Filabres**, essentially a continuation of the Sierra Nevada. The region is thinly populated, and few tourists venture this far, making it all the better for lovers of wild and dramatic scenery.

In the area around the villages of **Cóbdar** and **Albánchez**, wooded slopes and narrow valleys create a more intimate landscape, broken occasionally by great white scars cut by marble quarriers. One such quarry dominates the hillside above Cóbdar, and the rough road west of the village leads past another, with massive blocks of marble piled by the roadside.

Andalucían villages have a bizarre tendency to unilateral declarations of war. Huescar in Granada province took against the Danes (*see p279*), while **Líjar**, a few kilometres west of Albánchez, was officially at war with France from 1883 until 1983, supposedly sparked by an insult hurled at Alfonso XII as he passed through Paris.

South of the Sierra, the mountains give way to desert. Romantically desolate, this bone-bleachingly dry area has long drawn in filmmakers, who see in the majestic scale of its canyons and ravines, its polychromatic geology and weirdly eroded topography similarities with the American West.

Close to where the A92 from Guadix meets the A370 is **Oasys** (still signposted as Mini Hollywood), a film set turned tourist attraction. This was the original location for many classic Westerns, as well as for scores of other films that made use of the wild, lunar landscapes and crystalline air. It was here that Sergio Leone built the set for *A Fistful of Dollars*, which was later also used in *For a Few Dollars More* and *The Good, the Bad and the Ugly*. The set was subsequently bought by the local extras and run as a Western theme park. Now owned by the Playa Hoteles group, the site has been heavily commercialised (and is comparatively expensive), but is still fun, particularly if you time your visit to coincide with the Western show – a hammy but enjoyable 're-creation' of the demise of the James brothers. The most frustrating aspect of it is the lack of information about the cinematic classics filmed here – the potentially interesting 'Museum of Cinema' is no more than a load of old film cameras and posters. Tacked to the back of the park, incongruously, is a sizeable zoo. It's not badly done, but many of the cages and pens are very small, and how the animals cope with the blistering summer heat can only be imagined.

Oasys is not the only Western-themed tourist attraction in the area. Closer to **Tabernas** (overlooked by a romantically ruined castle) is **Texas Hollywood**, less commercialised than its better-publicised neighbour. The enjoyable English of its brochure proudly boasts the local filming of classics like '*One Dolar for the Deads*', '*The Long Way of the Revenge*' and '*The Seven Magnificients*'. Here you'll find a fly-blown Western town, an Indian settlement, a Mexican village, 'Fort Bravo' and the usual range of shows, plus bison, camels and 'the biggest horses in the world'. A third location, **Western Leone**, contains the ranch from the opening scene of *Once Upon a Time in the West* among its attractions.

From Oasys the main road towards Guadix and Granada brings you after 17 kilometres (11 miles) to **Gérgal**, with its fine castle. Behind here towers a mountain topped by the very *X-Files* **Observatorio de Calor Alto**, a further 23 kilometres (14 miles) by road. It's actually a series of German-Spanish observatories (home of the Max Planck Astronomy Institute) where, supposedly, stars can be seen more clearly than anywhere else in Europe. Cloud-free skies are assured for around 200 nights a year (four times what could be expected in northern Europe).

Back at Oasys, the main road heads south towards Almería city. Leading off it, the A348 winds westwards along the course of the River Andarax into the **Almerían Alpujarras**. A few kilometres along the road you'll see a sign to **Los Millares**, the largest Bronze Age settlement in Europe. Located on a spur-shaped plateau by the Andarax river (which was then navigable up to this point), the 19-hectare (47-acre) site was occupied between about 2700 and 1800 BC and consists of a necropolis containing 80 megalithic passage graves and a village protected by a complex defensive system.

West of Los Millares, the Sierra Nevada rises to the north and the Sierra de Gádor to the south as the main road leads from the harsher, barer landscapes of Almería to the higher, more heavily wooded Granadan Alpujarras.

Few of the villages along the route merit more than a quick refreshment stop (though **Canjáyar** is pretty and has a fine inn; *see below*), but the drive is spectacular. If you fancy exploring the area, the best base is **Laujar de Andarax**. The deposed Boabdil fled to Laujar after leaving Granada in 1492, but Fernando and Isabel reneged on the deal by which he was to rule an Alpujarran kingdom from the town, and within a year he was exiled to Africa.

Los Millares

Santa Fe de Mondújar (mobile 677 90 34 04). **Open** 10am-2pm Wed-Sun. **Admission** free.

Oasys (Mini Hollywood)

N340a, km464, Tabernas (950 36 52 36/ www.hvsl.es/lei/hojas/leio0002.htm). **Open** *Apr-Oct* 10am-9pm daily. *Nov-Mar* 10am-7pm Sat, Sun. *Wild West show* noon, 5pm (extra show 8pm in summer) Tue-Sun. *Can-can show* 1pm, 4pm (extra show 7pm in summer) Tue-Sun. *Parrot show* 11am, 3pm, 6pm Tue-Sun. **Admission** €17; €9 concessions. **Credit** DC, MC, V.

Texas Hollywood

N340a, km468, Paraje de Lunhay, Tabernas (950 16 54 58/www.texashollywood.topactive.com). **Open** *Apr-Nov* 9am-8pm daily. *Dec-Mar* 9am-7.30pm daily. *Shows* May-Nov 12.30pm, 2pm, 5.30pm, 7.30pm daily. Dec-Apr 12.30pm, 2.30pm, 5.30pm, 7pm daily. **Admission** €12.50; €7.50 concs. **Credit** MC, V.

Western Leone

C3326, km378, Tabernas (950 16 54 05/www. westernleone.com). **Open** *Apr-Oct* 10am-dusk daily. *Nov-Mar* 10am-dusk Sat, Sun. *Shows* 12.30pm, 2.30pm, 5.30pm, 7.30pm. **Admission** €9; €4.50 concessions. **No credit cards**.

Where to stay & eat

Places to stay are few in the Sierra de los Filabres. The **Hostal Amanecer** in the village of Albánchez (Avda Los Molinos s/n, 950 12 23 23, double €35-€40) is the best bet, with a lovely communal terrace.

In Laujar, try the **Hostal Nuevo Andarax** (C/Canalejas 27, 950 51 31 13, closed mid Dec-1st wk Jan, double €50) above a bar-restaurant, or the **Hostal Fernández** (C/General Mola 4, 950 51 31 28, double €36.40, closed mid Dec-1st wk Jan), with a terrace. For tapas, try **Bar Rodríquez** (Plaza Moajor de la Alpujarras 1, 950 51 31 10, closed Tue, €).

In Canjáyar, **La Posada de Eustaquio** (Plaza de la Iglesia 15, 950 51 01 77, www.posadaeustaquio.com, double €40-€60) is a real village inn; warm, inviting and stuffed with antiques; the best room is the suite with exposed beams and a balcony over the *plaza*.

A cheaper option is at the top of the hill at the **Hotel Restaurante La Piscina** (C/General González 86, 950 511 050, double €33-€35, restaurant €€, closed 1st 2wks early Sept), which does indeed have a swimming pool.

Getting there

By bus

Bus services in the interior are scant. There's a single daily bus from Almería to Láujar (Alsina Graells 950 23 81 97), a couple from Almería to Vélez Blanco (ALSA 950 28 16 60, www.alsa.es) and a few local services, but a car is enormously helpful.

By train

There are 4 trains daily from Almería to Guadix.

Directory

Features

Directory

Getting There & Around

By air

Log on to www.aena.es for info on all Spanish airports and live departure and arrival details.

Airlines

A vast number of airlines fly from the UK to Andalucía, and particularly to Málaga. Below is a list of the main scheduled operators. In addition, many charter companies offer flights to southern Spain. From North America, you'll need to connect in Madrid (or London).

Aer Lingus *(from Ireland 0818 36 50 00/from Spain 902 50 27 37/ www.aerlingus.com).*
Dublin to Almería and Málaga and Cork to Málaga.

bmibaby *(from the UK 0870 264 2229/from Spain 902 10 07 37/ www.bmibaby.com).* Birmingham Cardiff, Manchester, Nottingham East Midlands to Málaga.

Britannia *(from the UK 0870 607 6757/from Spain call Thomson's 24hr helpline 971 70 62 25/ www.britanniaairways.com).*
Seasonal flights from most UK airports to Málaga.

British Airways *(from the UK 0870 850 9850/from Spain 902 11 13 33/www.ba.com).* Gibraltar (from Gatwick); Málaga (Gatwick, Heathrow, Manchester); Seville (from Gatwick, Heathrow).

easyJet *(from the UK 0871 750 0100/from Spain 902 29 99 92/www.easyjet.com).*
Luton, Gatwick, Stansted, Belfast, Bristol, Liverpool, Nottingham East Midlands and Newcastle to Málaga; Gatwick and Stansted to Almería.

Flybe *(from the UK 0871 700 0123/from Spain 00 44 139 226 8519/www.flybe.com).*
From Birmingham, Exeter, Norwich and Southampton to Málaga.

GB Airways *(from the UK 0870 850 9850/from Spain 902 111 333/www.gbairways.com).*
This BA franchise operator flies to Gibraltar from Gatwick, Heathrow; Málaga from Heathrow, Gatwick, Manchester; and Seville from Gatwick.

Iberia *(from the UK 0845 601 2854/from Spain 902 40 05 00/ www.iberia.com).*
Heathrow to Seville and Málaga.

JMC *(from the UK 0870 010 0434/ www.jmc.com).* Seasonal flights from most UK airports to Málaga, and Gatwick, Birmingham, Glasgow and Manchester to Almería.

Monarch Airlines *(from the UK 0870 040 5040/from Gibraltar 350 47 477, flight info 350 73 026/ Spain flight info 914 14 15 03/www. flymonarch.com).*
Almería (from Manchester); Granada (from Gatwick); Málaga (from Aberdeen, Birmingham, Blackpool, Gatwick, Luton, Manchester, Newquay).

MyTravelLite *(from the UK 0870 238 7710/www.mytravellite.com).*
Málaga from Birmingham, Exeter, Newcastle, Norwich, Southampton.

Ryanair *(from the UK 0871 246 0000/from Ireland 0818 30 30 30/from Spain 807 22 00 32/www.ryanair.com).*
Stansted to Almería, Jerez, Seville and Granada, Liverpool to Seville and Granada, Dublin to Málaga.

Thomsonfly *(from the UK 0870 190 0737/from Spain 914 14 14 81/www.thomsonfly.com).*
To Málaga from Coventry, Gatwick, Luton and Manchester.

Airports

Almería

AL12, km9, Almería (950 21 37 00/flight info 950 21 37 90/97).
Almería airport is 10km (6 miles) east of the city. There are regular flights to and from Madrid and Barcelona, scheduled flights are twice weekly from London with GB Airways, and flights from Stansted with Ryanair. However, in high season, Almería airport is used by many charter companies. Local bus 20 runs to and from the airport and C/Doctor Gregorio Marañon, at the north-eastern edge of Almería city centre, every half hour on weekdays and every hour on weekends and holidays, from around 6.30am to about 10.30pm (for information, call 950 62 47 35). One-way tickets cost 85¢. The journey time is approximately 30mins. Taxis are also available: a fare to the centre costs approximately €10.

Gibraltar

956 77 30 26.
Gibraltar airport, which is run by the Royal Air Force, is a couple of kilometres from the town centre, near the frontier. British Airways flies to Gibraltar from Gatwick, and Monarch from Luton and Manchester. There is a bus service every 15-20mins from around 6.30am to 8pm. A single costs 60p and the journey takes 5mins. A taxi into town will cost about £5.

Granada

A329, Granada (958 24 52 00/ Iberia flight info 958 24 52 37/38).
Granada airport is located about 16km (10 miles) west of the city. It is now served by Ryanair from the UK, as well as domestic flights. The airport bus (958 49 01 64, €3 single) is scheduled to coincide with flights and takes about 25mins from the airport to the city centre. A taxi to the centre costs about €18-€20.

Jerez

A4-E5, km631, Jerez de la Frontera (956 15 00 00).
Jerez airport is 7km (4 miles) north-east of the city. There are about 5 flights a day to Madrid, Barcelona and Gatwick and Stansted. There's no public transport into Jerez – you'll need to take a taxi (about €11).

Málaga

Avenida García Morato, Málaga (952 04 88 38/44).
By far the region's busiest point of entry, Málaga's Pablo Picasso airport is 6km (4 miles) south-west of the city, just off the A7. A train service (902 24 02 02) runs from outside the international terminal to Málaga every 30mins (airport to Málaga/ Málaga to airport 7am-10.40pm, journey time 12mins, €1.10-€1.20 single) and south-west to Fuengirola every 30mins (airport to Fuengirola 6.45am-10.40pm, Fuengirola to airport 5.50am-11.40pm, journey time 32mins, €1.75-€1.85 single). There's a half-hourly bus service (No.19, 902 52 72 00) between the Paseo del Parque in the centre of Málaga and the airport (airport to Málaga 7am-11pm, Málaga to airport 6.30am-11pm, journey time 20mins, €1 single). Ten daily buses (more July-Sept) run between the airport and Marbella (902 14 31 44, airport to Marbella 6.15am-11pm, Marbella

to airport 5.30am-10.30pm, journey time 45mins, €3.92 single). A taxi from the airport should cost around €12-€15 to Málaga or Torremolinos, €27-€32 to Fuengirola and €55-€65 to Marbella.

Seville

A4-E5, km532, Seville (954 44 90 00/tickets 954 98 91 84).
Seville's San Pablo airport is 5km (3 miles) east of the city. From the airport, a bus service operated by Los Amarillos (902 21 03 17) – look for an 'Aeropuerto de Sevilla' sign on the front of the bus – runs every half hour on weekdays and every hour on weekends and holidays between the airport and C/Palos de la Frontera, via Santa Justa train station and C/San Francisco Javier (6.45am-11.30pm Mon-Fri, less frequently at weekends, journey time 20-25mins). It costs €2.50 for a single ticket. A taxi to the town centre from the airport will cost a flat fee of €18.50 on weekdays and €21 on weekends and holidays.

By bicycle

Despite their love of the car, the Spanish are absolute cycling fanatics; each and every weekend you'll see smaller roads clogged with stern-faced lycra-clad pedallers. Out of high season, cycling is a lovely way to see the back routes of the region, and you'll be shown a surprising amount of consideration by drivers. You can take your bike on to many trains. Tip: don't even consider cycling around Andalucía in the summer – the heat is too fierce.

For further information and route maps contact the **Spanish Cycling Federation** (Real Federación Española de Ciclismo, 915 40 08 41, www.rfec.com). For information on mountain biking holidays, *see p315*.

By boat

There are no direct ferries from the UK to Andalucía, but there are two services to the northern Spanish coast: Portsmouth to Bilbao and Plymouth to Santander.

The **Portsmouth–Bilbao** service is operated by **P&O Ferries** (from the UK 08705 20 20 20, from Spain 944 23 44 77, www.poferries.com) and runs twice weekly (less frequently Jan-Mar); the 35-hour outward crossing involves two nights on board, while the 29-hour return means one night aboard.

The **Plymouth–Santander** service is run by **Brittany Ferries** (from the UK 08705 360 360, from Spain 942 36 06 11, www.brittanyferries.com), with twice weekly sailings (three weekly late June to early September) and takes 18 hours.

If you fancy taking the boat and then the train, there's one daily direct service from Bilbao to Córdoba (11hrs 30mins) and Málaga (14hrs 40mins), although it's quicker to take one of the three daily trains to Madrid (7hrs 30mins) and to change to the high-speed AVE there (*see p311*). No direct trains run from Santander to Andalucía, though there are three daily services to Madrid (5hrs 35mins-8hrs 35mins). For info, see www.renfe.es/ingles.

By bus

Eurolines (from the UK 08705 80 80 80, www.eurolines.co.uk) runs several services from London to destinations in Andalucía, including Algeciras, Málaga, Seville, Granada and Córdoba, with a journey time of around 35 hours. For services from other European countries, see www.eurolines.com.

Andalucía's bus services are generally excellent and probably the best way to get around the region if you don't have a car. Most buses are comfortable, clean and air-conditioned and they connect almost every obscure village as well as all the major cities. There are dozens of companies providing services (see the 'Getting There' section at the end of each chapter). You can buy tickets at the station or sometimes on board.

By car & motorbike

From the UK you can take one of the two car ferries to Spain (*see above*), and drive down from Bilbao or Santander, or cross the Channel and drive down through France.

Driving around the south of Spain is usually easy and stress-free. The main roads are generally well maintained and pretty empty outside the cities. You are highly unlikely to find a traffic jam on a motorway (*autopista*). Having said that, the narrow, twisting roads in many small towns and villages can make driving pretty hairy.

MOTORBIKES AND SCOOTERS

This is a great way of seeing the region, especially inland, where you'll have many roads almost to yourself. If you plan on doing some serious touring, you will need a decent-sized bike to get up the steep hills, but for a few days pottering along the coast, a scooter is fine. Most resorts will rent scooters and there's also a good network of major-name franchises. Be sure to take out full insurance cover.

Helmets are compulsory. Speed limits are enforced on an ad hoc basis. The police are hot on headlights, which should be set on half-beam at all times.

Legal requirements

- In order to drive in Spain, you'll need a valid driving licence and third-party motor insurance. Theoretically, all valid UK driving licences should be accepted, but older all-green licences and Northern Ireland licences issued prior to 1 January 1991 do not conform to the EU model and may cause confusion. Photo driving licences from other European countries and North America are usually accepted, though you might like to obtain an International Driving Permit as a further guarantee.

- The minimum age at which you may drive a temporarily imported car and/or motorbike (over 75cc) is 18. Most rental companies require the driver to be at least 25 years old.
- Severe penalties, including fines and the withdrawal of your driving licence, may be enforced if the level of alcohol in your bloodstream is found to be 0.05 per cent or above.
- Fines are issued on the spot and can be steep: always ask for an official receipt. A 20 per cent reduction is usually available for foreigners.
- Seat belts are compulsory for front and rear seat occupants, if fitted.
- Children under 12 cannot travel as front-seat passengers unless a suitable restraint system is used.
- By law you must carry a fluorescent warning triangle, which must be set up on the hard shoulder some way behind the car if you break down. You must also carry a spare set of headlight bulbs.

Speed limits

On major roads and motorways the speed limit is 120kph (75mph); in built-up areas it is 50kph (31mph); on other roads it is either 90kph (55mph) or 100kph (62.5mph).

Roads & tolls

Map reading in Spain can be something of an endurance test. Roads are frequently reclassified and reappear in different forms, sometimes in different places, and, confusingly, many of the major routes have two different classifications.
A recent reclassification has left most Spaniards (even cartographers) perplexed. All *carreteras nacionales* (N-roads) have been renamed to begin with an A (standing for *autopista* – motorway), or AP if it's a *peaje* (toll road); in some cases the road number has changed too (*see below*).

ROAD CLASSIFICATIONS

E = European route. Major highways that, in theory, connect Spain with the rest of the continent. The E1 runs from Seville almost to the border with Portugal; the E5 runs from Cádiz, through Seville, and on to Madrid, Burgos and beyond; the E15 runs west from Estepona and then north to Barcelona and the border with France. They are all very fast, good-surface toll roads.

A/AP = Autopista. These are inter-region highways (often toll roads – peaje – prefixed AP), which are of the same standard as the E roads. In fact, E and A roads are often the same thing and will be signposted accordingly. Toll roads are often very quiet.

A/C = provincial roads. You can work out the standard of these roads by the number of digits following the letter prefix (the fewer, the better). C roads usually have two lanes.

AL/CA/CO/GR/HU/JA/MA/SE =local roads. The two-letter prefix relates to the province (SE = Seville, CO = Córdoba, etc). These roads are generally narrow (sometimes only a single track) and vary in quality.

RECENT ROAD CHANGES

A4 Seville–Cádiz toll motorway is now AP4

A7 Málaga–Guadiaro toll motorway is now AP7

NIV Madrid–Seville motorway (and Jerez A48) is now A4

N332 Bailén–Linares motorway becomes A32

N340 Barcelona–Algeciras motorway is now A7

N323 Bailén-Motril motorway becomes A44

A44/N331 Variante Aguilar/ Antequera–Málaga becomes A45

N340/A4 San Fernando–Algeciras is now A48

N344 eastern access road to Almería becomes AL12

N432 northern access road to Córdoba changes to CO31
H49 access road Huelva is now H31

N340 eastern access road to Málaga via La Araña becomes MA24

N351 access road to Gibraltar changes to CA34

NIV San Fernando–Cádiz highway becomes CA33

N354 access road to the Málaga port is now **MA22**

Breakdown services

If you take your car to Spain, get breakdown cover before setting out. For UK drivers,

Drive time

Approximate driving times within Andalucía (hours:minutes).

	Almería	Cádiz	Córdoba	Granada	Huelva	Jaén	Málaga	Seville
Almería		5:30	3:50	1:50	5:10	2:30	2:20	4:20
Cádiz	5:30		2:40	3:30	2:10	4:00	3:00	1:20
Córdoba	3:50	2:40		2:10	2:30	1:30	2:10	1:30
Granada	1:50	3:30	2:10		3:30	1:00	1:20	2:30
Huelva	5:10	2:10	2:30	3:30		3:40	3:00	1:00
Jaén	2:30	4:00	1:30	1:00	3:40		2:00	2:50
Málaga	2:20	3:00	2:10	1:20	3:00	2:00		2:20
Seville	4:20	1:20	1:30	2:30	1:00	2:50	2:20	

the AA (0800 085 2480, www.theaa.co.uk) and RAC (0800 55 00 55, www.rac.co.uk) are good.

Driving tips

- Don't expect drivers to allow you into a lane in heavy traffic. Instead, wait for a gap or simply barge your way in.
- Do not hold back from using your horn – it is not regarded as offensive in Spain.
- Look out for cars tail-gating you at 120kph before overtaking with hardly any space before the oncoming vehicle.

Signs & terms

- *ceda el paso* – give way
- *usted no tiene la prioridad* – you don't have the right of way
- *dirección única* – one way
- *cambio de sentido* – indicates a junction that allows you to change direction
- *recuerde* – remember
- *ronda de circunvalación* – ring road (around cities)

Fuel

Most fuel stations employ attendants to fill your car (tipping is not expected). Only unleaded petrol (*sin plomo*) and diesel (*gasoil*) are available; both much cheaper than the UK.

Parking

Parking is a nightmare. In the smaller villages, park on the outskirts rather than navigating the tortuously narrow roads. In towns, head for the nearest *aparcamiento* (car park; they're never expensive). If a parking space is blocked, you can often push the offending car out of the way – many Spanish drivers leave the handbrake off for this reason – or just sit on your horn till the culprit arrives.

Car rental

Renting a car is cheap in compared to the rest of Europe. There's lots of competition so shop around. Local firms are usually cheaper than the big internationals, but check for hidden extras before signing. At Málaga airport there's a huge choice of companies; the cheapest compact car should cost around €130 a week, all inclusive. Also check whether your airline has special deals with any rental company. Most companies require drivers to be 25 or over and to have held a valid licence for at least a year. You'll need to present your licence and a credit card when you hire the car.

As well as the companies below, **Holiday Autos** (0870 400 4461, www.holidayautos.co.uk) offers very competitive rates, as does the helpful, English-speaking **Bravo Car Hire** (966 46 04 18, www.bravocarhire.com), which acts as a broker for many local companies.

Avis

www.avis.com
From the UK *0844 581 0147.*
Almería airport *950 29 82 21.*
Granada airport *958 44 64 55.*
Jerez airport *956 15 00 05.*
Málaga airport *952 04 84 83.*
Seville airport *954 44 91 21.*

Budget

www.budget.co.uk
From the UK *0844 581 2231.*
Jerez City *956 33 80 54.*

Europcar

www.europcar.com
From the UK *0870 607 5000.*
Almería airport *950 29 29 34.*
Granada airport *958 24 52 75.*
Jerez airport *956 15 00 98.*
Málaga airport *952 04 85 18.*
Seville airport *954 25 42 98.*

Hertz

www.hertz.com
From the UK *0870 844 8844.*
Almería airport *950 29 27 83.*
Gibraltar airport *956 66 83 25.*
Granada airport *958 24 52 77.*
Jerez airport *956 31 00 15.*
Málaga airport *952 23 30 86.*
Seville airport *954 51 47 20.*

Local companies

Almericar *Almería airport 950 23 49 66/www.almericar.com.*
Autopro *Málaga airport 952 17 60 30/www.autopro.es.*
Crown Car Hire *Málaga airport 952 17 64 86/www.crowncarhire.com.*
Dany Car *Málaga airport 952 24 50 80/www.andalucia.com/danycar.*
Helle Hollis *Málaga airport 952 24 55 44/www.helleholis.com.*

By train

There are no direct trains from other European countries (except Portugal) to Andalucía. If you want to arrive by train, head to Madrid and then take one of the 21 daily high-speed AVE services from there to Córdoba (1hr 42mins) and Seville (2hrs 30mins).

For Eurostar tickets between London and Paris, call (from the UK) 08705 186 186 or see www.eurostar.co.uk. For European rail tickets, contact Rail Europe (from the UK 08708 371 371, www.raileurope.co.uk).

Andalucía relies upon a fairly comprehensive and generally reliable, though complicated, train system. Fares are cheap by UK standards. The network is operated by **RENFE** (information and reservations 902 24 02 02; some staff speak English). For information (in English) on train times, route planning and fares, consult RENFE's useful website **www.renfe.es/ingles**. You can also book tickets online via the site for many services.

The pride of the network is the **AVE** (Altitud Velocidad España – 'high speed Spain'), which connects Seville to Madrid via Córdoba in less than two hours 30 minutes. (The line is currently being extended to Málaga; due to be completed in 2007.) The rest of the region is criss-crossed by a variety of different train types, the best of which are the **Talgo** and the **TER** services, which are smart and speedy and connect the major cities. Slower but more picturesque are the (misleadingly named) **expreso** and **rápido** services, which tend to stop everywhere.

Where to Stay

There is an enormous range of places to stay in Andalucía, from luxury hotels to someone's spare bedroom. Outside the resorts, accommodation is plentiful and good value, and you shouldn't have difficulty finding a room except during specific high-profile events, such as Carnaval in Cádiz, Semana Santa and the Feria de Abril in Seville. Resorts are likely to be packed in July and August, but should have rooms available at other times of year.

Prices vary a great deal depending on the season, and it's possible to get some real bargains off peak. In most places in Andalucía, and certainly in the resorts, high season is from 15 June to 15 September. You may pay even more during Semana Santa, when rooms are at a premium throughout Andalucía, and during major festivals. The rest of the year generally counts as low season, although some places may have mid-season rates. Some hotels – particularly those in resorts – close between late November and January. Note, however, that July and August are regarded as low season for inland cities such as Seville, Jerez and Córdoba.

Prices are generally cheaper than in much of the rest of Europe, except in the major cities, in particular Seville. Most places will display the tariff at reception and behind the door of your room. It is unlikely you will ever be ripped off, but there is always a *libro de reclamaciones* (complaints book) 'at your disposal' at reception.

Value-added tax, known as **IVA**, will be added to your final bill at the rate of **seven per cent**, though it may or may not be included in the prices you are quoted – always check. Breakfast (*desayuno*) may or may not be included in the rate.

In this guide **we have added IVA** to room prices where relevant, so **the price listed should be the price you pay** (at the time of going to press).

Hotels

Most of the hotel chains in Andalucía are Spanish. They include the upmarket **AC** (902 29 22 93, www.ac-hoteles.com) with 12 hotels, and **Sol Meliá** (902 14 44 40, from the UK 0800 962 720, from the US 1888 55 63542, www.solmelia.com) with 31 hotels; mid-market **NH** (902 11 51 16, www.nh-hotels.com) with ten hotels, and **Husa** (902 10 07 10, www.husa.es) with 20 hotels.

There are five grades of hotel, from one star to five; 'GL' beside the five stars means that the hotel is 'Gran Lujo' ('grand luxury'), which is even posher. Stars correspond to facilities, size of room, and so on, and are regularly inspected, but don't reflect quality of service, atmosphere or location.

At the one-star level expect a simple room, usually with en suite shower and little else. This level isn't much different from a decent *hostal*, and you may pay more simply for a phone in the room. At two stars you are likely to find all rooms en suite and with facilities such as TV and perhaps air-conditioning. From three stars you can expect all mod cons, maid service, often a restaurant or café and perhaps a swimming pool. Four- and five-star hotels are as you would expect worldwide, with prices to match; four stars does not guarantee a pool.

'HA' denotes Apartment-Hotels, graded one star to four and offering self-catering facilities such as a kitchen.

PARADORES

The 86-strong *parador* chain (915 16 66 66, from the UK Keytel International 020 7616 0300, from the US Marketing Ahead 212 686 9213 or 1-800 223 1356, www.parador.es) was founded in 1928 and consists of state-run, subsidised hotels that are, for the most part, located in converted historical buildings such as monasteries, castles, palaces or stately homes. They range from three to four stars, and, despite their often fabulous locations, are always much cheaper than the commercial equivalent. The idea behind the scheme was to generate tourism in places people did not generally visit. Hence, you will find them in mountain villages and market towns and not, for example, in Seville or Marbella. There are 16 *paradores* in Andalucía.

Although *paradores* have many advantages, they are part of a chain, so you may not get the level of character and personal service you might find in the best privately owned hotels; also, their restaurants tend to be formal, pricey and of variable quality.

All *paradores* in Andalucía are individually listed under the relevant chapter. Check the website for details of discount schemes and loyalty cards.

Hostales & pensiones

Hostales (and *hostal-residencias*) are graded in the same way as hotels, with one or two stars. Most offer simple rooms with en suite facilities at reasonable prices. Some have a restaurant or café attached, and most are family run. *Residencia* simply means that no meal other than breakfast is served.

There is little difference between a *hostal* and a *pensión*, although *hostales* perhaps have the edge in terms of quality. At the lowest level a *pensión* is going to be pretty basic. *Pensiones* are also graded with one or two stars, but there's little difference between the categories.

Casas huespedes, fondas & camas

You don't often see the letters 'CH' (*casa huespedes*), but they signify basic accommodation, often not much more than a room in someone's house. You'll be lucky to have a sink and are likely to be sharing the bathroom with the owners. *Fondas*, denoted by 'F', are of a similar quality. '*Camas*' indicates that the homeowner rents beds for the night.

Villas turisticas

Villas turisticas are self-catering apartments in rural areas run by the regional government. They usually have a reception and all the facilities you would expect at three- or four-star level, with prices to match. Despite their unpromising name, they are often very tastefully appointed. For a list of all *villas turisticas* in the region, contact the **Centro Internacional de Turismo de Andalucía** at C/Compañía 40, 29008 Málaga, 902 20 00 37, www.andalucia.org).

Turismo rural & villa hire

Turismo rural is the Junta de Andalucía's way of getting more tourists away from the coast and into the countryside. There has been significant growth in this area, with many UK tour operators offering rural dwellings for rent. In high season you will probably have a minimum-stay requirement of a week, but out of this period you can usually negotiate the length of your stay.

A *casa particular* (guest-house) is the equivalent of B&B-style accommodation in Britain. You'll stay in someone's farmhouse or country cottage, with the advantages of home cooking and a distinct lack of tourists. A full list is available from the **Red Andaluza de Alojamientos Rurales** (Apartado de correo 2035, 04080 Almería, 950 26 50 18, 902 44 22 33, www.raar.es).

Other organisations that can book characterful rural accommodation are the **Asociación de Hoteles Rurales de Andalucía** (Avenida Niceto Alcalá Zamora 12, 14800, Priego de Córdoba, Córdoba, 957 54 08 01, www.ahra.es), **Rural Andalus** (C/Montes de Oca 18, 29007 Málaga, 952 27 62 29, www.ruralandalus.es) and **Rustic Blue** (Barrio la Ermita, 18412, Búbion, Granada, 958 76 33 81, www.rusticblue.com).

Casa Andaluza (956 45 60 53, www.casa-andaluza.com) specialises in villas in western Andalucía, while **Anda-Luzia-Reisen** (956 44 62 75, mobile 676 87 42 81, www.anda-luzia-reisen.com) focuses purely on the Costa de la Luz. For the eastern Costa del Sol around Nerja, try **James Villa Holidays** (from the UK 01622 655 900, www.jamesvillas.co.uk).

Youth hostels

There are 20 *albergues juveniles* in Andalucía and one in Gibraltar, open to anyone with an IYHF (International Youth Hostel Federation) card. They are well maintained and many have pools. In rural areas they offer an excellent cheap accommodation option, and in July and August you can also camp in the grounds for a few euros a night. In city areas, however, youth hostels are often a bus ride away from the city centre, so you be might be better off in a *pensión*.

Inturjoven manages the network of hostels and seasonal camping grounds across Andalucía. Bookings can be made either with the hostel direct, from the central booking number (902 51 00 00) or online (www.inturjoven.com).

Camping

There are around 130 official campsites in Andalucía, the majority of which are along the coast. You can camp elsewhere, but use your discretion: urban areas, private farmland and tourist beaches are off-limits; if you camp here you are liable for a fine.

Most campsites are well maintained with showers and functioning toilets; many also have bars attached or are within walking distance of restaurants. They won't cost you much more than €4 per person per night, plus €4 per night for the tent and the same for a caravan. The Junta de Andalucía publishes an official *Guía de Camping*, available from many tourist offices, which details all the officially recognised sites and prices.

Refugios

Mountain refuges, or *refugios*, are dormitory huts with washing and cooking facilities situated on popular hiking or climbing routes. You will find them dotted around the sierras, particularly the Sierra Nevada (where there are 12). They are usually indicated on maps, but for a full list contact the **Federación Andaluza de Montañismo** in Granada (Camino de Roda 101, Edificio Atalaya, piso°1 Oficina 7G, 958 29 13 40, www.fedamon.com).

Sport, Activities & Special Interests

Sport

Bullfighting

Despite international opposition, bullfighting remains popular in Spain, and particularly in Andalucía. The region has around 70 permanent bullrings and many village *ferias* climax with a *corrida*. The most renowned venues are the beautiful old ring in Ronda (built in 1785), which is regarded as the birthplace of bullfighting, and Seville's famed Maestranza, dating from 1761, which attracts the country's top matadors. The bullfighting season runs from April to October. For information on what to expect at a *corrida*, *see p72* **The unspeakable in pursuit of the edible**. The website http://mundo-taurino.org is packed with *toro*-related information.

Football

Football (*fútbol*) is an obsession in Spain and by far the country's best-loved sport. You'll see it on TV in every bar in every town and village during the season, which lasts from September to June. The three big Andalucían teams are **Seville**, its (traditionally working-class) city rival **Betis** and **Málaga**. Seville and Betis have maintained solid mid-table form in the first division over the past few seasons, while Málaga was relegated in 2006. **Recreativo Huelva** (Spain's oldest club, founded by the British workers in the Rio Tinto mine) was bumped up into first division. Regional teams in the second division are **Cádiz**, **Polideportivo Ejido**, **Córdoba**, **Xerez** and **Almería**. Unless it's a big match, tickets are available on the gate until kick-off, starting from €15. Trouble is rare and the atmosphere is generally friendly.

Activities

Aerial sports

For details of skydiving, parachuting, paragliding and other aerial sports, contact the **Federación Andaluza de Deportes Aereos** (Avenida San José 5, 41012 Sevilla, 954 23 58 64, www.feada.org).

One recommended paragliding school is **Fly Spain** (contact: Rob Mansley, mobile 651 73 67 18, www.flyspain.co.uk), based in Algodonales in north-eastern Cádiz province, which offers a range of flights and courses for beginners.

Birdwatching

Andalucía is one of Europe's premier spots for twitchers. For some prime sites, *see p198* **Birdwatching spots**.

Climbing

Serious mountaineers head to the Sierra Nevada, the highest mountains in Spain (*see p280*), which offer some of the best climbing outside the Alps. Its peaks (topped at 3,482m/ 11,424ft by Mulhacén) are snow-capped for most of the year. For information, contact the **Federación Andaluza de Montañismo** in Granada (Camino de Roda 101, Edificio Atalaya, planta 1, Oficina 7G, 958 29 13 40, www.fedamon.com).

Cycling & mountain biking

For information on getting around Andalucía by bike, *see p309*. Mountain biking in the region's rugged terrain is becoming increasingly popular. For mountain-biking holidays, *see p315*.

Diving & snorkelling

Diving off the Andalucían coast is not spectacular, but it does offer a few surprises. Perhaps the most exciting dives are to be had around Gibraltar (*see p167*), where the water is clogged with sunken warships. If you are after clear waters and an abundance of marine life, head to the Cabo de Gata nature reserve in Almería. There are a number of good dive schools here offering courses and shore and boat dives (*see p298*). For a full list of dive centres consult the local tourist office.

Fishing

Sea fishermen head to the Andalucían coast for spectacular swordfish fishing from July to September; another draw is open-sea tuna fishing. Marinas up and down the coast can supply information. Freshwater fishermen are attracted primarily by the excellent trout fishing. One of the best (year-round) spots is Río Frío, near Loja in western Granada province; trout have been caught here since at least the 17th century. For information and permits, contact the **Alberge de Pescadores de Río Frío** (Riviera de Río Frío s/n, 18300 Loja, 958 32 31 77). Look out for Turismo Andaluz's useful booklet *Sport Fishing* in tourist offices.

Golf

Andalucía's warm climate means that you can play golf year-round. Here you'll find more than 60 golf courses (a third of all the golf courses in Spain), around 40 of which are on the Costa del Sol. The choice of Valderrama in Sotogrande as the venue for the 1997 Rider Cup sealed the reputation of the 'Costa del Golf' as one of Europe's premier golfing destinations. There are so many courses, in fact, that prices are fairly keen and you can get a round at some of the smaller ones for as little as €30. Many resort hotels even have their own courses. For companies offering golfing holidays, see *below*. For more on the courses, see www.andalucia.com/golf/home.htm.

Horse riding

Andalucíans love horses and breed some of the finest in the world. The varied landscapes lend themselves perfectly to riding. For horse-riding holidays, *see below*.

Sailing

There are marinas all along the coast, and sailing is big business in this part of the world. Most of the boats you'll see berthed along the Costa del Sol are for pleasure purposes only but there are plenty of sailing clubs too. Consult the website www.andalucia.com/sailing for details. General information is also available from the **Royal Spanish Sailing Federation** (Luis de Salazar 9, 28008 Madrid, 915 19 50 08, www.rfev.es).

Skiing

Skiing is confined to the Sierra Nevada ski resort (Pradollano; *see p281*), about an hour's drive from Granada city. The resort is the most southerly in Europe and is small by Alpine standards. However, there are more than enough runs of varying standards (four green, 18 blue, 18 red) to keep you entertained for a weekend, which is about the length of time most people spend here in season. For details, see www.tuspain.com/travel/sierra.htm.

Surfing, kitesurfing & windsurfing

All three of the above are hugely popular activities on the windy Costa de la Luz in Cádiz province. The beach of El Palmar near Conil de la Frontera is favoured by surfers, while kite- and windsurfers flock to the beaches north of Tarifa. For more information, see www.tarifainfo.com/en/surfing.html.

Walking

Andalucía's varied and often spectacular landscapes make for wonderful walking and hiking. Guy Hunter-Watts' book *Walking in Andalucía* is a useful guide. For general information about hiking in Andalucía (and Spain) contact the Barcelona-based **Federación Español de Deportes de Montaña** (Federation of Mountain Sports, 934 26 42 67, www.fedme.es). For hiking maps, *see p319* **Maps**. For companies running walking holidays, *see below*.

Specialist interest holidays

Archaeology

Earthwatch International
(01865 318 838/from the US 1-800 776 0188/www.earthwatch.org/expeditions/gibert.html).

Birdwatching

Limosa Holidays *(from the UK 01263 578143/www.limosaholidays.co.uk).*

Cookery

Buenvino Cookery Courses
(from Spain 959 12 40 34/www.fincabuenvino.com).

Madrid and Beyond *(from Spain 917 58 00 63/www.madridandbeyond.com).*

Culture

ACE
(from the UK 01223 835055/www.acestudytours.co.uk).
Martin Randall Travel
(from the UK 020 8742 3355/www.martinrandall.com).

Dance

Dance Holiday Company
(from the UK 0870 2866000/www.danceholidays.com).

Golf

For information tailored to golfing visitors, see www.golfholidays.net.
Executive Golf Marbella
(from Spain 952 83 85 56/from the UK 0871 871 4905/www.executivegolfholidays.com).

Horse riding

Natural Horse Riding in Spain
(from Spain 952 72 02 71/www.naturalhorseridinginspain.com).
Rancho Los Lobos
(from Spain 956 64 04 29/www.rancholoslobos.com).
Rustic Blue *see p284.*
Rutas Alternativas Cabalgar
(from Spain 958 76 31 35/www.ridingandalucia.com).
Spirit of Andalucía
(from the UK 0845 230 1220/www.spirit-of-andalucia.co.uk).

Painting

Andalucian Adventures
(from the UK 01453 834137/www.andalucian-adventures.co.uk).
Andalucian Painting Holidays
(from the UK 01382 553736/www.langeart.co.uk).

Walking/trekking

Andalucian Adventures
see above.
Explore Worldwide
(from the UK 01252 391100/www.explore.co.uk).
Headwater Holidays
(from the UK 01606 720099/720033/www.headwater.com).
Ramblers Holidays
(from the UK 01707 331133/www.ramblersholidays.co.uk).
Rustic Blue *see p284.*
Sherpa Expeditions
(from the UK 020 8577 2717/www.sherpa-walking-holidays.co.uk).
Waymark Holidays
(from the UK 01753 516477/www.waymarkholidays.co.uk).

Wine

Winetrails
(from the UK 01306 712111/www.winetrails.co.uk).

Resources A-Z

Addresses

These are written street first, number second. In other words: C/Andalucía 7. Flat addresses are written according to the floor and which side of the block the flat is on: dcha = *derecha* (right); izda = *izquierda* (left); cto = *centro* (centre). Piso 1° dcha would therefore translate as first-floor flat on the right. The odd moniker s/n means *sin número* ('no number'). *Código postal* is the five-figure postcode and should always be included. Most Spanish street names are preceded by 'Calle', often abbreviated to 'C/' and not marked on many street maps.

Age restrictions

The minimum legal age for smoking and drinking is 16, but this is not strictly enforced. The age of consent for both hetero- and homosexuals is 13, one of the lowest in Europe. Due to the fact that many young Spaniards live at home until they marry, casual sex and teenage pregnancy are relatively rare. To drive a car you need to be 18.

Attitude & etiquette

The Spanish are far more tactile than northern Europeans; the common greeting between members of the opposite sex is a kiss on both cheeks. Personal space is much less guarded than in the UK or USA so do not be fazed if you find someone crowding you or bumping into you without apologising. It's the same with queuing, which is a largely alien concept in Spain.

Noise levels are also much higher than you may be used to – the first time you go into a bar you'll notice the TV, radio, coffee-maker and numerous high-volume conversations all going on simultaneously.

Children

The Spanish love children – so much so that they take them with them wherever they go at almost any time of day or night. The Spanish are also much less strict about keeping control of their kids than northern Europeans.

Bars and restaurants will bend over backwards to look after children or babies, even if they have no special facilities, and most hotels accommodate kids at reduced rates.

In terms of facilities and amusements, the best place is the Costa del Sol, which has water parks, theme parks, aquariums and other child-oriented attractions.

Consulates

Australia

C/Federico Rubio 14, Seville (954 22 09 71). **Open** 10am-noon Mon-Fri.

Canada

Edificio Horizonte, Plaza Malagueta 2, 1°, Málaga (952 22 33 46). **Open** 10am-1pm Mon-Fri.

Ireland

Plaza de Santa Cruz 6, bajo A, Seville (954 21 63 61). **Open** 10am-2pm Mon-Fri.

UK

Edificio Eurocom, bloque Sur, C/Mauricio Moro Pareto 2, 2°, Málaga (952 35 23 00/www.ukspain.com). **Open** 8.30am-1.30pm Mon-Fri.

USA

Edificio Lucía 1°C, Avenida Juan Gómez 'Juanito' 8, Fuengirola (952 47 48 91). **Open** 10am-1pm Mon-Fri.

Plaza Nueva 8, Seville (954 21 87 51). **Open** 10am-1pm Mon-Fri.

Consumer

Each municipality in Spain has its own 'OMIC' (Oficina Municipal de Información al Consumidor) office that aims to keep consumers informed of their rights and responsibilities. Ask at the local town hall for details.

Customs

There are no restrictions on the import/export of duty-paid goods into Spain from any other EU country, provided the goods are for personal consumption only. Amounts qualifying

Travel advice

For current information on travel to a specific country – including the latest news on health issues, safety and security, local laws and customs – contact your home country's government department of foreign affairs. Most have websites with useful advice for would-be travellers.

Australia
www.smartraveller.gov.au

Canada
www.voyage.gc.ca

New Zealand
www.safetravel.govt.nz

Republic of Ireland
http://foreignaffairs.gov.ie

UK
www.fco.gov.uk/travel

USA
http://travel.state.gov

as personal consumption are as follows. (If you import more than these amounts, you may be asked to prove that the goods are solely for your use.)

- up to 800 cigarettes, 400 small cigars, 200 cigars or 1kg loose tobacco.
- 10 litres of spirits (over 22 per cent alcohol), 90 litres of wine (under 22 per cent alcohol) or 110 litres of beer.

If you are travelling into Spain from outside the EU, the limits are as follows. You are advised not to break these or you will risk a very heavy fine.

- 200 cigarettes or 100 small cigars, 50 cigars or 250g loose tobacco.
- 1 litre of spirits (over 22 per cent alcohol) or 2 litres of wine and beer (under 22 per cent alcohol).
- 50g perfume.
- 500g coffee; 100g tea.

These limits also apply if you are entering mainland Spain by boat from the Canary Islands or the Spanish protectorates of Melilla and Ceuta in Morocco, or from Gibraltar.

When you enter Spain from Gibraltar, expect to be stopped and searched at the border for illegally imported goods. You may also find yourself subject to a search if you are coming back from Morocco into Algeciras, Tarifa or Gibraltar. You are likely to be offered hashish in Morocco: do not try and bring it into Spain – although attitudes to personal possession within Spain are fairly relaxed (*see below* **Drugs**), smuggling is regarded as a serious offence and you're likely to face jail or a huge fine.

Disabled

Andalucía is not very well geared up for disabled travellers and you will not find many facilities, particularly on public transport. Trains are better than buses in this respect, with wheelchairs usually available at most stations. Some car-hire companies offer specially adapted cars for hire. Disabled parking bays are denoted by a blue wheelchair sign.

Most public buildings and monuments, certainly in the cities, have disabled access and facilities by law. This also applies to larger hotels, including most *paradores*. Youth hostels in Andalucía also tend to have adapted access and accommodation, but smaller hotels and *pensiones* are unlikely to be equipped for disabled visitors. Larger restaurants and service stations in tourist areas will have disabled access, but away from the main routes, facilities are scarce.

In terms of accommodation, it's worth getting hold of the *Guía de Hoteles y Pensiones de Andalucía* from tourist offices; all wheelchair-accessible accommodation is marked with a wheelchair symbol.

Organisations

Get a list of wheelchair-friendly accommodation and useful disabled tips about Andalucía before you go from the Spanish National Tourist Offices around the world (*see p324* **Tourist information**).

Access Travel

6 The Hillock, Astley, M29 7GW (01942 888844/ www.access-travel.co.uk).
Tour operator that organises holidays for disabled people.

Holiday Care

2nd floor, Imperial Building, Victoria Road, Horley, RH6 9HW (0845 124 9971/www.holidaycare.org.uk).
Can provide a guide to accessible accommodation and other facilities for the disabled in Spain.

RADAR

250 City Road, London EC1V 8AF (020 7250 3222/Minicom 020 7250 4119/www.radar.org.uk).
The Royal Association for Disability and Rehabilitation has useful travel tips and information.

Drugs

Andalucía's proximity to Morocco means it is the main gateway for drugs coming into Spain and Europe from North Africa. Cannabis (known here as *chocolate*) is plentiful and cheap in the south of Spain and you may well find yourself offered some as you walk around. Tolerance towards soft drugs has become stricter since the heady days of the late 1980s when it was perfectly acceptable to smoke in parks and public spaces and in many bars and cafés. Today, you might still see people smoking joints (*porros*) in certain areas, but it's no longer commonplace.

Cannabis possession is illegal in Spain, but if it's a matter of just a few grams the police are unlikely to be concerned. Much more than that and you'll get a fine and a possible court appearance. If you are found in possession of any other drugs, you are looking at big fines and a prison sentence.

Electricity

Spain operates on a 220V, 50-cycle AC grid and uses two-pin plugs. You will need an adaptor if you are bringing British electrical appliances with you. Visitors from the USA will need to bring an adaptor and a transformer if they intend to use appliances from home.

Emergencies

If you're caught in any kind of emergency situation while you're in Spain, call the **Servicios de Urgencias** on 112; the multilingual operators on that number will then connect you to the fire, police or ambulance services, as the situation demands.

Gay & lesbian

Homosexuality was illegal in Spain when Franco was in power, but attitudes to same-sex relationships took a long time to relax. In 2005, however, homosexual marriages became legal. Attitudes to gays and lesbians in Andalucía have markedly improved in the last few years, and you'll find big scenes in Seville, Granada, Málaga, Marbella and, particularly, in Torremolinos, where there's a good drag scene and at least 20 gay bars. In rural villages, however, it's an entirely different matter; as a gay visitor you may be met with outright hostility, especially if you are trying to get a room with your partner.

For advice contact one of the local gay and lesbian groups. These include **COLEGA** (www.colegaweb.net, Almería 950 27 65 40, Cádiz 956 22 62 62, Córdoba 957 49 27 79, Granada 958 26 38 53, Huelva 959 28 49 55, Jaén 953 22 26 62, Málaga 952 21 71 99, Seville 954 50 13 77) and **NOS** in Granada (958 20 06 02/www.asociacionnos.org) Information on the gay scene is available in the following publications: *Guía Gay Visado* and *Spartacus España*.

Health

In 2006 the E111 form (the result of a reciprocal agreement to provide care for travellers from other countries within the EU) was phased out and replaced with the EHIC (European Health Insurance Card), which entitles them to free or reduced cost medical and hospital treatment from any doctor or hospital within the Spanish health system. The form is available from post offices in the UK, or you can apply online (www.dh.gov.uk; for information, call 0845 605 0707).

However, all travellers are strongly advised to take out comprehensive travel health insurance that will cover medical costs and repatriation, if required.

In a non-emergency, be aware that pharmacists are very well informed and can often offer advice for minor complaints and injuries (*see below*). **In case of a medical emergency, call 112**.

Contraception

Condoms (*condones* or *preservativos*) can be bought from pharmacies and also from vending machines inside the toilets of some bars. The female contraceptive pill (*la píldora*) can be bought at most pharmacies without a prescription, while the morning-after pill (*píldora del día siguiente*) requires one.

Doctors & dentists

Medical treatment covered by the EHIC reciprocal health agreement is only provided by practitioners within the Spanish national health service, and in some parts of rural Andalucía you may have to travel some distance to attend a participating surgery (*consultorio*), health centre (*centro sanitario*) or hospital clinic (*ambulatorio*). If you require treatment, you will need the EHIC card to give to the doctor. Anyone without an EHIC card who gets medical treatment in Spain (including all non-EU visitors) will need a doctor's signature in order to make an insurance claim. Dental treatment is not usually free of charge and you are unlikely to be able to claim back the costs unless you have comprehensive travel health insurance.

In Spain, doctors, health centres and hospitals have separate surgery times for private patients. If you are asked to pay for treatment, be aware that you are not being treated under the health service and that your EHIC will not be accepted. If you need to call out a doctor in an emergency, make it clear that you have an EHIC and you want to be treated under the EU arrangements.

Hospitals

Urgent medical treatment is free at a public hospital for EU citizens who can present a valid EHIC.

Opticians

You can get a replacement pair of spectacles or order new contact lenses at any opticians (*optica*) as long as you bring along your prescription.

Pharmacies

Farmacias, denoted by an illuminated green cross, can be found in most villages and all towns and cities. Pharmacists are highly knowledgeable and will often be able to save you a trip to the doctor. Pharmacies are usually open 10am to 2pm and 5pm to 8pm Monday to Saturday, but also operate a rota system so there is always one in the vicinity that is open 24 hours, as listed at the back of the local paper under '*Farmacias de guardia*'.

Prescriptions

Holders of an EHIC will be expected to pay up to 40 per cent of the cost of a prescription unless they are a pensioner, in which case it is free. All other visitors have to pay full prescription charges.

STDs, HIV & AIDS

Spain's high death rate from AIDS is falling, but the HIV virus continues to spread in many groups, such as drug users and heterosexuals. The national AIDS helpline can provide further information in English (freephone 900 11 10 00). There is also an Andalucía helpline (freephone 900 85 01 00). Some of the operators speak English.

Helplines

These are official lines run by the Junta de Andalucía and likely to be in Spanish only. Numbers prefixed with 900 can be dialled free of charge.

Citizen's advice 902 50 55 05.
Child abuse 900 85 18 18.
Drugs 900 84 50 40.
Elderly 900 85 83 81.
General emergencies 902 50 50 61.
Teenage/juvenile 901 40 00 40.
Women 900 20 09 99.

ID

You are meant to carry some form of ID with you at all times in Spain; the Spanish have identity cards, but a passport is ideal for most foreign visitors. If you are stopped by the police and are not carrying valid ID, you will probably get a warning, although you may be liable to an on-the-spot fine. Valid ID (passport) is essential when checking into a hotel, hiring a car, exchanging, or paying with, travellers' cheques and collecting poste restante.

Insurance

All travellers should take out personal travel insurance to cover trip cancellation, emergency medical costs and loss or theft of baggage, money or travellers' cheques. If you're planning on taking part in horse riding, skiing, scuba diving, moutaineering or paragliding, for example, you should also consider additional 'dangerous sports' cover. Keep a record of your policy number and the emergency telephone number with you.

Internet

You'll have little difficulty finding an internet café; often even small villages have web facilities. The bigger towns and cities are full of them, so prices tend to be reasonable. See the 'Resources' section at the end of relevant chapters in this guide. Many hotels and even *hostales* have a web page, often with online booking facilities, but only the bigger establishments are likely to have online computers for guest use and the prices will be high.

Many ISPs (such as Wanadoo, 902 01 19 02, www.wanadoo.es) offer free basic access, while others (like ONO, 902 50 00 60, www.ono.com) or Ya (902 90 29 02, www.ya.com) give a slightly better service for a monthly fee. Be warned that this is all relative and Spain lags behind most other European countries in terms of internet cost and customer service.

For useful websites on Andalucía, *see p329*.

Left luggage

Consignas are available at most bus and train stations and airports for a few euros a day.

Legal help

Consulates (*see p316*) can assist tourists in emergencies, and provide a list of English-speaking lawyers/interpreters.

Libraries

Municipal libraries open 9am to 9pm Monday to Friday and 9am to 2pm on Saturday. Most stock some books in English and provide free internet access. Ask at *ayuntamientos* or tourist offices for addresses.

Lost property

If you lose something in your hotel, report it to the concierge. There are lost property offices at most train or bus stations and at airports. Otherwise, go to your nearest police station (see 'Resources' at the end of the relevant chapter).

Maps

All *turismos* (tourist offices) supply free city-centre maps that list the main sights. Regional *turismos* stock maps of the province. Be warned: major roads were renumbered in 2004, and maps have been slow to update. Website www.barrabes.com sells walking and hiking maps for specific areas. Of the topographical maps available, the most reliable are those produced by SGE (Servicio Geográfico del Ejército). The Spanish Cycling Federation publishes cycling route maps on its website (www.rfec.com).

Media

Newspapers & magazines

In Spain newspapers and magazines are sold from *kioscos* – kiosks on the street. The Spanish press is generally serious and pretty dry; you won't find anything equivalent to the British tabloids. This may well account for the low circulations of most newspapers and for the fact that Spaniards tend to rely on the radio for their news.

The biggest seller on a national level, with a circulation of about 400,000, is the left-of-centre *El País*, which has the best foreign coverage and political analysis. The regional edition has a daily Andalucía supplement inside. *El Mundo* and *Diario 16* are both good centrist alternatives, while *ABC* is solidly conservative and reactionary.

The cities each have their own newspaper: *Diario de Sevilla*, *Diario de Cádiz*, *Diario de Córdoba*, *Ideal* (Granada) and *Sur* (Málaga). All of these have excellent listings and are particularly useful during big festivals, when they run supplements that include route maps and details of the events. *Sur* also publishes a good English edition with local news, which is useful for classifieds.

There are numerous expat-orientated newspapers and magazines along the Costa del Sol, which carry little news but lots of property ads. Among them are *The Entertainer*, *Lookout* and *Marbella Life*. Many British newspapers also print a Spanish edition, which is distributed in the resorts of the Costa del Sol. Otherwise, many British and US newspapers are available the same day in the larger cities, and the following day in smaller towns.

Celebrity gossip is confined to the magazines – in fact, Spain pioneered the genre with the sycophantic glitz of *¡HOLA!*. Parents should note that Spain's laissez-faire attitude towards pornography means that you will find hard-core porn magazines next to *National Geographic* and within easy reach of children.

Radio

The Spanish are avid radio fans; you'll hear radios blaring out of bars, cafés, buses and taxis. **Radio Nacional de España** is the main public broadcaster, with four stations. The main commercial broadcaster is **SER** (Sociedad Española de Radiofusión), with four networks: SER, a news network and music channels. There are an enormous number of talk radio stations with endless discussions about current affairs.

For music, by far the best station is, surprisingly, state-owned **Radio 3** on 98.6 FM, which plays a fantastically eclectic range of rock, pop, jazz, hip hop, blues and world music. Otherwise, for pop there are **Onda Cero** and **Cadena Cuarenta**, which play about two Spanish songs to every three English-language ones and are full of ad breaks. **Radio Olé** is fun for flamenco, and **Radio Clasical** is a relaxing alternative. The official local radio station in Andalucía is **Canal Sur**.

Along the Costa del Sol you'll also find a few English channels, and as you approach Gibraltar you will be able to pick up British forces radio and **Radio Gibraltar** – each as dire as the other. US forces radio can be picked up further west, around Rota.

Television

Spanish television is shockingly poor, but you'll find it dominating almost every bar or café you visit. There are five main channels, which pump out an endless diet of tacky game shows, talk shows, really bad imported *telenovelas* (soaps) from South America and badly dubbed American movies. Just about the only redeeming feature is the news, while **Canal 2** does show some good documentaries and films. Andalucía also has its own regional channel, **Canal Sur**, which shows plenty of bullfighting action during the season.

In most hotels with three or more stars you should be able to get BBC World and CNN. Cable channel Canal Plus offers premium sport and music.

Money

Spain is part of the euro zone. Each euro (€) is divided into 100 cents (¢), known as *céntimos* in Spain. Notes come in denominations of €500, €200, €100, €50, €20, €10 and €5. Coins come in denominations of €2, €1, 50 cents, 20 cents, 10 cents, 5 cents, 2 cents and 1 cent. Euro travellers' cheques are widely accepted. In Gibraltar the pound is still legal tender but you will find that most tourist outlets also accept the euro.

ATMs

Almost every bank has an ATM (Automated Teller Machine) that can be used to withdraw cash. ATMs accept most credit cards as well as debit cards that display the Cirrus symbol and they are usually the most convenient way to get hold of local currency. For both credit and debit cards you will need a valid PIN number in order to withdraw money. Your card issuer is likely to charge you a fee for using an ATM abroad.

Banks

You will find a bank in even the tiniest rural community, usually with an ATM. Banks invariably offer better rates of exchange than bureaux de change. For opening hours, *see p321*.

Credit cards

Credit cards, especially MasterCard and Visa, will be accepted in all major hotels and many upmarket restaurants in Andalucía, as well as in supermarkets and petrol stations. Note that, restaurants excepted, you may be asked to show your passport or driving licence when paying by credit card. However, smaller shops, bars, *hostales* and restaurants in rural areas are unlikely to have credit card facilities. If your card has a Maestro symbol, you can use it as payment in shops and hotels.

Tax

Value-added tax (IVA) at seven or 16 per cent is included in the price of all consumer goods and will be added on to the total bill in hotels and restaurants. (Be aware that it is often not included in initial quotes for rates in hotels.) IVA is non-recoverable for EU citizens. Visitors residing outside the EU should pick up a form at the airport and keep all receipts in order to get an IVA refund.

Natural hazards

- In summer beware the strength of the sun and temperatures that can reach 50°C (122°F) inland.
- In the mountains, watch out for rockfalls, flash flooding and avalanches in the winter.
- If you are swimming, beware the strong currents in the Strait of Gibraltar.
- Take extreme care not to walk through a field of *toros bravos* (fighting bulls), especially during mating season. Look out for signs reading *¡Peligro!* (danger) or *¡No Pasar!* (no entry).
- Beware semi-wild dogs in the rougher parts of the cities, in small villages and on farmland.
- Mosquitoes can be a problem in low-lying areas, especially in the Doñana National Park, and around inland reservoirs when it's warm or muggy.

Opening hours

Banks

Opening hours are 9am to 2pm Monday to Friday. Banks in towns and cities are also open 9am to 1pm on Saturdays from October to April.

Bars & cafés

Bars and cafés usually open at about lunchtime and stay open until midnight or 1am. Some cafés may open as early as 5.30am or 6am, depending on their clientele. *Bares de copas*, where the emphasis is more on drinking, rarely open before 7pm and may continue serving until 4am. Discoteca-bars start later still and do not close until after dawn at 6/7am.

Museums & monuments

Opening hours vary, although a siesta period in the afternoon is not uncommon. Most sights are also closed on a Monday.

Post offices

Correos are open from 8am to noon and again from 5pm to 7.30pm, although those in big cities do not close in the afternoon. Some offices are also open on Saturdays.

Restaurants

Restaurants are generally open from 1/2pm until 4/5pm and again from 8/9pm until midnight/1am at weekends. In tourist areas along the coast UK opening hours will apply. Note: most restaurants have a *día de descanso* (rest day), usually Monday or Wednesday and sometimes Sunday evening. Away from the coast they may close for the holidays in August (*cerrado por vacaciones*).

Shops

Most shops are open from about 9.30/10am until 1/2pm, when they close for a siesta until 5pm. In the evening they stay open until 8pm. Some smaller shops such as bakers (*panadería*) and greengrocers (*frutería*) will open much earlier, at 7/8am, and big department stores and supermarkets stay open all day, sometimes until 10pm.

Police & crime

There are three types of police in Spain: the *policia municipal* operate on a city or town level, directing traffic and dealing with intra-urban crime; the *policia nacional*, who wear brown uniforms, patrol the areas outside the cities; while the *Guardia Civil* spend most of their time on highway patrol handing out speeding tickets. The *Guardia Civil* were once the most feared men in uniform in Spain, acting as Franco's private police force, but they're not so scary these days.

Postal services

For opening hours, *see above*. There is usually just one post office per urban area, often characterised by endless queues, so if you are only after stamps (*sellos*) you are better off going to a tobacconist (*estanco*), which is recognisable by its brown and yellow *tabacos* sign.

Stamps for letters and postcards up to 20g (1oz) cost 29¢ within Spain, 57¢ within the EU and 78¢ for other international destinations. For items between 20g and 50g (2oz) the costs rise to 41¢, €1.26 and €1.66 respectively.

Post can take days just to go to the next town. Airmail within Europe usually takes at least five days, but often longer; to a destination outside Europe airmail will take at least ten days.

Poste restante

Poste restante is available at any post office. Letters should be addressed to the recipient at '*Lista de correos*'. You will need to take your passport when you want to collect your post. AmEx offers the same service.

Religion

Andalucía is a strongly Catholic region – certainly the strongest in Spain – and Sunday church services are well attended. However, as elsewhere in Europe, church-going is dominated by the older generation.

It is also worth noting that religious festivals, such as Semana Santa and the *romerías*, are almost pagan in their idol worship, with the emphasis more on ritual than on the actual tenets of Catholicism.

Having said that, some aspects of the Catholic doctrine are still quite closely adhered to in Andalucía, including no sex before marriage or, in the Spanish variation, sex only with the person you are going to marry.

Safety & security

Serious crime is rare in Andalucía, although drug-related crime is on the increase. Petty crimes such as bag-snatching, pickpocketing and opportunistic theft are also on the rise, particularly in the cities of Seville and Granada. For this reason you should take reasonable precautions when you're out and about:

- Don't flash around wads of cash or indeed carry a lot of cash on your person; lock it in your hotel safe instead.
- Conceal cameras and other valuables.
- Keep a tight grip on your handbag, both when walking and when sitting in a café or restaurant. (A good tip is to slip the strap of your bag under your chair leg.)

Theft from hotel rooms is more common in cities in the lower-end establishments. Again, it generally tends to be opportunistic, so don't leave mobiles or wallets lying around when you leave your room. Either put them in the safe or give them to the hotel reception for safe-keeping.

Cars are vulnerable when parked, or in stationary traffic with the window open, when scooter riders can snatch belongings from the passenger seat. Overnight, try and park in a hotel garage or a patrolled public garage.

If you are the victim of theft, report the incident at the nearest police station. You're unlikely ever to see your bag or camera again, but you'll need the police report in order to make an insurance claim. Be warned, though: the police rarely speak English, especially in rural areas, and the form-filling (which is likely to be in Spanish) takes ages.

If you are unlucky enough to have your passport and/or all your cash and credit cards stolen, contact your nearest consulate (*see p316*).

Smoking

Cigarettes in Spain – not matter whether international or local brands – are extremely cheap by UK standards and attitudes towards lighting up are relaxed, though the laws changed in 2006, requiring larger bars and restaurants to provide non-smoking areas. Those under 100sq m (about 1,000sq ft) must state on the door whether or not smoking is permitted inside. The only other places you'll find no-smoking areas are on public transport and in parts of the airports. If you are a non-smoker, some hotels have no-smoking floors and some smarter restaurants have designated areas. If you ask for a no-smoking room, it might mean no more than that the staff remove the ashtray.

Study

If you want to learn Spanish while you are in Andalucía, it's a good idea to check out the website for the **Instituto Cervantes** (www.cervantes.es). This provides a full list of the courses on offer throughout Spain. You'll also find useful links to a variety of language schools at www.andalucia.com/language/schools.htm.

Universities

The Erasmus student exchange scheme and Lingua project are the main parts of an EU programme to help students move between member states. Contact the Erasmus co-ordinator at your home college; information is available in the UK from the **UK Socrates-Erasmus Council**, Rothford, Gilles Lane, Canterbury, Kent, CT2 7LR (01227 762712, www.erasmus.ac.uk).

Universidad de Almería *Carretera Sacramento s/n, La Cañada de San Urbano, Almería (950 01 55 70/www.ual.es).*

Universidad de Cádiz *C/Ancha 16, Cádiz (956 01 50 00/www.uca.es).*

Universidad de Córdoba C/Alfonso XIII 13, Córdoba (957 21 80 33/www.uco.es).

Universidad de Granada C/Cuesta del Hospicio s/n, Hospital Real, Granada (958 24 30 25/www.ugr.es).

Universidad de Huelva *C/Doctor Cantero Cuadrado 6, Huelva (959 01 81 02/www.uhu.es).*

Universidad de Jaén *Campus Las Lagunillas s/n, Jaén (953 01 26 22/www.ujaen.es).*

Universidad de Málaga *Avenida de Cervantes 2, Málaga (952 13 10 00/www.uma.es).*

Universidad de Sevilla *C/San Fernando 4, Seville (954 55 11 46/www.us.es).*

Universidad Pablo de Olavide *A376, km1, Seville (954 34 92 00/www.upo.es).*

Telephones

The Spanish phone network (Telefónica) is efficient and fairly cheap for all but calls to mobiles.

Dialling & codes

Phone numbers in Andalucía consist of nine numerals, divided into the three-figure area code and then six numbers. When calling a number in Spain you always need to dial the area code, even if you are phoning from within that region.

To phone Spain from abroad

Dial the international access code (0011 from Australia; 00 from Ireland, New Zealand and the UK; 011 from the USA and Canada), followed by the country code for Spain (34), followed by the area code and the number.

To make international calls from Spain

To call abroad from Spain, dial 00 plus the international country code (Australia 61, Ireland 353, New Zealand 64, UK 44, USA & Canada 1), area code and number. Remember to omit the initial 0 from the area code.

To phone Gibraltar from anywhere in Andalucía except Cádiz province dial 956 7; from Cádiz province dial 7.

Public phones

It's much cheaper to make a call from a phone box than from a hotel. There are plenty of phone boxes in towns and villages; most will take coins (you'll need a fistful) and phonecards (*tarjeta telefónica*). Phonecards are the simplest option and can be bought at most *kioscos* (kiosks) and *estancos* (tobacconists) as well as from phone shops. Many bars also have pay phones.

To make a call from a public phone, lift the receiver, insert the card or coins, then dial the number (including the area code). If you wish to make another call and you have change left, press the 'R' button and dial again rather than hanging up.

You can also make calls from *locutorios*, which are small rooms full of phone booths where you sit down to talk and pay at the end. These often double as internet cafés and you can also send a fax from here. Faxes may also be sent from hotels and stationery shops (*papelerías*).

Operator services

In most phone boxes operator services will be denoted by little buttons with signs on the main phone panel. You will usually have to insert a coin even to make a free call, although it will be returned when you hang up. English is not commonly spoken or understood by Spanish phone operators, although English is spoken by international operators and international directory enquiries.

Useful numbers

National operator 1009.
National directory enquiries 11818.
Operator for calls to EU 1008.
International operator 1005 (call for international reverse-charge/collect calls, other than to Europe and North Africa, in which case you call 1008).
International directory enquiries 11825.
Weather reports 807 17 03 65.
Speaking clock 093.

Telephone directories

These can occasionally be found in telephone boxes but more often you will find them in *locutorios* or post offices.

Mobile phones

Mobile phones (*móviles*) on the 900 MHz or 1800 MHz GSM frequencies are common in Spain. If you're travelling to Spain from the UK, your phone should be compatible; if you're travelling from the US, you'll need a tri-band handset. Either way, check your phone is enabled for international roaming, and that your home service provider has a reciprocal arrangement with a Spanish provider.

If you're in Andalucía for more than a few weeks, you might be better off buying a pay-as-you-go package when you arrive and then top-up cards; the initial outlay will be around €80. Spanish service providers include Vodafone (mobile 607 123 000, www.vodafone.es), Amena (1474, www.amena.es) and Movistar (1485, www.movistar.es).

Time

Spain is an hour ahead of Greenwich Mean Time and six hours ahead of Eastern Standard Time. The clocks go back in the last week of October and forward in the last week of March.

Tipping

Waiter service is rarely included in the bill, but in most establishments tipping around five to ten per cent is customary. However, if you have had poor service, don't feel you have to pay. Many Spaniards do no more than round bills up to the nearest euro.

You are not expected to tip at the bar but you might wish to if the same barman has served you all evening. Taxi drivers expect a small tip for longer journeys. Hotel staff don't rely on tips to supplement their wage and will not expect them. Having said that, it is perfectly acceptable to reward particularly good service.

Toilets

In bars and restaurants toilets can be pretty basic, though often they're perfectly acceptable. They tend to be less private than in the UK or USA, with sometimes just one door rather than two giving on to the facilities. In rural areas women are advised to bring their own toilet paper with them. Public toilets are rare and generally not well maintained, but most bars are happy to let you use their facilities.

Toilets are known as *servicios*, *aseos*, *baños* or *lavabos*, and are usually denoted by 'S' or 'D' for ladies (*señoras* or *damas*) and 'C' for gentlemen (*caballeros*). Sometimes, however, you'll find an S on both doors, denoting *señoras* and *señores*.

Tourist information

Andalucía is well geared up for tourists and has an excellent network of tourist offices (*turismos*) run by the Junta de Andalucía, even in the smallest places (for details in each particular area or city, look under 'Resources' at the end of the relevant section of each chapter).

Tourist office staff are usually helpful, although they may only speak a little English outside major tourist areas. As well as supplying (usually free) maps and pamphlets with information on the local area, they can also help you find accommodation and provide lists of hotels and restaurants.

In towns and cities *turismos* are open throughout the day and at weekends. In villages they often close for siesta and at weekends. Out of season, village and resort *turismos* may operate a winter timetable with reduced hours.

If there is no actual tourist office in the place you are visiting, it is always worth trying the *ayuntamiento* (town hall). In most cases they should be able to supply you with some basic information and maps.

If you want to get hold of tourist information before you leave your own country, contact your local Spanish National Tourist Office (SNTO, www.tourspain.es).

Spanish tourist offices abroad

Australia *Spanish Tourism Promotions, Level 2, 221 Queen Street, Melbourne (1800 81 78 55/03 96 70 7755/www.spanishtourism.com.au).*

Canada *SNTO, 2 Bloor Street West, 34th floor, Toronto, Ontario M4W 3E2 (1-416 961 3131).*

UK *SNTO, 2nd floor, 79 New Cavendish Street, London W1W 6XB (020 7486 8077).*

USA *OK Spain, 8383 Wilshire Boulevard, Suite 960, Beverley Hills, CA 90211 (1-323 658 7188/www.okspain.org); Water Tower Place, Suite 915 East, 845 North Michigan Avenue, Chicago, IL 60611 (312 642 1992); 1395 Brickell Avenue, MIAMI, Florida 33131 (305 358 1992); 666 Fifth Avenue, New York, NY 10103 (212 265 8822).*

Visas & immigration

If you are a citizen of an EU country, the USA, Canada, Australia or New Zealand, you do not need a visa to enter the country and for stays of up to 90 days. For longer stays, citizens of EU countries no longer require a residency permit, but it is advisable to register with your local *ayuntamiento* (town hall).

Visa requirements are subject to change, so check the latest information with your country's Spanish embassy before leaving home.

Weights & measures

Spain uses the metric system.

Conversions

1 kilometre (km) = 0.62 miles
1 metre (m) = 3.28 feet
1 litre (l) = 1.76 UK pints or 2.12 US pints
10 grams (g) = 0.35 ounces
1 kilogram (kg) = 2.2 pounds
(9/5 Celsius temperature) +32 = temperature in Fahrenheit

What to take

There's likely to be very little you need to bring from home that you can't get in Andalucía.

When to go

The best time to visit Andalucía is in the spring when the blossom is out, the sun is not too fierce and the fiesta season is just beginning. At this time, prices (except during Semana Santa or the Feria de Abril) are still low but the weather is often warm enough to enjoy a beach holiday. Inland, however, it can still be a bit damp and chilly, so come prepared.

From mid June prices and temperatures begin to rise steeply and by July and August Andalucía is a furnace. Villages empty as people head for the coast, which quickly becomes packed. If you are touring inland at this time, you may find many places closed as Spaniards tend to take their main holiday in August.

By mid September high season is officially over and prices and temperatures start to fall. This is a good time to visit as the fine, mild weather often stretches into late October.

November to February is officially Andalucía's winter but on the coast it's often more like a mild English summer. Inland it's a different matter, though, especially in the hills where sub-zero temperatures are not uncommon. This is also the rainy season and sudden downpours after months of near drought can lead to flash floods. The Sierra Nevada gets its snow at this time and the ski season begins.

Climate

Andalucía enjoys one of the mildest climates in Europe with a year-round average temperature of 18-20°C (64-68°F) on the coast and an average of over 300 days' sunshine throughout the year. For average monthly temperatures, *see p325* **Weather in Andalucía**.

Public holidays

The Spanish enjoy more public holidays than any other country in Europe. In Andalucía there are also holidays specific to the region and, of course, local fiestas. If a holiday falls midweek, the Spanish will often take the following day(s) as holiday, too, turning it into a long weekend. On national and regional holidays, banks, post offices and public buildings close down and many museums and monuments operate Sunday opening times. Note, too, that many Spaniards take off the whole of August as holiday and that many restaurants and shops away from the resorts will close for the whole month. Gibraltar follows the UK holidays with a couple more thrown in for good measure.

Holidays in Andalucía

1 Jan *Año Nuevo* (New Year's Day)
6 Jan *Epifanía* (Epiphany)
28 Feb *Día de Andalucía* (Andalucía Day)
Mar/Apr *Jueves Santo* (Maundy Thursday)
Mar/Apr *Viernes Santo* (Good Friday)
1 May *Día del Trabajo* (Labour Day)
25 July *Día de Santiago* (St James's Day)
15 Aug *Asunción* (Assumption)
12 Oct *Día de la Hispanidad* (Columbus Day)
1 Nov *Todos los Santos* (All Saints' Day)
6 Dec *Día de la Constitución* (Constitution Day)
8 Dec *Inmaculada Concepción* (Immaculate Conception)
25 Dec *Navidad* (Christmas Day)

Holidays in Gibraltar

1 Jan New Year's Day
2nd Mon in Mar Commonwealth Day
Mar/Apr Good Friday
Mar/Apr Easter Monday
1st Mon in May May Day Bank Holiday
Last Mon in May Late Spring Bank Holiday
11 June Queen's Birthday
Last Mon in Aug Late Summer Bank Holiday
10 Sept Gibraltar Day
25-26 Dec Christmas Day & Boxing Day

Women

Attitudes towards women in the south of Spain would probably be considered fairly macho compared to the rest of Europe. However, as a tourist you are unlikely to encounter any more harassment than you would at home. Women encounter few problems when travelling alone; you may be approached if you are sitting on your own in a bar or café, but if you make it clear that you are not interested, you are likely to be left alone. Sex crimes are very rare compared to the UK and the USA, but do use your common sense. As in the rest of Europe, some areas of major cities such as ports or red-light districts are best avoided at night.

Working in Andalucía

Citizens of EU countries have the right to live, work and study in Spain for an indefinite period without having to apply for residency. If you do want to make a voluntary application for a *tarjeta de residencia* (residency permit) for any reason, you should be able to do so at any police station.

People coming from countries outside the EU, however, will need to get a special visa from a Spanish consulate in their home country; this can, of course, be a lengthy process. Contact your own consulate for further information.

By far the easiest and most usual way of finding work in Andalucía is as an English teacher. The smallest town will often have an *academia de inglés* and the cities each have numerous language schools. You do not even have to speak Spanish to become an English teacher (many schools prefer it, in fact, if you don't) but most places will want you to have a TEFL qualification (Teaching English as a Foreign Language).

Weather in Andalucía

Average daytime temperatures (minimum/maximum in °C)

	Almería	Cádiz	Córdoba	Granada	Huelva	Jaén	Málaga	Seville
Jan	8/16	8/15	4/14	1/12	6/16	5/12	8/16	6/15
Feb	8/16	9/16	5/16	2/14	7/18	5/14	8/17	6/17
Mar	10/18	11/18	8/19	5/18	9/20	8/17	10/19	9/20
Apr	12/20	12/21	10/23	7/20	11/22	10/20	11/21	11/23
May	15/22	14/23	13/26	9/24	13/25	13/24	14/24	13/26
June	18/26	18/27	17/32	14/30	16/29	17/30	17/28	17/32
July	21/29	20/29	19/36	17/34	18/32	21/34	20/30	20/36
Aug	22/29	20/30	20/36	17/34	18/32	21/34	20/30	20/36
Sept	20/27	19/27	17/31	14/29	17/29	18/29	18/28	18/32
Oct	16/23	16/23	13/24	9/22	14/25	13/22	15/24	14/26
Nov	12/19	12/19	8/19	5/17	10/21	9/16	12/20	10/20
Dec	9/17	9/16	5/14	2/12	7/17	5/12	9/17	7/16

Vocabulary

Like other Latin languages, Spanish has different familiar and polite forms of the second person (you). Many young people now use the familiar *tú* form most of the time, but, as a foreigner it's wise to use the more polite *usted* with people you do not know, and certainly with anyone over 50. In the phrases listed here all verbs are given in the *usted* form.

For help with a Spanish menu, *see p42* **Food glossary**.

Pronunciation

c, before an **i** or an **e**, and **z** are like th in **th**in (though in Andalucía, it is more commonly pronounced as an 's')
c in all other cases is as in **c**at
g, before an **i** or an **e**, and **j** are pronounced with a guttural **h**-sound that does not exist in English – like ch in Scottish lo**ch**, but much harder
g in all other cases is pronounced as in **g**et
h at the beginning of a word is normally silent
ll is pronounced almost like a **y**
ñ is like **ny** in ca**ny**on
a single **r** at the beginning of a word and **rr** elsewhere are heavily rolled

STRESS RULES

In words ending with a vowel, **n** or **s**, the penultimate syllable is stressed: eg ba**ra**to, **vi**ven.

In words ending with any other consonant, the last syllable is stressed: eg exteri**or**, universi**dad**.

An accent marks the stressed syllable in words that depart from these rules: eg estaci**ó**n, **t**ó**nica**.

Basics

hello *hola*; **hello** (on the phone) *hola, diga*
good morning, good day *buenos días*; **good afternoon, good evening** *buenas tardes*; **good evening** (after dark), **good night** *buenas noches*; **goodbye/see you later** *adiós/hasta luego*
please *por favor*; **thank you** (very much) *(muchas) gracias*
you're welcome *de nada*
do you speak English? *¿habla inglés?*; **I don't speak Spanish** *no hablo español*
I don't understand *no entiendo*
what's your name? *¿cómo se llama?*
speak more slowly, please *hable más despacio, por favor*
wait a moment *espere un momento*
Sir/Mr *señor (sr)*; **Madam/Mrs** *señora (sra)*; **Miss** *señorita (srta)*
excuse me/sorry *perdón*
excuse me, please *oiga* (how to attract someone's attention, politely)
OK/fine/(or to a waiter)
that's enough *vale*
where is...? *¿dónde está...?*
why? *¿porqué?*, **when?** *¿cuándo?*, **who?** *¿quién?*, **what?** *¿qué?*, **where?** *¿dónde?*, **how?** *¿cómo?*
is/are there any...? *¿hay...?*
very *muy*; **and** *y*; **or** *o*; **with** *con*; **without** *sin*
open *abierto*; **closed** *cerrado*
what time does it open/close? *¿a qué hora abre/cierra?*
pull (on signs) *tirar*; **push** *empujar*
I would like... *quiero...* (literally, 'I want...'); **how many would you like?** *¿cuántos quiere?*
I like *me gusta*
I don't like *no me gusta*
good *bueno/a*; **bad** *malo/a*;
well/badly *bien/mal*; **small** *pequeño/a*; **big** *gran, grande*;
expensive *caro/a*; **cheap** *barato/a*;
hot (food, drink) *caliente*; **cold** *frío/a*
something *algo*; **nothing** *nada*
more/less *más/menos*
the bill/check, please *la cuenta, por favor*
how much is it? *¿cuánto es?*
do you have change? *¿tiene cambio?*
price *precio*; **free** *gratis*; **discount** *descuento*; **bank** *banco*; **to rent** *alquilar*; **(for) rent, rental** *(en) alquiler*; **post office** *correos*;
stamp *sello*; **postcard** *postal*;
toilet *los servicios*

Getting around

airport *aeropuerto*; **railway station** *estación de ferrocarril/estación de RENFE* (Spanish Railways)
entrance *entrada*; **exit** *salida*;
car *coche*; **bus** *autobús*; **train** *tren*;
a ticket *un billete*; **return** *de ida y vuelta*; **bus stop** *parada de autobús*;
the next stop *la próxima parada*
excuse me, do you know the way to...? *¿oiga, señor/señora, sabe como llegar a...?*
left *izquierda*; **right** *derecha*; **here** *aquí*; **there** *allí*; **straight on** *recto*;
to the end of the street *al final de la calle*; **as far as** *hasta*; **towards** *hacia*; **near** *cerca*; **far** *lejos*

Accommodation

do you have a double (single) room for tonight (one week)? *¿tiene una habitación doble (para una persona) para esta noche (una semana)?*
where is the car park? *¿dónde está el parking?*
we have a reservation *tenemos reserva*
an inside/outside room *una habitación interior/exterior*;
with/without bathroom *con/sin baño*; **shower** *ducha*; **double bed** *cama de matrimonio*; **with twin beds** *con dos camas*; **breakfast included** *desayuno incluído*;
air-conditioning *aire acondicionado*; **lift** *ascensor*;
swimming pool *piscina*

Time

morning *la mañana*; **midday** *mediodía*; **afternoon/evening** *la tarde*; **night** *la noche*; **late night/early morning** (roughly 1-6am) *la madrugada*; **now** *ahora*;
later *más tarde*; **yesterday** *ayer*;
today *hoy*; **tomorrow** *mañana*;
tomorrow morning *mañana por la mañana*; **early** *temprano*; **late** *tarde*;
delay *retraso*; **delayed** *retrasado*
at what time...? *¿a qué hora...?*
in an hour *en una hora*; **the bus will take 2 hours** (to get there) *el autobús tardará dos horas (en llegar)*;
at 2 *a las dos*; **at 8pm** *a las ocho de la tarde*; **at 1.30** *a la una y media*;
at 5.15 *a las cinco y cuarto*; **at 22.30** *a veintidós treinta*

Numbers

0 *cero*; **1** *un, uno, una*; **2** *dos*;
3 *tres*; **4** *cuatro*; **5** *cinco*; **6** *seis*;
7 *siete*; **8** *ocho*; **9** *nueve*; **10** *diez*;
11 *once*; **12** *doce*; **13** *trece*; **14** *catorce*; **15** *quince*; **16** *dieciséis*;
17 *diecisiete*; **18** *dieciocho*;
19 *diecinueve*; **20** *veinte*;
21 *veintiuno*; **22** *veintidós*;
30 *treinta*; **40** *cuarenta*; **50** *cincuenta*; **60** *sesenta*; **70** *setenta*;
80 *ochenta*; **90** *noventa*; **100** *cien*;
1,000 *mil*; **1,000,000** *un millón*

Days, months & seasons

Monday *lunes*; **Tuesday** *martes*;
Wednesday *miércoles*; **Thursday** *jueves*; **Friday** *viernes*; **Saturday** *sábado*; **Sunday** *domingo*
January *enero*; **February** *febrero*; **March** *marzo*; **April** *abril*; **May** *mayo*; **June** *junio*;
July *julio*; **August** *agosto*;
September *septiembre*;
October *octubre*; **November** *noviembre*; **December** *diciembre*
spring *primavera*; **summer** *verano*;
autumn/fall *otoño*; **winter** *invierno*

Glossary

Architecture

artesonado wooden inlaid ceiling of Moorish design
atalaya watchtower
azulejo glazed ceramic tile
Churrigueresque elaborate 17th-/18th-century baroque style named after the Churriguera family of architects and artists
coro central part of a church, built for the choir
Isabelline ornamental late Gothic style, named after Queen Isabel I.
mihrab prayer niche facing towards Mecca in a mosque
Mozarabic Christian style developed under Moorish rule
Mudéjar Muslim-style of decoration and architecture in Christian buildings
muqarna Moorish ceiling ornamentation resembling stalactites
patio inner courtyard
Plateresque ornate, decorative late 15th- and early 16th-century architectural style reminiscent of silverwork (*platería*)
puerta gateway
reja window grille
retablo carved altarpiece
rococo light, florid late-baroque decorative style
sacristía/sagrario sacristy

Around town

alameda tree-lined promenade
alcazaba Moorish castle
alcázar fortified Moorish palace
ayuntamiento town hall
bar de copas night-time bar (unlikely to serve tapas)
barrio quarter or district
bodega wine bar/cellar
calle street
capilla chapel
carmen villa with a garden (used only in Granada)
cartuja Carthusian monastery
casa particular guesthouse
castillo castle
chiringuito beachfront seafood eaterie and/or bar
colegiata collegiate church
convento convent/monastery
correos post office
ermita hermitage
hammam Moorish bathhouse
iglesia church
judería Jewish quarter
medina Moorish town
mercado market
mezquita mosque
monasterio monastery/convent
palacio mansion
parador a member of the government-owned chain of luxury hotels
parroquia parish church
paseo promenade
peña semi-private flamenco club
plaza square
plaza de toros bullring
plaza mayor main square
posada inn
puente bridge
puerto port
turismo tourist office
urbanización housing development

Culture

cante jondo 'deep song'; the most emotionally charged form of flamenco
corrida de toros bullfight
duende the soul/passion of flamenco
feria annual fair
gitano gypsy
juerga gypsy party
Junta de Andalucía regional government
mantilla traditional scarf or shawl worn by women to cover the head and shoulders
matador principal bullfighter
matanza traditional pig slaughter
paso float for carrying holy images during Semana Santa processions
romería religious procession/pilgrimage
Semana Santa Holy Week
solera method of blending sherry and brandy
tablao flamenco show

History

Almohads Berber Muslims who ruled Andalucía in the late 12th/early 13th centuries
Almoravids Berber Muslims who ruled Andalucia in the 11th and 12th centuries
converso Jew who converted to Christianity
Falange Spanish fascist party
morisco baptised Muslim Spaniard who was subject to Christian rule
mozárabe Christian Spaniard subject to Moorish rule
Mudéjar practising Muslim Spaniard under Christian rule
Reconquista Christian conquest of southern Spain in the 13th-15th centuries
los Reyes Católicos 'The Catholic Kings': Isabel I of Castilla and Fernando V of Aragón
taifa small Moorish kingdoms that developed after the fall of the Córdoban Caliphate

Landscapes

arroyo stream
autovía/autopista motorway
barranco steep gorge
campiña flat countryside
carretera main road
cerro mountain, hill or peak
ciudad town or city
cortijo rural farmhouse
coto de caza hunting reserve
cuesta slope/hill
cueva cave
dehesa partially cleared area of forest
embalse reservoir
latifundio large estate
marisma marshland
mirador viewpoint
pueblo village
puerta mountain pass
río river
sierra mountain range
vega cultivated fertile plain

Further Reference

Books

Fiction

Alarcón, Pedro de *The Three-Cornered Hat & Other Stories*
Tales of 18th-century Spanish life by a 19th-century writer born in Guadix, Granada.

Ali, Tariq *Shadows of the Pomegranate Tree*
A Granadan family saga set in the last years of the Nasrid Kingdom.

Barea, Arturo *The Forging of a Rebel Trilogy (The Forge, The Track, The Clash)*
Covering the war in Morocco and the Civil War.

Cervantes, Miguel de
Don Quixote
The quintessential Spanish novel.

Day, Douglas *Journey of the Wolf*
The experiences of a Civil War fighter who returns 40 years later to his home in the Alpujarras.

Hemingway, Ernest
For Whom the Bell Tolls
The experiences of a young American volunteer fighting in the Civil War.

Hewson, David *Semana Santa*
The Easter celebrations form a vivid backdrop for this crime novel.

Irving, Washington
Tales of the Alhambra
Fanciful but influential stories and anecdotes inspired by the writer's residence in the Alhambra in the early 19th century.

Jiménez, Juan Ramon
Platero & I
Lyrical novel by the Nobel Prize-winning poet, which takes the form of conversations between the narrator and his donkey, Platero.

Maalouf, Amin *Leo the African*
Evocative historical novel based on the eventful life of a 15th-century Moorish traveller and diplomat, starting with the fall of Granada in 1492.

Machado, Antonio
Juan de Mairena
Based on the writer's experiences of teaching in Baeza, Jaén.

Pérez Reverte, Arturo
The Seville Communion
Superior crime tale involving priests and politicians, set in Seville.

Rushdie, Salman
The Moor's Last Sigh
Complex epic that uses the fall of Moorish Granada as the starting point for a multifaceted account of modern India.

Food & wine

Casas, Penelope *The Food & Wine of Spain/Tapas: The Little Dishes of Spain*
Comprehensive, readable overviews of Spanish and Andalucian cuisine.

Jeffs, Julian *Sherry*
All you need to know about Andalucía's famous drink.

Luard, Elizabeth
Flavours of Andalucía
Recipes for all the local favourites.

General reference

Baird, David *Inside Andalusia*
A fascinating and perceptive introduction to the region.

Elms, Roberts *Spain: A Portrait After the General*
Unromantic, witty look at modern-day Spain.

Gibson, Ian *Federico García Lorca/The Assassination of Federico García Lorca/Lorca's Granada*
An in-depth biography; an account of the forces that led to the poet's murder; and an exploration of the city through a series of detailed walks.

Hooper, John *The New Spaniards* Authoritative survey of contemporary Spanish life.

Jacobs, Michael *Andalucía*
An exemplary overview that reaches far beyond the usual clichés in its entertaining coverage of Andalucía's cultural, historical and sociological background. A useful gazetteer is included.

History & architecture

Brenan, Gerald
The Spanish Labyrinth
Study of the background to the Civil War: politics and social history with a personal slant.

Burckhardt, Titus
Moorish Culture in Spain
A classic study of the 700 years of Moorish dominance in southern Spain.

Elliot, JH
Imperial Spain 1469-1716
Entertaining, well-written study of Golden Age Spain.

Fletcher, Richard
Moorish Spain
Entertaining and provocative introduction to the history of the Moors in Spain.

Fraser, Ronald *Blood of Spain*
Oral accounts form the basis of this impressive book on the Civil War.

Fraser, Ronald *In Hiding*
Account of the Republican mayor of Mijas, who spent 30 years in hiding following the Civil War.

Fraser, Ronald *The Pueblo*
Follows the trials and tribulations of a mountain village on the Costa del Sol in the early 1970s.

Goodwin, Godfrey *Islamic Spain*
An architectural guide to the most significant Moorish buildings in Spain.

Irving, Washington
The Conquest of Granada
The last days of the Nasrid Kingdom as described by the 19th-century American diplomat.

Irwin, Robert *The Alhambra*
Arabist Irwin's take on Granada's palace on the hill.

Jacobs, Michael *Alhambra*
Beautiful photos and authoritative text in a guide to the most iconic of Andalucía's monuments.

Preston, Paul *Concise History of the Spanish Civil War*
Reader-friendly text and striking illustrations provide an excellent guide to Spain's darkest days.

Watt, WH & Cachia, PA
History of Islamic Spain
The low-down on al-Andalus.

Plays & poetry

Arberry, AJ *Moorish Poetry*
Translations of classic Hispano-Arab verse.

García Lorca, Federico
Romancero Gitano/Three Tragedies/Selected Poems/Poem of the Deep Song
Works by Andalucía's greatest playwright and poet.

Machado, Antonio
Eighty Poems
His best-known works, in English.

Travelogues

Borrow, George
The Bible in Spain
The amusing, idiosyncratic travels and travails of an unconventional 19th-century salesman.

Boyd, Alastair *The Sierras of the South/The Road from Ronda*
Boyd lived in Ronda during the 1960s; these two titles record landscapes and life in the Serranía de Ronda during that time.

Brenan, Gerald
The Face of Spain
Travels through Franco's Spain in 1949.

Brenan, Gerald
South from Granada
Superb depiction of the author's isolated life in a small village in the Alpujarras during the 1930s.

Ford, Richard
A Handbook for Travellers in Spain & Readers at Home
The classic 19th-century guide and travelogue: entertaining, opinionated and erudite.

Gautier, Théophile
A Romantic in Spain
Lucid and elegant account of a French traveller in 1840s Spain.

Hemingway, Ernest
Death in the Afternoon
The American's depiction of Spanish bullfighting.

Hewson, Gerald
The Flamencos of Cádiz Bay
Detailed and unrivalled account of an Englishman learning the flamenco lifestyle.

Jacobs, Michael
The Factory of Light
Affectionate and perceptive hymn to an obscure yet remarkable village in southern Jaén province.

Lee, Laurie *As I Walked Out One Midsummer Morning*
Well-observed trek through Spain on foot just before the Civil War.

Lee, Laurie *A Rose for Winter*
Lee returns, 15 years on, to many of his old 1930s Andalucía haunts in this vivid though slight and sometimes cloying travelogue.

Stewart, Chris
Driving Over Lemons/A Parrot in the Pepper Tree/The Almond Blossom Appreciation Society
Enjoyable good-life-abroad tales of one-time Genesis drummer Stewart's attempt to set up a farm and a new life in the Alpujarras.

Webster Jason
Duende: A Journey in Search of Flamenco/Andalus: Unlocking the Secrets of Moorish Spain
A rites-of-passage tale that follows the author from Alicante to Madrid to Granada, and a quest to trace the influence of the Moors in modern Spain.

Walking & nature

García, Ernest & Paterson, Andrew *Where to Watch Birds in Southern Spain*
Essential guide for twitchers in one of Europe's richest regions for birdwatching.

Grunfeld, Frederic & Farino, Teresa *Wild Spain*
There's a chapter on Andalucía in this summary of Spain's national parks and wildlife.

Hunter-Watts, Guy
Walking in Andalucía
Excellent guide to more than 30 walks across the region.

Oldfield, John & Christine
Andalucía & the Costa del Sol
Twenty-three detailed walks for all abilities.

Websites

General reference

www.andalucia.com
This comprehensive website has subsections dedicated to each province, plus general information on Andalucían customs and culture.

www.andalucia.org
Official tourist website for the region, with useful information on just about every significant village and town of Andalucía.

www.andalucia2.com
Amateur-looking, but with wide-ranging, useful links to other sites.

www.idealspain.com
Thinking of relocating to Spain? This site has all you need to know.

www.juntadeandalucia.com
Regional government website.

www.livinginspain.co.uk
Info for the English-speaking expat community.

www.okspain.org
Spanish tourist board's representative for the USA.

www.parador.es
Official guide to Spain's state-run *parador* hotel chain.

www.red2000.com
Useful tourist guide to Spain.

www.renfe.es/ingles
Official Spanish rail website.

www.tourspain.es
Another official tourist website – this time for the whole of Spain.

Leisure & culture

www.arrakis.es/%7Ejols/tapas/indexin.html
Comprehensive guide to Spanish tapas.

www.asoliva.com
All you need to know about Spanish olive oil.

www.flamenco-world.com
Details of this quintessential Andalucían art form all over the globe.

http://mundo-taurino.org
Links to bullfighting websites.

www.parquesnaturales.com
Information about Spain's Natural Parks.

www.sherry.org
Low-down on Andalucía's favourite tipple.

Towns & cities

www.aboutgranada.com
City guide to Granada.

www.almeria-turismo.org
Tourist guide to Almería.

www.aboutsevilla.com
City guide to Seville.

www.cadiznet.com
Provincial guide to Cádiz.

www.costasol.com
Tourist information about the Costa del Sol.

www.gibraltar.gi
Best internet resource for the Rock.

www.guiadehuelva.com
Provincial guide to Huelva.

www.malaga.com
City guide to Málaga.

www.marbella.com/eng/
Hotels, golf courses, real estate and restaurants.

www.sevilla.org
Sevilla city and its province.

www.turiscordoba.es
Tourist guide to Córdoba.

Index

Note: page numbers in **bold** indicate section(s) giving key information on a topic; *italics* indicate photos.

Advertisers' Index

Please refer to the relevant pages for contact details